Putting on CHRIST

A Road Map for Our Heroic Journey to Spiritual Rebirth and Beyond

By Steven Anthony Bishop

Putting on CHRIST

Second Edition****

Elite Online Publishing is committed to publishing works of quality and integrity. In that spirit, we are proud to offer this book to our readers. The author certifies that the spiritual material found in this work is true and includes both the author's own subjective experiences and those who have agreed to share the same with him and the reader in order to more clearly highlight a spiritual pathway that is referred to in scripture as "straight and narrow." The author, in no way, represents any individual, company, corporation, or brand mentioned herein. The views and opinions expressed in this book are solely those of the author, and not of Elite Online Publishing.

The content in this book is not intended to be a substitute for professional, medical or other advice, diagnosis, or treatment. Always seek the advice of your physician or other qualified health provider with any questions you may have regarding a medical, mental, emotional, or other condition. All content contained or made available through this book is for general information purposes only. VESCOVO BUONARROTI ART, LLC AND STEVEN BISHOP ARE NOT RESPONSIBLE NOR LIABLE FOR ANY ADVICE OR OTHER INFORMATION THAT YOU OBTAIN FROM THIS BOOK.

VESCOVO BUONARROTI ART, LLC
41 E. 400 N. #321
Logan, Utah 84321
PuttingOnChrist.com

In association with:
Elite Online Publishing
63 East 11400 South Suite #230
Sandy, UT 84070
EliteOnlinePublishing.com

Front Cover Artwork by renowned artist Joseph Brickey

All financial yield from this work shall go towards the work's advancement into the world at large as well as towards imparting temporal substance intended to provide for "every needy, naked soul" (Mos. 18:28).

Abbreviations: "Teachings" = Teachings of the Prophet Joseph Smith; JD or JOD = Journal of Discourses; "Lectures" = *Lectures On Faith*; NKJV = New King James Version; HC = History of the Church; New Witness = A New Witness For The Articles of Faith; D&C = Doctrine & Covenants; DBY = Discourses of Brigham Young; and JSH = Joseph Smith History.
All male pronouns found in this work are intended to rightfully include female pronouns. Every experience alluded to in this work is available to men and women equally.

Printed in the United States of America
ISBN: 979-8559574318 (Amazon)
ISBN: 978-1513660578 (Paperback)

Contents

"Wherefore the law was our schoolmaster to bring us unto
Christ, that we might be justified by faith.
But after that faith is come,
we are no longer under a schoolmaster.
For ye are all the children of God ***by faith*** in Christ Jesus.
For as many of you as have been baptized into
Christ have *put on Christ*.
And if ye be Christ's, then are ye Abraham's seed,
and heirs according to the promise."
(Galatians 3:24-27, 29)

Preamble

As long as we make the offering of a broken heart through surrender, in contriteness to God from the altar of our souls, entering the depths of repentance, while having received of His ordinances, and demonstrate that diamond-hard, committed willingness to risk everything to know Him—to emulate and be "all in" with Him from our hearts throughout eternity, ***IT IS ULTIMATELY HIS BESTOWAL OF FAITH AS AN ENDOWMENT OF POWER THAT SAVES****. This salvation arises through that catalyst of "falling down and crying out to Him" with all that we have and are—one whom we have never before seen with our natural eyes though nevertheless is real, allowing our desperate plea for his atoning blood to both heal and cleanse. Through this very personal journey, we will have been led to a mini-Gethsemane of our own to further appreciate and comprehend of His offering, while* ***RELYING ALONE UPON HIS MERITS, MERCY, AND GRACE****. In an instant, the promised gift of the Father can then be received through an inner commitment to abandon one's self and one's will to God. This is when we completely surrender and 'let go'...into His ineffably loving arms. It is by way of this ultimate expression of submission that we will have found oneness and spiritual union in Him, together with unspeakable joy in the Holy Ghost. This is the fulfillment of the promise of the Father. This is salvation. This is "putting on Christ."*

"And of tenets thou shalt not talk, but thou shalt declare ***repentance and faith on the Savior****, and* ***remission of sins by baptism, and by fire****, yea, even the Holy Ghost" (D&C 19:31).*

Preface

Knowing about God versus the Perfect Knowledge of God

In April of 2013, I received an indescribable tender mercy—an understanding of the importance of the knowledge *about* something versus the absolute knowledge *of* something. That difference is best represented in the very real and ongoing spiritual battle that is being waged over the hearts of men. For example, we may know a great deal about Christ but until we come to the actual knowledge of Christ, our lives may be in spiritual jeopardy—for how good is any knowledge if in the end it does not profit us unto salvation. The Light of Christ and inner awareness over the state of our hearts provides us protection against the adversary as he tries to harden our hearts against God, thereby preventing us from obtaining this necessary life-saving knowledge and guidance. The Prophet Joseph Smith taught,

> *"The principle of knowledge is the principle of salvation... The principle of salvation is given us through the knowledge of Jesus Christ"*[1]

The principle of knowledge that saves begins with coming to the knowledge "of" Jesus Christ and not merely knowledge "about" Him. The actual knowledge of Christ is the gateway to all other knowledge necessary for a "more sure" salvation, including that of entering His presence in mortality.

While the knowledge *about* Jesus Christ (God the Son) is different than the knowledge *of* Him, they are not mutually exclusive. For example, in 1820, fourteen-year-old Joseph Smith was determined to know, at least in part, which of the many religions he should join. He read a passage in the Bible instructing any who lacked wisdom to "ask of God" (James 1:5). Clearly, what he learned from his readings was knowledge *about* Christ—and that he could pray to God and have his prayer answered. Having faith in that new knowledge *about* God, Joseph decided to put it to the test. He went to a secluded wood to ask God which church he should join. According to his account, while praying he was visited by two "personages" who revealed themselves to be God the Father and Jesus Christ. In that visitation, Joseph had new knowledge, not merely *about* Christ but now *of* Christ, together with a knowledge *of* God the Father, and additionally, knowledge *of* the total Godhead. In that instant, Joseph's life was changed forever because of that one glorious experience—knowing God.

Moving from knowledge *about* something to knowledge *of* something is more common than one might realize. Those who have experienced a spiritual rebirth in Christ—being "born of the Spirit"–and the many who have had near death experiences are two examples. Each of these severally, yet in their singular experiences, came to the perfect knowledge that there is first and foremost a God, as well as a life after death. Admittedly, before those who underwent a near death experience passed through the veil, their beliefs about that subject greatly varied. But after that uniting experience, they all concluded and *knew* that mortal death is not the end of life. To a person, they no longer feared death. Some might have even longed for the peace and beauty they found in death. Moving from a belief *about* God to an undeniable knowledge *of* God is what this earthly experience is all about. In fact, it is paramount to our salvation. Obtaining this level of knowledge *is* our heroic journey.

Elder Bruce R. McConkie stated:

> *This true witness of the Holy Ghost is pure and absolute, and that a man can know with a **perfect knowledge**, by the power of the Holy Ghost, that Jesus Christ is the son of the living god, who was crucified for the sins of the world. This **unshakeable certainty** can rest in his soul even though he has not seen the face of the Lord.*[2]

Like Joseph, allow the seedlings of desire and faith in what you have learned *about* God to grow until you obtain a perfect knowledge *of* Him. Read on and see the steps that are available to those who desire this level of knowledge, for that is what this book is all about: the journey that will help us to move from where we are in our belief and understanding *about* God to the actual knowledge *of* God. Indeed, this is salvation.

[1] *Teachings of the Prophet Joseph Smith,* Section Six 1843-44, p. 297).

[2] *The Promised Messiah,* p. 592.

Introduction

Write the things which ye have seen and heard, save it be those which are forbidden.

And behold, all things are written by the Father; therefore out of the books which shall be written shall the world be judged (3 Nephi 27:23, 26).

This book is a hybrid of "self-help" and an analysis of the first principles and ordinances of the gospel of Jesus Christ. It is about the individual, experiential, and heroic journey in following the straight and narrow path that leads to spiritual rebirth and thereafter, through pressing forward in faith, communing with the Lord through the veil. This "communing" gives us the actual knowledge of our standing before God, together with the right and blessing, through faith, to lay hold upon the "more sure" promise of eternal life—the greatest gift of heaven. And with this promise, we obtain additional spiritual knowledge, together with an obsessive desire to "seek His face," "rend the veil," and enter the Divine Presence while yet in mortality.

Those whose overriding desire is to actually know God in mortality and who diligently and consistently act on this desire will find Him and will be given a place at His right hand. Those who put other priorities ahead of this preeminent one will find themselves at His left. If we truly desire to know Him, we will be unrelenting in our quest to both seek and find Him. The process of coming unto Christ cannot be described in simpler terms.

God's "end game," if you will, is that when our hearts inevitably break (and they most certainly will), that we be led to cry out for His mercy to heal, cleanse, and make us pure, and thereby become walking, breathing, embodiments of His love, as new creatures in Him. It is up to us, through God's gift of agency, to offer or give our hearts *fully* to Him and become sanctified through His blood. As we become full to overflowing with love for God, which is the first and great commandment, obeying the second great commandment will happen of its own accord, naturally spilling over onto all of our beloved brothers and sisters within the body of Christ.

The Journey to God

The path to God is an inner journey that involves the purification of the heart and the sanctification of the soul, with the final objective being to know God and enter His presence while we are yet in mortality. The path is real. It is akin to a profound love story that involves finding, knowing, and eventually returning to that God who gave us breath. The path, though we may discuss it in symbolic terms, is a completely experiential and living one. It is a journey of personally growing in God's light, truth, and love in the inner man. The journey cannot truly begin in power until we receive the First Comforter and are born of God, which is when we depart from the mere knowledge *about* God to the perfect knowledge *of* God. The path cannot be travelled alone—without God's power and guiding grace. Christ and His restored gospel is the power by which our brokenness, complete cleansing and mighty change of heart, "mighty offering," and other sacred endowments can happen in full. The doctrine of Christ, which leads us to actually put on Christ and become born again, is this book's primary focus.

This journey involves following the Light of Christ in our hearts and souls until we, through faith and broken-hearted repentance, are cleansed by spiritual fire and thereby receive a mighty change of heart and a new life in Christ. This is when we "put on Christ" and are born of God, or born again. Being born again is what Christ referred to when he said that we must be "born of the Spirit" to enter the kingdom of heaven. This is when we receive the actual companionship of the Holy Ghost or First Comforter, who will lead us to additional endowments of God's light and knowledge.

Eventually, those who endure in Christ after being born again will be led to what I refer to as the "mighty offering" and other sacred endowments. Lecture 6 of *Lectures on Faith* refers to it as "the same sacrifice." (Note: These lectures were considered as doctrine when published as part of the Doctrine and Covenants until 1921. Though they were removed from canonized scripture then, they are still available worldwide and published as a separate booklet). The Lectures teach that once this holy consecration or "sacrifice" is accepted by Deity, we can receive "the knowledge...that [we] are accepted in the sight of God" (*Lectures on Faith* 3:5; 6:9; emphasis added), and "that the course of life which [we] pursue is according to the will of God..." (*Lectures on Faith* 6:2).

The Role of the Holy Ghost

The above spiritual knowledge can give us the added power through faith to obtain other vistas, including that of laying hold of the "more sure" word of promise through prophecy of eternal life while in mortality (*Lectures On Faith* 6:7, 6:10). This "more sure" promise of eternal life is also known as the more sure word of prophecy (see chapter 11, "The More Sure Word of Prophecy"). As a general rule (and there are exceptions), this "more sure" word of promise is a condition precedent to seeing the Lord while in mortality, should we be so fortunate. I, for one, cannot imagine a more beautiful and tender vision to hold to in this life. "Where there is no vision, the people perish" (Proverbs 29:18). I believe this level of knowledge must come through a suspension of all "unbelief," achieved through our cumulative faith and spiritual knowledge. The *Lectures On Faith* contain important keys to fully eradicate our unbelief. To receive these glorious endowments, it is necessary that we begin by receiving the First Comforter, whose influence is given to abide ***in us*** (Moses 6:61).

President Wilford Woodruff and Elder Bruce R. McConkie, regarding the reception of the actual endowment of the Holy Ghost, have said:

> *"I have had the administration of angels in my day and time... and holy messengers... the room was filled with light. He laid before me as if in a panorama, the signs of the last days... But with all these, I have never had any testimony since I have been in the flesh, that has been greater than the testimony of the Holy Ghost" (Wilford Woodruff, "Administration of Angels," 3 March, 1889, in Stuy, Collected Discourses, 1:216-218).*

> *"The promised receipt of the Holy Spirit,* ***as on the day of Pentecost,*** *is the greatest gift a man can receive in mortality" (Bruce R. McConkie, Doctrinal New Testament Commentary, Vol. III, pp. 333-334; emphasis added).*

Why did Elder McConkie refer to this endowment's reception as the greatest gift? Because *without this gift, we are unable to receive the "greater things" which are hid up because of unbelief* (see Ether 4:13-16).

Orson Pratt, in speaking of the reception of the Holy Ghost, said,

> *"The gift and power of the Holy Ghost given to an individual is the greatest evidence that he can receive concerning God, Godliness, and the kingdom of heaven set upon the earth. There is no evidence equal to it.... It is given expressly to impart to mankind a knowledge of the things of God. It is given to purify the heart of man" (Journal of Discourses: 7:178-179).*

Notice that "it is given to purify the hearts of man." And we are also told that "the pure in heart shall see God." As stated by Elder McConkie, it is through receiving the Holy Ghost or First Comforter that we receive this sure, absolute, perfect knowledge and absolute certainty (i.e., "the knowledge of God"), which thereafter "can rest in his soul even though he has not seen the face of the Lord" (*The Promised Messiah,* 592). This ***perfect knowledge*** given to us through the witness of the Holy Ghost (or Comforter) is one of the ways in mortality by which we can truly "know God."

The Lord said, "It is I that granteth unto him that believeth unto the end a place at my right hand. For behold, in my name are they called; ***and if they know me***, they shall come forth, and shall have a place eternally at my right hand" (Mosiah 26:24; emphasis added). The Lord elsewhere defined those who know Him. Those who "receive the [actual] gift of the Holy Ghost…shall know me" (D&C 39:23; emphasis added). And a prerequisite to its reception is the "laying on of hands" performed under the authority of the Melchizedek Priesthood, because this greater priesthood "holdeth the key…, even the key of the knowledge *of* God" (D&C 84:19).

Those who receive the actual Holy Ghost, which is to be born of both water and the Spirit, obtain this "perfect knowledge" of God while in mortality, and endure to the end are those who "know Him" and receive eternal life as promised by the Father (2 Ne. 31:20). In his commentary, the Prophet Joseph says that "being born again comes by the [reception of the] Spirit of God through ordinances" (*Teachings of the Prophet Joseph Smith,* 162; emphasis added).

Now come the "greater things" referenced in Ether 4:13-16. Elder McConkie informs us that

> *"those who have this witness of the Spirit [or that 'perfect knowledge' given at the time of the spiritual rebirth] are expected, like their counterparts of old,* ***to see and hear and touch and converse with the Heavenly Person****, as did those of old" (The Promised Messiah, 592; emphasis added).*

The Holy Ghost can cleanse, sanctify, and make holy through the Lord's direction, for "no unclean thing" can enter the Lord's kingdom. Testimony alone is insufficient. We must be completely cleansed by God Himself.

> *"John answered, saying unto them all, I indeed baptize you with water; but one mightier than I cometh, the latchet of whose shoes I am not worthy to unloose:* ***he shall baptize you with the Holy Ghost and with fire****" (Luke 3:16).*

Receiving the ordinance called "the gift of the Holy Ghost" by the laying on of hands is insufficient to get us there. We must be truly converted, which is when we receive the *actual manifestations of the Holy Ghost* during spiritual rebirth and are both cleansed and healed. President Joseph Fielding Smith explained why many members never receive the gift *and enjoyment* of the Holy Ghost in power:

> *"It is my judgment that there are many members of the Church who have been baptized for the [intended purpose of a] remission of their sins, and who have had hands laid upon their heads for the [intended purpose of receiving the actual] gift [and enjoyment] of the Holy Ghost, but who have never received that gift—that is,* ***the manifestations of it.*** *Why? Because they have never put themselves in order to receive these* ***manifestations.*** *They have never humbled themselves. They have never taken the steps that would prepare them for the companionship of the Holy Ghost. Therefore, they go through life without that knowledge" ("Seek Ye Earnestly the Best Gifts," Ensign, June 1972, 3; emphasis added).*

To more easily understand the ordinance and doctrine of baptism, it would be more accurate to describe baptism as "baptisms," in its plural form, since by definition we must be completely "immersed and overwhelmed" in both elements, water and Spirit. Otherwise, the ordinance is incomplete. A man with proper authority performs the prior and God performs the latter, subject to the fulfillment of the requirements associated with the promised blessing. Or in other words, the actual gift comes through obedience to that law upon which the promised blessing (in this case, the reception and enjoyment of the Holy Ghost in power) is predicated.

Crying Out in Surrender and Commitment

I believe that one of the greatest stumbling stones for us as Latter-day Saints in receiving this "unspeakable gift" of the Holy Ghost and its accompanying perfect knowledge of God arises out of our lack of understanding that although we may belong to His true Church and although we may have received every ordinance available by proper priesthood authority, we must still cry out to Him for His mercy and redemptive power in pure faith, with our entire soul and in complete surrender. The Lord refers to this "crying out" as "calling on my name" (see D&C 39:10; see also Romans 10:13). Tied to this "cry of the soul" (now this is key) is a required *willingness* to consecrate our all, having a rock-solid intention, commitment, and determination to serve Him until the end, irrespective of the sacrifices that may be required of us. And we must then demonstrate our willingness out in the world. The process leading to spiritual rebirth (a powerful, "mighty change of heart") is the process of reaching this level of committed willingness to be "all in," a "risk everything" type of willingness to surrender and commit our very lives to Him—often facilitated by a personal, spiritual crash or other rock-bottom experience. In other words, we will typically find Him in our extremities. How and why else would we come to cry out in surrender with the requisite faith on this level? His mercy and grace require our desire to know Him as intensely as a drowning man desires air.

I had never caught hold of the above principle and never did understand it until after I had received of this gift's influential power in my life. I had thought that through obedience alone, I could be saved. I had assumed salvation would happen of its own accord, over time, if I were just obedient and "endured to the end" through Church service. I now know otherwise. This is a great deception, however, originating from the wicked one. Now is the time for man to prepare to meet God. Literally, here and now. Pay close attention here to Alma's words: "And *never, until* I did cry out unto the Lord for mercy, did I receive a remission of my sins" (Alma 38:8).

How many people do we know (ourselves included) who have "cried out" *with their entire souls* to Christ in complete surrender for His mercy and redemption to both heal and cleanse? How many do we know who have been led to such an experience? And what if it were absolutely required to "cry out" from our whole soul or "call upon His holy name" for mercy, only we just didn't know about it? In my experience, this cry of the soul occurs within a greater context that includes a perpetual yearning of the soul for the Lord's mercy and grace to cover us.

Hear now the word of the Lord: "And all that *call upon the name of the Lord*, and keep his commandments, shall be saved" (D&C 100:17). Zenos, the prophet, in speaking of praying to the Lord, said, "Yea, thou art merciful unto thy children *when they cry unto thee*" (Alma 33:8; emphasis added). This same principle is likewise confirmed in Helaman: "Thus we may see that the Lord is merciful unto all who will, in the sincerity of their hearts, *call upon his holy name* (Helaman 3:27; emphasis added). Amulek taught us to, "**call upon his holy name**, that he would have mercy upon [us]; Yea, cry unto him for mercy; **for he is mighty to save**" (Alma 34:17-18).

Before Adam had been quickened in the inner man and born of God, Enoch says, "Adam *cried unto the Lord*, and he was caught away by the Spirit of the Lord" (Moses 6:64; emphasis added). If the Saints, through the Lord's grace, can understand this prerequisite to spiritual rebirth (and there are others), we as the children of Zion will make great strides in furthering our own salvation and that of those closest to us.

The self-help portions in some of the earlier chapters of this book are designed to lay a foundation for our ability to first become more aware of the Light of Christ within us, thereby facilitating our ability to connect with that Light. Many in the world refer to this Light as "Energy," "Qi" (pronounced "Chee"), "Life Force," Universal Consciousness," "Inner Light," "Buddha-Nature," "Divine Intelligence, "Brahman," "Supreme Cosmic Spirit," "Universal Mind," or "The Tao." In Christianity, it is referred to as "the Holy Spirit" or "Light of Christ."

The self-help portion in mainly chapters 1 and 4 is mostly about creating an increased awareness surrounding the dichotomy between the "higher self" and its opposite, the natural man (or Ego), and the tools to empower the prior and tame the latter. We are all a blend of these two aspects of ourselves stemming from the Fall. The objective is for the prior (or the divine aspect of ourselves) to lead the latter in this relationship. These self-help devices are not meant to replace the reception of the First Comforter that is given to abide in us at the time of spiritual rebirth, but, rather, as tools to prepare us until such time as we are able to qualify for the same. This occurs by way of executing the doctrine of Christ, which will be explored in detail in chapter 7.

Notice that in order to issue forth this cry of the soul in surrender to be saved, we must have first viewed ourselves in an "unsaved" or "unsafe" condition. King Benjamin referred to this as both our "awful situation" (Mosiah 2:40) and as having "viewed [ourselves] in [our] own carnal state, even less than the dust of the earth" (Mosiah 4:2). Without this awareness and the commitment to sacrifice all that may be required of us, the perpetual cry of the soul remains unissued, and conditional salvation is therefore unobtained.

We must desire the redemption of Christ with our whole soul and both ask and plead for deliverance. After entering "the gate" or "door" leading to eternal life we will continue to follow the Light of Christ and the additional endowment of the gift of the Holy Ghost or First Comforter. This gift is given so that we may come to be "perfect in Him" in this life and come to the measure of the stature of the fulness of Christ in the next. Both occur through and by His grace.

A Personal Experience

In late April of 2013, I came to the knowledge of God the Father and God the Son through a manifestation of the Spirit in power, even a knowledge on the same level *as if* I had seen Them. I was forever changed by Christ's redeeming grace, and, as a result, I have not since been able to think much of anything outside of that experience. But this is not just my experience. It is the experience of many today and is available to all who have heard the directive, "Receive the Holy Ghost." Leading up to this perfect knowledge of God or of Their living reality, I had been forced to confront my own mortality, having been led to believe that I was physically dying... and in this extreme spiritual cris-is, I learned that Christ is. This knowledge had been preceded by over two decades of actively seeking Him. I told God in my heart that if He revealed Himself to me, I would do whatever He would ask of me. Through a perpetual cry of the soul to know Him, I experienced a oneness with God and with (seemingly at least) all of His natural creation, which is beyond description.

Jesus Christ is indeed He whom the prophets through the ages have testified that He is. The resultant fruit arising out of this experience left me weeping with gratitude seemingly every night for months. I spoke with a new tongue, issuing forth words of poetic praise to my God. The tears would not let up. Even if there were heavenly license to relate the overall experience, there would simply be no words in any earthly language to convey it.

> *And although we are told to "marvel not" (Mosiah 27:25), I just could not, nor will I ever, cease from marveling. Never did I anticipate such an overwhelming witness in power. Yet through the experience, I had been given the directive to bear testimony as to the holy and sacred reality of spiritual rebirth, known also as being born of God or partaking of the fruit of the Tree of Life, whose fruit is able to fill the human soul "with exceedingly great joy" and is "desirable above all other fruit" (1 Ne. 8:12). The Lord said, "But he that believeth these things which I have spoken, him will I visit with the manifestations of my Spirit,* ***and he shall know and bear record****" (Ether 4:11).*

This work known as *Putting on Christ* is not merely a book to be read, but one to be ***experienced and lived.*** It is my life's calling to write. And of the exceedingly joyful taste of this glorious fruit, I bear record. This work will join other books of a similar nature, all of which are written to bear witness to the Way, the Truth, and the Life, that is Jesus Christ.

The Need for Spiritual Rebirth

As a result of the above personal experience, my whole desire has been to humbly aid in any way within my faint and meager power any who seek to know the Lord. This then is the primary purpose of this book–to introduce people to the process and subsequent "spiritual birthing" by which we can be baptized into Christ (Gal 3:27) and thereby "Put on Christ." The reception and actual enjoyment of this gift, however, is not a guaranteed rite of passage or a forgone conclusion for us as members of the Church. M. Catherine Thomas put it this way:

> *"It seems that there are two parts to any Priesthood ordinance: the receiving of the ordinance and the obtaining of the power associated with that ordinance"* ("King Benjamin and the Mysteries of God," Neal A. Maxwell Institute of Religious Scholarship, see www.publications.mi.byu.edu).

This power is the bestowal of faith as an endowment of power by God, which is made manifest to the candidate of salvation in fulfillment of the Father's promise, resulting in a "mighty change" experience. It is referred to as "the gate" or entrance to the path that leads to eternal life. Most significant is that although there is a large multitude who obtain the fulfillment of the Father's promise overall, there are regrettably few (comparatively speaking) who will find this gate, and even fewer still who will thereafter endure to the end. Christ reaffirmed this truth when he said, "Strive to enter in at the *strait gate*: for many, I say unto you, will seek to enter in, *and shall not be able*" (Luke 13:24; emphasis added).

With that said, take heart and keep this truth and hope in mind. God is not a respecter of persons, and indeed cannot be. We are all on equal footing before Him, and He giveth to all liberally. If we *diligently seek Him*, we shall find and know Him, according to a law and a promise from our Father, covenanted and confirmed upon us through the laying on of hands. It does not matter if we are seeking "the right way," per se. It matters only that *our intention is sincere and authentic in our quest to find the true and living God* and that we are seeking to know Him diligently and steadfastly. Dr. David R. Hawkins suggests that "if inner alignment is with integrity, and inner honesty prevails, the outcome is aligned with the prevailing intention" (David R. Hawkins, "Discovery of the Presence of God," p. 77).

We must seek and learn by study and also by faith, which occurs by going directly to the source of all truth for spiritual direction and knowledge. Our most significant spiritual attainments in this life arise out of this spiritual birthing; this gate. It is the most crucial of all of Heavenly Father's gifts, for all other life-saving gifts or endowments arise out of this one gift—the actual gift of the Holy Ghost, not just the ordinance by the same name. The actual enjoyment, gifts, power, and companionship of this gift as the Holy Ghost or Comforter, is given to abide in us as we pass through the gate.

When Joseph Smith visited the president of the United States during his day, he was asked the difference between the LDS faith and all other Christian religions. Joseph's answer? "The gift of the Holy Ghost." Legrand Richards said, "You take the Holy Ghost out of this Church, and this Church would not be any different than any other Church" ("The Gift of the Holy Ghost," *Ensign,* Nov. 1979, 76). This gift is the most crucial because the Holy Ghost will cleanse, sanctify, and "show [us] all things that [we] should do" so we can know how to make our way back home into God's presence. "The principle of salvation is knowledge," beginning with the knowledge of Jesus Christ. And entering that Divine Presence is likewise attainable in this life, as many have proven in our modern day, the days of Kirtland, and throughout history as recorded in scripture.

Joseph Smith said, now hear it well, "It is the first principle of the Gospel to know for a certainty the Character of God, and to know that we may converse with him as one man converses with another" (*Teachings of the Prophet Joseph Smith,* 345). Do we believe the Prophet? If not, our progress is already being halted. This level of knowledge is one of the "greater things" (see Ether 4:13-16) we can achieve in mortality. Yet in order to obtain any of these "greater things," we must first receive the actual gift and be born of God.

After we are spiritually born again, there is a further sanctifying process, grace for grace and grace to grace, as we endure to the end. This enduring to the end is so much more than being active in the Church. After being "filled with the love of God," we must "endure" in welcoming the sanctifying influence of His Spirit and love so as to be made like unto Christ. As we continue to partake of portions of His light and glory, experienced as inner, spiritual, quickening feelings, we will become infused with more of His attributes in order to attain His "likeness." What makes the gospel come alive for us is experiencing these endowments and heavenly "vistas" while travelling this strait path during our mortal existence.

Imagine two felons who have gone to prison for the same crime. One just "does his time" and leaves prison more hardened than when he went in. He "checked the boxes," if you will. The other does the same time, and yet leaves with a soft and tender spirit and with the love of God in His heart. How did each endure? True, they both "endured" their time in prison. But how did they make use of that time? One chose to further harden his heart and continued to blame circumstances external to him for his predicament. The other turned directly to God through the yearnings of the soul, was given heavenly direction, and followed it.

The Search for Truth

God is leading us through the strivings of His Spirit to give Him our hearts by degrees until we give our hearts in full, which is when we will become fully converted and born of God.

Seeking truth may either consciously or unconsciously become initiated through the inner contemplation of a very subtle yet burning, nagging question. This question will likely be accompanied by an uneasy or unsettling feeling.

That question is…

"*Am I Right with God?*"

To answer this question will require a diligent and ongoing search for truth, even at times from the soul level. When we seek diligently the answer to this question, we will be guided through a spiritual journey of self-discovery, even unto obtaining the actual knowledge as to God's living reality—a knowledge beyond that of faith.

The whole process begins by seeking truth, both from within the Church and without, wherever found. President Brigham Young said, "The truth and sound doctrine possessed by the sectarian world, *and they have a great deal*, all belong to this Church.… There is no truth but what belongs to the Gospel.… If you can find a truth in heaven, earth or hell, it belongs to our doctrine. We believe it; it is ours; we claim it" (*DBY,* 2, 3).

It is my belief that seeking absolute truth wherever it may be found is purposefully designed to keep us in a state of maintaining an open mind. Having an open mind makes us "relatable" to others and allows others to be relatable to us. This facilitates being able to more easily share the gospel of love with others. I believe that an open mind is an attribute and characteristic that is encouraged by God, to be developed in us. Without an open mind, we could not consistently receive the requisite personal revelation that is necessary to be led unto individual salvation. Truth, in all circumstances, is absolute—and Christ is the embodiment of that Truth.

A Disclaimer

You will find many aspects of the Truth found in this work that come from outside the LDS community. Truth, however, is truth, regardless of where it is found. President Brigham Young taught that "it is our duty and calling, as ministers of the same salvation and Gospel, to *gather every item of truth* and reject every error. Whether a truth be found with *professed infidels*, or with … any other of the various and numerous different sects and parties, all of whom have more or less truth, *it is the business of the Elders of this Church … to gather up all the truths in the world* pertaining to life and salvation … *wherever it may be found … and bring it to Zion*" (DBY, 248; emphasis added). So are we doing it? Are we gathering all Truth from throughout the world to bring it to Zion?

I personally took President Young's admonition to heart, and many statements by the non-LDS authors quoted herein stem from my seeking Truth anywhere it can be found. Yet in this regard, I have one word of caution: Although there may be books and authors from which I may quote, it deserves to be plainly and rightfully understood that I do not endorse all things spoken by these authors or all things taught in their respective books. The things I do reference, however, I believe to be Truth, subject to the context in which the specific statements are referenced or discussed. I make no overall or encompassing endorsement of any of these books, with the exception of our canonized, LDS scripture. I leave it to the reader to discern Truth from falsehood by following the same Light of Christ that is freely given to all.

The Prophet Joseph said, "I want the liberty of thinking and believing as I please. It feels so good not to be trammeled" (*DHC,* 5:340). In accord with that stance, I have placed my thoughts and beliefs on these pages. If I happen to err from your perspective, please throw a cloak of charity over any of my perceived failings and I will do the same for you as reader. My views, opinions, beliefs, and, in some cases, actual knowledge are mine alone, for which I take full and complete responsibility. You need not believe or adopt my opinions. In all cases, instead of casually absorbing what I may have to say as being truth, I encourage you to ask God directly, and by this means draw your own conclusions, supported by your own personal revelation. I have no earthly endorsements, nor do I desire, anticipate, or seek any.

The path to God is both straight and strait. "Straight" is directional. "Strait" speaks to the narrowness of the way. The path is both simple and complex. Simple, because even a child can understand it. Simple, because we are being led to know each member of the Godhead, in a specific order: first, the Holy Ghost or the First Comforter; second, Jesus Christ or the Second Comforter; and third, the Father, who is "revealed" by the Son. An actual knowledge of our Deity can happen for all Latter-day Saints, while in mortality and in our individual lifetimes. In fact, I believe it is essential.

Now to the complexity part. The path is complex, because although not overly cumbersome, it takes persistence, steadfastness, and diligence. This "seeking journey" of the actual Christ must become a way of life through desire, and must predominantly occupy our consciousness, every day of our lives. As our gaze is constantly fixed on Him, we are spiritually creating His eventual manifestation, likely even unknowingly, so the knowledge of His reality and power might thereby come to fruition and be fulfilled in our lives. Joseph Smith declared:

> *"The extent of [our] knowledge, respecting His (God's) character and glory, will depend upon [our] diligence and faithfulness in seeking after him, until … [we] shall obtain faith*

> *in God and power with him, to behold him face to face," and "that it was human testimony, and human testimony only, that excited this inquiry ... in [our] minds" and through the credence given to that testimony, "the inquiry ... always terminated when rightly pursued, in the most glorious discoveries and eternal certainty" (Lectures On Faith, 2:55-56).*

This requisite human testimony is one of the reasons why this book contains many modern-day testimonies, in addition to the testimonies of apostles and prophets, which will naturally "excite this inquiry." This diligence and faithfulness in "seeking Christ" cannot be overstated or over-emphasized.

To find "the gate" or entrance to the path, which is both straight and strait, can potentially take decades, even for those who are honest and sincere. That said, finding the gate can also be instantaneous, depending solely on the candidate's level of faith and intensity in seeking, coupled with whole repentance. I believe the latter to be the exception to the rule as the Lord will want to test our willingness first through testing our level of resolve.

Elder Bruce R. McConkie said: "All men must receive the (actual) Holy Ghost in order to be saved. All have power to gain this holy gift, but *few there be that find it"* (*A New Witness* p. 273; emphasis added). In other words, the knowledge of God doesn't just automatically happen. Joseph Smith spoke of the awful situation in the next life, specific to those of us who had not chosen to diligently seek the Lord while in mortality: "The disappointment of hopes and expectations at the resurrection would be indescribably dreadful" *(Teachings of the Prophet Joseph Smith,* p. 336*)*.

This unmet expectation of salvation arises, at least in part, from the "all is well in Zion" numbing prescription that the adversary keeps writing us. And we keep buying what he's selling, and proceed unaware, like lambs to the slaughter. Unless of course, we awaken to our "awful situation." To awaken begins with an initial arousal of our overall awareness of and desire to know our standing before God. Thus, awareness will be the first focus of our spiritual journey.

I liken the effort in finding "the gate" to the energy it takes for a space shuttle to launch from the gravity of our earth into orbit. The Atonement of Jesus Christ provides the faith (power) and His grace (ignition and subsequent fuel) needed to exit the restraints of our natural man's "gravity." Once we make it into "orbit" through our spiritual birthing, we are set free from the previous strength and "gravity" restraints of the natural man and his heavy-laden burdens. Our journey, however, still takes us years of endowments of faith and further sanctification, thereby making us not just clean, but holy men walking this earth. Yet unless we are set free, we cannot make the journey. I have learned that the difficulty is not so much in travelling the straight and narrow path but mostly in actually finding it. The reception and enjoyment of the Holy Ghost is a gift of God unto all those who "diligently seek Him" (1 Ne. 10:17).

Looking back, I now realize I had gone down every rabbit hole imaginable in my own seeking journey, and each time had come up empty handed. For some, there may not be a whole lot here for them, but undoubtedly for others there will surface a treasure of "aha's" and "wow's" that may have otherwise remained hidden. The points discussed in this book are based on my consciousness level. I'm sure I will present ideas that I may enhance, modify, or add to down the road. I view this as personal development.

Regardless of the portion of truth that you may resonate with, what I can assure you is that this book is written with only the purest of intentions and love for my brothers and sisters, fellow seekers of Christ, in that these words will highlight some of the waymarks or guideposts I have encountered along my own journey. I pray they prove helpful within your own seeking journey as well. If you find any statement or point herein that does not resonate with the Light of Christ found in your heart and soul, I would admonish you to disregard it immediately and move on to those that do.

The points of doctrine and my own personal insights have been validated and confirmed to me on countless occasions by way of the spiritual assurances provided me experientially and subjectively, through the Holy Spirit. Given the fact that I had never previously received the Holy Ghost in power in my younger years, I had decided to look elsewhere in my seeking journey, in addition to within my own LDS faith. Looking back, I now know that I had been (mostly) following the Light of Christ within me all along. And even though I had been fairly active in "the Church" throughout my life, I was definitely guilty on occasion of "going through the motions" and "checking boxes" within the overall program of the Church.

My Inner Guide

I was dedicated and consistent in my seeking journey, however flawed that may have been. I sought diligently in the Light of Christ, my inner guide, deep within my soul. This inner guide is sometimes referred to as our intuition or conscience. The word conscience, comes from the Latin word conscientia, or "knowledge within oneself" (https://en.wiktionary.org/wiki/conscientia). Shakti Gawain gives an example of the knowledge that can be accessed through this Light of Christ in her book *Developing Intuition:* "You may ask for an intuitive message in your meditation one morning, but not receive any information. That evening … you may have the impulse to go into a bookstore … and find that you are drawn to a certain table of books. You pick up one of the books, open it randomly and read a paragraph. Suddenly you realize that you are reading exactly what you need to hear at this moment in your life. In fact, this is the answer to the question you had asked that morning."

Many times this impulse and inner yearning may go unnoticed in our conscious minds. This inner yearning, in my opinion, is what was deeply implanted in us to find and experience the love and oneness with God we once knew. This inner yearning, and the impulse to go into a bookstore, was God's light, leading and guiding with that inner spiritual nudge to act. But we must become more aware of these nudges. And then we must act, or else we are not valuing the gift of revelation that has come. And if we don't value these gifts, the gifts will eventually cease coming with the same frequency, or cease coming at all.

This Light of Christ or intuitive voice referenced above is the same Light that awoke me one morning as I was writing this book, with two words that came into my mind. They were "Shakti Gawain." I hadn't read any of Shakti's books for well over 15 years, but this is how the Spirit works. My journey involves, coincidentally, the exact example given by Shakti Gawain of being spiritually led to go into a bookstore. So I obeyed the light in me, walked directly to the self-help section where I was energetically or spiritually drawn, like a laser tractor beam, to one book. In fact, it is the only book in the entire bookstore that I even touched that day.

The book was about allowing our higher self to lead in the relationship within the dichotomy of the ego (natural man) and our higher or divine spirit within. The name of the book was *Your Sacred Self,* by Dr. Wayne W. Dyer. As I continued perusing the book, *an aliveness came over me* which I now know to have been the Light of Christ. I knew that this book was what I needed at this precise time in my life. I knew that the "God force" within me had lovingly nudged me to go to that exact bookstore at that exact time in order to obtain that exact book. This book was not *the* beginning, but it was certainly *a* beginning. What I learned over time is that we can, through using various tools, tame the beast of the natural man (ego), but because of the tenacity of the ego, there is only one who could completely overcome it, and that person is Jesus Christ.

Further along my spiritual journey, I learned other truths. For example, I learned we are coming unto Christ in a very literal way. We are to seek Him. The Church is the scaffolding needed to work on the temple of "us." *We are the temple of God.* We need to receive his gospel in order to be saved. The Church of Jesus Christ of Latter-day Saints provides the necessary ordinances with the required priesthood authority, without which we could not receive the fullness of the "exceeding great and precious promises" available that were referenced by the apostle Peter (see 2 Peter 1:4). "Therefore, in the ordinances thereof, the power of godliness is manifest" (D&C 84:20-21). And for those who may have not been afforded access to these ordinances in mortality, a perfectly loving, fair, and just God shall provide the same opportunity to those in the spirit world, "that they might be judged according to men in the flesh, but live according to God in the Spirit" (1 Peter 4:6).

Some who are struggling with issues they may have with the Church, parts of its history, or its culture (as many have had) may feel upset about the notion that the ordinances for salvation and exaltation can only be obtained from those holding the requisite Priesthood keys, performed by those holding actual authority from God. Was it any different in the primitive Church? It can definitely be a stumbling stone. We see the dysfunction within the culture of the Church and our people, and tend to, unfortunately, lump them together with the Church, its traditions, the gospel, or all three. As a result, many of us end up throwing the baby out with the proverbial bath water. I strongly caution all to stay the course. We can all overcome any issues we may have with any past negative experiences with the Church, its history, its members, leaders, or its culture by keeping our lives focused on Christ. Jesus Christ is the rock upon which we must build. "And now, my sons, remember, remember that it is upon the rock of our Redeemer, who is Christ, the Son of God, that ye must build your foundation" (Helaman 5:12).

For those of us who may be struggling with their testimony for one reason or another with the Church, we have two choices. We can either choose to remain in and make a difference for the better or choose to fall out. If we choose to be out, our influence may be completely marginalized and our ability to effect change and bring people to Christ almost nil. We may also, more likely than not, even lose our inheritance. Study 4 Nephi intently. Even when after 200 years since Christ's visit the wheels were coming off the cart of the Church, so to speak, the three Nephites *never left the Church.* They stayed on task, lifting the members wherever they could, even until the time in which "there were none [within the church] that were righteous save it were the disciples of Jesus" (4 Ne. 1:46). This is the type and pattern for us as well.

If we choose to be in, we can inspire and make a huge impact and difference on many. If the old ship Zion is taking on water, find the holes and plug as many of them as you possibly can. Then start bailing water with all your might! Remember. It is His Church. Do all within your power, then turn any concerns you may have back over to God, in quiet acceptance and peace. Simply choose to be part of the "few, who are the humble followers of Christ" (2 Nephi 28:14).

The Children of Zion under Condemnation

And what will our Lord say, He who has acknowledged his displeasure with us, placing all of us as the children of Zion under condemnation (see D&C 84:54-56)? He would say what He already has said: Treasure all scripture you have been given (D&C 84:57) and "*concern yourselves not with the affairs of my Church.*" Your job is to "*purify your hearts before me.*" (See D&C 112:23-28; emphasis added). In other words, He is saying, "I am God. I've got this. This is *My* Church. When expedient in me, I'll steady the ark and Church of God, as God." We must never lose sight of this. We can either make it about "out there" (i.e., "the Church," the world, and all that we may perceive as wrong with it) or we can place our focus on that which we do have control over—purifying what's "in here," or within our own hearts, accomplished by surrendering to and loving God. Stay the course. We have more than enough to be concerned with in purifying our own hearts, rather than worrying about all the perceived wrongs we may see in our Church, our community, and in our world. Christ said, "If they have not charity, it mattereth not unto thee, thou hast been faithful;

wherefore, thy garments shall be made clean" (Ether 12:37; emphasis added). Focus on cleansing "the inside of the cup" rather than on the distractions that come from highlighting the imperfections of others, whether within or without the Church.

Instead of criticizing, we may first want to focus on *being the change* we would wish to see in the overall membership of the Church and thereby inspire others to *be* that same change, starting at the ward level and expanding outward. Then as the children of Zion, we can work to expand that mindset, awareness, and love to the stakes, regions, and finally to the ends of the earth throughout the entire Church. The change needs to happen first within the hearts of us, the individual members. This is where Zion begins. We need to stop relying on "the Brethren" or the Church alone to spiritually spoon feed us. This is what Isaiah's prophecy was speaking to when he addressed Ephraim's need to be "weaned from the milk, and drawn from the breasts" (Isaiah 28:9). And this, by the way, is not a knock on "the Brethren" or the Church. It's a knock on us, the children of Zion and body of Christ. We only need turn to God, the author and finisher of our faith. As we do, the wearied traveler continues his very personal journey to Christ, and all the while the caravan of the gospel program, administered by Christ's restored Church, moves on…

> *What does it matter if a few barking dogs snap at the heels of the weary travelers? Or that predators claim those few who fall by the way? The caravan moves on.*
>
> *Is there a ravine to cross, a miry mud hole to pull through, a steep grade to climb? So be it. The oxen are strong and the teamsters wise. The caravan moves on.*
>
> *Are there storms that rage along the way, floods that wash away the bridges, deserts to cross, and rivers to ford? Such is life in this fallen sphere. The caravan moves on.*
>
> *Ahead is the celestial city, the eternal Zion of our God, where all who maintain their position in the caravan shall find food and drink and rest. Thank God that the caravan moves on! [Bruce R. McConkie, "The Caravan Moves On," Ensign, Nov. 1984, p. 85].*

We have the scriptures before us. The power is within us. We have the Light of Christ speaking to us, all the day long, whether we are aware or not. Many have the amplified version of this light through the Comforter given at the time of spiritual rebirth. A select few "have also a more sure word of prophecy," which if we "take heed" and follow the "light that shineth in a dark place," the day [will] dawn, and the day star arise in [our] hearts" (2 Peter 1:19). We have the ordinances performed by proper authority. The promises contained in the ordinances are given to us. The Prophet Joseph Smith reinforced Isaiah's prophecy when he spoke to our slothfulness in not turning directly to God ourselves instead of becoming overly dependent on himself as the prophet. Joseph told the early Saints "that the people should each one stand for himself, and ***depend on no man***... that righteous persons would only deliver their own souls (through faith in Christ), [and] ... said if the people departed from the Lord, they must fall—***that they were depending on the Prophet*** [meaning, "***alone*** on the Prophet," without the accompanying confirming witness of the Holy Ghost], hence were ***darkened in their minds***" (*Teachings of the Prophet Joseph Smith,* p. 237; emphasis added).

As we seek and obtain the coveted spiritual rebirth, we will become securely reliant upon God through the reception, enjoyment, and power of the Holy Ghost or Comforter, who will "show unto [us] all things that [we] should do" (2 Nephi 32:5). Thereafter, no one will ever again need remind us to minister to a select few. We will desire to minister to the entire world.

My Experiential Journey to Spiritual Rebirth

As for my personal journey, I had arrived at a place where I decided that I would put all my belief systems on the shelf, with the exception of God. I wanted to start all over with a clean slate. Every belief system that had been poured into me since childhood was reevaluated. I just wanted to learn what the truth was from God directly so I could then follow it. I started with the temporary removal of all belief systems (and I don't recommend this as there is an easier way—that of purposefully executing the doctrine of Christ), and I began to seek God and the Truth in earnest.

After many years, despite consistent reading of spiritual works and engaging in meditation, I eventually found myself in a spiritual panic, one of total desperation and despair. I intensely desired to know the truth and the true Messiah, yet I continued to still come up empty in my search. This despair was preceded by three trips to the emergency room spanning a period of about 18 months. On each occasion in the emergency room, I wholly believed that I was dying as I had feelings of sharp pins and needles throughout my entire body. The doctors performed EKGs, CT scans, and MRIs. They found nothing. Yet the symptoms persisted, and *I just knew I was dying.* This belief that I was literally facing the end of my own mortality instilled in me the desperate need to be right with God—at any and all cost. My standing before God became the only thing that mattered.

I finally committed to pin all of my hopes for salvation on one man—Jesus Christ of Nazareth. If I were wrong about Him and ended up "going down with the ship," so to speak, I could think of no other man as good and as kind as Jesus with whom I would rather perish, if I was to perish at all. I had been diligently seeking answers as to who or what God was for over two decades. I continued to cry out (mostly subconsciously) within my soul to God to know who or what the truth was so that I could follow it. I had desired so much and for so long to know the truth and the true Messiah, that I was "willing" to do anything and everything He asked—if He would only reveal Himself to me. I had to know Him, perhaps even to the degree that my own sanity depended upon it. My internal "soul cry" was very similar to that of King Lamoni's father: "Yea, what shall I do that I may be born of God, having this wicked spirit [of the natural man] rooted out of my breast, and receive his Spirit, that I may be filled with joy, that I may not be cast off at the last day? Behold, said he, I will give up all that I possess, yea, I will forsake my kingdom, that I may receive this great joy" (Alma 22:15).

Notice how this level of consecration, sacrifice, commitment, and "willingness" ties into our sacrament prayer: "that they may... witness... that they are willing to take upon them the name of thy son." I had finally gone into the depths of humility within my repentance process and held nothing back. I stood before God figuratively naked. I eventually decided to pin *all my hopes for salvation on one man, Jesus Christ the person, to the extent that if I were wrong about Him, I would rather not exist*. I "burned all my boats," so to speak, making it impossible to retreat. There was one way, and one way only, and that was through. I would have preferred annihilation, or at least so I thought. *I just had to know Him*. This extreme desire of *having to know Him* is what led me into my spiritual panic, as the knowledge of Him had not come, even after so many years of seeking. I was growing weary in my mind, and ready to spiritually faint.

Unbeknownst to me at the time, I fulfilled a requirement in some law that had previously remained hidden from my view. I guess you could say that I had exercised, through the grace and gift provided, whole, pure, and perfect faith in Jesus Christ, *relying alone upon His merits*. Another way of saying this is that I did not rely, in any degree, upon my own merits or works. For years I had persistently cried out, but it had never been previously tied to the requisite "willingness" and commitment to be "all in" with Him.

After having exercised full purpose of heart in both my repentance process and in exercising that sufficiency of faith required, the Truth was finally found. He was found! And in finding the Truth, I received unspeakable joy. I learned with a perfect brightness and clarity, a revealed perfect knowledge, through an unmistakable experience lasting several days and nights, that Jesus Christ was that Truth I had been seeking. I could speak with a new tongue. I had tasted of God's quickening influence. Tears were shed, words of praise spoken, and even more tears flowed.

For months, I could not stop myself from daily weeping in gratitude. I was weary and had found rest to my soul. I now KNEW! I wanted to shout it from the rooftops! Praise, tears, and more praise! I now knew with a *perfect brightness* of knowledge that I had been redeemed—that I had received a complete remission of all of my sins and that Jesus Christ and the Father live and are real! Christ was and is the promised Messiah! I knew that if I endured to the end in this same state of purity of heart and righteousness with which the Holy Ghost wrought in me, I would obtain eternal life. I experienced the same unspeakable joy and knowledge as delivered by King Benjamin, "that thereby whosoever should believe…, the same might receive remission of their sins, and rejoice with exceedingly great joy, *even as though he had already come among them"* (Mosiah 3:13; emphasis added).

Joseph Smith referred to the Holy Ghost, as *the same* (i.e., experientially identical or "alike") as given on the day of Pentecost: "There are two comforters spoken of. One is the Holy Ghost, *the same* as given on the day of Pentecost" (*Teachings of the Prophet Joseph Smith,* p.149; see also Acts 2). This was my experience. The Second Comforter, as we know, includes the personal visitation of Jesus Christ.

My son-in-law Mark asked me if I would share again my rebirth or full conversion story with him. This is what I wrote back to him, and I wish to share it with you as well:

> *I need to write down in depth that which led up to it, but there is really no way to describe the experience in words. The word Pentecostal is what was revealed to me at the time, having inquired of the Lord from my heart to know, but prior to that I had never had any experience even remotely close or similar to this one, and certainly not "Pentecostal-like." Other words that most closely describe it but totally fail are "Manifestation," "Partaking of his Glory," "Indescribable Joy and Peace," "Knowing God," "Overwhelming Love of God," Partaking of a "Christ Consciousness," and experiencing "Spiritual Union with God." It is the "taste of Oneness" for which Christ prayed to the Father for us to receive" (John 17:19-26). And through enduring to the end, we might not only taste of His everlasting glory, but have a fulness thereof throughout all eternity.*
>
> *Would this mighty experience not create a "mighty change" in all of us? Nothing else but Him thereafter would even ever matter! Even the words "mighty change" would seem like the greatest understatement ever uttered. It makes me long to return and not even remain here, Mark. I miss Him.*

(Perhaps that's the whole point, by the way. Perhaps God wants us to miss Him so badly that we'd never desire to stray thereafter).

Then I shared these verses with Mark from Christ out of the New Testament:

> *"And for their sakes I sanctify myself, that they also might be sanctified through the truth. "Neither pray I for these alone, but for them also which shall believe on me through their word; "THAT THEY ALL MAY BE ONE; as thou, Father, art in me,*

and I in thee, THAT THEY ALSO MAY BE ONE IN US, that the world may believe that thou hast sent me. "And THE GLORY which thou gavest me I have given them; that they may be ONE, EVEN AS WE ARE ONE: "I in them, and thou in me, that they may be made perfect in one; and that the world may know that thou hast sent me, and hast loved them, as thou hast loved me."

"And I have declared unto them thy name, and will declare it: that the love wherewith thou hast loved me may be in them, and I in them" (JOHN 17:19-23, 26; emphasis added).

Allow me to draw our attention to a question and answer by Joseph Smith as found in the *Lectures On Faith* that highlight this Oneness:

> *"Do the believers in Christ Jesus, through the gift of the Spirit [i.e., the actual reception of the Holy Ghost], become one with the Father and the Son, as the Father and Son are one?" Smith's Answer: "**They do**"* (see Lecture 5:19).

Christ Himself spoke to the above. "And I will pray the Father, and he shall give you another Comforter, that he may abide with you for ever; Even the Spirit of Truth; whom the world cannot receive, because it seeth him not, neither knoweth him: but ye know him; for he dwelleth with you, *and shall be in you*. At that day ye shall *know* that I am *in* my Father, and ye *in* me, and I *in* you" (John 14: 16-17, 20).

This Oneness spoken of is to partake of a God Consciousness—to partake of Their Consciousness (see David O. McKay, "Consciousness of God, Supreme Goal of Life," Conference Report, April 1967). It is not only to become "one in purpose," as I had been taught my whole life. And although this heightened level of consciousness does not remain as a permanent endowment, at least in my experience, it can be enjoyed by all when we receive the Holy Ghost as a gift.

I then shared some additional insight with Mark that, although it is not all that I experienced, it is what I can at least attempt to share, since there are no words that can convey the experience:

> ***The Oneness experienced was not just with the Deity, as we know Them to be, and They are real, but a Oneness seemingly with all of nature and the physical and spiritual world around me as well. The trees, the plants, the birds, and every living thing, at least in my immediate environment, seemed to be communing with me, and I too with them, through this unseen love and light which seemed to permeate all things. Everyone and everything appeared radiantly beautiful to me.***

Ultimately, spiritual rebirth can only really be described as "indescribable." Nothing else can compare to it in this world. It includes being filled with God's love to the degree that I became seemingly in love with all things living. My personal will seemed to have become completely intertwined with the Divine will. I wanted to hug everyone, including complete strangers, and share what I was feeling inside with them. And I often did, which truly startled some. The experience also included and was followed by an immense and profound peace that the scriptures refer to as "the peace of God, which passeth all understanding" (Philippians 4:7).

During this experience, I felt so perfectly ready to be taken from this earth. And although I longed for my heavenly home, had I been given the option, I would have chosen to remain here to assist my family to find this same gate and to partake of the same fruit that I had enjoyed.

> *The remission of sins and sure promise of eternal life as part of the Redemption of Christ when one is born of God, together with the oneness with and perfect knowledge of the Deity, particularly in terms of Their absolute, manifested reality, are the preeminent gifts obtained during spiritual rebirth. This is full conversion, even as on the day of Pentecost. This is "the knowledge of God" or "the knowledge of the Lord" spoken of in scripture that we may all obtain in mortality.*

To bake this cake of actual knowledge will require the three ingredients of intensely desiring to know God, exercising faith in Him as a real, exalted being (not one of past or future but the very Christ found in our "now" or present moment), and diligently seeking Him until He is found. We must find Him as part of our "present," so that we may ultimately dwell in His Presence. When this "cake" is baked properly, the knowledge *of* God will be obtained, not just *about* God. Joseph taught, "For there is a great difference between believing in God and knowing Him—knowledge implies more than faith" (see *Lectures On Faith*, p. 77). And so it is.

This knowledge is obtained through the experiential oneness for which Christ yearned and prayed in His great intercessory prayer. In my own experience, even though I "knew" exactly what was happening to me, the following words still came to my mind: *"You are being born of the Spirit."* I found these words to be extremely self-evident as well as revealing. These words were obviously not my own thoughts, because they started with the word *You*. Some third party was actually speaking to my mind as I was experiencing this transcendent *manifestation* which filled me with spiritual fire. Was it the Father? Was it the Son? Was it the Holy Ghost? Since they are one, we could accurately affirm that the answer to the above questions to be yes, yes, and yes!

Experiencing this oneness and obtaining the knowledge of God is what President Ezra Taft Benson meant when he said, "When you choose to follow Christ, *you choose to be changed.*" He described this "changed feeling" as indescribable and as something "real." And he was right on both counts. He also described it as "*one of the most widespread of Christ's modern miracles*" (Ezra Taft Benson, "Born of God," general conference, October, 1985). Jacob suggests, "For why not speak of the atonement of Christ, and attain to a perfect knowledge of him…"? (Jacob 4:12). I say, great question! Why not?

By way of my own witness, I was not consciously seeking to know whether the "Church was true." I was just searching to know God or who "the Truth" was. I had found so much deception, conning, and lies in this world, and so many different religions and philosophies originating from who knows where, that I had to know Him and couldn't leave it alone. I remember on several occasions just weeping while lying in my wife's lap telling her that I just wanted to know the Truth and who God was. I believe in part that it was in my refusal to "let it go" or give up on seeking to know the truth of God that brought me to a point of desperation, despair, and spiritual panic. It was shortly after this process that I found Him. And if I were to be completely honest with myself, I really had hoped deep down that Jesus was indeed that Truth, for I had loved Jesus deep within my heart all of my life.

> *He is "the Way" by means of the light that we follow within our hearts and centers of our souls (beginning as our intuition or conscience). He is the Truth, because all truth rests, abides, and is centered in Him and in His light forever. And that light is literally found in us and throughout the immensity of space, permeating all things. He is the Life, because if it were not for His light that is in us (and in everything), together with His offering through the Atonement, none of us could abide, "for in him we live, and move, and have our being"* (Acts 17:28).

This, my first endeavor in writing, started out as a labor of love for my wife, four beautiful daughters, sons-in-law, extended family, and posterity. Then the directive came, followed by many spiritual assurances, that I was to make this available to a much broader audience. The Lord often uses the weak of the world to further his purposes.

If we open ourselves to Christ and His light in faith, we will be guided *experientially* through the process, which will leave us all eternally weeping as a result of God's merciful and amazing grace, a grace for which so fully He proffers us. Oh, it is wonderful, indeed.

Eyes to See

For those with eyes to see, the temple endowment is symbolic of our own heroic, spiritual journey leading to the veil and the literal, tear-soaked feet of Christ while yet in mortality. It requires that our gaze be purposefully and squarely placed on the path that lies beyond the veil—our true home. Our view of this world must fade into the background. At some point during this spiritual journey, we will feel many angels around us. Our homes will feel much more like a temple than a home. If we are to spiritually understand the scope and beauty of this majestic path, and receive true vision, we must acquire eyes to see and ears to hear. This hearing and seeing starts with desire, which may be preceded by the practice of loving God as well as self-introspection and honest, inner self-inquiry. This inquiry further promotes our desire, awareness, and the softening of our hearts and the opening of our minds in a greater degree to God so that we can receive His light and spiritual understanding. It promotes the desire to be right with God at all costs.

> *This is where we pause. This is where deep contemplation occurs. This is where we decide whether we're in or out. The Lord is patiently awaiting our decision in choosing the level of consecrated sacrifice and "willingness" that is required. When we choose to be "all in" with Him, He chooses to receive us by adopting us into His family as his sons and his daughters.*

We must be willing to let go of all that we think we know. Our hearts and minds must remain open to receive the light, just as little children. As this increased light and faith expands within us, it will lead us to "act in gospel belief" and actually do the things Christ did by emulating Him, or in a way, "pretending" as would a little child, that we are just like Jesus. We will be led to comfort those who mourn, to succor the weak, to lift up the hands which hang down, and to strengthen the feeble knees, and by this means we will come closer unto Christ. (See D&C 81:5-7.) These "hands on" experiences, together with proper broken-hearted repentance, then promote and bestow on us a living faith as a gift or endowment from God, through the fulfilling of the law associated with the promised blessing.

Through this faith and light, along with our inner longing and desire to know God and His Truth, we can be led through a process to the climatic heights of full conversion and become born of God. After spiritual rebirth, we connect with and hold to a newfound yet curiously familiar spiritual feeling. We become filled with Christ's light, and the scales fall quickly from our eyes so that we see things as they really are. We are then able to receive spiritual knowledge and understanding and grow in sanctification, grace *for* grace, and grace *to* grace. We literally become spiritually taught by God, no longer by the arm of the flesh. The path becomes deliciously real to us, and our hungering and thirsting for Christ becomes insatiable. This then leads us to acquire, through the gift of grace, additional faith. Faith is then heaped upon faith. And this mounting, cumulative faith continues to build into an eruption of spiritual knowledge. This cycle repeats itself and gradually rids us of all unbelief, while at the same time revealing the spiritual waymarks and knowledge of the straight and narrow path, which leaves us emotionally spent and spiritually in awe, unable to express in any language the shear wonderment that God, through His grace, has mercifully allowed us to behold. The ultimate step is one that each one of us must take on our own, for no one else can take it for us. And that step is to rend the veil and actually know God, eye to eye, here and now. This too is not for the faint of heart.

I pray that these words and the intention and spirit behind them may through God's grace find their way into your hearts, that we may all receive of "that joy which is unspeakable and full of glory" (Helaman 5:44). Alma's words are therefore my words, from the depth of my soul: "Yea, and from that time even until now, I have labored without ceasing, that I might bring souls unto repentance; that I might bring them to taste of the exceeding joy of which I did taste; that they might also be born of God, and be filled with the Holy Ghost" (Alma 36:24).

Chapter 1

Ground Zero - The Battle Over the Heart.

"The Holy Ghost is a revelator." "No man can receive the Holy Ghost without receiving revelations." (Teachings of the Prophet Joseph Smith, p. 328).

On May 16th of 2015, during the process of writing this book and a little more than two years after my spiritual rebirth, I received a beautiful, tender mercy in the form of a gift of spiritual knowledge. Unexpected yet impactful, it involved the very real and ongoing spiritual battle over my heart and involved the heart's ability to intuitively feel in order to be led. The purpose of this knowledge, as I now see it, was to provide the theme, context, and initial chapter of this book. It is a continuation of the battle that began for us all in our pre-earth life as spirit children. Although the information was intended for my own personal walk, the principles involved can profit all on this mortal journey.

The majority came by way of a linear diagram, which I will discuss in detail later in this work. It includes the following principles: Each of our individual spiritual battles involve the ongoing, daily fight to maintain our hearts—soft, tender, and open to God—so that we might ultimately receive ongoing spiritual knowledge through contact with the Light of Christ (experienced mostly as spiritual perception, including impressions that arrive by way of intuitive feelings), guiding us through faith to the knowledge of God and salvation. Said in simpler terms, *obtaining the knowledge of God and salvation through His light (by faith) requires that we acquire and preserve an open and tender heart*. Doing so will allow us to sense His guidance and feel our way back to Him.

The adversary and his followers are intent on hardening our hearts by any means at their disposal, thereby preventing us from being able to intuitively feel. Feeling, which enables us to acquire most *life-saving knowledge*, comes by way of an open and tender heart. As outlined in the preface, "The principle of salvation is given us through *the knowledge of Jesus Christ*" (Joseph Smith, *Teachings of the Prophet Joseph*

Smith, p. 297). Salvation comes through receiving the knowledge *of* Jesus Christ, not merely knowledge ***about*** Him. The actual knowledge *of* Christ is the gateway to all other "knowledges" necessary for a ***more sure*** salvation, including that of entering His presence in mortality. Joseph Smith taught:

> *"Having power by faith to obtain **the knowledge of God**, they could **with it** [meaning, the knowledge of God, which when received, sanctifies the recipient and brings the enjoyment of the Comforter] obtain <u>all other things</u> which pertain to life and godliness" (Lectures On Faith, 7:18; emphasis added).*

"Accordingly, those who are saints indeed, those who have been born again, those who are so living as to be in tune with the Spirit—they are they who receive revelation, personal revelation, revelation which is the mind and will of God to them as individuals. They know there are apostles and prophets directing the kingdom who receive revelation for the Church and the world. But they as individuals receive personal revelation in their own affairs. *And there are no restrictions placed upon them; there are no limitations as to what they may see and know and comprehend.* No eternal truths will be withheld, if they obey the laws entitling them to receive such truths" (Bruce R. McConkie, "Rock of Salvation," Conference Report, October 1969, pp. 79-84).

"All other things," as referenced in *Lectures On Faith,* are revealed line upon line to the recipients of salvation because the Comforter, whom they have fully received, is He who "showeth all things," beginning with His witness of the Father and the Son. "And then cometh the baptism of fire and the Holy Ghost, even the Comforter, which *showeth all things*" (D&C 39:6). In other words, it is through the Comforter, Who accompanies this witness, that we obtain "conditional" salvation. This is when we are born of God. "The knowledge of God" is synonymous with having received the Holy Ghost or *First Comforter*. To receive one is to receive the other. And when we receive the Holy Ghost, He bears record through a manifestation *in power* as to the reality and divinity of the Father and the Son in an unmistakable, soul-changing way: hence the term *mighty change* (see Alma 5:12-14). Notice Joseph Smith's translation: "And in that day, the Holy Ghost fell upon Adam, *which beareth record of the Father and the Son*" (JST Genesis 4:9; emphasis added).

When the Holy Ghost "beareth record" by way of a heavenly manifestation, we receive *the knowledge of God.* The revelatory light given through the Comforter, when received in power as our constant companion then becomes the dynamic, living, and indwelling "roadmap of our heroic journey to spiritual rebirth and beyond" because, in addition to its cleansing and purifying effect, it opens up the way to obtain "all other things." These *other things* include all we need to know to make our way back to the Father. Or, as Elder McConkie taught us, "The Lord wants his saints to receive... truth upon truth, revelation upon revelation, until we know all things and have become like him" ("Rock of Salvation," Conference Report, October 1969, pp. 79-84). No "arm of the flesh" can lead us there. Even well-intentioned, holy, and inspired men can only lead us (individually speaking) so far along the straight and narrow path. At some point, our hungering and thirsting must of necessity transcend into *direct experience with Deity*. The Prophet Joseph Smith insisted that "*true religion was one of individual participation in revelation [or in other words, "personal experience"] from God*" (*The Words of Joseph Smith,* p. 21, emphasis added). If we hunger and thirst, the Lord has promised that we shall be blessed by being "filled with the Holy Ghost" (3 Ne. 20:27). There is no other experience like it, and once received we will never again be the same.

The battle over the hearts of men is considered "Ground Zero" in the spiritual war that began in our pre-earth life. We need to remain in a state that allows us to "feel our way" back to God. The adversary, on the other hand, wants us to become past feeling in our hearts. That's why the heart is at the epicenter of this war and is the focus of both sides of the battle today. Without being able to *feel our way*, we will become lost. By continuing to follow the Light of Christ, we can be led to experience the great healing power of Jesus Christ Himself and have our hearts healed and natures changed by Him in a mighty way.

And what is our part in this battle? Simply this: anything we can do to get people to soften their hearts towards God, to get them to come unto Christ by receiving His gospel and enduring through faith in His light, is to work in alignment and in divine partnership with Him.

Almost immediately after learning this important truth, I heard an interview of former atheist Howard Storm as he told of his life-changing near-death experience. While physically dead and on the other side of the veil, an angel taught him:

> *"God works by changing people's hearts, and God wants all of us to be working towards the same end.... What God wants is conversion of the heart"* ("Stunning and Life Changing NDE, 2001," Minutes 1:09:30 & 1:11:38, Youtube).

Wow—here was another witness! We are to be engaged in facilitating a change in people's hearts—even a conversion! The questions that subsequently arise are: "What does that change look like?" and, "What type of involvement is God looking for from us in facilitating this change?"

Ultimately, God wants us to maintain soft and open hearts so that we may be guided through feeling our way to ultimately experience or taste of His grace and salvation—how we ultimately become converted to the Lord. This guidance will come line upon line, precept upon precept, and may culminate in an experience wherein we obtain the perfect knowledge of the reality of the Father and the Son. Will all experience it? No. But it is available for all. (One method of amplifying our efforts is to sincerely embrace the first and great commandment and seek God from our heart during meditative "alone time" with Him.)

As we experientially "practice loving God," as we would practice any art form, we will not only become proficient, but our hearts will remain as fertile soil in which He may plant within us portions of faith and spiritual knowledge.

The Word of God is often that personal revelation which reaches us through the *still small voice* in the form of the quiet whisperings within the heart and soul of man (D&C 8:2-3). But if that heart is not tender and open, we will not be able to feel, and since the Spirit works *through feelings* in our heart, the requisite spiritual knowledge will not be able to find its intended destination. We must remain aware and vigilant, holding to this understanding as with a vice-grip.

An awareness over the state of our heart, including a constant, self-monitored awareness of our ability to perceive and intuitively feel from the same, is essentially necessary for our individual salvation.

We will, therefore, now turn to a greater understanding of awareness, specifically the awareness over the state of our hearts and of our hearts' ability to intuitively *perceive, feel, and sense* Truth and God's loving direction in our lives.

Awareness

"Awareness, according to an online dictionary, is the ability to perceive, *to feel*, or to be conscious of events, objects, thoughts, emotions, or sensory patterns. In this level of consciousness, sense data can be confirmed by an observer without necessarily implying understanding. More broadly, it is the state or quality of being aware of something. Awareness is a sister to living consciously" (see "Awareness," Wikipedia).

Our agency involves choosing either more awareness or less awareness. We may choose to remain asleep and adopt less awareness because we think that in so doing, life will become easier. We may choose less awareness because we may not want to face the pain associated with the truth that we see in our character—the truth that we are not living in alignment with the very God of Truth who created us. We may subsequently attempt to run and hide from the truth and the pain, thinking that it will just miraculously go away of its own accord.

But ultimately, we find out that it doesn't always just go away. Our issues and pain often become further magnified and compounded. We will eventually come to realize that any and all spiritual error will eventually be manifested through some form and degree of pain. Anything that we may be holding on to that is not in alignment with the truth and purpose of our creation will manifest this way. Pain, then, can become a blessing, for it can provide an opportunity to ask God of that pain's cause, which is typically a "truth" that has been buried and not allowed to surface to our conscious awareness. With our commitment to awareness, however, we are then able to confront the issue tied to our pain head on, ultimately "undoing" or resolving the core issue and root cause of the pain, be it spiritual or emotional.

We use all types of avoidance mechanisms to stay unconscious and bury our pain. Some of those mechanisms include overindulgent work habits and zoning out with excessive television, media, social media, or any number of mechanisms in which we may distract ourselves. We may also do it by taking a deep dive into various addictions. Shakti Gawain says that "we avoid the things that we're afraid of because we think there will be dire consequences if we confront them. But the truly dire consequences in our lives come from avoiding things that we need to learn about or discover" (*Path of Transformation,* p. 172). Truly, the only way out is through. We must confront our issues head on, as painful as that process may seem or appear.

Joseph Smith said, "All will suffer until they obey Christ himself." This statement allows for one of the greatest realizations ever granted us. We will continue to suffer, and watch the same movie repeating itself over and over again throughout our lives, unless and until we become aware of the voice of God within us and heed its promptings. The Prophet Joseph Smith's statement, by the way, is not some cleverly devised way to scare us into submission. God does not work this way. His statement is merely a statement of fact. How much pain are we willing to endure until we are willing to finally surrender to the One who can give us peace and freedom in this world and immortal glory in the world to come? The Lord has said, "My people must needs be *chastened until they learn obedience*, if it needs be, *by the things which they suffer*" (D&C 105:6; emphasis added). In other words, if we learn to become obedient to that inner voice that steers us clear of impending physical, spiritual, and emotional dangers, we may suffer less.

We intuitively know that it is not beneficial to remain unaware or unconscious. In fact, it is much more difficult to live a life devoid of awareness. So we are constantly presented with a choice of becoming more aware or less aware, more conscious or less conscious. Our decision to live in awareness, often arising out of immense suffering, is the signal to God that we are finally ready to listen, be taught, and be led. We will have finally begun to *open our minds and let go of what we think we know.* We will have then begun to finally *open our hearts* to understand His divine will for our destiny, which includes that fulness of joy which is in store for the elect who heed His voice and follow His light.

An Introduction to the Three Essential Stations of Awareness unto Salvation

We will now focus our attention on three essential stations of awareness facilitating our salvation: (1) awareness of the current state of our hearts, (2) awareness of dark influences, and (3) awareness of God's involvement in our lives.

Our ability to feel is the first station. It begins with the awareness of the current spiritual state of our heart, whether hard or soft, using our awareness to sense whether we are able to intuitively feel. This may include asking ourselves if we feel a connection to our own soul or inner self. This awareness is absolutely essential if we are to both find the gate of spiritual rebirth and endure to the end. We must remain vigilant and aware so as not to allow darkness to infiltrate and harden our hearts, thereby closing off our minds in unbelief. When a hardening of the heart happens, we lose our ability to perceive, sense, and feel our way. Gerald N. Lund taught: "...carefully assessing the condition of our hearts is one of the most essential things we can do in this life" (Gerald N. Lund, "Opening Our Hearts," 2008 General Conference).

God said to the Prophet Joseph, "Behold, thou art Joseph, and thou wast chosen to do the work of the Lord, but because of transgression, *if thou art not aware*, thou wilt fall" (D&C 3:9; emphasis added). The same goes for us. If we are not aware, we too will fall. *This preeminent awareness concerning the ongoing battle to keep our hearts soft and tender is not just a one-off; it is a lifelong endeavor.* By maintaining a soft heart, we maintain our ability to feel, which gives the Light of Christ constant access to our hearts.

This leads to our second essential station of awareness unto salvation, which is an awareness of "any energy or feelings of darkness of any kind" in our surroundings that may infiltrate our hearts and souls. It includes *an awareness of how these energies and stimuli make us feel.* There are spiritual energies and forces, good and bad, and from both sides of the veil, that frequently act on us. Media also produces a "feeling," for example, that will either uplift and inspire or bring us down. In fact, every thought that we have is not just a thought, but contains a spiritual energy-signature of sorts. Said another way, *thoughts and words* are "real things." They have an *effect on how we feel.* They influence how we feel because we too are composed of energy or Spirit (D&C 93:23). And how we feel influences how we act and what we intentionally and unintentionally create for ourselves in life.

Anything that uplifts and inspires is of God and is light (see D&C 50:24). Any word, thought, or feeling that does not uplift or inspire is not of God and is darkness (see D&C 50:23). Our job is to consciously direct our thinking towards uplifting words, mental images, and scenes that make us *feel good* spiritually. It may seem counterintuitive to think and speak kind and loving thoughts and words when we don't feel kind and loving, but that's precisely how they and we are transmuted into something much greater. I find that listening to uplifting music with inspired lyrics is the greatest catalyst for this. We must consciously direct our thinking and our words to be the antithesis of our (sometimes degrading and depressing) self-talk, thereby creating how we may negatively feel. We must continually watch and monitor ourselves (Mosiah 4:30).

The third and last essential station of awareness unto salvation involves constantly looking and waiting with expectancy (i.e., a component of faith) to see God's hand in our lives through tender mercies—to recognize that we are surrounded by His light and love. It is also important to recognize that His hand is constantly being extended and offered to us, if we will only first *see* and acknowledge, then receive of His offering. This awareness enhances gratitude for God (which can become a form of worshipful prayer) and builds immense belief unto a bestowal of that living faith necessary for life and salvation. This is how we begin to build and subsequently "see" the unique tapestry of our lives as we come further unto Christ.

Self-Observation, Personal Inventory, and Self-Inquiry

Elder Robert Hales admonishes us to spend time in "personal counsel," or personal inventory. We need to check where we are headed and "come to ourselves" just as the prodigal did. This happens first through an awareness of the state of our hearts within, or our ability to feel connected with our authentic selves. We must *question our every motive* through this inner awareness and personal inventory. This process can take many, many years. It can also go quickly, depending upon how much we are unconsciously or unknowingly trying to hide the truth of our current spiritual standing before God from ourselves.

Other questions we may ask through the process of this self-inquiry are, "Can I feel the truth of who I really am and of my divine mission, calling, and purpose in this life? Can I feel God's direction in my life? Can I even feel anything at all?" If the answer to any of the above is "no," then we are at least in part lost in the "mists of darkness," with our hearts partially obscured or hardened. To reconnect with the Light of Christ, we must consciously slow down the pace of our lives and find some quiet time in order to still the monkey chatter of our restless mind. Be alone. Be still. This is how we listen to God. This is how we spend our one-on-one time with the Father. When we slow down our restless minds, we are in more of a creative state of being and can more easily connect with Him, eventually being led to commune with Him.

If we are unable to "feel after God" (see Acts 17:27) so that we become aware of and feel God's Light within us, or if we feel disassociated from ourselves, then we have no way of ultimately filling the measure of our creation (see D&C 88:18-19). We will not come to the knowledge of God and conditional salvation, which can open to our view the mysteries of godliness. We will become a ship without a rudder, "tossed to and fro, and carried about with every wind of doctrine" (Ephesians 4:14). This is when we may enter down forbidden paths and become lost.

The Diagram of the State of Our Hearts Leading to Salvation

Notice the structure and diagram of the state of our hearts leading to salvation (hereinafter, "Diagram") and the fruit that the tender/open heart ultimately yields. Although the below Diagram is displayed in a linear fashion for easier comprehension, the Diagram may unfold experientially in a non-linear, non-sequential way as well:

*Desire →Tender/Open Heart →Spiritual Sight/"Seeing" →Belief (Light) →Acting in Gospel Belief→**Faith** →Spiritual Knowledge/Understanding **(Hope)** →Salvation **(Charity)****

**Salvation includes an experience of being filled with the Love of God [charity], an actual knowledge as to the reality of the Father and the Son manifested in power, receiving a remission of sins as though by spiritual fire, and receiving the sure promise of Eternal Life, subject to enduring to the end.*

Below is a view of the Diagram shown above, only now in a numbered fashion and with additional context:

1. The Desire to find and know God leads to a "Tender or Open Heart," which enhances Spiritual Sight or "Seeing."
2. This Spiritual Sight or "Seeing" leads to Belief and additional, spiritual awareness (Belief is a synonym of Light).
3. Belief and additional, spiritual awareness can then lead to "Acting in Gospel Belief" (which is a demonstration of one's personal resolve and commitment to follow Christ out in the world).
4. Acting in Gospel Belief is ultimately about following the Christ's Light, which leads to a living Faith (and said faith is bestowed as an endowment) as a direct result of one's obedience to the doctrine of Christ, including having made the "all-in" commitment to God and to "cry out" or "call upon the name of the Lord" for mercy (see Romans 10:13). This soul cry is tied to a willingness to consecrate all that we have and are. *This "all in" commitment, in my opinion, is the state of heart obtained and found by*

the true seeker, which will include a willingness to not only "believe," but also to die for the cause of Christ.

5. Faith (as a perfect, living, spiritual endowment of power bestowed by God Himself, resulting from an "all in" commitment and willingness to sacrifice our all for Him during and after broken-hearted repentance) leads to Spiritual Knowledge or Understanding, beginning with the knowledge of God with absolute certainty, a remission of sins, and the sure promise of eternal life subject to enduring to the end. Note: This "knowledge" is also referred to at times as Hope in the scriptures.
6. Spiritual Knowledge or Understanding (Hope), including the most critical of all knowledge, or the knowledge of God, precedes and accompanies the sure promise of eternal life and salvation and being filled with God's love (Charity).
7. Salvation includes an experience of being filled with the love of and oneness with God (Charity) lasting up to several days and nights, an actual knowledge of the reality of the Father and the Son by way of a manifestation in power by the Holy Ghost, receiving a remission of sins as though by spiritual fire, and receiving the sure promise of eternal life, subject to enduring to the end. This is when we are ***redeemed*** of the Lord.

*Notice the last 3 steps of our Diagram (5 through 7) are clearly Faith, Hope, and Charity. If and when we receive the endowment of a living, perfect faith (2 Ne. 9:23), we will see the endowments of the other two. Said another way, to receive the first, or a perfect faith (which can only be delivered by a perfect God), is to receive all three. For how could we be given perfect faith (or power) by God Himself to become his sons or daughters and not obtain the fruits promised that would arise out of that faith? (See John 1:12). Moroni says it this way:

> "Wherefore, there must be ***faith;*** and if there must be faith there must also be ***hope;*** and if there must be hope there must also be ***charity***" (Moroni 10:20).

When the living endowment of a perfect *faith* or *power* (see John 1:12) is bestowed through true and whole, broken-hearted repentance by a perfect God, and we issue the cry of surrender and complete commitment to Christ, *there must also be* the hope (which is a knowledge) of God and of His promise to us of eternal life. And if we have received this knowledge and accompanying promise, *there must also be* an experience wherein we are filled with God's love, also known as *charity*. In other words, the endowment of *faith* by God Himself or "*power* to become the sons of God" (see John 1:12), creates a ripple effect that brings the reception of the other two endowments—and they all occur in succession. In effect, they are three endowments received in close proximity (speaking relative to man's time) to one another. Hence, if there is the first, *there must also be* the other two. This knowledge is part of the "other things" that the Lord promises to give to us line upon line through the Comforter.

A verse in the Book of Mormon reinforces this same pattern, which highlights and is amazingly compatible with our Diagram. We will begin by this verse, followed up a second time with my commentary:

> *"And now, my brethren, I desire that ye shall plant this word in your hearts, and as it beginneth to swell, even so nourish it by your faith. And behold it will become a tree, springing up in you unto everlasting life. And then may God grant unto you that your burdens may be light, through the joy of his Son. And even all this can ye do if ye will. Amen" (Alma 33:23).*

"And now, my brethren, I desire [note that nothing happens unless preceded by desire, which is the first rung on the ladder of our Diagram] that ye shall plant this *word* in your hearts [this word is "Belief," a synonym of light], and as it beginneth to swell [which occurs by "Acting in Gospel Belief"] even so nourish it by your faith. And behold [through this nourished faith] it will become a tree [of spiritual knowledge or understanding of having received the conditional, yet sure promise of eternal life or 'hope,' together with the First Comforter], springing up in you unto everlasting life [being filled with 'charity' and a Oneness with God, thereby becoming branches of the true Vine]. And then may God grant unto you that your burdens may be light, through the joy of his Son [Second Comforter]. And even all this can ye do *if ye will* [which takes us full circle once again to 'desire"]. Amen" (Alma 33:23; emphasis added).

Notice that the Tender or Open Heart is what allows us to spiritually see so we can be guided by God and ultimately led to salvation. So the question then arises, what can we do to soften our hearts? Here is what I find works best for most, which I will refer to as "Tools to Soften the Heart." Feel free to find what works best for you.

The first and most reliable is to yearn for and ask God in solemn prayer (while at times even involves perpetually crying out to Him), in the name of His Son, that we might receive of His grace so that our hearts might be softened. This is an ongoing prayer of the soul in earnest, or as my daughter Ashlyn suggests, to "pray our guts out." Others include immersing ourselves in spiritually uplifting music and lyrics (especially music of worshipful praise, which facilitates the exercise of authentic love and gratitude for God); enjoying media that uplifts and inspires the heart; practicing meditation in the stillness (which simply means seeking to connect with God through our "heart space"); involving ourselves in contemplative prayer; heeding (as best we can) the voice of the Spirit in our hearts and acting on those promptings; immersing ourselves in both his written word and "the Word" of His revelatory light; losing ourselves in compassionate works of service toward others; speaking positive affirmations about ourselves founded in truth in order to counteract any negative subconscious programming by way of negative self-talk; acknowledging God's hand in all things through expressions of gratitude, being accountable (which is to practice personal responsibility), practicing humility by remaining open to be taught at all times; conscientious and broken-hearted repentance while partaking of the sacrament weekly, attending the temple, and, perhaps the one that gets delayed the most, truly forgiving all who have trespassed against us, including that of forgiving our own selves.

Remember that Nephi did "cry unto the Lord," and the Lord "did soften [his] heart that [he] did believe" (1Nephi 2:16). Notice that in our Diagram, Belief (a synonym of light) directly follows a softened heart. Coincidence? Notice also that when we "cry unto the Lord," *He* softens our hearts unto acting in gospel belief.

Laman and Lemuel's hardness of heart prevented them from understanding their Father. "For he [Lehi] truly spake many great things to them, which were ***hard to be understood***, save a man should inquire of the Lord; and they being ***hard in their hearts***, therefore they did not look unto the Lord as they ought" (1Nephi 15:3; emphasis added). Notice that because they had a hardened heart, the word was "hard to be understood." In short, they could not receive spiritual knowledge and understanding. It simply could not "sink in." They didn't spiritually "see it" or rightly "perceive." Christ said, "Because they seeing see not; and hearing they hear not, neither do they understand" (Matthew 13:13).

Our awareness of the current condition of our hearts, through our ability to intuitively "feel" or "sense" for God's direction, can truly become a moment-to-moment endeavor.

Ground Zero of the battle of good vs evil, God vs. Satan, light vs. darkness, is to get us to choose to either harden or soften our hearts, thereby affecting our ability to sense, perceive, and feel God's revelatory direction, whether aware or not.

Why is this so critical to understand? Why is this battle over the heart "Ground Zero"? For one, it is something the whole world knows of and can relate to, stemming from the horrific events of 9-11 in New York City. Bottom line: If our hearts become hardened, we will become lost, because it requires knowledge from God (which is mostly made available through our ability to feel) to be led to salvation. And if we "harden not [our] hearts," (Alma 12:37) we shall be saved because we will have been led through God's light of personal revelation. It is so simple and plain, *yet I fear that most will discard this information and the importance of monitoring our ability to intuitively sense, perceive, and feel through our hearts (using awareness) as a thing of naught, because of its plainness and simplicity.* This, however, has been and shall be our ongoing battle throughout mortality. Our salvation will actually depend on how well we implement this principle.

Apathy and a Hardened Heart Ultimately Result in Our Becoming Lost

It can be helpful to view our lives from the perspective of the Diagram's opposite. Notice the fruit that the hardened or closed heart yields, especially when aided by the slow death of the soul I call *apathy*, which we all know is the antithesis of *desire*:

Apathy →Hard/Closed Heart →Spiritual Blindness →Unbelief (Darkness) →Acting in Unbelief →Fear →Loss of Spiritual Knowledge/Understanding →Condemnation

The adversary is focused on the heart because this is ground zero of the spiritual battle. He whispers to us to build a wall around our hearts, to distrust God, and to close ourselves off from His light. He sometimes does this by getting us to focus on the seeming "failings" within His Church, or seeming failings with some of its policies or leaders, and then gets us to lump them together as one, even together with God Himself! In this way he may get us to think, "It's all God's fault." Or we may think, "Well, if the Church is not true in this one thing, then I can't believe anything to be true, or that there is even a God." The adversary's game is one of deception, lies, and trickery. One of the greatest and most cunning tools of the adversary is to get us to close off from God through our preoccupation with "the cares of this world," for he knows that these cares will choke the revelatory light of His Word (and His Word is spirit), even by using our own agency and volition. He knows that no knowledge or instruction from God can make its way to our souls without God's Light, and without being able to feel it or Him, we will inevitably perish. Nephi exclaimed,

"How is it that ye will perish, because of the hardness of your hearts?" (1Nephi 15:10).

Wow! Nephi's answer is actually framed in his question! They will perish *because of* the hardness of their hearts. To perish is synonymous with spiritual condemnation from our Diagram, is it not? Alma said, "Then *if our hearts have been hardened*, yea, if we have hardened our hearts against the word ['and my word is Spirit'], insomuch that it has not been found in us, then will our state be awful, for *then we shall be condemned*" (Alma 12:13).

Inasmuch as we turn away from God to any degree, it is to this same degree that we will end up hardening our hearts. If that evil one can get us to harden our hearts, he knows that will create spiritual blindness in us, like "mists" over our "seeing" hearts. In short, *we will no longer care or feel the need to draw close to God or believe we even need God*, and we will likely not even know why. But we now know why on a conscious level: It occurs through our inability to feel stemming from when we betray our own intuition, which is God's light given to every man.

This inner betrayal occurs by getting us to focus on the cares of this world which "choke the Word" of His Spirit. The adversary gets us to accuse our brethren, take credit for our "righteousness" (i.e., pride), betray those close to us (including ourselves), and entice us through the flesh to sin. These choices give place for that evil one to gain access to our hearts. The resultant hard heart and spiritual blindness create unbelief and fear, which is the exact opposite of what is needed for salvation. Notice these words from the days of Alma and Amulek. In the account, we are told that "the Lord did pour out his Spirit...to prepare their hearts to receive the word,...that they might not be ***hardened,***...that they might not be ***unbelieving***" (Alma 16:16-17).

Notice in the prior scripture above how "unbelief" follows having a "hardened heart" and tracks our Diagram perfectly. Coincidence? This is precisely why the heart is ground zero in the battle between the forces of good and evil, including that of eternal salvation and condemnation. Remember, His "Word" is not only the written word, but is referred to as "Spirit"! The Spirit is rarely perceived first through the analytical mind, just like you would not attempt to intellectually dissect a beautiful painting or intellectually enjoy a piece of soul-lifting music. Beautiful art and music simply bypass the intellectual prowess of the natural man. Said another way, perceiving through the Spirit is an experiential phenomenon, arrived at typically through intuitive feelings, and beyond the capacity of the five senses.

Unbelief: The Antithesis of What Is Needed for Salvation

Unbelief is a spiritual synonym for "darkness of mind," which promotes both doubt and fear. Unbelief, doubt, and fear are the antithesis of faith, which is needed for salvation, for we are saved by grace through faith (see Eph. 2:8). Joseph Smith said, "For where doubt is, there faith has no power" (*Lectures On Faith* 3:44). And where faith has no power, there can be no creation nor salvation. Unbelief creates a loss of spiritual knowledge. We actually become spiritually dumb. Alma says, "And thus we can plainly discern, that after a people have been once enlightened by the Spirit of God... and then have fallen away into sin and transgression, they become more hardened, and thus their state becomes worse" (Alma 24:30). The Lord taught, "...for unto him that receiveth [i.e., more of My Spirit and spiritual knowledge, made possible by having an open heart and mind] I will give more; and from them that shall say, we have enough [by having a hardened or closed heart and mind] from them shall be taken away even that which they have" (2 Nephi 28:30; emphasis added).

You'll notice that a hard or closed heart (whether due to sin, unresolved emotional pain, anguish, turmoil, darkness, or as a byproduct of living in a fallen world, etc.) can create the equivalent of "spiritual blindness" or "blindness of heart" (D&C 58:15). The various levels of a spiritually darkened wall surrounding our hearts, although invisible to the eye, are real and directly affect our ability to keep hold of the rod of personal revelation.

Some may cry foul at times and say, "But I am not responsible for my emotional trauma, abuse, and pain! I did not create this!" Well, that may be true, but here's the deal: As adult, aware, and accountable beings, it is our responsibility to do everything within our power to seek healing in order to become whole once again. Whether we are responsible or not for the initial injury, at least in my experience, it is best that we approach everything that occurs in our personal world from strictly an accountable perspective (whether "our fault" or not) and do all within our power to heal and soften our hearts so that we can be guided.

I have noticed that part of the search to become healed ourselves of emotional wounds and traumas runs parallel to our desire to become more authentic and to find and know the living Christ. Is He not the Master Healer? Most of us, once we have tried everything within our scope and ability to find relief from spiritual and emotional pain or suffering, will inevitably appeal to God's mercy and grace to make up the difference. Failing to seek any and every Christ-centered healing modality available to us, however, is to keep our heads buried in the sand. It is to deny the power of our spirit and intellect, given as a gift to us from God. It is to fail to find any and all truth in the world, wherever found. We will occasionally go out into the world and get emotionally and spiritually beaten down. This is all part of the fallen world in which we live. *Yet it is purposeful in that it teaches us about the life that we don't want.* Notwithstanding the fact that we may become unjustly bruised or scarred emotionally or spiritually, we also learn that we must come back to our sacred spaces and "closets" in the safety and security of our own homes to facilitate our healing. We can light a candle, play some celestial soothing music, and turn to God with all our hearts to petition that His grace both attend us and attend to us. In these moments, we can also be ministered to by those on both sides of the veil who sincerely love us as themselves. When we do these things and petition God for His assistance in healing, He may put people in our paths to help us or He may heal us directly in a miraculous way. It is all dependent upon our faith and His holy will and grace.

The denial to seek healing for ourselves from the servants of God or from God directly, arising out of unbelief or even false beliefs, will keep us in our own hardness of heart. And this hardness of heart will keep us in spiritual blindness and cause our internal compass to function improperly or to fail altogether. In Helaman we read that, "The Spirit of the Lord began to withdraw from the Nephites, because of the ... hardness of their hearts" (Helaman 6:35). Notice again the words of Nephi: "How is it that you will perish, because of the hardness of your hearts?" (1 Ne. 15:10).

With spiritual blindness, we become a ship without a rudder. The softening of our hearts allows our internal GPS to function again, thereby opening up moment to moment guidance in our lives. For those with cell phones, it may be like going from 1 bar to 3 or 4 bars in reception. I would be willing to bet that for most of us, if our ability to have actual cell phone reception were tied to keeping our hearts tender and open so that we could feel after God, we would all maintain perfect tenderness of heart. Why would we not equally monitor our hearts and prevent any signs of early hardening when tied to our own salvation?

Now as previously mentioned, our Diagram does not always unfold in a linear or sequential direction. For example, "unbelief" can actually happen first, thereby causing the heart to harden. This verse in Mosiah illustrates this point: "because of their unbelief they could not understand the word of God; and their hearts were hardened" (Mosiah 26:3).

Spiritual Cataracts

Many cataracts begin as small spots or specks in the lens of the eye (i.e., "distractions" or "cares of the world"). These spots or specks interfere with light rays that pass through the lens to be focused as an image on the retina in the back of the eye. The greater the number of specks, the more obscure the image. These specks can become so dense that the entire lens becomes milky white, and the light rays can't pass through the lens, resulting in blindness. *But it is important to remember that the light is still there; it just can't pass through the lens of the eye.* This is similar to the "hardening of our hearts," which inhibits our ability to feel and thereby delays our finding the tree of life and gate of salvation, or keeps us from finding them altogether.

In certain circumstances of self-protection or emotional self-preservation, we may unconsciously shut down our ability to feel, and in so doing, we may unknowingly and unwittingly close ourselves off from God's love and direction in our lives as well. God tells us to "chase darkness" from among us. And darkness includes the "ungodliness" from which we are to deny ourselves (Moroni 10:32). I like to think of darkness as *any thought, word, or feeling, including any fear, doubt, unbelief, worry, confusion, or despair in any degree which is not in tune with or compatible with the Light of Christ.*

While it is true that we can actually be successful in walling ourselves or our hearts off from feeling any future pain as a defense mechanism, which is actually quite normal and natural, we may at the same time keep ourselves "walled off" from experiencing true joy, peace, and fulfillment. Thus, the decision (performed mostly unconsciously) to shut down or close off our hearts in order to protect ourselves produces the experience of a double-edged sword. There is a better way.

Our Ability to Feel and Perceive Is Necessary to Be Led by God

The use of our agency to not feel by shutting off our hearts, acts like a drug. As Nathaniel Branden puts it, "What is blocked is the capacity to experience feeling." He likens the blocking effect of some drugs to our emotional "stuffing" or repression. "What remains true for everyone is that to diminish one's capacity to experience pain is to diminish also one's capacity to experience pleasure [i.e., joy]" (*The Art of Living Consciously*, p. 145). This is why *we MUST be absolutely and staunchly committed to our own healing process so that our hearts can feel for however long as that journey might take.* Seek healing and relief through any and all means available, as guided by the Spirit. As we follow and seek the healing in our hearts and the Light of Christ within, the Savior will guide us through our desire and faith to the ultimate healing experience, even the rebirth of the spirit. Remember again the Savior's question to the Nephites: "Will ye now not return unto me, and be converted, that I may *heal* you?" (3 Ne. 9:13).

Talk Back To Negative Thinking

The resource booklet given to all full-time missionaries by the Church entitled "Adjusting to Missionary Life," addresses how we can talk back to negative thinking. It could just as appropriately be called "Adjustment to Mortal Life." Published by the Church, it addresses tools to counteract the often-unconscious practice of negative self-talk, such as positive affirmations. The small segment of the following chart is taken from this booklet and I would invite everyone to review all of them whenever time permits:

Talk back to negative thinking. Right now, or before bed tonight, list your negative thoughts from today on paper; then rewrite them to be more hopeful, truthful, and encouraging.

MY THOUGHTS	MY REWRITE
I can't learn this language.	If I keep practicing, I'll learn it well enough to do my job and teach with the Spirit. The Lord will help me.
Sister Smith must think I'm an idiot.	I can't read her mind so I don't know what she thinks, but I can ask if I've upset her and apologize.
I hate having to get up so early. (See Author's note #1 below).	I don't have to like it. I think I can do this. Once I get up and start moving, I'll probably feel better. (See Author's note #2 below).

Author's Note #1: As I tell my children, never use the word *hate* because of the spiritual energy and negative feeling associated with that word. We could instead use the words, "I'm not a fan of having to get up so early." Close your eyes and say it both ways and notice how it feels. Can you notice a difference?

Author's Note #2: Affirmations should not include any doubt, whether we feel doubt or not. Remember, thoughts and words carry a spiritual marker, energy, or signature. Words and phrases like, "don't have to," "I think," "Once," and "Probably" still references "negative speak" and doubt. And doubt is darkness and kills faith. I have performed a rewrite on a couple of these above in order to provide an example to demonstrate how all "rewrites" might be patterned. My re-write might look something like this: "I desire and choose to arise early to seek my God. I know I can do all things in and through Christ, who strengthens me. I commit to get up every morning and start moving. I know that in doing so, I shall without a doubt feel energized, especially with the Lord's Spirit!"). Notice the difference in words like *shall* instead of *perhaps* or *probably*. There is no power in *probably*, because the word *probably* always allows for a back door. And back doors are a pathway to darkness and unbelief, the opposite of faith, which is the power needed to overcome in and through Christ.

So what we think about all day long will eventually find its way as "feelings" into our hearts. And these *feelings*, especially when coupled with deep emotion, will then attract (i.e., restore or "bring back" again, per Alma 41:13) more of the same types of thoughts and patterns of thinking. And if these thoughts and patterns are negative, they will create a "feeling" that is negative, which may in turn, "attract" or "bring back" negative behaviors and experiences. This is how we unknowingly create many of the deteriorating conditions in our lives. As we understand this better, we will become increasingly aware that we ourselves are mostly responsible for creating these conditions, beginning with the choices we made about the thoughts that we allowed to remain within our conscious minds. We can marinate in the good feelings or the bad, depending on what we allow into our inner and outer environments.

Someone born in poverty, through positive thinking, can pull themselves out of the slums of depression and despair and find complete success, both spiritual and temporal. Conversely, someone born with all the advantages inherited of temporal and spiritual blessings, can, through a choice to adopt negative thinking patterns, find themselves in the slums of depression and despair. But here's the important thing to understand and keep in mind as to spiritual creation: It's not as much about the thought itself. It's about the spiritual imprint and deeply imbedded feeling and emotion associated with or tied to that thought… which can in turn spiritually restore "back again" to us that which we may have either knowingly or unknowingly sent out through feelings in our hearts.

Dr. Dyer often taught that "what [we] focus on, expands." Again, given that all things are created spiritually before naturally (meaning they are "created" in our world of form through the beginnings of thoughts, feelings, emotions, and the spoken word), all of these will increase how we feel and what we'll subsequently attract. Good feelings carry a certain spiritual flavor which will return to us more of the same until these eventually become manifest as "blessings" from a benevolent God. *It is a law. I like to think of it as how we spiritually create a type of spiritual boomerang for ourselves, either for good or for bad.* Alma spoke of the law in its simplicity: "For that which ye do send out shall return unto you again" (Alma 41:15).

Watch, Pay Attention to and Guard Your Inner Selves

King Benjamin admonished his people to "watch yourselves," including their thoughts. We are admonished that if we do not "watch [ourselves]," we will ultimately perish. If we look back on the Diagram, we will see that if we choose to continue with a hard heart, we must unavoidably become condemned and ultimately perish. The Lord through King Benjamin admonished, "But this much I can tell you, that if ye do not watch yourselves, and your thoughts, and your words, and your deeds, and observe the commandments of God, and continue in the faith of what ye have heard concerning the coming of our Lord, even unto the end of your lives, ye must perish. And now, O man, remember, and perish not" (Mosiah 4:30).

Why did the Lord mention watching our thoughts and words? Because as part of what we are learning about our second station of awareness, our thoughts and words carry a spiritual flavor associated with them which will influence us in either feeling positively or negatively. And these "feelings" and subsequent emotions will later end up in the reservoir of our hearts and thereby influence our words and deeds in a repetitive cycle. Jesus said, "For out of the abundance of the heart, the mouth speaketh" (Matt. 12:34). Positive, new ways of being then will become habitual, beginning with positive words and affirmations until these sink into our hearts. And if they become habitual, a new character will be built, either for good or for bad. This new character, amazingly, will have arisen out of something so seemingly insignificant as our original "tiny, little, harmless thoughts" which prior to this new awareness had been left unchecked. Do we see now why we must watch ourselves and direct our conscious selves through positive and purposeful thinking patterns, words, and affirmations?

Our Thoughts, Words, and Deeds Are Being Recorded

Scientific research has revealed compelling evidence specific to the reality of words and thoughts leaving a type of spiritual marker, signature, or imprint. As we become more aware of this, we will be much more careful of the thoughts we think, the words we speak, and the actions we take. This becomes especially true when we understand that all our thoughts, words, and deeds are being recorded. I like to think of this "recording" as part of "the record of heaven" described by the prophet Enoch in Moses 6:61. Elder Bruce R. McConkie has likewise said that "Every thought, word, and deed has an effect on the human body; all these leave their marks, marks which can be read by Him who is Eternal, as easily as the words in a book can be read" (*Mormon Doctrine,* 2nd ed. [1966], p. 97). And I would submit they most assuredly leave an imprint on spiritual consciousness as well. Dr. Hawkins appears to validate McConkie's words when he said: "By consciousness calibration research, it is demonstrable that every thought, action, word, or deed is *recorded forever, beyond time, in an infinite field of consciousness for eternity*" (David R. Hawkins, *Discovery of the Presence of God,* p. 159).

The above is sobering, is it not? To further highlight the reality of these "spiritual imprints" associated with thoughts and words, I would invite you to check out the research performed by Dr. Masaru Emoto. You can find him on YouTube. Watch the video entitled, "Water, Consciousness & Intent: Dr. Masaru Emoto." In it, Emoto says that "water was a 'blueprint for our reality' and that emotional 'energies' and 'vibrations' could change the physical structure of water." Emoto has also said, "Water is the mirror that has the ability to show us what we cannot see. It is a blueprint for our reality, *which can change with a single, positive thought.* All it takes is faith, if you're open to it."

Emoto's book *The Hidden Messages of Water* was a *New York Times* bestseller. Emoto's water crystal experiments consisted of exposing water in glasses to different words, pictures, or music, and then freezing and examining the aesthetics of the resulting crystals with microscopic photography. Emoto makes the claim that water exposed to positive speech or thoughts—and intention—will result in "beautiful" crystals being formed when that water is frozen, and that negative intention and words tend to yield "ugly" frozen crystal formations. (Resource: https://drjoedispenza.net/blog/general/the-passing-of-a-legend-dr-masaru-emoto-the-water-doctor-dies/).

As of the time of my viewing of the above-referenced video found on Youtube, it had received over 3.3 million views. The most interesting phenomena observed in studying Dr. Emoto's life is not about his findings, but in the immense amount of energy that others have spent in attempting to discredit him. Why would this relatively unknown individual from Japan become the focus of such antagonistic opposition? I believe it's because he was on to something. I'm not a scientist, but his research is compelling. You can watch his full documentary on YouTube. (https://www.youtube.com/watch?v=PDW9Lqj8hmc). He also exposes water, which he later freezes and studies under a microscope, to beautiful uplifting music composed of positive lyrics, which likewise form beautiful crystalized art patterns. In his documentary, he states his belief that "music is a form of healing before it is an art." If words and thoughts (which is really more about the spiritual imprint associated with or tied to those words and thoughts) can influence the water molecules around them and by freezing them in water form beautiful crystalized art, what does this mean for us, being that our bodies are made of 70% water? For me it means that we must be both aware and careful as to what we "take in" in the form of the spiritual properties inherent in what we think, see, hear, say, do, and experience.

Awareness and the Number Three

To demonstrate the workings of awareness, let's look with awareness at the spiritual significance and symbolism behind the number 3. (I will refer to this number again and again to facilitate a deeper understanding regarding the importance of our awareness.) Obviously, our awareness should encompass not only patterns with numbers and symbols but also all things which "happen to us" and all things having a "likeness to Christ" (Moses 6:63).

The number 3 is a perfect number and represents completeness, perfection, and wholeness. There are other perfect numbers as well. Let's explore, however, the number 3 further: after the deluge were the righteous patriarchs Abraham, Isaac, and Jacob. Jesus prayed 3 times in the Garden of Gethsemane before His arrest. There were 3 hours of darkness that covered the land while Jesus was suffering on the cross from the sixth hour to the ninth hour. Christ was dead for 3 days and 3 nights before the Resurrection. The apostle Paul saw the third heaven. There are 3 degrees of glory. There are 3 members of the Godhead. There were 3 witnesses to Christ's transfiguration on the mount—Peter, James, and John. There are 3 members of the First Presidency on earth. There were 3 witnesses to the golden plates and the angel Moroni. This list could go on and on. You get the idea.

The Lord uses numbers to highlight things that we should view as highly important. Have you ever noticed that ***after*** you buy a car or bike, you then see the same car or bike seemingly everywhere? This happens out of an increased awareness. As our awareness increases, so does our faith through the awareness of the "evidences" made manifest. We are to continuously seek for and expect (which is faith in action) evidences of God's hand in our lives within our personal journey. As more and more of these evidences come into view, our awareness of and faith in God increases—until that day when we come to know Him and obtain "peace in this world" (D&C 59:23). Awareness acts as a component in exercising faith unto salvation as a principle of power.

As our spiritual awareness increases, we will find that it builds on itself. Through the revelation of added pieces to our life's puzzle, God unveils more and more, revealing His guiding and loving hand, which promotes an increasing love for and faith in Him. As a fun example of this principle, in the movie *Evan Almighty,* certain signs from God kept revealing themselves in an almost ridiculously amazing manner. I say "ridiculously amazing" because the assurances would come so frequently that it would become almost *ridiculous to not believe* that God's almighty hand was guiding Evan's life. This too is a type for our own journey.

Through our exercise of faith, aided by the awareness of God's hand in our lives, we may begin to view and believe more deeply in these tender mercies and assurances; alternatively, we may cast them aside and discard them as mere coincidence. And yet coincidently (pun intended) in geometry, two angles are said to coincide when they fit perfectly together. This act of casting aside things of "coincidence" is called "unbelief." And unbelief is a synonym of and is referred to in scripture as…wait for it: darkness! This explains the Lord's admonition to "chase darkness" from among us (D&C 50:25). Notice again the antithesis of our Diagram:

Apathy →Hard/Closed Heart →Spiritual Blindness →Unbelief (Darkness) →Acting in Unbelief→Fear →Loss of Spiritual Knowledge/Understanding →Condemnation.

This unbelief or spiritual darkness keeps us from living in the world of *real magic*. As we remove our "unbelief consciousness helmets," we develop more and more faith until the perfect day dawns. It is always more advantageous to "over believe" than to "under believe," especially when it comes to spiritual matters. Joseph Smith said, "I never hear of a man being damned for believing too much; but they are damned for unbelief" (*Teachings of the Prophet Joseph Smith,* p. 373). So, if we were to "err" it would be wise to take the side of belief, not unbelief. As a tenet of our faith boldly professes, "We believe all things." If someone cons us into believing more in God, and the resultant fruit within us ends up being an enhanced faith and love for God, wherein have we been wronged? Have we not been conned all our lives by the world to not believe in God and to doubt His existence, even though His reality is all around us, yea, even *in* us? The directive is to "believe in God; believe that he is, and that he created all things, both in heaven and in earth; [to] believe that he has all wisdom, and all power, both in heaven and in earth" (Mosiah 4:9; bracketed addition, mine).

As we pay close attention, using awareness, noticing and truly valuing these spiritual evidences to our hearts and minds that are all around us, and as we look inwardly for their spiritual significance and meaning, God notices and rewards us with more assurances of the same. Whenever possible, we write them down, demonstrating that we value them. This added awareness, coupled with gratitude and faith, dispels unbelief and promotes light (a synonym of belief), thereby leading us to act in our gospel belief, even obtaining a living faith through these repeated spiritual assurances that the Father's promises are indeed available to us specifically and individually. It is then that we experience the love of God, and our proverbial cup runneth over with inexplicable and inexpressible gratitude. It's easy for us to believe that the *precious promises* are available for apostles and prophets. It's another thing to believe they are available for the rest of us, meaning, the *seemingly insignificant* you and me.

The greatest patterns for spiritual rebirth are found in the Book of Mormon. I have often said that the Book of Mormon could have easily been called, "How to Be Born of God." Perhaps this is the reason why President Benson urged us to read and study the Book of Mormon so frequently. In his talk "Born of God," Benson taught that "when we awake and are born of God, a new day will break.... May we be convinced that Jesus is the Christ, choose to follow Him, be changed for Him, captained by Him, consumed in Him, and born again" ("Born of God," General Conference Report, April, 1962).

Seeing Our Weakness through Inner Honesty and God's Grace

> *"And it came to pass that the Lord said unto me: If they have not charity it mattereth not unto thee, thou hast been faithful; wherefore, thy garments shall be made clean. And BECAUSE THOU HAST SEEN THY WEAKNESS, thou shalt be made strong, even unto the sitting down in the place which I have prepared in the mansions of my Father (Ether 12:37).*

Through radical inner honesty and self-introspection, if we will first "check" ourselves and then chasten ourselves, we can auto-correct through heeding the voice of the Spirit, who will have allowed us to see our weakness in the first place. Most of us are accustomed to unintentionally and subconsciously hiding our weaknesses from ourselves because they are painful to view. We know what to confront when we find anything that "gets under our skin" or manifests in the form of emotional triggers or pain. These uncovered, painful signals are merely sending us a message, informing us to pay closer attention and uncover not just the symptoms but also their root cause. These messages will also be teaching us that we still have more work to do in our spiritual journey of overcoming. When we notice that there are no more "triggers" or "buttons" that can be pushed by others, we will find that we are well on our way to feeling more whole once again, and more pleasing in God's sight.

The Ongoing Battle Within

Elder F. Enzio Busche provided insight to the ongoing battle within: "This war is a war that has to be fought by all of Heavenly Father's children, *whether they know about it or not*. But without a keen knowledge of the plan of salvation, and without the influence of the divine Light of Christ to bring us *awareness*, this war is being fought subconsciously, and therefore its battlefronts are not even known to us and we have no chance to win" ("Truth Is the Issue," *Ensign,* Nov. 1993; emphasis added).

Notice what Elder Busche is saying here. In essence, *without spiritual awareness*, we will eventually succumb to that wicked one. He continues: "Wars in the inner self that are fought subconsciously, with unknown battlefronts, lead to defeats which also hurt us subconsciously. These defeats are reflected in our conscious life as expressions of misery, such as a lack of self-confidence, lack of happiness and joy, lack of faith and testimony, or as overreactions of our subconscious self, which we see then as pride, arrogance, or in other forms of misbehavior—even as acts of cruelty and indecency. No! There is no salvation without Christ, and Christ cannot be with us unless we pay the price of the *constant fight for self-honesty*.... The only way to find truth is through uncompromising self-education toward self-honesty to see the original 'real me,' the child of God, in its innocence and potential" ("Truth Is the Issue," *Ensign,* Nov. 1993; emphasis added).

Adhering to Reality through a Dedication to Truth

Finding truth is often delayed in life because of avoidance mechanisms we may have unconsciously established in order to avoid pain. Dr. M. Scott Peck wrote: "Truth or reality is avoided when it is painful. We can revise our maps only when we have the discipline to overcome that pain. To have such discipline, *we must be totally dedicated to truth.* That is to say that we must always hold truth, as best we can determine it, to be more important, *more vital to our self-interest, than our comfort.* Conversely, we must always consider our personal discomfort relatively unimportant and, indeed, even welcome it in the service of the search for truth. Mental health is an ongoing process of dedication to reality at all costs" (*The Road Less Traveled*, M. Scott Peck, p.50).

Elder Daniel Wells, of the original Twelve Apostles in Joseph Smith's day, made this statement on September 30, 1860: "*The inward monitor*, if we will let him have full play, will teach us many things that are applicable to ourselves. And if we inquire more fully into ourselves, we shall find that we are not always acting from the best of motives those things that we do in regard to others" ("Privileges of the Saints," *JD,* vol. 9:94).

We all have this "inward monitor." But we must allow it to have *full play*, that is to say, *to inquire more fully into ourselves as to our desires and motives*, whether purely intended and without guile or not. In a way, we are to become a private investigator of sorts into our own motives and actions. It takes radical inner honesty. It almost goes without saying that it would become literally impossible for our "inward monitor" to have full play if our hearts were walled off.

The Great Undoing

As we surrender and commit to "undoing" the characteristics and attributes of our false self through consistent introspection and unrelenting self-honesty, our true self begins to be revealed. This will aid us in connecting with and finding God. David R. Hawkins puts it this way: "The Realization of the Presence of Divinity unfolds of its own when the ego and its perceptual positionalities are surrendered" (*Discovery of the Presence of God,* p. 38).

An example of this is found in the work of the worldwide renown sculpture called *La Pieta*, by Michelangelo. Michelangelo began his work at the age of 22, using a process of "subtraction only." If he had gone too far and removed too much stone, he would have likely ruined his work of art. Michelangelo is suggested to have said of his works that he could "visualize" or "see" the final masterpiece that was locked inside the stone, and that through sculpting he just needed to release the image that was being held captive. Is this not a "type" of what Christ does with us?

For example, Joseph Smith referred to himself as a rough stone rolling. As he encountered adversity, a chip here and a chip there would fall or break off so that he could eventually be made smooth by the Master's skillful hand. This polishing will inevitably involve some forms of suffering. Christ is likewise performing His works in us. He is our inner and outer sculptor. M. Scott Peck wrote: "One measure of a person's greatness… is the capacity for suffering. Yet the great are also joyful… So if your goal is to avoid pain and escape suffering, do not seek higher levels of consciousness or spiritual growth…why desire to evolve at all?" (*The Road Less Traveled*, M. Scott Peck, p. 89).

Understanding with the Heart and Applying Our Heart to Understanding

In the scriptures, this spiritual, revealed knowledge is referred to as "hope." There is the popular definition of the word *hope* that precedes faith, and there is another type of hope that follows faith. The first meaning is what we normally think of when we hear the word *hope.* The hope that precedes faith becomes the "desire" in our Diagram, only now joined with a spiritual assurance, as witnessed by the Light of Christ as to any truth—including the reality and power of Christ and His gospel. This type of hope is part of testimony. It testifies that salvation is both available and attainable "for me." The latter is an actual, spiritual knowledge, now beyond that of faith. As it pertains to spiritual rebirth, this latter type of hope is the actual knowledge of the reality of God, together with the knowledge that our sins have been remitted, that we have been redeemed of the Lord, and that we have been given the sure promise of eternal life, subject to enduring to the end. This is why the latter type of hope is described as a "perfect brightness." Here's a question to consider: If we didn't know we had received the sure promise of eternal life, could its description rightly be portrayed as "sure" or a "perfect brightness"?

Abinadi told the corrupt king Noah, "Ye have not *applied your hearts to understanding*; therefore, ye have not been wise" (Mosiah 12:27; emphasis added). Notice that Abinidi did not say, "Ye have not applied your brains and analytical minds to understanding." He was clearly referring to a type of spiritual understanding that can only come to us through a softened heart, which also yields an open mind and a cognitive comprehension obtained through spiritual means. Abinidi continued, "And now, did they understand the law? I say unto you, Nay, they did not all understand the law; and this *because of the hardness of their hearts*; for they understood not that there could not any man be saved except it were through the redemption of God" (Mosiah 13:32; emphasis added).

For one to spiritually understand is therefore to "get it." To not spiritually understand is synonymous of one who "doesn't get it." He hears, he sees, but he still does not spiritually comprehend the deeper meaning. "Seeing they may see, and not perceive; and hearing they may hear, and not understand" (Mark 4:12). It is absolutely impossible to spiritually perceive or comprehend God's revelatory light if our hearts are hardened. The Lord reaffirmed this truth when He asked His own Apostles, "Perceive ye not yet, neither understand? *Have ye your heart yet hardened?*" (Mark 8:17; emphasis added).

King Mosiah implored his people to "open your ears that ye may hear, and your hearts that ye may understand" (Mosiah 2:9). These verses teach us that it is nearly impossible to gain spiritual knowledge and understanding for solving any question or problem unless we can first spiritually "see" or "get" what is being taught, which is made possible through an open and tender heart. This is reaffirmed in the book of Mark: "For they had not understood about the loaves because their heart was hardened" (NKJV, Mark 6:52).

Repentance and a Soft or Tender Heart Enables Us to Be Led through Faith in Christ unto the Promised Remission of Sins

With this understanding, here's something we can all both see and "get." If we repent with Godly sorrow, seek Christ in faith, and soften or open our hearts (which is the same as "hardening not our hearts"), we will be led to mercy and a remission of our sins, and enter His "rest" should we endure to the end. And His rest is to ultimately receive a fulness of His Glory, which is exaltation: "Therefore, whosoever repenteth, and hardeneth not his heart, *he shall have claim on mercy* through mine Only Begotten Son, *unto a remission of his sins*; and these shall enter into my rest" (Alma 12:34; emphasis added).

So how is it possible for the Lord to have given such a lofty promise as the gift of the Holy Ghost and the conditional promise of eternal life for something so seemingly simple as repenting and softening our hearts? Answer: Because the Lord knows that through obtaining soft hearts, we shall "hear His voice," and through persistence, be led to salvation. To "hear His voice" is to feel, sense, or perceive through the Light of Christ. And as we "feel our way," the answers will come by way of an intuitive perception, a peace found in the stillness, or as an inner "knowing." Through this guidance, we will be continually led until we obtain of the salvation spoken of in holy writ. Notice these verses:

> "As it is said, today if ye will hear [i.e., feel, sense, or perceive] his voice, ***harden not your hearts***" (Hebrews 4:7; emphasis added).
>
> "For mine elect hear my voice and ***harden not their hearts***" (D&C 29:7; emphasis added).

Can we not see the battle that is raging is over the hearts of men? The mists of darkness surface through the walls, barriers, and other various levels of obscurity of the heart created through sin, neglect, distractions, and other effects from living in a fallen world. These mists can cause apathy and unbelief. It is imperative that we awaken to this unseen battle. When our hearts are hardened, we lose our grasp of the iron rod and end up getting lost. Notice how the heart wall can also lead to a brain wall (i.e., a closed mind), and vice versa. Neither obstruction or obscurity is conducive to receiving personal revelation. With this understanding, notice the interpretation of the "mists" given to Nephi:

> "And the mists of darkness are the temptations of the devil, which *blindeth the eyes, and hardeneth the hearts* of the children of men" (1 Ne. 12:17; emphasis added).

More On Being Staunchly Committed to Our Spiritual and Emotional Healing

Shakti Gawain said, "If we want to experience the full range of our being in this lifetime, we need to commit ourselves to heal the emotional wounds from our childhood and early life." She then added, "Our feelings are an important part of the life force [i.e., the Light of Christ] that is constantly moving through us. If we don't allow ourselves to fully experience our emotions, we stop the natural flow of that life force. Energy gets blocked in our physical bodies and may remain that way for years or even a lifetime, unless it is released. This [blockage] leads to emotional and physical pain and disease, by the way. Repressed feelings = blocked energy [of Christ's light] = emotional and physical ailments" (The Path of Transaformation, Pg., 121-122; bracketed additions, mine).

By suppressing our emotions, we may unknowingly and inadvertently create unseen, spiritual heart walls that cause us to become "past feeling," unknowingly making our inner, spiritual compass, inoperable. It could be likened to losing cell phone reception. This is exactly the adversary's objective. When our vision and inner guide is no longer functional, we become lost in the mists of darkness, relying on our natural man, the enemy to God, to lead us back to God. Do any of us see a problem with this?

Shakti also points out the way to health and well-being: "Experiencing (good) feelings = Free-flowing energy = Emotional and physical health and well-being." (The Path of Transformation, Pg., 121-122; parenthetical addition, mine). Now let's look at the opposite of the above. Experiencing (bad) feelings = Energy-flow blockage = Emotional and Physical sickness, dis-ease and illness.

Unless we surrender and release our repressed feelings, not only are we harming ourselves emotionally and physically, but also spiritually. Those unresolved feelings remain with us and contribute to the layers of our heart walls and our overall inability to feel, which we now know inhibits our ability to spiritually see. The pain or uneasiness in our body will help by pointing us in the direction of the unresolved emotional or spiritual issues. For an awareness of the unbalanced emotional and spiritual causes of physical symptoms in the body, I strongly recommend "Heal Your Body," by Louis Hay. "And as all have not faith," sometimes a Christ-centered specialist in emotional release work can effectively help you release the dam of blocked or trapped emotions that may have been building for decades. Be prayerful and seek guidance with regards to your spiritual and emotional healing. All truly sincere, Christ-centered healing modalities can only help in removing the heart walls that have been built up over time. Consistent prayer and repeated pleadings for God's grace is most helpful when our faith is sufficient, however. Remember, we are never alone, although we will inevitably feel otherwise at times. We will be led as we sincerely and consistently seek divine guidance and direction from the Lord. We must never give up!

It would really serve (speaking of us men) if we were to get more in touch with our "feminine side." The adversary has culturally tweaked this "in-touch-ness" as being something weak or un-masculine. Most all of us men need to soften. *The most powerful being in the universe is also the most tender.* His mercies are called "tender" for a reason.

Spiritual Heart Plaque

The hardened shell around the heart is like plaque around teeth. The plaque is there, and sometimes we don't even see it ourselves or are even aware of it until we are told by the dentist. The clearing away of our "heart plaque," obtained over a prolonged period of time through neglect or abuse, may require some help. Shakti states, "If you feel really blocked for a long period of time, you probably need to do some emotional healing work. When we are holding our emotions inside us, it can be difficult or even impossible to contact our intuitive feelings" (*The Path of Transformation,* p. 88). These "intuitive feelings" are how we interface with God, so to speak.

As previously mentioned, do not be afraid to seek those professionals who work in Christ-centered emotional release work, the healing arts, and other emotional healing modalities. I love Elder Holland's wise counsel on the matter:

> *"If things continue to be debilitating, seek the advice of reputable people with certified training, professional skills, and good values. Be honest with them about your history and your struggles. Prayerfully and responsibly consider the counsel they give and the solutions they prescribe. If you had appendicitis, God would expect you to seek a priesthood blessing and get the best medical care available. So too with emotional disorders. Our Father in Heaven expects us to use all of the marvelous gifts He has provided in this glorious dispensation" (Jeffrey R. Holland, "Like a Broken Vessel").*

If you feel you need this extra help, meet with and interview various practitioners in the various fields of healing therapies; when you receive the green light through the Spirit, you'll have God's approval to move forward. Many of these practitioners have endured their own severe trials and adversity, which is why they were led to learn how to first minimize their own pain themselves and thereby help relieve the suffering of others. Elder Orson F. Whitney, said: "To whom do we look, in days of grief and disaster, for help and consolation? … They are men and women who have suffered, and out of their experience in suffering they bring forth the riches of their sympathy and condolences as a blessing to those now in need. Could they do this had they not suffered themselves?" (*Improvement Era,* Nov. 1918, p. 7).

Never Give Up

Becoming more in touch with Christ's Light, including His suffering, will help us to become prepared by Christ to eventually surrender all we have and are to Him. He is leading us to experiences that will ultimately either break or melt the spiritual walls, barriers, or shells surrounding our hearts, which will thereby allow the life-saving Light to come from behind the obscured clouds of fear, darkness, and despair. Once we are truly committed to our own healing journey, we will be given the added faith and direction from Christ Himself, which is what is ultimately needed to produce the miracle of His grace in our lives.

Never give up. Not ever! God is always there. In fact, He is everywhere present and will help us with what we need. If God notices the fall of the sparrow, which is His creation, how much more will He notice His offspring, a son or a daughter? Know that we are never alone! Know it to the core of who you are! We must press forward with the work of healing the heart within us at all times until the Master Healer, by grace and through faith, heals us completely.

In monitoring my own heart the last couple of decades, through inner awareness and Alma's "great check" (see Alma 15:17), I would often notice if I were able to feel, get emotional, or even cry. My inability to do so was always a signal to me to focus on softening my heart. Remember that crying is spiritually and emotionally healing and cleansing. It doesn't mean you're weak. It is like a mini shower for the soul. His light and love is constantly flowing to us. We need only allow its entrance by maintaining a softened heart. Then it is our gift to be able to share of that light and love by having it flow from our hearts to all our brothers and sisters within the body of Christ. Notice how the fruits of abiding in the first commandment, naturally fulfills the second. The heart and seat of our soul act both as a reservoir and as a conduit for charity, the pure love of Christ, to flow to the body of Christ and beyond, just as the physical organ of our heart acts as the reservoir and conduit (through the arteries) to carry the life-giving blood and oxygen to the needed places within our physical body.

Christ's light and love is leading us to having the hard shell over our hearts either "broken open" or at least melted so that we can be filled with charity. In order to have a healed and purified heart, our hearts must first break before the Lord, and then be offered to Him in complete surrender, having made the eternal commitment to always do His will (2 Nephi 2:6-7).

There once was a certain eunuch of great authority under Candace, queen of the Ethiopians, who desired to be baptized of Phillip. Phillip required only one thing of him: "If thou believest ***with all thine heart***, thou mayest" (Acts 8:37; emphasis added). To believe "with all thine heart" is much more than mere believing. It involves an inner oath—a commitment of the soul we intend to carry out.

In the next chapter, we will continue to explore Christ's light and how we are ultimately being guided to make this level of commitment, including how we can follow His course, light, and guidance to our own "promised land" of salvation.

Chapter 2

The Light of Christ

In the beginning was the Word, and the Word was with God, and the Word was God. (New Testament, John, John 1:1).

"The Word" is another name for the Christ, and/or His Light, which is Spirit. This Spirit is spiritual light and intelligence which fills the immensity of space. To use the Star Wars analogy, it is "the force." He gives life to all things. "He" is in and through all things, including us. Without this light, no living thing could abide. Hence, "***in him*** we live and move and have our being" (Acts 17:28). And one could appropriately say that, "In us, He lives and moves and has His being." This Christ Light is also "the Lord," in addition to the Lord who was born of Mary and became the physical manifestation of this love and light. This physical manifestation is whom we know as Jesus of Nazareth, who lived and atoned for all of our sins. But He is much, much more. Elder Holland, in referencing the many powerful figures found in the Book of Mormon, referred to Jesus as "the *omnipresent* central figure…" (See Elder Jeffrey R. Holland, "The Message, The Meaning, and the Multitude," October General Conference, 2019). I like this phrase offered by Elder Holland because it makes me think of the Lord in another context than perhaps what was intended by him.

For example, the light of the omnipresent Christ is also referred to as "the Lord" that inhabits our physical bodies or temples (only in smaller degree), and is referenced throughout scripture as such as well. Notice the following:

"Ye are the temple of God"

*"**The Lord**...dwelleth not in unholy temples" (Mosiah 2:37)*

*"...**the Lord** hath said he dwelleth not in unholy temples, **but in the hearts of the righteous** doth he dwell..." (Alma 34:36).*

*"Now **the Lord is that Spirit**..." (2 Cor. 3:17).*

*"And I heard a great voice out of heaven saying, Behold, **the tabernacle of God is with men**, and he will dwell with them, and they shall be his people" (Rev. 21:3).*

"And what agreement hath the temple of God with idols? For ***ye are the temples of the Living God****; and God hath said,* ***I will dwell in them****, and walk* ***in them****; and I will be their God, and they shall be my people."*
(1 Cor. 3:16-17 and 2 Cor. 6:16).

"In whom ye also are builded together for ***an habitation of God through the Spirit****" (Ephesians 2:22).*

"One God... who is above all, and through all, and ***in you all****"*
(Eph. 4:6).

"But Christ is ***all in all****" (Col. 3:11).*

"... the fullness of ***Him who fills all in all****" (Eph. 1:23).*

"Abide in me, and ***I in you****" (John15:4)*

"He that descended is the same also that ascended up far above all heavens, that ***he might fill all things****" (Eph. 4:10).*

"... and thou shalt abide in me, and ***I in you****, therefore walk with me"*
(Moses 6:34).

*"...****I am*** *the true* ***light*** *that is* ***in you****..." (D&C 88:50).*

"He became like me so I could receive him, He thought like me so I could become him and I did not tremble when I saw him, for he was gracious to me. He took on my nature so I could learn from him, ***took on my form so I would not turn away****"*
(The Odes of Solomon, Ode 7).

Too often we think of the Father and the Son as solely perfected, glorified and exalted beings…and They are. But "the Lord" is also referred to as this Christ Light or Spirit of Truth, that literally lives in us, only in a smaller degree or portion. Ammon taught that "*a portion of that Spirit dwelleth in me…*" (Alma 18:35). Because "the Lord" (at least in this context) is everywhere, He may appear to the natural man as being nowhere. The understanding of the Lord being everywhere, however, will keep us in the right state of mind and awareness, or that of forever being alert and on guard as to our desires, thoughts, and actions. It is to recognize that we are a part of that Spirit of Intelligence that is Omnipotent, Omniscient, and Omnipresent. We are "a part" of Him, and He is "a part" of and in us.

The purpose of the gospel of Jesus Christ is to provide mankind the channel, through priesthood authority and keys by way of ordinances, to be "filled" with a fulness of this "Lord" or "Spirit" and "Glory" of the Father, subject to obedience to gospel law, even until such time that we become exalted ourselves by Them and thereby become connected to the same Spirit that exists throughout the immensity of space which proceedeth forth from the presence of God (D&C 88:12). The Prophet Joseph taught that, "the Melchizedek Priesthood...***is the channel*** through which all knowledge, doctrine, the plan of salvation, and every important matter is revealed from heaven" (HC, IV, p.207). It is through this channel (by way of the ordinances) through which we are able to receive of this described "fullness" of His Spirit, also referred to as a "fulness of the glory of the Father" in the *Lectures On Faith*. Why is this? Because the power of this "channel for all knowledge," including the actual knowledge of God, comes to us from the King of Righteousness Himself. "Melchi" means "King of" and "Zedek" means "righteousness." The Melchizedek Priesthood, or "The Priesthood after the Holy Order of the Son of God" (D&C 84:18), or the Priesthood after the Holy Order of the King of Righteousness, is after the holiest order of God. Were it not for this holiest order of the Priesthood, and the necessary ordinances required to be performed by one administering this Priesthood under the direction of those holding Priesthood keys, no man could ever come to the requisite degree of faith to be saved, no matter how intently or intensely he "believed." There would simply be no "channel" and without this requisite channel, the power could not flow as needed. The ordinances by proper authority are *that* essential. How could we obtain the benefits of performing on a contract with the Deity without even having entered into such a contract?

The Great "Principle" of the Deity Within Us

Brigham Young said, "*The Deity within us* is the great *'principle'* that causes us to increase ('principle', meaning, the 'source of Light' or 'Spirit of Intelligence'), and to grow in grace and truth..." (Brigham Young, JD 1:93) He also called it, "*the eternal 'principle'* that governs the Intelligence of all the gods" (JD 26:27). Gods are governed? In this sense, I believe they are—yet willingly so. And if we are to become as Them, we too must practice living in full alignment with this same *principle* of Divine Spirit.

There are two primary definitions of the word "principle." One is, "a fundamental truth or proposition that serves as the foundation for a system of belief or behavior." This is the definition that is thought of by most but is *not* the definition to which President Young is referring. President Young is eluding to a second definition of "principle," described as "*a fundamental source of something*." In this case, this "source" is the Spirit of Intelligence, Spirit of Truth, or Spirit Principle of the Father. This is the spiritual "source element" (or "principle") from which I believe our spirit beings were organized or created. This is likewise what I mean when I refer to the

"Father principle," which is "*the Deity within us,*" referenced by President Young. He also said that it is this "great principle" that causes us to increase, and to grow in grace, light and truth…" (Ibid; parenthetical addition, mine). President Harold B. Lee saw it the same way:

> *"Our existence is eternal. We use words rather loosely when we speak of the 'life before this, and this life, and the next life,' as though we were a cat of nine lives, when as a matter of fact, we only have one life. This life we speak of did not begin with mortal birth. This life does not end with mortal death. There is something that is not created or made. The scriptures called it "Intelligence," which at a certain stage in the pre-existence was organized into a 'spirit.' After that spirit had grown to a certain stature it then was given the opportunity by an all-wise Father to come into another stage for its development. It was added upon, and after having lived its span and having attained to its purpose in mortality, another change took place. We go, not into another life, in fact, but into another stage of the same life. There is something which was not created or made (i.e., Intelligence, Glory, Light and Truth), and something which does not die, and that something shall live on forever" (Harold B. Lee, The Teachings of Harold B. Lee, page 74; parenthetical addition, mine).*

Our objective then, is to become filled with the same "Lord," "Deity within us," "Light and Truth," or "Glory of the Father." This is, at least in part, how we can become "One" in Them, and eventually, by grace and through faith and continued obedience, receive of a fulness of this glory of the Father ourselves. This "principle," or what apostles and prophets refer to as "the Great Eternal God," was not created or made and has always existed. Elder Charles Penrose, an apostle and counselor in the First Presidency to both Joseph F. Smith and Heber J. Grant said:

> *"The individual, the organized person may have had a beginning, but that spirit of which and by which [the individual was] organized never had a beginning…The works of that eternal spirit of intelligence,* ***the great Eternal God****, manifested to us in our Father and through Jesus Christ, never had a beginning" (Charles W. Penrose, Journal of Discourses, 26:27, Nov16, 1884).*

The Prophet Joseph taught that through this same Spirit of Intelligence, we too are co-equal (meaning, co-eternal) with God (Teaching, pg. 353), for we came from this same source or Father principle of Spirit. He also said, "The intelligence of spirits had not beginning, neither will it have an end" (ibid). The Lord said, "Ye were also in the beginning with the Father; *that which is Spirit*…" (D&C 93:21, 23).

The Great Eternal God is another name of the "fundamental source" or "principle" of this Spirit and Divine Intelligence which fills the temples or tabernacles of the gloried, resurrected, and exalted beings who are the Father and the Son, as well as all other gods. These Beings are filled with this spirit and glory of the Father *principle*, from which President Harold B. Lee said we were all derived, and through attaining unto this fulness ourselves by the grace and will of the personages of the Father and the Son, we can then be connected (in a way incomprehensible to finite, mortal man) with the same fullness of light and love that fills Them as well as the Oneness and connectedness They enjoy with all creation throughout the immensity of space—filling all in all.

To the degree that we are filled with the Spirit of the Great Eternal God is the same degree to which we can be One with the Father and the Son, and They in us. Now read this verse again with new eyes:

> *"And the Father and I are one. I am in the Father and the Father in me; and inasmuch as ye have received me (and He is the Light and Spirit of Truth), ye are in me and I in you" (D&C 50:43: parenthetical addition, mine).*

I like to think of the whole heart and soul of our gospel plan as growing or expanding this "Great Eternal God" or Spirit of Intelligence, love, and light within man through faith and adherence to the laws and ordinances of the gospel. Our training on this earth is to see if we will "follow the Spirit" or the "Great Eternal God," which is to follow the directives of this Spirit of Intelligence that our Father Elohim (the Father that spoke our spirit beings into existence) is filled with and connected to throughout the immensity.

This glory of the Father *principle* or original source of that Spirit of the Father's divine Intelligence, light and truth is that which I believe Jesus referenced when he said, "…but *the Father* that dwelleth within me, He doeth the works" (John 14:10).

Brigham Young appears to concur with President Lee and Elder Penrose and taught that,

> *"We must have the same spirit within us that our Father in heaven is in possession of," and referred to it as "**the predominant principle**" that has been planted in us by God (See JD 3:355).*

Following the Light of Christ: Practice Makes Perfect

The reason we follow this principle of Spirit, this Light of Christ, is to make practice, perfect. It is intended to be practiced here in mortality so that we might demonstrate our willingness and prove our ability to do so in the eternal world. This aligning our will with His occurs through a synchronization through this Spirit or Light until, as Elder Busche has said, "He ('The Lord' within us) has become the doer of all our deeds and He has become the speaker of all our words" (F. Enzio Busche, "Truth is the Issue," Conference Report, Oct., 1993). This is what Christ meant when he said, "I can of mine own self do nothing: as I hear (the Father's voice within), I judge (i.e., discern): and my judgement is just (because it comes from the Father's voice who can only speak truth); because I seek not mine own will, but the will of the Father hath sent me" (John 5:30; emphasis added). And the Father's will…is ALWAYS that "eternal principle" of Intelligence, Spirit and Light that governs all of the gods.

Brigham Young speaks more on this source or *governing principle*:

> *"…One eternal 'principle' governing and controlling the intelligence that dwells in the persons of the Father and the Son. I have these* ***principles within me****, Jesus has them within him, and* ***you have them within you****. I am governed and controlled by them, my elder brother, Jesus, is governed and controlled by them, and his Father is governed and controlled by them. He learned them, Jesus learned them, and* ***we must learn them in order to receive crowns of glory, immortality, and eternal lives****" (JD 3:355).*

It is through having become filled with this "predominant principle" of divine Intelligence that the gods become connected with the ether or matrix (if you will) of this all-pervading, immensity-filling Light, which makes them One, and of the same Mind, Spirit, and Consciousness.

By understanding the above, it is easier for finite man to understand the "foretaste" of that Oneness with the Father and the Son, as well as with all living creation that is experienced and enjoyed during Spiritual Rebirth, even *the same* or "like" experience as given the early apostles on the day of Pentecost. The Lord said, "Then shall ye know that ye have seen me, that I am, *and that I am the true light that is in you*, and that you are in me, otherwise ye could not abound" (D&C 88:50). Those who obtain a manifestation of the Lord to themselves through Spiritual Rebirth and receive of this Oneness and Pentecostal-like outpouring, experience a taste of a Christ Consciousness. "All Saints are expected to be of one mind and that mind is to be 'the mind of Christ'" (Mormon Doctrine, 2nd edition, p. 502). This "mind of Christ" does not remain for an extended period of time but the experience leaves one wanting more and more…so that through our continued longing, we shall desire to press forward in faith until the perfect day.

A brief description of this foretaste of experiential Oneness with God was expressed to my son-in-law, Mark, found in the Introduction:

> ***The Oneness experienced was not just with the Deity, as we know Them to be, and They are real, but a Oneness seemingly with all of nature and the physical/spiritual world around me as well. The trees, the plants, the birds, and every living thing, at least in my immediate environment, seemed to be communing with me, and I too with them, through this unseen love and light which seemed to permeate all things. Everyone and everything appeared radiantly beautiful to me.***

The Oneness referenced above is so much greater than what I had been taught my whole life in the Church—that the Father and Son are "one in purpose." Notwithstanding this being *true*, the Oneness described by Christ is infinitely more. The Father and Son are filled, as we too may become through Their grace, with the "Great Eternal God" or "predominant and governing principle" composed of love and light, which is that Spirit of Intelligence that cannot be created or made, and which has always existed. "Intelligence, or the light of truth, was not created or made, neither indeed can be" (D&C 93:29). During my own Rebirth, *it's as if this Divine Spirit of Intelligence were also welcoming me home.* Just prior to his crucifixion, Christ spoke of that day when the apostles would partake of *His Consciousness, in effect,* and experience a Oneness in Him, which occurred on the day of Pentecost. This is also when they were experientially *converted* unto the Lord. "***At that day*** ye shall ***know*** that I am ***in*** my Father, and ye ***in*** me, and ***I in*** *you*" (John 14:20).

After partaking of a mere portion of His glory and Oneness in my own life through God's grace, everything I observed in nature was experienced as if for the very first time. For example, when I looked upon a tree in my backyard, I didn't just see a tree. In an indescribable way, it would be more accurate to say that I "experienced" or "perceived" the tree. It was the same with all living creation, at least in my immediate environment. I became awestruck by the overwhelming beauty of every living thing that God had created. I think the apostle Paul said it best: "Old things are passed away; behold, all things are become new" (2 Cor. 5:17). It was as if for a time (seemingly, at least), the natural man in me had become completely obliterated. And this continued for what seemed to be many, many months. The enjoyment does not remain indefinitely at the same amplified level (at least in my experience), which I believe to be by the purpose, design and will of God. It is withdrawn by degree at times in order for us to further strengthen ourselves and our resolve through continued opposition, until we are able to overcome the world, which can only happen in and through Christ.

The Mind of God

The Prophet Joseph taught that the "Mind of God" is the Holy Spirit (*Lectures On Faith* 5:2). The Father and Son are possessed with, I believe, the same Spirit of Intelligence and Consciousness, notwithstanding their being separate, individual personages, having glorified bodies. They became One, not just in purpose, but one through being filled with the same divine principle of Intelligence and light which all the gods inherit in full, having overcome by way of strict adherence to the light, the laws, and the ordinances of the gospel. Elder McConkie spoke to this unity and oneness: "This unity among all the saints, and between them and the Father and the Son, is reserved for those who gain exaltation and inherit the fulness of the Father's kingdom. Those who attain it will all know the same things; think the same thoughts; exercise the same powers; do the same acts; respond in the same way to the same circumstances…enjoy the same eternal fulness… All this is the eventual unity that is to be achieved" (Mormon Doctrine, 2nd edition, "Unity," p. 814-815).

Christ said that, "No unclean thing can enter into His kingdom; therefore nothing entereth into his rest save it be those who have washed their garments in my blood, *because of their faith*, and the *repentance of all their sins*, and their *faithfulness* unto the end" (3 Ne. 27:19). Christ and His doctrine, which is the doctrine he received from His Father, is the only way to achieve this oneness. Anyone who climbeth up some other way, as the Savior has said, "is a thief and a robber." In short, this particular climber shall fail miserably in the attempt.

In cases involving those who have undergone a near-death experience ("NDE") in their lives, you may notice that most witness to having found themselves (at least at some point) surrounded by and immersed in an indescribable peace and love of and in God. Their expression and description of peace and love is seemingly identical, to me at least, to the moment in which we partake of a portion of God's glory in power when we enter His Presence (or He enters ours) during Spiritual Rebirth and are purified by Him. When we enter God's Presence, whether through an NDE or through that of Spiritual Rebirth, the ineffable peace, love and oneness experienced is described as very much the same. Why would it be different? God's glory is… God's glory is… God's glory. In either scenario, a mighty change will have assuredly happened to the recipient(s), and the actual knowledge of God will have been gifted through an act of grace. And in either scenario, the fear of death will have been removed from the recipients because they will have "seen behind the curtain," so to speak. They would now *know*. When I refer to coming to *the knowledge of God* in Putting On Christ, the above description as to the degree and level of knowledge, is precisely what I mean by it. There is absolute, crushing certainty, through seemingly, ever-flowing tears. This gives us greater context from which to build when we speak of acquiring the knowledge of God and the critical nature of obtaining the same. To be Born of God is to receive an experiential knowledge of God, obtained through a manifestation of the Lord's Spirit and an immersion in the predominant principle of the heavenly element of God's love and light, by grace. It is a holy anointing referenced in scripture (1 John 2:27,29). We thereby obtain unto a perfect knowledge of God. As the Prophet Joseph taught, "*knowledge implies more than faith*" (Joseph Smith, *Lectures On Faith* 7:18).

The experience of total immersion in God's love and light forever changes the one having received it. For one having partaken of Spiritual Rebirth (in contrast to the NDE recipient), the candidate of salvation ***additionally receives*** a sure and rock-solid knowledge (described by Nephi as "a perfect brightness") as to having been conditionally redeemed (past tense), having received a complete remission of all sins, having received the sure promise of eternal life, having had his soul filled with God's, love, and having received the promised gift and ongoing enjoyment & companionship of the Comforter. This gift of the Comforter is designed to further sanctify and lead each recipient unto holiness, in order to one day be prepared to enter His Divine Presence, even while yet in mortality. Paul referred to this process as the "inward man" being "renewed day by day" (2 Cor. 4:16). These gifts are all available to those members of the Church who seek diligently, believe… and receive.

Preach My Gospel says that when we receive the gift of the Holy Ghost (and not just the ordinance by the same name), we receive a "***foretaste*** of eternal joy and a promise of eternal life" (see Preach My Gospel, pg. 65; emphasis added). This sure promise (although conditional at the time) can be made "more sure" through a subsequent endowment obtained through our ongoing diligence and obedience. Hence the term, "the *more sure* word of prophecy." Describing this *foretaste* of immortal glory (Moses 6:59) is like describing salt to one who has never tasted it. It cannot adequately be done. We all rely on our own experiences in order to relate. This is why I liken the knowledge of God obtained through Spiritual Rebirth in many ways to an NDE because it is helpful for the one who has not yet experienced this level of knowledge to at least have a concept as to what it might be like. Notwithstanding, this *foretaste* mentioned above is a "sampling" of that future spiritual union and "Oneness" with God and His glory which its recipients "come to the knowledge of" in mortality (Mosiah 4:11; 1 Ne. 10:14) and will yet *hope* for in the eternities. It is that Oneness the Lord referenced, "*That they all may be one*; as thou, Father, art in me, and I in thee, *that they also may be one in us*."

This "foretaste," arising through a manifestation of God's glory as part of the mighty change experience, is described by seven individuals in their own words (four known to me personally), who all live or have lived in our latter day (see Chapter 8, "Seven Born Again in Our Latter Day"). You will see both the uniqueness in their experiences as well as their commonality, revealing a pattern to aid us in our own spiritual journey to help us know if and when we have been Born of God. This understanding will facilitate our growing from faith to additional endowments of faith, until we were to receive the actual knowledge of God ourselves, even on the same level "as though he had already come among [us]" (See Mos. 3:13).

The Iron Rod described in Lehi's dream is "the Word" (i.e., the Christ Light or Spirit) of God that arrives to our hearts as personal revelation to guide us along the path. His word is not only the written word delivered using symbols of man-made languages, but the voice to the soul via His Spirit or Light, experienced by way of intuitive feelings and promptings which many refer to as spiritual "knowings." This Christ Light may also manifest itself as an inner desire to act, without any concrete knowledge as to why we may even have this desire. This was the case when I had the overwhelming desire to go to a bookstore, referenced in Chapter 1.

This "Word of God" then is also this Spirit that is directing our path through personal revelation through an intuitive, inner knowing that we must do some act of service or act in a specific way. *The purpose of the gospel of Jesus Christ, then, is to grow the smaller portion of this Light or Spirit of Christ already within us, unto an overflowing fullness, through faith, and by His grace.*

The Savior said, "the *words* that I speak unto you, *they are Spirit*... and they are life. (New Testament, John, John 6). *Notice His words are Spirit*! That means that when his "word" or "words" come to us, they most often come by way of a divine energy, element, or contact, prompting or encouraging us through feelings to act in doing good—to love and serve God and our fellow man.

They will also inevitably lead us to godly sorrow and broken-hearted repentance in order to receive the Father's promise which was confirmed upon us as members of His Church by the laying on of hands. These "words" are intuitively known and felt. The Spirit typically works through these feelings. They come as spiritual comprehension that will often bypass the natural and/or analytical mind altogether and become infused directly into the soul.

The written word of God found in scripture was first received by prophets (prophets, meaning, those who partook of the tree of life, received the Holy Ghost, and who may or may not have additionally held Priesthood keys). These prophets later recorded His "words of Spirit" into the letters and characters within a specific language, as originally found in ancient manuscripts, which then became translated into various other languages of the world to aid our efforts in obtaining faith unto salvation ourselves.

If we are to come unto God and truly live (by being constantly nourished by His Light unto Eternal Life), we must also hearken unto the nourishing "word" of His Spirit, whose primary contact is found within the deep recesses of our heart and center of our soul. Elder Uchtdorf likens this Word or Spirit of Christ to a "light within," a "powerful…instinct for home," and to an "inner guidance system" (Elder Dieter Uchtdorf, October 2017, General Conference, Saturday morning session). One of the purposes of the Diagram in Chapter 1, as already discovered, is to allow us to see how a hardened heart will inevitably get in the way of this "inner guidance system" and its ability to function properly and efficiently, or even function at all.

The Word of the Lord is Spirit

In the Doctrine and Covenants, we are taught, "For the word of the Lord is truth, and whatsoever is truth is light, and whatsoever is light is Spirit, even the Spirit of Jesus Christ. (D&C 84:45). The short version of the above is encapsulated in the phrase, *"the Word of the Lord is Spirit"!*

If the Word=Truth, and Truth=Light, and Light=Spirit, then the Word=Spirit also.

The "Word" is the Spirit of Jesus Christ. It is also referred to as His "voice." This Spirit is truth and it is light. And everything that is light is Spirit, or the very Christ Light.

We are told that we are to live by every "word" that proceedeth forth from the mouth of God. (D&C 84:44). Given the fact that His "words" are Spirit (again, not merely symbols or characters found in an earthly language) and that they are constantly being broadcast to us, it is incumbent upon us to attune ourselves to this, His spiritual wave length, if you will. This is what Christ meant when he said, "...how often would I have gathered thy children together, even as a hen gathereth her chickens under her wings, and ye would not! (Matthew 23-37).

The Difference Between the Light of Christ and the Holy Ghost

For the purposes of this work, when referring to the Holy Spirit, Spirit of God, or Spirit of Jesus Christ, I will be referring to the Light of Christ which is "given to every man that cometh into the world" and that is "in all and through all things" (see John 1:9; D&C 88:6). When using these terms, it will not be in reference to the personage of Christ or the personage of the Holy Ghost who is the third member of the Godhead. When referring to the personage of the third member of the Godhead, I will refer to Him as the Holy Ghost. I wanted to define these terms up front so that we are all on the same page together on this journey of discovery. Having defined these terms early on, it will keep things clear for our collective comprehension.

The differences between the Holy Ghost and the Light of Christ are often confusing to Latter-day Saints and Christians in general, and with good reason. To start, the Light of Christ is also known by many other names. It is referred to as The Spirit, our Conscience, Intuition, Light of Life, Light of the World, Light of Truth, and the Spirit of the Lord.

Elder McConkie elucidates our understanding on the differences between the Light of Christ and the Holy Ghost in Stephen R. Covey's book, the Divine Center. In it, Covey says that McConkie used the following illustration or metaphor as follows:

> *The Holy Ghost is analogous to a radio transmitter; you and I may be compared to radio receivers; and the Spirit of Christ may be likened to the radio waves." Covey then adds, "He didn't say this, but I think it would be appropriate in this comparison to think of the Father and the Son as the radio announcers, since the messages originate with them (Stephen R. Covey, "The Divine Center," p.262).*

The Godhead primarily communicates to mankind through the Holy Spirit or Light of Christ. The illustration below highlights what McConkie taught as well as how it all works. The announcer's message is transmitted through the Holy Ghost, which relies upon the existing matrix of light as the "radio waves" through which this spiritual information will travel. If our hearts are tender and open, we will "receive" the spiritual messages which had originated from the Father and Son and our minds will become elucidated and gradually enlightened. The above looks something like this:

The Father & Son:	**Holy Ghost:**	**Light of Christ:**	**Hearts of Men:**
Radio Announcers	Radio Transmitter	Radio Waves	Radio Receivers

Said in perhaps more simple terms, the Holy Ghost "transmits" what he hears from the Father and the Son through the agency and existing *ether or matrix* of the Light of Christ, and this Light of Christ is already in and through all things throughout the vast immensity of space. "The Spirit of Christ (i.e., the light of Christ) is the agency through which the Holy Ghost operates" (Mormon Doctrine, 2nd edition, "Gifts of the Spirit," p. 314; parenthetical addition for clarification).

To this point Elder Orson Pratt said,

> *"We do know, so far as light is concerned, that it is **transferred from world to world by the vibrations of the waves of a luminous ether** intervening between world and world; consequently, if these waves can proceed forth from thousands and thousands of millions of miles, it proves to us that all space is filled with an ether, which we cannot see, and yet we know it must exist, in order to transfer light" (Orson Pratt, A lecture delivered in Ogden City, Tuesday, January 27, 1874: JD 16:353).*

All of God's creations obey this Omniscient, Omnipotent and Omnipresent Spirit which fills the immensity of space as part of this ether or matrix. All of course, but us, the Father's offspring. This is why when we are disobedient, we are considered even "less than the dust of the earth. For behold, the dust of the earth moveth hither and thither...*at the command of our great and everlasting God*" [and yet we as His offspring, sadly, do not]. (see Helaman 12:7-8; bracketed addition, mine).

The Holy Ghost

"The Holy Ghost is the third member of the Godhead. The Father is the Creator by whom all things are: the Son is the Redeemer by whom all of the terms and conditions of the Father's plan are put into full operation; and the Holy Ghost is their minister and their messenger, the one who does, at their bidding, what must be done for men to make them fit candidates to go where God and Christ are." (Bruce R. McConkie, New Witness, pg. 254).

The Holy Ghost does not need to condescend every time He needs to communicate a message to the children of men from the Father and the Son. He mostly works through the existing, all-pervading ether or matrix of Intelligence, light and love. In the case of the Baptism of Fire and of the Holy Ghost, however, the Holy Ghost may actually condescend and "rest upon" or *dwell in* the one who has qualified through whole faith and repentance as an act of grace. For the gentile at least, who is not of the seed of Abraham naturally, how could this not be noticeable? Remember, the Holy Ghost "is a personage of Spirit. Were it not so, the Holy Ghost could not *dwell in us*" (See D&C 130:22). When one actually receives the Holy Ghost, the candidate for salvation is filled and cleansed as though by spiritual fire and is "quickened in the inner man" (see Moses 6:65), which is to be "quickened by a portion of the celestial glory" here in mortality (see D&C 88:29). He likewise experiences "a mighty change of heart" and is filled with *the love of God* (or charity, which is to partake of the fruit of the tree of life) and salvation (see Moroni 7:48).

When we receive this *promised gift of the Father* (Elohim) made possible by the laying on of hands performed by those possessing the higher Priesthood, we experience "exceedingly great joy." During this honeymoon period of experiential bliss and Oneness in God through Spiritual Rebirth, opposition is completely non-existent, having been completely obliterated by God's power. Would this experience not make us all joyous? We come to truly know what the early settlers of Kirtland knew when they were filled with the Holy Ghost, even as on their "like" day of Pentecost, which occurred for most (if not all) present during the dedication of the Kirtland temple. There would be little difference from their experience and our individualized experience today. God is not a respecter of persons. This "fruit" of knowledge and heightened joy comes when we are baptized by fire and of the Holy Ghost. It is also when we pass through our spiritual birthing canal known as "the gate." Elder Delbert L. Stapley of the Twelve Apostles taught that,

> *"Too many are skeptical about the actuality of the Holy Ghost or lack faith in it and thus deny themselves of its powers and blessings. God is not a partial God but is the same yesterday,*

today, and forever ***to those who love and sincerely seek him****"*
(Conference Report, Oct. 1966, pp. 111-114).

Amen, Elder Stapley! Elder McConkie says that "there is nothing as important as having the companionship of the Holy Ghost"…and that "*there is no price too high, no labor too onerous, no struggle too severe, no sacrifice too great*, if out of it all we ***RECEIVE and ENJOY*** the gift of the Holy Ghost" (Bruce R. McConkie, *A New Witness for the Articles of Faith*, p. 253). Why would he say this? Because *we cannot continue our journey to the veil without its guidance* nor would it be possible for us to continue the journey of *ongoing sanctification and in retaining a remission of our sins* without it. This is so crucial since we need to be made pure in heart and like unto Christ before entering His Divine Presence. Remember, "no unclean thing can enter the kingdom of heaven."

More On The Light of Christ

The Light of Christ, also known as "The Spirit" or "The Holy Spirit,"

> *"…defies description and is beyond mortal comprehension. It is in us, and in all things; it is around us and around all things; it fills the earth and the heavens and the universe. It is everywhere, in all immensity, without exception: it is an indwelling, immanent, ever-present, never-absent spirit…It may be that it is also priesthood and faith and omnipotence, for these too are the power of God." "…****the Holy Ghost uses the Light of Christ to transmit his gifts****. But the Spirit of Christ (aka, the Light of Christ) by which the Holy Ghost operates, is no more the Holy Ghost himself than the light and heat of the sun are the sun itself." (Bruce R. McConkie, New Witness, pg. 258; parenthetical addition, mine).*

I like Elder McConkie's analogy. The sun is likened unto the Personage of the Holy Ghost, in this context, and the light and heat of the sun, likened unto the Light of Christ. It is important for us to understand that our contact with God, the Father, is through this "i*ndwelling Spirit*." This is why we must quiet the ego chatter of the natural mind and "turn inward," feeling after It, in order to connect with It. Notice that "It" is capitalized. That's because this "It" (referred to as "He") is revealed in Holy Writ as "God." This "It" is an extension of the Father Elohim which proceedeth forth from His Tabernacle to fill the immensity of space. This "indwelling Spirit of the Father principle" is what is inside each of us, only in a relatively small degree. This is why I believe we have often heard we are gods in embryo. It is by ordinances performed through the channel of the higher Priesthood authority (which "channel" possesses the key to obtaining the actual knowledge of God in mortality; D&C 84:19) that this "indwelling Spirit of the Father principle" may be expanded within us, degree by degree, even unto an eventual fulness. Indeed, to be exalted is to be endowed of a fulness of this divine element of Intelligence or "glory" which is centered in Christ (which He received from His Father) and be connected with all that is. This is only made possible through the grace of the exalted beings of the Father and the Son as we exercise faith in Them.

B. H. Roberts teaches us that all the gods are incarnations of the One God of Divine Essence or Spirit which fills the immensity of space, and...

> *"is also God, even the Spirit of God, or of the Gods, for it proceeds forth or vibrates or radiates from all the Gods—from all who have partaken of the One Divine Nature—Hence, "The God of all other Gods," mentioned by our prophet of the New Dispensation, 'The God of Gods', 'The Lord of Lords' proceeding forth from Them, to extend the one God into all space that He might be in and through all things; bearing all the powers and attributes of God... He continues, "United in this Divine Essence or Spirit is the mind of all Gods: and all the Gods being Incarnations of this Spirit, become God in Unity: and by the incarnation of this Spirit in Divine personages, they become the Divine Brotherhood of the Universe, the One God, though made of many" (B.H. Roberts, "The Last Seven Discourses of B. H. Roberts pgs. 99-100).*

It is this same Light of Christ which gives life to all things, including us, and which dwells in our hearts. Hence the words of Ammon when he said that, "*a portion of that Spirit dwelleth in me*, which giveth me knowledge, and also power according to my faith and desires which are in God" (Alma 18:35). Elder McConkie states that, "It (the Light of Christ) is the instrumentality and agency by which Deity keeps in touch and communes with all his children...It is *the agency through which the Lord strives with men*, through which he encourages them to forsake the world and come unto Christ, through which *good desires and feelings* are planted in the hearts...It is the agency through which ***the Lord himself*** *influences, entices and enlightens* mankind" (Bruce R. McConkie, New Witness, pg. 259).

Notice that Elder McConkie here references a distinction between the Light of Christ (i.e., The Holy Spirit) and the actual reception of the Holy Ghost. The Spirit which gives unto us spiritual knowledge by revelation, does so in order to lead us to partake of the fruit of the tree of life, which is to be filled with the Holy Ghost, receive a remission of sins, and the sure knowledge as to the promise of eternal life to ourselves individually. It is at this juncture that we are able to enjoy the companionship of the Holy Ghost, or as the Sacrament ordinance reaffirms, "that [we] *may* always have His Spirit to be with [us]." "The Spirit," in this context, is the Holy Ghost or First Comforter given to abide *in us* thereafter (Moses 6:61).

The Spirit or Light of Christ has other names. It is also known as 'the voice', 'the voice of the Spirit', 'the law', the 'law of Christ', 'the Father', and 'the law of the Celestial Kingdom'. "And everyone that hearkenth to the voice of the Spirit cometh unto God, even the Father" (D&C 84:47). But he that "breaketh a law, and abideth not by law, but seeketh to become a law unto [himself], and willeth to abide in sin, and altogether abideth in sin, cannot be sanctified..." (D&C 88:35; bracketed addition, mine).

The Greatest Revelation Pertaining to The Light of Christ

Now to the greatest revelation ever given in the history of the world concerning this all-pervading and ever-reaching Light of Christ. *A portion* of the Light of Christ is a free gift to every man, woman, and child who cometh into the world, member and non-member alike, and irrespective of our cultural, racial, or ethnic backgrounds. It is best described by the Lord Himself in the Doctrine and Covenants:

"He that [a]ascended up on high, as also he [b]descended below all things, in that he [c]comprehended all things, *that '**He**' might be in all and through all things*, ***the light of truth***; (Author Commentary: "He" is the Light. To descend below all things means that Christ experienced all of our collective and cumulative suffering, agony, remorse, guilt, shame, etc., arising out of the sin, affliction, and the emotional and spiritual pain of all men and women from the beginning of the world through the end thereof. There is nothing that he doesn't "get" about us. He willingly chose to go into these "depths" out of His infinite love for us, so that He could, a) know how to succor us, his people, having suffered temptations although never giving heed to them, b) provide a heavenly channel whereby we could all receive a complete remission of sins and further sanctification necessary to return to the Father, subject to gospel law, c) be "relatable" to us, having literally experienced our every pain, suffering, agony, remorse, guilt, shame, etc., and d) provide a way whereby we could become a clone or replica of Himself, and receive of His character, perfections, and attributes, by grace and through obtaining a living faith in Him. He did all of this so that "*'He' might be in all and through all things*, the Light of Truth." And He is).

"Which truth shineth. This is the light of Christ. As also 'He' is in the sun, and the light of the sun, and the power thereof by which it was made. (Author Commentary: This Light is everywhere present, including in us. 'He' is the light and power of the sun and 'He' is the light within us that gives us life, "for in Him we live and move and have our being." (See Acts 27:17). And 'He' is that portion of the "indwelling Spirit Element of Intelligence" found within our being).

"As also 'He' is in the moon, and is the light of the moon, and the power thereof by which it was made;

"As also ('He' is) the light of the stars, and the power thereof by which they were made;

"And ('He' is in) the earth also, and the power thereof, even the earth upon which you [a]stand.

"And the light which shineth, *which giveth you light, is through him* who enlighteneth your eyes, which is the same light that quickeneth your understandings; (Author Commentary: He is the light that shineth in darkness [i.e., not only our dark world, but in the darkness of our flesh and Natural man] and we live day to day mostly unawares, which is what the Lord meant (at least in part) when he said "and the darkness comprehended it not" [John 1:5]. Any spiritual vision or enlightenment we receive comes by way of His light and His light only).

"Which light proceedeth forth from the presence of God to fill the immensity of space—The light which is in all things, which giveth life to all things, which is *the law by which all things are governed*, even *the power of God* who sitteth upon his throne, who is in the bosom of eternity, who is in the midst of all things." (Commentary: Here we learn that He [i.e., Christ's light] is in all things and only that Christ Light can give life and make alive all things. We also learn that His light is "the law" that we are to follow, *the power of God* through which all movement and activity occurs, and that He (Christ's light) is in the midst of all things, including us. I liken His light to water surrounding the fish in the ocean or the invisible air we breathe that surrounds us at all times. Since "He" is in the midst of ALL THINGS, there is no place in which "He" is not. That's why He and the Father can notice the fall of the sparrow, because they are both filled and connected to this matrix, if you will, of all truth, intelligence, and light which permeates all and extends throughout the immensity of space. That is why when we pray, we needn't try to reach out into the stratosphere, far, far away. Before you can even as much as whisper, He can hear you. Know this to the core of who you are.

The Companionship of the Holy Ghost is Likened by Apostles and Prophets, to the Increased Rays (or Higher Endowment) of the Light of Christ.

When we receive the First Comforter, and enjoy the actual Holy Ghost as a gift, its continued influence will be dependent upon keeping the commandments, and will be experienced in our souls as *an* amplified version of the Light of Christ, or as President Young taught, "*the increased rays of that light which lighteth every man that cometh into the world.*" (see Journal of Discourse, 6:315). Elder Charles W. Penrose of the Twelve Apostles and First Presidency similarly taught that a person who receives the gift of the Holy Ghost receives "*a greater and higher endowment of the same spirit* (i.e., Light of Christ) which enlightens every man that comes into the world." (Journal of Discourses 23:350; parenthetical addition, mine). What he is saying is that the gift and companionship of the Holy Ghost is, at least experientially speaking, the same as the Spirit or Light of Christ, *only now as an increased, amplified and enhanced endowment.* The prophet Alma taught that the purpose of entering into the covenant of baptism with the Lord was so "that he may pour out his Spirit *more abundantly* upon you" (Mosiah 18:10).

President Joseph F. Smith said: "The spirit of God may be enjoyed as a temporary influence by which divine light and power come to mankind for special purposes and occasions. But the gift of the Holy Ghost, which was received by the apostles *on the day of Pentecost…* is a *permanent witness and higher endowment*" (in James R. Clark, comp., *Messages of the First Presidency of The Church of Jesus Christ of Latter-day Saints,* 6 vols. [1965–75], 5:4). President John Taylor seems to concur with President Smith: "We have something more than that portion of the Spirit of God (i.e., Light of Christ) which is given to every man and it is called the gift of the Holy Ghost… and it *differs very materially* from the portion of the Spirit that is given to all men to profit withal" (John Taylor, Journal of Discourses 23:321; emphasis added).

The "Gift of the Holy Ghost" (meaning, *the ordinance by the laying on of hands*) is different and separate from *the reception and enjoyment of the actual* "Gift of the Holy Ghost." The latter comes in fulfillment of the promised blessing by way of the ordinance at the time that we fully give of ourselves and of our hearts "without restraint" to Jesus Christ (see Mormon Doctrine, 2nd Edition, "Born Again"). The confusion for many often arises because both "the name of the ordinance received" and "the receipt and enjoyment of the Holy Ghost" are both referred to as "the Gift of the Holy Ghost." It is called a gift because when the Holy Ghost is actually received, it comes to us by God as a gift, and as an act of grace.

Elder McConkie summed up the above this way: "Men are born again by following the light of Christ to the point where they receive the *actual enjoyment* of the gift of the Holy Ghost" (Mormon Doctrine 2nd Edition, "Light of Christ," p. 447). He also taught that, "the baptism of fire is not something in addition to the receipt of the Holy Ghost; rather it is the actual enjoyment of the gift" when first received, since the baptism of fire happens only once in our mortal lives (see Bruce R. McConkie, Mormon Doctrine, 2nd edition, "Baptism of Fire," p. 73). The Lord taught that remission of sins "comes by baptism and by fire, yea, even the Holy Ghost (D&C 19:31). After the baptism of fire, we still have the ongoing flame of His Spirit as a companion as we endure in its sanctifying influence to the end of our mortal lives through obedience.

Fellow seeker: The initial immersion in God's light is what happened to King Lamoni, when he was Born Again. The specific account reads that,

> *the glory of God, which was a marvelous light of his goodness—yea, this light had* ***infused*** *such joy into his soul!*

Do we all now "get" that we are not the ones who perform this "infusion of light" or "upgrading of our soul" in us, by some type of superhuman willpower of our own? Man cannot glorify or sanctify himself, by himself. The apostle Paul said, "And you *hath **He** quickened*, who were dead in trespasses and sins" (Ephesians 2:1). Too many of us are unknowingly trying to save or sanctify ourselves, by ourselves, through our own works and merits. This powerful "infusion" can only happen when we come to recognize our *complete and utter, spiritual bankruptcy before God*—that we can do nothing to deliver our broken selves, by ourselves, from our awful situation and spiritual deadness. Through following the rod of iron of personal revelation through the Light of Christ, we will be led to finally fall on our faces, and make the eternal commitment to do His will, by crying out to the Lord with the same desire as a drowning man wants air, and thereby receive the salvation the Savior intended. My dear brother John Pontius said that,

> *"The course to eternal life may at times seem overwhelming. But know this, and do not despair: even though your goals and aspirations...seem unreachable, the way to accomplish them is truly simple...Take hold of the rod of iron of personal revelation and obey the law of the celestial kingdom. God does not require us to perfect ourselves, or to develop godly attributes by our own labors. He will give us all those marvelous things. He will change us in a mighty way. He will exalt us, if we obey Him. Hear it again. He will exalt us. He will work the changes. He will purify us. He will cleanse us—if we obey Him" (John Pontius, "Following the Light of Christ into His Presence, p. 452, e-book).*

Pontius speaks further as to the adversary's lie that we must overcome of our own willpower. He said the lie was,

> *"...that we must, of our own strength, and by our own efforts (i.e., law of performances or works), overcome all our sins, obey every commandment, and when we are finally perfect, the Lord will apply the Atonement, and we will be exalted. It is that baptism (of water) alone constitutes the rebirth of the Spirit. The lie wants us to believe that casual performances and halfhearted obedience will exalt us. It is that being a member of His true Church (being a virgin) is in itself enough. It persuades that being married in the temple, without further justification and sanctification will give us claim to the*

> *promises. It is that 'All is well in Zion, yea Zion prospereth,' when in fact, all is not well in Zion. Zion is under attack. It is circled about by its enemies, and their war is being successfully waged while we swagger about securely unaware that we are under siege." (Excerpt From: Pontius, John. "Following the Light of Christ into His Presence, pg. 142, ebook, CFI, 2011. iBooks; parenthetical additions, mine and by John Pontius).*

Does the above not provide those of us comfort, at least in some degree, who have been trying to perfect ourselves, by ourselves? Are we to become like Christ solely through personal development and self-help techniques? Are we to do it by hyper activity in the Church? Are we to do it through excessive good works alone? Note the words of Paul: "But *God… hath quickened us…*, (by grace ye are saved;)" (Eph. 2:5). Fellow seeker, it is ultimately the bestowal of a living faith by God Himself that saves, so long as we have first met or fulfilled the requirements of the law required for such an endowment.

The "Principle" of Jesus Christ

Our surrender to God will lead us to the knowledge and desire for our tabernacle to be more fully inhabited in this life (as well as in the resurrection) by *the principle* of Jesus Christ, and growing the same, through abiding by every word (both the written letter and "word" of His Spirit) which proceedeth froth from the mouth of God. This "principle" contains the attributes and consciousness or mind of Christ.

The prophet Brigham Young said:

> *"I heard brother John Taylor preach in the Tabernacle one of the most heavenly discourses ever spoken, upon* ***the 'principle' of Jesus Christ being in man*** *a well of living water. If people will live to the light they have, and to* ***every manifestation*** *from God, they will arrive at* ***such a state of perfection that God (this 'principle', or source of His Light) will dwell in them*** *a well of everlasting life—a fountain of living water that will dispense life wherever they go. Whatever they do, every act, thought, and word will be full of life, and they will grow into eternal lives in the kingdoms of our God. It is your privilege to so live that you are constantly filled with the light of revelation,* ***that Jesus Christ (i.e., this 'principle') may be within you*** *as a fountain of living water continually springing forth and yielding life eternal"*

(Remarks by President Brigham Young, made in the Bowery, Great Salt Lake City, July 15, 1860; JD 8:120; parenthetical additions, mine).

Our Light in the Wilderness

And Christ truly said unto our fathers,

> *"And I will also be your light in the wilderness; and I will prepare the way before you, if it so be that ye shall keep my commandments; wherefore, inasmuch as ye shall keep my commandments ye shall be led towards the promised land;* ***and ye shall know that it is by me that ye are led****" (Book of Mormon, 1 Nephi, 1 Nephi 17:13).*

That wilderness consists, at least in part, of the darkness or evil of the flesh, the Natural man, and the enticements and distractions of the world that must be overcome through following Christ's light found within each of us.

This Light is the same light that most if not all of the major religions of the world teach their adherents to connect with, only they may call it by different names. But the fact remains, and I bear witness, that the Buddha is not the one; Allah is not the one; neither are the Hindu Pantheon of gods. Fellow seeker: Jesus Christ is the Son of the Living God, the Promised Messiah, the Savior of all mankind, the Chosen One. He is The Way, The Truth and The Life. He is our Lord, Savior, God, and King. He lives within us through the extension of His Spirit. No man cometh unto the Father, except by and through Him. He is the Holy One of Israel. He is the keeper of the gate and employeth no servant there, and cannot be deceived, for the Lord God is His name. He has been exalted from On High by the Father and He eternally retains His rightful place, even at the right hand of God. There is no other name given under heaven whereby man may be saved in the kingdom of God, only in and through the name of Christ, the Lord Omnipotent. Any who attempt to climb some other way, other than through Him, is a thief and a robber. Those who are truly Born of God and obtain the knowledge of Him will obtain the same testimony of Jesus as obtained by Elder Christofferson, when he proclaimed:

> *"It is Spiritual Rebirth through Jesus Christ that is the context of my witness of Him" (Elder D. Todd Christofferson, "Born Again," 2008).*

The Essential Tool of Meditation and Getting Still

David O. McKay said that, "*we pay too little attention to the value of meditation*, a principle of devotion. In our worship there are two elements: One is '*spiritual communion arising from our own meditation*'; the other, instruction from others, particularly from those who have authority to guide and instruct us." Fellow seeker, those who have "authority to guide and instruct us" are our Priesthood Leaders, including Apostles and Prophets. Now pay close attention. President McKay then adds, "*Of the two, the more profitable introspectively is meditation*" (David O. Mckay, "Consciousness of God: Supreme Goal of Life," Conference Report, April 1967, pp. 84-88).

Consider what the Prophet just said here. What is more profitable to us individually and *introspectively* is the guidance and personal revelation that we can receive through meditation, even over that of our leaders. Why is that? Because in spiritual communion with God, it is God speaking directly to us individually in its purest form, in accordance with our own specific, individual needs, in the precise moment that His direction is needed for our personal journey. In other words, it is a tool which facilitates our contact with God through ***direct experience***. God guides the Church through His Prophet. God guides the individual, primarily through the word of His Spirit. That's why His Prophet consistently counsels us to seek the Lord and follow the Spirit.

President McKay continues: *"Meditation is the language of the soul."* And "language" is a means as to how we can communicate with God. McKay defines mediation as "a form of private devotion, or *spiritual exercise*, consisting in deep, continued reflection on some religious theme. *Meditation is a form of prayer.* Meditation is one of the most secret, most sacred doors through which we pass into the presence of the Lord." (David O. Mckay, "Consciousness of God: Supreme Goal of Life," Conference Report, April 1967, pp. 84-88). Sounds kind of like abiding in that secret place of the Most High (Psalms 91:1). The Prophet Joseph said that,

> *"If thou wilt lead a soul unto salvation...**thou must commune with God.**" (Teachings, pg. 138)*

This holy communing with God then becomes the secret place where we learn of God's immense love for us. This is the secret place where miracles reside. This is the secret place where nearly endless tears flow from a seemingly bottomless ocean of His grace. This is the secret place where we receive glimpses into Their plan for us into the eternities. This is the secret place where the experiential witness and reality of His ineffable peace passeth all understanding. This is the secret place where we learn that we are "accepted in [Their] sight." This is the secret place where we "abide under the shadow of The Almighty" (Psalms, 91:1).

After our daily meditation, we then elect to write down the thoughts and impressions that have come to us, because of their immense value. This is how we enhance growing in knowledge as to the things of God, given through personal revelation. This is also how the tapestry and full view of our life's mission and calling will come into view!

Being Born Again and Growing in the Principle of Jesus Christ

When we receive the ordinances by the proper authority and through faith, become spiritually Born Again, we will grow in the *principle* of Jesus Christ. President Benson says it this way:

> *"Besides the physical ordinance of baptism and the laying on of hands, one must be spiritually born again to gain exaltation and eternal life" (Ezra Taft Benson, Born of God, 1985 General Conference).*

In order to return to God, we must first overcome. But it is impossible to overcome, unless we are first Born Again, thereby becoming purified by the Deity and given the Comforter to abide *in us* to give us the further sanctification and guidance we need to make our way back to the Father. The Prophet's primary calling is to point us to Christ and His Gospel so that we might be saved by coming under covenant directly with Him, who is the only being whose calling it is to save us. Without the ordinances of our religion, we cannot receive the promised blessings, starting with being Born Again. This is precisely why the prophet of the restoration cried out from his soul these words:

> *"Here it all ye ends of the earth... Repent! Repent! Obey the Gospel.* ***Turn to God****, for your religion won't save you... and you will be damned! (Teachings of the Prophet Joseph Smith, pg. 374).*

The above quote by the Prophet Joseph is sobering, direct, and truthful. And lovers of truth will receive it because it will bring them to the light. What the prophet of the restoration was saying, effectively, was this—if I may be so bold:

> *Yes, we need the ordinances performed by proper authority, but the ordinances found in our religion (alone) cannot save us. It's when we "turn to God" with "full purpose of heart" that these ordinances can be "justified" (meaning, approved) by the Deity and sealed by the Holy Spirit of Promise. In other words, we can have all the ordinances performed on our heads; we can attend all our meetings; we can perform all our duties under the law of performances—our "schoolmaster," we can check all the boxes on our checklist, but unless and until we BELIEVE and TURN TO GOD with all of our hearts for His redeeming grace, our progress may become halted. We must LOOK TO GOD, relying on Him alone, and by this means, truly live.*

As we "continue in God" (or as He continues in us) by following His light after the Rebirth, doing the compassionate works that Christ did, that light within us expands more and more and gets brighter and brighter until the perfect day.

> *"That which is of God is light; and he that receiveth light (and doth not reject that light through hardened hearts of unbelief) and continueth in God (meaning, by remaining in sync with His light and heeding its directives and promptings), receiveth more light (by grace, through faith); and that light groweth brighter and brighter (through accrued "portions" of His light and glory infused into the soul) until the perfect day." (D&C 50:24; parenthetical additions, mine).*

The Lord refers to this growth as receiving portions of "Him" (or the Christ Light) in ourselves, by using the word "inasmuch":

> *"And the Father and I are one. I am in the Father and the Father in me; and* ***inasmuch*** *as ye have* ***received me****, ye are in me and I in you. (Doctrine and Covenants, D&C 50:43).*

Said another way:

> *"That level and degree to which you have received of My Spirit, Glory, and Consciousness in you, it is to this same level and degree that you are in me, and I am in you."*

Fellow seeker: Being Born of God entails a heavenly *manifestation of God whereby we are immersed in His light and love and experience a Oneness in Them.* The change is mighty. It is the same as given on the day of Pentecost that the Prophet Joseph teaches that "all Saints (may) receive after faith, repentance, and baptism" (*Teachings of the Prophet Joseph Smith,* p.149; emphasis added). The words used in various dictionaries to define the word "mighty" are "extremely," "exceedingly," "enormously," "immensely," "tremendously," and "hugely." Does this sound like the type of change that would be unnoticeable? Remember, the change (as previously mentioned) is so *impactful*, that as many of the Lamanites that had experienced this immersion in Spirit, "never did fall away" (Alma 23:6).

The Attunement of Jesus Christ: The Vibrations Are There

Since Christ is the light, and since all light emanates or gives off a vibration, reason would dictate that Christ, too, emanates a certain spiritual vibration, which we mortals experience and refer to as "feelings"—these "*inward and invisible sensations*" referenced by President Young (see DBY, 421-22). Experientially speaking, these "feelings" originating from Christ are real. To the degree that we remain attuned to, resonate with, and heed that light which emanates from Christ, remaining in sync with Him, is the same degree in which we may receive portions of His Spirit and be "One in Him" and He, "One in us"—even unto the reception of an eventual fullness. This fullness of the Spirit is to obtain the same Mind, Consciousness, and Oneness with God… "which Spirit is shed forth upon all who believe on his name and keep his commandments… being filled with the fullness of his glory, and become one in him even as the Father, Son and Holy Spirit are one" (Joseph Smith, *Lectures On Faith*, Lecture 5:2).

We accomplish this growth through receiving periodic endowments of Light and Truth (also called His "glory") as an act of grace through faith, until we receive of a Fulness of His Light, Truth and Spirit (See D&C 93:26-28). The reception of portions of this Light and Truth can be subjectively experienced as these sensations and feelings. These "sensations" are revealing something to us. They are revealing God's ongoing spiritual sanctification and maintenance of our "inner man." God will upgrade the souls of all those who love Him and "marinate" in these spiritual vibrations or "sensations" which stems from Him. I like to refer to this type of ongoing sanctification with God as ***the Attunement of Jesus Christ***.

Elder Faust spoke of an "*unerring vibration*" in an April, 1896, General Conference talk referring to when our own inspiration comes: "Your own inspiration will be ***an unerring vibration through the companionship of the Holy Ghost***" (Elder James E. Faust, The Responsibility Rests with me and my family, General Conference talk, April, 1986).

"President David O. McKay said, "And let me say in this regard, that *communion with the Holy Spirit* is *just as real* as your connection through the radio with the unheard voices and music that fill the air. ***The vibrations are there.***" (David O. McKay, Teachings of David O. McKay, Teachings of Presidents of the Church*: David O. McKay*, (2011), 112–23).

President Spencer W. Kimball alluded to these vibrations as well, when he said, "Is there no sound because ears do not perceive it? ***Are there no vibrations in the air because no receiver sets are in tune?*** Does God not speak because our ears are closed? And does He not appear when eyes are leaden? Some people hear a noise. Others think it thunders, ***while others hear and understand the voice of God and see him personally***" ("Prayer," First Presidency Message, March, 1980).

Elder Delbert L. Stapley of the Twelve Apostles, said: "The Holy Ghost, as a personage of spirit, has the power and capacity of touching the spirit of man (spirit to spirit) and influencing him for good and righteousness ***if he is tuned to its spiritual wave length.*** ("The Holy Ghost," Conference Report, October 1966).

The lyrics in some of our early hymns also reference the experiential reality of these vibrations: For our purposes, I offer one for our consideration, found as hymn number 158: "Before thee, Lord, I bow my head and thank thee for what has been said. ***My soul vibrates***; my poor heart sings, ***when thy sweet Spirit strikes the strings***" ("Before Thee, Lord, I Bow My Head," Hymns, 158).

Orson Pratt taught: "Let me here observe, that the people of God can be united only upon ***that principle that vibrates*** *from the very bosom of heaven*" (JOD, Vol. 1, p. 121). Pratt later gave us additional insight regarding these vibrations of celestial intelligence: "If we will be united as the heart of one man, and that general union of spirit, of mind, be fastened upon the Lord Jesus Christ, we shall draw down *celestial intelligence* by the Spirit of God,... ***an electric wire through which and by which intelligence comes from heaven to mortals***" (Ibid., p. 127).

B. H. Roberts teaches us that all the gods being incarnations of the One God of Divine Essence or Spirit which fills the immensity of space…"is also God, even the Spirit of God, or of the Gods, for it proceeds forth or ***vibrates*** or radiates ***from all the Gods***—from all who have partaken of the *One Divine Nature…*" (B.H. Roberts, "The Last Seven Discourses of B. H. Roberts pg. 99).

Keep in mind that any frequency that gets amplified requires a source. The amplifier can only propagate a frequency stemming from that source. In this case, the source is Christ. We need to connect with the vibration-like "feeling" of Christ. This feeling becomes more noticeable, amplified, and prominent after Spiritual Rebirth when we have received the Comforter to abide in us (see Moses 6:61; see also Teachings, pg. 362). Whenever we become attuned to Him through these "feelings," a connection is made. We are the spiritual tuning fork "sons" that are to become in tune with the spiritual frequency, if you will, which emanates from Christ, our spiritual father through adoption. It is He, through these feelings, who is leading us along. This is how we walk with Him. He is the vine and we are the branches. "And God hath said, I will dwell *in* them, and walk *in* them" (2 Cor. 6:16). As we become "in tune" with Him, we will begin to resonate with this Christ vibration. Again… although tough to describe, it is real, just as He is real.

This "spiritual wave length" spoken of by Elder Stapley of the Twelve will lead us into the Lord's Presence if we *endure* in maintaining this type of connection with Him. We must remain hyper vigilant, however, of any and all thoughts or spiritual influences in our environment that might not be compatible with Him. That is why we are commanded to "deny [ourselves] of all ungodliness" (Moroni 10:32)—for if we do not, the darkness will gain ground and the effects of these feelings through the

Comforter, will dissipate. If we leave our minds unchecked, or expose ourselves to the source of lower, slower, or darker influences, the devil may seize the moment to enter in. If we allow virtue to garnish our thoughts unceasingly, then will our confidence truly wax strong when we are allowed a divine audience with our Lord.

Renting a Car and Getting a Truck

In all my years renting cars, this is the first time that a larger airport (in this case, Eugene, Oregon) did not have a car available for me. I could have a small truck or a large truck. I chose the smaller one.

Before heading to the Oregon coast, I ran into some missionaries in town walking to what I later discovered to be a distant bike shop. I had them get into my truck to take them to the bike shop to retrieve their bikes which had just been repaired.

Anyway, the "why" of the truck phenomenon became apparent when it started to rain just after the missionaries had picked up their repaired bikes. They put them in the back of the truck and off we went to their apartment. Anyway, as a result of having a truck, the missionaries arrived completely dry to their apartment. These are the small tender mercies that can be every day occurrences when we are on the Lord's errand. But we must constantly be aware of and looking for opportunities to serve God. I bore witness to the missionaries for about 40 minutes that day about the reality and power behind the doctrine of Christ leading to salvation and of Christ's divine mission.

I am now currently sitting in a studio apartment that I rented right on the ocean along the pristine Oregon coast. A "thick" portion of His all-pervading Spirit has been here with me the entire time. I had finished this Chapter 2 on the Light of Christ late the night before and decided that I needed to make it to town to make a phone call since I had no cell reception at my location. I'd been staying at a beautiful studio about 15 minutes south of Yachats, Oregon, which is a quaint little village, with a small population of less than 800 people. South of where I had been staying by about 30 minutes was the town of Florence, Oregon. I had driven about half way to Yachats when I saw a homeless man, on the two-lane 101 Highway, making his way in the opposite direction as mine (south to Florence). Nightfall was fast approaching and I knew he wouldn't make it to Florence with any daylight left. He appeared to be in his mid-sixties. I saw him and didn't think a lot about it, at least not at first. Then what came to my mind was what I had just written the night before about "the voices" that come to us.

The following question then came to my mind that I had just written the night before. "Brother Bishop, how do I know if it is my own thought or a revelation directly from God? My answer would be, 'why would it matter'?" Well, here is where the rubber met the proverbial road. I began "pinging God" from my heart to know His will. Although I was sensing as much as I could for a "feeling" or "prompting" as to what to do, nothing came. This happened in all of about 15 seconds; all while trying to make a decision on whether to turn around or not. I thought, "this is what I just wrote about late last night." You can't tell me that God does not have a sense of humor. "God, don't you know how busy I am? I'm here to write a work… for you, God." But nothing. Nothing came. At least not at first.

So I determined that I had better practice what I had just preached the night before in writing this chapter. Did the thought, regardless of its provenance, invite me to do good? "Check." To Love God through loving my fellow man? "Check." The thought then came, "Steve: What if this were your own brother, meaning, a member of your immediate family? *Then the voice came again.* "He ***is*** your brother." I swiftly turned the truck around and started heading back south, which was going to be insanely out of my way. I knew that this would take me about an hour and a half of driving round trip in getting him to the next town and back.

When I came upon him, I asked him if I could help him out by giving him a ride. He said he was trying to make it to Coos Bay and said that it would be great if I could just get him to Florence. So we threw his stuff in the back of my truck, and off we went. It hit me again later. In 53 years of my life, I had never been told at a major airport that they could not give me a car, but that they only had the choice between 2 trucks for me. And yet, when I went out to the rental car parking area at the airport, there was a literal sea of rental cars. Anyway, this was the second time I had had the opportunity to use this truck in a way to assist another. But remember, things seem to happen in "three's" for me. So off we went. During my conversation with this brother, I noticed that he had some serious mental deficiencies. He told me that he had been in Russia when they had the nuclear plant leak nuclear toxicity at Chernobyl and he happened to be working and living there at the time. He started talking to me about government surveillance, etc., and that he thought he was being followed. He talked to me about how he had been beaten up several times before and of other unsettling things.

About 1/3rd into our journey, we had just come through a tunnel, when we happened upon another gentleman, who had a bike with 3 sets of saddle-bags attached to it, pushing it up an incline in the road. I thought to myself, "wait, I have a truck!" So I pulled over to the side of the road and asked the gentleman if he could use a ride. He gratefully accepted. The Lord works in mysterious ways. We loaded his bags into the back seat and as we loaded his bike in the back of the flatbed, he told me that this was the third time he had seen this same homeless man in the past 48 hours, the same man who I had already picked up. It seems as though things worked in three's with this brother as well!

We continued on our journey and eventually made it to Florence, Oregon. I had one homeless guy with me, and another "houseless" guy. I have learned a lot from the "houseless guy." He told me there is a difference between the two. And the difference was one of choice. Ever since he had been fourteen years old, he had been mostly on the road, traveling the life of an adventurer. He had many trade skills. He knew anything and everything there was to know about construction. When he would run out of money, he would just go to a town, hold a sign up that said, "Handyman for hire" (at a local hardware store), and he would get work every time. But he would never spend his money on a place to stay. When it was time to sleep, he would "get out of dodge," as he called it, leave to the outskirts of town and then find any tree covered area. As long as it was secluded, it had his name on it. There he would set up his tent for the night.

He had lived this lifestyle for about a decade. He was now 31. He is a very aware person; a deep thinker; one who follows the light of Christ and thinks constantly on spiritual themes. He told me that, for example, most of the other "homeless people" out there would drink alcohol. He told me that in order for him to stay alive, the Spirit had told him to not drink alcohol, so he complied. He had been talking to God a lot. When you are living that type of a lifestyle, there is nowhere else to turn but upward. There are no friends to speak of, other than those other travelers you happen upon briefly. There are none of the regular "distractions" from TV, Media, or phone, etc. It was just him, the stars, and God. He had traversed the entire country multiple times. He knew every spot. His faith amazed me. I asked him what it was like to live that life style. He told me that it made him "relatable," that he could talk to almost anyone and find something in common with them. I could relate with his "relatability" because of my having journeyed to foreign lands and having studied the religions of the world myself. This study made it so that I too, could become "relatable" to others not of my faith.

I called to line up a bus ride for the homeless person but he refused and said he wanted to stay a couple of days in Florence. He had told me that he would go through garbage to find things to eat—to survive. Well, he wasn't going to eat out of garbage cans, at least not that day while on my watch. The houseless person, who I will refer to as Christian to protect his privacy, asked to stop at MacDonald's and we all agreed that MacDonald's would be our final stop. The difference of the houseless vs. homeless person, I am told by Christian, is that a houseless person is not destitute, but lives without a house by choice. Christian is an adventurer; a traveler; a "wanderer in a strange land."

Anyway, the homeless person wanted a number 4 meal at McDonald's. We supersized it and he was a happy camper. In my mind, I knew I couldn't reach this brother with the gospel because of his mental disabilities and since he wouldn't accept my help anymore, I gave him about 1/3rd the cash I had on my person and bid him God's speed. When I got home that evening, I thought of him again and wept. The next morning when thinking on him, I wept again. I still pray to this day that God bless that dear brother (my brother) and keep him safe.

After leaving McDonald's, I told Christian that I had wanted to have him join me for dinner, and he accepted. We talked about spiritual things and I was amazed at the depth of his thinking. I could tell that this was a spiritual young man, who loved God and had deep faith in Him. After dinner, we sat in my truck and I taught him the

Doctrine of Christ, the First Vision of Joseph Smith, and of the restoration of the Priesthood. I bore witness to him that we all are to be immersed in water and in the Spirit to return to live with God again. He told me that he knew that what I was saying was true, because ***he could feel it.*** He told me that when he was a young boy, he remembered an experience where he felt the "vibrations" (his word, not mine) of the Spirit in a very impactful way. He told me that he had been feeling those same vibrations while I had been witnessing to him of my own Rebirth experience. He told me that he knew that it was true! As he was talking, I was amazed at Christian's spiritual depth and insight. I was enthralled by him. I was inspired by him. Part of me wanted to actually *be* him and take it on the road! My heart went out to him and I knew by the Spirit that I was to bring him back to Arizona with me, but said nothing about it at first.

We continued our conversation that night at a hotel room that I had gotten for him. He couldn't get enough. In all, we spent at least 5 hours together talking about the gospel of Jesus Christ. He told me in not so many words, that he knew he needed to follow the example of Jesus Christ and get baptized, even though he had been baptized once before, so that he could have it performed by proper authority.

Then he shared the following story: He told me that he had traveled on foot all the way to the northern coast of Washington because he desired to go to Alaska. He told me that he was on the dock, in front of the large vessel that was about to depart, and he had a strong impression that he was not to get on the boat. Most would have invalidated that impression after traveling 350 miles by foot and hitchhiking, but not Christian. He has always lived close to the Spirit and always followed that "voice" when he heard it. He then ended up buying a bike and had begun his trek south along the Washington coast and into Oregon.

Fast forward about 4 weeks. Christian made his way south to Florence, Oregon with a buddy he had met on the road. They were traveling towards California to beat the winter weather that was soon approaching. When he arrived to Florence, he "felt" that he should not continue heading south with his traveling companion, so they said their goodbye's and his companion continued without him. Christian thought to go north again along the Oregon coast. He told me he rarely "backtracked" because of the Lord's admonition in the Bible to "never look back." He stayed around the area for another 4 weeks doing odd jobs, retrieved some items north of where I was staying that he had left behind, and then began to make his way south again. He told me that the day before meeting me, he had pulled into a coffee shop in Depoe Bay, Oregon and the person that served him coffee was a Pakistani that he had never met before, but found him to be a man who was very "in tune." As soon as the Pakistani took Christian's order for coffee, the Pakistani said abruptly,

> *"You are done! This life you have been living is over! You've already seen it and done it, and now you are just spinning your wheels! You're not going to live on either coast anymore. You*

need to live away from the coast. You've been living this life of the adventurer and God has a new plan for you! It is now time for you to start a new life, settle down, and establish some roots. This much I know: You are done!"

Christian was dumbfounded. As we were sitting in my truck talking, at one point I saw himself hold his hands over his face. He had recollected the 3 times that he had seen the homeless guy. He had recollected the vibrations of the Spirit as a child that had been witnessed to him in similar fashion. He had remembered the whisperings of the Spirit to not get on the boat in Washington after having travelled 350 miles to get on that very boat. And he had just remembered the strange, unsolicited spiritual direction coming from this seeming prophet from Pakistan. "You are done!" Christian knew, beyond any doubt, that our encounter had been orchestrated by his loving Father in heaven.

Here's one of the things I had relearned through this experience with Christian. We are to look for the language of God through other people with whom we come in contact. The Spirit of God is given to every man who cometh into the world. Those who are more connected with God's light within them, regardless of any religious background, will offer us pearls of wisdom that are not to be ignored or discounted. God is everywhere. He is "all in all." He is, by way of His light, speaking to us "all the day long," including through other people.

When I told Christian's story to my father tonight, he said to me, "son, you didn't go to Oregon to write a book. You went to Oregon to find Christian and bring him home." I said, "Dad, I already have a flight booked for him on my same flight home. We broke down his bike and shipped it out yesterday." Then as I went to check both of us in tonight, Christian had not paid for assigned seating, which means that the "airline" did the assigning for him. As I went to check us in, the thought came to me, "what if God puts us right next to each other on the flight home? That would most certainly give this story the miraculous 'cherry on top' that it deserves. That and of course, a picture standing next to Christian, all dressed in white." So I checked in Christian first: 11E. I had been assigned to 11D. I booked my flight 3 weeks ago, and only booked Christian's flight yesterday. Coincidence? This story will be continued, but this much I know. Christian will be baptized and confirmed a member of the Church of Jesus Christ of Latter-day Saints. He will receive the ordinances by proper authority and thereby come under heavenly contract with God. He will receive the "promise of the Father" by the laying on of hands, and if faithful, will be able to receive the actual Holy Ghost and be cleansed as though by fire; and endowed with power from On High.

Tonight as Christian and I were sitting on a bench overlooking the ocean in Yachats, Oregon, I said, "Christian." Then I paused until he looked over at me. When he turned my way, I said, "I love you, Christian. You're my brother." He said, "I love you, too, Steve," and spoke it with the purest of sincerity back to me. I told him that

God was about to completely blow up his entire life, only in a very good way. He smiled and then said, "Wow, I feel those vibrations again." Christian looked at his arms, with a gesture to look at his goose bumps. "I can't wait!", he said.

Fellow seeker and sojourner. Here's what I'd like to impress upon the reader of these words. God gave an unworthy creature a simple test that could have easily been flunked. There was no angel. There was no trumpet sounding in the background. There was only a thought that enticed me to do a single good deed for another person; "A brother." That's it. This one, unheralded and seemingly unnoticed good deed turned into a "chance meeting" with a man who had been following the voice of Christ for years, under the stars of heaven, in the "literal wilderness." He had been prepared by God for a new life in Christ. Christian, I'm confident, will be baptized, and I happen to know a guy who can baptize him. I love Christian. And more importantly and profoundly, I love God. And I love God for sending me such a special gift in the form of a true seeker and truth seeker; a man whose heart had been being prepared to receive the witness of the restored gospel for many years. Through Christian's "cry in the (literal and figurative) wilderness" from his heart, God had answered his plea, and will deliver salvation unto Him, by and through His amazing grace! Our promised land is salvation. And what God says and makes available to one, He says and makes available to all. But we must continue to diligently seek, by making our seeking journey a way of life.

While following this Light of Christ in the wilderness *prior to my having met him*, Christian wrote these words which will give you a feel for his prior connectedness to God:

> *"Spiritual revelation given through the Spirit on earth while under contract with the Almighty: Knowing we're born into the wilds of this world by the Father to experience all things holy ourselves, given no tools, no map and no instructions;* ***only knowledge of a beautiful story of love between a Father and son****. Each spirit being planted in this new and bright vessel, to be tested by time, giving us a choice. Creating all living that we see, He could only create our vessel empty, giving it to us to fill through free will. A battlefield we were born in, to test and to be strengthened or to test and be broken It is in His light of knowledge, we will find Him." (Spiritual Writings of Christian, the wanderer, prior to my first encounter with him along the Oregon Coast).*

Remember the pattern: Desire…Ask, Seek, Knock—Receive. Then repeat.

UPDATE: Christian was baptized by water in October, 2017. The following day, I had the great honor of confirming Christian a member of The Church of Jesus Christ of Latter-day Saints so that the Father's promise could be confirmed (effectively sealed) upon him. Now it is up to Christian to "receive the Holy Ghost," the Father's promised blessing, and thereafter endure to the end. All glory, honor and praise be to God for His endless mercies and goodness.

Chapter 3

The Creation, Fall, and Atonement.

Before coming to this earth, "there was war in heaven: Michael and his angels fought against the dragon; and the dragon fought and his angels, and prevailed not, neither was their place found any more in heaven" (See Rev. 12:7-9).

It was important that there was a world wherein the Father's spirit children might dwell and be tested. That world is the world in which we now live. Everything that was created was first formed in the mind of God. After the creation of the world, the world existed in a state of paradise. Adam and Eve were made from the dust into living souls and given commandments. They transgressed these commandments and thereby introduced the fall of the world from its paradisiacal state and also introduced the fallen nature in man. This fallen nature has been incorporated in us as part of our journey in mortality. It is through our fallen nature that the devil operates and gains access to our souls, to torment and bring us into captivity and unto destruction.

The transgression by Adam and Eve brought about their fall from grace, and in a way, ours as well. In other words, this "fall" was passed on to their seed, of which we are all a part. The fall of Adam brought about Physical and Spiritual death. And although we did not inherit Adam's transgression, we still inherited in a very real way, the consequences of that transgression. So let's go deeper.

Physical Death, which occurred immediately following Adam's transgression, wrought a change in Adam and Eve's physical bodies (making them mortal) which would likewise introduce the very necessary Natural man to their entire posterity, which includes all of us. This change in their bodies caused us to become mortal and susceptible to disease, sickness and death. This is called physical death. Spiritual death is when Adam and Eve were expelled from God's presence. This condition of being separated from God's presence was likewise passed on to us. We will remain spiritually dead or outside His presence until we come alive in Christ and are born of Him.

The fall of Adam also created the law of the opposites wherein man began to experience opposition in all things, and man's initial struggle to overcome the Natural man's nature within himself. Consider the following, if you will: As the seed of Adam, how do we return to be in the Presence of God once more and how do we reverse the existing terminal illness we are all looming under called mortality? Simply put, how do we overcome these deaths which began from the fall? The answer is found in the perfect Atonement wrought by a perfect Lamb:

The purpose of Christ's Atonement was to reverse the effects of the Fall of Adam, which created our fallen condition of both Physical and Spiritual death.

Please re-read the previous sentence until it completely sinks in. It is important to understand that all will receive physical life again through the Atonement. Yet not all will live with God again. Elder McConkie taught the following:

"Adam and Eve chose to estrange themselves from God through their disobedience. They were told to depart from the garden and the divine presence; they sought the toils and trials and tests of mortality, all with a purpose, to see if they could overcome the world and prove worthy of eternal blessings. They were cast out of the presence of God—and died spiritually.

"The divine plan also called for a savior, a chosen vessel... All of this is the foundation for the doctrine of advocacy, of intercession, and of mediation. To be saved man must be reconciled with God. He must rise above the Natural man and become a saint. He must be freed from the chains of sin. He must return again in harmony, love, and peace to the eternal family circle.

"But how can it be? Who will ransom and atone? Who will pay the penalty for man's sins? Who will satisfy the demands of divine justice? Who will intercede for fallen man before the Father's throne? Who advocates his cause in the courts above? Who will mediate the differences between him and his maker, so that once again he can have peace and harmony with his God? Verily, it is Christ. He is our Advocate, Intercessor, Mediator." (Bruce R. McConkie, The Promised Messiah, p. 328.) Elder McConkie says that, "As justice is the child of the fall, so mercy is the offspring of the atonement" (Bruce R. McConkie, The Promised Messiah, pg. 245).

The Doctrine of Christ leads us to the steps we can take to reverse the effects of our Spiritual Death, or being outside the Presence of God. Christ's Atonement and Resurrection is what reverses Adam's (and our) Physical Death by providing all mankind with the free gift of resurrection ourselves, regardless of our individual sins or choices, whether good or bad, made here in mortality. All men will resurrect because Christ did, and will live again eternally in perfected, immortal bodies.

Notwithstanding this, not all men will live with God again. To live with God requires being cleansed and purified, and remaining in that state through the companionship of the Comforter through Christ's atoning grace, "for no unclean thing can dwell… in his presence (Moses 6:57). And this "purification" can only happen one way, and one way only. It is prescribed by God, and this prescription must be followed to the letter. This letter entails following His doctrine through first receiving 2 baptisms, and thereafter enduring to the end. Following our baptism of water, we can be justified by the Spirit and "cleansed by the blood of mine Only Begotten…" (Moses 6:59).

The apostle Paul highlighted the purpose of the fall and Christ's Atonement with these words: "For as by one man's disobedience many were made sinners, so also by one Man's obedience many will be ***made*** righteous" (Rom. 5:19; parenthetical addition, mine). Note that we do not become righteous through a personal iron will, but in fact, *made* righteous by the King of Righteousness Himself. This comes as a reward or gift from having exercised both whole and pure faith unto repentance in complete surrender.

The second baptism is referred to as the baptism of fire and of the Holy Ghost. This is when we are Born Again, Born of God, or Born of the Spirit. These are synonymous. Thereafter, we must still endure to the end, through faith and faithfulness. Being (spiritually) born of God only happens if and when men choose to be obedient and completely adhere to the Doctrine of Christ. This being spiritually reborn is preceded by following God's prescription. More specifically, it is preceded by Faith in Christ similar to having cashed in all our valued relationships, earthly treasures and possessions, and placing them all at risk by way of a heavenly wager that Jesus was in fact, the very Messiah, as well as our personal Savior and Redeemer. With such a spiritual wager, we would either lose it all or gain it all. It is preceded by confession and a complete, broken-hearted repentance with godly sorrow, among other pre-requisites. It is preceded by the continual cry of the soul in petitioning for His grace to save, rescue and heal us through the actual reception of the endowment which was promised of the Father and *confirmed* upon us (D&C 84:48) when hands were laid on our heads.

After the reception of the Comforter which is given to abide in us (Moses 6:61), the promise of eternal life and the experience of a complete purification of the soul, we are then required to "endure to the end," which is to remain yoked to Christ the remainder of our mortal lives. Spiritual Rebirth is the gate that although many will find, they will still be few in numbers as compared to the overall membership of Christ's Church. This heroic journey to Spiritual Rebirth and beyond can only happen through executing Christ's doctrine.

Lay Hold Upon the Doctrine of Christ

Mormon spoke to laying hold upon the Doctrine of Christ:

> *And he hath brought to pass the redemption of the world, whereby he that is found guiltless before him at the judgment day hath it given unto him to dwell in the presence of God in his kingdom, to sing ceaseless praises with the choirs above, unto*

the Father, and unto the Son, and unto the Holy Ghost, which are one God, in a state of happiness which hath no end.

Therefore repent, and be baptized in the name of Jesus, ***and lay hold upon the gospel of Christ****, which shall be set before you... and if it so be that ye believe in Christ, and are baptized, first with water, then with fire and with the Holy Ghost... it shall be well with you in the day of judgment. Amen (Mormon 7:7-8, 10).*

So we are all to be baptized "first by water, then with fire and with the Holy Ghost." We all have the water part of this two-part ordinance of baptism down. But we must press forward in faith until the subsequent baptism is performed by God Himself.

We cannot possibly understand the need to be regenerated in Christ through laying hold upon His doctrine, until we first understand the way in which we got here—meaning, to our fallen state and condition. The natural man in us which was introduced through the fall of Adam, is real. So is the divine. They are enmeshed or blended together but they must become unblended, with the prior to become weakened and eventually abolished.

The brother of Jared said to the Lord in prayer that "*because of the fall, our natures have become evil continually.*" This, our fallen nature, was instituted as part of the divine plan wherein through Adam's transgression, "the Lord appointed us to fall" (Joseph Smith, "The Words of Joseph Smith," Ehat & Cook, p. 63). What was that? Yes, "the Lord appointed us to fall" (Ibid). It was He who appointed, ordained, or decreed that we must fall and inherit the Natural man in us and be separated from Him which began as a consequence of those choices made by Adam and Eve. So through their choices, we were likewise "appointed to fall." But here's the good news of Christ and His gospel. Just as we were *appointed to fall*, we were also *appointed unto life*, through our full and whole reliance upon a redeemer. Enter Jesus Christ of Nazareth.

Nephi says, "Wherefore, all mankind were in a lost and in a fallen state, *and ever would be save they should rely on this Redeemer*" (who could then cleanse us and change our very natures and desires away from that of the natural, "fallen man"). Keep in mind that Adam and Eve did not produce "seed" until *after the fall*. This is why our individual natures are fallen as well, because we are of their seed—a fallen seed. Joseph Smith taught that when we obtain the Spirit of God through the ordinances, we will become the *actual seed* of our new father Abraham. And it appears that we must obtain this *conversion* at some point during mortality, and thereafter "endure" in order to obtain a "more sure" salvation. This is why Spiritual Rebirth is such a big deal. It is the only way given in scripture that we may come alive again (here) so that we may live with God again (there), "for no unclean thing can dwell there, or dwell in his presence…" (Moses 6:57). It is a big deal because when received, we are promised to become "joint heirs with Christ" (Romans 8:17), subject only to enduring to the end, which in its simplicity means *to maintain the aliveness of His Spirit* within our souls the remainder of our mortal sojourn on earth.

The resultant affect through the fall of Adam introduced the beginnings of a dichotomy given to all mankind born into this world. This dichotomy includes the Natural man and the divine part of us. We need to slay the Natural man aspect of ourselves, but we cannot do it by ourselves. It can only be done by, in and through Christ. We must recognize this or else we may never rely 100% upon His merits, mercy, and grace. "And since man had fallen, *he could not merit anything of himself*; but the sufferings and death of Christ atone for their sins, through faith and repentance, and so forth…" (Alma 22: 13, 14).

Nephi tells us that we must rely "***wholly*** upon the merits of him who is mighty to save" (2 Nephi 31:19). Moroni tells us that we must rely "***alone*** upon the merits of Christ, who was the author and finisher of [our] faith" (Moroni 6:4). Abinidi taught the people of his day, "...If you believe on His name, ye will repent of all your sins, that thereby ye may have a remission of them through *His merits*" (Helaman 14:13). To rely in *any degree* upon our own merits disqualifies us from receiving Spiritual Rebirth. That said, irrespective of our worthiness or lack thereof, we all are entitled to approach the throne of grace for redemption and at any time through the authority provided us by our faith in Christ.

The doors of the kingdom of heaven only open themselves to those who abandon all human effort as a means of "saving themselves" or overcoming the natural man. It comes when we perform the inner-surrender to Christ in full. This submission is what it means to have a "contrite spirit." It means we cease trying to "earn our way in" by way of our own work, effort or merit. When this happens, and we issue forth the "cry of the soul" tied to that requisite willingness to sacrifice and surrender our all, including our very lives to Him, we can be born of Him through the grace, power, and will of God. Or as the apostle Paul suggests, it is "not only to believe in Him, but also to [be *willing* to also] suffer for His sake" (Phil. 1:29; bracketed additions, mine).

As mentioned above, when we are born again into the family of Christ, we become the "actual seed of Abraham" (Joseph Smith, Teachings, pg. 149), in fulfillment of the oath that God swore, that in Abraham and his seed, all the nations of the earth would be *blessed*, through obedience to the laws and ordinances of the gospel. This being "blessed" is code for receiving the baptism of fire and of the Holy Ghost, the remission of sins, being born again, being conditionally saved, receiving the sure promise of eternal life and being filled with God's love. When the above endowment happens, we will have then become the seed of Abraham. This is one mighty *blessing* indeed!

The Lord also confirmed the above doctrine when He said to Abraham, "for I give unto thee a promise that this right shall continue in thee, and in thy seed after thee (that is to say, *the literal seed, or the seed of the body*) shall all the families of the earth be *blessed* (now listen for the type of blessing), even with the blessings of the Gospel which are *the blessings of salvation, even of life eternal*" (Abraham 2:11; parenthetical addition, mine). When we receive the *blessings of salvation*, we are converted and healed. And this conversion from natural man to saint is real. We become saints when we are saint-ified by the reception of the Holy Ghost.

The Atonement of Christ, Together with Ordinances by Proper Authority, Open the Way for all Mankind to Re-Enter His Presence and be Spiritually Born of God

Brent Top, former chair of the department of Church history and doctrine at BYU, says this as to spiritual regeneration, being Born Again and overcoming the "fallen man" in ourselves.

> *"I can't overcome that spiritual death, that fallen mortal nature of my own, any more than I can resurrect myself!* ***It's going to require Christ to bring me back to life spiritually*** *and that is what we call Spiritual Rebirth." (Brent Top, Mormon Identity, "Born Again," Part I, Episode 16, as found on mormonchannel.org).*

Robert Millet, former Dean of Religion at BYU, in agreement with Brent Top's comment, adds the following:

> *"...it's not a matter of just behavior modification, or grit and willpower. What we're talking about [is] an infusion of spiritual strength,* ***a renovation of the human nature that has to come in a miraculous way. We're talking about a miracle here, the miracle of Spiritual Rebirth****, that comes by virtue of the Atonement but through the Holy Ghost." (Robert Millet, Mormon Identity, "Born Again," Part I, Episode 16, as found on mormonchannel.org).*

Brent Top, in emphasizing the doctrine of being born of the Spirit, says this: "Sometimes we misinterpret or at least misquote Jesus to Nicodemus and we interpret that, when he says 'except a man be born of water and of the Spirit...', and I've heard it where some people say, 'well, that means that a man must be baptized and confirmed'. *No, it means you have to be baptized and confirmed, one, and then have that (mighty) change of heart (wrought by the Holy Ghost in us)*. So they are really two different things." (Ibid., Parenthetical additions, mine). He continues,

"Ordinances are absolutely critical, ***but the ordinances by themselves, do not bring the Spiritual Rebirth****" (Brent Top, Mormon Identity, Born Again, Part I, Episode 16, as found on mormonchannel.org, runtime 23:14; parenthetical additions, added for context).*

Elder Bruce R. McConkie illuminates the doctrine further for us:

"Sins are remitted not in the waters of baptism, as we say in speaking figuratively, but when we receive the Holy Ghost. It is the Holy Spirit of God that erases carnality and brings us into a state of righteousness. We become clean when we ***actually receive*** *the fellowship and companionship of the Holy Ghost.* ***It is then that sin and dross and evil are burned out of our souls as though by fire****. The baptism of the Holy Ghost is the baptism of fire" (Elder Bruce R. McConkie, "A New Witness for the Articles of Faith," pg. 290).*

Of this remission of sins above, notice he does not say it is received necessarily when we are confirmed by the laying on of hands through the ordinance called the gift of the Holy Ghost, but in fact, when we ***actually receive*** the Holy Ghost. McConkie further adds to our understanding of this principle with these words:

"The baptized person becomes a new creature. He is baptized with fire, sin and evil are burned out of his soul, and he is born again."
(Bruce R. McConkie, A New Witness for the Articles of Faith, p. 291).

"All those who are saints in very deed and who seek salvation--all these desire above all else, to gain the companionship of the Spirit, the baptism of the Spirit, so they can stand spotless before the Holy One in the day of judgment."

(Bruce R. McConkie, "A New Witness for the Articles of Faith," p. 292)

Elder McConkie then asks the following questions and provides the answer: "When do we receive the remission of our sins? When are we changed from our carnal and fallen state to a state of righteousness? When do we become clean and pure and spotless so as to be able to pass by the gods and angels? ***What is the baptism of fire and of the Holy Ghost***?"

Notice some of these other quotes on Spiritual Rebirth, which is to be born of the Spirit:

"Baptism by water ***MUST be followed by baptism of the Spirit*** ***<u>or it is incomplete</u>****. Only when we receive baptism and the gift of the Holy Ghost can we receive a remission of our sins and become* ***COMPLETELY spiritually REBORN****" (Preach my Gospel, pg. 65).*

"Baptism by Immersion (in water) is "the introductory ordinance of the gospel, and ***MUST be followed by baptism in Spirit <u>in order to be COMPLETE</u>****" (LDS Bible Dictionary, "Baptism"; parenthetical addition, made for context).*

Notice that Spiritual Rebirth is likened unto *an experience* in the following 3 quotes:

"One is Born Again by ***actually receiving and experiencing the light and power*** *inherent in the gift of the Holy Ghost" (Marion G. Romney, The Light of Christ, April 1977 Priesthood Session, General Conference).*

"Gospel instructors should recognize that they do not teach lessons, they teach people. They do not merely present lessons about gospel topics, they invite seekers of truth to ***experience the mighty change of heart****" (David A. Bednar, "Acting In Doctrine," page 133).*

"I repeat that striving for the spiritual second birth, striving to know the Lord and to obtain his blessings and powers, is the ***most challenging, difficult, and yet exhilarating experience of mortal life****." (George Pace, Knowing Christ, Pg. 110).*

Our Baptism of Water is Incomplete Without the Other Half

Our worldwide missionaries are instructed to teach that, "*Baptism by water* ***must be followed by baptism of the Spirit <u>or it is incomplete</u>***" (Preach My Gospel, p.65). And if our baptism is incomplete until then, we must come to the realization that we may not have yet been completely or effectively baptized. Would this realization not drive us immediately to our knees? This is when we "awake to a remembrance of the awful situation of those that have fallen into transgression" (Mosiah 2:40), as referenced by King Benjamin. The remission of sins and initial spiritual cleansing by way of this "spiritual fire" (and the subsequent enduring to the end in that state of purity and holiness through the Comforter thereafter), should be the overriding objectives for us in mortality.

This book you are reading is about the process leading to Spiritual Rebirth or Putting on Christ. It is about the path leading to the baptism of water and of the Spirit; partaking of the fruit of the tree of life and then enduring in faith, hope, and charity until the end of our mortal lives. To "endure" involves the simplicity of following our Lord and Savior by emulating Him and maintaining the Comforter's influence in us. Said another way, it is about receiving 2 baptisms and then enduring to the end by increasing in sanctification unto holiness. The apostle Paul said: "But now being made free from sin, and become servants to God, ye have your *fruit unto holiness*, and the end everlasting life" [Rom. 6:22]).

In Moses, we read: "And in that day the Holy Ghost fell upon Adam, *which beareth record of the Father and the Son*, saying: I am the Only Begotten of the Father from the beginning, henceforth and forever, *that as thou hast fallen thou mayest be redeemed*, and all mankind, *even as many as will*. And in that day Adam blessed God and was filled, and began to prophesy concerning all the families of the earth, saying: Blessed be the name of God, for because of my transgression my eyes are opened, and in this life I shall have joy, ***and again <u>in the flesh</u> I shall see God*** *(Moses 5:9-10; emphasis added)*. Adam's pattern is our pattern. In effect, we are Adam, and are traversing the same path of salvation as he did.

The scripture states, "And this is life eternal, that they might ***know thee*** the only true God, and Jesus Christ, whom thou hast sent" (John 17:3). There are only 2 ways that we can "know" God or receive a perfect knowledge of Him in mortality. One is through the reception of the First Comforter, or Holy Ghost, even "***the same*** as given on the day of Pentecost" (*Teachings of the Prophet Joseph Smith,* p.149; see also Acts 2). The other is via the Second Comforter, which includes the visitation of the personage of Jesus Christ to us personally and individually.

Aaron Teaches King Lamoni's Father How To Be Purified and Reconciled To God

We'll all recall the miraculous conversion of King Lamoni's father, including his whole household. There are a few things that stand out in it for me. How many of us have asked ourselves, "*What shall I do that I may be born of God*?" Alma inquires if we have asked this same question in Alma, chapter 5, which is the chapter outlining Spiritual Rebirth or being Born Again. He says,

"And now, I ask of you, my brethren of the Church, have ye spiritually been born of God... ***have ye <u>experienced</u> this mighty change*** *in your hearts?*

Notice to whom Alma was directing his question. It was to "my brethren of the Church." In other words, the question was posed to all those who had been baptized and who had previously had hands laid on their heads, thereby receiving ***the promise*** *of the Father for the Holy Ghost*. Why would he ask the members of the Church this question? The answer could only be that many had not yet tasted or experienced this mighty change in their hearts.

President Benson made this pertinent statement: "Just as a man does not really desire food until he is hungry, *so he does not desire the salvation of Christ until he knows why he needs Christ*." And we only come to realize that we need Christ when we see our hopelessness; when we awaken and realize our "awful situation." It is through this one desire of having to be right with God at all costs that we will eventually arrive at a *spiritual crash site of our own* and cry out in an urgent plea in faith to Christ for his atoning blood to cleanse and purify us.

Notice the lyrics in the below hymns. "Out of my *stony griefs* Bethel I'll raise; So *by my woes* to be nearer, my God, to the Nearer, my God, to thee, Nearer to thee!" (LDS Hymn, "Nearer, My God, to Thee"). John A. Widtsoe said it this way in his lyrics: "Eternal Father, gentle Judge! Speed on the day, ***redemption's hour*** ... From grim confusion's awful depth, the wail of hosts, *faith's urgent plea*: Release our anguished, weary souls; swing wide, swing wide the gates, and set us free!" (LDS Hymns, Number 126, "How Long, O Lord Most Holy and True").

Fellow Seeker. These hymns contain the pattern of being Born Again. It is made possible through Christ's Atonement. It includes the awful depth of "grim confusion," and the anguished crying out in pure faith unto Christ through the woes of a wearied soul. And so long as this "crying out" for mercy is tied to an absolute, committed "willingness" to be "all in," the promised blessing is received during redemption's hour. It is referenced throughout scripture repeatedly. The simplicity of this pattern is found in Mosiah 4:1-3:

> *"And now, it came to pass that when king Benjamin had made an end of speaking the words which had been delivered unto him by the angel of the Lord, that he cast his eyes round about on the multitude, and behold they had* ***fallen to the earth****, for the* ***fear of [their fallen condition before] the Lord*** *had come upon them.*
>
> *"And they had* ***viewed themselves*** *in their own carnal state,* ***even less than the dust of the earth****. And they all cried aloud with one voice, saying****: O have mercy, and apply the atoning blood of Christ*** *that we may receive forgiveness of our sins, and* ***our hearts may be purified****; for we believe in Jesus Christ, the Son of God, who created heaven and earth, and all things; who shall come down among the children of men.*
>
> *"And it came to pass that after they had spoken these words the Spirit of the Lord came upon them, and they were filled with*

> *joy, having received a remission of their sins, and having peace of conscience,* ***because of the exceeding faith which they had in Jesus Christ*** *who should come, according to the words which king Benjamin had spoken unto them."*

This fear of the Lord that caused King Benjamin's people to fall to the earth arose out of having *viewed themselves in their own fallen and carnal state*, even less than the dust of the earth. And if we are to receive the same endowment, we too must see ourselves in this same dilemma and "fall to the earth." The experience this people endured was their collective crash site, which came as an act of grace. This collective crash site will also happen with the inhabitants of the entire world when we all collectively *fall to the earth and cry out for a Savior* when the calamities reach a heightened climax prior to the Savior's return, the earth's baptism of fire, and the earth's receiving of its paradisiacal glory.

Pay close attention now to the words of Elder Faust, reaffirming this principle of our *extremities* and *spiritual adversity* being preparatory to becoming born anew and Spiritual Rebirth:

> *"**In our extremities**, it is possible to become **born again, born anew, renewed in heart and spirit**. We no longer ride with the flow of the crowd, but instead we enjoy the promise of Isaiah to be renewed...*
>
> *Trials and adversity can be preparatory to becoming born anew. **A rebirth (arising) out of spiritual adversity causes us to become new creatures**. From the book of Mosiah we learn that all mankind must be born again—born of God, changed, redeemed, and uplifted—to become the sons and daughters of God. (See Mosiah 27:24–27emphasis added).*
>
> *Out of the refiner's fire can come a glorious deliverance. It can be **a noble and lasting rebirth**. The price to become acquainted with God will have been paid."*
>
> *("The Refiner's Fire," Elder James E. Faust, 1979 Annual General Conference; parenthetical addition, mine).*

Lorenzo Snow stated that,

> *"It is necessary that we **suffer in all things**, that we may be **qualified and worthy to rule and govern all things**, even as our Father in heaven and his eldest son Jesus" (Millennial Star,*

Dec. 1, 1851, 363). (Lorenzo Snow, The Teachings of Lorenzo Snow, p. 156. Bold in original).

Fellow seeker, our souls are imprisoned by the Natural man; the enemy to God. The only way out of this prison, and to become forever free of this evil wrought in our flesh, is through Christ. But we have to first demonstrate to Him, the only one who can free us, that we want it bad enough. So how much do we want it? What are we willing to sacrifice and endure to get there? What are we willing to go through to receive such an endowment? King Lamoni's father had similar questions. He asked, "What shall I do that I may have this eternal life of which thou hast spoken? Yea, what shall I do that I may be born of God, having this wicked spirit rooted out of my breast, and receive his Spirit, that I may be filled with joy, that I may not be cast off at the last day? Behold, said he (now notice the level of his willingness to sacrifice all), ***I will give up all that I possess*, yea, *I will forsake my kingdom***, that I may receive this great joy" (Alma 22:15). Notice his level of willingness! He did even "prostrate himself" just as those in King Benjamin's day who had "fallen to the earth, for the fear of the lord had come upon them." The account reads that he "cried mightily," just as those in King Benjamin's day who "cried aloud" saying, "O have mercy, and apply the atoning blood of Christ…" (Mosiah 4:1-2; parenthetical addition, mine). "That they may… witness… that they are *willing* to take upon themselves the name of thy Son."

In Mosiah we learn that the people "were desirous to be baptized as a witness and a testimony that they were *willing* to serve God with *all their hearts*" (Mos. 21:35). *The promised blessing of the Holy Ghost comes, at least in part, when we actually demonstrate this willingness out in the world, conditioned upon our consecrated sacrifice being joined with all our hearts—surrendering our all to Him.* The question we must individually ask ourselves is, "what is my own level of willingness"? Willingness is directly tied to sacrifice, which in the end is tied to love. What am I willing to endure and sacrifice to know Him? To arrive to this level of "willingness" is why it is essentially necessary to desire to know Him—even as a drowning man desires air.

A brother close to me shared the following about his own experience leading up to his Spiritual Rebirth: He said, "I just knew I had to be right with God. I feared the possible breakup of my marriage and family stemming from possible Church action. All that truly really mattered to me, however, was to be 'right with God' at all costs. It was like having to breathe; like a struggle for spiritual survival. There was no other way, other than *actually knowing* that I was right before God." Fellow seeker, this brother found rest unto his soul. He now has an absolute knowledge, born in fire, that he was redeemed and cleansed in power by the Deity.

The Prophet Joseph lays it out in simplicity and plainness:

"Adam was made to open the ways of the world, and for dressing the garden. Noah was born to save seed of everything,

> *when the earth was washed of its wickedness by the flood; and the Son of God came into the world to redeem it from the fall.* ***But except a man be born again, he cannot see the kingdom of God. THIS ETERNAL TRUTH SETTLES THE QUESTION OF ALL MEN'S RELIGION****. A man may be saved, after the judgment, in the terrestrial kingdom, or in the telestial kingdom, but he can never see the celestial kingdom of God without being born of the water and the Spirit." (Joseph, the Prophet, HC, I, p. 283).*

When we are Born Again, we are baptized and immersed in Spirit. Without this immersion, we would not be able to later endure God's presence, either while in the flesh, or in that eternal world. Is this not sobering? What is it going to take for us to awaken? Let's not allow Christ's blood to be wasted on our behalf. Because if we as members of His true Church are not Born Again, meaning now, in this life, we may never see or enter the kingdom of God ever again. This should be enough to at least ask ourselves the question which the father of King Lamoni asked: *"Yea, what shall I do that I may be born of God?"*

For Baptized and Confirmed Members of the Church, the Clock is Ticking

Amulek likens *the day of this life* to mortality. He testifies that [we] should "work out [our] salvation with fear before God...". We read that now is the time to prepare to meet God. Now! Are we prepared? "For behold, ***this life*** is the time for men to prepare to meet God; yea, behold *the day of this life is the day* for men to perform their labors. And now, as I said unto you before, as ye have had so many witnesses, therefore, I beseech of you that ye do not procrastinate the day of your repentance until the end; for after *this day of life*, which is given us to prepare for eternity, behold, if we do not improve our time ***while in this life***, then cometh the night of darkness wherein *there can be no labor performed*" (Alma 34:32-33).

When I found myself in the Emergency Room on three separate occasions spanning an 18-month period and while wholeheartedly believing I was dying each time, I was literally preparing to meet God. I was preparing to die and meet my Maker. This is the type and degree of preparation to which Alma was referring. Prepare as if you're dying and going to meet God, here and now. This can bring a deeper level of understanding to Alma's pleading to prepare to meet God *now*. "Now is the time and day of your salvation" (Alma 34:31).

Here now is perhaps the most sobering of all truths. Those of us who have come under heavenly contract with God through the ordinances by proper authority, are in desperate need to "fall down" and "cry out" to God from the very depths in order for Christ's atoning blood to save us. Or as it says in the Psalms, "Out of the depths have

I cried unto thee, O Lord" (Psalms 130:1). This is what it means, at least in part, to "call upon His name."

> *We must desire to know Him with our all and cry out with our whole souls for this Savior in our brokenness—tied to a willingness to sacrifice our all, and to surrender our very lives. His grace unto a complete remission of sins does not happen of its own accord, even for those of us who are faithful and fully active our entire lives in His Church. This is one of the most important things that remains undiscovered by most of us.*

As President Uchtdorf said, "It is a most wondrous thing, this grace of God. *Yet it is often misunderstood.*" Elder Uchtdorf further says that, "*we cannot purchase salvation with the currency of obedience*" (i.e., through integrity of service or good works in the Church alone*)*. For, said he, "Do we understand our indebtedness to Heavenly Father and plead *with all our souls* for the grace of God?"

As a general rule for us Latter-day Saints, I wholly believe our remission of sins (even as though by spiritual fire) needs to happen in mortality. I say "as a general rule" because if we are taken by God early through His holy will, and we would have received the gospel and his Spirit had we been permitted to remain, then I believe we can still be saved in the kingdom of God. Those who know not the gospel and have not partaken of these ordinances are not yet under contract or at risk. We, the Latter-day Saints, are the ones under contract. This is what the whole "All is well in Zion" statement means. We are the ones who are not necessarily safe. And this knowing that we are not necessarily safe, is purposeful to understand. Without this understanding of our own predicament and "awful situation," we may procrastinate our repentance until our time is expired; even when it is perhaps, "everlastingly too late" (Hel. 13:38). That's why Joseph Smith said (relative to some) of the Latter-day saints, that "*the disappointment of hopes and expectations at the resurrection would be indescribably dreadful*" (Teachings of the Prophet Joseph Smith, pg. 336).

President Benson, in speaking to the members of the Church in his talk, "Born of God," referred to being Born of God as one of *Christ's most prevalent modern-day miracles*. In the below scripture, I have substituted the words "miracles are wrought" with the words "man is Born of God," since to be born of God is a miracle wrought by God. "For it is by faith that man is born of God... For no man can be saved, according to the words of Christ, *save they shall have faith in his name*; wherefore, if these things have ceased... awful is the state of man, *for they are as though there had been no redemption made*" (Moroni 7:38).

The Savior taught: "Enter ye in at the strait gate; for strait is the gate, and narrow is the way that leads to life, and ***few there be that find it***; but wide is the gate, and broad the way which leads to death, and *many there be* that travel therein, ***until the***

night cometh wherein no man can work *"* (3 Ne. 27:32). And what is this strait gate that we are to find during the day of this life wherein our labor can be performed? It is the reception of the First Comforter, which happens when we receive the baptism of fire and of the Holy Ghost. Hence the directive in the next verse from Amulek where he directs us "that [we] contend no more against the Holy Ghost, but that [we] *receive it, and take upon [us] the name of Christ...(through spiritual adoption)" (Alma 34:33,38; parenthetical additions, mine).*

It is critical that we come to the realization of our "awful situation," for this will lead us to descend into *the depths* of true and whole repentance with Godly sorrow. Those of us who may be trying to earn our way in by our own efforts, or who alternatively may feel entitled to or make erroneous assumptions about salvation merely through faithful activity in His true Church, may be making a blundering error or soul-saving miscalculation. President George Q. Cannon spoke to this:

> *"... we find, even among those who have embraced the Gospel, hearts of unbelief. How many of you, my brethren and sisters, are* ***seeking*** *for these gifts (of the Spirit attending the Rebirth) that God has promised to bestow?... How many of you* ***ask*** *the Father, in the name of Jesus,* ***to manifest Himself to you through these powers and these gifts****? Or do you go along day by day like a door turning on its hinges, without having any feeling upon the subject, without exercising any faith whatever;* ***content to be baptized and be members of the Church, and to rest there, thinking that your salvation is secure because you have done this****? I say to you, in the name of the Lord, as one of His servants, that you have need to repent of this" (Elder George Q. Cannon, Millennial Star, Apr. 1894, pp. 260–61; parenthetical addition, mine).*

In the end, I believe that all *we* can do to be saved is to fall on our faces in offering our broken hearts in whole repentance and cry out in whole faith for His mercy and redemptive power to save us. Christ patterned the same for us in Gethsemane and requires that we consider ourselves "fools before God," with absolutely no feeling of entitlement to his grace by belonging to His true Church, or through any attempts to earn our way in by our own good works, in *any degree whatsoever*. This includes those called to leadership capacities within the Church. Titles and positions may falsely lead many of us to believe that we are special; to lift us up in the pride of our hearts in feeling better than our brothers and sisters. This is what Isaiah spoke of referring to us as the Latter-day "drunkards of Ephraim" (see Isaiah 28), drunken in our own pride. Instead, we must become *humble, even as little children*. Elder McConkie says it this way:

"True greatness in the Lord's earthly kingdom is measured, not by positions held, not by pre-eminence attained, not by honors bestowed by mortals, but by intrinsic merit and goodness. Those who become as little children and acquire the attributes of godliness for themselves, ***regardless of the capacity in which they may be called to serve****, are the 'greatest in the kingdom of heaven'" (Bruce R. McConkie, Doctrinal New Testament Commentary, Vol. I, pg. 415).*

Is it possible that the following words from our Lord were also intended, not as much for the heathen, but for those found within His own Church? "Many will say to me in that day, Lord, Lord, have we not prophesied in thy name? And in thy name have cast out devils? And in thy name done many wonderful works?" (Matthew 7:21-22).

Fellow seeker, do these truths from the Prophet Joseph, George Q. Cannon, Amulek, and the Savior not cause us to realize our *awful situation* and time critical predicament? Alma inquired, "…is it expedient that I should awake you to an *awful reality* of these things" (2 Ne. 9:47)? The day of this life is the time we are given in which to perform our labor. The day of this life is the day of our salvation. Does this not cause us to want to be right with God at all costs and as soon as possible? We must cry out to God "with fear and trembling before Him," calling upon his name for mercy with and from our whole souls and continue this pattern until He answers our cry and petition. The Lord gave us further insight through the Prophet Joseph Smith as to our time-sensitive predicament relative to the days of our probation:

"Wherefore, I, the Lord God, caused that he (Adam) should be cast out from the Garden of Eden, from my presence, because of his transgression, wherein he became spiritually dead, which is the first death, even that same death which is the last death, which is spiritual, which shall be pronounced upon the wicked when I shall say: Depart, ye cursed.

"But, behold, I say unto you that I, the Lord God, gave unto Adam ***and unto his seed****, that they should not die as to the temporal death, until I, the Lord God, should send forth angels to declare unto them* ***repentance and redemption, through faith*** *on the name of mine Only Begotten Son.*

"And thus did I, the Lord God, appoint unto man the days of his probation—that by his natural death he ***might*** *be raised in immortality unto eternal life, even as many as would believe;*

"And they that believe not unto eternal damnation; for they cannot be redeemed from their spiritual fall, ***because they repent not****" (D&C 29:41-44).*

The verses above are applicable to those who are under contract ("covenant") with the Almighty through the ordinances by proper authority. In other words—we the people of His Church. If we who have the restored gospel of Jesus Christ choose not to exercise *faith unto repentance* during the days of our probation, the first death which is spiritual, may also become an enduring death—meaning, that we may remain for eternity outside the presence of God, other than when we are brought before Him to be judged. Of those that do not avail themselves of this "*space* granted unto man, in which he might repent" and turn to God with full purpose of heart, Alma affirms: "Then cometh a death, even a second death, which is a spiritual death; then is ***a time*** that whosoever [notice the timing] *dieth in his sins, as to a temporal death*, **shall also die a spiritual death**; yea, he shall die a spiritual death" and "shall be as though there had been no redemption made" (Alma 12:24; 16-18).

I will close this segment by presenting this thought-provoking question: If we did not need to be born again or born of the Spirit in this life (which by divine law must be preceded by *broken-hearted repentance*), why would the God of heaven have **prolonged** or **lengthened** the days of Adam's posterity? Here is the definitive answer from Nephi, which applies to us all:

> *"The days of the children of men were **prolonged**, according to the will of God (why?), **that they might repent** (when?) **while in the flesh**, wherefore, their state became a state of probation, and **their time was lengthened**... For he gave commandment that all men must repent (while in the flesh); for he showed unto all men that they were lost..."*
> *(2 Ne. 2:21; emphasis added).*

The Redemption of God

The redemption of God requires that we not only perform our duties under the gospel law (which, by the way is insufficient for salvation), but that we *desire and seek to know Him* with our whole heart and soul, tied to an unbending willingness to do anything that He were to ever ask as a condition prior to finding Him—to be "all in," if you will. Then through this surrender in contriteness and the offering up of our broken hearts in pure and whole faith, we may in our spiritual desperation and despair, issue forth the cry of the soul and be accepted in His sight, being justified through Christ by way of complete repentance, while *relying wholly and alone upon His merits*.

"And moreover, I say unto you, that *salvation doth not come by the law alone*; and were it not for the atonement, which God himself shall make for the sins and iniquities of his people, that they must unavoidably perish, *notwithstanding the law of Moses*.

"And now I say unto you that it was expedient that there should be a law given to the children of Israel, yea, even a very strict law; for they were a stiffnecked people, quick to do iniquity, and slow to remember the Lord their God;

"Therefore there was a law given them, yea, *a law of performances* (note: this can be likened unto the proverbial "checklist" that many focus on *exclusively*, often without any involvement of the heart, and thereby "miss the mark") and of ordinances, a law which they were to observe strictly from day to day, to keep them in remembrance of God and their duty towards him…". (note: This "law of performances" is purposeful, however, and is part of the "training wheels" we use until we are made free—no longer subject to the law of performances but guided and governed exclusively by the law of Christ).

"But behold, I say unto you, that all these things were types of things to come.

"And now, did they understand the law? I say unto you, nay, *they did not understand the law*; and this *because of the hardness of their hearts*; for they understood not that there could not any man be saved *except it were through the redemption of God*" (Mosiah 13:28-32; parenthetical additions, mine).

The apostle Paul referred to this law of performances as our "schoolmaster" or teacher. "Wherefore the law was our schoolmaster to bring us unto Christ, (for what purpose?) that we might be *justified by faith*" (Gal. 3:24), which is when man is acquitted from the weight of God's justice followed by being sanctified through the blood of Christ.

Said another way, by trying to perfect ourselves by ourselves (through the works of the law alone) by adhering exclusively to "the law of performances" (without the required involvement of the heart in perfect surrender), we are not relying solely in faith upon the merits of Christ, which is a pre-requisite for justification by His grace and the subsequent Spiritual Rebirth and adoption into the family of Christ. For when this were to happen, we will have been found "willing to take upon [us] the name of [His] son." Is this not what we reaffirm each week by participation in the Sacrament Ordinance? Do we understand this? In relying in any degree upon our own efforts or merits, we have in effect, perhaps *unknowingly even, been trying to save ourselves by ourselves*. In doing so, we will have disqualified ourselves from receiving His atoning grace to the degree that we could have been afforded otherwise.

The Law of Performances Joined With the Involvement of the Heart

As discussed, the law as our schoolmaster (including the "law of performances") is purposeful and necessary. It is purposeful because *as we provide compassionate service to others from the heart and through our righteous desires to alleviate suffering, we are given "portions" of faith*, as an endowment or gift. Notice it must involve the heart space. This is reaffirmed in the Book of Mormon by the actions of some of the Lamanites who joined the Anti-Nephi-Lehi's. They knew that the law of Moses and works therein alone could not save them, but that "the law of Moses did serve to ***strengthen their faith*** in Christ (which "faith" had, in fact, saved them); and thus they did retain a hope (ie., "knowledge of God and promise of eternal life, etc., how?") ***through faith*** unto salvation" (Alma 25:16; parenthetical additions, mine). Notice the pattern of the Diagram here. Hope, in this context is an actual, spiritual knowledge (no longer a belief) that one has come to the knowledge of God, and has had the promise of eternal life extended to him or her. How was it done? Through an endowment of a perfect faith by God. And in our Diagram, what follows hope (as to the fulfillment of the promise of eternal life and other spiritual knowledge received)? Salvation, or charity.

*Desire →Tender/Open Heart →Spiritual Sight/"Seeing" →Belief (Light) →Acting in Gospel Belief→**Faith** →Spiritual Knowledge/Understanding **(Hope)** →Salvation **(Charity)****

**Salvation includes an experience of being filled with the Love of God [charity], an actual knowledge as to the reality of the Father and the Son manifested in power, receiving a remission of sins as though by spiritual fire, and receiving the sure promise of Eternal Life, subject to enduring to the end.*

Remember, to retain an actual, Spiritual Knowledge of God and in his promise to us of eternal life (which we "hope" to receive a fullness of in the resurrection because of the actual knowledge of having received the promise from Him here), necessitates having first obtained said knowledge of salvation which happens by faith. Or as said another way in the book of Ether, "… ***which hope cometh of faith***…" (see Ether 12:4). This "hope" is also for the future permanency and fulness of that portion of "glory" which we "tasted" during Spiritual Rebirth which we may be granted in the resurrection, subject to enduring to the end. The apostle Paul teaches we are to "rejoice in hope of (what?) the *glory* of God" (Rom. 5:2; parenthetical addition, mine). We rejoice in the hope of His glory because we already experienced a taste of it, which then gave us the right to obtain a fulness of the same in the resurrection through enduring to the end. This is the "hope" referred to in the phrase, "Faith, Hope, and Charity."

The accumulation of spiritual light in us works the same way and parallels our accumulation of that spiritual element called "faith" which we accrue as well, per the example above. We accrue "more and more light until the perfect day," just as we do with increments of faith. These accrue through compassionate service with the intention of serving our God. The works of service alone however, without the involvement of the heart, may be considered "good" by man, yet may be considered as only "having a form of godliness" by God. In other words, the "outer forms" may end up becoming stale or hollow, and most people will notice our inauthenticity, since all have been given the Light of Christ, and through it, will be able to spiritually discern our authenticity or lack thereof.

This is a huge distinction that deserves to be highlighted and understood. It's not just about the works or "law of performances," but it's about the works, blended with the involvement of our hearts being engaged in our service. When the progress slows in the Church, it is because our hearts as members, may be becoming more and more hardened…even unto the degree of becoming potentially "past feeling." If this were to occur, we would then run the risk of becoming a religious group of "past feeling doers," patterned after some of the cultural traditions of our fathers, and potentially become the proverbial blind following the blind.

As to these traditions, Lorenzo Snow has warned: "If the people here have not received the miraculous blessings promised (i.e., the reception of the Holy Ghost and accompanying gifts and manifestations of the Spirit) in connection with their obedience to the Gospel... *they are perpetuating upon their children and their children's children and...* ***binding a yoke of tradition upon them*** which, in its consequence, is beyond the power of language to express. The people are guilty of the most gross offense before the Almighty, for they are not only injuring themselves, but they are ***destroying the happiness of unborn generations***" (Discourse by Lorenzo Snow, delivered in the Tabernacle, Salt Lake City, January 14, 1872; JD 14:300). Snow's words, sadly, are plainly visible in our day. Elder Maxwell warned: "For those either untaught or unheeding of the essential gospel truths, ***the lapse of faith in Christ is just one generation away***" ("The Children of Christ," Neal A. Maxwell, BYU Speeches).

When these hollow forms and works (including those that have arisen out of tradition) are witnessed by those investigating the Church, the work of the Lord will unavoidably cause the progress of the church to slow to a mere crawl (Alma 4:11). These *hollow forms* may even repel those investigating the Church from ever joining. Regrettably, we may observe the same becoming increasingly visible in the many wards and branches within the true Church of God, but this is not the purity of the gospel. Yet through all of this, those who are on the path within the confines of His Church must still continue to "press forward" with a steadfastness of faith in Christ and in so doing, be able to experience a plethora of missionary successes and aid others in coming unto Christ as well.

In Alma chapter 4 referenced above, the hardness of heart in the members of the Church came as a result of wickedness. Hardness of heart creates enmity which was described in Chapter 1 as an unseen, spiritual "heart barrier." Enmity is a form of pride. And this pride (aka, "wickedness") found within the Church in Alma's day exceeded those who did not belong to the Church. This pride became "a great stumbling-block to those who did not belong to the Church; and *thus* the Church began to fail in its progress" (Alma 4:10). In Helaman it says it this way: "the pride which began to enter into the church—not into the church of God (notice the distinction), ***but into the hearts of the people who professed to belong to the church of God***" (Helaman 3:33; parenthetical addition, mine). If the Church *thus* failed in its progress in Alma's day, could it not create the same for us in our day?

Do we see a "type" of this today in our modern-day Church? Of course we do. There have been these types of challenges in every dispensation wherein the Lord's Church, priesthood keys and ordinances have been made available. Yet as we see the "old ship Zion" taking on water, our job is to plug the holes and bail as much water as quickly and as best we can as humble servants of Christ. Our job is to "choose in" and work even harder, lifting where we stand and uplifting those we can. We will accomplish this through that ever-growing and ever-expanding Light of Christ in our souls.

In an interview with Adam S. Miller, author of "Future Mormon: Essays in Mormon Theology," Dr. Miller counsels the new generation of Latter-day Saints thus:

> *"Every generation must work out their own salvation. Every generation must live its own lives and think its own thoughts and receive its own revelations. And, if Mormonism continues to matter, it will be because they,* ***rather than leaving****, were willing to be Mormon all over again...and* ***make it their own*** *in order to embody Christ anew in this passing world."*

Well said, Dr. Miller. Kudos to you, and a resounding Amen!

Too often our primary focus may be on the Church. This can be a stumbling stone, because the Church, although "true," is an organization full of imperfect mortals, ourselves included. This focus is not necessarily bad, it's just that there's another focus that's even better. We go to Church to serve the Lord. He must be and remain our focus. Keep in mind that salvation is an individual, one on one journey to Christ. If we lose Christ as our focus, we will lose our footing, and may inevitably stumble. Let go and surrender in full all concerns to God, notwithstanding the actions of imperfect people both in and out of the Church. Focus on Christ and don't get sidetracked by those who may offend. The Lord said, "If they have not charity, what mattereth that to thee; *thou hast been faithful; wherefore, they garments shall be made clean*" (Ether 12:37). Again, ***we are not coming unto the Church, we are coming unto Christ!*** Dr. Miller says it this way:

> *"If I think that Mormonism is about Mormonism, I'll get stuck in the same trap. I'll miss what it means to be Mormon. In my experience, Mormonism comes into focus as true and living, only when I stop looking directly at it, and instead aim my attention (and intention) at Christ. Instead of aiming at Mormonism, I have to aim at what Mormonism is aiming at, otherwise I'll miss what matters most." He continues, "...what*

if instead of looking at the hand pointing at the moon, I look straight at the moon?... Mormonism, when it is true to itself, is about Christ" (Adam S. Miller, "Letters to a Young Mormon, Unplugged," Youtube; parenthetical addition, mine).

This, fellow seeker, is why we are to build upon the rock of our Redeemer, who is Christ the Lord, so that when the tests come, we may still stand.

When we "aim our attention," as Miller puts it, and build upon any other foundation other than upon Christ, or if we even focus more on His Church or its leaders *than on our God Himself*, our progress as a Church will slow in its progress. And this "slowing in the Church's progress" (per Alma 4) is precisely why we must do all we can to find the gate and partake of the fruit of salvation by being Born of God ourselves, so that witness after witness may be borne by those who know. This is how we can "embody Christ anew in this passing world."

"Brother Lawrence," said it this way: "I engaged in a religious life *only for the love of God*, and I have endeavored *to act only for Him*; whatever becomes of me, whether I be lost or saved, I will always continue to act purely for the love of God. I shall have this good at least, that *till death I shall have done all that is in me to love Him*" ("The Practice of the Presence of God," copyright 1895 by Fleming H. Revell Comapy, p. 7). I love this man!

So anything not about Christ, is about tenets. And tenets are those principles and teachings within the Church that may be good and true, but perhaps not life-saving. The Lord clearly teaches where to "aim our attention," so that we might obtain salvation:

"And of tenets thou shalt not talk, but thou shalt declare repentance and faith on the Savior, and remission of sins by baptism, and by fire, yea, even the Holy Ghost" (D&C 19:31).

When we receive of this baptism by fire, we shall obtain the eternal witness of ***the knowledge of God*** we seek, that can never again be taken from us. It is when we are purified (or made pure as though by fire) so we may return to God. *We must make sure that we seek the blessings of salvation ourselves, through the first Comforter, so that we can bear witness to its existence and His existence, in all reality. This is done in order to instill in others the belief and faith to then seek, follow, and do likewise.* And as the apostle Paul suggested, any "imaginations [i.e., arguments] and every high thing that exalteth itself against ***the knowledge of God***" should be cast down (2 Cor. 10:5; bracketed addition, mine).

Elder Packer, in speaking of obtaining the blessings of salvation, stated that "when one has received that witness, and is called to testify, for him to dilute, to minimize, to withhold would be grossly wrong. It is in the face of this that I feel the urgency to bear witness. And I bear my solemn witness that Jesus is the Christ" (Boyd K. Packer, "Can I Really Know?", Conference Report, October 1964, pp. 126-129).

Receiving of this "witness" and concurrent ***manifestation*** and purification in power by the Holy Ghost (also known as full conversion) is the primary purpose of all programs and instruction within the Church and gospel of Jesus Christ. Elder Bednar taught that,

> *"Fundamentally, ALL GOSPEL TEACHINGS and activities are centered on RECEIVING the Holy Ghost...." (Elder Bednar, "Receive the Holy Ghost," General Conference Talk).*

And since the most glorious of all "end games," if you will, in mortality is to see the face of God, how else could we possibly be prepared and sanctified sufficient to being made like unto Him (a requirement for most to enter His Presence), void of this gift? It would be impossible. Can we see the critically important nature and necessity of receiving this gift of the Holy Ghost?

Without the Involvement of the Heart, All "Forms" are Hollow

In Moroni 7:9, the above-mentioned point with regards to "hollow forms" is drilled down extensively with regards to prayer. And yet it is not just prayer that needs the involvement of the heart. It is any Christ-centered action that we provide within the Church and gospel program. Notice the admonition:

> *"And likewise also is it counted evil unto a man, if he shall pray (substitute here the word "pray" for any other service or "works") and not with real intent of heart; yea, and it profiteth him nothing, for God receiveith none such. (Moroni 7:7-9; parenthetical addition, mine).*

Hence the purpose of the words delivered to Joseph during the first vision, where Joseph was told by the Lord Himself that, "they draw near to me with their lips, but their hearts are far from me, they teach for doctrines the commandments of men, ***having a form of godliness*** (through the "law of performances" or "works of the law" with little involvement of the heart), but deny the power thereof" (JSH 1:19). Jeremiah taught that,

> *"...External service is **useless** where there is no devotion of heart..." (See "Jeremiah," Bible Dictionary).*

This is precisely why "checking boxes" doesn't work and is woefully insufficient in the Lord's eyes. The Lord Himself said, "Behold, the Lord ***requireth the heart*** and a willing mind; and the willing and obedient shall eat the good of the land of Zion in these last days" (D&C 64:34). In the Odes we read: "Open, open your hearts to the exultation of the Lord, and let your love abound from the heart…" (The Odes of Solomon 8:1). Notice it begins with the heart. The heart must be involved in all that we do, or it may be said that "it profiteth [us] nothing." Works of the law, without the involvement of the heart, is one of our many cultural stumbling stones.

Through compassionate acts of service *performed sincerely from our heart space*, faith is then added upon faith (as a gift bestowed from God by grace) until we receive of that "sufficiency of faith" that saves. Brigham Young said, "When you believe the principles of the Gospel and attain unto faith, *which is a gift of God*, he adds more faith, adding faith to faith. *He bestows faith upon his creatures* ***as a gift***…" (Discourses of Brigham Young, p.154). Notice that faith is attained (how?) as a gift bestowed of and from God.

Faith then, which is a gift of God, is preceded by doing the things that Christ did from our hearts (not by just checking a box); by "acting in gospel belief," which affords us the opportunity to demonstrate to God our belief by our very works and not just through lip service. We must "act in gospel belief" from our hearts to receive the endowment of that spiritual substance called "faith." "Yea, come unto me and bring forth works of righteousness (which, when joined with whole repentance and doing the compassionate acts of service from the heart, is to act in gospel belief) and ye shall not be hewn down and cast into the fire (Alma 5:35). Once our "faith cup" begins to fill, even to overflowing, we will receive actual, spiritual knowledge of God and partake of the fruit of the tree of life and salvation.

Lip service is a hollow form, without the compassionate works from the heart to back it up. And to do the works from the heart truly requires a willingness and commitment beforehand to follow Christ. Connecting from our heart space is imperative. This is what set the apostles apart from the Pharisees and Sadducees in Christ's day. The apostle Paul said it this way: "But God be thanked that though you were slaves of sin, *yet you obeyed from the heart* that form of doctrine which was delivered you" (Rom. 6:17).

Christ said, "Wherefore, follow me, and **do** the things which ye have seen me **do**." He also said, "Verily, ye know the things that ye must **do** in my Church; for the works which ye have seen me **do** that shall ye also **do**; for that which ye have seen me **do** even that shall ye **do**. Notice that the most prevalent word in the above verses by Jesus Christ is the word "do." This is what true "ministering" is. "To minister is to act in the name and place and stead of another person in teaching those truths and performing those acts which are necessary for the salvation of those on whose behalf the ministerial service is rendered" (see The Promised Messiah, pg. 474). Dr. Hawkins reinforces the Lord's admonition to "do His will" and suggests that, "it is not just spiritual truth but the degree of one's devotion to it that empowers it to become transformative" (Dr. David R. Hawkins, Transcending the Levels of Consciousness, p.336). The Savior said, "Why call me Lord, Lord, and do not that which I say?"

The Interdependency of Faith and Works

Remember that the "doing" is not what saves us, although the doing can lead us to endowment upon endowment of faith unto an eventual sufficiency of faith necessary for salvation. Ultimately, *it is faith and faith alone that saves, subject to having fulfilled the pre-requisites under the law of God* (including whole repentance and 'acting in belief' or doing 'the works of righteousness') found in His gospel. Brigham Young says it this way:

> *"...No living, intelligent being, whether serving God or not, acts without belief. He might as well undertake to live without breathing as to live without the principle of belief. But he must believe the (gospel) truth, obey the truth, and practice the truth (ie., consistently act in gospel belief), to obtain the power of God called faith" (DBY,153). (Faith in the Lord Jesus Christ, Teachings of the Presidents of the Church, Brigham Young, Pgs. 54-59; parenthetical additions, mine).*

The law of Moses together with the law of performances ("works of the law") from the heart are preparatory for many future endowments of faith unto salvation. (Note: This preparation is a kin to the preparation of receiving the Aaronic Priesthood [known as the "preparatory priesthood"] to receive of the higher or Melquisedec priesthood).

After Spiritual Rebirth, we do the works of righteousness because much of our individual will becomes interwoven in the Divine will. In other words, we do the works because it has now become our nature, passion, love, and strongest desire. This is the place where true freedom is found. The partition between us and God is leveled as we are reconciled to Him. The inner battle is no longer an overwhelming one because now our desire coincides with God's desire. The above demonstrates the interrelatedness between works and faith. In the final judgement when the books are opened, we will be rewarded according to our works (see Rev. 20:12), which are the "fruit" we are to bring forth. As we do these works of love and compassion in mortality from the heart, we "continue in God," which is to say, we continue in His love and light, through the work and service of alleviating (as best we can) the suffering of mankind. In doing the "like" works that Christ did, we shall accrue more and more light, faith, and knowledge until the perfect day dawns when we are prepared to rend in totality the veil of unbelief, and enter the Divine Presence.

The Perfect Faith Bestowed by God

Through these incremental portions of faith that builds unto an explosion of faith, we will eventually "see" that the miracle of salvation is being offered and extended to us individually. This is when we may first "see the Kingdom of God." Through this faith that comes alive on our heads and within us, we begin to truly ***know*** that we can actually receive "immortality and eternal life" ourselves, which is God's work and His glory. When this occurs, unbelief slips away and vanishes. And the feeling is undeniably real as this spiritual element of a living, perfect faith is bestowed. This is when our faith is *profoundly awakened*. "Faith is the *substance* (i.e., both a spiritual element of a 'living faith' and spiritual assurance) of things hoped for…". (Author Commentary: It is my opinion that many times in scriptures, the word "faith" is used in the context that would really be more closely associated with the word "belief," and vice versa. We would do well to follow the Spirit to know which context of the word "faith" or "belief" is being used when reading the scriptures. Words are pointers only and often fail us. It is beneficial for the seeker to be spiritually discerning so as to better understand the scribe's, apostle's, or prophet's original intent behind the word being used, in order to understand the word of God on perhaps, a much clearer and deeper level).

In conclusion then, it is important for us to fully recognize that the tests as to our level of "willingness" will continue through the above-mentioned schoolmaster until, through the intended purpose of our heartfelt works or "performances" under the law, we attain unto that *sufficiency and quality of faith* needed to be redeemed, healed, and saved. This initial salvation is, of course, preceded by having descended into the depths of despair through whole repentance in offering up of our broken hearts, which is all a part of our "works" as well.

The requisite desperation and despair arising out of our unrelenting need to find and know God, is unveiled as the climax of our unfulfilled yearning to know Him and to be saved and purified by Him. It's part of our breaking point in anguish which also ends up being a glorious catalyst to "cry out" to Him for mercy from our souls, with the requisite sufficiency of faith. Elder Orson Pratt referenced this anguished cry of the soul:

> *"The arguments brought forth in the first Christian sermon after the resurrection of Christ were sufficient to send conviction into the hearts of many thousands of people.* ***They believed... and <u>cried out, in the anguish of their hearts</u>*** *(notice their crash site), "Men and brethren, what shall we do?" (Acts 2:37). As much as to say... now we are convinced that he is the Holy One, and that he has indeed risen from the dead; and is there any salvation for our nation, seeing that it has put Jesus to death? These were the feelings of sincere, sin-convicted persons on that occasion..." (Orson Pratt, "The Day of Pentecost—The Gifts of the Spirit—Cornelius," JD 14:173, delivered June 18, 1871; parenthetical addition made for added clarity).*

As it was with them, even so it is with us, if we are to be born of God. We must arrive at this point of a sincere, sin-convicted state by sufficient degree that we too, may *cry out in the anguish of our hearts* for His mercy and grace to redeem and cover us. It is a cry heard only by God. It needn't necessarily manifest as a vocal cry. It is most often the crying yearning of our hearts in faith to know God, to know the Truth, and to be rescued, healed, and redeemed. Do we have eyes to see? Can we not see that there is more to salvation than just having hands laid on our heads and attending Church? Remember Alma's words: "... And **never, until**, I did *cry out unto the Lord Jesus Christ for mercy*, did I receive a remission of my sins" (Alma 38:8).

When *the sufficiency of faith is reached and comes alive as a living force or "perfect faith" (2 Ne. 9:23), bestowed as an endowment from God*, and as we steadfastly cry out from our souls to be redeemed (which must be tied to our absolute willingness to sacrifice all that we have and are), we can one day, through God's will and grace, receive the Holy Ghost in power, even *the same* as was given on the day of Pentecost. This power is the power and endowment of faith referenced in John. To wit, "To them gave He *power* to become the sons of God" (John 1:12). Who gave the adopted sons of God this "power" or faith to be saved? God Himself did. Can we, of ourselves alone, develop or bestow upon ourselves this *perfect faith*? God forbid! Only a perfect being could bestow such a faith. When this living endowment of faith is *received*, it will be in fulfillment of the promise of the Father, conferred by the laying on of hands, as a gift. "For *by grace are ye saved* ***through faith***; and that not of yourselves: it is the gift of God" (Ephesians 2:8). And when we are saved, there will certainly be signs that will follow this power or living faith in us, just as one of our Hymns affirms. "And signs shall follow ***living faith***, down to the latest day" (LDS Hymn, "Come Listen To A Prophet's Voice").

Remember, the "end game" or purpose for us in our "*receiving*" His gift of the Holy Ghost is, "...that through the power and manifestation of the Spirit, ***while in the flesh***, [we] may be able to bear his presence in the world of glory" (D&C 76:118). Said another way, we must be cleansed and purified through the manifestation of His Spirit, while in our flesh, and retain that remission of sins and sanctification by the Comforter's influence thereafter, to later stand once again in the presence of God, both here in mortality (should we be so fortunate) and within His Kingdom in the world to come. Christ referenced the phrase "purified in me" three times in two consecutive verses in 3rd Nephi Chapter 19 to get this point across. Without being ***purified in Him*** through this manifestation referenced, we cannot enter and remain in His Presence.

The Longing to Know God leads us through Desire and Faith to find The Knowledge of God by way of Direct Experience

I have frequently pondered over the fact that seemingly very few that I have ever met have had the desire and yearning to actually know God in the most literal of ways, while in mortality. The majority appear to view this Heavenly Gift as either an impossibility or as too much work. Just as there are many that would not be able to comprehend anyone who would sincerely have a desire to know God, I cannot comprehend anyone who would not. These thoughts had then led me to the question as to whether or not it was even possible to either unearth that desire (so to speak) in another, or have such a desire instilled in a man who had not previously contemplated such a miraculous journey for himself.

In my search for answers, two things have stood out to me. First, I have found that adversity and pain are often great catalysts in unearthing the desire to know God which parallel's our own personal journey to be healed of our emotional and spiritual pains, traumas, and afflictions. This makes sense since Christ is the Master Healer. Second, in his book entitled "Discovery of the Presence of God," Hawkins speaks to self-inquiry as a secondary source for finding this desire: "*Self-observation* leads to *awakening* which then motivates the desire to learn, grow, mature, and evolve. *Self-inquiry leads to discovery and the unfolding of the layers (ie., "barriers" or "walls") that obscure the (higher) Self.* With self-inquiry, one examines the basis for faith and beliefs, and by instituting spiritual techniques and criteria (i.e., executing the doctrine of Christ which includes whole faith and repentance with Godly sorrow), *proceeds to discover the inner validation of spiritual truths for oneself" (*i.e., it becomes experiential*)*. Hawkins then adds, "There is a difference between having 'heard' a truth and having discovered it as an *inner reality. The way to 'be it' is to own it as an experiential reality*." (David R. Hawkins, Discovery of the Presence of God, pg. 58; parenthetical additions, mine).

This is what Heber C. Kimball meant when he spoke of the latter-day sifting that was to take place amongst the latter-day saints. He said that, "the difficulties will be of such a character that the man or woman who does not possess a personal knowledge or witness (of Jesus Christ and the Father) will fall. If you have not got this testimony (i.e, this witness yourself), you must live right and *call upon the Lord*, and **cease not until you obtain it**" (Heber C. Kimball of the First Presidency, May 1868, in Deseret News, 23 May, 1931, see also Conference Report, Oct. 1930, pg. 58 & 59; parenthetical addition added to clarify). He continues by saying that, "no man or woman will be able to endure on borrowed light. Each will have to be guided by the light within themselves. If you do not have *the knowledge that Jesus is the Christ*, how can you stand?" (Heber C. Kimball of the First Presidency, May 1868, in Deseret News, 23 May, 1931, see also Conference Report, Oct. 1930, pg. 58 & 59; parenthetical addition, mine).

President Hunter said: "Science has done marvelous things for man, but it cannot accomplish the things he must do for himself, ***the greatest of which is to find the reality of God.*** The task is not easy; the labor is not light; but as stated by the Master, 'Great shall be their reward and eternal shall be their glory'" (D&C 76:6). (Teachings of the Presidents of the Church, Howard W. Hunter, chapter 21, 'Faith and Testimony').

This *experiential knowledge of God's reality* is crucial. Marion G. Romney of the First Presidency also spoke of the quest of obtaining the knowledge of the reality of God for ourselves. "If we will but ask [God] in sincerity and faith, he will make known to each of us ***the reality of himself***" (Marion G. Romney, "The Living and True God, *Conference Report*, October 1964, pp. 48-52). The apostle Paul taught, "And He gave some, apostles; and some, prophets… For the perfecting of the saints, for the work of the ministry, for the edifying of the body of Christ (until when?) Till we all come in the unity of the faith, and of ***the knowledge of the Son of God***…" (Eph 4:11-13).

Elder D. Todd Christofferson had this to say about our seeking journey: "In the Church we not only learn divine doctrine; *we also experience its application… we have to go beyond concepts and exalted words and have a real 'hands-on' experience…*" (D. Todd Christofferson, "Why the Church?", Oct, 2015). Sri Nisargadatta Maharaj taught that, "Your book knowledge is useful to begin with, but soon it must be given up for ***direct experience,*** which by its very nature is inexpressible." In a very simplistic way, he adds: "To have the direct experience of a country, one must go and live there…trust-test-taste." (I Am That, Maharaj, pg. 143, 170). To *trust* is to believe the word and then decide to "risk" acting in gospel belief. To *test* is to act in gospel belief out in the world, doing the works of compassion that Jesus did by emulating Him. To *taste* is to experience the power of godliness, including the fruits of the Spirit through true conversion and those endowments made part of enduring to the end. This is exactly what the Savior meant when he said, "If any man will do his will, he shall know of the doctrine, whether it be of God, or whether I speak of myself" (John 7:17). This *direct experience* or as Hawkins put it, "*to own it as an experiential reality,*" is what the power of our living and restored Church and gospel, with its accompanying ordinances and authority, is all about. Elder McConkie spoke of the same this way:

> *"I have sufficient background and understanding that I could reason these things out from the revelations. I could read the scriptures and ascertain that all this is accurate and sensible, that it is logical and rational, but what I am now saying is something that is in addition to that. It is very helpful to have a knowledge of the gospel and be able to reason on the principles of eternal truth; it is helpful in that it leads to a testimony of the divinity of the work. But what I am now saying is that* ***I am a witness of the truth and the divinity of the work…*** *" (Bruce R. McConkie, "Rock of Salvation).*

If we will but *desire* to obtain the knowledge of God and to seek His face as our preeminent goal—our "vision," we will be led (if we have not already) to receive of the requisite ordinances by the proper priesthood authority in order that we might manifestly *experience the power of Godliness, while in the flesh.* We too shall become "a witness of the truth and the divinity of the work." The baptism of water possesses an essential key and sign to God, but the laying on of hands by the authority of the Higher Priesthood is the channel through which this power is able to be made manifest to men in the flesh.

> *"And this greater priesthood holdeth the key...* ***of the knowledge of God****. Therefore in the ordinances thereof, the power of godliness is manifest. And without the ordinances thereof, and the authority of the priesthood, the power of godliness is not manifest unto men in the flesh" (D&C 84:19-21).*

I bear solemn witness that the preceding verses are true and faithful and can be *experientially known.*

The baptism of water is "a sign to God, to angels, and to heaven that we do the will of God..." [Joseph Smith, Teachings of the Prophet Joseph Smith, Section Four 1839-42, p.198]). Our confirmation, given through priesthood authority, provides the right whereby man *can* receive the power of godliness in the flesh. These two ordinances by the proper authority create "the channel" or conduit, through which this power can flow. That said, the power does not automatically start flowing just because the channel has been established. It takes our participation. When hands are laid upon our heads at the age of eight, for example, we receive *the promise only* of the future reception of the Holy Ghost and eternal life. The fulfillment of that promise happens in our "*riper years*" (Joseph Smith, "Teachings," Section Six 1843-44, p.314) when we wholly repent and are faithful (or full of faith). When we fulfill the law tied to this blessing, we will receive the Holy Ghost and his guidance on a level which Harold B. Lee likens unto Adam's experience when walking and talking with God. And as we all know, Adam partook of the glory of God before the time in which he fell. When God's power flows thus, through the established channel, we will have been spiritually reborn. Harold B. Lee describes this miraculous guidance this way:

> *After baptism, hands are laid upon the head of the baptized believer, and he is blessed to receive the Holy Ghost.* ***Thus does the one baptized receive <u>the promise</u>*** *or gift of the Holy Ghost for the privilege of being brought back into the presence of one of the Godhead,* ***by obedience*** *to whom and through his faithfulness one so blessed* ***<u>might receive</u> the guidance and direction of the Holy Ghost*** *in his daily walks and talks,* ***even as Adam walked and talked in the garden of Eden with God,*** *his Heavenly Father.* ***<u>To receive such guidance and such direction from the Holy Ghost is to be spiritually reborn.</u>*** *Unfortunately, there are many of those who are blessed to receive the Holy Ghost and that companionship of one of the*

Godhead in their mortal lives who fail of their blessings (Harold B. Lee, Conference Report, Oct. 1947, pp. 63-67).

Harold B. Lee lays out "the gift of the Holy Ghost" in plainness for us. When hands are laid upon our heads during our confirmation as children, we do not receive the Holy Ghost but ***the promise*** for the same subject to fulfilling the law entitling us to receive the promised endowment. Children have no sins to remit at eight years old for they are "alive in Christ." Lee describes there are many of those upon whom *the promised* gift of the Holy Ghost is made (which happens when we are confirmed) who fail to receive the fulfillment of the actual promised blessing given by God. Much more is needed beyond that of just the receiving of the ordinances. The receiving of the ordinances is the relatively easy part that can be performed by men having Priesthood authority through Priesthood keys.

To simplify the above for our understanding, I will liken the electrical wiring provided for electrical current to flow in a home, together with its outlets, to that of our receiving the ordinances of God by proper authority—and more specifically, the ordinance called "the gift of the Holy Ghost." For the purposes of this example, the master switch or main breaker that powers the entire house will be set in the off position.

When we receive the laying on of hands after our baptism of water, it would be comparable to say that we will have instantaneously had all of the "channels," conduit and electrical wiring installed in our homes so that we could then have the right and ability to receive the power. But to receive this power, the main breaker must be switched on. To actually receive the power of godliness while in our flesh will require much more than the events of testimony given throughout our lives. The spiritual experiences which strengthen a testimony are preparations to make the eternal commitment to surrender our will to God which will lead us to become truly converted, and changed from natural man to Saint by God Himself. We must fulfill all the prerequisites under the law which are tied to receiving the promised blessing. Otherwise, the power of godliness is not made manifest to men in the flesh.

We're talking about receiving God's power here. It is a real power. It involves an initial visit of the Lord by way of a manifestation of His Spirit. It is to have a third member of the Godhead condescend and even "rest" upon us in order to purify us, quicken us, and prepare us to enter the Lord's Presence and see His face, both here and in that eternal world. It is no small thing. And although there is a process leading to it, there is also an experience of reconciliation available to us in which we can be spiritually reborn, and know it. And when we know it, we will "know Him."

So how do we flip this master switch on so that the power or "electrical current" might flow through this "channel"? It is done by whole, gut-wrenching repentance and performing the spiritual ordinance of the soul in consecrating our broken hearts in full to Him in faith, tied to a commitment to do His will forever. The apostle Paul said it this way, "For behold this selfsame thing, that ye sorrowed after a godly sort"

(2 Cor. 7:11), "For godly sorrow worketh repentance to salvation" (2 cor. 7:10). This level of consecration will likely be preceded and joined by a continuous cry of surrender to Him in faith to do His Will, while holding nothing back.

It is not an easy process to arrive at such a commitment. That's why the Lord has said, "few there be that find it." Should redemption be as easy as just receiving the outer forms by way of the ordinances? Or should we have to really, really desire it, seek it, and yearn for it in order to receive and experience the inward change? Close your eyes and ask God. Feel for the answer. When we demonstrate the requisite level of desire with a willingness to sacrifice our all to Him forever, the "switch is turned on," and the power of godliness is made manifest. And those who receive this power are those who come ***"to the knowledge of their redeemer***; yea, and how blessed are they, for they shall sing to his praise forever" (Mosiah 18:30).

Fellow seeker. When this power comes, we will be baptized by fire and of the Holy Ghost. We will experience that Oneness prayed for by Christ to the Father. We will become a new creature—changed mightily by God and born of Him, even like unto that which was experienced by the early apostles on the day of Pentecost. Orson Pratt, spoke to this experience:

"... for (Peter, on the day of Pentecost) had just told them that it was the effects of the Holy Spirit which they had been witnessing, and they, no doubt, *felt anxious to receive the same*, for the Holy Spirit was that which would enable them to (notice the fruits) *prophesy, see visions, dream dreams, and guide them into all truth, reveal unto them the things of the Father, and show them things to come...*" (The Day of Pentecost—The Gifts of the Spirit—Cornelius, Orson Pratt, delivered in the New Tabernacle, Salt Lake City, June 18, 1871; parenthetical addition, for context).

Pratt then personalizes it more for Saints: "Supposing this congregation had been present eighteen centuries ago at Jerusalem at the first Gospel sermon preached after the ascension of Christ, and that, in the anguish of your hearts you had inquired what you must do to receive the pardon of your sins and how you could obtain the Holy Ghost, and what effects that Holy Ghost would have had upon you, *would you not have expected to receive something **precisely similar*** to what the hundred and twenty had received upon whom it was poured out? ***Could you have expected anything else*? No**" (Ibid).

Pratt proceeds to further explain the fruits of the First Comforter outlined above and how we reject it in our lives: "If you can tell me any way by which the power of godliness can be more effectually denied than to do away the effects of the Holy Spirit ***as they were manifested on the Day of Pentecost*** and in all the Christian churches so long as there were any on the earth; I say if there is any more effectual way of denying the power of godliness than to do away with this power *and say it is not necessary, I do not comprehend it.* I, myself, should not know how to deny the power of godliness..." (Ibid).

As to faithful execution of the Doctrine of Christ which makes the effects and gifts of the Spirit manifest to those who "believe," Pratt adds:

"...it is the same doctrine [of Christ] that tens of thousands have received. Do they receive the promises? Is the Holy Ghost given? If it is, all these gifts are given; ***and if the Latter-day Saints are not in possession of these gifts, they are not in possession of the Gospel… Well, Latter-day Saints, you are no better if you have not these gifts... and I think you know whether you have them or not.*** If you have, blessed are ye; but if you have them not, it is time you waked up and began to hunt around for the Gospel..." (Ibid; parenthetical additions, mine).

In order to experience of this "power of godliness" while in the flesh, we must first receive the ordinances by proper authority as referenced. These ordinances, however, are external forms only and require our participation through a foundation of desire and faith. Through our ongoing and expanding desire and faith, we are then able to have those ordinances justified (i.e., "approved and ratified" by the Holy Spirit of Promise) on our behalf, and thereby, ***experientially known and received***. This is what Christ meant when speaking of having the "inside of the cup" cleansed vs. becoming "whited sepulchers," referring to the outside only. After we have fulfilled the tenets of the law tied to the promised blessing confirmed upon us, we are ultimately saved by grace, through faith. "And if by grace, then is it no more of works: otherwise grace is no more grace" (Rom 11:6). Without perfect faith as an endowment from Him, received through our broken-hearted repentance and "all in" commitment to do His will, His saving grace will not come, no matter how much waiting on the Lord we may do.

Sri Nisargadatta Maharaj says that "***mere longing…pure, concentrated longing, will take you speedily to your goal***" (I Am That, Maharaj, pg. 172). This desire for Christ, and consistently acting on this desire to connect with His presence from our heart space, is the seeking that yields the fruits of our desire.

I believe that this desire or "longing" to know God, with a diamond-hard resolve to find Him, at least as a general rule, is essentially necessary to receive the power of godliness in its various forms, degrees, and manifestations.

Sri Nisargadatta Maharaj says that "*spiritual practice is will asserted and re-asserted*" ("will," meaning "desire") and adds, "*unwillingness* born out of fear is the only obstacle." (I Am That, Maharaj, pg. 172; parenthetical addition, mine). Our Sacrament ordinance reaffirms the covenant we make each and every week… *to be born again and adopted by Christ Himself*: "That they may… witness… that they are *willing* to take upon them the name of thy Son…". Remember, our spiritual practice is the desire to know Him, which is to be asserted and re-asserted until we find Him. Desire… Ask, Seek, Knock… Receive. Then repeat.

Chapter 4

The Great Dichotomy in Man: - The Divine Self vs. The Natural Man (Ego)

I came out alone on my way to my tryst. But who is this me in the dark?
....I move aside to avoid his presence but I escape him not.
....He makes the dust rise from the earth with his swagger;
....He adds his loud voice to every word I utter.
....He is my own little self, my lord, he knows no shame;
....but I... I am ASHAMED! to come to thy door... in his company.

("The Ego," Labidranath Tagore, 1864-1941)

Through the fall of Adam, a dichotomy arose that became inherent in each of us. Once we reach the age of accountability, we begin to develop two significant aspects of ourselves. One aspect is a false persona known as the natural man (aka, the "ego") and is tied to the flesh. The other, our higher or divine self, was created by God. It is our true, eternal identity. The apostle Paul refers to this dichotomy in us this way: "For I delight in the law of God after the inward man: But I see another law in my members, warring … and bringing me into captivity to the law of sin which is in my members" (Rom. 7:22-23).

A main purpose of Christ's condescension was to give us all, through faith, the power by grace to put off the natural man and the "enmity" inherent within this dichotomy. It is Christ's grace that gives us the possibility of abolishing the influence of the natural man—this "warring . . . in our members,"—in order to live predominantly in harmony with the divine aspect of ourselves. Speaking of Christ's power to this end, Paul says, "Having abolished in his flesh *the enmity … for to make in himself of twain one new man, so making peace*" (Eph. 2:15; emphasis added). Paul also counseled "Ye *put off* concerning the former conversation *the old man*, which is *corrupt* according to the deceitful lusts; And be renewed in the spirit of your mind; And that ye ***put on the new man***, which after God is created in righteousness and true holiness" (Eph. 4:22-24; emphasis added). This "new man" we put on is Christ.

Without the infinite Atonement of Christ and His power, this enmity would forever remain. "And our spirits must have become like unto him [the devil], and we become devils, angels to a devil, to be shut out from the presence of our God, and to remain with the father of lies, in misery, like unto himself" (2 Ne. 9:9). To ensure this would never happen, we have been commanded in accordance with our self-interests (whether aware or not), to exercise *faith unto repentance.* A detailed process of how we are to exercise "faith unto repentance" is found in the Twelve Steps of Alcoholics Anonymous. I invite all to intently study them. *Be sure to approach and execute step 8 as if you only had weeks to live.* Our *faith unto repentance* will necessarily include making sure that everything and every consideration in this world be totally surrendered that stands in the way of our path to God. When we do so, we will experience oneness with God and His love as spoken of in scripture, and, should we endure faithfully, even be "found possessed of it at the last day" (Moro. 7:48). This experience can only arise out of a miraculous power, by grace and through perfect faith in Christ, bestowed as a gift through whole repentance and complete surrender. "But as many as *received* him [Christ], to them gave he *power* [that is to say, 'having *perfect faith* in the Holy One of Israel'; see 2 Ne. 9:23] to become the sons of God, even to them that believe on his name" (John 1:12; emphasis added).

King Benjamin made reference to this ego spoken of by Tagore (calling it "the natural man") in an address to his people, but also explained the attributes we could acquire by "putting off" the natural man and its inherent enmity: "For the natural man is an enemy to God, and has been from the fall of Adam, and will be, forever and ever, unless he yields to the enticings of the Holy Spirit [i.e., follows the Light of Christ in order to be led to partake of the tree of life and salvation], and [in so doing] putteth off the natural man and becometh *a saint* through the atonement of Christ the Lord [which is when we are born of the Spirit, or born of God], and becometh as a child, submissive, meek, humble, patient, full of love, *willing to submit to all things* which the Lord seeth fit to *inflict* upon him, even as a child doth submit to his father" (Mosiah 3:19; emphasis added).

Through Christ's power and grace, we are able to become *converted* and "Saint-ified" through the reception of the Holy Ghost. Until we experience this power in our lives, however, the sympathies of the natural man and the divine in us remain mostly blended or enmeshed together. The natural man is an enemy to God, which is that aspect of ourselves which is fallen—also known as the false self. The natural man is directed by the "will of the flesh and the *evil which is therein*, which giveth the spirit of the devil power" (2 Ne. 2:29; emphasis added).

Only God can unwind the natural man and thereby unbind the divine self so we may flourish. This spirit lives within us and is, in a very literal way, the true "us." The fight between these two aspects of ourselves, spirit vs. flesh, always rages inside. It's the battle of good and evil, wherein our agency is constantly at play. That is, at least until the Savior slays the dragon of the natural man and we are set free from his tenacious hold. Without the Lord's intervention, this battle may always continue to rage in the devil's favor. As mortals, we will never break completely free on our own. But we can continue to try until we come to the realization and knowledge that we cannot succeed by ourselves. This is when we turn to Christ in full and wave the white flag of surrender. Until we receive our new life in Christ, we are sure to continue being enslaved through sin unless and until we yield to the Savior's guidance and liberating power. The *battle within* is truly about which of these blended sympathies will overcome and ultimately prevail over the other. For the divine aspect in us to overcome, we must turn to Christ and execute His doctrine in full. It can happen by *no other way* (2 Ne. 31:21).

Brigham Young said: "The spirit which inhabits these tabernacles naturally loves truth, it naturally loves light and intelligence, it naturally loves virtue, God and godliness; but being so closely united with the flesh *their sympathies are blended…* the spirit is indeed subject to be influenced by the sin that is in the mortal body, and to be overcome by it and by the power of the Devil, unless it is *constantly enlightened* by that spirit which enlighteneth every man that cometh into the world [i.e., the Light of Christ given to all men], and by the [amplified] power of the Holy Ghost [through the Comforter when we are born again] which is imparted through the Gospel" (DBY, 422–23; emphasis added).

The true divine part of us within is who we are. The flesh is but a garment, albeit a very powerful one. Until our spirit is able to take control in this relationship, meaning, between the two aspects of ourselves, our lives will likely end up in chaos, confusion, and ultimate defeat. The natural man will, of course, win many of the battles in us. But at some point, we will eventually tire of the futility and uselessness of the mundane and worldly payoffs, and perhaps through our pain and anguish, consciously and more intelligently search for a relief that endures and a better way.

As we nourish our spirit more, the light within it grows and influences the flesh by sanctifying and enlightening it. This is how our spirit gains more power in the relationship between the two. Conversely, as we nourish the flesh more, the evil and darkness within it influences our spirit (in a negative and spiritually contaminating way). Brigham Young taught that, "*The spirit is influenced by the body, and the body by the spirit*" (Discourses of Brigham Young, 69-70).

John Wesley's mother (note: John Wesley was a prominent theologian) reputedly has given us this: "Would you judge of the lawfulness or unlawfulness of pleasure? Take this rule: Now note—whatever … *impairs the tenderness of your conscience*, obscures your sense of God, takes off your relish for spiritual things, whatever increases the authority of the body over the (spiritual) mind, that thing is sin to you, however innocent it may seem in itself" (*Teachings of Presidents of the Church: David O. McKay* (2011), p. 198, emphasis added). Anything that "impairs the tenderness of [our] conscience" is the same as the "mists of darkness" that gradually form a spiritually darkened wall around our hearts so that our spiritual GPS and signal to God becomes "impaired," perhaps even nonfunctional.

Introduction of the Natural Man in Mortality and Its Purpose

We are told that "it must needs be, that there is an opposition in all things" (2 Nephi 2:11). The Fall of Adam and Eve, which brought about our *fallen man syndrome*, was purposeful to this end, meaning, to bring the law of the opposites and the introduction of the opposition in all things (2 Ne. 2:15). How could we prize the good without knowing the bitter? And without the enticements of the opposites, the good and the bad, the sweet and the bitter, how could we effectively choose?

The Intellect Alone Can Only Take Us So Far

Dr. David R. Hawkins, a very enlightened man himself, developed a scale or map of consciousness, using arbitrary numbers of between 0 and 1,000, with 0 representing no consciousness (i.e., "no light") and 1,000 representing the higher states of enlightenment. He discovered that he could use muscle testing or kinesiology as a conduit to knowing all "current and past" truth by tapping into the Light of Christ found in the human body. Using his technique, he was able to validate his findings through his own scientific research.

The purpose for my discussing Hawkins's map of consciousness, however, is not to convert you into believers of kinesiology or his map of consciousness, especially since the "tests" are primarily a subjective exercise and can be influenced and made unreliable by one's own biases and non-integrous motives, among other things. The main purpose is to make the point that Hawkins was able to demonstrate that mortal and fallen man could only attain a certain level of spiritual consciousness (i.e., "en-light-enment") by way of the intellect, which is tied to the flesh.

Said another way, "the way of the intellect" could only take humanity so far in its spiritual progression.

Hawkins's research revealed that even the greatest minds of history were capped at a consciousness level of 499, based on his scale of 1,000, with 1,000 (or higher) being an enlightened being, such as Jesus Christ.

In his map of consciousness, Hawkins determined that the consciousness level of right versus wrong was at the level of 200. He also discusses that "the scale of consciousness may be seen in one aspect as a scale of ego [natural man], with the level of 200 being *the fulcrum at which selfishness begins to turn to selflessness*" (David R. Hawkins, *Power vs. Force,* p. 145). He writes: "Statesmen represent true power, ruling by inspiration, teaching by example and standing for self-evident principle. The statesman invokes the nobility which resides within all men [i.e., "the light given to every man who cometh into the world"] and *unifies them through what can best be* *termed **the heart**.*" He adds: ***"Though the intellect is easily fooled, the heart recognizes truth.** Where the intellect is limited, **the heart is unlimited** [which makes sense since this is our primary contact with the Light of Christ]; where the intellect is intrigued by the temporary, the heart is only concerned with the permanent"* (*Power vs. Force,* p. 128; emphasis added).

Again, the key point Hawkins is making is that the maximum level of consciousness we can attain to by way of reason or intellectual strength alone, has a ceiling of 499. No wonder we were told by Elder McConkie that *"we do not come to a knowledge of God and his laws through intellectuality, or by research, or by reason"* ("The Lord's People Receive Revelation," 1971 Annual General Conference). No wonder we are told by Elder Neil Anderson that "*using our mind without our heart will not bring spiritual answers.*" ("Faith Is Not by Chance, but by Choice," 2015 Semi-Annual General Conference). This is because spiritual understanding acquired solely through the intellect or through reason is capped at less than 50% of the total scale of consciousness.

Dr. Hawkins and his group is said to have performed over 30 million calibrations using kinesiology. He was definitely not "winging it." His research tends to validate what Brigham Young explained:

> *"When men are in the habit of philosophizing upon every point, only relying upon what we call **human reason**, they are constantly liable to error" (JD 7:157).*

This is validated, is it not, by the fact that we have thousands of Christian churches today using the same Bible and there is still not a unity of the Christian faith. *The intellect can only take us so far in our seeking journey to find and know God, as well as in our journey of becoming like our Heavenly Father.* That is why I have and will continue to focus on "getting out of our heads" so we can more easily feel the voice of God and obtain our own individual revelation. Meditation facilitates this.

Through Dr. Hawkins's research, Hawkins teaches that the "'ego/mind' [aka, the natural man], by virtue of its structure and design, is intrinsically **incapable** of being able to differentiate truth from falsehood (essence from appearance)" (Discovery of the Presence of God, p. 63; emphasis added). Hawkins adds,

> *"Consciousness research indicates that the human ego/mind is constitutionally unable to differentiate truth from falsehood by virtue of its construction. The mind is like the hardware of a computer that will play back anything for which it has been programmed" (Discovery of the Presence of God, p. 68).*

This is the reason why we need to intentionally fill our minds with things that uplift and inspire, using our own agency and power to choose, and doing so consciously.

This is also why so many people swear by the benefits of saying positive affirmations or by listening to Christ-centered music with uplifting lyrics before retiring to bed.

Have you ever gone to bed having just listened to a song, with that song having been "played" in your subconscious until awakening the next morning? Can you image what saying positive affirmations and listening to spiritually uplifting music filled with positive lyrics could do for us just before bed every night? Let us then give our subconscious "computer" the material or "recordings" to play back those materials which we feel to be congruent with the things of God, or those things that we consider "virtuous, lovely, or of good report or praiseworthy."

Getting Lost in Our Compulsive Thoughts

We have learned from Chapter 1 that our inability to spiritually hear or see is due to a hardened heart. The Savior taught that the "cares of the world" choke *the word* (which is Spirit)! When our heart becomes hardened, we lose our compass and connection to God's light, the awareness of who we are and our overall direction. *We get lost in our thoughts*, we get lost in our work, we get lost in our busyness, we get lost in the world, and ultimately, we get lost, period. Eckhart Tolle suggests that "Knowing yourself, is to be rooted in Being, instead of being lost in your mind" (*A New Earth,* p. 186). In other words, we need to slow down at least once a day and quiet the mind in order to effectively "listen" and hear His voice found in the stillness of our souls.

Reaching for the Savior with Intensity

President Russell M. Nelson spoke to the value of *reaching for the Lord and His power* in the April 2017 general conference:

> *"Many of us have* ***cried out*** *from the depths of our hearts.... When you reach up for the Lord's power in your life* ***with the same intensity that a drowning person has when grasping and gasping for air****, power from Jesus Christ will be yours. When the Savior knows you truly want to reach up to Him—When He can feel that the greatest desire of your heart is to draw His power into your life... When you spiritually stretch beyond anything you have ever done before, then His power will flow into you" ("Drawing the Power of Jesus Christ into Our Lives;" emphasis added).*

When we exhibit the same level and intensity in our desire to know the Savior as a drowning person desires air, then we will be given the knowledge and complete cleansing purification by the Deity we seek. Are we not all spiritually drowning without

Him? In order to receive of this power and cleansing, we must faithfully execute the doctrine of Christ.

Becoming a Law unto Ourselves

The Lord said:

> *"That which [he who] breaketh a law, and abideth not by law [meaning, the law of Christ in heeding the still, small voice], but seeketh to become a law unto [himself], and willeth to abide in sin, and altogether abideth in sin, cannot be sanctified by law [which is His light], neither by mercy, justice, nor judgment. Therefore, they must remain filthy still" (D&C 88:35).*

We all know that if we remain filthy still after our mortal sojourn is completed, "that same body which doth possess [our] bodies at the time that [we] go out of this life, that same spirit will have power to possess [our] body in that eternal world" (Alma 34:34).

It is important to understand that the willingness to surrender our all will typically happen when our pain becomes excruciating enough to arrive to that point of commitment wherein we choose to turn to God in full.

> *Suffering causes us to realize that the way of "going it alone" or "doing it our way" is not the way of peace. The only way to lasting peace, joy, and happiness is through our total surrender to the Prince of Peace.*

We must come to completely understand, with every fiber of our being, that the only way to truly obtain that oneness and peace that passeth understanding is to surrender our all to His will and direction, as found in that Light which is constantly whispering to our souls, and broadcasting over His frequency.

> *We often don't hear "God's voice" because the natural man can never get enough of hearing its own loud, narcissistic, ego chatter, opinions, and positionalities. And because of its fear and insecurity, it does not want to relinquish its perceived reins to the directives of the beautifully meek and soft voice of that portion of God located within the soul of man.*

The reason meditation is so powerful and essential is that it trains us to quiet and relax the mind long enough to be able to hear or feel (through "sensing") the faint whisperings of the still and small voice. Meditation can lead to a holy communion with God, which I find is facilitated by finding the gap (as best we can) between waking and dreaming consciousness. This is where we can find God in "the now" or present moment. The Prophet Joseph taught that "the past, the present, and the future were and are, with Him, one eternal 'now'" (*Teachings,* p. 220). The Lord also informs us that He resides "on a globe like a sea of glass and fire [meaning, light and glory], where all things for their glory are manifest, past, present, and future, and are continually before the Lord,... a great Urim and Thummim" (D&C 130:7-8). When we find him in *the now* or present moment, we will experience a holy communion. This holy communion is to have an experiential encounter with the heart, love, and Presence of God. Joseph Smith taught, "***the only way*** to obtain truth and wisdom **is *not to ask it from books, but to go to God in prayer and obtain divine teaching*"** (Ehat and Cook, *The Words of Joseph Smith,* p.77; emphasis added). To go to God and obtain divine teaching *is* what it means to *learn by faith.*

The Value of Meditation and Becoming the Compassionate Witness

There are tapes running incessantly in our heads. As an experiment, take 10 minutes out of any part of your day and spend those ten minutes doing nothing but observing the thoughts that race across the screen of your mind like characters of a play entering and exiting a stage. You may be dumbfounded to learn how ridiculous your thoughts can actually become when carefully observed. You may even be horrified.

Tolle likewise talks about "watching the thinker" or being the "witnessing presence." In other words, he invites us to not only become aware of any particular thought but of ourselves as the witness of the thought. *This witness is your higher self, your divine self, the intelligence inherent in the child of God.* The bottom line is this: As long as you are identified with solely your natural mind, the ego (which is part of the natural man) may end up running your life.

The Church-produced booklet titled *Adjusting to Missionary Life*, given to all full-time missionaries, talks about the benefit of relaxation for relieving stress, but its benefits can go much deeper (see Adjusting to Missionary Life Resource Booklet, pages 18-19, churchofjesuschrist.org). This booklet is a godsend for missionaries, but the information it contains can also be a godsend for us. Here are some examples, which I will expand into further detail below and in another chapter. The breathing and relaxation exercises can set the table for entering the sacred stillness of God's peace and holiness:

Breathing Exercise

- Sit in a comfortable position or stand quietly. Take a few deep, slow breaths through your nose, pausing after each one.
- Relax your shoulders and try to breathe so your stomach moves, not your shoulders.

- Continue to breathe slowly and calmly for five minutes or until anxious feelings ease up.

Progressive Relaxation Exercise

Deep relaxation helps your body recover from stress. Practice this at night before you sleep to train your body to relax. Do a shorter version of this exercise during the day any time you feel overstressed.

- Lie or sit comfortably and close your eyes.
- Concentrating on one part of your body at a time, look for any tension. Consciously relax that part of your body. Feel all the tension draining away, like sand running through your fingers. Then move on to the next part of your body. Take your time. If you are not sure if there is still tension, tighten that part of your body for 10 seconds; then completely relax for 10 seconds before moving on.
- Focus on these areas, one at a time: 1. head and face; 2. eyes; 3. jaw; 4. neck; 5. shoulders and back; 6. arms; 7. hands and fingers; 8. chest and abdomen; 9. legs; 10. feet and toes.
- Mentally scan your body for any remaining tension. Completely relax.
- Choose a "personal scene"—a memory or an *imagined setting*—that brings you joy and peace. Try to imagine this scene as vividly as possible.

(End of the Progressive Relaxation Exercise).

Try not to get backed up about the word *meditation* and what it should look like. No "lotus position" is necessary. No hand positions are necessary. Just be still and sit upright in a comfortable chair, *with the intention of connecting with your Creator*. Meditation can be viewed as a simple tool we use to maintain a sure grip on the rod of iron, thereby facilitating personal revelation. The Lord said, "Enter into thy closet, and when thou hast *shut thy door*, pray to the Father which is in secret" (Matt. 6:6). In other words, go to your mental closet and "shut the door." Be alone. Be present. Be still. *Shutting thy door* begins by shutting out the world and the inner monkey chatter of the egoic mind. This is accomplished by shutting out all distractions, including the hyper activity of the natural and analytical mind in order to get "still" so that you might then connect with God through spiritual impressions and feelings within the inner stillness and seat of your soul.

Meditation is a tool we can use to connect with God's light. It is also a practice which gives more power to the divine aspect of ourselves, which can effectively "starve" the natural man of (similar to fasting) the nutrients he needs to maintain his control. In essence, connecting with God's light is the natural man's "kryptonite." Increasing in Light weakens the false in us.

To me, meditation is a form of prayer—a deep inner contemplation and striving to connect with the Presence of God through feelings and yearnings in the Spirit in order to experience a holy communion in Him. Meditation is about getting inwardly quiet and still so we can experience Him. Through this practice we can better notice and feel the still small voice. Don't get backed up about the word meditation. Come up with your own. Words are only pointers. As my daughter Chelsea suggests, "You don't have to be a Buddhist monk to meditate." Meditation is simply a practice wherein we *turn inward* and connect with the Presence of God through *feeling after Him* (see Acts 17:27). This is how we "seek diligently *in* the Light of Christ" (See Moroni 7), because that's where our connection with the Light of Christ is primarily found. Still the restless mind and *turn inward* to know.

Putting Theory into Practice

We will now dive headfirst into more of the self-help portion of this book. After reading down to the next italicized heading, close your eyes. We begin by closing our eyes because it allows us a time in which we are *not* constantly reminded of being "in this world." It allows us to "image in" or ***imagine*** the world from which we came—a heavenly world. This is how God allows us to be involved in spiritual creation with Him as well. Some refer to this word *imagine,* as "I'm-a-Gine"—like the genie in a bottle where we get our wishes fulfilled. Through meditation, we can go *there*. We too can have our wishes fulfilled through this childlike exercise called imagination (agreeable of course to the will of God) and can experience a taste of what we once knew. Henry David Thoreau reinforced this idea when he taught "that if one advances confidently *in the direction of his dreams*, and endeavors to live the life which he has *imagined*, he will meet with a success unexpected in common hours" (*Walden,* p. 253).

I'm going to now use my own words to guide us through a sample of the breathing and relaxation exercise highlighted in *Adjusting to Missionary Life.*

Take in deep, relaxing breaths. Inhale through your nose as deeply as you can in the beginning and exhale slowly through the mouth by using gentle back pressure with your lips to lengthen and extend your exhale which often helps to relax more deeply. Do this for 5 minutes, and don't rush it. This time is when you let down the walls that may have been unconsciously building. It is a time of surrender—your alone time, an exclusive time with just you and God. He longs for this time, and so should we. Our focus should be on relaxing every part of our physical body, starting at the crown of our head, then our forehead, face, and neck; making our way down through our shoulders, back, abdomen; and continuing down to the souls of our feet.

Remember that when we are tense, we are assuming a posture of resistance. When we are completely relaxed, we open ourselves up to God from a vulnerable space and simply "allow." Remember our objective is to spiritually connect with the presence of God—to practice loving Him. This is facilitated by not having our "guard up" ("stiffened necks") towards Him. This is one reason why we are to focus on any areas in the body that are stiff or tense, until the tension in that area, through attention and intention, becomes fully relaxed. Fully relaxing ourselves can be an expression of our trust and vulnerability towards God as part of our body language. This vulnerability is akin to when my little yorkie dog, Gracie, turns over and completely exposes her belly to be rubbed. Her action, at least to me, demonstrates an expression of the type of vulnerability to which I am referring.

As we go deeper into our awareness of the Light within us, we begin to connect with the God light or light of Christ, which I like to think of as an extension of God's love and tender feelings for us. Our connecting with Him is not only a form of prayer, but from my perspective, true prayer. Prayer is best approached with the intention of having an exchange or interchange of feelings and may not even involve words. The more we "go away in God" into His world, the more we will disconnect and lose interest in our own. Our hearts will be *there*. As we keep our hearts there, He will keep His heart "in here" within *the heart and seat of our own soul*—to abide in us. "Abide in me, and I in you. As the branch cannot bear fruit of itself, except it abide in the vine; no more can ye, except ye abide in me" (John 15:4). "He that *dwelleth in the secret place* of the most High shall abide under the shadow of the Almighty" (Psalm 91:1; emphasis added). Guess what? This place is no longer a secret.

The greatest example I have found of what meditation "looks like" is patterned for us by Mary, the mother of Jesus, in the video called, "An Angel Foretells Christ's Birth to Mary," found on churchofjesuschrist.org. The specific segment begins at 1:12 of the video and ends at 1:35 of the same. Play this segment multiple times and notice how Mary connects with God. You can tell that there is a bond that Mary is able to establish through her feeling after God. Notice the stillness that arises just before the appearance of the angel Gabriel. Notice also that when Mary opens her eyes at the end of this short segment, it appears as though she has had an "aha" moment or spiritual revelation. This is the same type of personal revelation we can all find in this same place of inner, sacred stillness. This is the same stillness to which we too will arrive as we "grow in grace, and in the knowledge of our Lord" (2 Pet. 3:18). And this stillness will precede our very intimate and direct experiences with God.

President Nelson has recently taught: "The voice of the Lord is not 'a voice of a great tumultuous noise, but… it [is] a still voice of perfect mildness, [like] a whisper, and it [pierces] even to the very soul.' In order to hear this still voice, ***you too must be still!...*** we can use our time to hear the voice of the Lord whispering His guidance, comfort, and peace. ***Quiet time is sacred time…*** time that will facilitate personal revelation and instill peace" (Russell M. Nelson, "What We Are Learning and Will

Never Forget," April, 2021 General Conference; emphasis added). Said another way, quiet time is meditation time. Now we'll again rejoin our meditation.

After your body is completely relaxed, gradually revert back to your normal, more shallow levels of breathing, while maintaining the awareness of this light of Christ within you as you do so. Remember, there is no right or wrong way to meditate. It's all about getting relaxed and still, with the pure and determined intention of connecting with God. Feel for His Presence. Feel for Him. Allow your head, mind, and neck to go "limp" even more—while relaxing the "thinking" mind. This is best accomplished by relaxing the muscles and tension in your forehead, face, neck and back—letting it all go. Now notice that your ego mind may be screaming at you right now as to how weird this may seem. The ego may also be telling you that this is a waste of your time. Notice how uncomfortable or "awkward" you may be feeling about it. Notice the judgments towards me or even yourself that you may be experiencing as well. These thoughts may suggest, "This is bizarre, weird, strange." Notice that you may be experiencing judgment that "a Christ-centered book" should not have anything to do with weird meditation or getting inwardly quiet and still. This, by the way, is an entirely normal reaction for the egoic, natural mind. Now tell that "compulsive controller" (the natural man part of you) to "be quiet and take a back seat"—that it is no longer in charge.

What is the purpose of getting still by quieting the thinking mind? To connect with God's Presence, or the divine Light within which is an extension of Him. "Brother Lawrence," a monastic worshiper from the 1660's said, "I cannot imagine how religious persons can live satisfied without *the practice of the presence of God*" ("The Practice of the Presence of God," copyright 1895 by Fleming H. Revell Comapy, p. 27; emphasis added). Meditation is a form of this same practice. Meditation can become a powerful form of worshipful prayer. Any practice, exercise, or device that brings us closer to God, to love and connect with Him must, by Moroni's definition, be "inspired of God," even "sent forth by the power and gift of Christ" (see Moroni 7:13, 16).

Now that you're breathing well and ready, take the posture in meditation suggested by Dr. Hawkins, which is to "merely assume the attitude of being too lazy to bother to think" (Discovery of the Presence of God, p. 247). Relax your brain, especially the analytical, thinking part of your mind. Surrender the mental chatter and all the preoccupations with what is going on in your "outer world" to God so there are absolutely no distractions. For some, spiritually relaxing music may be a distraction, but for others it is an absolute necessity in quieting the mind. You may begin with music in the beginning stages and then later, remove it from your meditational practice altogether. Stick with whatever helps you best connect with God.

Remember that spiritual and sacred music (especially joined with intention in turning our hearts to God) has healing properties that will aid in melting the heart walls that will have naturally surfaced through living in a fallen world. The prior sentence cannot be over-emphasized. Allow me to suggest a few songs for you to try to get to that place of stillness: "How I Love You," by Christy Nockels; "Oh God, You Are My God," by Fernando Ortega; and "I Won't Forget," by Brian Johnson. If you enjoy these, you will likely add many others down the road. For non-lyric music, I'd recommend trying different songs by Paul Cardall, especially from his 2011, "New Life" CD or his 2016, "A New Creation." "Still, Still, Still," by Jon Schmidt is also a very peaceful one. One of my favorites is the "End Credits," by Alan Silvestri, from the "Cast Away" CD.

I will often play a particular song with gospel-centered lyrics on repeat for up to several hours in order to go really deep into it to feel its depths and ponder its various layers and meaning. Many revelations have surfaced for me during this time, especially in the late evening or early morning hours. Try it and you will know. The meditation described in this chapter is not necessarily "the" way, but merely "a" way, intended to get the spiritual seeker started in finding that place we might refer to as "sacred silence" or "sacred stillness." This is where we will best "hear Him."

Pay Attention to the Messages Received

Lose yourself in "feeling after God" to perceive His spiritual directives. When you arrive at that place of peace and inner stillness, pay attention to any messages you receive. Then during the latter part of or after your meditation (also known as the missionary's "Progressive Relaxation Exercise"), write them down and later act upon them. Writing down personal revelation demonstrates to God that we take His word seriously, and as something sacred that we value. With persistence in meditation, we will find ourselves just in between waking and dreaming consciousness. This is "the wormhole," "the gap," or "secret place" of stillness to which we desire to arrive—a state of pure being-ness and revelation. Voilà! You're now meditating.

I like to think of prayer as mostly my "outbound" communication with God, and of meditation as an experiential practice that more fully allows the "inbound" intuitive voice of God's direction, love, and will for me on a much deeper level.

Silence the phones and devices during this time. Go into thy closet and *shut thy door!* This *reverential practice* may be viewed as a sacrifice in the beginning, but I can promise you it will later become an unquenchable need—perhaps even become essential for spiritual survival. It is also a demonstration of our love for God, which coincidentally is the first and greatest of all commandments. President David O' McKay said,

> *"These secret prayers, these conscientious moments in meditation, these yearnings of the soul to reach out to* ***feel the presence of God****—such is your privilege and mine.... I pray...*

that through worship, meditation, communion, and reverence we may sense the reality of being able to have a close relationship with our Father in Heaven" ("Consciousness of God, Supreme Goal of Life," Conference Report, April 1967, pp. 84-88; emphasis added).

Keep in mind that when eyes are closed during meditation, one does not know if one is in a castle, a primitive hut, or in a cardboard box. Through meditation, pure joy can still be found in any environment, regardless of our external circumstances.

Salvation Requires Knowledge, Obtained through His Light

Salvation requires spiritual knowledge and direction. And this knowledge can only come by spiritual means, through being guided by the inner light and intuitive voice within. If we do not maintain this connection, we will let go of the rod of iron.

> President Mckay referred to meditation as *"the language of the soul,... 'a form of private devotion, or* ***spiritual exercise,'****... a form of prayer." As a preface to that description, he explained that the "spiritual communion arising from our own meditation" is* ***"more profitable introspectively" than being taught by "those who have authority to guide and instruct us****"* (*Teachings of the Presidents of the Church: David O. McKay,* pp. 31-32).

Once you find yourself in this sacred space or "gap," we must go deeper and deeper *still* (pun intended) into our meditative experience. The deeper we go into the stillness, the closer we will come to that secret place of the Most High unto a holy communion. As we continue to practice meditation and "getting still," we will be able to arrive at a heavenly place quickly and with frequency. It takes practice. Keep pressing forward and never give up!

Relaxing the Brain

While making my way through the airport one day, I "happened upon" a book called *Flight to Heaven.* It is about a pilot's plane crash, near-death experience (NDE), and miraculous return to physical, mortal life. I was pleasantly surprised at the parallels found in his book and the concepts discussed in this chapter. I noticed that the memories of his experience with God and the revelations given during his NDE could not be accessed if he "thought too much." What a confirmation! Remember, the born again experience is similar to that of a near-death experience as it relates to obtaining the absolute knowledge as to God's reality. In both cases, there is a heavenly manifestation of God's light and love which is *infused* into the soul through a complete immersion in that unspeakable love, which then powerfully delivers a knowledge of Him beyond that of faith. The candidate who is born of God, in contrast to the NDE recipient, additionally receives a complete remission of sins (i.e., through the "redemption of Christ"), the Holy Ghost as a companion, and the (conditional) sure promise of eternal life. Thereafter, one can never be the same. He or she is changed mightily, hence the term "mighty change of heart."

Captain Dale Black had this to say about his ability to recall memories he had enjoyed during his near-death experience:

> *"The memories I am about to share came back sequentially. These are not memories I could summon on command. They bypassed my conscious brain. If I thought too much, they resisted revealing themselves.* ***I had to let my brain relax*** *and allow my heart to take over" (Flight to Heaven, pp. 97-98; emphasis added).*

Captain Black gives us more insight about refusing our ego thoughts and comments:

> *"I wasn't used to giving up control easily, but I had no alternative.* ***They wouldn't come*** *[i.e., the memories of his NDE],* ***if I didn't let go and tune into my heart****" (Flight to Heaven, pp 97-98).*

Notice that the "tuning" happens through the tuning device, which is *not* found above the neck. Some of the Lord's first words to Joseph during the First Vision were, ""they draw near to me with their lips, *but their hearts are far from me*"" (Joseph Smith—History 1:19; emphasis added). Obviously, the Lord had an issue with the fact that their hearts were far from Him. And the same issue He had with them in Joseph's day, He likewise has with us today.

Salvation Is the Same Today as in Ancient Days

Regarding the First Comforter, the Prophet Joseph Smith taught:

> *"There are two comforters spoken of. One is the Holy Ghost, <u>the same</u> as given on the day of Pentecost" (Teachings of the Prophet Joseph Smith, p. 149; emphasis added. See also Acts 2.).*

We can receive this First Comforter only *after* pure and whole faith, repentance, baptism of water, and the laying on of hands (see *Teachings of the Prophet Joseph Smith,* p. 151). Through this manifestation, even as on the day of Pentecost as experienced by the apostles of old, we can be entirely cleansed by the Deity, completely healed of all spiritual and emotional wounds, and have all addictions miraculously lifted from us. We are then "converted unto the Lord," as was the apostle Peter. I bear personal witness of such an unspeakable miracle. Elder Bruce R. McConkie said:

> *"If I do not receive* ***the same*** ***testimony of our Lord's divine Sonship that Peter gained****, if I do not know by the power of the Holy Ghost that Jesus is Lord, that is,* ***if I do not have the testimony of Jesus,... I shall have no abiding inheritance in that church and kingdom****" ("The Rock of Revelation," Conference Report, 1969, pp. 79-84; emphasis added).*

What witness did Peter gain? When was Peter converted? He gained the knowledge of God when God filled him with Himself on the day of Pentecost, by the power of the Holy Ghost.

Through our own conversion, we receive a sure witness, not originating from this world but by way of a heavenly manifestation from the unseen world, that Jesus Christ is the Son of God—the Way, the Truth, and the Life. We speak with a new tongue, or like the very angels of heaven with words of pure praise. This is an experience we can actually have during our lifetime. We likewise receive a *sure witness* that the Father is real and has been directing His work this entire time. We experience oneness in Them and seemingly, at least, with all living creation. *We experience and receive a "portion of the celestial glory" (D&C 88:29; emphasis added), and a "quickening in the inner man,"* while in the flesh (Moses 6:65; emphasis added). We are immersed and overwhelmed in the Spirit Element, the influence and light of God's glory by the power of the Holy Ghost. We receive "a foretaste of eternal joy and a promise of eternal life" (*Preach My Gospel,* p. 65). We become "of one heart and of one mind" (Moses 7:18) and "stand fast in one spirit, with one mind" (Phil.1:27). We become "one in [Him], a son of God" (Moses 6:68). We "*receive alike*, that [we] may be one" (D&C 51:9; emphasis added). We come to the perfect knowledge of God (now beyond that of faith). "And this greater priesthood administereth the gospel and holdeth the key... *even the key of the knowledge of God*" (D&C 84:19; emphasis added). This is full conversion. Our process in coming to know God leads to reconciliation and a perfect knowledge of Him.

The apostle Erastus Snow spoke to the effects of the new birth as being the same today as anciently—that the work of God is the same in all ages:

> *True, there are many who affect to believe that they must be born again, and teach the doctrine of the new birth, the spiritual birth. But how little they seem to comprehend what is meant by that birth, and the effects that follow it.... The Holy Spirit, when overshadowing the people born of the water and of the Spirit produces certain fruits, certain effects, that are* ***the***

> ***same today as anciently****, and will be* ***the same among all people in all ages and times when people receive that Spirit****....* *It is this Spirit...which is the witness of the Holy Ghost of the Father and of the Son.... They cannot be turned away from the light of the Gospel and the liberties they enjoy in Christ Jesus" ("Work of God the Same in All Ages," JD 25:68; emphasis added).*

To experience the new birth is to "put on Christ." It involves an *unyielding commitment* to follow and serve Him in complete surrender the remainder of our days and into eternity. *This is the covenant of obedience* performed out of love and demonstrated through our willingness to offer sacrifice. There is no coercion involved. This pattern for "Putting on Christ" is the purpose of this work. My witness, and I pray that it be delivered by the Spirit to the hearts of all who desire to receive it, is that all may know and receive a witness to themselves that these words are true, and more important, that this experience of a mighty change can happen for themselves. God is not a respecter of persons.

I witness that the "exceedingly great joy" referenced in holy writ is available to each and every Latter-day Saint, if we will only first plant the seed of belief in our hearts and follow that Light that is given to every man (John 1:9), and heed His direction and counsel through "feeling our way." Seek this Jesus. He lives. He is real. The process leading to reconciliation and the mighty change experience are all tests of our willingness to surrender and sacrifice all that may be required of us. Lorenzo Snow stated that we may even

> *"be compelled to make the most serious sacrifices of wife, children, houses and lands, spoiling of goods, and even life itself, perhaps....*
>
> *"No persons are prepared to enter upon this new life* ***until they have formed within themselves this resolution****" ("The Gospel, Discourse by Lorenzo Snow," JD 13:284; emphasis added).*

During a tumultuous time for the early Saints, the Lord said to Joseph, "I have heard their prayers, and will accept their offering; and it is expedient in me that they should be brought *thus far* for a trial of their faith" (D&C 105:19; emphasis added).

> *These trials of our faith are the tests of our willingness to sacrifice all that we have and are, including life itself. When, through our brokenness, we arrive at that state of pure and whole "willingness," and we subsequently cry out in surrender in whole or perfect faith, we will then be born of God, subject to His holy grace, will, and timing.*

In my experience, this ***birth*** will happen at 11:59 p.m., or at the bottom of the 9th inning, to use the baseball analogy. It will not come easily. It will *always come after the trial of our faith*. Our hearts must break in preparation for this endowment. The need for a broken heart is more literal than one might think, but everyone's "brokenness" will occur in a very personalized way, specifically tailored for them individually. It must break in order to then be reconstituted and regenerated by Christ, with the attributes and increased depth of compassion towards our fellow man. *For the true seeker and truth seeker, there is no avoiding this brokenness. It's coming.* As my brother said at my mother's funeral, "I do not know what trials you currently face, or what trials you will yet face. But this much I do know: face them you will until your dying day, because the very purpose of this life is to be tried and tested. As Christ told his ancient apostles: 'In the world ye *shall have tribulation*: but be of good cheer; I have overcome the world'" (John 16:33). With all of this, however, take heart. Any tribulation, heartache, or pain we endure will be swallowed up and fully lifted—even transmuted into "exceedingly great joy." This is just as true as that which a pregnant mother experiences after the birth of her newborn baby. Her pain is immediately forgotten and swallowed up in the exceeding joy of her newborn babe. Alma spoke to these "afflictions" that could be "swallowed up in the joy of Christ" (Alma 31:38). Believe me when I say that the reward will far exceed the required price.

Our "Awful Situation": A Fearsome, Spiritually Induced View of Our Fallen Condition

M. Catherine Thomas explains:

> *"Part of man's earthly tutorial seems to be that he be brought to see his **true condition ["awful situation"]**, develop a deep desire to be delivered from it—seeing sin as the greatest enemy to his happiness—**feel keenly his own inability to deliver himself after repeated tries**, and finally in abject humility come to taste the grace of Jesus Christ" ("Alma the Younger [Part 2]: Man's Descent," Neal A. Maxwell Institute of Religious Scholarship).*

Speaking of this, our "*true condition,*" and while referring to the people of King Benjamin's day, Catherine Thomas says that,

> *"Notwithstanding the spiritual dangers, the people courageously crossed the threshold of spiritual experience into **a fearsome, spiritually induced view of the reality of their fallen condition**" ("King Benjamin and the Mysteries of God,"*

Neal A. Maxwell Institute of Religious Scholarship, see www.publications.mi.byu.edu; emphasis added).

Thomas taught the very purpose of our distress and how we might escape our awful situation:

*"One's distress would create the **desire** to escape the Fall and **reach out for a Savior**" (M. Catherine Thomas, "Alma the Younger (Part 2): Man's Descent," BYU Publications).*

When we consecrate *our all*, we will find the pearl of great price called Spiritual Rebirth and be born of Him. Elder Delbert L. Stapley of the Quorum of the Twelve spoke to the price required of possessing this pearl:

*"The price of possession is **one's all**. No individual can become a citizen of the kingdom of God by partial surrender of his earlier allegiances. He must **renounce everything foreign to the kingdom**, or he can never be numbered therein. **If he willingly sacrifices all that he has**, he shall find that he has enough. The cost of the hidden treasure and of the goodly pearl is not a fixed amount alike for all; **it is all one has**, and the poorest may come into enduring possession. **His all** is a sufficient purchase price*
("This Pearl Beyond Price," Conference Report, October 1965, pp. 11-16).

Christ said, "Do the things which ye have seen me do." This directive takes our "doing" from the realm of lip service into actual service. Constant repetition of the words of the affirmation below during meditation, although short, are deceptively powerful. After reading them, I'd invite you to feel (with eyes closed and filled with all the desire you can muster) and actually experience them. They were given to us in scripture for a reason. Ready?

***"I will give up all that I possess… to know thee"** (Alma 22:15, 18; emphasis added).*

This affirmation (especially when offered repeatedly during meditation) may seem simple, but I believe *the practice of it will bring salvation to all who truly mean it and persist in it!* "All that [we] possess" is the level of our willingness to sacrifice to which we must arrive in our *desiring* process. "All that we possess" will include not only our intention and willingness to give up any and all temporal possessions, but also our broken hearts, our vices, our sins, our false "persona," our pride, our purported "righteousness," our past, and our very lives, when or if called upon to do so. It is a willingness to "sacrifice" or offer up to God all that we have and are by turning solely to Him. *Why would we not be willing to give back all that was His to begin with?* This willingness is a similitude or type of that offering that Christ made to the Father.

To Die as to the Natural Man Through a Willingness to Sacrifice All

We must be willing to take upon us the name of Jesus Christ during mortality through complete surrender. If we do not, our awful situation may morph into an *awful crisis*, which may become "the night of darkness wherein there can be no labor performed" (Alma 34:33).

When I described in the introduction my feeling the need to be right with God, what I had effectively decided, was to fully and whole-heartedly repent in order to "prepare to meet Him." In other words, I was literally preparing to die and meet my Maker face to face. This is what I believe Alma meant. We are to prepare ***as if*** we're dying ***now*** and going to meet Him. This approach brings a deeper understanding—a more profound level of sentiment and meaning behind Alma's words when he said: "Now is the time to prepare to meet God."

This figurative "dying before we die" is to find that space or feeling state that those who were on the *Titanic* felt in the darkness after being told that their "unsinkable" ship would inevitably drown into the depths of the sea—that there were insufficient life rafts on board to save them all. It would be a very solemn, deep, and *sinking feeling* indeed, which must have included their turning to the heavens with "full purpose of heart, acting no hypocrisy and no deception before God, but with real intent, repenting of [their] sins, witnessing unto the Father that [they were] willing to take upon [them] the name of Christ" (2 Ne. 31:13) through a willingness to sacrifice their all for Him. To be born of God, we must all find a similar *sinking feeling* state of being—this solemn spirit of surrender in our brokenness.

Finding Our Crash Site and Crying out: A Necessary Prerequisite

Fellow seeker: When we find our crash site, we must *cry out*, which is to call upon His name from the depths of our souls in order to be redeemed. For those of us who persist in our own carnal wills, it will be "as though there was no redemption (and atonement) made" (Mosiah 16:5), "*having never called upon the Lord* while his arms of mercy were extended towards [us]" (Mosiah 16:12). We must continue to cry out until we have *actual knowledge* as to our status before God and are born of Him, so we can "enjoy the words of eternal life" and have *peace in this world* (Moses 6:59; D&C 59:23). His grace is not an automatic rite of passage just because hands were laid on our heads after being baptized by water.

For the purposes of this work, when I mention "mini-Gethsemane," I am referring to an experience that is meant to reference the symbolic "border lands" of Gethsemane, not to making our refiner's fire comparable to the level of Christ's. There is no equivalence to be found. That said, what I will say is that our own mini-Gethsemane will still be huge for us personally. When I went through my own rock-bottom experience, I could not function in the world, and was not even able to open a piece of mail for many years. This is how broken I was. Did I atone for the sins of the world? Of course not. I could not even atone for my own. But the experience, nevertheless, was still a monumental ordeal for me personally, especially when compared to my own limited capacity to deal with my then emotional brokenness.

The crash site (or personal, mini-Gethsemane), and the subsequent exquisiteness of our pain wrought by our having allowed the natural man in us to have steered our soul's ship into seeming destruction produces in us the "willingness" to finally surrender and do whatever God asks, to execute absolute obedience in following Christ to the letter, and to sacrifice whatever is required, including all things temporal and spiritual, even all that we have and are.

In order to produce the level, amount, or sufficiency of faith required to be saved, we must be willing to sacrifice all things. The Prophet Joseph taught: "Let us here observe, that a religion that does not require ***the (willingness to) sacrifice of all things*** never has power sufficient to produce the (perfect) faith necessary unto (eternal) life and salvation" (Lectures On Faith, 6:7; emphasis added).

This is the purpose of our individual crash site or mini-Gethsemane, for it leads to the willingness to sacrifice all things which ultimately yields the bestowal of a *perfect faith* unto salvation by God Himself. This is the purpose of our seemingly intolerable and exquisite pain in our moment of *desperation and despair*. This desperation and despair will likely, if not always, precede being born of the Spirit.

The desperation, despair, and spiritually induced panic arising out of our unrelenting need to find and know God are unveiled as the climax of our unfulfilled yearning to know Him. It's part of our breaking point, which becomes a glorious catalyst to "cry out" to Him for mercy for our salvation, tied to the requisite sufficiency of faith. It is the cry of the soul heard only by God.

Our Mini-Gethsemane: A Very Real Mental and Emotional Anguish

The Savior Himself refers to this rock bottom "spiritual and emotional crash site" as coming "down into the depths of humility" (3 Ne. 12:2). Jacob insists that if we do not "come down in the depths of humility," the sole keeper of the gate, who is "the Lord, the Holy One," will "not open unto [us]" (2 Ne. 9:41-42). In Mosiah we read that the people "did humble themselves even in *the depths of humility*; and they did cry mightily unto God" so that "their God… would deliver them…" (Mosiah 21:14). Think on these two words—*the depths*. These *depths* are the godly sorrow we must pass through. They are the labor pains experienced before our spiritual rebirth. They are part of our very own mini-Gethsemane.

> *"Where in my need to know... where is the quiet hand to calm my anguish? Who, who can understand? He, only One. He answers privately,* ***reaches my reaching in my Gethsemane****" ("Where Can I Turn for Peace?" Hymns, 129; emphasis added).*

Remember the pattern Christ requests of us. When Christ entered the garden of Gethsemane and while He was agonizing over the sins of all mankind, He said, "My soul is sorrowful, even unto death." Our mini-Gethsemane is how we join Him in this sorrow (as if it were happening in the present moment and perhaps for the very first time), both for our own sins and for the pain and anguish that our sins caused Him who knew no sin.

Why did the Lord require the broken heart and the contrite spirit to "satisfy the ends of the law" in order for us to be redeemed? (see 2 Nephi 2:7) I believe He wants us to symbolically join Him, *at least in some measure or as much as we can*, by experiencing a minute portion of what He experienced. In Gethsemane and on Calvary, our Lord's heart broke from the magnitude of the plight of the human condition and our collective, deplorable situation. It broke because of His all-consuming love for us—seeing us in our awful, unredeemed state. Our mini-Gethsemane is just that: mini, as in miniscule. It simply allows us the ability to "relate" to His sacrifice on a deeper level by experiencing an *infinitely smaller version of our own.* None were with Him then, but now we can get at least a glimpse of the depth of His suffering on our behalf.

> *What He is doing, at least in part, is inviting us to join Him now,* ***at the level that we are able****, so that our comprehension and appreciation of His offering can be understood at a much deeper level than ever before.*

President Ezra Taft Benson spoke of what leads to our mini-Gethsemane as a *very real mental, emotional and spiritual anguish.* He said, "Godly sorrow is a gift of the Spirit. It is a deep realization that our actions have offended our Father and our God. It is the sharp and keen awareness that our behavior caused the Savior, He who knew no sin, even the greatest of all, to endure agony and suffering. Our sins caused Him to bleed at every pore. This very real mental, emotional and spiritual anguish is what the scriptures refer to as having 'a broken heart and a contrite spirit.' … *Such a spirit is the absolute prerequisite for true repentance,"* and, I would add, subsequent rebirth ("A Mighty Change of Heart," *Ensign,* Oct. 1989; emphasis added).

Listen how Alma the Younger describes his "spiritual and emotional crash site" with such phrases as "after wading through much tribulation, repenting nigh unto death," "the gall of bitterness and bonds of iniquity," "in the darkest abyss," and having his "soul racked with eternal torment" (Mosiah 27:28-29). Enos referred to "the wrestle which [he] had before God, ***before*** [he] received a remission of [his] sins" (Enos 1:2; emphasis added). He "cried unto him" in mighty prayer and supplication for his own soul. Enos "knew" of his awful situation, meaning, that he had not yet been "saved" or born again. That's why the wrestle was so important.

What if Enos had been taught his whole life that spiritual rebirth was a process over a lifetime, void of any type of reconciliation with God? What if he had been taught that he was to, perhaps, not stress it so much—that "all is well"—or had the idea planted in his mind that salvation would all just come of its own accord simply by being an active member of the Lord's true Church? Does this not run contrary to the whole "now is the time for man to prepare to meet God" tenet, that "if we do not improve our time ***while in this life***, then cometh the night of darkness wherein there can be no labor performed?" (Alma 34:32-3). Does this not also put us potentially in a position wherein our time may unintentionally run out on us, while at the same time, hoping that our "process over a lifetime approach" (void of reconciliation) will be sufficient to save us? Perhaps Enos may have been born of God another way or even at a different time had he not "wrestled with the Lord" when he did, but my guess is he would have missed out on glorious promises and blessings had he chosen to take the more casual approach.

Strive for All That Is Possible, All That Has Been Promised

Elder Holland affirmed that

> "change, growth, renewal, and repentance can come for you as **instantaneously** as it did for Alma and the Sons of Mosiah" ("For Times of Trouble," Jeffrey R. Holland, ChurchofJesusChrist.org; emphasis added).

Do we believe Elder Holland? God is not a respecter of persons, and we are all on equal footing with Him. In the *Lectures On Faith*, we are given an immutable truth: "*whatsoever constitutes* ***the salvation of one*** *will constitute* ***the salvation of every creature*** *which will be saved*" (*Lectures On Faith*, Lecture 7, p. 72; emphasis added).

In the Doctrine and Covenants, we are specifically told that "all covenants, contracts, … not made and entered into and sealed by the Holy Spirit of promise, of him who is anointed… are of no efficacy, virtue, or force in and after the resurrection from the dead; for **all contracts that are not made unto this end have an end when**

men are dead" (D&C 132:7; emphasis added). In other words, it appears that the ordinances performed on our heads may need to be sealed by the Holy Spirit of Promise, here and now, in mortality! Are we not also told that "**it is impossible for a man to be saved in ignorance**" (D&C 131:6; emphasis added)? For me, I'd want to absolutely know that my sins had been remitted in full and not remain in mystery about it. To know for certain for ourselves individually, we are to go to God and ask of Him directly, fervently, and in faith. It is my belief that we are to never give up our petitioning until we know. And once we know, the Comforter (also referred to at times as, "the Spirit of truth") will guide us into all truth (John 16:13).

Through Spiritual Rebirth, we will obtain a new life in Christ as a new creature. The fetus cannot remain in the mother's womb forever. It must continue to receive nourishment, increase in development, and eventually pass through the birthing canal—"the gate." But we must eventually be birthed. We are not physically birthed as a process over a lifetime void of passing through *the gate* of the birth canal. At some point, we must actually pass through the birth canal into life—the temporal likened to that of the spiritual. The natural birth involves a mother and infant "in labor." We must likewise labor in passing through our own sorrow, pain, and suffering as we endure our own refiner's fire and come to more deeply feel of Christ's suffering and sacrifice for us. Greater compassion and individual authenticity arises out of our suffering. And the labor we may encounter in our own desperation, despair, and crying out occurs through our inner, ongoing seeking to find and know God—to ultimately be healed and converted.

The mother is willing to pay the price of the labor involved in child birth because she knows the joy and prize found in the reward. Spiritually speaking, we are likewise willing to endure any and all trials, because we too know of the "exceedingly great joy" and prize to be found in Christ.

The Mighty Change Experience

The mighty change experience during spiritual rebirth, even "*the same* as given on the day of Pentecost" (*Teachings of the Prophet Joseph Smith,* p.149; see also Acts 2), is so gloriously and powerfully real that it brings exceedingly great joy to the soul with lasting effects into the eternities. It gives us actual knowledge of God's reality.

E. Richard Packham, in his book *Born of the Spirit*, asked, "Will we know when we receive the birth of the Spirit? Does it come gradually so that we may have received it already and do not recognize it?" Packham then unveils the following:

> *"There's no question that spiritual preparation to receive this new birth could be a long, gradual process. But the distinctive change spoken of by Alma leads me to believe that one cannot receive such an experience without a powerful awareness of it.*

*Like the witness of the spirit, **we will easily recognize this gift when it comes, and we will know the day and the hour we receive it**" (p. 17; emphasis added).*

William W. Phelps and Parley P. Pratt reinforce this sentiment in the lyrics of two of our hymns:

*"Now let us rejoice in **the day of salvation**. No longer as strangers (now fellow citizens with the Saints) on earth need we roam" ("Now Let Us Rejoice," William W. Phelps, Hymns, no. 3; emphasis added).*

*"New life impart to us **this day**, And bid the sinners **live**.... Let us **receive** through covenant, The Spirit's heav'nly flame.... Baptize us with the Holy Ghost, And seal us as thine own, That we may join the ransomed host And with the Saints **be one**" ("Father in Heaven, We Do Believe," Parley P. Pratt, Hymns, no. 180; emphasis added).*

Does this "knowing the day and the hour" not coincide with the words of King Benjamin unto his people after they had partaken of the fruit of spiritual rebirth, in which the entire multitude present received the Holy Ghost in power?

*"For behold, **this day** he hath spiritually begotten you; for ye say that your hearts are changed [this day], through faith on his name; therefore ye are born of him [this day], and **have become** his sons and his daughters" (Mosiah 5:7; emphasis added).*

Notice the words "this day," "the day, "the hour," and "have become." They did not receive the rebirth as a process over a lifetime, void of reconciliation with God, although there may have been a long and gradual process leading to it. Elder Renlund of the Twelve Apostles referred to this process as one that leads us to a specific destination, even "*a process that leads to reconciliation*" (Oct. 7, 2018 general conference). And there is such a process. Please note, however, that *reconciliation with God has either happened in our lives or it has not*. In King Benjamin's address, you'll notice that they received it (i.e., the baptism of fire and of the Holy Ghost) *that day*. In similar fashion, we do not participate in our natural birth as a process over a lifetime void of a birthing. The process involves an actual experience—a birth. The entire pregnancy involves a process leading to the actual birth. The seed planted in the mother could be likened to the seed(s) planted in our hearts that need to be nurtured from *belief*, to *faith*, and then to actual *knowledge*. And after the actual spiritual rebirth, a process of further sanctification unto holiness and growing up in Christ continues. But the birth itself is an actual birth. Can you imagine the horror of a never-ending pregnancy, be it physical or spiritual? What other purpose would there have been for Enoch, who walked and talked with God for over 300 years prior to being translated and taken up, to have likened spiritual rebirth to the natural birth?

Richard Packham concludes,

> *"Another reason I believe we will know when the birth of the Spirit comes is that at that point our sins will be cleansed from us—**an experience** described by such words as 'fire' and 'burning'. Surely such an inward purging will be noticeable" (Born of the Spirit, p. 17; emphasis added).*

Fellow seeker. At some point within the process of feeling our way towards the tree of life, holding to the guidance of the "rod" of God's light or "word," we will come to a point of having been spiritually birthed. In the natural birth, there is a nine-month gestation period—a process. This process leads to excruciating labor. (Note: Christ experienced "labor pains" for us in Gethsemane while bleeding from every pore so that we all might have the opportunity of being spiritually birthed by Him.) The gestation period does not last a lifetime, neither does our birth last a lifetime. After our spiritual "birthing," which is when we are reconciled to God, we thereafter grow up in Christ unto eternal life by pressing forward with a steadfastness in Him (**faith**), having a perfect brightness of **hope** (in the promise given to us by God Himself of eternal life), and having been filled with the love of God and of all men (which is the fruit of the tree, the pure love of Christ or **charity** that will entirely fill us, per Moroni 7:48). *Faith, hope, and charity.* If we thereafter feast upon both the written and living "word" of Christ (for "my word is Spirit") and endure to the end, we are given eternal life. This is the plan of salvation unto all men. "For by the water ye keep the commandment; by the Spirit ye are justified, and by the blood ye are sanctified" (Moses 6:60).

Elder Charles. W. Penrose, a prior member of the First Presidency under two prophets, said of his born again experience, that he knew exactly what had happened to him and that his experience had a commonality with "the experience of others." He said that his spiritual rebirth had

> *"brought to me that which is called in the Scriptures, 'the peace of God that passes all understanding'. The joy, peace, the satisfaction that it brought to me could not be described in words. I knew that my Redeemer lived; **I knew that I was born again**; I knew The Holy Spirit was working in my heart. Truths were manifested to me that I had never heard of or read of, but which I afterwards heard preached by the servants of the Lord; all this was testimony to me that I had received the truth. I make mention of this because **I know this to be the experience of others**" (Journal of Discourses, 23:351; emphasis added).*

Full Conversion

Our modern-day apostles and prophets have also referred to a "full conversion," "whole conversion," and "true conversion." These descriptive words intimate and suggest that there is another type of conversion that perhaps falls short of the "full," "whole," or "true" type. May I suggest that "full" conversion is when we are *fully reconciled to God*, which is when we have been *redeemed* of the Lord (meaning redeemed from sin) through having *received* a complete remission of sins. This can only happen when we have likewise received the Holy Ghost or First Comforter in power, even "the same as on the day of Pentecost," as Joseph Smith himself defines its reception (see *Teachings of the Prophet Joseph Smith,* p.149). President Marion G. Romney describes it this way:

> *"When one is **wholly converted**, desire for things contrary to the gospel of Jesus Christ has actually died, and substituted therefor is a love of God with a fixed and controlling determination to keep his commandments" (Conference Report, Oct. 1963, 23; emphasis added).*

Elder D. Todd Christofferson also spoke to this full conversion. "The temptations and tribulations we experience, plus any testing that the Lord sees fit to impose, can lead to our *full conversion and healing*. But this *happens* [please note, that full conversion and full healing "happens"] if, and only if, we do not harden our hearts or stiffen our necks against Him. If we remain firm and steadfast, come what may, we achieve *the conversion the Savior intended* when He said to Peter, 'When thou art converted, strengthen thy brethren,' ***a conversion so complete that it cannot be undone*"** ("Firm and Steadfast in the Faith of Christ," October 2018 general conference; emphasis added). Said another way, when we experience *full conversion*, we shall encounter an experience like unto that which was had by Peter, which occurred on the day of Pentecost.

President Joseph Fielding Smith likewise said, "Through the Holy Ghost the truth is ***woven into the very fibre and sinews of the body so that it cannot be forgotten***" (*Doctrines of Salvation,* vol. 1, p. 48; emphasis added). President Kimball provided us an additional witness when he said, in speaking of Enos's journey, which we are to liken to our own: "He had now come to realize that no one can be saved in his sins, that no unclean thing can enter into the kingdom of God,… that ***there must be a purging, a new heart in a new man***. He knew it was not a small thing ***to change hearts, and minds, and tissues*"** ("Prayer," *New Era,* March 1978, p. 14; emphasis added). Lorenzo Snow spoke to the impactful nature of having obtained the above truth and knowledge: "You cannot take this knowledge from us by imprisonment or any kind of persecution. We will stand by it unto death..." (Discourse by Lorenzo Snow, delivered at the General Conference, held in the Tabernacle, Salt Lake City, Oct. 6, 1879). Elder James E. Faust emphasized the above when he said that, "The Holy

Ghost bears witness of the truth and impresses upon the soul the reality of God the Father and the son Jesus Christ ***so deeply that no earthly power or authority can separate him from that knowledge***" (Apostle James E. Faust, "The Gift of the Holy Ghost—A Sure Compass, 1989 Annual General Conference).

Ponder the phrases above. Do they sound like something received, void of the candidate's awareness of having been impacted in a spiritually significant way? Ask of God for this spiritual purification and knowledge, and don't stop until He reveals Himself to you. Turn to Him directly in faith—filled with the overwhelming desire to know Him.

The Prophet Joseph said, "We believe in it [this gift of the Holy Ghost] in all its *fulness, and power, and greatness, and glory*" (*Teachings of the Prophet Joseph Smith,* p. 249; emphasis added). Why would the prophet of the restoration use words to describe the reception of the actual Holy Ghost with words such as "fulness, and power, and greatness, and glory"? My immediate answer would be "because it is that." But don't rely on my words, turn to God and ask Him directly.

Jacob inquired, "Will ye reject…and deny…the power of God, and the gift of the Holy Ghost?" (Jacob 6:8).

The Lord said, referring to Joseph,

> *"After it was **truly manifested** unto this first elder that he had **received** a remission of sins [which happens by fire and the Holy Ghost by way of a heavenly manifestation], he was entangled again in the vanities of the world" (D&C 20:5; emphasis added).*

The above words in bold depict that Joseph's remission of sins was *truly manifest unto him*. In other words, he absolutely knew it had happened! What joy would there be in the giver of the gift if the receiver of the gift had no knowledge of having received it? Recall to memory the Prophet Joseph's words: "***Whatever constitutes the salvation of one will constitute the salvation of <u>every creature</u> which will be saved***" (*Lectures On Faith, 7:9).* In other words, how one receives salvation is similar, at least, to how all will receive salvation. Joseph also taught,

> *"the gospel has always been **the same**; the ordinances to fulfill its requirements, **the same**, and the officers to officiate, **the same**; and **the signs and fruits resulting from the promises, <u>the same</u>**" (Teachings of the Prophet Joseph Smith, p. 271; emphasis added).*

The apostles Charles Penrose and Orson Pratt spoke to this "sameness" as well:

> *These were the fruits of the spirit in the days of the Apostles. Now, if this same spirit is given to people today, through obedience to the Gospel, **it will bring forth the same fruits**. [And what are those?] The gift of tongues will be enjoyed; the gifts of interpretation, of healing, prophecy, discerning of spirits, etc., and people will be united together in spirit and be filled with love, joy, peace, patience and charity, and be baptized by one spirit into one body" 1 Cor. 12:13 ... **and all the gifts of the spirit anciently enjoyed are the fruits of the spirit today...**" (Discourse by Elder Charles W. Penrose, delivered in the Tabernacle, Salt Lake City, Sunday Afternoon, July 17, 1881; JD 22:155). Elder Pratt said: "And it is again just as reasonable that they should receive the same gospel and the same spirit, and that **the same effects should be produced among them, as among these at Jerusalem**" (Discourse by Elder Orson Pratt, delivered in the Fourteenth Ward Assembly Rooms, on Sunday Afternoon, Dec. 2, 1877).*

In my experience, and in talking with people who have not experienced of this power and fruit-yielding "exceedingly great joy," I do not get a sense that the more casual approach demonstrates the power referenced by Nephi. Again, the solution is simple. Don't rely on me or any other man, for "cursed is he that putteth his trust in man, or maketh flesh his arm" (2 Ne. 28:31). Ask of God. Inquire of Him. Turn to Him. He giveth to *all* men liberally and upbraideth not, so long as we ask in faith, nothing wavering. If we keep pleading, He will give us the spiritual knowledge we seek, sometime, somewhere. The answer may or may not be as immediate as a Google search. It may happen in short order or may take years, perhaps even after a decade or two of seeking. This I know through the crucible of personal experience.

David O. McKay, while serving as a missionary in Scotland, received this spiritual manifestation in power of the Holy Ghost, which seems to accord:

> *"Never before had I experienced such an emotion.... It was a **manifestation** for which as a doubting youth I had secretly prayed most earnestly on hillside and in meadow. It was an assurance to me that sincere prayer is answered 'sometime, somewhere'." (Francis M. Gibbons, David O. McKay, p. 50; emphasis added).*

The Cloud of Darkness; A Pattern Precedent to Spiritual Rebirth

Many, including King Lamoni, experienced a "cloud of darkness" that preceded their rebirth. (Alma 19:6). Joseph Smith experienced this "thick darkness" right before obtaining the First Vision and experiencing the glory of God (Pearl of Great Price, JSH 1:15). Father Lehi experienced "a dark and dreary waste" before seeing the tree of life (1 Ne. 8:7). The people in King Benjamin's day "had fallen to the earth" (Mosiah 4:1). Note that these faithful souls had not viewed themselves as "special" or "true saints" just because they were members of the Church, but they saw themselves as, "even less than the dust of the earth" (Mosiah 4:2).

In Helaman, the "cloud of darkness" would not disburse until they did "cry unto the voice" (Helaman 5:41, 42). The dark cloud is symbolic of our emotional and spiritual "crash site" or our own personal, mini-Gethsemane. It is the dark abyss. It is likened unto "depths of humility" that Christ invites us to participate in as part of our repentance process. It is when our souls are racked with torment. "And it came to pass the Lamanites said unto him: What shall we do, that this cloud of darkness may be removed from overshadowing us? And Aminadab said unto them:

> *"You must repent, and **cry unto the voice**, even **until ye shall have faith in Christ**; ... and when ye shall do this, the cloud of darkness shall be removed from overshadowing you" (Hel. 5:40-42; emphasis added).*

And we all know the rest of the story. A group of about 300 souls all received the baptism of fire and the Holy Ghost, were born again, and received that joy which is *unspeakable and full of glory*. (Please note: Although this happened to them concurrently as a group, salvation occurred for each individually, in a very intimate way and on a very personal level.) Thereafter, they were all able to "speak forth marvelous words" (Helaman 5:44-45). It must have been akin to "speaking with the tongue of the angels" (2 Ne. 31:13, 14). When we are baptized by water, we bear witness to the Father and Son that we are willing to follow them. When we are baptized by the Spirit, the Father and Son bear witness back to us, by the *power* of the Holy Ghost, that they are real and that they accept the offering of our broken heart and contrite spirit performed from the altar of our souls as a spiritual consecration.

President Lorenzo Snow, just prior to his miraculous rebirth, found himself "under the oppressive influence of a gloomy, disconsolate spirit, while an *indescribable cloud of darkness* seemed to envelop [him]" (*Biography and Family Record of Lorenzo Snow*, comp. Eliza R. Snow, pp. 7-9; emphasis added). Are we seeing a pattern here?

I have been asked by many: "Must there be an emotional and spiritual crash site that is inflicted upon us? Is this absolutely required?" My answer would be yes and no. Our hearts must indeed break and be offered up. This is the "yes" part. Yet apart from some external catastrophe or crisis in our lives which may bring it all to a head, if and when we are willing to submit to God's will by going into the depths of our repentance process, with godly sorrow, whether "inflicted" to do so or not, is this still not a "type" of His offering? Is this not a way in which we, through crying out in our brokenness, can spiritually join Him in some small degree? In doing so, we will have fulfilled the law (see 2 Ne. 2:6-7) and will have become qualified or eligible, according to His holy will, grace, and timing for justification and salvation. Notwithstanding the above, I believe that most will be led through broken-hearted experiences, individually tailored for each of us, ultimately designed to facilitate our crying out in full for His mercy.

Conclusion

In this chapter, we have learned about the great dichotomy in man. We have learned that there are two aspects of ourselves that are blended. We have learned that it is the divine aspect of ourselves which is intended to lead in the relationship in this dichotomy. The natural and analytical mind (which is part of the body) is there to aid in a supportive role to that divine light found in our hearts and is to become perfectly aligned with it. Brigham Young seems to concur:

"Recollect, brethren and sisters, ... that when evil is suggested to you, when it arises in your hearts, it is through the temporal organization. When you are tempted, buffeted, and step out of the way inadvertently; when you are overtaken in a fault, or commit an overt act unthinkingly ... and wish to yield to it, *then stop and let the spirit, which God has put into your tabernacles, take the lead.* If you do that, I will promise that you will overcome all evil, and obtain eternal lives. But many, very many, let the spirit yield to the body, and are overcome and destroyed" ("Faithfulness and Apostasy," *Journal of Discourses* 2:248, April 6, 1855).

Allowing the Spirit to lead may look different at times, especially when it comes to the spirit and the intellect. For example, if my spirit or higher self directs me to start a nonprofit organization to help emotionally wounded veterans from the war or to start an orphanage, my intellect is there to guide me primarily through the logistical processes. My intellect will inform me that I am going to need a business plan of action, a commercial space to rent, a phone system, utilities turned on at my new office address, employees, a financial endowment structure that may, perhaps, perpetually fund the endeavor, and so on. You get the idea. But the decision to move in that direction came through "sensing" the whisperings of the Holy Spirit to my soul. The Spirit needn't instruct me as to how to get utilities turned on. The Spirit gives the overall direction, and the intellect assists in executing the plan of action, but always in perfect alignment and in a supportive role, becoming unified and one with the directives through the Spirit which have been communicated to our spirit. This "intellect" needs to be brought into subjection (or "at one") with that light found in our hearts and center of our souls. This is a "type" of the At-one-ment, intellect and spirit, knitted and working harmoniously together, and perfectly aligned.

Chapter 5

Lehi's Dream: - The Type and Pattern of Our Spiritual Journey.

In order to best understand our journey in mortality, it is helpful to understand Lehi's dream, as it is a type and pattern for our own (see 1 Nephi 8). Almost the first thing that father Lehi observed in his dream was a man in a white robe who came and stood before him, spoke to him, and bid him to follow, which Lehi did.

While following this man, Lehi spoke of finding himself in a dark and dreary waste. After remaining in this state for some time, Lehi cried out for mercy. This prolonged darkness was part of Lehi's emotional and spiritual crash site. He was weary and needing rest. He turned to God for mercy and deliverance and prayed to have this darkness removed from him. (Note: Does this not sound like the same experience had by Nephi and Lehi in Helaman, wherein the people were admonished to pray that the "dark cloud" might be dispersed?) And shortly thereafter, Lehi beheld a large and spacious field. Within a specific clearing in the field, "he beheld a tree, whose fruit was desirable to make one happy." Lehi partook of the fruit, which he described as being "the most sweet," above anything before that [he] had ever before tasted. This fruit is the fruit of salvation. It is the fruit experienced at the time of our spiritual rebirth when we actually "take upon [ourselves] the name of Christ," wherein Christ writes His name on our hearts and adopts us into his family. This is when we become His sons and His daughters.

Lehi then says that "as [he] partook of the fruit thereof it filled [his] soul with exceedingly great joy." These words "exceedingly great joy" are "code" for being born of God or born again. And as a natural consequence of experiencing this level of joy, which created a mighty change in his very nature and heart, he desired all in his family to receive it. This is likewise my desire and the reason why I chose to write *Putting on Christ*. As Lehi cast his eyes about for his family, his eyes were opened to the treacherous journey that he had undertaken and that his family was still about to undertake for themselves. Lehi "beheld a river of water; and it ran along, and it was near the tree of which [he] was partaking the fruit." Lehi looked a "little way off" to the head of the river, and beheld Sariah, Nephi, and Sam who all appeared to be lost, not knowing wither they should go.

Lehi "beckoned unto them; and [he] also did say unto them with a loud voice that they should come unto him, and partake of the fruit, which was desirable above all other fruit." In essence, Lehi was witnessing to them of Christ's reality, having come to *a perfect knowledge of the Lord* while in the flesh. Sariah, Nephi, and Sam did come to Lehi, partook of the same "exceedingly great joy" of salvation, and were filled with the love of God (Moroni 7:48). In doing so, they obtained *a perfect knowledge of God* themselves and *knew*. Lehi was hopeful that Laman and Lemuel would also come to him, but they would not.

Lehi then "saw numberless concourses of people, many of whom were pressing forward, that they might obtain the path which led unto the tree by which [he] stood." Many were pressing forward in faith to obtain or find the path leading to the tree. And many did come forth and commence on the path leading to the tree. Both the tree and its fruit represent "the love of God" that we are to be filled with when we are born of God or born of the Spirit. This love of God is bestowed on those who fulfill gospel law, namely, broken-hearted repentance with godly sorrow and relying in whole faith upon the merits, mercy, and grace of the Holy Messiah—surrendering all to Him.

Then father Lehi observed that for many people who had initially caught hold of the rod of iron, "there arose a mist of darkness; yea, even an exceedingly great mist of darkness" to such a degree "that they who had commenced in the path did lose their way" and became lost. I believe these mists of darkness are, at least in part, the layers of hardness that gradually form over the heart through various life's experiences and misguided choices as highlighted in chapter 1, when critical heart maintenance is not pursued. This hardening often involves listening and heeding the wisdom and things of man rather than the wisdom and things of God. It also involves turning to "the cares of the world." Lehi saw others pressing forward in faith "*through the mists of darkness*, clinging to the rod of iron, even until they did come forth and partake of the fruit of the tree," being filled with the love of God (emphasis added). We later learn that these mists of darkness also represented the cunning of the adversary, his deceptions, temptations, and distractions placed in our path in an effort to redirect our course away from God, harden our hearts, and thereby inhibit our ability to come unto Him to partake of His salvation and our own redemption. When we turn from God by even small degrees, a small layer or film of hardness (unseen yet noticed) develops over the heart, and our signal or connection with Him is diminished. Without this connection, we can become lost.

Now after many had partaken of the fruit of the tree, many "did cast their eyes about as if they were ashamed." In other words, they allowed *the approval of men* to be more important than *God's approval* of them, and a select few later turned back to the world. Throughout scripture, we are admonished and warned that "no man, having put his hand to the plough, and looking back, is fit for the kingdom of God" (Luke 9:61-62). It certainly didn't work out well for Lot's wife. This is what the Lord was warning us about, that after partaking of spiritual rebirth and the love of God, we are to never again turn back to the world.

Lehi then "beheld on the other side of the river of water, a great and spacious building; and it stood as it were in the air, high above the earth." This building is symbolic of something that wasn't real, lasting, or enduring. The building was "in the air," suggesting that it was not "grounded" upon our true foundation, which is Christ. And this building was "filled with people, both old and young, both male and female." "For wide is the gate, and broad is the way, that leadeth to destruction, and many there be which go in thereat" (Matt. 7:13). Could this building also be the place where a few of us who have received of God's ordinances may possibly find ourselves?

The dream further revealed that those in the great and spacious building had a manner of dress that was "exceedingly fine," and "were in the attitude of mocking and pointing their fingers towards those who were partaking of the fruit." This reveals the important truth that we must not ever become debilitated by what others may think of us, including those found within our own families or the Church of Christ. We must never submit to "approval based" behavior out of our desire to fit in or to be "liked"—even accepted. Many of these approval-based partakers of the fruit later "were ashamed" and "fell into forbidden paths and were lost." This information teaches us that even after spiritual rebirth, "let those who are *sanctified* take heed also" (D&C 20:33-34).

Lehi then sums up that "he saw other multitudes pressing forward [in faith]; and they came and caught hold of the end of the rod of iron; and they did press their way forward, continually holding fast to the rod of iron [of personal revelation through the Light of Christ], until they came forth and [note it well] *fell down* and partook of the fruit of the tree" (1 Ne. 8:30; emphasis added), which is to be filled with the light and love of God. This *falling down* is symbolic of our own individual, emotional, and spiritual *crash site*, thereby facilitating the broken heart and contrite spirit that must be offered to God from the altar of our souls as part of our complete surrender—being "sacrificed," as it were. This type of sacrifice is required under the law (2 Ne. 2:6-7) in order to qualify for the exceedingly great joy of spiritual rebirth or First Comforter, which the Prophet Joseph defines as "*the same as given on the day of Pentecost*" (*Teachings of the Prophet Joseph Smith,* p. 149; emphasis added; see also Acts 2).

Falling Down: A Pattern Preceding Spiritual Rebirth

The Lord said, "My soul is exceeding sorrowful, even unto death" and he "*fell on his face*" in Gethsemane, giving us the pattern for ourselves. Joseph, the Prophet of the Restoration, *fell to his knees* prior to his encounter with darkness and the subsequent light and love of God that burst upon him and filled his soul. The lyrics of "Oh, Holy Night" invite us to "fall on our knees" while we experience our "night divine." Jacob's people "*fell to the earth*" and the "love of God" was "again among the people." Enos described a "wrestle" he had before God, and that he "*kneeled down*" before his Maker and "*cried unto him*" in mighty prayer. Alma the younger, after being called to repentance by the angel, "*fell...to the earth*" "for the fear of the Lord had come upon [him]." King Lamoni *cried for mercy* unto the Lord and "*fell down*" as if he were dead, symbolic of the death of the natural man. Lamoni's entire household fell into a trance, and the queen also "*sunk down*" prior to being filled with joy. Peter *fell or "sunk"* while on the water when his fear, doubt, and unbelief overcame him before *he cried out, "Save me, Lord*"! King Lamoni's father went as far as to "*prostrate himself* upon the earth" just before he "*cried mightily.*" The saints in King Benjamin's day "*fell to the earth*" because they recognized themselves and their awful situation or things "as they really [were]," and viewed themselves not as "righteous" members of the Church, but rather "even less than the dust of the earth" in their own carnal state and in desperate need of Christ's saving grace and atonement. ***Those of us who do not reach this level of awareness as to our need for Christ's atonement may likely never fall down, cry out for mercy, and thereby receive from Him that perfect endowment of faith (2 Ne. 9:23) that can save us.***

This falling down and crying out is a type and pattern preceding our spiritual rebirth and salvation. It may be best described in the Psalms: "I cried with my whole heart; hear me, O Lord: [now notice the covenant] *I will keep thy statutes.* I cried unto thee; *save me*, and I shall keep thy testimonies" (Psalm 119:145-46; emphasis added). He cried out because he realized his *awful situation.* Perhaps he realized that receiving the ordinances alone (even by proper authority) was not enough and did not entitle him to salvation.

Father Lehi concluded his dream by stating that he also saw other multitudes making their way "towards that great and spacious building," and "that many were drowned in the depths of the fountain; and many were lost from his view, wandering in strange roads." The multitude that did enter into that strange building was great and they did "point the finger of scorn" at Lehi and others partaking of the fruit or love of God, but [note it well], says Lehi, "we heeded them not."

This was the end of Lehi's dream. Have we caught hold of the rod yet? Have we partaken of the fruit? If we have, have we been dissuaded from *staying by the tree* in order to continually partake of the light and love of God? Or have we gone back to the world, and perhaps even to the great and spacious building because we cared more of what man thought of us than what God thought of us? The Savior said that the cares of the world "choke" the word, which is His revelatory light to our hearts that guides us. Christ also has said that "pride and the cares of the world" are ways in which we reject Him (D&C 39:9).

The Rod of Iron Led Me to Desire a New Life

One Sabbath day (not coincidentally, Resurrection Sunday), prior to my family's move to Arizona, I felt the impulse to go to my mother's grave site in Delta, Utah. This, His light, was whispering to me to "come home," as my false god up until that time had been the god of money. I informed my wife where I intended to go that Sabbath day, and away I went. I spent about five hours in Delta at my mother's grave. The weather was overcast and slightly rainy, but I did not get rained on that day. I spent the time reading scriptures, talking out loud to my mom and to my Heavenly Father. In my prayer that day, I asked God for a new life. I didn't want to live any more with this hatred and anger inside of me. It was killing me. In fact, as mentioned in the Introduction, I had previously found myself in the emergency room on three separate occasions thinking I was literally dying. I had symptoms of pins and needles going throughout my entire body. It was through this blessed crisis and my knowing that I was dying (or so I wholly believed), that I would later end up turning to God in full.

A Cash Buyer Is on His Way Now!

On my drive home, my thoughts turned to my biggest concern about moving, and that was the fact that I had a large mortgage I could not pay off because of a down real estate market as well as my inability to collect on monies owed to me that would have more than satisfied my home loan. I decided to turn to God. I spent the next 2 hours on my drive home saying affirmations and praying to God that he would send me a cash buyer to purchase our home. This occurred at the lowest point of the real estate market since the Great Depression. I still remember the repetitive affirmation: "A cash buyer is on his way now!" I'm sure God thought that my little affirmation was cute (and perhaps more than a little presumptuous). I alternated the above affirmation with a vocal prayer to God that I delivered with all of the emotion, feeling, and spiritual intention I could muster.

"Father in Heaven, please send me a cash buyer." Why the cash buyer? Because I wanted it to be a sure deal. I know—it was silly. Anyway, this is where I proceeded to outline all my reasons to Him to grant my request, but the reasons didn't matter to God. What mattered was that I was praying from my entire soul, and it aligned with His will. *I embedded the desires and feelings of my heart within the deepest part of my emotions.* (Note: *I have found this to be a key to any miracle that I have ever been a part of throughout my life.*) So back and forth I went. Affirmation, prayer, affirmation, prayer, affirmation, prayer—and this lasted two hours during the drive home. Joseph Smith taught us that "it is by faith that the Deity works" and that "when a man works by faith, he works by mental exertion instead of physical force. *It is by words* … which every being works when he works by faith" (see *Lectures On Faith*, 7:2-3; emphasis added). The Lord said, "Let there be light," and there was light.

Fast forward two days. I was in my office, which was located over our detached garage, and I saw a man approach the front door of our home. I hadn't told my wife of my prayers and affirmations, especially the part where I was very specific in my request that the Lord send me a cash buyer. Our home had been worth a significant amount of money at one point, but because of the great recession in 2010, there were little to no buyers to be had in our price range, and certainly not "cash buyers."

So after I saw this gentleman leave our home, I received a call from my wife. She informed me that he had asked if we were interested in selling our home. He then stated that he was a cash buyer and wanted to close as quickly as possible. I knew God had heard my prayer. I remained there alone in my office—weeping.

From this I learned (once again) that God was aware of me personally, that He had heard my cry and petition, and that He was not only supporting me but was completely backing me in the move of my family to Arizona. As I write these words, I feel His deep love for me, and He feels mine, along with my immense gratitude.

This experiential love and gratitude, which surfaces in seeing the Lord's hand in our lives through awareness, is what additionally helps us melt the walls that may form over our hearts through years of spiritual neglect. It is also the third essential station of awareness discussed in Chapter 1. I believe this also to be the primary purpose behind the first and great commandment of loving God. God knows that as we "practice" loving Him (like any developed art form), we will be able to keep the channels of His Light and Love open to our hearts so that we can be led to salvation by Him through the iron rod of personal revelation.

Fellow seeker, the above story began with a sincere desire in my heart. If the desire is good and has a good intention, or invites or entices us to come unto God, to love God, to learn of God, to speak or write of God, or to love or serve our fellowman, *then it is of God,* and we have an eternal "green light" to pursue, follow, and even chase after this desire. It is interesting that "desire" is the first step on our diagram in Chapter 1, is it not? This is the same desire described by Enos: "And my soul hungered." It was this same desire, delivered through the Light of Christ or "word of God" that led me to my mother's grave and my request that God send me "a cash buyer."

The Light of Christ Leads Us to Christ Being Formed in Us

As we follow the Christ Light by turning inward through meditation, prayer, and seeking for spiritual answers, and as we continue to soften our hearts, we will be led to fall down and cry out, tied to a committed willingness to do anything He were to ever ask. We will experience the Mighty Change. We will experience that "joy which is unspeakable and full of glory" (1 Pet. 1:8). We will receive this Comforter spoken of in Moses 6:61, which is given to abide *in us* (see also *Teachings of the Prophet Joseph Smith,* p. 362). Thereafter, this Comforter will be experienced as an *amplified portion* of the Light of Christ. This was the mystery, which is no longer. The apostle Paul referenced "the riches of his glory of this mystery" when he said, "Christ in you, the hope of glory" (Col. 1:27). When we receive the Holy Ghost or First Comforter, we receive a "perfect brightness of hope" (2 Ne. 31:20), through the portion of Their Glory received, that we have been *redeemed of the Lord* (past tense), have been given the sure promise of eternal life, and have *received* a remission of sins.

Elder McConkie spoke to this mystery: "This doctrine that man crucifies his old, sinful self so that Christ can dwell in him, and that man as a consequence has *power, through faith*, to inherit all things, is truly a mystery to spiritually untutored souls." Elder McConkie continues, "What is the mystery? It is that *Christ dwells in the hearts* of those who have crucified the old man of sin [or rather, 'dwells in the hearts of those in whom He, Christ Himself, had crucified the old man of sin' in man], and that as a consequence they have a *hope [i.e., actual, spiritual knowledge] of [the promise given of] eternal glory*! Such is what the Lord requires of his children in working out their 'own salvation with fear and trembling' before Him. (Phil. 2:12.) And it is in this connection that Paul says, somewhat caustically, 'But if our gospel be hid, it is hid to them that are lost.' (2 Cor. 4:3.)

"Hidden from the world, but revealed in the hearts of those who are enlightened by the Spirit, *this doctrine becomes the measuring rod by which the saints determine whether they are faithful and true* [and whether or not they are inside the strait gate]" (*The Promised Messiah,* pp. 124-125; emphasis added).

Paul elaborated more on this when he said: "And if Christ be *in you* [meaning, if we've been born of God and have received the Comforter and His initial cleansing as well as His inner, ongoing influence], the body is dead because of sin; but the Spirit is life because of righteousness. But if the Spirit of him that raised up Jesus from the dead *dwell in you,* he that raised up Christ from the dead shall also *quicken your mortal bodies by his Spirit that dwelleth in you*" (Rom. 8:10-11; emphasis added). Let me just add here that, for the true disciple, Christ is not only living "in the hearts of those who are enlightened by the Spirit" (after the rebirth), but is also in a very real, private, and undivided way living out the pattern of His life again, only now in and through us. Said differently, through spiritual rebirth, the "Word" (once again) becomes flesh, if you will. We are the vessels which can become filled with "Himself." To live in Christ is to live a life that has become new and "alive" and an experiential awareness of that ongoing "aliveness" within us. It is to have Christ "formed" anew in us.

The lyrics to the song "Remembrance," by Hillsong Worship, speaks to this:

"I'll walk salvation's road
With fear and trembling
Your way borne as my own
As Christ is formed in me."

In the Odes we read: "And He has caused to dwell *in me* His immortal *life,* and permitted me to proclaim the fruit of His peace" (The Odes of Solomon 10:2; emphasis added).

Elder F. Enzio Busche summarized it most beautifully when he said: "We will not be satisfied until we have *surrendered our lives* into the arms of the loving Christ, and until He has become the doer of all our deeds and He has become the speaker of all our words" ("Truth Is the Issue;" general conference, Apr. 1993; emphasis added).

Surrendering Our Will and the Price of the Promised Reward

Most of us may not inherently desire to sacrifice our control over our lives. From my own personal experience, I believe that most of the delay in our coming unto Christ and surrendering all is the inaccurate fear of losing control or losing our own personal will or identity, as well as the fear of knowing that by "choosing in" to this complete surrender, there may arise a more difficult journey. Take heart. Our will does not get lost when Christ comes alive and is formed in us. We still possess our own individual will. It just becomes strengthened, enhanced, and *blended* in His will through that indwelling "God principle of Intelligence." We will eventually become filled with a spirit and oneness with that God who is all in all, adding to the taste or portion we received during spiritual rebirth. "The elements are the tabernacle of God; yea, man is the tabernacle of God, even temples" (D&C 93:35). Through this indwelling God principle or source, we become one in having the same desired end as the Father and Son, which is the work of eternal salvation. In other words, we find a joy in the work that never expires.

Christ said, "If any man will come after me, *let him deny himself*, and take up his cross, and follow me" (Matt. 16:24; emphasis added). Deny himself of what? Well, the natural man part of himself as well as the cares of this world which choke the word or His guiding light. Yes, it's going to require a sacrifice. This is without question. Was Christ's road easy? Of course not. But was it worth it? Look at Him now! All that He has achieved, the Father and Son are now offering to us as well, even that of becoming joint heirs in all that the Father has. Do we believe it? Do we trust God and His precious promises?

Elder McConkie said, "No one can pursue such a course until he knows of its existence. No one will ever make the sacrifice necessary to gain eternal life until he believes in his heart that the reward is worth the price" (The Promised Messiah, p. 132; emphasis added). Are we willing? Is the reward worth the price? Each will have to decide this for himself. But an absolute willingness to sacrifice all is required or we cannot attain. Mortality is the vehicle for these tests of our willingness. And we must faithfully execute the doctrine of Christ as Nephi lays it out in plainness (see 2 Nephi 31 and 32), or as Jacob taught, "these things are manifested unto us plainly [for what purpose?], for the salvation of our souls" (Jacob 4:13; parenthetical addition, mine). "There is none other way" (2 Ne. 31:21).

The Road to Salvation Goes through Man's Own Mini-Gethsemane

Elder Holland insightfully said:

> *"I know that in my own life, that* ***salvation is not a cheap experience.*** *That no one is going to have rich and abundant experiences for minimal effort.... God's opportunity is man's extremity (i.e., man's crash site)... When we come to know the Savior, it's when we've been out somewhere, at least in the border lands of Gethsemane.* ***The road to salvation always goes through Gethsemane.*** *And it will always require a journey to the summit of Calvary" ("Missionary Work and the Atonement," from a talk given at the Provo [Utah] Missionary Training Center on 20 June 2000, Ensign, Mar. 2001; emphasis added).*

This "extremity" referred to by Elder Holland is the crash site or mini-Gethsemane that I have referred to throughout this work. Elder Holland continues,

> *"If we say we are disciples of Christ, we walk where he walked, we feel what he felt, we pray the way he prayed and we shed the tears he shed.* ***At least in some proportion; at least in some symbol...*** *Now it isn't always like that and it is isn't supposed to always be like that, and we're a little self-pitying if we act like it's always like that. But* ***some parts of the discipleship require 'that walk,' basically, His walk****" ("For Times of Trouble," as found on Youtube; emphasis added).*

Passing through our own crash site or mini-Gethsemane is also reinforced by Elder McConkie. He said that we must be "broken down with deep sorrow for sin, to be humbly and thoroughly penitent." This is how we are to spiritually and emotionally join Christ in Gethsemane. Elder McConkie spoke of the *broken heart and contrite spirit as being pre-requisites to our own individual salvation*, and they are (see 2 Ne. 2:6-7). He specified that this "*status* is a condition precedent to a valid baptism and consequent membership in the earthly kingdom of God" (*Mormon Doctrine,* "Contrite Spirit," p. 161).

In a letter from Truman Madsen to his friend, he wrote:

> *The Hebrew root I have learned of the word "**contrite**" is the equivalent of **shattered, pulverized, broken into bits, separated, disheveled, bruised, battered, and driven as by a wave**. Is this the self-awareness the Master asks us to bring to his altar? I thought not. Life, I supposed, was to build strength, or define the point of no return. **I know now that there is no ascent without descent.** God bless you, my brother, to come naked and open to the nurturing link with Christ. He who locked step with you in pre-mortality and who accepted the whole gamut of your anticipated burdens as you with matching intensity accepted His. He has yet to say to you "in all your afflictions I was afflicted." **Holiness will come through worthy humiliation in pain**. God will help you to be **delivered into sanctification**. For that is His will. And I know it.*

In referring to the required prerequisite of a broken heart and contrite spirit, Elder McConkie tells us, "Indeed, it was primarily for *those in this condition of heart and mind that the very atoning sacrifice of Christ was worked out.*" And then he adds (now pay close attention), "*And the sacrifice the Lord, in turn, <u>requires</u> of his saints is that they offer him a broken heart and a contrite spirit.*" (Remember, "it is a condition precedent to a valid baptism," which will include that of both water and Spirit.) McConkie adds, "The Lord's Spirit is sent forth to *enlighten the contrite [and broken hearted only, for it is a law]*, ***and they are the ones who gain the [actual] gift of the Holy Ghost*** (ibid; emphasis added). Mark it well! Those of us who make this offering (see 2 Ne. 2:6-7) from the altar of our souls to God with pure intent and all sincerity of heart are the ones who gain, through faith, the gift of spiritual rebirth and are adopted by Him into His family! But we must be "all in," having a committed "willingness" and determination to follow His will (which becomes our own) to the end of our mortal lives and into eternity.

Notice this verse:

> *"Wherefore, redemption cometh in and through the Holy Messiah; for he is full of grace and truth.*
>
> *"Behold, he offereth himself a sacrifice for sin, to answer the ends of the law, unto all those who have a **broken heart and a contrite spirit; AND UNTO NONE ELSE** can the ends of the law be answered" (2 Ne. 2:6-7; emphasis added).*

Joseph Smith stated that when a man is born of the Spirit (i.e., born again or born of God), there are certain effects that occur to a gentile: "The effect of the Holy Ghost upon a gentile is to *purge out the old blood and make him 'actually of the seed of Abraham'*, that man that has none of the blood of Abraham naturally ***must have a new creation by the Holy Ghost***" (see Teachings of the Prophet Joseph Smith, p. 149). And for those not being the actual seed of Abraham, the experiential manifestation would be much greater, and therefore, more easily recognizable.

George A. Smith spoke to this as well:

> *"I have always heard it suggested that as the spirit of 'Mormonism' gathered together the seed of Abraham—mostly the sons of Abraham that are mixed among the nations, that the Holy Spirit falling upon men, who are not of the pure blood, who had the predominance of other blood in their veins,* ***that the manifestation is greater****" (Journal of Discourses, 11:1).*

This is the power inherent in the gospel that is hidden from most of us. This power is felt physiologically in our bodies at the time of our spiritual rebirth, having a commonality to that same experience which was had by the ancient apostles on the day of Pentecost through a heavenly manifestation of the Lord's Spirit. (Note: During this *manifestation*, we will likely experience and believe that *the veil is seemingly ready to burst and that we will be surrounded by hosts of angels, even anticipating the appearance of the Lord of glory Himself.)* During the days of Kirtland, "The Lord had endowed the Saints with power, and Kirtland was flourishing beneath the towering steeple of the Temple. The visions and blessings that season had given them a *foretaste* of Heaven. *The veil between earth and heaven seemed ready to burst*" (Saints, p. 243; emphasis added). The hymn "The Spirit of God," which is all about the "baptism of fire" and other heavenly endowments, confirms that this "power of God" was indeed expanding with the Saints and that "*the veil o'er the earth [was] beginning to burst*" ("The Spirit of God," LDS *Hymns,* p. 2; emphasis added).

During our *manifestation* of the Spirit of God to us individually in power, there is a purging of sin as though by spiritual fire. This purging and new creation of us comes in fulfillment of the oath that God swore, that through Abraham all the nations of the earth would be *blessed.* In other words, our rebirth is the initiation into receiving the blessings of Abraham relative to salvation. These blessings are the fulfillment of receiving the promise of eternal life, thereby becoming the seed of Abraham, adopted into his family and that of Christ. "For as many as receive this gospel [see D&C 39:4-6] shall be called after thy name, and shall be accounted thy seed, and shall … bless thee, as their father" (Abr. 2:9-10).

Lorenzo Snow calls the reception of the gift of the Holy Ghost, together with its "***supernatural gifts***" accompanying it as (now pay close attention)—

*"being **unchangeable** in its nature and operations," ... "reasonable, consistent, and scriptural **to anticipate the same gifts and blessings [as 'in the apostolic age'];***

*"whenever a man will... conform to the whole order of the gospel of Jesus Christ, then there is nothing beneath the celestial worlds that will operate against claiming and receiving the gift of the Holy Ghost **and all the blessings connected with the gospel in the apostolic age**" ("The Only Way Way to Be Saved," London, England, 1841,p p. 9-10; emphasis added).*

God is not, indeed cannot be, a respecter of persons. If we fulfill the same law, we will receive the same or "like" blessings and fruits as those received on the day of Pentecost, even "*all the blessings connected with the gospel in the apostolic age" (ibid).*

John Taylor reaffirmed that the signs and fruits resulting from the promises, including the wonderful manifestations of the Holy Ghost, are the same (or at least can be) for all:

*"I want the doctrines that were promulgated by the disciples of Jesus **on the day of Pentecost**, through obedience to which **men may gain the power and inspiration that were enjoyed by them**, in accordance with the promises which Jesus had made....*

*"When the people saw these **wonderful manifestations**, they said, "Men and brethren, what shall we do?" [Acts 2:37] I have often reflected upon this saying....*

*"I have reflected upon these matters a good deal.... When they asked on the day of Pentecost what they were to do to be saved, said Peter, 'Repent, and be baptized every one of you in the name of Jesus Christ for the remission of your sins, and you shall receive the Holy Ghost.' (Acts 2:37-38). This was the command to all—to the doctors, lawyers, Pharisees, and pious people, as well as to the harlot, publicans, and thieves. This was the doctrine of the Apostolic Church. **The question with me is, "If this was the true Gospel 1,800 years ago, is it not the same today? ...***

*"**The Gospel of Jesus Christ produced certain results then** [i.e., 'signs and fruits resulting from the promises' as being **the same**, per Joseph Smith], and it will produce **the same today, <u>or</u>***

it is not the Gospel" *(Discourse by John Taylor, delivered in the Old Tabernacle, Salt Lake City, March 14, 1869; emphasis added).*

The Knowledge of God Comes through a Holy Manifestation, When Redeemed

President Howard W. Hunter taught, "Science has done marvelous things for man, but it cannot accomplish the things he must do for himself, ***the greatest of which is to find the reality [i.e., knowledge] of God.*** The task is not easy; the labor is not light; but as stated by the Master, 'Great shall be their reward and eternal shall be their glory' (D&C 76:6)." (*Teachings of Presidents of the Church: Howard W. Hunter,* chapter 21, "Faith and Testimony;" emphasis added).

For the purposes of this book, the phrase "the knowledge of God" or "the reality of God" is understood as synonymous with "knowing God" or spiritual rebirth, which occurs when we partake of a portion of His glory through a heavenly *manifestation* of His Spirit in power and are purified as though by spiritual fire, lasting several days and nights.

When this visit through a heavenly *manifestation* is experienced, we are then truly and fully converted unto the Lord and Born of God. As stated in the preface of this book, the knowledge *of* God is different than the knowledge *about* God. As Joseph stated clearly, "*knowledge implies more than faith*" (*Lectures On Faith,* p. 77; emphasis added). Lorenzo Snow gives his witness of this faith-surpassing knowledge and endowment: "There followed the *same testimony* and the *same experiences* so far as the *knowledge of the divinity of these principles* was concerned. The heavens were opened over my head and the power of God and the light of *the Holy Ghost descended and elevated my whole being* and gave me ***the most perfect knowledge* that Jesus was the son of God.** It was not the result simply of opinion or belief, as is the case in many other things, but ***it was a knowledge far beyond that of belief* or opinion** [or, as Joseph Smith suggested above, 'Knowledge implies more than faith'].

I knew that God sent His angels and restored the fullness of the gospel *as taught in ancient times*—that he sent angels to authorize Joseph Smith and gave him *authority* to administer in the ordinances of the gospel and *to promise the Holy Ghost* to all who would be obedient" (*Testimony of Lorenzo Snow,* transcribed from a video by the same name, as found on Churchofjesuschrist.org; emphasis added).

When this *manifestation* happens, we become cleansed and purified by the Deity—we come to *"the most perfect knowledge of God"* and receive a perfect brightness of hope as to the sure promise of salvation having been extended. **We *experience the redemption of Christ,*** which is likewise when we are born of the Spirit and grafted in, becoming once again His sons and daughters through adoption.

The apostle Charles Penrose in the early days of the restoration stated that the reception and enjoyment of the gift of the Holy Ghost was "*not merely an influence which made them feel good; that exalted their spiritual natures so as to make them happy, contented and peaceful (as is experienced with the Light of Christ),* but it was ***a manifestation of the power that comes from God***" (*Journal of Discourses,* 25:40-41; emphasis added).

Elder McConkie enlightens us further as to the type of knowledge we are to acquire: "From an eternal perspective, what each of us needs is a *Ph.D. in faith* and righteousness. The things that will profit us everlastingly are *not the power to reason, but the ability to receive revelation; not the truths learned by study, but the* ***[spiritual] knowledge gained by faith****; not what we know about the things in the world, but our [spiritual] knowledge of God* and his laws"" ("The Lord's People Receive Revelation," 1971 Annual General Conference, Ensign; emphasis added). Notice his words here. It is the spiritual "*knowledge gained by faith which profit us,*" even everlastingly. This is the "learning by faith" referenced in scripture, which can only happen as we turn directly to God for divine instruction.

President Joseph F. Smith stated:

> *"The greatest achievement mankind can make in this world is to familiarize themselves with divine truth, so thoroughly, so perfectly, that the example or conduct of* ***no creature living in the world can ever turn them away from the knowledge that they have obtained****.... From my boyhood I have desired to learn the principles of the gospel in such a way and to such an extent that it would matter not to me who might fall from the truth, . . . who might fail to continue to follow the example of the Master, my foundation would be sure and certain in the truths that I have learned. . . . I know of but One in all the world who can be taken as the first and only perfect standard for us to follow, and he is the Only Begotten Son of God" (Gospel Doctrine, pp. 3–4).*

Fellow seeker, this knowledge referenced by President Smith, such that "no creature living in the world can ever turn [us] away," can only come through full conversion and spiritual rebirth. It's not so much about conversion to the true Church of Jesus Christ (although that certainly may come as one of its fruits), but to Jesus Christ and the power inherent in His atonement and gospel.

President Kimball likewise spoke to the importance of acquiring spiritual knowledge, above and beyond that knowledge of a secular or temporal nature. He said,

> *"The treasures of both secular and spiritual knowledge are hidden ones—but hidden from those who do not properly search and strive to find them. . . Spiritual knowledge is not available merely for the asking; even prayers are not enough. It takes*

> ***persistence and dedication of one's life.*** *The knowledge of things in secular life are of time and are limited; the knowledge of the infinite truths are of time and eternity. Of all treasures of knowledge, the most vital is* ***the knowledge of God****" (Teachings of Spencer W. Kimball, pp. 389–90; emphasis added).*

Think about what our beloved prophet said: "It takes persistence and dedication of one's life" to find the most vital of knowledges, that of ***the knowledge of God!*** As has been repeatedly stated within this work, *we must make seeking Christ a way of life.* This knowledge is obtained through Spiritual Rebirth, which is very similar in nature as what occurred on the day of Pentecost and was received by the early apostles in the Lord's day. Nephi refers to this "persistence and dedication of one's life" a bit differently. He said that the Holy Ghost was a gift of God… "unto all those who **diligently seek Him**!" (1 Ne. 10:17; emphasis added).

The knowledge of God is knowing His absolute reality by way of a heavenly manifestation while in our flesh. This is conditional salvation. Elder McConkie said, "But the thing that we are concerned with here in mortality, is to have the Holy Ghost reveal to us the things of God, ***the knowledge that God is our Father, that Jesus Christ is his Son (see 2 Ne. 31:18)***, literally born of Him in the flesh… that we with the ancients, might be heirs of the fullness of the Father's kingdom. We believe that *it is life eternal to know God and Jesus Christ*, whom he has sent… John 17:3, and that *these glorious beings are manifest by the power of the Holy Ghost [which is what brings the 'knowledge'].* We believe that man is saved no faster than he gains knowledge, ***meaning knowledge of God***" (Bruce R. McConkie, "The Holy Ghost—A Revelator," Conference Report, April 1953, pp. 74-76; emphasis added).

This knowledge of God I'm speaking of is not the "gentle stuff" as is the case with the still small voice. It is given us through a manifestation of His Spirit ***in power*** by the Holy Ghost and is called the First Comforter.

The Lord "Visits Us" During Spiritual Rebirth

President Joseph F. Smith has said: "Then if we would *know the Lord Jesus Christ...* we must enjoy the light of the Spirit of the living God *individually.* The possession of this ***heavenly knowledge*** is absolutely necessary to keep us in the paths of life and truth... and although we may be in fellowship with the Church, fully believing the counsels of our brethren to be dictated by wisdom, ***yet without something more than mere belief or supposition we cannot stand***" (JOD 19:20). And what is this "something more than mere belief?" It is the "heavenly knowledge" of the Lord Jesus Christ that President Smith laid out for us in plainness.

Nephi tells us that he had "*great desires* to know the mysteries of God," and that when he did "cry unto the Lord," the Lord "did ***visit*** [him]*"* (1 Ne. 2:16-17; emphasis added*)*. He spoke of "the things which the Lord had *manifested* unto [him] by his Holy Spirit" (ibid; emphasis added). Mormon, when only fifteen years of age, was "***visited*** of the Lord, and ***tasted*** **and** ***knew*** of the goodness of Jesus" (Mormon 1:15; emphasis added). Fellow Seeker, when the Lord "***visits us***," we too shall know God or obtain the knowledge of Him ourselves—just as they had, for God is no respecter of persons.

> "Where are the individuals that can say that they know that Jesus lives?... To me it is certain, that no man lives on the face of the earth--no woman lives that can say this, ***except those to whom Christ has revealed Himself***' [through this manifestation spoken] (Brigham Young, JOD 1:37; emphasis added).

Notice now the words from the Savior Himself:

> *"And behold, whosoever believeth on my words,* ***them will I visit*** *with the manifestation of my Spirit and they shall be born of me, even of water and of the Spirit" (D&C 5:16; emphasis added).*

In addition to the *manifestation of the Lord's Spirit*, His ***"visit"*** may also include (all in accordance with His holy will), the actual ***visit*** in the form of His personage, yet shrouded by the veil. Or His ***visit*** may be through an extension of His glory by way of a spiritual manifestation of Himself. To those fully *converted unto the Lord*, the overwhelming impression received when one is born of God is that the Lord is most definitely present in the form of His personage (yet shrouded by the veil), and the expectation of that candidate who is being baptized by fire is that the Lord Himself is going to appear. There may arise a wall of fear in that moment. And this, not because we fear the Lord, but we may not feel spiritually ready to receive Him on this level, nor do we know exactly what to expect in the form of the unknown, or what may actually happen next. I remember trying to push through this fear with as much faith as I could possibly muster, wholly expecting to see Him—and not only Him but a host of other heavenly beings perhaps as well. And of course, the reality was that this was not to be. He did not intend to manifest Himself in the form of His Personage on this occasion, but it is at least a very real, *experiential knowledge* of what we can expect in some degree when He does. Hence the difference between the Two Comforters spoken of—the First and the Second.

I believe that the endowment wherein the Lord ***visits*** us through a powerful ***manifestation*** of His Spirit is part of that promised blessing when hands were laid on our heads through confirmation. This is when our broken hearts (which have been offered to Him) are "comforted" by the Comforter. The sons of Mosiah experienced this comfort and witness in order to preach the word in power. Therefore, "the Lord did **visit** them with his Spirit… and they were comforted" (Alma 17:10). I witness that these same ***manifestations*** which accompany this ***"visit"*** are within our grasp as spiritual seekers so that we too might be sanctified and preach the word even as the sons of Mosiah. Why take the risk in not pursuing such an endowment?

Lorenzo Snow, who was personally tutored by the Prophet Joseph, seems to see it the same way. It appears that thousands received these ***Pentecostal-like manifestations*** in the early days of the Church, as many do today. Pay close attention here to his words found below. They are from an apostle of the Lord who was taught by the man who communed with Jehovah and who later saw and spoke with the Lord of glory Himself after the death of Wilford Woodruff.

Lorenzo Snow's talk entitled "The Gospel" (delivered in the Tabernacle, Salt Lake City, Sunday, Jan. 23, 1870; see *Journal of Discourses,* 13:284-292), is in my view arguably *the single greatest discourse on the experiential fruits of spiritual rebirth spoken in plainness that has ever been uttered from the pulpit by any man*, saving only Christ Himself. You may decide what the fruits of spiritual rebirth looked like for the early Saints, and with God being an unchangeable God, what they reasonably might look like today. This is the same priesthood leader, who, as President of the Church, issued these words: "The Spirit of the Lord rested *mightily* upon me—*the eyes of my understanding were opened*, and *I saw* as clear as the sun at noonday, *with wonder and astonishment, the pathway of God and man.* I formed the following couplet which expresses the revelation, as it was shown me…: As man now is, God once was. As God now is, man may be" ("Lorenzo Snow," on www.history.lds.org).

By spiritually discerning the words taken from his talk, it is easy to conclude that Lorenzo Snow knew whereof he spoke. He was a man of God, and as such, we should pay very close attention and not take lightly his words. He refers to the *perfect knowledge of God* that can be obtained by any man who has received the Holy Ghost through the ordinances of baptism by water and the laying on of hands to confer its gifts, revealing its miraculous and powerful spiritual manifestations. In it, President Snow references these attendant blessings and signs which come to those who "believe" with the words "manifestations," "perfect knowledge," "divine knowledge," "same knowledge," "knowledge of its divinity," "promised knowledge," "tangible knowledge," "tangible form," "knowledge of this work," "divine authenticity," and "divine power," a whopping 28 times in total. The words "divine manifestations" or "manifestations" are referenced a total of 11 times. Do you think he was trying to send us a message as to what it is like to receive the Holy Ghost in power? All of these words describe the experiential fruits that accompany the reception of the Holy Ghost which were had by the ancient Saints, the early Saints of the restored Church, and the fruits that every member of the Church may receive today, *if diligently sought for with honesty and integrity of heart.* Please find this talk in the *Journal of Discourses*,

13:284-292, and read it now. You may even want to highlight any word or phrases having the words knowledge, divine, and manifestation. Then we'll continue.

All done? Ready?

To receive this *knowledge of God*, we must first become *willing* to make "the most serious sacrifices of wife, children, houses and lands, spoiling of goods, and even life itself, perhaps" (ibid). When this manifestation comes, lasting several days and nights in varying degrees, we will have obtained this knowledge of God, or "come to the knowledge of the Lord" as though he had already come among us in the flesh (see Mosiah 3:13). It will be accompanied with the "peace of God which passeth all understanding" (Philip 4:7). We will experience an unspeakable oneness with God. We will even partake of His Consciousness. Can you imagine this? We will have eyes to see and ears to hear. This ongoing manifestation in power of the Holy Ghost is when we truly come to "know God" or "know the Lord" in mortality for the very first time (and not merely that of having a testimony of Him as delivered and witnessed through the Light of Christ). The experience is also when we receive and know Him "in the world" (D&C 132:23).

Spiritual rebirth is like finding our "promised land" of salvation. The Lord said,

> "After ye have arrived in the promised land [i.e., received of these manifestations], YE SHALL ***KNOW*** THAT I, THE LORD, AM GOD; and that I, the Lord, did deliver you from destruction."

This destruction spoken of is literal on every level, and the battle being waged is real. And without the remission of sins by fire and the Holy Ghost, which is part of a manifestation of His Spirit, we do not pass through the gate and must be left in the courtyard, still awaiting passage. *It is during spiritual rebirth that the revelation (or revealing) of Jesus Christ unto a perfect knowledge is made manifest—**a knowledge which is then beyond that of faith***. This is what President Joseph F. Smith meant when he stated that we need "something more than mere belief and supposition" (JOD 19:20). It is given through *"the administration of the Comforter, shed forth upon them **for the revelation of Jesus Christ**" (D&C 90:11)*.

The very purpose of the administration of the Comforter is to have Christ and the Father made manifest and *revealed* to us individually. This is when we can truly say, "*I know* that my Redeemer lives," and ***really know***. This is what Brigham Young meant when he said that no man can know Jesus Christ lives, "except those to whom Christ has revealed Himself" (JOD 1:37).

This revelation of Jesus Christ, or *unshakeable certainty* of Him, leaves such an impression on the soul that it has been described by Joseph Fielding Smith as even more deep or impactful than that of seeing the face of the Savior. Could this be?

"Therefore, the seeing, even the Savior, does not leave as deep an impression in the mind as does the testimony of the Holy Ghost to the spirit… the impressions on the soul that come from the Holy Ghost ***are far more significant than a vision.*** It is where spirit speaks to spirit, and the ***imprint upon the soul is far more difficult to erase***" (*"Seek Ye Earnestly"* [Deseret Book Co., 1970], pp. 213-14).

By definition, faith is believing without having a perfect knowledge. This is why the knowledge we obtain when we are immersed in spiritual fire is beyond faith: we then will have obtained for ourselves a "perfect knowledge" and "unshakeable certainty" (*The Promised Messiah,* p. 592), as referenced by Elder McConkie. This is the oil in the lamps that the virgins will need to have to enter the wedding feast.

Brigham Young spoke to being filled with this "knowledge of the Lord." He said, "The eye, the ear, the hand, all the senses may be deceived, but the Spirit of God cannot be deceived, and when inspired with that Spirit, ***the whole man is filled with knowledge.***" "What I know concerning God … I have received from the Heavens.… It is all by the power of God, and by *intelligence* received from Him" (*Journal of Discourses,* 16:46). This intelligence is preceded by but not gained by book knowledge. It is that spirit of intelligence, light and truth, and taste of God's glory that we partake of during Spiritual Rebirth. "The glory of God is intelligence, or in other words, light and truth" (D&C 93:36).

As to this knowledge we seek, Marion G. Romney said the following:

> *There is also* ***knowledge of divine things*** *which comes through* ***direct revelation****—religious knowledge, it is sometimes called. And there are two aspects to religious knowledge. One of them concerns the great store of religious knowledge which we have in the scriptures.... The other aspect to religious knowledge is the* ***personal witness available.... To know God our Eternal Father and Jesus Christ*** *(see 2 Ne. 31:18), whom he sent, one must, as did the Apostles of old, learn of them through the process of divine revelation.* ***One must be born again****" (Marion G. Romney, "Except a Man Be Born Again, general conference, Oct. 1981; emphasis mine).*

In other words, being born again is when we *know Him* or "come to the knowledge of the Lord" through a revelatory experience, *just as did the apostles of old.* When this happens, we too shall be *filled with knowledge.* Notice these other scriptures that speak of being brought to "the knowledge of the Lord their God," "the knowledge of the truth," "the knowledge of their Redeemer," "the knowledge of the glory of God," and more, to the salvation of their souls:

> *"They shall be brought to* ***the knowledge of the Lord their God,*** *who hath redeemed them" (3 Ne. 20:13; emphasis added).*

[Notice the word "redeemed" is past tense. There must have been some type of experience that occurred.]

"And thus they were instruments in the hands of God in bringing many to ***the knowledge of the truth****, yea, to* ***the knowledge of their Redeemer*** *(Mosiah 27:36; emphasis added). [Notice that being brought to the knowledge of the "truth" was the same as being brought to the knowledge of Jesus Christ, their Redeemer.] Is He not the Way, the Truth, and the Life?]*

"That they might impart the word of God to their brethren, the Lamanites—

"That perhaps they might bring them to ***the knowledge of the Lord their God****,... that they might also be brought to* ***rejoice in the Lord their God****, that they might become friendly to one another [because they will have been filled with the Oneness and love of God], and that there should be no more contentions in all the land which the Lord their God had given them. Now they were desirous that salvation should be declared to every creature" (Mosiah 28:1-3; emphasis added). [Notice that the experiences of rejoicing in the Lord and receiving exceedingly great joy are likened to* ***the knowledge of God****, which is when we are* ***born of God during spiritual rebirth and experience salvation****, subject to enduring to the end.]*

"...after having had so much light and so much ***knowledge given unto them of the Lord their God.... Having been visited by the Spirit of God****; having conversed with angels, and having been spoken unto by the voice of the Lord; and having the spirit of prophecy [see Rev. 19:10], and the spirit of revelation, and also many gifts, the gift of speaking with tongues, and the gift of preaching, and the gift of the Holy Ghost" (Alma 9:19-21). [Note that this being "visited" is the manifestation of the Spirit of God, which we receive when we are born of God and obtain the perfect knowledge of Him.]*

"For because of the [greater portion of the] word which he has imparted unto me, behold, many have been ***born of God****, and have* ***tasted as I have tasted*** *[First Comforter], and have seen eye to eye as I have seen [Second Comforter]; therefore they do know of these things of which I have spoken, as I do know; and the* ***knowledge*** *which I have is* ***<u>of God</u>****" (Alma 36:26; emphasis*

added). [Notice his knowledge was not about God, but ***of God****—meaning the perfect knowledge as to His living reality. Notice also that to be born of God requires having "tasted" or* ***experienced the knowledge of God****.]*

"...yea, and convinced many of the error of their ways, and brought them to ***the knowledge of their God unto the salvation of their souls****" (Alma 37:8; emphasis added). [Notice here that to be brought to the knowledge of God is to be saved.]*

"... for the edifying of the body of Christ, till we all come to the unity of the faith ***and of the knowledge of the Son of God****" (Ephesians: 4:13; emphasis added). [Notice that the end game of having a church with apostles, prophets, evangelists, and so on is for its members to ultimately obtain* ***the knowledge of God****. This is because the church of God provides the necessary ordinances by proper authority to obtain such knowledge through* ***diligently seeking the Son of God****.]*

"They shall again be brought to ***the true knowledge which is the knowledge of their Redeemer****, and their great and their true Shepherd, and be numbered among his sheep" (Helaman 15:13; emphasis added).*

"And again I say unto you as I have said before, that as ye have come to ***the knowledge of the glory of God*** *[through a heavenly* ***"visit"*** *by way of a* ***manifestation*** *of His Spirit], or if ye have known of his goodness and have* ***<u>tasted</u> of his love****, and have* ***<u>received</u> a remission of your sins****, which causeth such* ***exceedingly great joy*** *in your souls" (Mosiah 4:11; emphasis added). [Notice all the synonymous expressions of the same experience here: Having come to "the knowledge of the glory of God," having "tasted of his love," having "received a remission of your sins," and having experienced "exceedingly great joy." This verse is packed with revelatory light and knowledge as to the experiential reality of spiritual rebirth and being born of God. Notice also the past tense verbs "****tasted****" and "****received****," which points to an* ***actual reconciliation*** *that had occurred.]*

The Melchizedek Priesthood, together with the ordinances, acts as the channel through which this gift and manifestation of the Holy Ghost can be received in power, enabling us to thereby find the gate of salvation and come to the knowledge of God ourselves. In my opinion, this is the primary purpose and reason for the Church of God. The Church that is true is not a "perfect" Church, because it is run by flawed (although righteous) mortals. The Church is said to be true because its authorized servants possess the priesthood keys and authority to administer the priesthood ordinances to its members, allowing those who receive them a way to come under heavenly contract with God and thereby be saved, through fulfilling His law(s) and having those same ordinances justified by the Holy Spirit of Promise.

Elder McConkie stated: "The Melchizedek Priesthood is ***the key to the knowledge of God*** because it is in and through this priesthood *and its ordinances* that men receive the gift of the Holy Ghost. And those who *grow in the knowledge of God* ... [through this ongoing, sanctifying gift of the Comforter and obtaining additional experiences of God's reality that reaffirm the prior knowledge of Him obtained through spiritual rebirth] *cannot be kept within the veil* and they are permitted to see the Lord" (*Mormon Doctrine;* emphasis added. See also D&C 84:19-21).

Stay In the Ark of God

We may awaken to our "awful situation" as the children of Zion within the Church and be tempted to "climb up some other way." We need to be reminded that there is "none other way." Peter inquired, "Lord, to whom shall be go?" We should view those who are in the mists of darkness (which at times will also include ourselves) as our brothers and sisters who need our love, support, and encouragement. It's similar to how teenagers may initially view the purported "ineptness" of their parents. With time and experience, those same teenagers, now adults, can later view their parents from a different perspective—one of compassionate love and understanding, having experienced similar adversity of their own. We need to choose the restored gospel. Case in point, many critics of the Church would have been more influential preaching the sound doctrine of Christ within the boat of the old ship Zion instead of taking positions that they must have known would have abruptly ended their boating journey.

With regards to the Church and its purpose, many might exclaim, "But Brother Bishop, I don't really get a whole lot out of going to Church." My answer to that is that we go to Church not so much to be lifted as to lift. It's not as much about "us," as it is about those we can lift through our heartfelt words of compassion and encouragement. We are to "mourn with those who mourn, comfort those who stand in need of comfort," are we not? And when we do so, we too are lifted. Additionally, we go to Church to partake of the bread and the water, symbols of His infinite sacrifice wherein we are permitted to reaffirm our willingness to sacrifice all that may be required of us in obedience to His Spirit, to take upon ourselves His name, and if so fortunate, to receive of His Spirit to be with us always as an ongoing companion thereafter.

It is this author's opinion that the Church of Jesus Christ shall remain and not dive into apostasy, similar to what has been apostasy's predominant theme throughout history. Remember that although the ride may get bumpy, the priesthood keys and authority of God will remain within the Lord's Church, allowing us to *individually find the knowledge of God and salvation* (irrespective of what others within the same may choose), and thereafter endure to the end. The Prophet Joseph saw it the same way:

> *"My feelings at the present time are that, inasmuch as the Lord Almighty has preserved me until today, He will continue to preserve me, by the united faith and prayers of the Saints, until I have fully accomplished my mission in this life and [which is to]* ***so firmly established the dispensation of the fullness of the priesthood in the last days, that all the powers of earth and hell can never prevail against it*** *" (Teachings of the Prophet Joseph Smith, p. 258; emphasis added).*

Fellow seeker: Even though our numbers will be relatively few compared to the population of the world, the restored Church and gospel of Jesus Christ, the latter-day kingdom, the stone cut from the mountain without hands, will fill the whole earth. "And in the days of these kings shall the God of heaven set up a kingdom which shall never be destroyed: ***and the kingdom shall not be left to other people***... and **it shall stand for ever**" (Dan. 2:44; emphasis added). If we are experiencing a crisis of faith, we are to immerse ourselves in the scriptures and in connecting with God, truly connecting from the heart space, facilitated by mighty prayer and deep meditation. Remember, what we focus on expands, for good or for bad.

Put down and silence the machines and devices and "be still." Stay away from all media unless its contents are godly. Beware of not just the media we watch, but the energy inadvertently absorbed into our beings stemming from any and all media, or even individuals, irrespective of the various locations in which we may find ourselves. This may even be in our homes. E. Richard Packham said that, "the soul is like a sponge. It absorbs that to which it is exposed" (Born of the Spirit, p. 37).

Pay attention to how you feel at all times through awareness. Trust that! If you are getting "creeped out" or feel any darkness of any kind from whatever source, move away as quickly as possible. This is part of "denying ourselves of all ungodliness" (Moroni 10:32), as anything dark is ungodly. Notice the words of George Q. Cannon with respect to this issue:

> *"There are [energetic or spiritual] influences in the atmosphere that are invisible to us that...we ought to resist with all our might, mind, and strength" (Journal of Discourses, 11:29).*

Feel after God for the spiritual answers delivered through the impressions and feelings you receive. Secular knowledge obtained through logic, reason, or a Google search, including the pervading anti-LDS propaganda that exists, even if originating from the best intellectual minds, is what we aviation pilots refer to as a ***sucker hole.*** Beware of false prophets who say that the Lord's anointed are out of the way, while at the same time keeping our gaze fixated on Christ. The apostle Paul admonishes us to "mark them which cause divisions and offences contrary to the doctrine … and avoid them," for these by their "good words and fair speeches deceive the hearts of the people" (Rom. 16:17-18).

We are to stay the course until additional light, faith, and knowledge is bestowed on us individually by God Himself. And while we're waiting, perhaps these words by Dr. David R. Hawkins can help us off the ledge, so to speak, and assist us to focus on the positives of not just our religion, but religion in general. He said, "A religiously integrous lifestyle is satisfying and results in the healthy self-esteem as well as respect for others. Traditional religion provides dependable, practical morality and a set of ethics and guidelines for behavior, values, and character formation. The diehard skeptic might ask, 'But what if God and religion are not true or real?' The answer, of course, is that then they will have lived a good life of virtue for its own reward" ("Discovery of the Presence of God," p. 188). I love this.

Stay in the ark of God, yet all the while looking to God for direction through personal revelation. If we jump out of the ark, would we not be found in the ocean with hungry sharks? I fear we might also run the risk of becoming "sifted as wheat" or "devoured" (see 1 Peter 5:8). "O Remember, remember" that the primary purpose of the Church is to provide the priesthood authority that allows us to come under heavenly contract individually with God through ordinances administered to us by imperfect men, yet holding perfect priesthood keys. ***The rest is a one-on-one journey to Christ.*** It is then that all the responsibility subsequently shifts to us! To paraphrase Adam S. Miller, "We can either look at the hand pointing to Christ or we can look directly to Christ." I would add to Miller's brilliant assessment that all too often we get caught up in obsessing about the warts on the hand that is pointing to Christ. It's not about the hand or the warts. It's about Christ. Don't be fooled by another fool. Look to God *directly* and live.

Trust that God will handle the affairs of [His] Church and will not need your help or mine to right any purported wrongs. It's not our Church, it's His. He is God. We are not. The apostle Orson Hyde said, "*It is for me to live my religion and honor my God*, and let Him steady His own ark [see D&C 85:8]. Let me do *my duty* [notice the focus] and all will work for the best" (*Journal of Discourses,* 13:179). By holding to Hyde's philosophy, it is doubtful any of us would ever be led astray.

Fellow Seeker: Follow no arm of the flesh unless you absolutely know by the Spirit that God is speaking through that flesh. President J. Reuben Clark said, "We can tell when the speakers are moved upon by the Holy Ghost *only when we, ourselves, are moved upon by the Holy Ghost.* In a way, this completely shifts the responsibility from them to us to determine when they so speak" (*Church News,* July 31, 1954; see also Ezra Taft Benson, *"An Enemy Hath Done This,"* p. 295). This responsibility of our knowing truth through the Holy Ghost includes the words spoken by any man, whether the prophet and President of the Church, the person assigned to minister to us, or the homeless person we may encounter on the street corner. God can speak to us through any man or by any means, *but we ourselves must be in tune to know* if it is the man speaking or whether God is speaking through that man. We will perceive truth given to us through an intuitive feeling or knowing—a part of what we may term our sixth sense.

The Apostle Delbert L. Stapley saw it the same way as President Clark. He said,

> *"If prophets speak by the power of the Holy Ghost then the Holy Ghost is required to interpret correctly the teachings of holy men" (Conference Report, October 1966, pp. 111-114).*

Be one of the few who are the humble followers of Christ. Walk the daily disciple's walk, in meekness, marinating in His Spirit. Let us not become accusers of our brethren. Remember that "accuser" can be another name for the devil (see Rev. 12:10). Too often we may find fault with the Church, its leaders, or its members as an avoidance mechanism to distract ourselves from the excruciatingly hard and painful work of facing inward to view the impurities found within our own souls that may be, perhaps, too uncomfortable for us to confront.

Bottom Line: We are to build our foundation upon the Rock of Jesus Christ and revelation from Him through the gift received of the Holy Ghost once we receive this gift. Our job is simple: *To "trouble not [ourselves] concerning the affairs of [His] Church,"* but to *"purify [our] hearts before [Him]"* (D&C 112:27-28).

A Personal Experience and Pattern for Rending the Veil and Knowing God

I'd like to relate a very personal story regarding a type and pattern for making Christ our rewarding obsession and meeting Him in this life. It involves the world-renown author, Dr. Wayne Dyer, or as my wife likes to call him, "The Wayn-er." After I had read *Your Sacred Self,* as referenced in chapter 1, I began to read most of Dr. Dyer's other books. I bought his tapes. I became a mini version of Dr. Dyer. In short, I followed his spiritual journey, read much of what he read, patterned my life after his, and desired to be more like him. At one point along this journey, I bought a book that he had published on "manifesting" miracles in our lives. It included tapes that taught meditation and visualization techniques that resonated with me in having "an eye of faith." I began to practice what he spoke about and decided that I would put Dr. Dyer to the test. You will notice the pattern and parts of the Diagram from chapter one in my story: Desire and an open heart… which leads to belief and "acting in the belief "and exercising faith… which leads to the miracle and "spiritual knowledge" that I will describe. Dr. Dyer taught that whatever we visualized in meditation, if held to, would eventually come to pass or become "manifest" in our lives. I love Wayne. Dr. Dyer was very influential in my emotional healing process as well. He helped me in so many ways along my healing journey because much of his teaching is grounded in universal truths.

With the heart and resolve of a pure little child, I had decided that I was now going to "manifest" Wayne Dyer himself into my life, that I was going to meet him personally in a "chance meeting" simply by putting to test his words on how to manifest. This process did not happen overnight. It took persistence and diligence. It is important for all who are now reading these words to understand that I truly believed this would happen for me. I removed all doubt. "What things soever ye *desire*, when ye pray, *believe that ye receive them, and ye shall have them*" (Mark 11:24; emphasis added). I expected that "energy," or what we call the Spirit of God and His grace, would go before me and orchestrate this "chance" encounter. I didn't care what it looked like because I knew that other than God no one else knew of my intention; therefore, no one could mock, deride, or make fun of me. Not even my wife knew. I treasured this *expectancy* in my heart.

For the next 18 months, I spent time almost every day in meditation, visualizing my meeting with Wayne Dyer on a beach somewhere. It was akin to a romantic love story. It was sincere. It was pure. The "where" didn't really matter to me. In my meditation, I saw Dr. Dyer walking towards me on a beach from the opposite direction, and we proceeded towards each other until we came to within a few feet of each other in order to engage in conversation. I "saw" or visualized with an eye of faith that I had been given the opportunity to speak to Dr. Dyer (just he and I, one on one) for about 45 minutes.

Fast forward after now having visualized this encounter with Dr. Dyer almost every day for 18 months. I received an invitation from my pediatrician neighbor, John, who lived across the street from me, to go on a trip to Maui, Hawaii, together with our wives. He was going there for some continuing medical education. Every day he would have half of the day to do whatever he liked. I was self-employed and financially able, so I saw no impediment to making this happen. Who wouldn't want to go to Maui, Hawaii? I hadn't been to Maui for about 20 years and have not been back since, which is now well over 20 years ago.

So I'm walking in Whaler's Village in Kaanapali, Maui, Hawaii. It's an outdoor, open air shopping area located *on the beach*. I walked past a gentleman that looked similar to Dr. Wayne Dyer. He was wearing gym shorts, white socks, and tennis shoes … but no shirt. That was it. My wife said to me, "That man looked like Wayne Dyer." I said, "I saw him, but I don't think it's him." Notice my lack of faith! I had a momentary stint of *unbelief*. Then I told her that I knew one way for certain to know if it was him. ***I knew his voice***. I knew that if I could get within range to ***hear his***

voice, I would know immediately because of all of the tapes I had listened to of his. ***I knew and loved that voice***. I knew and loved Wayne Dyer. *I felt I knew him intimately because of all the study that I had done of his life and of his having overcome the adversities and challenges he had faced.* (Note that we are to do the same with Christ). He was an inspiration to me because he became a success against all odds, and he had helped me overcome some of my own personal obstacles. He was raised in various orphanages and without a father. Later in life, he went on a search to find his father: through a series of miraculous events, Wayne found his father's grave and spoke to him in tears, lasting several hours, while feeling his father's literal presence at the grave site. After this emotional purging and forgiveness of his father, he returned to his home, visited the university where he was employed, and abruptly quit his job. He actually gave up the security of his highly sought-after "tenure" as a college professor. He then flew to Florida, checked himself into a hotel room, and wrote his very first book, which flowed through him and onto many pages, a future best seller called *Your Erroneous Zones* (standing for our "erroneous ways of thinking"). He travelled the United States selling books out of the trunk of his car and had an iron-clad resolve to get his message out to the world. This first book has since sold over 100 million copies.

I soon positioned myself within earshot of his voice as he spoke on the phone with his publisher, Hay House, out of Carlsbad California. I immediately knew. I hovered for a bit and waited for his call to end. After he hung up the phone, I approached him and said, "You do not know me, but I think I have read nearly every book you have ever written." He responded, jokingly, "So you're a mini me!" I was speechless. I could hardly believe that this was in fact happening.

What I had been visualizing for 18 months was precisely how it had occurred. I was on a beach. We had approached each other from opposite directions, just as I had visualized. And we spoke to each other for 45 minutes, just as I had seen it play out in my mind's eye. He asked if I wanted to buy any of his books at a bookstore within a short walking distance and that he would wait for me so he could sign them. I straightway did as he had suggested. When I returned, he was still speaking to my wife and our neighbor friends we had travelled with from Utah. But then it became just him and me, one on one. When I gave him the books, he wrote a personalized message in the front of each one and then turned to the back. In the back he proceeded to write his home phone number as well as his mobile number. He told me to call him anytime. He then invited my wife and me to his home that evening to have dinner with his family. Are you kidding me?

Now as I write this, even after all of these years, my eyes fill with tears of gratitude, not so much because I was able to meet Wayne Dyer, but more important, because I recognize from whom this blessing came. It was a tender mercy from my Father in Heaven. He knew the significance that this "chance meeting" would have for me personally, and He delivered. Gratitude is the only appropriate response to any and all manifested blessings in our lives. Our Father loves to see and feel our gratitude!

Shortly after this unanticipated encounter that day, we made our way back to our hotel. The sun began to fade away until it was almost dusk. From our hotel room, I went out on the balcony, which had a beautiful view to the ocean, and watched God's finishing touches of His sunset going down. I was completely overcome with emotion—so full of love and gratitude to and for God that I could hardly speak. I was completely overwhelmed with this feeling. My cup was running over. The tears flowed like a river because once again, *I knew* that God was aware of me personally. I had known this through prior experiences, but now I knew it on a much deeper level. God actually knew me! And now I could feel it within, beyond any reasonable doubt. I will never forget this tender mercy. Words cannot express the gratitude I will forever feel for His tender mercy to me, nor will the tenderness of that experience ever fade from my memory or the deep feelings of my heart that I have for God.

So why am I telling you all this very personal story? Because it became more than clear to me that this encounter with Dr. Dyer was a type and pattern for our own encounter with the Son of God while here in mortality. Can there be anything more significant or beautiful throughout the universe? All of the components for our "chance encounter" with our Lord are found in it. We must become a "mini Jesus" instead of a mini Wayne Dyer. We must have the belief and faith of a little child in coming to Him. We must learn everything about His life, just as I did with Wayne. We must come to ***know His voice***. I'm sad to say this, but I had made Wayne to be somewhat of an idol at the time. But in the end, it was extremely purposeful because this encounter would be the type and pattern for the encounter of all encounters we can all have with our Lord, which is further highlighted in chapter 12 of this work concerning the reality of the Second Comforter.

We must diligently and steadfastly hold to this vision of meeting Christ, just as I had held to the vision of meeting Dr. Wayne Dyer through 18 months of visualizing my encounter with him with an eye of faith during meditation. It was this desiring and longing in my soul, coupled with a loving Father who felt my yearning, that manifested its fruition in a "chance encounter" as an act of grace.

And now this is my witness. I know through the constant spiritual experiences and assurances that have been given to me that we can all experience the true reality of meeting our Lord while in this mortal sphere. We must visualize it with an eye of faith. God is not a respecter of persons! It is up to us to hold to this vision and to remove the weeds of doubt ourselves (i.e., unbelief) in order to manifest this supreme encounter in our lives, subject to our faith and faithfulness, together with God's holy will and timing. What could be greater?

This is life eternal—***to know Him***. And the result will be so much more glorious than that "chance meeting" I experienced with Dr. Dyer many years ago now. ***Desire and faith are the foundation for its realization, having an unrelenting longingness in our soul unto its fruition.*** *This is what will carry us to His manifestation and appearance unto us individually, one by one.* As a general rule, the reception and enjoyment of the Holy Ghost (and subsequent calling and election made sure) precedes this reunion, because in order to enter His literal presence we must first be made like unto Him. In a word, we are to be made inwardly clean and holy ourselves, by and through this gift of the Comforter, received by His grace.

This explains the primary reason why obtaining the First Comforter is the purpose and focus of this book. The Comforter will sanctify us and lead us into all truth and the needed sanctification unto holiness. And Christ is that Truth. But we must first obtain a diamond-hard will and determination to obtain this Comforter until we receive it. Know this as your future reality if it has not already been enjoyed! God is faithful and so are His promises. I trust our God to come through on His every word for us all, for He is a God of love who cannot lie. As we love Him with all our heart, might, mind, strength, and even our whole soul, He shall manifest His love to us in return in miraculous, unspeakable ways. Of this I witness and know of it experientially. This is His will for us, not just our own. His work and His glory are to bring to pass ***our*** immortality and eternal life. It really is! He is faithful and true to every word He has ever uttered.

Our Own Treasure Hunt and Holy Grail

We are all on a treasure hunt seeking Christ, the very Personage of Glory, through His Light. He is the Heavenly Gift we are seeking (Ether 12:8; Hebrews 6:4). The Heavenly Gift is one of His names. Remember that with very few exceptions, only seekers become finders. This treasure hunt is one of the primary purposes for our existence in this, our second estate. It involves growing in faith and spiritual knowledge. All distractions are purposely designed by the adversary to sidetrack us from *this very objective.* There is nothing greater or more worthy an endeavor than to be "quickened in the inner man" and sanctified in our flesh in order that we might one day see our Master eye to eye. We are seeking the Holy Grail, who is the very Christ. In physical terms, the Holy Grail is generally considered the cup that the apostles and Christ drank from during the last supper. It is also generally considered in greater Christendom to be the cup which Joseph of Aramathea used to catch Christ's blood as he was crucified on the cross. Spiritually, the Holy Grail represents that living water which springs up unto everlasting life. It represents an infinite abundance of spiritual sustenance, grace, eternal youth, and everlasting joy, which is promised to the faithful. All these blessings are available through Christ, our Holy Grail.

In the time and legend of Arthur, the Holy Grail represented the *highest spiritual pursuit and aspiration.* We are the royal knights who must achieve the Holy Grail. As knights, we are spiritual warriors—warriors who have an extreme dedication to the truth, no matter what. These knights had to be willing to die for the truth or they were not "invited in." As with them, we too must be willing to die for the truth. As anyone knows, knights can only be knighted by the King, and if we as knights are proven true and faithful in all things to our Heavenly King, we will be *crowned* by Him later ourselves. This is why we were foreordained and called to come to this earth—to find the gate which leads to this Holy Grail. We are given a spiritual map or "map from our spirit" and from "the Spirit" to help lead and guide us along our heroic journey towards spiritual rebirth and beyond. Once we find the gate of spiritual rebirth, the clarity of our purpose comes into focus and view. We are given additional insight as to our mission and calling, further instilling in us the requisite faith and knowledge to find that Holiest of all Grails, the Heavenly Gift.

As knights, we put on the breastplate of righteousness, the helmet of salvation, having our loins girt about with the truth. We carry with us the shield of faith and the sword of His Spirit, with our feet shod with the preparation of the gospel of peace. In short, we put off the natural man by putting on Christ. But in truth, it is not us that puts off the natural man. It is Christ who overcomes the natural man in us. We overcome through our faith in Christ and thereby partake of His grace. We can become perfect in Him and by Him! The only ones who can overcome the travails of this journey are those who have passed through the gate and have received the gift of pure charity or that love of God stemming from the partaking of the fruit of the tree of life, and later endure in the quickening influence of the Spirit to the end.

James Russell Lowell's nineteenth-century poem, "The Vision of Sir Launfal," gave to generations a notion of "*the Grail quest as something achievable by anyone who is **truly charitable***" (The Holy Grail, Symbols and Motifs, "The Camelot Project," part of Robbins Library Digital Projects). This "charitable nature" comes through the bestowal of the "love of God" and the "change in our natures" that is given at the time of our spiritual rebirth, instilling in us the desire "to do good continually" while removing any "disposition to do evil" (Mosiah 5:2). It is obtainable by those of us who "pray unto the Father with all the energy of heart, that [we] may be filled with this love [or charity, the pure love of Christ], which he hath *bestowed* upon all who are true followers of his Son, Jesus Christ [to what end?]; that [we] may become the sons of God" (Moroni 7:48; emphasis added).

Armed now with this love and the Comforter's influence to abide in us, we are able (in fact, it becomes our mission), through faith and having previously partaken of the ordinances provided in the temple, to find this Holy Grail. By heeding the Comforter's gentle directives, we will traverse dangerous terrain, but with a peace and confidence instilled through the Light of Him who is the "author and finisher of our faith" to ultimately arrive at the precise veil separating us from the living, resurrected Christ and to then enter therein. This is the heroic pursuit in which the true knights are engaged. And He is the gift that keeps on giving—our eternal spring of living water, our very own rewarding obsession.

To find this Holiest of Grails, the preparation for our mission begins with our thoughts and the observation and awareness of those thoughts. We begin to center those thoughts on God, desiring to truly know Him. We become willing to take a serious look at the truth of our current standing before Him. We seek the truth of that standing, hiding nothing. We become willing to do whatever is necessary to become right before Him, irrespective of the personal sacrifices required. Our hearts break, and we surrender to Him as a submissive little child. We cry out to Him with a willingness to do His will that is unbreakable, and we come to taste the grace of Christ and know Him. We experience unspeakable joy in the Holy Ghost, and we put on Christ. The author of the Odes summarizes it succinctly: "Therefore, put on the name of the Most High and *know Him*" (The Odes of Solomon 39:8; emphasis added).

Chapter 6:

Desire to Find the "Knowledge of God": Ask, Seek, and Knock

"My son, if thou wilt, ... incline thine ear unto wisdom, and apply thine heart to understanding. Yea, if thou ***criest after knowledge****, and liftest up thy voice for understanding; If thou* ***seekest her as silver****, and* ***searchest for her as for hid treasures****; Then shalt thou understand the fear of the Lord, and* ***find the knowledge of God****" (Proverbs 2:1-5).*

The fulfillment of every ambition and goal begins with *desire*. Enos said of his desire, "My soul hungered" (Enos 1:4). Finding the gate begins by *finding the desire* to find and know the Lord and then allowing that desire to become activated within us—allowing it to "ferment," if you will. As Alma suggested, "Let this desire work in you." We allow the "desire to work in [us]" unto the manifesting of the object of our desire, when this "fermenting" is allowed to thrive. But here is a crucial awareness that ties back to Chapter 1, "Ground Zero: The Battle over the Heart." ***Desire is the fuel for our journey to salvation***. As we "let this desire work in us," we increase our faith. Desire will lead to endowments of faith that accrue in us, thereby acquiring spiritual knowledge, which likewise removes unbelief, even that same unbelief which acts as a veil, keeping us separated from the presence of God. And when our hearts become obscured with "clouds," which inhibit the Christ Light from entering, this desire dissipates to the point of our becoming apathetic, or even worse, past feeling. So with no desire, there is no fuel. And with no fuel, we cannot make it to the gate of salvation, let alone beyond the gate.

As we keep our hearts open to Christ's love and light, we will find and stay connected with this *desire*, which will fuel our journey and expand both desire and faith within us. This rising desire will, however, be offset by the sacrifices that will be required to get us to the gate of salvation and beyond, which will affect our level of willingness to sacrifice whatever may be required in order to pursue and obtain the necessary outcome. This *willingness* is that which is spoken of in our sacrament ordinance.

Some are "willing" because their level of desire to find and know the Christ EXCEEDS the requisite sacrifices, which include passing through certain tests. These individuals will be found at His right hand. Some are "unwilling" because their level of desire mentioned FALLS SHORT of these requisite sacrifices. These shall be found at his left.

Most of the tests that we encounter in mortality will surround this, our willingness to sacrifice our all for God. Elder McConkie stated, "No one will ever make the sacrifice necessary to gain eternal life *until he believes in his heart that the reward is worth the price*" (*Promised Messiah,* p. 132). It's all about our willingness to sacrifice and pay whatever price may be required to get us there. He put his life on the line for us. We must be willing to do the same for Him. When we do so, or at least become wholly willing to do so, we will find a new life in Him.

We will inevitably sacrifice and take up our cross in order to obtain as He did (through His grace), but this will prepare us for a world of glory where suffering and pain is no more. As the hymn so eloquently states of our Exemplar, "Once all things he meekly bore, but he now will bear no more" (*LDS Hymns,* "Jesus, Once of Humble Birth," no. 196). Ultimately, as the Lord has said, "if any man will come after me, let him *deny himself*, and *take up his cross daily*, and follow me" (Luke 9:23; emphasis added).

The "sifting" spoken of in holy writ is ultimately tied to our sufficiency of desire and faith in coming unto Christ and obtaining the knowledge of Him while in mortality, and thereafter enduring to the end, irrespective of the cost or level of sacrifice that may be required of us. Consecrated sacrifice or "offerings," then, is the way in which we demonstrate our love for God.

The level and degree of our overall willingness to make consecrated offerings through sacrifice to God is ultimately the measure against which we may know the level and degree of our love for God.

The Redeemer's mission involved that of allowing his *body and soul to be offered up* to the Father and to experience unspeakable physical and spiritual agony, including the offering of His physical life upon the cross. As he offered his life in sacrifice for us, we too must be (at least *willing*) to offer our lives in return to Him by way of compassionate service, and if required, our mortal lives as well, if necessary. "This is the reason that the Former-day Saints knew more, and understood more, of heaven and of heavenly things than all others beside" (*Lectures On Faith,* 7:20). ***Again, our level of "willingness" to sacrifice is where all the tests in mortality are centered.*** And that willingness, in my opinion, includes our willingness to lay down our life for God, which may even include "to suffer death in its most horrid forms" (*Lectures On Faith,* 6:3). Dr. Hawkins speaks to this level of willingness:

> *"Within yourself already exists that which is willing to lay down its life for God. It's not something you acquire, not something you have to develop.* ***It's something you locate within yourself****. Because that question will come up over and over again in the spiritual pathway. Am I willing to surrender this to God? Am I willing to surrender that to God? And you will then locate within yourself that there is a capacity to lay anything down for God....*
>
> *"If... Jesus stood here and said, 'Would you lay down your life for me', you would say, 'Yes, O Lord'. So you find within yourself, that which would say, 'Yes, O Lord', to that request....* ***That within you which is willing to lay down its life for God, locate that within yourself now****, when you don't need it, because the final moment arises unannounced.... And there is where you need the conviction. You reach within yourself, 'with thee O Lord I lay down my life itself'. And then you summon forth the very core of devotion, because* ***there is within you already, that which loves God more than the personal self****" (YouTube, David Hawkins - Lay Down Your Life for God, Dec. 29, 2014).*

As to our willingness to sacrifice at this level for Him, the Lord said,

> *"Let no man be afraid to lay down his life for my sake; for whoso layeth down his life for my sake shall find it again. And* ***whoso is not willing to lay down his life for my sake is not my disciple****" (D&C 103:27-28; emphasis added).*

Could this level of *willingness* possibly be a divine law and prerequisite for spiritual rebirth? Lorenzo Snow said of the Prophet, "I knew Joseph Smith to be an honest man, a man of truth, honor and fidelity, *willing to sacrifice everything he possessed, even life itself*, as a testimony to the heavens" (*The Teachings of Lorenzo Snow*, p. 73; emphasis added). Here's another confirmation and pattern of the type of individual the Lord is looking to adopt within His family.

Keep in mind that for most of us, there is a long and arduous process leading to this level of *willingness* from which arises the reception of the actual gift of the Holy Ghost promised by the Father when hands were laid on our heads. And there is a similar, continuing process leading forward and upward from that state. And our offering will include the *willingness* to demonstrate our commitment out in the world (which in my opinion means, not just church assignments we may have been given, but assignments of service by God Himself, given through the Spirit). *By these offerings through sacrifice, we demonstrate our love for God* and our willingness to become and subsequently remain His sons and His daughters. We must be built up as "a spiritual house … to offer up *spiritual sacrifices* acceptable to God through Jesus Christ" (1 Peter 2:5; emphasis added).

After sealing upon Joseph his exaltation, the Lord told him, "I have seen your *sacrifices* in obedience to that which I have told you" (D&C 132:50; emphasis added). Notice these words through the lens of the afore-mentioned perspective on desire, willingness, and sacrifice:

> *"That they* ***may… witness… that they are willing*** *to take upon them the name of thy son."*
> *Or said another way,*
>
> *"That they* ***may… witness… that they are willing*** *to offer up the broken heart, and surrender their whole life unto thy service as a consecrated offering of sacrifice, even to the laying down of one's life for God, if required."*

So the question is, how bad do we want it? How bad do we desire to know the Lord and not just casually believe in Him? What are we willing to sacrifice and endure in order to know Him and become like Him? *Those who have the requisite level of desire to find and know God, which exceeds the sacrifices that may be required to successfully prevail, will diligently seek Him (while never giving up), and shall find Him.* It is a law and a promise from our Father!

Elder Lawrence E. Corbridge nails it!

> *"Pay whatever price you must pay, bear whatever burden you must bear, make whatever sacrifices you must make, in order to get and keep in your life the spirit and power of the Holy Ghost. Everything depends on that" ("Stand Forever," BYU Devotional, Jan. 22, 2019).*

When we receive the Holy Ghost in power, we will then know God and experience the reception of the Holy Ghost, also called the First Comforter. Why is this cleansing and sanctification received through this Comforter so crucial? Because we cannot be made clean nor be prepared to receive the next, or Second Comforter, without it. "For without this no man can see the face of God, even the Father, and live" (D&C 84:22). We are told in scripture that it is "through the power and *manifestation* of the Spirit, *while in the flesh*, [that we] may be able to bear his presence" (D&C 76:118; emphasis added). This includes His presence in the world of glory both in this life and in that world of glory in the next. Keep in mind that wherever the personage of God is found is also found a world of glory, for glory surrounds Him at all times.

After the reception of the Holy Ghost (see Moses 6:61; see also Teachings, pg. 362), the Comforter will then be given to abide *in us*, further sanctifying us and leading us unto all truth, including The Truth, which is Christ. Marion G. Romney of the First Presidency, in his talk entitled, "The Key to Peace" (April Conference Report, 1970, pp. 66-69), referenced a "clear and certain knowledge of God" that we can obtain in mortality through a *manifestation* given which yields a *transformation,* and that this transformation arises out of "seeking to find the true and living God."

I'd like to emphasize the fact that once God reveals Himself to us through "this clear and certain knowledge of God," and through "these manifestations which God has given *of himself*," we will then *know Him* because we will have experienced a *transformation* from natural man to Saint, having "become quickened in the inner man" (Moses 6:65). Through this experience and Oneness obtained in Them, we will have tasted of a profound and indescribably joy and peace in this life—even a perfect Oneness. Inherent within that peace is to "enjoy the words of eternal life *in this world*" here, which "words" are the promise of eternal life obtained from God directly, "and eternal life in the world to come, even immortal glory"—there, or in that world which is to come (Moses 6:59). And these unspeakable blessings arise out the foundation which consists of the desire to find the Christ, and the sufficiency of faith to receive Him.

Notice below that there are several verses of scripture pertaining to this law of promise afforded us through *diligently seeking Christ.* The Lord, through the prophet Jeremiah, gave us a grand key: "And ye shall seek me, and find me, *when ye shall search for me with all your heart"* (Jer. 29:13). Notice that it is our heart that is tied to love and that the act of seeking equates to love. If we did not truly love Him, why would we seek in the first place? Do we have anything to do of greater value than making the commitment to seek, find, and know Christ while here in mortality and to become as close a replica of him as possible, and then working to perform on that commitment?

There are various ways and means in which we may seek Him. We *seek him* by first learning all about His life and devouring His word (be it written or "the word of His Spirit"), through approaching Him in mighty prayer and connecting with Him through deep meditation, through doing the compassionate works that He did, and through the inextinguishable *desiring, yearning, and longing* in our souls to come unto Him and know Him on a very personal level while here in mortality.

Seeking to connect with God in meditation and prayer through our heart space—*feeling after Him*, His love, *His Presence*, and incorporating the same as a way of life, is to *diligently seek Him*. It is to find that space or gap between this world and His world which allows that connection to thrive. In doing so, would our all-knowing God not know our intention? And would He not then reward us accordingly?

The seeking journey will likely begin through an intellectual endeavor because in order to have faith, we must hear and learn the word. But at some point, book knowledge must take a subordinate role to that direct knowledge acquired through "learning by faith" which yields power and learning from on high.

Nephi and others spoke to the diligence required in seeking, and it all began with *desire*. This desire cannot be overstated, for as we have discussed it is our fuel to get us to our destination of the grace of Christ and salvation, and thereby know Him. Notice the pattern that begins with inner desire and is continued by diligently seeking and finding in the below verses when the Lord "visits" us:

> *"And it came to pass that I, Nephi ... having* ***great desires*** *to know of the mysteries of God, wherefore, I did cry unto the Lord; and behold* ***he did visit me"*** (1 Ne. 2:16; emphasis added).

> *"Therefore, I was* ***visited*** *of the Lord, and* ***tasted*** *and* ***knew*** *of the goodness of Jesus"* (Morm. 1:15; emphasis added).

> *"I, Nephi, was* ***desirous*** *also that I might see, and hear, and know of these things, by the power of the Holy Ghost, which is the gift of God unto* ***all those who*** *DILIGENTLY SEEK HIM, as well in times of old as in the time that he should manifest himself unto the children of men. For he that DILIGENTLY SEEKETH SHALL FIND; and the mysteries of God shall be unfolded unto them"* (1 Ne. 10:17, 19; emphasis added).

> *"For every one that asketh, receiveth, and* ***he that seeketh, findeth****, and to him that knocketh, it shall be opened"* (3 Ne. 14:8; emphasis added).

> *"My elect ones have walked with me,* ***and my ways I will make known to them who seek me; and I will promise them my name.*** *Hallelujah"* (Odes of Solomon 33:13; emphasis added).

> *"****Seek me diligently*** *and ye shall find me"* (D&C 88:63).

> *"****Seek the Lord*** *thy God, thou shalt find him"* (Deut. 4:29).

> *"Those that* ***seek me early*** *shall find me"* (Prov. 8:17).

> *"Whoso* ***findeth me*** *findeth life"* (Prov. 8:35).

As to the above admonitions to seek the Lord, Sterling W. Sill once said: "The greatest tragedy of our world remains the fact that so many never attain this all-important objective. And yet only he who fails to seek fails to find." ("We Would See Jesus," Sterling W. Sill, *Conference Report*, April 1968).

All Are Accountable to Seek Christ

> *"**All who know of Christ and all who should know** because the opportunity is available **have the responsibility to seek him out**. Men have an obligation to seek truth. The Spirit of Christ is given to every soul born into the world; its function is to guide them to that light and truth which saves, and all who follow its enticings and promptings come unto Christ and salvation" (Bruce R. McConkie, The Promised Messiah, p. 301).*

The Holy One of Israel said, "Behold, here is the agency of man, and here is the condemnation of man; because that which was from the beginning is plainly manifest unto them [yea, even that Light of Christ which is in, around, and through us], and they receive not the light [by hardening their hearts]. And every man whose spirit receiveth not the light [which is Christ] is under condemnation" (D&C 93:31-32; emphasis added).

You'll notice that in this book I refer to you, the reader, as a fellow seeker. All of mankind is seeking to find something. We are seeking for something that is difficult to pinpoint or put words to, yet nevertheless is real. Perhaps it's a desire or feeling. It may even be a craving or a need. This life-saving search from our soul level is real for all of us, whether we are aware of it or not. It is something innately recognizable to our spirits but may have remained elusive throughout our lives. Perhaps what we are seeking for is a peace, a bliss, or a euphoria of some kind. We often won't know until we find and obtain it. And those who are of the elect, who "hear his voice," will continue to search high and low until this "thing," whatever it is, is found.

Some may attempt to find it through financial freedom. Some, through the short-term highs of illegal drug use or through living promiscuous lives. Wherever our seeking takes us, it will inevitably end in disappointment unless and until we *find the knowledge of God* and experience spiritual oneness in Him. What most of us do not realize is that we are both longing for Him and our true home. He is love. It is this, His love, the love of God, that I believe we are all unconsciously seeking. What we ultimately desire, perhaps unknowingly, is to find that all-encompassing love and peace of God that is already familiar to us. This makes sense since our spirits came from the presence of Divine Beings filled with and surrounded by this divine love.

Our most basic human need is that of love—to both love and be loved. Our need is to likewise be accepted, valued, and understood. When we *find God and truly know Him*, we will experience *spiritual union and a oneness with Him* through becoming filled with His *love* and a *peace* which passeth all understanding by way of a heavenly manifestation. We will experience a holy communion lasting several days and nights. But to experience this love and spiritual union, we must first get in touch with this inexpressible and unexplainable *desire to find and know God*, which may be buried deep within us. The *desire* to find this spiritual knowledge of God and the experiential oneness with seemingly all that is must become an ever-consuming effort in our lives or it may never become fulfilled or realized.

Everything pertaining to life and Godliness hinges first on finding that buried desire which, through nurturing, can lead the candidate of salvation to that sufficiency of faith which saves.

Without desire, we cannot be led to deepened belief nor living faith. And here is the simplicity of all of it. Ready? God gives us the desires of our hearts, *according to our wills*. That's the good news. The bad news is… God gives us the desires of our hearts, according to our wills. Or in other words, He gives us the desires of our hearts, even for evil designs and destructive ends. Notice these verses:

"I know that [God] granteth unto men ***according to their desire****, whether it be unto death or unto life; yea, I know that he allotteth unto men, yea decreeth unto them decrees which are unalterable, according to their wills,* ***whether they be unto salvation or unto destruction****" (Alma 29:4; emphasis added).*

"Wherefore, he gave commandments ... placing themselves in a state to act, or being placed in a state to act ***according to their wills and pleasures****, whether to do evil or to do good " (Alma 12:31; emphasis added).*

"O Lord, thou hast given us a commandment that we must call upon thee, that ***from thee we may receive according to our desires****" (Ether 3:2; emphasis added).*

In Alma we read: "The one raised to happiness *according to his desires* of happiness, or good *according to his desires* of good; and the other to evil *according to his desires* of evil; for as he has *desired* to do evil all the day long even so shall he have his reward of evil when the night cometh. And so it is on the other hand. If he hath *repented of his sins, and desired righteousness until the end of his days*, even so he shall be rewarded unto righteousness. [And what is that reward?] *These are they that are* ***redeemed of the Lord***; yea, these are they that are taken out, that are *delivered from that endless night of darkness*; and thus they stand or fall; for behold, *they are their own judges* [stemming from that which they desired most], whether to do good or do evil. Now the decrees of God are unalterable; therefore, *the way is* *prepared that whosoever will [according to his desires for happiness and good works] may walk therein and be saved*" (Alma 41:5-8; emphasis added). In Mosiah we learn that the Lord, "did deliver them because they did (now notice) *humble themselves* before him; and because they *cried mightily* unto him…" (Mosiah 29:20; emphasis added). This is a "type" of how we can ultimately become "delivered" and redeemed ourselves as we descend into *the depths* of our individual repentance.

A Process That Leads to Reconciliation.

We must all yearn and strive for the baptism of the Spirit and become "redeemed of the Lord." That's why we must clearly understand the context of the word *process* relative to spiritual rebirth. Sure, the whole journey is a process, even a process of achieving the measure of the fulness of the stature of Christ. After we have been born of God and have been adopted as His son or daughter, would we still be in the process of being born again or will we have already been birthed? After we receive our calling and election made sure, are we still in the process of receiving our calling and election? After we meet the Savior while in the flesh, which is to receive the Second Comforter, will we still be in the process of meeting Him? There are certain "encounters" with the Son of God that we can all experience as we journey through the overall process of becoming a replica of Him. Notice the past tense use of the words below in italics:

> *"Therefore,* ***the redeemed of the Lord*** *shall return, and come with singing unto Zion" (2 Ne. 2:8).*

> *"For, said he, I have repented of my sins, and have been* ***redeemed of the Lord****; behold I am born of the Spirit" (Mosiah 27:24).*

> *"These are they that are* ***redeemed of the Lord****; yea, these are they that are taken out, that are delivered from that endless night of darkness" (Alma 41:7).*

Notice the words *been born, received,* and *experienced* from Alma below:

> *"And now behold, I ask of you, my brethren of the church, have ye spiritually* ***been born*** *of God? Have ye received his image in your countenances? Have ye* ***experienced*** *this mighty change in your hearts" (Alma 5:14)?*

Fellow seeker: The above words were asked of members of the Church in Alma's day. Are most of us who are striving for the second birth gradually receiving more and more light, thereby becoming prepared to receive this mighty change experience? Of course. Are we to grow grace for grace and grace to grace thereafter? Of course.

That is also part of the process of coming unto Christ. The point I'd like to make here is that there can be a *mighty change experience*—an actual reconciliation with God that happens through entering the depths of repentance, crying out, and exercising whole and pure faith in surrendering our lives to Christ through our *willingness to sacrifice all that we have and are.*

When we partake of the fruit of the tree of life, and are *redeemed* of the Lord, we become a new creature in Christ. Our hearts are *changed* by Him in a mighty way. This is when we are born of Him, born again, born of the Spirit, or born of God. These are synonymous. Elder Hales says it this way: "Our Savior knows the heart of each of us. He knows the pains of our hearts. If we seek the truth, develop faith in Him, and ... sincerely repent, *we will receive a spiritual change of heart* ***which only comes from our Savior***. Our hearts will become new again (Richard D. Hales, "Healing Soul and Body," general conference, Oct. 1998).

In Moroni we read: "And *after* they had been received unto baptism *and* were *wrought upon* and *cleansed* by the power of the Holy Ghost. ..." Notice the words *after* with the past tense word *cleansed* relative to having been "wrought upon" by the power of the Holy Ghost." We find use of the word *after,* together with the past-tense usage of several verbs to connote that something had already occurred:

"But *after* that the kindness and love of God our Saviour toward man appeared. Not by works of righteousness which we have done, but according to his mercy he *saved* us [how?], by the washing of regeneration, and the renewing of the Holy Ghost; Which he *shed* on us abundantly through Jesus Christ our Saviour; That being *justified* by his grace, we should be made heirs according to the hope of eternal life" (Titus 3:4-7; emphasis added).

There is a process leading up to this cleansing, regenerating, and renewing power of Christ through the Holy Ghost, which makes us a new creature. There is also a process leading therefrom, "to keep us continually watchful unto prayer, relying alone upon the merits of Christ, who was the author and the finisher of our faith" (Moroni 6:4).

Consider these questions, if you will: After the Lord saved Peter from drowning, was he still drowning? After Lehi partook of the fruit, was he still curious as to what the fruit tasted like? For those raised in the Church, is this not what we have been taught our whole lives, that we cannot survive on borrowed light? Once we are brought to the actual knowledge of God through a manifestation of His Spirit, even a knowledge on the same level as if we had seen Him, would we still be in mystery as to His reality, or would we now know Him?

Fellow seeker, we are either a caterpillar or a butterfly. We are either a cucumber or a pickle. We are either still in the womb or we have been birthed. Once we are a butterfly, we cannot go back to being a caterpillar. Once we are a pickle, we cannot go back to being a cucumber. We are either a natural man, or we will have been awakened by God as a reborn, adopted son.

Our natural birth does not occur over a lifetime and neither does our spiritual rebirth. Physical birth is preceded by a gestation period—a process. And this process leads to an actual birthing. It is the same with spiritual rebirth. Yet after we are spiritually "birthed"—meaning, fully redeemed from sin and reconciled to God—*we are newborn babes who must still grow up in Christ.* In other words, the process continues. Growing up in Christ is the process of being made like Him through the reception and ongoing companionship of the Comforter. As we abide in Him thereafter in righteousness, He most literally will abide *in us* through His indwelling presence. Or as Paul said, "Nevertheless I live, yet not I, but Christ liveth in me" (Gal. 2:20). Notice the past tense of the following verbs used by Alma in bold below, as well as He who actually changes us:

*"Behold, **He** **changed** their hearts; yea, **He** **awakened** them out of a deep sleep, and they **awoke** unto God" (Alma 5:7).*

After God changed their hearts, were their hearts still unchanged? *After* God had awakened them out of a deep sleep, were they still asleep? *After* we have been cleansed and purified by the Deity, are we filthy still? *After* we have been given "*power*" in the form of a perfect faith from God, and have been "born, not of blood, nor of the will of the flesh, nor of the will of man, but of God" (John 1:12-13), and have become the sons of God through adoption into His family, are we still striving to be adopted? *After* we have been reconciled to God, which we are commanded to do, are we still seeking reconciliation? Are we seeing this? Anyway, I think by now we all can see the point being made. It is clear, at least to me, that spiritual rebirth does in fact involve a process. But that process is leading us to something. And that "something" is a birth—an actual reconciliation with God.

The words of Christ to the apostle Peter, "When thou are converted, strengthen thy brethren," reference a culminating and climactic point in time in which Peter would no longer be in the process of conversion, but would in fact be converted (past tense). This conversion occurred through an experience of being immersed in the heavenly element by the power of the Holy Ghost, just as occurred on the day of Pentecost (see Acts 2). Now keep in mind that the day of Pentecost occurred six months *after* Peter witnessed the transfiguration of Jesus, saw Moses and Elijah, and heard the audible voice of the Father say, "This is my beloved Son, in whom I am well pleased; hear ye him" (Matt. 17:5). Do you think you and I would have been converted had we heard the actual voice of Elohim and had witnessed the transfiguration of Christ? One might think so, but it would be inaccurate. The account of the Lord's transfiguration reads, "and his face did shine as the sun, and his raiment was white as the light" (Matt. 17:2). And at that time, think of it, Peter had still not been converted. Can one think of having a greater "testimony" than Peter had after witnessing the transfiguration of

Jesus on this mount, and yet still not be truly converted? So even with having had all of these witnesses (i.e., "events of testimony," if you will), not to mention his having witnessed all the miracles of Jesus' ministry, *Peter had still not been converted*!

Peter was not converted unto the Lord until he received the Comforter or Holy Ghost and power from on high six months later. This occurred for Peter on the day of Pentecost, and this is ***exactly*** when he was converted. Peter's experience of conversion corresponds with the Prophet Joseph's definition of the First Comforter, or "***the same*** as given on the day of Pentecost" (*Teachings of the Prophet Joseph Smith,* p.149; see also Acts 2) . We are converted when we are filled with that third member of the Godhead and obtain the fulfillment of the second birth, even becoming new creatures, born of God.

Fellow seeker. Receiving the Holy Ghost was not an automatic endowment for Peter and will not be an automatic endowment for us either. And it is this witness in power by the Holy Ghost which truly converts us and brings the *sure "knowledge of God."* From the above, it is plainly evident that *events of testimony (i.e., those times we have clearly "felt the Spirit") are not conversion but are those experiences that increase our faith and prepare and lead us to the full conversion that the Savior intended.* Notice the difference between Elder Faust's having had *a testimony his entire life* and that of *an overpowering witness* that came into his soul during the latter part of his life. I cannot know for absolute certain, but when I read his statement below, I'm confident that he received the *full conversion* and *sure witness* like that which was obtained by Peter on the day of Pentecost—of which we too may be partakers when we fulfill the *same law*:

> *"**I have had a testimony all of my life**. Recently however, there has come into my soul **an overpowering witness** of the divinity of this work. This **sure witness** is more certain than ever before in my life. Of this I testify" ("The Weightier Matters of the Law," general conference, Oct., 1997).*

Notice that even though Elder Faust had had a testimony all of his life, there was still *something more* which gave him what I believe to have been "the knowledge of God" through "an overpowering witness." And through this *sure witness*, he became a living witness and witnessed to us so that we could be strengthened and press forward in faith ourselves, and likewise obtain *something more.*

The Lord's admonition to Peter was, "When thou are converted, strengthen thy brethren." Clearly the Lord also contemplated that there would be a point in Peter's life wherein he would be truly converted, which was on the day of Pentecost. "And behold, I send *the promise of my Father* upon you: but tarry ye in the city of Jerusalem, *until* ye be endued with power from on high" (Luke 24:49; emphasis added). Every individual who has had hands placed upon his or her head for the bestowal of the gift of the Holy Ghost has had this same "*promise of [the] Father*." And as with Peter, so can it be with us. The main thing holding us back is our own unbelief that the same redemption and perfect knowledge is available to us personally and individually.

Fellow seeker: God is not a respecter of persons. And once we are *changed* by God, we are changed. *We cannot ever be the same thereafter,* and should we dare to deny the knowledge obtained through the *overpowering witness* received in power by the Holy Ghost, we would become sons of perdition. This is the level and surety of the witness we will have received, just as I believe Elder Faust received. Through our *redemptive experience*, we will have obtained the *sure witness* in our souls that our forefathers sang about with the words, "The Spirit of God Like a Fire Is Burning." And after this mighty (not subtle) change, our desires will continue in God for we will have experienced that taste of Oneness and immersion in God's peace, love, and light similar in many ways to that of some who have had a near-death experience (without having to go unconscious or leave our bodies)—it can never be forgotten, undone, or duplicated by the world. We will continue in God through our continued steadfastness in the faith of Christ and growing in the knowledge of Him, even unto that knowledge of Him in the form of His personage, see as we are seen, and *know* as we too are known. This is full redemption from the Fall.

We Must Experience Being Born of Water and of the Spirit

I raise my voice with Lehi's: "Wherefore, *how great the importance to make these things known unto the inhabitants of the earth*" (2 Ne. 2:8). Let us not become numbered among those who are flattered by the devil, nor pacified and lulled away, thinking we have plenty of time, especially in light of the many voices chanting, "All is well in Zion." Doctrinal concerns and questions may be discussed at length. But there is one which is plain, straightforward, and not open to any private interpretation whatsoever: ***We must be born of both water and of the Spirit to enter the kingdom of God—****period, full stop.* Elder D. Todd Christofferson affirmed: "We know that our physical bodies have a divine origin and that ***we must experience*** both a physical birth and a ***spiritual rebirth***" ("The Moral Force of Women").

It would be advantageous to *know* if we have been born of both water and Spirit in order to have peace in this world, would it not? Therefore, we must inquire of God, and keep inquiring until we know. If we do not know, or if we think we are safe because we are members of Christ's true church, I fear the devil may be cheating our souls. Brigham Young, just as Nephi of old, speaks in plainness about the necessity of our being born of the Spirit:

> *Jesus... said to Nicodemus, "Except a man is born of the spirit, he cannot see the kingdom of God." Shall we admit that Jesus spoke the truth, or shall man say that his doctrine is true and Jesus spoke that which is not true? Which shall we do? There is*

no alternative but to admit that Jesus is true, and will ***save on no other condition*** *than that laid down in the Scriptures, and that* ***all who preach any other doctrine take the testimony of men instead of the testimony of Jesus****, or that the Christian world with their varied opinions and creeds are true and that Jesus is untrue.*

This is plain talk, my friends. Can you mistake it? Can you gain any idea from what I say except what I mean*—let God be true, if it makes every man a liar. I think my words are so pointed and emphatic that no person can mistake them. Did Jesus say, "Except a man is born of the water and of the Spirit, he cannot enter the kingdom of God?" Yes, all Christians will admit that. Then* ***do you think there was one plan of salvation for Nicodemus and another for you and me?*** *It is all folly for any person to expect any such thing! ("The Gospel of Jesus Christ," Journal of Discourses, 13:328; emphasis added).*

Elder Orson Pratt spoke to the restoration of the gospel, which was accompanied by the same gifts as those experienced in ancient days as on the day of Pentecost, so that we too might know of a surety *when* we had received the Holy Ghost:

"It was absolutely necessary that the Gospel should be restored, together with the authority to administer its ordinances, baptism for the remission of sins, and the laying on of hands for the baptism of fire and the Holy Ghost; authority to build up the Church and kingdom on the earth, ***that the Holy Ghost might again be poured out [how?] as in ancient times [as was patterned for us on the day of Pentecost]****, that the people might receive the gifts thereof,* ***and that they might know of a surety, when they had received the Holy Spirit****" (Journal of Discourses, 16:284; emphasis added).*

When we receive that promised remission of sins as in ancient times, made possible by *the promise of the Father* through the laying on of hands, we will gain that knowledge of having been immensely *blessed* through adoption by God Himself. Zacharias prophesied that his son John would go before the face of the Lord, who would subsequently give "*knowledge* of salvation … by the *remission* of sins" (Luke 1:77; emphasis added). In other words, when we receive the remission of sins, which comes by fire and the Holy Ghost, we will have that *sure knowledge* that we have had something transformative happen to us. And this "something" is to have been saved and redeemed by God Himself.

We are to fall in love with Christ, the object of our obsession, even like that of a beautiful love story between a father and son. Any love, interest, or love interest that stands between us and Him could be considered an idol, at least to some degree. We must make Christ the aim, goal, and preeminent focus of our lives. We must love God with all our heart, might, mind, strength and soul. All other considerations must become subordinate to this one love—the love of God. We arrive at this place by "practicing" the art of loving Him. Emotional and spiritual inner-honesty will tell us where we stand in terms of our love for God if we seek earnestly the answers. Those answers will be revealed when we persistently search diligently in the light of Christ found by turning within and tuning in to that point of contact where He is found—that inner place of stillness of the soul. This is facilitated by slowing down and quieting our minds. When we turn inward and maintain an awareness of that inner light, while diligently seeking Him in the stillness, we will be led to Him and eventually find Him. My own seeking journey took me more than 2 decades of diligently seeking Him. Yet I'll confess, had I focused merely on the Doctrine of Christ, I am convinced I would have found Him early on in my journey. But my path was purposeful in that I am now able to relate with any seeker of almost any faith or spiritual persuasion. And for that, I am indeed grateful.

The White Dove in Hawaii

Awareness is key to assembling the pieces of a celestial puzzle for ourselves and ridding ourselves of unbelief. I'd like to share a quick experience. While on vacation on Oahu, Hawaii, shortly after my rebirth, my wife, Rebecca, and our daughter Ashlyn were reading out loud from a book wherein the author was witnessing of the Second Comforter, or the personal visitation of Jesus Christ to an individual. Immediately, out of seemingly nowhere, there appeared a perfect white dove, which had gracefully descended and perched itself on the balcony railing (located about 15 stories high), less than an arm's length from where my wife and daughter were sitting. The close proximity was startling, but that was not the extent of the unanticipated surprise. This perfect white dove remained for ***3 minutes***, with no fear whatsoever, as if the dove were being tutored by the truth of the message being read. The Prophet Joseph taught:

> *"The sign of the dove was instituted before the creation of the world, a witness for the Holy Ghost, and the devil cannot come in the sign of a dove. The Holy Ghost ... does not confine itself to the form of the dove, but in sign of the dove,... but the sign of a dove was given to John to signify the truth of the deed, as the dove is an emblem or* ***token of truth*** *and innocence" (Teachings of the Prophet Joseph Smith, p. 275; emphasis added).*

The visit of this dove was the token of truth as to the reality of the Second Comforter. After the dove flew away, my wife and daughter were dumbfounded. To this day they can scarcely believe it. They made it a point immediately following this "visit" to look at every balcony for any other white doves, and none were to be found, including for the rest of our vacation. I know this to be true because I witnessed this through the partitioned glass and afterward helped them look. These "coincidences" in life are pieces to a puzzle that we must first recognize through awareness, and later put together as part of assembling the full picture of our divine puzzle or tapestry as we gain further light and knowledge from the Lord. As we believe and look for spiritual meaning in these seemingly random occurrences, more of the same show up. As we discard them as a thing of naught, the experiences stop coming. These experiences are there to build testimony, if we'll only allow them. And these events of testimony, if you will, are leading us to eventually fall down and partake of the fruit of the tree of life—or the "mighty change" experience of salvation for ourselves.

Events of Testimony Lead to Full Conversion, or the Second Birth

Elder McConkie noted that "the Latter-day Twelve, *long after they had testimonies* of the gospel, and more than two years after their calls to the apostleship, were promised that if they would be faithful, they would *yet be converted*" (*Mormon Doctrine,* "Conversion," p. 163; see D&C 112:12-13). If our early apostles struggled to receive this gift in the early days of the Church, why would any of us view it as an automatic endowment for ourselves? Elder Bednar has taught: "Strong testimony is the foundation upon which conversion is established. Testimony alone is not and will not be enough to protect us in the latter-day storm of darkness and evil in which we are living. ***Testimony is important and necessary but not sufficient*** to provide the spiritual strength and protection we need" (David A. Bednar, "Converted Unto the Lord," Oct. 2012 General Conference Talk).

Fellow seeker: We can have the greatest belief and testimony on planet earth, but if we have not yet been born of the Spirit, we have not therefore become fully converted like Peter of old, who prior to his conversion had denied the Christ three times. Peter first needed to be "born of the Spirit," as do we. This is the elephant in the room, is it not? "The devils also believe, and tremble" (James 2:19).

I like to think of *conversion as immersion*—immersion in the Lord's Spirit. This immersion is part of a manifestation. To be fully converted in such a miraculous way is to be born of God and receive the second birth. It appears Orson Pratt and Matthew Cowley, both apostles of our Lord Jesus Christ, saw it the same way. When referring to the apostle Peter's words on the day of Pentecost, Pratt defined what it meant to be truly "converted":

> *"'Repent, and be converted.' Notice now what this sentence means. The word '**converted**' has been construed to be '**born of God**, or to become a **new creature**'" (Journal of Discourses, 15:312).*

Matthew Cowley reaffirmed this principle:

> *"Of those who sought the kingdom of God, Christ required* ***complete conversion****, or* ***the second birth*** *as explained by him to Nicodemus" ("Seek Ye First the Kingdom of God," Conference Report, October, 1946, pp. 103-108).*

Preaching the Purity of the Gospel of Christ

The number one question I get from people with whom I share the purity of the doctrine of Christ is "Why aren't the Brethren teaching us this?" The fact is...the brethren are teaching it. The problem is that we're either hard of hearing or just not paying close attention. We can help them, however, and here's how. We first need to learn the pure doctrine ourselves by opening our eyes and ears to what the Brethren, the scriptures, and instructions from the Holy Spirit are telling us. And once learned and truly understood, we begin teaching the true and pure doctrine in our wards and stakes throughout the Church. This can be a top down as well as a bottom up, approach. The true doctrine of Christ includes faith, broken-hearted repentance, baptism by water, confirmation, reception of the actual Holy Ghost or First Comforter (delivered when we cry out and fully surrender and consecrate our lives to God) and enduring to the end. That's it. There is much work to do. We need only "choose in."

To illustrate the above, allow me to quote from the words of these two apostles, starting with Elder Bednar, who said:

> *"Following our baptism, each of us had hands placed upon our head by those with priesthood authority and was confirmed a member of The Church of Jesus Christ of Latter-day Saints, and the [gift of the] Holy Ghost was conferred upon us. The statement 'receive the Holy Ghost' in our confirmation was a* ***<u>directive to strive</u>*** *for the baptism of the Spirit. The Prophet Joseph Smith taught, 'You might as well baptize a bag of sand as a man, if not done in view of the remission of sins and getting of the Holy Ghost. Baptism by water is but half a baptism, and is* ***<u>good for nothing without the other half</u>****--that is, the baptism of the Holy Ghost.' We were baptized by immersion in water for the [purpose and intent of a] remission of sins. We must also be baptized by and immersed in the Spirit of the Lord, 'and THEN cometh a remission of your sins [how?] by fire and by the Holy Ghost'" ("The Baptism of the Holy Ghost," ChurchofJesusChrist.org; emphasis added).*

Question: Why would we be directed to strive for something we had already received unless we hadn't already received it? And why would we seek for something if we believed we had already received it? And if seeking is required to finding… well, I trust you get what I'm conveying here.

So then according to Elder Bednar's statement above, by what power comes the remission of sins? Answer: By fire and the Holy Ghost, sent by the will of the Father through Jesus Christ His Son, "unto the fulfilling of *the promise* [*of the Father]* which He hath made, that if ye entered in by *the way* [i.e., "the gate"] ye should receive" (see 2 Ne. 31:18). And when was this promise of the Father confirmed upon us? Answer: During our confirmation into the Church and the laying on of hands, through priesthood authority, providing the "channel" through which this divine power and knowledge of God could come to us and be enjoyed. Remember, the Melchizedek Priesthood must be held by the one who performs the ordinance by the laying on of hands because this same priesthood, "holdeth … the key to the knowledge of God." And to arrive at this knowledge is to not only believe that He is, but to know with an absolute, perfect certainty, of His reality.

This knowledge does not allow its recipient to let go of the fruit easily after he or she has partaken. For they will have experienced being filled with God's love, a spiritual oneness with Him, as well as having partaken of His consciousness. Most endure to the end thereafter because they now have an experiential knowledge as to *what the prize is "behind the curtain," so to speak, and what it feels like to abide in Their love.*

The second statement I'd like to share is from Elder Christofferson:

> *"Knowing why we left the presence of our heavenly Father and what it takes to return and be exalted with Him, it becomes very clear that nothing [hear it again: nothing], relative to our time on earth, can be more important than physical birth [already accomplished] and spiritual rebirth: the two prerequisites to eternal life!" ("Why Marriage, Why Family," general conference, April, 2015; emphasis added).*

And since all in mortality have already experienced physical birth and therefore can "check that box," there is only one other priority left as a prerequisite to eternal life, which is that of spiritual rebirth.

The Worst and Best of All Human Conditions

> *"Of all the problems you encounter in this life, there is one that towers above them all and is the least understood.* ***The worst of all human conditions in this life*** *is not poverty, sickness, loneliness, abuse, or war—as awful as those conditions are.... It is to die. It* ***is to die spiritually. It is to be separated from the***

***presence of God**, and in this life, His presence is His Spirit or power. That is the worst.*

*"Conversely, **the best of all human conditions in this life** is not wealth, fame, prestige, good health, the honors of men, security.... It **is to be born again**, to have the gift and companionship of the Holy Ghost, which is the source of knowledge, revelation, strength, clarity, love, joy, peace, hope, confidence, faith, and almost every other good thing. Jesus said, 'The Comforter, which is the Holy Ghost, . . . shall teach you all things.' It is the power by which we 'may know the truth of all things.' 'It will show . . . [us] all things . . . [we] should do.' It is the fountain of 'living water' that springs up unto eternal life" ("Stand Forever," Lawrence E. Corbridge, BYU Devotional, Jan. 22, 2019).*

"Must Yet Find the Path"

Elder McConkie also speaks to the essential nature of spiritual rebirth:

*"The baptism of the Holy Ghost, the baptism of fire, the birth of the Spirit, is absolutely essential to salvation in the kingdom of God. Those who receive this endowment are on the path leading to eternal life, while those not so blessed must yet find the path **before they can gain peace in this world** and eternal life in the world to come" (Doctrines of the Restoration, page 104).*

The Promise of the Father Is the Promised Reception of the Holy Ghost, Remission of Sins, Promise of Eternal Life, and Other Endowments, Subject to Fulfilling Divine Law.

The promise of the Father includes a promise of the Holy Ghost (received as a gift) or First Comforter, with its accompanying gifts of the Spirit. This promise of being endowed with "power from on high" was referenced by Christ when he said, "***but wait for the promise of the Father***, which, saith he, ye have heard of me." How do we know that this "promise of the Father" to which Christ was referring was the Holy Ghost, received as a gift? Because in the very next verse the Lord provides the context: "For John truly baptized with water; but ye shall be baptized with the Holy Ghost not many days hence" and "*ye shall receive power [from on high], after that the Holy Ghost is come upon you"* (Acts 1:4-5, 8; emphasis added).

This power from on high was made manifest through the gift of the Holy Ghost, received through the channel of the priesthood, promising "the knowledge of God" by way of the "key" provided through this authority by the laying on of hands. Notice the Prophet Joseph's words: "The first principles of the Gospel, as I believe, are, faith, repentance, baptism for the remission of sins, *with the promise of the Holy Ghost*" (*Teachings of the Prophet Joseph Smith,* p. 328). And this promise is confirmed and sealed upon us by the authority of the Melchizedek Priesthood during our confirmation. Peter reaffirmed that this... "*promise is unto you, and to your children, and to all that are afar off, even as many as the Lord our God shall call*" (Acts 2:39) and that... ***"this promise is just as good as it was on the day of Pentecost** when the Holy Ghost was poured out so mightily upon the apostles*" (Discourse by Elder John Morgan, delivered in the Tabernacle, Salt Lake City, on Sunday Afternoon, Aug. 17, 1879; JD 20:277; emphasis added).

In Luke, the Lord addresses the same: "And, behold, I send ***the promise of my Father*** upon you: but tarry ye in the city of Jerusalem, until ye be *endued with power from on high*" (Luke 24:49). This is why, when certain Jews, exorcists, took upon them to cast out the evil spirit by saying, "We adjure you by Jesus whom Paul preacheth," "the evil spirit answered and said, Jesus I know, and Paul, I know; but who are ye?" (Note: These certain Jews had not received priesthood authority nor the enjoyment of the gift of the Holy Ghost, which would have enabled them to possess this "power from on high"). As a result of their having not obtained these spiritual gifts, the evil spirit knew them not and "*prevailed against them*, so that they fled out of that house naked and wounded" (Acts 19:13-16). The Savior instructed the early saints that through this power and gift of the Holy Ghost, the gates of hell shall "*not prevail against you*" (see D&C 33:11-13).

Referring to this same power from on high, the Prophet Joseph stated, "We also believe in prophecy, in tongues, in visions, and in revelations, in gifts, and in healings; and that [now pay close attention] *these things cannot be enjoyed without the [reception and enjoyment of the] gift of the Holy Ghost*" (*Teachings of the Prophet Joseph Smith,* p. 249; emphasis added). This same principle is confirmed and reaffirmed by the apostle Charles Penrose. He said that "the Elders when they are sent forth to preach are instructed to preach nothing but the first principles of the Gospel—to preach nothing but repentance to this generation. Why? Because the people ***cannot comprehend further advanced principles***" without first obtaining the actual gift and enjoyment of the Holy Ghost (*Journal of Discourses,* 25:212; emphasis added). And I would add that without the reception and enjoyment of the gift of the Holy Ghost, the elders themselves cannot comprehend further advanced principles either.

The priesthood authority, together with the *promise of the Father*, with its attending blessing of "power from on high," is further clarified by the Lord: "That they themselves may be prepared... taught more perfectly, and have experience [in order to preach the word]... *And this cannot be brought to pass until mine elders are endowed with power from on high*" (D&C 105:10-11; emphasis added). To be endowed with power from on high refers to priesthood authority and various gifts of the Spirit, including "signs" which "follow them that believe." Examples include these: "in my name shall they cast out devils; they shall speak with new tongues; they shall take up serpents; and if they drink any deadly thing, it shall not hurt them; they shall lay hands on the sick, and they shall recover" (Mark 16:17-18). "Faithful persons are expected to seek the gifts of the Spirit with all their hearts" (*Mormon Doctrine,* 2nd edition, "Gifts of the Spirit," p. 314).

This power from on high also encompasses "certain knowledge, powers, and special blessings," and "any ministers or missionaries in any age—***are not fully qualified to go forth, preach the gospel, and build up the kingdom, unless they have the gift of the Holy Ghost and also are endowed with power from on high***" (Bruce R. McConkie, *Doctrinal New Testament Commentary,* 1:859; emphasis added). Wow! Take a moment and let what we just read sink in. Please go back and re-read the portion in bold italic. Take an additional pause. Now, can you imagine what strides we would make in our missionary work if we had all received the actual *manifestation* of the Holy Ghost, having received the actual knowledge of God by having received this heavenly bestowal and enjoyment of this gift, with its ongoing influence and companionship, prior to our missionary service? The apostle Moses Thatcher seems to concur with the above: "No man has authority to preach the Gospel and administer its ordinances without a commission from Jesus Christ; and the seal of such commission has always been, and always will be the gifts, blessings and endorsement of the Holy Ghost, *which, not only leads to the form, but also to the power of godliness*" (Moses Thatcher, JD 23:197, delivered at a General Conference, Saturday, April, 1882).

President Ezra Taft Benson spoke to this as well: "Would not the progress of the Church increase dramatically today with an increasing number of those who are spiritually reborn? Can you imagine what would happen in our homes? Can you imagine what would happen with an increasing number of copies of the Book of Mormon *in the hands of an increasing number of missionaries who know how to use it* ***and who have been born of God***? When this happens, we will get the harvest President Kimball envisions. *It was the 'born of God' Alma who as a missionary was so able to impart the [purity of the] word* ***that many others were also born of God*** [see Alma 36:23-26]" ("Born of God," general conference, October 1985; emphasis added).

This gift of the Holy Ghost, Elder McConkie tells us, "offers certain blessings provided there is full compliance with the law involved; **everyone upon whom the gift is bestowed <u>does not in fact enjoy or possess the offered gift</u>**." Wow again! Now let's allow this one to sink in as well. Elder McConkie refers to the actual gift this way: "In the case of the apostles, the actual enjoyment of the gift was delayed *until the day of Pentecost*" (Doctrinal New Testament Commentary, 1:857; emphasis added). And so it is with us. Through our individual compliance in full with the gospel law involved, it can likewise be **enjoyed** by us, as "there is nothing an apostle can receive that is not available to every elder in the kingdom" (Bruce R. McConkie, The Promised Messiah, p. 595).

This enjoyment can be received as part of our own personal, individual "day of Pentecost"—our own day of salvation unbeknownst to anyone else. Notice the words of an ancient prophet: "For behold, ***this day*** he hath spiritually begotten you" (Mosiah 5:7; emphasis added). The actual enjoyment of the gift is given by God to the individual without any knowledge or fanfare of the world, after whole repentance and receiving of that "living faith" from the Lord, which is the "power to become the sons of God" (see John 1:12).

More on the Promise of the Father

"This Comforter is **the promise** which I give unto you **of eternal life**, even the glory of the celestial kingdom" (D&C 88:4; emphasis added).

Elder Alvin R. Dyer, an ordained apostle who served as a member of the First Presidency under President David O. McKay, said that being born of the Spirit *"is attained by covenant and promise," which means that when man "progressively pursues this avowed determination" to "conform his life to the laws of righteousness,"* ***then*** *"man becomes the beneficiary of '****the promise of the Father****' by receiving the guiding and enlightening influence and the powers [from on high] bestowed by the Holy Ghost." Elder Dyer further declared: "From this third member of the Godhead, or the Holy Ghost, there is bestowed upon mankind* ***varying degrees of light and intelligence, speaking of intelligence as a spiritual power*** *pertaining to spiritual laws which are eternal, in accordance with man's ability to receive it" ("Who Am I?" pp. 318-319; emphasis added).*

When Christ was personally with His apostles, He acted as their comforter: "Nevertheless I tell you the truth; it is expedient for you that I go away: for if I go not away, the Comforter will not come unto you; but if I depart, I will send him unto you" (John 16:7).

Joseph Smith stated that "the Gift of the Holy Ghost by the laying on of hands, cannot be received through the medium of any other principle than the principle of righteousness, ***for if the proposals are not complied with, it is of no use***" (*Teachings of the Prophet Joseph Smith,* p. 150; emphasis added). These proposals are the foundational tenets of the doctrine of Christ. These principles of righteousness, or proposals, are the *preliminary requirements* for the second baptism, or an immersion in spiritual fire and the Holy Ghost.

As Elder James E. Talmage has said:

> *"And the words of the resurrected Savior to the Nephites come in* ***plainness indisputable****, and with* ***authority not to be***

***questioned**, proclaiming the baptism of fire and the Holy Ghost unto all those who obey the preliminary requirements" ("Articles of Faith," p. 133).*

The Father's Promise of the Holy Ghost and Eternal Life Is "Confirmed" on Us by the Laying on of Hands

This gospel covenant gets confirmed on us during our confirmation after the baptism of water. In other words, the "promise of the Father" gets sealed on our heads by the authority of the Melchizedek Priesthood, which is when this covenant and right to receive of the promised blessing is actually confirmed upon us (hence the term *confirmation*). This happens after having received the "key" of the baptism of water. *Thereafter, it is up to us to fulfill and receive the promised blessing (which is the actual Holy Ghost) associated with that gospel covenant.* Notice the following:

*"And every one that hearkeneth to the voice of the Spirit cometh unto God, even the Father. And the Father teacheth him of the **covenant** which he has renewed and **confirmed upon you**, which is confirmed upon you for your sakes" (D&C 84:47-48; emphasis added).*

The elders confirm the promise of the Father upon us. When we abide by any covenant, there is a law irrevocably decreed before the foundation of this world which guarantees us of the associated, promised blessing, subject to fulfilling the law involved. In this specific case,

The promise of the Father, by gospel covenant, is the baptism of fire and reception of the Holy Ghost, as a gift, which is accompanied by the absolute reality as to the knowledge of God, and the sure promise of eternal life, subject to enduring to the end.

During the Kirtland Temple dedication and after singing the words, "The Spirit of God like a fire is burning," Lydia [Knight, wife of Newel Knight] *felt the glory* of God fill the temple. Rising to her feet with the other Saints in the room, she joined her voice with theirs as they shouted, 'Hosanna! Hosanna! Hosanna to God and the Lamb!'

"After the temple dedication, ***manifestations*** of the Lord's Spirit and power ***enveloped Kirtland.*** On the evening of the dedication, Joseph met with church leaders in the temple, and the men began to speak in tongues, as the Savior's apostles had done at Pentecost. Some at the meeting saw heavenly fire resting on those who spoke.

Others saw angels. Outside, Saints saw a bright cloud and a pillar of fire rest over the temple."

Three days later the manifestations continued when "ministering angels appeared to some men, and a few others had visions of the Savior.

"Outpourings of the Spirit continued until the early morning hours. When the men left the temple, their souls were soaring from the wonders and *glories they had just experienced.* They felt endowed with power [through having received the baptism of fire and the Holy Ghost, ***as on the day of Pentecost***] and ***ready** to take the gospel to the world*" (See "*Saints,*" The Church of Jesus Christ of Latter-day Saints, pp., 237, 239; emphasis added).

These manifestations *were not just amazing, spiritual experiences*. That is not our objective, nor God's. It is really about becoming *cleansed and purified by God*, for as it is written, *no unclean thing can dwell in His presence*. This is the point to never lose sight of as we press forward in faith.

Notice that the intended purpose of confirmation by the laying on of hands is "for the baptism of fire and the Holy Ghost," without which we would most certainly remain "filthy still" (2 Ne. 9:16). Does it get much plainer than this? If we truly received the promised blessing or actual gift and enjoyment of the Holy Ghost (i.e., baptism of the Spirit) at the time of our confirmation when we were eight years old, for example, what purpose would there be to continue to "strive" or to fight vigorously to receive it in our more mature or riper years? And why would we receive the actual gift and remission of sins at eight years old, when we have no purported sins to remit, since Christ's Atonement covers all of us through the age of accountability? Lastly, whether we receive the ordinances at eight or later in life, the condition of faith and repentance will always be in play. To truly, whole-heartedly repent, we must be of riper years to fully understand the importance of our broken-hearted offering, as well as the "all in" commitment being made to God. The Prophet Joseph speaks to these points:

> *"Baptism is for remission of sins. Children have no sins... Children are all made alive in Christ, and those of **riper years** through faith and repentance" (Teachings of the Prophet Joseph Smith, p. 314).*

This *mighty change experience*, with its accompanying gifts of the Spirit, is part of that "power from on high" that the Lord himself referenced. This power and the accompanying gifts are what was given to the early apostles on the day of Pentecost. They are the same gifts and power that were given to the early Saints of Kirtland. If you read the *revealed prayer* given to Joseph Smith that the Lord Himself instructed Joseph to read at the Kirtland Temple dedication, the Lord refers to it yet again:

"Let it be fulfilled upon them [meaning, the promised gift that had been confirmed upon them by the laying on of hands], as upon those ***on the day of Pentecost*** *[i.e., which is when the promise was* ***received and enjoyed*** *by the apostles and subsequently others]" (D&C 109:36; emphasis added).*

The Rebirth of the Spirit Is Described by Prophets, Seers, and Revelators, along with the Savior Himself as the Same or "Like" Experience as Was Received on the Day of Pentecost

Allow me to share some other witnesses from the Lord and His modern-day apostles as to the Holy Ghost being likened to the early apostles' experience on the day of Pentecost:

"The Holy Ghost is the Holy Spirit; he is the Holy Spirit promised the Saints at baptism, or in other words, the Holy Spirit of Promise, this exalted name-title signifying that ***the promised receipt of the Holy Spirit, AS ON THE DAY OF PENTECOST****, is the greatest gift a man can receive in mortality." (Bruce R. McConkie, Doctrinal New Testament Commentary, Vol. III, pp. 333-334; emphasis added).*

Notice that all men can receive it in mortality. Why the greatest gift? Because it takes this gift to be prepared and led to all other endowments and knowledge, including that of entering the Divine presence while yet in mortality. Heber C Kimball witnessed:

"Under the ordinances of baptism and the laying on of hands, I received the Holy Ghost, as the disciples did in ancient days, ***AS ON THE DAY OF PENTECOST****, which was like a consuming fire. I felt as though I sat at the feet of Jesus" (as cited in Orson F Whitney, Life of Heber C. Kimball, p. 22; emphasis added).*

Lorenzo Snow refers to his rebirth, or to when he received the Holy Ghost, this way:

"It was a complete baptism—a tangible immersion in the heavenly principal or element, the Holy Ghost ... ***<u>the same</u> as in apostolic times****" (Eliza R. Snow, Biography and Family Record of Lorenzo Snow, p. 8; emphasis added).*

Lorenzo Snow also spoke the following:

> *"And God promised him (the Prophet Joseph) that whosoever should receive and obey his message, and whosoever would receive baptism for remission of sins, with honesty of purpose, should receive divine manifestations, should receive the Holy Ghost, should receive* ***the same Gospel and blessings*** *as were promised and obtained through the Gospel,* ***as preached (and received) by the ancient Apostles****" (Journal of Discourses, 13:284; emphasis added).*

Now we move to the witness of all witnesses, the Lord Jesus Christ Himself, spoken in the days since the restoration of His Church in the latter days:

> *"Thou didst baptize by water unto repentance, but they received not the Holy Ghost; But now I give unto thee a commandment, that thou shalt baptize by water,* ***and they shall receive the Holy Ghost*** *by the laying on of the hands,* ***even as the apostles of old****" (Doctrine and Covenants 35:5-6; emphasis added).*

And how did the Apostles of old receive the Holy Ghost? Answer: The same endowment and manifestation(s) as they received on the day of Pentecost (see Acts 2). Joseph Smith defines the reception of the First Comforter or Holy Ghost as "***the same*** *as given on the day of Pentecost*" (*Teachings of the Prophet Joseph Smith,* p.149; see also Acts 2; emphasis added), or as Lorenzo Snow puts it above, "*the same as in apostolic times" (ibid.; emphasis added).*

Obey the Same Law, Receive the Same Blessing, Regardless of Title or Position

Not everyone will receive the actual Holy Ghost, the same as was administered to the early apostles on the day of Pentecost—this is true. But that can only be true because the candidate for "the same immersion in Spirit" had not fulfilled the same law upon which the promised blessing was predicated. Elder McConkie states:

> *"All of the elders [and sisters] in the kingdom are expected to live the law as strictly as do the members of the Council of the Twelve, and if they do so live,* ***the same blessings*** *will come to them that flow to apostles and prophets" (The Promised Messiah, p. 594; emphasis added).*

This is so clear and plain that there can be little room for misinterpretation. God is not a respecter of persons. We are all on equal footing with Him, irrespective of our titles or positions in the world or in the Church. Oliver Cowdery, in speaking to the original twelve apostles of the restoration said, "God does not love you better or more than others," and that "the Lord loves people, not [because you may be] office holders. Every elder [and sister] is entitled to ***the same blessings and privileges*** offered the apostles" (as cited in *The Promised Messiah,* p. 594; emphasis added). And what are those same blessings and privileges provided to the apostles? I'll leave it to the seeker to ask God Himself and thus obtain his own answer.

Now as to my own testimony. I bear solemn witness from the deepest part of my soul to all who read these words, in all humility, that this experience and "power from on high," even ***the same*** experience as given on the day of Pentecost, is more real than the earth upon which we stand and is absolutely available to ***all*** who have had hands placed on their heads by proper authority and have heard the admonition to "receive the Holy Ghost." It is conditioned on having likewise *struggled and fought vigorously* for having obtained its commission through *an unbending, diamond-hard commitment and willingness* in our desire and faith to *find the knowledge of God* and the yielding of our hearts to Him in complete surrender. But it will require that we first view "[ourselves] in [our] own carnal state, even less than the dust of the earth" (Mosiah 4:2). I invite all to not just read these words, but to *feel them* and to then *experiment upon them.* We must *cry out* for His mercy and grace to fill us (see Mosiah 4:3), wholly repenting of our sins and *relying alone upon His merits, tied to a committed willingness and determination to do His will throughout our lives and into eternity.* It will not come easy. It may even require the bending of our souls to obtain it.

The apostle George Q. Cannon served in the First Presidency under four Presidents and Prophets of the Church—Brigham Young, John Taylor, Wilford Woodruff, and Lorenzo Snow. Speaking of the gospel, President Cannon said the following as to our ability to receive the same gifts and powers today as were administered to those who lived anciently:

> *"If we* ***obey the same form of doctrine obeyed by those who lived anciently****, and it is administered by those who hold authority from God,* ***the gifts and powers will most assuredly follow****, for God loves his children now as much as he loved them in any past age of the world" (Journal of Discourses, 15:111).*

If we fulfill the same law that governs its fulfillment, then we can absolutely expect to receive the same blessing, even ***the same*** that the apostles of old received on the day of Pentecost. "Or what man is there of you, who, if his son ask bread, will give him a stone" (3 Ne. 14:9)? I'll say it again. Any Church member who obeys *the same law* which allows one to qualify for a particular blessing may be permitted to receive *the same blessing* through adherence to the same law upon which the promised blessing was predicated. If this were not so, God would be in fact, a respecter of persons (which He is not).

President Cannon also spoke his mind in boldness when he said,

> *"We become spiritually alive through the influence of the Holy Ghost as we actively seek, receive, and act upon its promptings. If this [mighty] change does not take place,* ***it is because the person*** *who has been baptized and who has had the laying on of the hands for the gift of the Holy Ghost* ***has not sought for these blessings with diligence****" (Millennial Star, Apr., 1894, pp. 260-261; emphasis added).*

He also adds, that,

> *"Everyone who submits to the ordinances of the Gospel with sincerity and determination to serve God will undergo this change" (ibid).*

Elder Bruce R. McConkie said that "apostles and prophets are named as *examples and patterns* of what others should be." "*There is nothing an apostle can receive that is not available to every elder in the kingdom.*" And "every elder is entitled and *expected* to seek and obtain *all* the spiritual blessings of the gospel, *including the crowning blessing of seeing the Lord face to face*" (*The Promised Messiah,* p. 595; emphasis added). And, of course, any spiritual endowment that an elder can receive, a sister may likewise receive. Elder Ballard confirmed the same when he said that *every member* of the Church is entitled to and can "develop an apostolic-like relationship with the Lord" ("We Are Witnesses: The Twelve Apostles Today," July 2019 Ensign; found also on churchofjesuschrist.org).

Spiritual rebirth is such a transcendent, profoundly real, and emotionally overwhelming experience (with ripple effects that can last into eternity) that "those who have this witness of the Spirit are ***expected***, like their counterparts of old, ***to see and hear and touch and converse with the Heavenly Person***, as did those of old" (*The Promised Messiah,* pp, 592). And the knowledge obtained from spiritual rebirth is so "sure" and "certain" that if we were to deny it and become an active enemy against God thereafter, we would become sons of perdition.

As a general rule, without this unspeakable gift it would be impossible to reach that point of faith, knowledge, and sanctification unto holiness in which we might later "see and hear and touch and converse" with God. I love Elder McConkie's words on both the reception and maintenance of the Holy Ghost in our lives:

> *"Truly the Holy Ghost is a sanctifier and the* ***extent*** *to which men* ***receive and enjoy*** *the gift of the Holy Ghost is the* ***extent*** *to which they are sanctified (A New Witness of the Articles of Faith, p. 266; emphasis added).*

Given the truthfulness of the above, and knowing that there are many today (although few, perhaps, compared to the total Church membership) who are experiencing spiritual rebirth as the apostles of old experienced it, as well as those in the days of Kirtland, why would we settle for anything less? Why would we spend any of our waking energy arguing for our limitations as to why we *cannot* receive it? I'll answer this. I believe it is largely out of fear, unbelief, and many of the cultural traditions of our fathers" (see D&C 93:39). Yet fear is darkness and akin to unbelief. How often did the Savior of the world say, "Fear not"? Remember, fear is the opposite of that faith which saves. Is bowing to fear our greatness? We must ponder these things in our hearts and then ask of God. We must turn to Him and inquire for ourselves. Remember, He is not a respecter of persons, and He "upbraideth not" (James 1:5). Joseph said, "*He alone must be our protector and safeguard, spiritually or temporally, or we fall*" (*Teachings of the Prophet Joseph Smith,* p. 260; emphasis added). He alone.

Now a solemn word to my fellow seeker. I don't know if this spiritual rebirth can occur differently than how it has been outlined for us in plain English by Joseph Smith ("even as plain as word can be" [2 Ne. 32:7]), through whom the Lord has said we would receive His word in this generation (D&C 5:10) and through whom we should receive it as if from God's own mouth (D&C 21:5). But what I can attest, affirm, and witness to is that I don't know of any person in my circle of friends, associates, or acquaintances in our modern day (or any other day) who has truly, wholly, and fully been born of God who did not have either a miraculous experience which changed their very natures or whose soul and heart had not been touched in a most profound and mighty way, even though they may not have initially known what had happened to them.

Pay very close attention to the following words of Elder Bednar: "Elder Dallin H. Oaks has explained that in renewing our baptismal covenants by partaking of the emblems of the sacrament, we do not witness that we take upon us the name of Jesus Christ. [Rather], we witness that we are *willing* to do so. (See D&C 20:88.) The fact that we only witness to our *willingness* suggests that *something else must happen* before we *actually* take that sacred name upon us in the [ultimate and] most important sense" ("Taking upon Us the Name of Jesus Christ," *Ensign,* May 1985, 81; emphasis added).

Elder Bednar, in another talk, issued these words: "The baptismal covenant clearly contemplates **a future event or events** and looks forward to the temple" ("Honorably Hold a Name and Standing," general conference, April 2009; emphasis added).

I believe that the "event or events" referred to by Elder Bednar is when the Lord visits us through the *manifestations* of His Spirit in power when we are born of God.

Alma called it a "mighty change" for a reason, not to tease or entice us into striving for that which was unattainable. It is mighty, because this experience allows us to come to ***the***

***knowledge of the Lord while in our flesh**, with the same certainty and joy as if we had seen Him (see Mosiah 3:13).*

This certainty is there because we will have come into His presence and partaken of a portion of His glory, even while His personage was shrouded by the veil. And keep in mind that we can all come into His presence without Him necessarily standing right next to us in the form of His personage, although either way it will certainly feel like He is there. Remember, He is God. Spiritual rebirth is preparatory to being in His Presence both in this world and in the world of glory to come (see D&C 76:117-118).

Can we better understand why receiving the Holy Ghost as a gift is not the same as having experienced the peaceful influence of the Spirit (i.e., Light of Christ) in our lives, which aids us in gaining faith-promoting experiences of testimony? These experiences of testimony, although wonderful, are not the "end all" or even the intended destination. They are given to nudge us onward in faith until such time as we receive this absolute certainty and knowledge of God ourselves, which is likewise when we partake of the redemption of Christ. If we stop along our journey of faith merely because we have obtained a testimony, we might cheat ourselves and our God of additional wonderous blessings He desires for us to receive. Remember, testimony is dynamic and subject to constant change. It either increases or decreases in strength within us, depending on our diligence. And as we nourish our faith and allow it to grow, our testimony too will grow, even until such time as we obtain a perfect knowledge of God and *experience redemption*. Elder Christofferson taught: "The greatest service we can provide to others in this life... is to bring them to Christ through faith and repentance, ***so they may <u>experience</u> His redemption***" (Elder D. Todd Christofferson, "Redemption," April General Conference Address, 2013). I would invite all to allow Christofferson's words to sink deep within our souls.

Fellow seeker, to "come to the knowledge of God" *<u>is</u>* to be redeemed by Christ, and vice versa:

*"And my prayer to God is... that they... come to **the knowledge of God**, yea, **the redemption of Christ**" (Words of Mormon 1:8; emphasis added).*

To come to the knowledge of God is to be converted. To be converted is to be redeemed by Christ and to thereby *know Him*. This was revealed by God Himself to Joseph Smith, which was also spoken at the dedication of the Kirtland Temple: His words reaffirm the above: "That they may be ***converted and redeemed*** with Israel, and ***know*** that thou art God" (Doctrine and Covenants 109:70). These three are all part of the same experience—to be *converted, redeemed*, and *know* that He is God.

Elder Neal A. Maxwell references his own redemptive experience this way: "I had been *blessed*, and I knew that God knew, that I knew, I had been *blessed*" (as cited by Neil L. Anderson, "Overcoming the World," general conference, April 2017). Listen again to the words of Elder Holland from an earlier chapter: "I know that in my own life, that salvation is not a cheap *experience" ("Missionary Work and the Atonement,"* from a talk given at the Provo (Utah) Missionary Training Center on 20 June 2000, Ensign, Mar. 2001*;* emphasis added*)*. Fellow seeker: I have searched the Book of Mormon tirelessly and have not found one instance that describes the born of God experience as a process over a lifetime, void of reconciliation and this life-changing and nature-changing encounter with the Son of God. Joseph said, "We ***must*** have *a change of heart* to see the kingdom of God, and subscribe the articles of adoption to enter therein" (*Teachings of the Prophet Joseph Smith,* p. 339). And these articles of adoption are those found within the doctrine of Christ. It is my witness that the journey to spiritual rebirth can be a long and arduous process that can lead to actual reconciliation with God through a mighty change *experience*, and grace for grace. I know of no other way.

Notwithstanding the above, I'll confess the following. I really pray that there is another way. I pray for this because I have many family members who have not received of this endowment, as defined by the Prophet Joseph, even "***the same*** as given on the day of Pentecost" (see *Teachings of the Prophet Joseph Smith,* p. 149). I'd also say that I know that salvation is a very personal matter. It is between the candidate and God. And I am not going to attempt to put God in a box, nor is it my place to tell the Almighty how He can or cannot deliver salvation. My full intent is simple, which is to instill a hope, confidence, and faith in the Savior, such that through one insignificant man's witness (and others'), the candidate for salvation might, through his "brokenness" and "descending into the depths" of repentance, *cry out* to God in faith from the very core of his being for the Savior's mercy in order to be healed, cleansed, and sanctified, made possible and preceded by having a committed willingness and determination to serve Him to the end of his mortal life and beyond. This is how we can all receive of this *mighty change of heart experience* for ourselves. This level of *willingness* will most likely have been previously demonstrated through the offering of our broken hearts and by sacrificing our comforts in the world in doing the compassionate works that we saw Him do during His earthly ministry.

Fellow seeker: Being born of God involves a change. A change witnesses as to an experience. Something happens to create this change. We do not perform this change upon ourselves or obtain it merely through our own works, for as the apostle Paul said, "Not of works, lest any man should boast" (Eph. 2:9).

> *The Mighty Change is done* ***to us****, performed* ***on us*** *and* ***in us <u>by God Himself</u>****, through a powerful manifestation of His Spirit, as an act of grace! It's a mighty change; not a weak, unnoticeable change. It's a mighty change of heart, which changes our very natures and desires away from that of the natural man to do*

that which is good—even "to do good continually" (Mosiah 5:2).

Let Us Reason Together on Striving for Full Conversion and Its Fruit

The Savior said, "And now come … and … let us reason together … even as a man reasoneth with another face to face" (D&C 50:10-11). Yes, let us then reason. Fellow seeker, if there were another way to achieve salvation, and God only knows there "may be," why would we still not reach for the sun (the Son) and attain to what is possible and that which has been promised according to the definition of the First Comforter given by Joseph Smith himself? And why would I want to pin the hopes of eternal salvation for myself and my family on a "maybe" that is experientially unknown to those who are receiving *the same endowment today* as likewise was modeled for us throughout *the days of Kirtland*, the *days of the ancient Church and apostles*, and in the *Book of Mormon*? How could I possibly "enjoy the words of eternal life *in this world*" (Moses 6:59; emphasis added) without this knowledge or otherwise have peace *in this world* (see D&C 59:23)?

The "words of eternal life" are the voice and spirit of revelation from God given to the recipient of salvation regarding his or her own redemption and promise of eternal life, in fulfillment of the promise which the Father hath made pertaining to the same, subject to enduring to the end. How could anyone "be sanctified from all sin, and ***enjoy*** the words of eternal life ***in this world***" if the "words of eternal life" were not attainable nor permitted to be *enjoyed* in this world? (see Moses 6:59). Allow this question to be fully digested.

You will note that the first thing that father Lehi did after partaking of the fruit was to look around for his family. He did this because he desired with all his heart to have his family members "taste" or experience this mighty change and *exceedingly great joy* for themselves, and to know God with a "perfect knowledge" and "unshakeable certainty," per Elder McConkie. I have desired nothing less than the same for my family, and now for you, my extended spiritual family and body of Christ.

A dear brother whom I spiritually know yet never had the chance of meeting in this life describes partaking of the love of God and experiencing the "exceedingly great joy," with its accompanying gifts of the Spirit, this way:

"Having had your soul filled with the joy of pure charity (resulting from the Rebirth), and a bright awareness of the remission of your sins (and 'perfect brightness of hope' in the reality and promise of eternal life for ourselves, per 2nd Nephi 31:20), you feel such a profound sense of love that you soon seek the Lord in prayer. As you kneel in humble silence, the Holy Spirit burns within you, until you are consumed with

> *spiritual fire. You raise your voice as the Spirit gives utterance. Your words become pure praise and worship (this is "the speaking with the tongue of the angels," referenced by Nephi as a noticeable fruit which occurs during Spiritual Rebirth), and soon become an outpouring of worship so pure it transcends speech, eclipses poetry, and is more beautiful than music. It is the song of the angels and the incense of precious odors which ascends up before the throne of God day and night. It is the song of redeeming love, and is sung only by those divinely inspired to sing it. It is soul filling, and is pure, sustained revelation. It is a two-way exchange of love of the highest magnitude, and while seeming to be only moments long, may last many hours. It refines the soul as nothing else can, and leaves the participant both fulfilled, fed, and overjoyed. This is when you finally understand the phrase, "my cup runneth over." (Pontius, "Following the Light of Christ into His Presence," p. 159; emphasis added).*

This "speaking with the tongue of the angels" or speaking "forth marvelous words" were made manifest in the early days of our Church's history:

> *"The other quorums were more careful, and the quorum of the Seventy enjoyed* ***a great flow of the Holy Spirit****. Many arose and spoke, testifying that they were* ***filled with the Holy Ghost, which was like fire in their bones****, so that* ***they could not hold their peace****, but were* ***constrained to cry hosanna to God and the lamb, and glory in the highest****" (History of the Church, p. 392; emphasis added).*

This, fellow sojourner, is what Nephi meant when he referenced "speaking with the tongue of the angels" or as referenced in Helaman where many spoke forth "marvelous words."

I'd say one additional thing concerning this mighty change experience, which is witnessed as to having entered God's presence by partaking of a portion of His glory. I have several friends that I know who have received the spiritual rebirth as Joseph described—even as on the day of Pentecost. And at the time in which they received this holy endowment, they absolutely *knew* that they had been blessed in a most profound way. Their rebirth experience had lasted for several days and nights in power, with lasting fruits that exist to this day. They knew that their hearts and very natures had been changed in a mighty way as well, *but they did not know that what had happened to them was referred to in scripture as a "baptism of fire.*" They did not know they had been born again in that moment. In other words, "they knew it not," as described of the Lamanites in 3 Nephi, chapter 9. In fact, even though one of them had been inactive for many years and did not know the scriptures at all, he had always referred to his experience as his "baptism of fire."

This baptism of fire is experienced differently for a Gentile than, say, for one who is the natural seed of Abraham. This is why I have often referenced this distinction. In this example, the experience for one who is of the natural seed of Abraham, according to the Prophet Joseph, is more "calm and serene," which would make it less perceptible perhaps to the one receiving it. This could conceivably be the reason and give us further insight into those of the Lamanites (who were naturally of the seed of Abraham), who received the baptism of fire, yet "knew it not."

Again, salvation is a very personal matter between the candidate and God. We must ask Him if we have been born of Him or born of the Spirit, and keep asking until we know directly from Him, and not from what man may opine, so that we can have "peace in this world" (D&C 59:23). How could we have peace otherwise? For it appears that unless we (meaning, those who are members of Christ's Church) are born again during this mortal existence, we may not be able to return to where God is in the eternities. Pay close attention to these words from the Prophet Joseph on the subject:

> *"But except a man be born again, he cannot see the kingdom of God. This eternal truth settles the question of all men's religion. A man may be saved, after the judgment, in the terrestrial kingdom, or in the telestial kingdom, but* ***he can never see the celestial kingdom of God without being born of the water and the Spirit****" (History of the Church, 1:283; emphasis added).*

Remember also Elder McConkie's words. The extent to which we both receive the Holy Ghost and enjoy its fruits and companionship is the extent to which we become sanctified. The more sanctification, the better, correct? So let's shoot for the heavens and not be complacent with anything less than a mighty change delivered by God to our hearts! This mighty change was delivered to the saints in the Book of Mormon. This mighty change was delivered to the ancient saints on and after the day of Pentecost. This mighty change was delivered to the saints at Kirtland. And the same can be delivered to us, personally and individually even now, in the privacy of our own homes and within our own souls, if we diligently seek the Lord in faith. We are to latch on with all our might in seeking to obtain Him and His baptism of us, and never give up. Remember the pattern: Desire. Ask, Seek, Knock—Receive. Then repeat.

Let's Go for It!

Elder McConkie counseled us to ***go for it***! Said he, "Oh that we might rend the heavens and know what the ancients knew. Oh that we might pierce the veil and see all that our forebears knew.... Oh, that we might see, and know and *feel*... ***he who is no respecter of persons*** calls us with his own voice; if we will but attune our ears, we shall hear his words" (*Mortal Messiah,* p. 372; emphasis added). We can and must know by experience ourselves! Elder Maxwell provides this gem: "This life is not lineal, it is *experiential.* It is not really chronological, though we use clocks and calendars and wristwatches. *It is essentially experiential.* Someone said it well, 'we live in deeds, not years, in thoughts, not breaths, in feelings, not figures on a dial and we really should count times, by heart throbs' (Phillip James Bailey)" ("If Thou Endure Well," BYU Fireside, December 4, 1984).

We are told by the Prophet Joseph: "Reading the experience of others, or the revelation given to them, can *never* give us a comprehensive view of *our condition* and true relation to God. *Knowledge of these things [and our own condition before God] can only be obtained* **by experience** [made possible] through the ordinances of God set forth for that purpose" (*Teachings of the Prophet Joseph Smith,* p. 324; emphasis added).

Notice that the very purpose of the ordinances is to give us a comprehensive view of our condition and true relation to God through *experiential means.* Mark it well! The candidate of salvation receives it ***by personal experience***, which is made possible through the ordinances of God for the intended purpose of obtaining this actual knowledge of God, so that we no longer need remain in mystery as to our own standing before Him, or as to whether we have been born of Him or not. *We will know it because we will have experienced it.* How can we obtain any knowledge by experience without an awareness that the experience has even happened? "The Prophet insisted that ***true religion was one of individual participation in revelation [i.e., personal experience] from God***" (*The Words of Joseph Smith,* p. 21; emphasis added).

Step 6 of the LDS Addiction Recovery Program, entitled, "Change of Heart," says: "As you yield to the promptings of the Spirit and look to the Savior for salvation, not only from addiction but from character weaknesses, you can be assured that a new... character will grow out of your willing heart. [Now notice.] ***A growing desire*** *to be* <u>*sanctified by God*</u> *will make you ready for a change in your very nature" (see Step 6, "Change of Heart," found on https://addictionrecovery.churchofjesuschrist.org).* This change involves a process and leads the candidate of salvation to reconciliation. It begins with *desire, endures with faith, and culminates in a climactic, experiential change in our very nature.* I witness that this statement from the above program "Change of Heart" to be true by way of ***direct experience*** just as I know that I live, and that Christ lives. And it begins with the very first word of our Diagram from Chapter 1—that of *Desire.*

My daughter Chantelle Bishop, wrote and recorded a song as a gift to me and her mother for Father's and Mother's Day, respectively. It can be found on YouTube. I include the lyrics here which point to this desire to find and know God. Notice the perfect number in which she references the word desire. Her song is entitled, "Through Jesus Christ":

> *"Through all things, there is Christ. Inside of me is His light. I feel His love within my soul,* ***'I desire you Lord'****. Through my faith, He is leading me. Through my doubt, He still blesses me.*
>
> *"Through my pain, and my fears,* ***I desire… to draw nearer****, Oh nearer to my God.*
>
> *Through Jesus Christ, I am free, Oh Jesus has come to save me! Yes Jesus, has come to save me, granting His grace and peace.*
>
> *"Through the broken and the hopeless, through my prayers He shows me how he cares. I will give all to Him,* ***I desire… to draw nearer, and grow to know my God****.*
>
> *Through Jesus Christ, I'm made clean, Oh Jesus is here to save me! Yes, Jesus, is here to save me, granting His grace and peace. Peace. Giving His love to me. Tenderly comforting me. His angels surrounding me…"*
>
> *(Music and Lyrics of "Through Jesus Christ," by Chantelle Bishop; also found on Youtube.com. Make sure to also listen to "For You Alone," a song of the journey of faith to Spiritual Rebirth written and sung by my wife, Rebecca Bishop, found on PuttingOnChrist.com).*

Notice the progression in the above lyrics. Chantelle first desires her Lord. This leads her to the desire to draw nearer to her God. Then her desire to draw nearer transitions to a desire to know her God, which is to *come to the knowledge of Him by way of direct experience*. Jesus Christ is the Savior of all those who avail themselves of His offering through obedience to His gospel law. And as so eloquently stated by Chantelle, it all begins with the ***desire*** for our Lord, to ***draw nearer*** to our God, and then to ***know*** Him.

A Concluding Recipe for Spiritual Life—to My Children

I close this chapter with a recipe I have given my children to follow in order to find the knowledge of God for themselves. Those words found below in bold are by design.

1. ***Desire*** to actually know the Father, the Christ, and Their reality by first coming unto Christ and *desiring* to know and meet Him again. We met and knew

Him before the foundation of this world, and we must come to know Him again here. The circumstances of this meeting are of most importance. This belief and desire to know Them, if continually nurtured, will fuel our entire journey. As Alma suggests, "Let this *desire* work in you."

2. Be a lifetime, perpetual seeker of Christ. ***Make seeking Him a way of life***. Time is of the essence, for this life is the time for men and women to prepare to meet God. If we ask, seek, and knock, the promise is that we *shall find.* Remember, if we are not *diligent seekers*, we cannot be finders.

3. Practice experientially, ***daily loving God*** with *all* your heart, *all* your might, *all* your mind, and *all* your strength. Knowing to do this is not the same as doing it. The Lord loves and redeems those who love Him with *all*. Loving God is not done out of compulsion or some future reward. Loving God in the present moment ***is*** its own reward. This love will melt the heart walls and unseal the mind, making it possible for God to reach, contact, and direct us unto salvation.

4. Be wise by taking ***the Holy Spirit as your guide***. The Spirit or Light of Christ will lead us to the reception of both Comforters. The First Comforter, when received and consistently enjoyed, will prepare and sanctify us in order to receive the Second. Trust the unseen truths through the Spirit over the "proofs" or "evidences" of men, reason, or logic. The latter are mostly folly. By doing so, we will not be deceived and "shall not be hewn down and cast into the fire, but shall abide the day" when the Lord comes in glory (D&C 45:57).

It's all pretty straightforward. We just have to now choose to DO and LIVE it, 100%, "All In."

Chapter 7

Putting on Christ

And again I say, hearken unto my voice, lest death shall overtake you; in an hour when ye think not the summer shall be past, and the harvest ended, and your souls not saved. Listen to him who is the advocate with the Father, who is pleading your cause before him (D&C 45:2-3).

From the Preamble:

> *As long as we make the offering of a broken heart through surrender, in contriteness to God from the altar of our souls, entering the depths of repentance, while having received of His ordinances, and demonstrate that diamond-hard, committed "willingness" to risk everything to know Him—to be 'all in' with Him from our hearts, IT IS ULTIMATELY HIS BESTOWAL OF FAITH AS AN ENDOWMENT OF POWER THAT SAVES. This salvation arises through that catalyst of 'falling down and crying out to Him' with all that we have and are, one whom we have never before seen with our natural eyes though nevertheless is real, allowing our desperate plea for his atoning blood to both heal and cleanse. Through this very personal journey, we will have been led to a mini-gethsemane of our own to further appreciate and comprehend of His offering, WHILE RELYING ALONE UPON HIS MERITS, MERCY, AND GRACE. In an instant, the promised gift of the Father can then be received through an inner commitment to abandon one's self and one's will to God. This is when we completely surrender and 'let go'...into His ineffably loving arms. It is by way of this ultimate expression of submission, that we will have found Oneness and spiritual union in Him, together with unspeakable joy in the Holy Ghost. This is the fulfillment of the promise of the Father. This is Salvation. This is Putting On Christ.*

Notice in the following scriptures below the key principles of being saved by grace, through faith, and accompanied with true repentance.

"Yea, repent and be baptized, every one of you, for a remission of your sins; yea, be baptized even by water, and then cometh the ***baptism of fire*** *and of the Holy Ghost. Behold, verily, verily, I say unto you,* *this is my gospel;* ***and remember that they shall have faith in me or they can in nowise be saved"*** *(D&C 33:11-12).*

"By grace are ye saved, ***through faith****; and that not of yourselves:* ***it is the gift of God****" (Ephesians 2:8-9).*

"...the plan of redemption... ***according to their faith and repentance*** *and their holy works" (Alma 12:30).*

"And no unclean thing can enter into his kingdom; therefore nothing entereth into his rest save it be those who have washed their garments in my blood, ***because of their faith****, and the repentance of all their sins, and their faithfulness unto the end" (3 Ne. 27:19).*

"That the blessing of Abraham might come on the Gentiles through Jesus Christ; that we might ***receive the promise of the Spirit through faith****" (Gal. 3:14).*

"And I said: Lord, how is it done? And he said unto me: ***Because of thy faith in Christ****, whom thou hast never before heard nor seen" (Enos 1:7-8).*

"...that salvation might come unto the children of men even ***through faith*** *on his name..." (Mosiah 3:9).*

"...We are made alive in Christ ***because of our faith*** *and we keep the law because of the commandments" (2 Ne. 25:25).*

*"...****remission of sins through faith*** *on the Lord Jesus Christ" (3 Nephi 7:16).*

"...and nothing can save this people save it be ***repentance and faith*** *on the Lord Jesus Christ" (Helaman 13:6).*

"...for ye say that your hearts are changed ***through faith*** *on his name; therefor ye are born of him and have become his sons and his daughters" (Mosiah 5:7).*

"...and since man had fallen he could not merit anything himself; but the sufferings and death of Christ atone for their sins, ***through faith and repentance...*** *" (Alma 22:14).*

"And it came to pass that Nephi... went forth... and began to testify, boldly, repentance and remission of sins ***through faith*** *on the Lord Jesus Christ"*
(3 Ne. 7:16).

"...that they may be purified in me, ***through faith...*** *" (3 Nephi 19:28).*

"For ye are all the children of God by faith in Christ Jesus" (Gal. 3:36).

"... ***remission of sins*** *by Jesus Christ,* ***by the endurance of faith on his name...*** *" (Moroni 3:3).*

"And after that he came men also were ***saved by faith*** *in his name; and* ***by faith****, they become the sons of God..." (Moroni 7:26).*

" ***redemption, through faith*** *on the name of mine Only Begotten Son"*
(D&C 29:42).

"...rely upon the merits of Jesus Christ and be ***glorified through faith*** *in his name..." (D&C 3:20).*

"... ***salvation through faith*** *which is in Christ Jesus" (2 Timothy 3:15).*

"And whoso ***having faith*** *you shall confirm in my Church, by the laying on of the hands, and I will bestow the gift of the Holy Ghost upon them"*
(D&C 33:15).

"And the scripture, foreseeing that God would justify the heathen ***through faith****, preached before the gospel unto*

Abraham, saying, In thee shall all nations be blessed" (Gal. 3:8).

"But that no one is justified by the law in the sight of God, it is evident: for, The just shall live ***by faith****" (Gal. 3:11).*

"That the blessing of Abraham might come on the Gentiles through Jesus Christ; that we might receive ***the promise of the Spirit through faith****" (Gal. 3:14).*

"Yea, even he commanded them that they should preach nothing save it were ***repentance and faith on the Lord****, who had redeemed his people. "And thus he commanded them to preach.* ***And thus they became the children of God****" (Mosiah 18:20, 22).*

"... the Holy Ghost; which ***power*** *he received* ***by faith*** *on the Son of God"*
(1 Ne. 10:17).

"For the promise... was not to Abraham or to his seed through the law, but through ***the righteousness of faith****" (Rom. 4:13).*

"And of tenets thou shalt not talk, but thou shalt declare ***repentance and faith on the Savior****, and remission of sins by baptism, and by fire, yea, even the Holy Ghost" (D&C 19:31).*

"Wherefore the law was our schoolmaster to bring us unto Christ, that we might be ***justified by faith****.*
But after that faith is come, we are no longer under a schoolmaster.
For ye are all the children of God ***by faith in Christ Jesus****.*
For as many of you as have been baptized into Christ have put on Christ.
And if ye be Christ's, then are ye Abraham's seed, and heirs according to the promise."

(Galatians 3:23-27, 29)

Welcome to the most important chapter of this work, which is "Putting on Christ." We'll start with each line of the above scripture from Galatians chapter 3, and then I'll add commentary in an attempt to build upon it:

WHEREFORE THE LAW WAS OUR SCHOOLMASTER TO BRING US UNTO CHRIST

The "law" here refers to the law of Moses and other performances under the Jewish law, yet for our purposes will be likened unto the checklist of all the "to do's" (i.e., "works of the law") and other responsibilities we are expected to perform in the Church. John said that "the law was given by Moses, but grace and truth come by Jesus Christ" (John 1:17). These performances under the law for the law's sake are most critical until they are supplanted by a greater law.

What do I mean by that? At some point we will not be under the law of performances, but we will be led by following God through the Comforter given to abide in us (see Moses 6:61). "Do we then make void the law through faith? God forbid: yea, we establish the law" (Rom, 3:31). Paul also said it this way: "But if you are led by the Spirit, ye are not under the law" (Gal. 5:18). "The Spirit" in this context is referring to those who have received the Holy Ghost. Allow me to further elaborate. The "law" may suggest that we do our ministering visits to the two or three (or more) families that we have been assigned. The Comforter may lovingly direct us to minister to not only our assigned families but to also visit several more that may be spiritually hurting—and who may or may not be in our ward. The Lord is not confined by ward boundaries, and neither should we be. If we have a connection to someone who is hurting, the Spirit will bring that person to our heart, mind, and awareness, and we will immediately reach out to that person as an enlisted soldier in the Lord's cause.

The critical works are those required in order to "do the things which I have told you I have seen that your Lord and your Redeemer should do; for, for this cause have they been shown unto me" (2 Ne. 31:17). We can then become *justified by faith.* In the beginning, we might do the works strictly out of obedience, perhaps without even a desire to do so. But as we continue, faith begins to develop through grace until, through an accumulation of this faith, we are able to cry out and rely alone upon the merits of Christ and surrender all to Him. This is when we come under the One Law and abide in Christ and He in us. This is when we are no longer abiding under "the law of performances." Abinidi taught that although salvation (which includes justification and sanctification) did not come by the law, "*the law of Moses did serve to strengthen their faith in Christ*" (Alma 25:16; emphasis added). This faith then, through all things that build faith in us (including the works of the law), continues to build until a sufficiency of that living faith is bestowed, resulting in a change, even a mighty one. Then the Comforter will abide in us. This Comforter then becomes the rock upon which we are built, that rock of revelation which flows to us and in us as living waters.

After tasting of the glorious "fruit," however, and through the *Oneness* experienced with God and with seemingly all living things, our natures and desires become changed miraculously by God so that they become totally in alignment with His. When you have the same desire as God, service and loving your fellow man will no longer be a drudgery or a "have to"—it will then become part of your spiritual DNA. Obedience and service will be your pathway of joy! We will do what "we want to do," only it just so happens that what we want to do is what the Lord desires for us as well. What a blessing! This is why we needn't fear surrendering control of our lives to God. This is where true freedom comes from during spiritual rebirth, not the chains and shackles in "surrendering our will" in the sense of no longer having an individual will. Loss of identity is what the adversary of our souls whispers in our ears in order to scare us away from pursuing such a course. In other words, obedience is no longer confining, but liberating. It becomes our newfound authentic and true freedom because our personal will becomes intertwined in the Divine will. The conflict between our wants and God's wants are removed. The inner battle is obliterated—at least for a season. (But be wary—some of it will resurface later to test our resolve.)

Obedience to God is not designed to enslave us to any one or any thing. On the contrary, it is designed to generate and instill in us the *true freedom and independence of heaven.* Through our allegiance to the divine law of Christ and partaking of His ordinances, we can be rewarded with endowments of His Light and Truth (that Divine Spirit of Intelligence or glory) by degrees until we receive a fullness thereof. This is how we become a truly independent being of glory, in and through Him, *authentically free and freed from the constraints of the adversary and natural man.* This is how we are initiated by God and immersed in His mind during spiritual rebirth, one in Christ as He is one with and in the Father. This is how *in the resurrection* we may forever "become heirs of the heavenly kingdom, and joint heirs with Jesus Christ; *possessing the same mind*, being transformed into the same image or likeness, even the express image of him who fills all in all; being filled with the fullness of His glory…" (see *Lectures On Faith* 5:2; emphasis added).

It is therefore clearly in our own best interest to follow Christ's admonition and pleading by obeying the laws and ordinances of His revealed gospel. It is through this *freedom-yielding obedience* that we place ourselves in a position to grow grace for grace and grace to grace until we become like our Father, giving glory, honor, and praise to Him for all eternity because of the eternal joy we shall be experiencing through and in Him. It is through our bowels of eternal gratitude that we will willingly and joyfully yield our eternal obedience, allegiance, and praise to our God. And we do this, not on the basis of compulsion or coercion, but upon the principle of authentic love for Him, by and through our own free will, choice, and volition. Hence, the purpose of the first and great commandment.

The law as our schoolmaster is akin to the training wheels used when first learning to ride a bike. We must do the basics until such time as we are able to graduate to the next level. And that next level occurs when we "act in the [gospel] belief" that has been revealed to us by the Spirit or Light of Christ, thereby accumulating additional gifts of faith by grace until we reach that point of faith that brings forth the promised blessing of the Father—the baptism of fire and of the Holy Ghost, which both saves and redeems.

THAT WE MAY BE JUSTIFIED BY FAITH

Here the law of justification is introduced, which also arises out of faith. It is because of our ***exceeding faith in Christ***, while relying upon the merits of Christ alone, that we are justified. In Mosiah we read, "And it came to pass that after they had spoken these words the Spirit of the Lord came upon them, and they were filled with joy, having received a remission of their sins, and having peace of conscience, ***because of the exceeding faith which they had in Jesus Christ*** who should come, according to the words which king Benjamin had spoken unto them" (Mosiah 4:3; emphasis added). This faith is perfect and comes from a perfect God.

For us to be "justified" means that we must arrive at that point of faith where we, in fact, relied alone upon the merits of Christ and His atonement in fulfillment of divine law. As long as we receive the baptism of water and are given "the promise of the Father" confirmed upon us by the laying of hands, we can merit the fulfillment and bestowal of this promised blessing which is the reception of that sure promise of eternal life, the actual gift of the Holy Ghost, and other gifts of the Spirit—subject to satisfying the fullness of the divine law involved. In order to receive any promised blessing, the "covenant, contracts, bonds, obligations, oaths, vows, performances, connections, associations, or expectations" (D&C 132:7) "must be entered into *and performed in righteousness* so that the Holy Spirit can justify the candidate for salvation in what has been done" (*Mormon Doctrine,* "Justification," p. 408). *An act that is justified by the Spirit is one that is sealed by the Holy Spirit of Promise, or in other words, ratified and approved by the Holy Ghost*" (ibid, p. 408). This "act" is what allows the promised blessing of the Father to be bestowed, even by fire and the Holy Ghost. Elder McConkie adds that "ratification and approval by the Holy Ghost" "is to assure that no unrighteous performance will be binding on earth and in heaven, and that no person will add to his position or glory in the hereafter by gaining an unearned [or what I would term, an 'unmerited'] blessing" (ibid. p. 408).

The power of Christ and His atoning blood both initially justifies us and sanctifies us. Man being justified by the Spirit refers to the divine manner in which *man is led to obtain justification before the bar and law of God.* To be justified is to be made "righteous" by the Atoning One as an act of grace. This act of grace stems from man having received divine approval from the Deity, *protecting man from the full weight and force of the law of justice.* Justification deals mainly with man's "acquittal" from the demands of having broken God's law. "And we know that justification through the grace of our Lord and Savior Jesus Christ is just and true" (D&C 20:30).

In the context of partaking of spiritual rebirth, God will have approved and sanctioned man's faith and repentance, his full purpose of heart tied to an unbending willingness to serve Him to the end, the ordinance of baptism by water, and the ordinance by the laying on of hands for the reception of the Holy Ghost. We are fully justified when we are made "*just men in Christ,*" through His Atonement. The apostle Paul taught that "a man is not justified by the works of the law, but by the faith of Jesus Christ," and added, "for by the works of the law shall no flesh be justified" (Gal. 2:16). Father Lehi similarly declared, "By the law, no flesh is justified" (2 Ne. 2:5).

"And we know also, that sanctification through the grace of our Lord and Savior Jesus Christ is just and true [now take notice], *to all those who love and serve God with all their mights, minds, and strength*" (D&C 20:31). When we receive the gospel, we do so that we "may be sanctified ["Saint-ified"] by the reception of the Holy Ghost" and thereby become true Latter-day Saints, in all actuality, and be able to stand spotless before the judgment bar of Christ (3 Ne. 27:19-21). After spiritual rebirth, we are pure and newborn babes in Christ, yet there still is a further process of ongoing sanctification unto holiness through the Comforter which is given to abide in us throughout our journey of enduring to the end. God, by way of this Comforter (and through our works of grace for others by performing the compassionate works of and for Christ), cleanses and additionally *infuses* the attributes of godliness in us, grace for grace—even to an eventual fulness in the resurrection. "For salvation consists in the glory, authority, majesty, power, and dominion which Jehovah possesses and in nothing else; and no being can possess it but Himself or one like Him" (*Lectures On Faith,* 7:9).

Both justification and sanctification are gifts of grace from God. We cannot merit them in and of ourselves. We can only qualify for them through aligning our will to the holy will of God in following His gospel and to "live by every word ['for (His) word is Spirit'] which proceedeth forth from the mouth of God" (D&C 98:11).

BUT AFTER THAT FAITH IS COME, WE ARE NO LONGER UNDER A SCHOOLMASTER

"But after that faith is come…": notice that this faith *comes*. Who does it come from? It comes from God as a gift and an endowment of power. Why? Because we will have entered the waters demonstrating our faith, received the laying on of hands, and made the requisite offering of *our all* to God—that of a broken heart in complete surrender. What this verse is saying is that when we finally, after perhaps years of seeking, attain that bestowal of faith as an endowment of power that saves (from God Himself), arising out of our obedience to the gospel law, we will no longer be beholden to a schoolmaster, the law of performances, or checklist of "do's and don'ts." As the apostle Paul taught: "If you are led by the Spirit, you are not under the law" (Gal 5:18), for we will have received power from on high through a manifestation of the Lord's Spirit, which is liberating, not confining. President Ezra Taft Benson said, "When obedience ceases to be an irritant and becomes our quest, in that moment God will endow us with power" (as cited in Donald L. Staehli, "Obedience—Life's Great Challenge," *Ensign,* May 1998, 82). And so it is.

After the bestowal of faith comes as an endowment of power from God sufficient to save us, we will then be redeemed and adopted into the family of Christ, thereby becoming His sons and His daughters. We then walk after the Spirit. As the apostle Paul says, "That the righteousness of the law might be fulfilled in us, who walk not after the flesh, but after the Spirit" (Rom 8:4). Paul also says that through this bestowal of faith by God, "we have been delivered from the law, having died to what we were held by, so that we should serve in the newness of the Spirit and not in the *oldness of the letter*" (Rom. 7:6). "But after that faith has come," we will no longer need to be "commanded in all things" but will be led by God directly, through the power of the Holy Ghost, by way of the Comforter which has been given to abide in us (see Moses 6:61). "It will show unto [us] all things that [we] should do" (2 Ne. 32:5). God's intention is for all to become prophets. And prophets are all those who have in truth received the Holy Ghost. And by prophets I do not mean the various prophets who are called to guide the Church, but who through personal revelation so live as to continue to receive that personal guidance from God directly in order to be steered out of harm's way and brought safely and individually back to the Father.

Elder McConkie, whose words are confirmed by the Spirit, instructed us that "any person who receives the revelation that Jesus Christ is the Lord [i.e., obtains 'the knowledge of God'] *is a prophet* and can, as occasion requires and when guided by the Spirit, 'prophesy of all things'" (*The Promised Messiah,* p. 240). Hence, the apostle John revealed that "the testimony of Jesus is the spirit of prophecy" (Rev. 19:10). John Taylor said that, in regards to "the life and light and power and intelligence which the Gospel imparted [through the reception of the actual Holy Ghost], ... it shall place them in communion with God and enable them to have dreams and visions, to prophesy and see things to come; in other words, it will make them Prophets" (John Taylor, JD 16:301). Moses exclaimed, "Would to God that all the Lord's people were prophets, and that the Lord would put his spirit upon them!" (Num: 11:29).

Every man or woman who obtains the actual knowledge of God through spiritual rebirth is a prophet in this sense. That's why the Prophet Joseph said, "No man can receive the Holy Ghost without receiving revelations" (*Teachings of the Prophet Joseph Smith,* p. 328). I believe this is what the Book of Mormon was referring to, for example, when it says that "there came prophets in the land again, crying repentance unto them—that they must prepare the way of the Lord" (Ether 9:28). Enos also mentions that, "there were exceeding many prophets among us" (Enos 1:22). These prophets entered in *by the way* and received the actual Holy Ghost. The Lord desires all to be prophets to receive personal revelation to guide themselves so "that every man might speak in the name of God the Lord, even the Savior of the world" (D&C 1:20).

FOR YE ARE ALL THE CHILDREN OF GOD BY FAITH IN CHRIST JESUS

King Benjamin emphasizes the apostle Paul's words this way: "For ye say that your *hearts are changed through faith* on his name; therefor ye are born of him and have become his sons and his daughters" (Mosiah 5:7; emphasis added). After all gospel requirements have been met under the law, it is a bestowal of faith by God Himself as an endowment of power that saves. As we grasp hold of the iron rod of personal revelation, guided by the Light of Christ, we will be led to act in accordance with these promptings and feelings. In other words, the Spirit will lead us to repent with godly sorrow, forgive all who have wronged us, offer up the broken heart in contriteness, fall down (literally, figuratively, or both) in our brokenness, and cry out from our souls in pure and *perfect faith (which is a power bestowed), relying alone upon Christ's merits, mercy, and grace.*

Although works are a required and necessary component to arrive to this point of faith on many levels through that schoolmaster, especially those "works" of whole repentance together with a diamond-hard willingness to do the Father's will in all things, *it is ultimately His bestowal of faith as an endowment of power that saves and redeems us.* Obviously, the works of the law, law of performances, or "checklist," especially when performed from our heart space, contributes to that faith which allows us to arrive to that life-saving level and quality of faith. But ultimately, it is His bestowal of a perfect faith. When we receive an endowment of power from God called "faith" as a gift of grace, this is when we receive that "aliveness of faith" and are justified by the Holy Spirit of Promise and thus subsequently born again. This is when we "take upon [us] the name of [His] Son" (Mor. 4:3), and thereby become adopted into the family of Christ. John said, in referring to Christ, "to them gave he *power* to become the sons of God" (John 1:12; emphasis added). This power is that *faith bestowed which instantaneously comes alive in us.* We receive of this power or endowment of a bestowed, perfect faith when we are justified by the Spirit against the bar of God's law and justice. This is when the Comforter is given to abide *in us* (Moses 6:61). This is when we are then able to "put on Christ" through His grace. This is when we can then say, like the apostle Paul, "nevertheless I live; yet not I, but Christ liveth in me" (Gal. 2:20).

FOR AS MANY OF YOU AS HAVE BEEN BAPTIZED INTO CHRIST HAVE PUT ON CHRIST

Baptism means "immersion." The word stems from the Greek *baptizo,* which "means to immerse or overwhelm, and that sprinkle is from the Greek verb 'rantizo', and means to scatter on by particles" (*Teachings of the Prophet Joseph Smith,* p. 269). By definition, we must be both immersed or overwhelmed in water and immersed or overwhelmed in the Holy Spirit. Being baptized into Christ implies that we have been "immersed in Christ," having received the anointing of His light and thereby taking upon us His name by grace, through our faith, by having made the eternal, unyielding commitment to follow Him. Through a broken-hearted personal crisis of sorts, we will be led to broken-hearted repentance in order to "cry out" to Him from the depths of our souls for mercy and to receive a remission of sins in order to be saved and redeemed. This cry of the soul must be tied to a diamond-hard willingness to serve Him to the end of our mortal lives and beyond. This will not be because we feel compelled to do so but rather because we ourselves desire to do so. When we are immersed in spiritual fire, He changes our very natures. In fact, immediately after being born of the Spirit, there is no obstacle or person in this stage of our progress that could stop us in our spiritual flight, not even from the entirety of all the demonic forces in hell combined. We will have endured our schoolmaster and performances of the law, and we would now be ready to soar like the eagle. We will have experienced the true freedom of heaven because our desires will have been changed and would now be united and intertwined with God's desire and will. This will arise as part of the fruit of having been "baptized in His name."

Being "baptized in His name" has, at a minimum, a dual meaning. The most obvious, of course, is that the ordinance for the baptism of water is uttered with words that include being baptized in the name of the Son. Every ordinance is performed in His name or includes His name, either specifically, spiritually, or both. Another name for "the Son" is Christ. And Christ is "the Light." We do everything in the gospel and in the Church in His name. The name *Christ* means "the Anointed One" or "Holy Anointing." To be baptized in His name may also signify a holy immersion in His Light that we receive when we are spiritually born of God. This is when we are immersed "in His Name" or "in His Light," thereby receiving of His holy anointing by the power of the Holy Ghost. "But the anointing which ye have received of him abideth in you, ***and ye need not that any man teach you***: but as the **same anointing** teacheth you of all things, and is truth, and is no lie, and even as it hath taught you, ye shall abide in him [meaning, in His Light]. If ye know that he is righteous, ye know that every one that doeth righteousness is born of him" (1 John 2:27, 29; emphasis added). In other words, if God is your teacher, why would you need man to teach you, unless of course, God were speaking through that man. "Therefore, it is given to ***abide in you***, the record of heaven; *the Comforter*" (Moses 6:61; emphasis added).

Many Christian religions may "christen" a child when only a few months old, which in their tradition means to baptize the child. Another definition of christening involves either to name or to dedicate or set something or someone apart. "They christened the baby Anne Marie"; "They christened her the reigning Queen of Tennis"; or "They christened and dedicated the new naval ship, the *Ronald Reagan*." Notice the similarities. To christen is also to anoint. When we are "baptized into Christ" or "baptized in his name," we receive His holy anointing of light. We are baptized into Christ's light by complete immersion in it; we are thus spiritually born again, adopted into the family of Christ. We have taken upon us this new name of

Christ, by adoption. Our new spiritual "last name," if you will, now becomes "Christ" instead of our given surname, just as in most societies an adopted child takes upon himself the surname of the adoptive parent. We are then dedicated and set apart for a new life in Christ. We have been baptized into Christ or "in his name." This is when we "put on Christ" and are born again into His family, no longer estranged but now "reconciled to God."

To be reconciled is to have the relationship repaired that was initially severed or ruptured as a result of the fall of Adam and Eve. Being the seed of fallen Adam and Eve, we all inherited this relationship that is in need of being individually mended, through whole or perfect faith, together with a "godly sorrow" type of repentance, or, as Alma calls it, "repenting nigh unto death."

AND IF YE BE CHRIST'S, THEN ARE YE ABRAHAM'S SEED, AND HEIRS ACCORDING TO THE PROMISE.

The "mighty change" can be so mighty and the change so impactful, renewing, and regenerating that during the spiritual rebirth there is a reshaping of our physical composition as well. To quote Joseph Fielding Smith, "Through the Holy Ghost the truth is woven into the very fibre and sinews of the body so that it cannot be forgotten" (*Doctrines of Salvation*, Vol. 1, p. 48). Elder Christofferson refers to it as "***a conversion so complete that it cannot be undone*** ("Firm and Steadfast in the Faith of Christ," October 2018 general conference; emphasis added). Lorenzo Snow, a prophet of the Church and one who was personally tutored by the Prophet Joseph Smith, referred to spiritual rebirth as obtaining "*divine manifestations*" (Lorenzo Snow, "The Gospel," Jan. 23, 1870; Journal of Discourses 13:284; emphasis added).

If immersion in the Holy Ghost is impactful enough that it cannot be forgotten or undone through divine manifestations, it must be a mighty experience. Through full conversion, we experience a transformation of sorts in our blood, whereby we become "actually of the seed of Abraham" (*Teachings of the Prophet Joseph Smith,* p. 149). We are then no longer known as the "fallen man" or the "seed of man" through Adam and Eve. We become the seed of Abraham our father, born and reconciled sons of God. For as the apostle John witnessed, these newborn sons "were born, not of blood, nor of the will of the flesh, nor of the will of man, but of God" (John 1:13).

When that time comes, being born of God, at least for a gentile, should leave little doubt or mystery as to what is happening to us. Joseph says, "The effect of the Holy Ghost ***upon a Gentile***, is to *purge out the old blood*, and ***make him actually of the seed of Abraham***. That man that has none of the blood of Abraham (naturally) must have a new creation by the Holy Ghost" (*Teachings of the Prophet Joseph Smith,* p. 149; emphasis added). To undergo such a change would indeed have to be considered mighty by any standard. This being made "actually of the seed of Abraham" is in fulfillment of that "covenant the Lord made to our father Abraham, saying: In thy seed shall all the kindreds of the earth be blessed" (1 Ne. 15:18). The Father fulfills His covenant with Abraham when He pours out the Holy Ghost upon us through Christ. We will then become the seed of Abraham, according to the Savior's own words: "And after that ye were ***blessed*** [code for spiritual rebirth] then fulfilleth the Father the covenant which he made with Abraham, saying: In thy seed shall all the kindreds of the earth be blessed [how?]—UNTO THE POURING OUT OF THE HOLY GHOST THROUGH ME UPON THE GENTILES" (3 Ne. 20:27; emphasis added). When the Holy Ghost is poured out upon us, it is in fulfillment of the promise of the Father we receive when we are confirmed in Christ's Church and told to "receive the Holy Ghost." This is the spiritual gathering of Israel. And in the winding up scene of the last days, there will be a literal one as well.

For those who have not undergone this change, it may sound wholly unbelievable. But to those who have and who possess little or none of the blood of Abraham naturally, the change is both spiritually and physiologically experienced and is wholly undeniable, unto the praise and glory of God! This is why "it cannot be forgotten" or "undone." During this transformation in the inner man, we then speak with the tongue of the angels and cannot help but shout praises unto the Holy One of Israel! We experience a oneness in God through "the peace of God, which passeth all understanding" (Philip. 4:7). We obtain eyes to see and ears to hear. When we listen to the accounts of those who have been fully converted to the Lord through spiritual rebirth, we might inquire, "Can there be a greater experiential joy and peace granted any man in mortality?"

Elder Boyd K. Packer spoke to the joy obtained by way of his own rebirth:

> *"Almost mid-sentence it happened. I could not describe to you what happened if I were determined to do so. It is* ***beyond my power of expression****, but it is as clear today as it was 65 years ago.* ***I knew*** *it to be a very private, very individual manifestation. At last* ***I knew*** *for myself.* ***I knew for a certainty****, for it had been given to me. After some time, I crawled from that bunker and walked, or floated, back to my bed. I spent the rest of the night in a feeling of* ***joy and awe****" ("The Witness," April 2014 general conference; emphasis added).*

Coming into the presence of God during spiritual rebirth is when the promise and blessings of Abraham are given, wherein Abraham was promised that through him, all the nations of the earth would be blessed, which blessing specifically entailed the promised blessing of eternal life.

Christ's Teaching to Nicodemus: The Necessity of Being Born Again

"Jesus answered and said unto him, Verily, verily, I say unto thee, Except a man be born again, he cannot see the kingdom of God.

"Nicodemus saith unto him, How can a man be born when he is old? can he enter the second time into his mother's womb, and be born?

"Jesus answered, Verily, verily, I say unto thee, Except a man be born of water and of the Spirit, he cannot enter into the kingdom of God" (John 3:3-5).

In referring to the Lord's words to Nicodemus above, President Spencer W. Kimball said, "This is the simple total answer to the weightiest of all questions. ... To gain eternal life there must be a rebirth, a transformation" (in Conference Report, Apr. 1958, p. 14)

King Lamoni asked, "*Yea, what shall I do that I may be born of God*"? In this chapter, the answer to this question will be given through the doctrine of Christ. This doctrine was first introduced in the Book of Mormon in plainness by the prophet Nephi.

The Doctrine of Christ according to the Prophet Nephi (See 2 Nephi 31)

The gospel of Christ is synonymous with the doctrine of Christ. The question then surfaces: Why have we not heard much about this doctrine which Nephi calls the Savior's "only and true doctrine"? Well, the fact is we have. We were perhaps just not clear on what it was called. Elder Bruce R. McConkie, in speaking of attaining exaltation and eternal life and thereafter living the kind of life that the Deity live, made this profound statement: "It follows that any teaching, *any doctrine*, any dramatization that can keep the mind of man riveted on his goal [of entering the Divine Presence and receiving eternal life] and on what he must do to gain it, *any such device is the greatest of all teaching devices"* (Bruce R. McConkie, "The Promised Messiah"; p. 132; emphasis added). So what doctrine would be the best doctrine to keep the mind of man riveted on his goal of knowing God and obtaining eternal life? If during Nephi's time the Deity believed that the doctrine of Christ was the only and true doctrine, would it not stand to reason that this should be the doctrine to understand most fully and comprehensively? Would it not become incumbent on us to learn as much as we possibly can about this doctrine known as the doctrine of Christ? So, let's search together steadfastly and diligently, shall we?

The doctrine of Christ is simply this—and it largely parallels the fourth article of faith, penned by Joseph Smith—faith, repentance with godly sorrow (which includes the offering of a broken heart with a contrite spirit of complete surrender to God's holy will), baptism for the intended purpose of a remission of sins, the gift of the Holy Ghost (as promised by the Father), which is confirmed on us by the laying on of hands, the *reception and enjoyment* of the Holy Ghost (with its accompanying baptism of fire, which is so transformative that it allows us as one of its fruits to speak with the tongue of angels, which are *words of praise* to the Holy One of Israel), and enduring to the end. The reception and enjoyment of the Holy Ghost occurs when the candidate for salvation has qualified by complying with the law upon which the promised blessing was predicated. The crowning and most significant moment of the doctrine of Christ is to be born again or born of the Spirit, to experience this "baptism of fire" which creates in us a mighty change of heart—a change in our very natures. ***This is the gate.*** Thereafter, we are to endure to the end in the quickening influence of His Spirit, achieved through our continued faith and faithfulness, through living by every word which proceeds from the mouth of God.

Elder McConkie taught that "the word of the gospel is written in the scriptures; *the power of the gospel* is written in the lives of those who ***both receive and enjoy the*** *gift of the Holy Ghost*" (*Doctrines of Salvation,* p. 237; emphasis added). To be born of the Spirit (or to both *receive and enjoy the companionship of the Holy Ghost),* puts us within the strait gate, having partaken of the fruit of the tree of life. Elder McConkie says that "***everyone upon whom the gift is bestowed does not in fact enjoy or possess the offered gift.*** In the case of the apostles the *actual enjoyment of the gift was delayed* until the day of Pentecost.... If and when [we] are worthy [i.e., which occurs when we are justified through the Holy Spirit of Promise], [we] are then immersed in the Spirit [and its accompanying manifestations in power, being 'quickened in the inner man'], as it were, ***thus actually enjoying the gift***" (*Doctrinal New Testament Commentary,* p. 857; emphasis added).

It is Nephi, the son of Lehi, who delivers *in clarity* the doctrine of Christ and even gives us an interesting description of how we can know if we have received the actual Holy Ghost, which includes the baptism of fire and the Holy Ghost. This clarity is spelled out *in plainness* in 2 Nephi, chapters 31 and 32. We will commence reading this together, and I will offer commentary in brackets. We'll begin with verse 2 of chapter 31.

The Doctrine of Christ according to Nephi (2 Nephi 31:2-20)

2 Wherefore, the things which I have written sufficeth me, save it be a few words which I must speak concerning the doctrine of Christ; wherefore, I shall speak unto you plainly, according to the plainness of my prophesying. [Here Nephi introduces "the doctrine of Christ" for the first time in the Book of Mormon].

3 For my soul delighteth in plainness; for after this manner doth the Lord God work among the children of men. For the Lord God giveth light unto the understanding; for he speaketh unto men according to their language, unto their understanding.

[Here Nephi discloses his love of speaking plainly, using a short, simple, and straightforward way in communicating to us. He wants us to understand in a manner that cannot be misunderstood or misinterpreted.]

4 Wherefore, I would that ye should remember that I have spoken unto you concerning that prophet which the Lord showed unto me, that should baptize the Lamb of God, which should take away the sins of the world.

[Nephi is introducing here John the Baptist, the ordained forerunner who baptized the Son of God and whom Nephi saw in vision.]

5 And now, if the Lamb of God, he being holy, should have need to be baptized by water, to fulfil all righteousness, O then, how much more need have we, being unholy, to be baptized, yea, even by water!

6 And now, I would ask of you, my beloved brethren, wherein the Lamb of God did fulfil all righteousness in being baptized by water?

7 Know ye not that he was holy? But notwithstanding he being holy, he showeth unto the children of men that, according to the flesh he humbleth himself before the Father, and witnesseth unto the Father that he would be obedient unto him in keeping his commandments.

[Nephi tells us that if Christ was baptized—who knew no sin—how much more so do we, as sinners, have need to be baptized. Although it was not technically necessary for Jesus to be baptized to cleanse Himself, He fulfilled all righteousness by setting the example for all of us to follow, ***thereby leaving us without excuse to do the same.*** We too must humble ourselves before the Father and witness unto Him that we will obey His commandments.]

8 Wherefore, after he was baptized with water the Holy Ghost descended upon him in the form of a dove.

[Notice here how simple these words. Christ was baptized with water by one having authority to do so. Then the Holy Ghost descended upon Him. This is the part that most of us forget. We must strive to have this Holy Ghost likewise descend upon us! This can only happen when we have complied with the entire gospel law and have, as Elder McConkie has instructed, "given ourselves without restraint to the Lord" (see *Mormon Doctrine,* "Born Again."]

9 And again, it showeth unto the children of men the straitness of the path, and the narrowness of the gate, by which they should enter, he having set the example before them.

[The definition of "the gate" is plainly set forth in verse 17 below. It is also a synonym of "the way" and "the door," who is Christ, the keeper of the gate. The culmination of having passed through this gate is when the Holy Ghost condescends on the candidate for baptism in which sin, dross, and evil are burned out of the candidate by spiritual fire. From most accounts, this experience lasts several days and nights. Spiritual rebirth lasts several days and nights with effects of spiritual "aftershocks" (similar to physical aftershocks that typically follow an earthquake), lasting for up to weeks and even many months. Lorenzo Snow gave his personal account as follows: "That night, as I retired to rest, the same wonderful manifestations were repeated, and continued to be for *several successive nights.* This sweet remembrance of those glorious experiences, from that time to the present, bring them fresh before me, imparting an inspiring influence which pervades my whole being, and I trust will to the close of my earthly existence" (Eliza R. Snow, comp., *Biography and Family Record of Lorenzo Snow,* pp., 7-9).

10 And he said unto the children of men: Follow thou me. Wherefore, my beloved brethren, can we follow Jesus save we shall be willing to keep the commandments of the Father?

11 And the Father said: Repent ye, repent ye, and be baptized in the name of my Beloved Son.

12 And also, the voice of the Son came unto me, saying: He that is baptized in my name, to him will the Father give the Holy Ghost, ***like unto me***; wherefore, follow me, and do the things which ye have seen me do (emphasis added).

[The commandment of the Father is tied to a promised blessing that the Savior referred to as "the promise of my Father" (see Luke 24:49). When we repent and are baptized in the name of the Father's Beloved Son, we are then given the right to the promised blessing by the laying on of hands of eternal life. The fulfillment of the promise is when we receive the actual sure promise of eternal life (conditioned upon "enduring to the end") a remission of sins by way of the Holy Ghost received in power through an immersion in spiritual fire, and the Comforter to abide in us as our companion. This baptism of Spirit is performed not by "the will of the flesh, nor of the will of man, but of God" (John 1:13). Our reception of the Holy Ghost will be *like unto that same endowment of the Holy Ghost that Jesus Christ received* after His baptism of water. Hence, His words that the Father will give the Holy Ghost "***like unto me***" (2 Ne. 31:12; emphasis added). This is when we receive the First Comforter as our new companion to abide in us and are born again into the family of Christ.]

13 Wherefore, my beloved brethren, I know that if ye shall follow the Son, with full purpose of heart, acting no hypocrisy and no deception before God, but with real intent, repenting of your sins, witnessing unto the Father that ye are ***willing** to take upon you the name of Christ*, by baptism—yea, by following your Lord and your Savior down into the water, according to his word, behold, then shall ye receive the Holy Ghost; yea, then cometh the baptism of fire and of the Holy Ghost; and then can ye speak with the tongue of angels, and shout praises unto the Holy One of Israel" (emphasis added).

[In my opinion, this is the single greatest verse of scripture found anywhere in our entire standard works which outlines with specificity the doctrine of Christ and what we must do to be saved. Here we learn that we must follow the Son, doing the things that He has done with full purpose of heart. Notice the word *full* used by Nephi. Anything short of being 100% involved from our hearts will not get us there. Notice that Nephi does not say, "full purpose of intellect." Trying to find God through endless, intellectual pursuits alone can only take us so far. In the end, we must acquire spiritual knowledge by faith. The Lord said, "*and as all have not faith*...seek learning, even by study *and also by faith*" [D&C 88:118; emphasis added]. Most of us already have the "learning by study" part down. This pursuit or seeking knowledge "by faith" must become a way of life if we are to obtain all that is promised. Much of this spiritual knowledge comes by way of making our minds "still," or quieting our minds so that we may feel the voice of God within, which I believe is best achieved through meditation. Our intention of coming unto Christ must be pure, and our resolve, constant and unrelenting. We must repent of our sins with the requisite godly sorrow, crying out spiritually from our souls, offering up our broken hearts to Him, while at the same time witnessing unto the Father our "willingness" and committed resolve to take upon us the name of Christ. We must be *willing* to sacrifice all that we have and are and doing the things that He did through compassionate service and sharing the gospel the remainder of our lives. The Lord said, "whosoever he be of you that *forsaketh not all that he hath*, he cannot be my disciple" (Luke 14:33). The footnote for the word *willing* in the Book of Mormon brings up the word *commitment*. This word, or true *commitment*, is what being "all in" is all about. It's a willingness to *risk everything* to know Him just as He has risked everything and put it all on the line for us. Without the requisite *willingness* [i.e., true commitment] *and determination to surrender all that we have and are and serve Him to the end*, the requirements to spiritual rebirth will remain unfulfilled, as well as the receipt of the promised blessing of the Father, including the Holy Ghost, which is "confirmed upon us" by the laying on of hands. This *willingness* to take upon us the name of Christ also involves our willingness to overcome any and all opposition, obstacles, and distractions in mortality that may come in the way of our seeking journey, in finding and coming to the knowledge of God (which becomes then an absolute certainty beyond that of faith), and occurs at the time when we are born again or born of the Spirit. If we allow the world to take precedence, we will not become adopted into Christ's family. Hence why we are admonished to seek *first* the kingdom. Once we fulfill the above prerequisites with an unyielding faith in Christ, we are promised the Holy Ghost, yea, even a baptism of fire! Nephi also describes one of the fruits of the Spirit which accompanies the baptism of Fire and of the Holy Ghost, as that of *speaking with the tongue of the angels*. Speaking with the tongue of the angels is to speak forth words of praise (like the angels) unto the Most High God (while filled with the Holy Ghost) and is the first of three times that this "fruit" of spiritual rebirth is mentioned by Nephi (see 2 Ne. 31- 32). These two chapters in Nephi specifically outline the doctrine of Christ and how we are to become saved.]

14 But, behold, my beloved brethren, thus came the voice of the Son unto me, saying: After ye have repented of your sins, and witnessed unto the Father that ye are willing to keep my commandments, by the baptism of water, and have received the baptism of fire and of the Holy Ghost, and can speak with a new tongue, yea, even with the tongue of angels, and after this should deny me, it would have been better for you that ye had not known me. [This verse reinforces why the Father and Son, who are One, do not give the actual gift and enjoyment of the Holy Ghost out like candy. If we have received a perfect knowledge of God through a Pentecostal-like baptism of fire and of the Holy Ghost (a manifestation of the Lord's presence), including a complete remission of sins, if we have received the promise of eternal life and have spoken with the tongue of praise to the Most High God, and then were to later reject Christ's offering and gift and become an enemy to God, we would become sons of perdition. This level of knowledge qualifies us for such a condemnation. And sons of perdition would be unable to receive forgiveness in this life or in the world to come. Why? Because through having received the Holy Ghost in power, we would have received a perfect knowledge of Christ and the Father, which is a level well beyond that of testimony, belief, and faith. We would have become a living witness. We would have then "known God." Joseph spoke to this turning against God after having obtained this level of spiritual knowledge: "If men have received the good word of God, and tasted of *the powers of the world to come*, if they shall fall away, it is impossible to renew them again, seeing they have crucified the Son of God afresh, and put Him to an open shame" (*Teachings of the Prophet Joseph Smith,* p. 338; emphasis added).

I shudder to think or even contemplate the horror of what this would be like, to turn away from Christ after having received Him and known Him, along with possessing the clarity of our own redemption and promise of eternal life with absolute certainty, or as Nephi puts it, with a "perfect brightness of hope." This "crucifying the Son of God afresh" would lead to eternal hell and damnation. Alma explained that "if ye deny the Holy Ghost when it once has had place in you, and ye know that ye deny it, behold, this is a sin which is unpardonable" (Alma 39:6). The apostle Peter said it this way: "For if after they have escaped the pollutions of the world *through the knowledge of the Lord* and Saviour Jesus Christ, they are again entangled therein, and overcome, the latter end is worse with them than the beginning" (2 Pet. 2:20; emphasis added). The Prophet Joseph asked, "What must a man do to commit the unpardonable sin? He must *receive the Holy Ghost*, have the heavens opened unto him, *and know God*, and then sin against Him. After a man has sinned against the Holy Ghost, there is no repentance for him" (*History of the Church,* 6:314).

The Lord Himself has said: "Thus saith the Lord concerning all those who *know my power, and have been partakers thereof*, and suffered themselves through the power of the devil to be overcome, and to deny the truth and defy my power—They are they who are the sons of perdition, of whom I say that it had been better for them never to have been born; For they are vessels of wrath, doomed to suffer the wrath of

God, with the devil and his angels in eternity: Concerning whom I have said there is no forgiveness in this world nor in the world to come—Having denied the Holy Spirit *after having received it*, and having denied the Only Begotten Son of the Father, having crucified him unto themselves and put him to an open shame" (D&C 76:31-35; emphasis added). Thank God that there are relatively few who will partake of this misery. Joseph Fielding Smith reaffirmed this truth: "How fortunate it is that in the mercy of God there will be comparatively few who will partake of this awful misery and eternal darkness" (*Doctrines of Salvation,* Vol. 1, p. 49).

Notwithstanding the above penalties, let me point out that those who have experienced this spiritual fire, have spoken with this new tongue of praise, and have become filled with the love of God during spiritual rebirth will have had their "natures changed," instilling in them the desire to only do good continually thereafter. So, in essence, we need not fear seeking after and obtaining this knowledge. It would be an extremely rare event for any individual to completely turn against the witness of the Holy Ghost after having received this perfect knowledge of the Father and the Son.

Lorenzo Snow commented on having received this "perfect knowledge that God lives": "Oh, the joy and happiness I felt! No language can describe the almost instantaneous transition from a dense cloud of mental and spiritual darkness into a refulgence of light and knowledge, as it was at that time imparted to my understanding. I then received a perfect knowledge that God lives, that Jesus Christ is the son of God, and of the restoration of the holy priesthood, and the fullness of the Gospel," [To "turn against Him," I do not mean to suggest that we cannot sin or transgress ever again. We will inadvertently transgress God's law because we will continue to live and operate within a fallen world and will still be human. Repentance and divine forgiveness will likewise still be in play. What I mean here is to become an outright enemy of God and come out in open rebellion against Him after receiving the knowledge of God through spiritual rebirth, knowing all the while that we are doing so. Note that this verse contains the second reference of three total found in 2 Nephi, chapters 31 & 32, of the fruit of *speaking with the tongue of the angels*.]

15 And I heard a voice from the Father, saying: Yea, the words of my Beloved are true and faithful. He that endureth to the end, the same shall be saved. [Now we hear the witness of not just the Son but also of the voice and witness of the Father. The Father is reaffirming the words of His Beloved Son that if, after receiving this "baptism of fire," we were to "endure to the end," we would thereby be guaranteed eternal life, which is to become an exalted co-heir with Jesus Christ. Enduring to the end means that, upon receiving of this immersion in spiritual fire and the First Comforter, we are to endure in the sanctifying light of His Spirit thereafter, through our continued faith and faithfulness until the end of our mortal lives. This sanctifying influence of the Comforter given to abide in us (see Moses 6:61) is necessary for the ongoing "cleanliness maintenance" and upgrading of our souls unto holiness by way of its sanctifying light in order that we might come to that *point of faith* wherein we can

pierce the heavenly veil and see the face of God while still in mortality. Is it not written that He is "the author and the *finisher* of our faith?"]

16 And now, my beloved brethren, I know by this that unless a man shall endure to the end, in following the example of the Son of the living God, he cannot be saved. [To be saved in the end, we must first receive the Holy Ghost and then "endure to the end." Other components involved with enduring to the end include "to preach and persuade to the last" (Teachings of the Prophet Joseph Smith, p. 62) and to follow the example of the Son through Christlike, compassionate service that He exhibited when He lived on the earth. This, we are told in D&C 93, is how we are to grow "grace for grace" and grace to grace." As we extend "grace" by way of compassionate, Christlike service to others, we thereby receive "grace" from God in the form of increased endowments of His light and glory, which contain the attributes of Godliness (which includes faith or power) that become infused into us by Their grace. "For if you keep my commandments you shall receive of His fulness, and be glorified in me as I am in the Father; therefore, I say unto you,***you** shall receive grace for grace*" [D&C 93:20; emphasis added]. One of these commandments is to "do the things that ye have seen me do." As we increase in this, the light of His glory, also known as the "marvelous light of his goodness" [see Alma 19:6], we become more like Him. This is not a process of overcoming through grit or personal will power alone. It is a process whereby we receive gift upon gift of the light of His glory (containing His attributes), infusing in us the divine nature by degrees, thereby becoming "partakers of the divine nature" that the apostle Peter admonished us to receive (2 Pet. 1:4). This process of "grace for grace" continues until we are made like Him, even holy, and all unbelief becomes eventually dissipated in full.

The end of our *enduring* in mortality gives us the holy privilege to "rend that veil of unbelief (Ether 4:15)" so "that when he shall appear [to us literally, in mortality], we shall be like Him" (1 John 3:2), thereby allowing us to enter His Divine Presence. And what will we be like? We will be beings of perfected faith by Their grace and power, for as Joseph taught, "when faith is perfected, [we] are like Him" [*Lectures On Faith,* 7:8]. Remember that God does much if not most of the work *in us*. Our job is to merely surrender in love to His will, which is made manifest to us by His Spirit, as well as the additional, amplified influence of the Comforter we receive at the time of spiritual rebirth. In my experience, we must vigorously fight to maintain the influence of this Comforter just as we fought to maintain our connection with the light of Christ in coming to the tree of life to partake of its fruit in the first place. I believe that the Lord purposefully withdraws a portion of His spiritual influence during times of our lives so we will "dig deeper" in our seeking journey, just as He provides additional spiritual challenges and opposition *as a way of testing our resolve* while furthering our progression along the straight and narrow path. Pressing forward in faith connotes that there is something against which we are to press. This "something" entails the requisite trials and opposition that are there to test and strengthen us as we ultimately overcome them in and through Christ and are made perfect in Him.]

17 Wherefore, ***do*** the things which I have told you I have seen that your Lord and your Redeemer should do; for, for this cause have they been shown unto me, that ye might know the gate by which ye should enter. ***For the gate by which ye should enter is repentance and baptism by water; and then cometh a remission of your sins by fire and by the Holy Ghost*** (emphasis added). [Nephi is the prophet of "plain talk." There could be no words spoken with greater plainness than these about "the gate." And yet some of us still believe that when we were baptized by water at eight years old, or later as converts, we were made instantaneously clean. The scriptures are clear. The remission of sins comes "by fire and by the Holy Ghost" through a complete immersion in the heavenly element of spirit through the Holy Ghost. Little children are "alive in Christ" through the age of accountability, which means that all of their purported "sins" would have automatically been swallowed up in Christ through His atoning sacrifice. Notwithstanding this being true, these little children will grow up. And when they reach their "riper years," as Joseph called it (see "Teachings," Section Six 1843-44, p.314), they will need to seek the Lord and salvation through faith and broken-hearted repentance and in *doing* the things that He did through emulating Him.

After we have exercised true and whole repentance with godly sorrow, received water baptism by one having authority, and have received the promise of the Father confirmed on us by the laying on of hands, then we *may* receive a remission of sins by fire and by the Holy Ghost either concurrently at that moment (for those of us in our riper years) or at some point thereafter through faith and broken-hearted repentance, thereby fulfilling the law. There is very strong evidence to suggest that this endowment must happen between the time when we have received the laying on of hands, on the one hand, and the day we leave this mortal existence, on the other. [Note: Since little children are "alive in Christ," what point would there be for them to receive the remission of sins at the age of eight years old when there are no sins presumably to remit?] Now is the time for man to prepare to meet God by receiving a remission of sins and also an endowment of the First Comforter. Indeed, the very purpose of missionary work, as the Lord Himself has said, is to teach "that *repentance and remission of sins* should be preached in [His] name among all nations, beginning at Jerusalem" (Luke 24:37; emphasis added).

Once we have received this spiritual fire, which is to come into the Lord's presence while He is yet behind the veil, we will have received the remission of sins and would now find ourselves inside "the gate." Receiving both the immersion in water and this spiritual fire is referred to as "the gate." This gate, we are told by the Prophet of the Restoration, is an experience that is "***the same*** as given [the apostles and others] on the day of Pentecost" (*Teachings of the Prophet Joseph Smith,* p.149; emphasis added. See also Acts 2.). And we are told that "the keeper of the gate is the Holy One of Israel; and he employeth no servant there; and *there is none other way save it be by the gate*; for he cannot be deceived, for the Lord God is his name" (2 Ne. 9:41; emphasis added). In other words, Christ Himself decides who will come through this gate, which will be those who have come down into the depths of humility in their repentance process, having cried out in whole and pure faith to Him through a spiritual ordinance of the soul and an offering of a broken heart, having called upon His name for mercy to cover them, subject to having a committed ***willingness*** and determination to be "all in" with Him in serving Him until the end. He is the Holy One of Israel and "cannot be deceived" (2 Nephi 9:41). The reception of the Holy Ghost as part of the promise of the Father is not an automatic occurrence, no matter how many hands have been laid on our heads, or how much we may have served within the Lord's true Church and gospel. We must risk it all to know Him, and plead with our Lord to give us entrance, witnessing in our minds and hearts that we will thereafter be dutifully and resolutely committed thereafter. We must not stop seeking until we find and ***know Him*** and receive of that spiritual cleansing that is necessary to return to live in the presence of our Father Elohim and Christ Himself. Elder Christofferson further enlightens our understanding as to this soul-saving doctrine in that when we actually come to *the knowledge of the Lord* through this "cleansing" during Spiritual Rebirth, we will also (with surety) experience His redemption: "As authorized messengers (speaking of the missionaries), they offer the incomparable blessings of faith in Jesus Christ, repentance, and the gift of the Holy Ghost (i.e., the ordinance), *opening the way to Spiritual Rebirth and redemption*" (Elder D. Todd Christofferson, "Redemption," April General Conference Address, 2013; emphasis added)].

18 And **then** are ye in this strait and narrow path which leads to eternal life; yea, ye have entered in by **the gate**; ye have done according to the commandments of the Father and the Son; and ye have received the Holy Ghost, which witnesses of the Father and the Son, unto the fulfilling of the promise [of the Father] which he hath made, that if ye entered in by the way ye should receive (emphasis added). [Once we have been immersed in spiritual fire through this baptism performed by God, we have then (and not until then) entered through the gate or by the way which leads to eternal life. We will have fulfilled the directive given the day of our confirmation to receive the actual Holy Ghost as a gift (and not just the ordinance by the same name), by having done according to the Father's commandments, thereby fulfilling the Father's promise which He made and confirmed on us when hands were laid on our heads after water baptism. Elder McConkie taught: "Further, the fact that a person has had hands laid on his head and a legal administrator has declared, 'receive the Holy Ghost,' does not guarantee that the gift itself has actually been enjoyed.... Those who actually enjoy the gift or presentment of the Holy Ghost are the ones who are born again, who have become new creatures of the Holy Ghost" (Mormon Doctrine, 2nd ed., p. 313; see also Mosiah 27:24-26). During and after this immersion or baptism of Spirit occurs, we then enjoy the gift [per Elder McConkie] and are born of the Spirit, adopted into the family of Christ and have the Comforter to abide in us (Moses 6:61). Until this happens, however, we can be guided by the Light of Christ, which is given to every man of every background, religion, race, and creed, throughout the entire world.

19 And now, my beloved brethren, after ye have gotten into this strait and narrow path, I would ask *if all is done*? Behold, I say unto you, Nay; for ye have not come thus far save it were by the word of Christ [and His word is Spirit] with unshaken faith in him, ***relying wholly upon the merits of him who is mighty to save.*** ["If all is done?" is similar to the question contemplated in chapter 9, which is, "After the rebirth, now what?" Nephi admonishes us to continue to do the same things after rebirth that brought us to being born of God in the first place. He reminds us that we have come thus far through the "word" of Christ in faith, *relying wholly upon His merits. To rely wholly upon His merits means that if we were to rely even one percent on our own merits, we would be disqualified from receiving the gift of spiritual rebirth.* To follow the word of Christ is to follow the spirit of Christ, which is the Light of Christ we connect with in our hearts. The Lords tells us that "the word of the Lord … is Spirit, even the Spirit of Jesus Christ" (D&C 84:45). We connect with this Spirit by turning inward through inner awareness, "getting still" in meditation and prayer, and getting "in sync" with God by *feeling after Him*, which is to literally feel after any sign or intimation of His presence. (See Acts 17:27.)

20 Wherefore, ye must press forward with a steadfastness in Christ **[**i.e., **faith]**, having a perfect brightness of **hope**, and a love of God and of all men **[**i.e., **charity]**. Wherefore, if ye shall press forward, feasting upon the word of Christ, and endure to the end, behold, **thus saith the Father: Ye shall have eternal life** [emphasis added]. This scripture is loaded with spiritual gold. It is a mini sermon on faith, hope, and charity. The phrase "steadfastness in Christ" means faith. "Perfect brightness" is descriptive of the type of actual, spiritual knowledge of Christ and the Father we receive at the time of spiritual rebirth together with the actual knowledge that we have been given the sure promise of eternal life, which gives us a knowledge or "hope" for what we have been promised to come, subject to enduring to the end. Third, the "love of God and of all men," means charity, which is when we were immersed in the love and oneness of God when we are born again. This experiential reality is also referred to as partaking of the fruit of the tree of life or salvation. As mentioned in Chapter 1, the last three items of our diagram are faith, hope, and charity.

Remember, there are two kinds of hope. There is the hope that accompanies belief, which comes with an assurance born of the Light of Christ that the promises are indeed ***available*** to us personally and individually. And then there is the level of hope shown after "faith" demonstrated in our Diagram, which is now a knowledge [void of any doubt whatsoever, hence the term, "perfect brightness"] of the reality of God the Father and God the Son, of having received a remission of sins, having been redeemed, and having been promised eternal life. This latter "hope" referenced above, arising out of that living faith bestowed, is the knowledge of having been promised eternal life by God Himself. This latter "hope" is also highlighted for us in Alma: "While many thousands of others truly mourn for the loss of their kindred, ***yet they rejoice and exult in the hope*** *[now notice]*, ***<u>and even know</u>***, *according to the promises of the Lord,* [and what were those promises received by Him which gave them this "hope" or sure knowledge?] ***that they are raised to dwell at the right hand of God, in a state of never-ending happiness***" (Alma 28:12).

An actual, spiritual knowledge of God and of his promise of eternal life to us [i.e., "hope"] comes by that "perfect faith" and power bestowed by grace through choosing Christ with all of our hearts and outwardly acting in this new choice in the world. "And as many as received him, to them gave he power ('perfect faith'; see 2 Ne. 9:23) to become the sons of God" (John 1:12). This living faith is the power that leads to justification. And then, of course, when we are born of the Spirit, we are cleansed head to toe by spiritual fire, thereby coming to the knowledge of God and concurrently filled with the oneness and "love of God" (see Moroni 7:48). This love is that which then overflows to all men and women with whom we come in contact. The resultant fruit from this experience is that we will unavoidably love everyone. We will feel just like George Bailey felt in the movie *It's a Wonderful Life* after he had been given a second chance at life. That's because we too will have been given a second chance. A second chance at a new life in Christ! Will we squander this gift, or will we take every advantage of it and use the gift of the Holy Ghost to further us along our journey of coming to the literal feet of Christ while here in mortality? After we experience this living faith, hope, and charity, we are promised by the Father that if we continue to feast on the word or Spirit of Christ (which now includes the greater endowment of the Comforter given to abide in us) and ***endure to the end***, we *shall* have eternal life.

Elder Joseph B. Worthlin said, "The gospel of Jesus Christ includes enduring to the end as one of its bedrock doctrines. Some think of enduring to the end as simply suffering through challenges. It is so much more than that—it is *the process of coming unto Christ and being perfected in him*" (as quoted in *If I Am This Moment This Day,* by Marjory Wilcock and Renee Jacks, p. 70). The following is a more comprehensive list which facilitates a deeper understanding of the phrase "enduring to the end," which will also aid the spiritual seeker in *coming unto Christ* and being *perfected in Him.*

This list is as follows. We are to endure to the end…

1. In the sanctifying light of His Spirit that we experience as feelings, so we can "know the only true God and Jesus Christ whom [He] hath sent," increasing in His light and intelligence, also known as His glory, which contains His attributes. This is how we "*continue in God*" and grow grace for grace and grace to grace, receiving more and more light until the perfect day. This is how "the inward man is renewed day by day" (2 Cor. 4:16). It happens as we continue in His light, which is also referenced as "God" in scripture (D&C 88:13, 41). As we continue in this "God" or Spirit of truth, light, and intelligence, we grow brighter and brighter until the perfect day, which is (at least in part) when we are able to enter the divine presence of His personage—a perfect day. "That which is of God is light; and he that receiveth light, and *continueth in God*, receiveth more light; and that light

groweth brighter and brighter until the perfect day" D&C 50:24; emphasis added). "For if you keep my commandments you shall receive of his fulness [of His Spirit, light, power, and glory], and be glorified in me [and He is the light] as I [through this same light and divine consciousness] am in the Father; therefore, I say unto you, you shall receive [of this same light and divine consciousness] grace for grace" (D&C 93:20).

2. Through first partaking of His salvation and the power of His redemption through spiritual rebirth. "And now, my beloved brethren, I would that ye should come unto Christ, who is the Holy One of Israel [how do we do this?], and [1] partake of his salvation, and the power of his redemption [through the offering of a broken heart in complete surrender, which yields being born and coming alive in Him, which is how we "come to the knowledge of God"]. Yea, come unto him, and [2] offer your whole souls as an offering unto him, and continue in fasting and praying, and endure to the end; and as the Lord liveth ye will be saved" (Omni 1:26; emphasis added).

3. In faithfulness and faith on His name, increasing our faith cup, adding faith to faith unto overflowing spiritual knowledge, thereby eventually yielding the *dissolution of all unbelief in the present*, which allows us to rend the veil and arrive into His presence. "For therein is the righteousness of God revealed *from faith to faith*: as it is written, The just shall live by faith" (Romans 1:17; emphasis added). And, "It is I that granteth unto him that believeth [i.e., exerciseth faith] unto the end ... a place eternally at my right hand" [Mosiah 26:24]. Lastly, "I am mindful always in my prayers … that he, through his infinite goodness and grace, will keep you *through the endurance of faith on this name to the end*" [Moroni 8:3; emphasis added]. This "endurance of faith" is patterned for us, at least in part by Nephi, when he exclaimed, "my heart groaneth because of my sins; nevertheless, I know in whom I have trusted" [2 Ne. 4:19].

4. In bearing record of the name of Christ and doing His works until the end. "And I give unto you a commandment, that ye shall observe to do the things which ye have seen me do, and *bear record of me even unto the end*" [JST, Matthew 26:25; emphasis added]. To truly bear record of Him, even as a *living witness*, we must first receive that witness.

5. In following the example of the living God, in doing the things that He would and did do. "And now, my beloved brethren, I know by this that unless a man shall endure to the end, *in following the example of the Son of the living God*, he cannot be saved. Wherefore do the things which I have told you I have seen that your Lord and your Redeemer should do" [2 Nephi 31:16-17; emphasis added]. As the Savior "went about doing good," so should we for the remainder of our mortal lives.

6. In loving God (through experiential "practice") and denying ourselves of all ungodliness and the cares of the world. The cares of the world choke the Word, or His light, which provides guiding, personal revelation unto salvation. "Yea, come unto Christ, and be perfected in him, and deny yourselves of all ungodliness; and if ye shall deny yourselves of all ungodliness, and love God with all your might, mind and strength, then is his grace sufficient for you, that by his grace ye may be perfect in Christ; and *if by the grace of God ye are perfect in Christ*, ye can in nowise deny the power of God" (Moroni 10:32; emphasis added).
7. In always retaining in *remembrance* the greatness and goodness of God and *our own nothingness*. "Even so I would that ye should *remember*, and always *retain in remembrance*, the greatness of God, and *your own nothingness, and his goodness* and long-suffering towards you, unworthy creatures, and humble yourselves even in the depths of humility, calling on the name of the Lord daily, and standing steadfastly in the faith of that which is to come, which was spoken by the mouth of the angel" (Mosiah 5:11; emphasis added).
8. In "seeing Him who is invisible" through visualizing our future encounter with Him in mortality. "By faith he forsook Egypt, not fearing the wrath of the king: *for he endured, as seeing him who is invisible*" (Heb. 11:27; emphasis added).
9. In enduring His chastening of us and not denying Him. "My son, despise not thou the chastening of the Lord, nor faint when thou are rebuked of him: For whom the Lord loveth he chasteneth, and scourgeth every son whom he receiveth. If ye endure chastening, God dealeth with you as with sons; for what son is he whom the father chasteneth not?" (Heb. 12:5-7).
10. In and through the trials, adversity, and afflictions that must needs surely come to us all. "And thus we see that except the Lord doth chasten his people with many afflictions, yea, except he doth visit them with death and with terror, and with famine and with all manner of pestilence, they will not remember him" (Hel. 12:3). And if we "do always remember Him, we "may have His Spirit to be with [us]," per our Sacrament Ordinance.
11. In preaching and persuading to the last, as did the Apostle Paul. "No one, we presume, will doubt the faithfulness of Paul to the end. None will say that he did not keep the faith, that he did not fight the good fight, that he did not *preach and persuade to the last*" [Joseph Smith, *Teachings of the Prophet Joseph Smith,* p. 63; emphasis added].
12. In *preserving the purity of our hearts* through "heart purification and softening maintenance" so we may be continually guided by the Light of Christ and that amplified endowment of the gift and enjoyment of the

Holy Ghost. This is "Ground Zero: The battle over the heart," discussed in Chapter 1. The Comforter, which is the gift and companionship of the Holy Ghost, is what ***preserves our hearts in a purified state.*** "May we who know the sacred Name from every sin depart [the remission of sins as though by fire]. Then will the Spirit's constant flame [the companionship of the Holy Ghost or Comforter, which is given to abide in us thereafter], ***Preserve us pure in heart***" ("Sweet Is the Peace the Gospel Brings," *LDS Hymns,* verse 4, p. 14].

13. In laying down our individual will, over and over again, and yielding to His, until the end comes. We must also battle every day in an effort to maintain the influence of the Comforter within us so that we might continue to be sanctified unto holiness. "The men and women who desire to obtain seats in the celestial kingdom, will find that ***they must battle every day***" (Brigham Young, as quoted in *If I Am This Moment,* by Marjory Wilcock and Renee Jacks, p. 70; emphasis added).

14. In keeping the commandments of the Lord and walking in His statutes to the end. "That those who keep the commandments of the Lord and walk in His statutes to the end, are the only individuals permitted to sit at this glorious feast, is evident from … Paul's last letter to Timothy" (*Teachings of the Prophet Joseph Smith,* p. 63).

15. In desiring righteousness until the end of our days. "And so it is on the other hand. If he hath repented of his sins, and ***desired righteousness until the end of his days***, even so he shall be rewarded unto righteousness" (Alma 41:6; emphasis added).

16. In being obedient to the covenant we have entered into at baptism. "Therefore, I would that ye should take upon you the name of Christ, all you that have entered into the covenant with God that ye should be obedient unto the end of your lives" (Mosiah 5:8).

17. In going about doing good. "Jesus of Nazareth … went about doing good … for God was with him" (Acts 10:38).

18. In praying always. "What I say unto one I say unto all; pray always lest that wicked one have power in you, and remove you out of your place" (D&C 93:49).

19. In laying aside the things of this world, cleaving unto our covenants, and keeping His commandments continually. "And verily I say unto thee that thou shalt lay aside ***the things of this world*** and ***seek*** for the things of a better.… Wherefore … rejoice, and ***cleave unto the covenants*** which thou hast made.… Keep my commandments ***continually…*** And except thou do this (notice the warning), where I am you cannot come" (D&C 25: 10, 13, 15; emphasis added).

20. In finding Christ as "the end" of our journey of faith in mortality, while at the same time as the beginning of our journey in the eternities. To meet Him and see His face in mortality could be viewed by some as an endowment absolutely required to receive here or by others as perhaps just spiritual extra credit. Here's the real question to consider. Will the difference in seeing His face in mortality give us the advantage in this world and in the world to come? If so, why not seek for it? Each seeker must find the answer to this question for him or herself, directly from God. Yet what we can most assuredly know and agree with is that the endowment of the Heavenly Person is available to those who have received all the ordinances of God through His restored Church and who have had those ordinances justified by the Holy Spirit of Promise through fulfilling the law(s) associated with the same. Here's a question to consider once again. We know why Christ is the author of our faith, but why is Christ said to be *the finisher* of our faith? If "growing in faith" is the journey, what would it look like at the end of this journey? And is faith in Christ not designed to ultimately manifest the Lord of Glory Himself? And is the answer to the previous question what it is to travel the length of the path? Elder McConkie writes:

"To gain the promised inheritance in the celestial world it is necessary to travel the length of the path, a course of travel which consists in obedience to the laws and principles of the gospel. This process is called enduring to the end, meaning the end of mortal life (Mormon Doctrine, p. 228; emphasis added).

Joseph Smith taught the following: "The apostle [Paul] says this is eternal life, ***to know God and Jesus Christ***, who he has sent. If any man enquire what kind of a being is God,... if the declaration of the apostle be true, *he will realize that he has not eternal life, there can be eternal life on no other principle*" ("King Follett Discourse," *History of the Church,* 6:302-317; emphasis added).

Remember, the purpose of the Atonement is to reverse the effects of the Fall of Adam. One of the effects of the Fall is to be outside the presence of God. Not only do we need to be redeemed from sin, but our other objective is to be *redeemed from the Fall*. When the brother of Jared came back into the Lord's presence, he was told, "Because thou knowest these things ye are *redeemed from the fall*; therefore ye are *brought back into my presence*; therefore ***I show myself unto you***" (Ether 3:13; emphasis added). Remember also the words of Joseph Smith on the matter:

"It is the first principle of the Gospel to know for a certainty the Character of God, and ***to know that we may converse with him as one man converses with another****" (Teachings of the Pprophet Joseph Smith, p. 345).*

Elder McConkie may have brought the pieces of the puzzle together as to what "enduring" to the *final end* might actually look like.

"Any person who will search the scriptures, keep the commandments and ask in faith will get his heart so in tune with the Infinite that there will come into his being, from the still small voice, the eternal realities of religion. And as he progresses and advances and comes nearer to God, there will be a day when he will entertain angels, when he will see visions, and ***the final end*** *is to view the face of God" (How To Get Personal Revelation, New Era, June 1980, 46–50; emphasis added).*

[End of the author commentary on 2 Ne. 31:20 and enduring to the end]

21. And now, behold, my beloved brethren, this is the way; and there is none other way nor name given under heaven whereby man can be saved in the kingdom of God. And now, behold, **this is the doctrine of Christ**, and the only and true doctrine of the Father, and of the Son, and of the Holy Ghost, which is one God, without end. Amen (emphasis added). [Wow! This verse is very profound and creates in me a very deep-seated and solemn realization, which is that there is "**none other way"**! There is "none other way" to come unto Christ than by complying with the principles and ordinances found within this doctrine of Christ, so that we might be saved in the kingdom of God. As Joseph said, we must "subscribe the articles of adoption to enter" the kingdom of heaven, which is to exercise whole faith and repentance, partake of the ordinances by proper authority, and continue seeking and asking for the promised gift from the depth of our souls until the gift and its enjoyment is actually experienced in our souls as by fire. I bear witness that the words in this verse are true. I bear witness that they are not just words on a page but constitute the very way to salvation, and needs to be sought for strictly and diligently until the promised blessing is both received and experienced. As the Prophet Joseph has said, "Knowledge of these things **can only be obtained by experience** through the ordinances of God set forth for that purpose" (Teachings of the Prophet Joseph Smith, p. 335; emphasis added). If we have not experienced this exceedingly great joy and subsequent endowments, we are to continue seeking. Joseph taught, "Being born again, comes by [receiving] the Spirit of God [i.e., Holy Ghost], through ordinances" (Teachings of the Prophet Joseph Smith, p. 162). These divine signatures, tender mercies, or events of testimony obtained by experience invite us to search out the higher meaning, which

I believe is to obtain the knowledge of God. The spiritual experiences that build faith and testimony are what lead us to full conversion.

I like to think of our immersion in His Spirit, an experience like that given the apostles on the day of Pentecost, as full conversion. This is when we obtain the actual knowledge of God beyond belief and faith. And it is the same as was patterned for us by the apostle Peter when he was fully converted on the day of Pentecost. Elder Busche said: "In the course of my life the spiritual experiences that I have had, became for me *the instigators and the forces driving me to search out the higher meaning*" [F. Enzio Busche, "This Is Life Eternal," *BYU Speeches,* 1981, p. 2]. These experiences or events of testimony are the bread crumbs left out for us by our Father to find our way back to His home and dwell in His presence, which begins in power when we receive the First Comforter, and subsequently, the Second. Finally, I would also bear witness that the adversary's goal is to skew, distort, dilute, and conceal this doctrine of Christ from our view and turn it into a foolish and vain thing to even pursue. Why? Because this is the only doctrine that can save our immortal souls. His goal is to "get possession of the hearts of the people" so that he might "blind their eyes and lead them away to believe that *the doctrine of Christ* was a foolish and vain thing" (3 Ne. 2:2).

The Doctrine of Christ according to Nephi (Continued—see 2 Nephi 32:2-7)

2 Do ye not remember that I said unto you that after ye had received the Holy Ghost ye could *speak with the tongue of angels*? And now, how could ye *speak with the tongue of angels* save it were by the Holy Ghost? (emphasis added). [This verse constitutes the *third and last time* that Nephi describes speaking with the tongue of angels as one of the fruits arising out of spiritual rebirth. When God, through His holy prophets, feels the need to repeat Himself *three times*, we are to pay attention. I believe that the multiple references of this particular fruit, as well as this question posed by Nephi, is asked so that we might ascertain through self-inquiry whether we have *experienced* this fruit ourselves yet. For why would we continue seeking for something we had already found? We might turn inwardly and ask, "Have I ever felt so deeply towards God that I have broken out into pure words of praise to Him spontaneously, as if the words spoken were not even my own?" If not, perhaps we are to continue our seeking journey until we have, and thereafter continue to do as directed by our new companion, the Comforter. Remember, we do not know what we do not know. The description of this specific fruit [i.e., "speaking with the tongue of the angels"] is to help us become aware that perhaps there is more for us to both seek and find. Notice in this question whom the prophet Alma was speaking to when he inquired, "And now behold, I ask of you, *my brethren of the Church* [who have already received the promise of the Father by the laying on of hands for the intended reception of the Holy Ghost], *have ye spiritually been born of God*? Have ye

received his image in your countenances? Have ye *experienced* this mighty change in your hearts?" (Alma 5:14; emphasis added).]

3 Angels speak by the power of the Holy Ghost; wherefore, they speak the words of Christ. Wherefore, I said unto you, feast upon the words of Christ; for behold, the words of Christ will tell you all things what ye should do. [The only way to speak the words of Christ, in this context, is through the power of the Holy Ghost. The "word of God" is the "Spirit of God." The "words of Christ" are not only those words found in holy writ but also those words of Spirit which are communicated by way of personal revelation to the individual soul. This is what it means to hold fast to the iron rod. We are admonished to not just partake of the "words of Christ," or His Spirit, but to actually feast on that Spirit or "words." In doing so, we receive spiritual direction as to things next in our journey along the straight and narrow path leading back to the presence of our Father and His Only Begotten Son.]

4 Wherefore, now after I have spoken these words, if ye cannot understand them it will be because ye ask not, neither do ye knock; wherefore, ye are not brought into the light, but must perish in the dark. [I love Nephi's plainness and truth. Nephi is cutting to the chase. What he is saying, in essence, is this: "If you have no idea what I'm talking about when I describe this baptism of fire and one of its attendant fruits of *speaking with the tongue of the angels*, then you have likely not received it yet and must diligently continue pursuing it until you obtain it." Again, Elder Bednar: "The statement 'receive the Holy Ghost' in our confirmation *was a directive to strive* for the baptism of the Spirit" (David A. Bednar, *"That We May Have His Spirit To Be With Us," May Ensign, 2006,* ; emphasis added). Nephi is saying, in other words, "If you do not continue to ask, seek, and knock by your own volition and choice, because perhaps you don't value, love, and desire Christ and His offering enough to endure in doing so, you must ultimately perish in the dark, without ***receiving the manifestations*** of the Holy Spirit. This is what Joseph Fielding Smith meant when he said, "It is my judgment that there are many members of the Church who have ... never received that gift—that is, *the manifestations of it.* Why? Because they have never put themselves in order to receive *these manifestations....* Therefore, they go through life *without that* ***knowledge*"** [and the critical cleansing required, for no unclean thing can enter into His kingdom]. Remember the words of Alma, *'...and* ***never, until,*** *I did cry out unto the Lord Jesus Christ for mercy, did I receive a remission of my sins' [see Alma 38:8]"* ("Seek Ye Earnestly the Best Gifts," *Ensign,* June 1972, p. 3; emphasis added).]

The *manifestations* spoken of above are unspeakably real and, according to Joseph Smith, "*<u>the same</u> as given on the day of Pentecost"* (*Teachings of the Prophet Joseph Smith,* p.149; see also Acts 2). When we are born of the Spirit, we actually "come into the presence of the Lord," through partaking of a portion of His glory through *a manifestation of Himself* in power by the Holy Ghost. The Lord either directly or through His prophet describes it in a similar way:

"But he that believeth these things [i.e., "exerciseth whole faith"] which I have spoken, him will I ***visit*** *[including at times in the form of His personage, shrouded by the veil] with the* ***manifestations*** *of my Spirit, and* ***he shall know*** *and bear record. For because of my Spirit he shall know that these things are true" (Ether 4:11; emphasis added).*

"And that he ***manifesteth <u>himself</u>*** *[through a heavenly manifestation unto a perfect knowledge of Him] unto all those who believe in him [how?], by the power of the Holy Ghost; yea, unto every nation, kindred, tongue, and people, working mighty miracles, signs, and wonders, among the children of men according to their faith" (2 Ne. 26:13; emphasis added).*

"And behold, whosoever believeth on my words [i.e., exerciseth faith unto repentance], them will ***I visit*** *with the* ***manifestation*** *of my Spirit; and they shall be born of me, even of water* ***and of the Spirit*** *" (D&C 5:16; emphasis added).*

This actual knowledge given through the Lord's visit by way of a powerful manifestation is the perfect brightness of hope described by Nephi, beyond that of faith, relative to the reality of God, our remission of sins, and His sure promise of eternal life to us subject to enduring to the end. And those who now "know" are commanded to "bear record." Why? The *Lectures On Faith* tells us that it is "***human testimony, and human testimony only***, that excited this inquiry, in the first instance, in their minds. *It was the credence they gave to the testimony of their fathers* [who had already obtained the knowledge of God for themselves], this testimony [i.e., "this witness and knowledge"] having aroused their minds to inquire after [what?] the ***knowledge of God***; the inquiry frequently terminated, ***indeed always terminated when rightly pursued, in the most glorious discoveries and eternal certainty***" (*Lectures On Faith* 2:56; emphasis added). Although this particular section in the Lectures is speaking to seeing the Lord's face, it is also applicable to those who have obtained the same perfect knowledge of Him, yet shrouded by the veil].

5 "For behold, again I say unto you that if ye will enter in by *the way*, and receive the Holy Ghost, it will show unto you all things what ye should do" (emphasis added). [Christ is "*the way,* the truth, and the life" (John 14:6; emphasis added). "The way," which is another name for Christ, has specific reference here to "the gate" that Christ said few would ultimately find. This failure to find Him is caused, I believe, by a lack of desire and tenacity in asking Him, seeking Him and knocking at His door. The fulfillment of the promise of the Father is "the gate" or "the way." It includes (a) the promise of eternal life, subject to enduring to the end, (b) the reception of the promised blessing of the gift *and enjoyment* of the Holy Ghost, born in spiritual fire, and (c) portions of that power from on high spoken of by Christ, with its

accompanying gifts of the Spirit, attendant with receiving the Comforter (see Luke 24:49: D&C 45:8). Nephi said that "the keeper of the gate is the Holy One of Israel; and he employeth no servant there; and *there is none other way save it be by the gate*; for he cannot be deceived, for the Lord God is his name," and later added, "And whoso knocketh, to him will he open" (2 Nephi 9:41-42; emphasis added). Christ also refers to Himself as "the door," which is likewise synonymous with this "gate" or "the way." He is the door because we have to receive His holy anointing through His Light, in order to be saved. He is the door between this world of mortality and the kingdom of heaven. This Christ Light "anoints us" at the time of spiritual rebirth by the power of the Holy Ghost. Christ said, "I am the door: by me if any man enter in, *he shall be saved*, and shall go in and out, and find pasture" [John 10:9; emphasis added]. The adversary, through his wiles, may whisper to us, "Just be a humble man. Don't be ungrateful. Just take whatever the Lord sees fit to give you. You shouldn't be demanding with God. Don't ask to understand the greater things that you can't possibly obtain anyway." Fellow seeker, I will tell you that not only is this wrong, it is an evil lie perpetrated by that evil one. Christ implores us to ask, seek, and knock. The extent of our love for God is the same extent to which we will diligently seek Him. Our heightened, even excruciating level of desire in this endeavor is what our Lord is looking for in us. How bad do we want it? We are to beg, plead, even cry out to our God, who dwells in the heavenly realm, in order to demonstrate our earnest and sincere desire to know Him and receive the greater things of God. That's why Joseph told us to "continue to weary Him with your importunings, as the poor woman did the unjust judge" (*Teachings of the Prophet Joseph Smith,* p. 35).

We are best advised to follow the example of Abraham and his righteous *desiring*, who said, "having been myself a follower of righteousness, *desiring* also to be one who possessed great knowledge ... and to possess a greater knowledge, and to be a ... prince of peace, and *desiring* to receive [divine] instructions" [Abraham 1:2; emphasis added]. The greater our desire and faith for the things of God, the greater it appears will be our blessings. This is supported by Christ, who said to the three Nephites, "Behold, I know your thoughts, and ye have *desired* the things which John, my beloved ... *desired* of me. Therefore, *more blessed are ye*" for "ye have *desired* that ye might bring the souls of men unto me, while the world shall stand. *And for this cause* [meaning, because of this level of *desire*] ye shall have a fulness of joy; and ye shall sit down in the kingdom of my Father; yea, your joy shall be full, even as the Father hath given me fulness of joy; and *ye shall be even as I am*, and I am even as the Father; and the Father and I are one" (3 Ne. 28: 6-7, 9; emphasis added). In the end, because their *desires* were greater, their blessings were immeasurably greater as well. Remember ... "*More blessed are ye!*" (3 Ne. 28:7; emphasis added).]

6 "Behold, **this is the doctrine of Christ**, and there will be no more doctrine given until after he shall manifest himself unto you in the flesh. And when he shall manifest himself unto you in the flesh, the things which he shall say unto you shall ye observe to do" (emphasis added). [Here Nephi is informing us that this "doctrine of

Christ" is all we need to know and follow, at least until such time as He shall appear in the flesh during His visit to the Americas to establish His Church among the people of the Americas. Nephi may likewise be offering us an additional meaning, which would include doing the things that He commands us to do, until such time as we are given additional instruction at the visit of Jesus Christ, known as the Second Comforter.]

7 And now I, Nephi, cannot say more; the Spirit stoppeth mine utterance, and I am left to mourn because of the unbelief, and the wickedness, and the ignorance, and the stiffneckedness of men; for they will not search knowledge, nor understand great knowledge, when it is given unto them in plainness, even as plain as word can be. [Nephi here is truly mourning in the spirit of his soul. He wants so bad for the people to "get it," but many of the peoples' hearts are hardened and their minds sealed. This hardness of heart and blindness of mind is the fruit of unbelief. Unbelief creates wickedness, ignorance, stiffneckedness, and pride, which is enmity between people and God. Many are complacent and even recalcitrant, having no desire to earnestly seek Christ. And there is nothing Nephi can do about it except to feel godly sorrow for their blindness, despondency, apathy, and lack of interest in the things of God. The Spirit "stoppeth [his] utterance," because by telling them any more in plainness, he might be condemning them unnecessarily. This condemnation occurs because where more light is given, more accountability is required for failing to heed that light. Said another way, where much is given, much is expected. The Spirit admonishes him to now "pull back" by holding his tongue.

Clearly Nephi believed the doctrine of Christ to be simple and plain. Interestingly enough, so do our modern-day prophets, seers, and revelators. Listen to these words by D. Todd Christofferson, of the Quorum of the Twelve Apostles, regarding this doctrine:

"This is our message, the rock upon which we build, the foundation of everything else in the Church. Like all that comes from God, ***this doctrine is pure, it is clear, it is easy to understand—even for a child.*** With glad hearts, we invite all to *receive* it" (D. Todd Christofferson, "The Doctrine of Christ"; 2012 General Conference, emphasis added). This invitation to be born again is likewise patterned after the one given in Alma 5:49. We are told that it is to be taught to "every one that dwelleth in the land, yea, to preach unto all, both old and young, both bond and free, yea, I say unto you the aged, and also the middle aged and the rising generation; yea, to cry unto them that they must repent and be born again" (Alma 5:49). Question: When we include the teaching of our need to be born again to the old and young, the aged, the middle aged, and the rising generation, who does this leave out?

Every Sunday, most of us either unknowingly or unconsciously reaffirm our desire and willingness to be spiritually born again or born of God, which is to say, to "take upon [us] the name of [His] Son" (Mor. 4:3). How many of us ever clue in to this fact? The Lord said that there would be few who would find the gate of spiritual rebirth, which occurs by receiving the ***manifestations*** of God by the power of the Holy Ghost. This is because few are willing to *risk it all* or be "all in" pertaining to our willingness to sacrifice everything. President Joseph Fielding Smith spoke to these few who would find the gate when he spoke of "a great many members" who would not desire to find it on the level that is required: "We have a great many members of this Church that have never reached a *manifestation* through the Holy Ghost. Why? Because they have not made their lives conform to the truth.... That great gift of the Holy Ghost comes to us only through humility and faith in obedience. Therefore, a *great many members* of the Church should not have that guidance" (*Deseret News: Church Section,* November 4, 1961, p. 14). Notice how the antithesis to "a great many members of the Church" directly corresponds to the "few there be that find it." That said, all who subscribe to the articles of adoption will find the gate. We are all on equal footing. *The unquenchable desire to know God and the diligence in seeking Him through faith is the path that will lead us there.*

The level of willingness to find the gate requires that one seek Him diligently and have a diamond-hard resolve and determination to serve Him to the end, should He reveal himself to the candidate of salvation. Sadly, we are the ones holding ourselves back and refusing His grace. But know this. His arms are outstretched everlastingly to embrace us. Seek this Jesus! Desire... Ask, Seek, Knock—Receive. Then repeat.]

The Doctrine of Christ according to the Resurrected Christ (3 Nephi 9).
(See www.PuttingOnChrist.com for future release of this material.)
The Doctrine of Christ according to the Resurrected Christ (see 3 Nephi 11:22-41).
(See www.PuttingOnChrist.com for future release of this material.)

The Doctrine of Christ according to the Resurrected Christ (see 3 Nephi 12:1-2).

1 And it came to pass that when Jesus had spoken these words unto Nephi, and to those who had been called, (now the number of them who had been called, and received power and authority to baptize, was twelve) and behold, he stretched forth his hand unto the multitude, and cried unto them, saying: Blessed are ye if ye shall give heed unto the words of these twelve whom I have chosen from among you to minister unto you, and to be your servants; and unto them I have given power that they may baptize you with water; *and after that ye are baptized with water, behold,* ***I*** *will baptize you with fire and with the Holy Ghost*; therefore blessed are ye if ye shall believe in me and be baptized, after that ye have seen me and know that I am (emphasis added). [After describing three times the doctrine of Christ and the method of being saved, Christ laid His hands on the heads of His apostles in order to confer the holy priesthood upon them, giving them the authority to perform these ordinances themselves. Then he gave them a promise that those who receive the baptism of *water*

(notice that He specified the type of baptism), He himself would then baptize them "with fire and with the Holy Ghost." These are the required baptisms to enter the kingdom of God, and the "baptism by water is but half a baptism, and is ***good for nothing without the other half***—that is, the baptism of the Holy Ghost" (Joseph Smith, *Teachings of the Prophet Joseph Smith,* p. 314) The Prophet Joseph also stated: "The baptism of water, without the baptism of fire and the Holy Ghost attending it, is of no use; they are necessarily and inseparably connected. An individual must be born of water and the Spirit in order to get into the kingdom of God" (TPJS, p. 360)].

2 And again, more blessed are they who shall believe in your words because that ye shall testify that ye have seen me, and that ye know that I am. Yea, blessed are they who shall believe in your words, and come down into the ***depths of humility*** and be baptized, ***for they shall be visited with fire and with the Holy Ghost, and shall receive a remission of their sins*** *(emphasis added).* [Here the Lord breaks down the doctrine of Christ with more specificity and includes the words, "come down into the depths of humility." The "depths of humility" can be facilitated by a spiritual crash site or mini-Gethsemane of our own. The Lord also makes a distinction between those who had seen Him and those who should believe on the words of others who had seen Him [or those who had otherwise obtained the knowledge of God]. The latter He describes as "more blessed" should they believe. Then He issues the promise that these too who should believe on the words of others "***shall be visited with fire and with the Holy Ghost, and shall receive a remission of their sins.***" This is the ***third time***, by the way, that the Lord uses the phrase "fire and with the Holy Ghost," in 3rd Nephi, Chapters 11 & 12, a perfect number. Here the Lord also explains, just as Nephi did in 2 Nephi 31:17, that the remission of sins comes by way of "fire and with the Holy Ghost," not in the waters of baptism, although the baptism of water is a prerequisite and deemed a required ***sign to God.*** Joseph said, "Baptism is a sign to God, to angels, and to heaven that we do the will of God" (*Teachings of the Prophet Joseph Smith,* p.198).]

The Doctrine of Christ according to the Resurrected Christ (see 3 Nephi 27). (See www.PuttingOnChrist.com for future release of this material).

The Doctrine of Christ according to the Resurrected Christ through His Prophet (see 3 Nephi 30:1-2, which concludes 3 Nephi)

1 Hearken, O ye Gentiles, and hear the words of Jesus Christ, the Son of the living God, which he hath commanded me that I should speak concerning you, for, behold he commandeth me that I should write, saying:

2 Turn, all ye Gentiles, from your wicked ways; and repent of your evil doings, of your lyings and deceivings, and of your whoredoms, and of your secret

abominations, and your idolatries, and of your murders, and your priestcrafts, and your envyings, and your strifes, and from all your wickedness and abominations, and come unto me, and be baptized in my name, that ye may receive a remission of your sins, and be filled with the Holy Ghost, that ye may be numbered with my people who are of the house of Israel. [Why would the Savior through His prophet conclude with the doctrine of Christ? Because this is the *only way* we can be saved—the one and *only way*. There is *no other way*. He invites us to turn from sin and to come unto Him through repentance and turning to Him in faith so that we might be "baptized in [His] name" and "filled with the Holy Ghost." This is when we are born again and are "numbered with [His] people who are of the house of Israel." To endure to the end is to *remain numbered* with His people].

The Doctrine of Christ according to Enoch, Patriarch of the Translated City of Enoch (see Moses 6:50-68)

50 But God hath made known unto our fathers that all men must repent.

51 And he called upon our father Adam by his own voice, saying: I am God; I made the world, and men before they were in the flesh.

52 And he also said unto him: If thou wilt turn unto me and *hearken unto my voice*, and *believe, and repent of all thy transgressions*, and be *baptized,* even in water, in the name of mine Only Begotten Son, who is full of grace and truth, which is Jesus Christ, the only name which shall be given under heaven, whereby salvation shall come unto the children of men, *ye shall receive the gift of the Holy Ghost*, asking all things in his name, and whatsoever ye shall ask, it shall be given you (emphasis added). [Alma admonished his son Helaman to "look to God and live." To do this, one must "hearken unto [His] voice," which is Spirit (D&C 88:66). This "looking to God" through turning to the voice of His Spirit was reaffirmed by Joseph Smith when he told us to repent, obey the gospel, and "turn to God" directly, because, as he said, "*your religion won't save you*" (Teachings of the Prophet Joseph Smith, p. 361; emphasis added). In other words, our religion, although true, is not enough to save us. We are not members of an "automatic salvation factory," even in the true Church of Christ. This may be the belief which may "lull us away." The ordinances and authority found within our religion gives us "the opportunity for salvation" subject to our own "turning to God" directly, using our God-given agency. The directive is to "Draw near unto me and I will draw near unto you; seek me diligently and ye *shall* find me" (D&C 88:63; emphasis added). This "turning to God" requires our absolute belief and faith in Christ, repentance of all our sins, offering our broken heart upon the altar of our souls in complete surrender, the prior immersion in water, relying 100% upon the merits of Christ, and crying out for His mercy with the required willingness, commitment, and resolve (even as a desperate and panicked man who is drowning needs air) to "hearken" all the days of our lives to His voice thereafter.

Subject to the fulfillment of these conditions, together with the ordinance of the laying on of hands by those having authority (not mentioned, yet understood), we will thereafter be given the gift of the Holy Ghost, which is a "type" of that "director" or Liahona which is given to abide in us as the Comforter so that we can be made and remain clean and make our way back to the Father. Alma finishes the tender words to his son Helaman by saying, "O my son, do not let us be slothful because of the easiness of the way; for so it was with our fathers ... that if they would look [to God as the author and finisher of their salvation] they might live [i.e., be made alive in Christ, and by enduring to the end, receive eternal life]; even so it is with us. The way is prepared, and if we will look [to God] we may live forever" (Alma 37:46). This looking directly to God is paramount. Elder George Q. Cannon stated, "Perhaps it is his own design that faults and weaknesses should appear in high places in order that his saints may learn to trust in Him and not in any man or men," paralleling Nephi's warning to not put our "trust in the arm of the flesh" (as cited in Ezra Taft Benson, *An Enemy Hath Done This,* Bookcraft, p. 290;).]

55 And the Lord spake unto Adam, saying: Inasmuch as thy children are conceived in sin, even so when they begin to grow up, ***sin conceiveth in their hearts***, and they taste the bitter, that they may know to prize the good (emphasis added). [Because we are the seed of Adam, and because Adam fell, once we reach the age of accountability, this seed begins to naturally conceive and sprout sin in our hearts. In other words, it is at the age of accountability that we first begin to blossom as the natural, fallen man. This natural phenomenon of sin conceiving in our hearts happens to all of us automatically. The only way to reverse this is for a miraculous change to happen wherein we are no longer the seed of Adam but become the actual seed of Abraham and an adopted member in the family of Christ. This conversion happens when we receive the First Comforter, which is when we receive a baptism or "immersion" in Spirit. This helps us better understand the Prophet Joseph's words wherein he stated that "the effect of the Holy Ghost upon a Gentile, is to purge out the old blood, *and make him actually of the seed of Abraham. That man that has none of the blood of Abraham (naturally) must have a recreation by the Holy Ghost"* (*Teachings of the Prophet Joseph Smith,* p. 149). Surely such a mighty change experience for a gentile would be noticeable.]

56 And it is given unto them to know good from evil; wherefore they are agents unto themselves, and I have given unto you another law and commandment.

57 Wherefore teach it unto your children, that all men, everywhere, must repent, or they can in nowise inherit the kingdom of God, for ***no unclean thing can dwell there, or dwell in his presence***; for, in the language of Adam, Man of Holiness is his name, and the name of his Only Begotten is the Son of Man, even Jesus Christ, a righteous Judge, who shall come in the meridian of time (emphasis added). [Here God further introduces the doctrine of Christ in its simplicity: **No unclean thing can dwell with the Man of Holiness**. This is very clear. All that should consume our desire, thoughts, intentions, and time should be to answer the question as to how we

may become cleansed and purified by God while here in mortality in order to again dwell in His presence in the afterlife. For we cannot become clean by our own merits or individual willpower. ***Testimony or belief alone is insufficient to save us since our testimony may not have led us yet to actually being cleansed by the Deity.*** "Devils also believe, and tremble" (James 2:19).

Hence why we must turn to God and obey the gospel, repent in full, offer up our broken hearts in complete surrender, and cry out for His mercy and grace, tied to that committed willingness to be "all in" thereafter. What we are looking for is not just forgiveness of a few sins or even *many* sins. We are looking for a remission of *all* sins. This should be every individual's objective who comes into mortality. But there's a catch. We must find the organization on earth that possesses the keys and authority to perform these ordinances. That organization is Jesus Christ's alone, restored by His hand. So often I hear people recite that Joseph Smith restored the Church of Christ, but this is a fallacy. Christ restored His Church, working through Joseph Smith as an instrument. And had the Lord's "instrument" failed to perform in accordance with His will, the Lord would have replaced this instrument with another. For the Lord said that Joseph would continue to be His instrument "*if he abide in me*, and if not, another will I plant in his stead" (D&C 35:18; emphasis added). Hence it is not the Church of Joseph Smith, but rather The Church of Jesus Christ of Latter-day Saints. Is this not liberating when hearing "Lo here, and lo there" as to Joseph's purported sins and transgressions? Joseph was traversing the same path we are to traverse and was imperfect like unto us. As previously referenced, we become "true" saints when we are "Saint-ified" by the reception of the Holy Ghost in power through that baptism of spiritual fire referenced throughout holy writ. Everything received from God ultimately plays a part in leading us to this experience of reconciliation through a spiritual cleansing and purification.]

58 Therefore I give unto you a commandment, to *teach these things freely unto your children*, saying: (emphasis added). [We are told by God himself that we are to teach how we may go about becoming "clean" so that we might return to live with Him. We are to teach "these things freely *unto [our] children"* without holding anything back. And this directive is also given us by Alma: "Yea, to preach unto all, both old and young, both bond and free; yea, I say unto you the aged, and also the middle aged, and the rising generation, yea, to cry unto them that they must repent and be born again" (Alma 5:49).

Many in the true Church of Christ shy away from this term *born again*. I believe it is because of its affiliation with our Protestant friends known as "Born Again Christians." Nothing could be more imperative for us than being born again in this life! Nothing. For without this transformative experience of the heart, we will not have found nor known God on the level required to be saved. "The principle of salvation is given us through the knowledge of Jesus Christ," the Prophet states (*Teachings of the Prophet Joseph Smith,* p. 297). And this knowledge is "a knowledge of all things that pertain to life and salvation" (*Lectures On Faith,* Lecture 4:18), which preeminently includes *the knowledge of God* and of His reality. And this knowledge of God is a knowledge on the same level "as though he had already come among [us]" (Mosiah 3:13). And after it is received, this knowledge places us securely at a station beyond that of belief or testimony obtained through the Light of Christ. It is actual knowledge. "Strait is the gate, and narrow the way that leadeth unto the exaltation and continuation of the lives [meaning, to have eternal offspring as an exalted being in the eternities], and few there be that find it, ***because ye receive me not in the world neither do ye know me. But if ye receive me in the world, then shall ye know me***, and shall receive your exaltation; that where I am ye shall be also" (D&C 132:22-23; emphasis added).

Notice again that we must "receive Him in the world" in order to "know Him." D&C 39 outlines for us what it means to "receive [Him] in the world": "But to as many as received me [meaning, in mortality], gave I power [i.e., an endowment of power of a living faith] to become my sons; and even so will I give unto as many as will receive me, power to become my sons. And verily, verily, I say unto you, *he that receiveth my gospel receiveth me; and he that receiveth not my gospel, receiveth not me*" [D&C 39:4-5; emphasis added]. So here, the only thing that remains is to know how to receive His gospel, so that we can "receive Him." The next verse outlines how this "receiving His gospel" is to occur: "And this is my gospel—repentance and baptism by water, and ***then cometh the baptism of fire and the Holy Ghost, even the Comforter***, which showeth all things, and teacheth the peaceable things of the kingdom" [D&C 39:6; emphasis added]. ***This is the gate!*** Could there possibly be anything clearer than what we have read here in black and white, in our own language? This is the plain and simple answer as to how we can become clean and pass through the gate. It is through that baptism in spiritual fire by the Deity, which purges filth, sin, and dross out of the human soul. This is when we are born again ***and know Him***, even while *in the world.* Do not accept any of the erroneous teachings or traditions of some of our fathers as to how we are saved. Find the gate! We must not stop until we not only believe, but until we have come to receive the *actual knowledge of God*! Nephi said, "Wherefore, now after I have spoken these words, if ye cannot understand them it will be because ye ask not, neither do ye knock" (2 Ne. 32:4). Nor will we experience one of the fruits of spiritual rebirth, which is to *speak with the tongue of the angels while being filled with a member of the Godhead, shouting praises unto the Holy One of Israel,* until this knowledge is given us. Surely, if we had experienced something this transformative, we would know about it. If not, we must press forward with a steadfastness in Christ until the gift is received. I thoroughly believe our eternal salvation depends on it. The next verse likens spiritual rebirth to that of a natural birth. It lists the elements involved in both types of births, spiritual and natural, which is that of water, blood, and spirit.]

59 That by reason of transgression cometh the fall, which fall bringeth death, and inasmuch as ye were born into the world by water, and blood, and the spirit, which I

have made, and so became of dust a living soul, even so ye must be born again [spiritually] into the kingdom of heaven, of water, and of the Spirit, and be cleansed by blood, even the blood of mine Only Begotten; that ye might be sanctified from all sin, and ***enjoy*** the words (i.e., the promise) of eternal life ***in this world***, and eternal life in the world to come, even immortal glory (emphasis added). [In this verse, the Lord begins by teaching about the Fall, which brings "spiritual death," which is to be separated from the Father's presence. We are likewise made "fallen man," whereby we become a "natural man." Then He continues by likening the natural birth to that of the spiritual. We must be spiritually born again, beginning with the baptism of water. Joseph stated that, "Baptism [of water by priesthood authority] is a holy ordinance *preparatory* to the reception of the Holy Ghost; it is the *channel and key* by which the Holy Ghost will be administered" (*Teachings of the Prophet Joseph Smith,* p. 148; emphasis added).

The law of justice, which requires that we pay for our sins in full, is still in play. This requires that man be "justified through Christ," made possible by His infinite atonement. This justification is when we *obtain justification before the bar and law of God.* To be justified is to be "acquitted" and even made instantaneously righteous by the Atoning One as an act of grace. (Faith is "*the foundation of all righteousness*" [*Lectures On Faith* 1:1, 27]). This act of grace stems from man having received divine approval from the Deity, *protecting man from the full weight and force of the law of justice* (see *Mormon Doctrine,* p. 408; emphasis added). The words "might be sanctified" suggest that this sanctification is contingent on our being justified through Christ *and* having our ordinances approved by the Holy Spirit of Promise, after which we can then be born of the Spirit. This being born of the Spirit is what few find because few are willing to fully repent and "cry out" with that sufficiency of faith required, while possessing the requisite *willingness* to be "all in" with Christ thereafter. The Prophet Joseph taught, "The Gift of the Holy Ghost by the laying on of hands, cannot be received…if the proposals [meaning those proposals outlined within the doctrine of Christ and the patterns for their fulfillment found in scripture] are not complied with" [*Teachings of the Prophet Joseph Smith,* p. 148).]

60 For by the water ye keep the commandment; by the Spirit ye are justified, and by the blood ye are sanctified. [Here the Lord instructs Enoch that it is the act of entering into the water of baptism that gives us the possibility for entrance into His presence in a coming day. It is a sign. Joseph said, "Upon this same principle…baptism [of water] is a sign ordained of God, for the believer in Christ to take upon himself in order to enter into the kingdom of God,—for except ye are born *of water*, and *of the spirit* ye cannot enter into the kingdom of God, saith the Savior.… Baptism [of water] is a sign to God, to angels, and to heaven that we will do the will of God" (*Times and Seasons,* vol. 3, pp.751-752). The fulfillment of our objective to enter into the presence of God again is contingent on the ordinance performed by the laying on of hands on our heads, becoming "justified" as pertaining to the law and being cleansed and sanctified in power by the Holy Ghost—all made possible by the

shedding of the blood of Christ in Gethsemane and on Calvary. It is the blood of Christ which sanctifies us. As previously referenced, when we are "justified" by the Holy Spirit of Promise, we are immediately "made righteous." How is this possible? Because now the Father and the Son have approved the offering of our broken hearts in total submission through a contriteness of Spirit, in total repentance and surrender to Them in full, tied to an unbending commitment to serve Them until the end. The Lord "searcheth the hearts and the reins" (Rev. 2:23) and thereby knows when we have complied in full with the requisite proposals and divine law granting our justification, thereby nullifying the sin for which we otherwise would have been responsible to pay.

When this justification is sanctioned by the Holy Spirit of Promise, the actual gift of the Holy Ghost can then be received, and the candidate can be fully immersed or baptized in the Holy Ghost. This is when all dross, filth, evil, and sin is burned out of the baptized candidate, as though by spiritual fire. This is when we receive the remission of sins. This is when we are sanctified by the Spirit and become righteous "Saints," not just in word but in power and in all reality. This is also when Christ writes His name on our hearts (see Mosiah 5:11-12). This is full conversion (an "immersion" in His Spirit), just as the apostle Peter's conversion was on the day of Pentecost. Can this full conversion happen for all? The Prophet Joseph taught that "*whatsoever constitutes the salvation of one will constitute the salvation of* ***every creature*** *which will be saved*" (*Lectures On Faith,* p. 72).]

61 Therefore it is given to abide in you; the record of heaven; the Comforter; the peaceable things of immortal glory; the truth of all things; that which quickeneth all things, which maketh alive all things; that which knoweth all things, and hath all power according to wisdom, mercy, truth, justice, and judgment. [This verse constitutes the most significant and profound description of the endowments we receive at the time of our spiritual rebirth when we receive the First Comforter and gift of the Holy Ghost. Just as all men who come into this world have "implanted in them" a portion of God's light and Spirit called the Light of Christ, all "new creatures" of the Holy Ghost receive an amplified influence of guiding and enlightening powers and endowments which are implanted, bestowed, and infused through the Comforter.

Each expression within the above scriptural verse refers to a specific endowment of the Spirit within man. I like to think of the "record of heaven" as twofold: a record of all thoughts, feelings, and actions by which we will be judged, and a "record" that brings all truth to our remembrance. The peaceable things of immortal glory are what the apostle Peter called "the divine nature," which is infused in us through the periodic endowments of portions of God's light and glory as a gift of grace. These "peaceable things" of His nature are the portions of His attributes we receive grace for grace as we do "the works which ye have seen me do," thereby growing in light and truth, from grace to grace. The "truth of all things" is that Spirit element referred to in scripture as "the Spirit of truth." That which "quickeneth all things" is that element of God's glory which we experience as the "quickening in the inner man" which sanctifies us through the Comforter. That which "maketh alive all things" is this same Spirit or light that fills the immensity. And contained within this light is that which "knoweth all things, and hath all power according to wisdom, mercy, truth, justice, and judgment." Through receiving a fulness of this light, we can "discern" or "judge" perfectly, because all will be "known." This transformation all takes place within the "inner man" and is not necessarily discernable to anyone looking on the outside, although the eyes and countenance of one born of the Spirit often reveal it. Membership in the Church and kingdom of God on earth alone is not sufficient for man to be born again and obtain salvation, which would include the accompanying spiritual endowments as outlined above. Man must *look to God* in order to spiritually live. Man must realize that he cannot "merit anything of himself; but the sufferings and death of Christ atone for [his] sins, *through faith and repentance*, and so forth" (Alma 22:14; emphasis added).

Orson Pratt spoke about gifts imparted by the Comforter when he said, "This knowledge… when persons receive this, they then have for themselves an assurance that no earthly argument or philosophical demonstration can possibly impart.… What can be a stronger evidence to any man than an evidence of this kind? It affects his inner man…it is ***a part of God*** imparted unto man…giving him… *an assurance that no person has, and that no person can have, unless they adopt* ***the same*** *means, in order to partake of* ***the same*** *blessings or to be administered to in* ***the same*** *way, and receive through* ***the same*** *medium,* ***that same*** *spirit of intelligence which nothing but the Holy Ghost can impart"* (*Journal of Discourses,* 3:178-179). Joseph Smith defined this gift of the First Comforter as "**the same** as given on the day of Pentecost" (*Teachings of the Prophet Joseph Smith,* p.149; see also Acts 2; emphasis added).]

62 And now, behold, I say unto you: This is the plan of salvation unto **all men**, through the blood of mine Only Begotten, who shall come in the meridian of time (emphasis added). [Or as Nephi said, "***This is the way; and there is none other way nor name given under heaven whereby man can be saved in the kingdom of God.*** And now, behold, ***this is the doctrine of Christ***, and the only and true doctrine of the Father, and of the Son, and of the Holy Ghost, which is one God, without end. Amen" (2 Ne. 31:21; emphasis added). It is made possible through the blood of Christ shed in Gethsemane and on Calvary, providing the opportunity for all, "that whosoever will believe might be saved" (Hel. 14:29). Salvation is made available to all, subject to man's compliance with the full gospel law. When man fulfills the whole of the law, the promised blessing of the Holy Ghost is then received as a gift.]

64 And it came to pass, when the Lord had spoken with Adam, our father, that Adam *cried [out] unto the Lord [for mercy and redemption]*, and he was caught away by the Spirit of the Lord, and was carried down into the water, and was laid under the water, and was brought forth out of the water (emphasis added). [This is the baptism or immersion in water, which is a sign by man that he will follow God. Crying

out to God from the soul for mercy during our own mini-Gethsemane (or broken-hearted repentance) is a prerequisite demonstrated throughout scripture and necessary to be born again.]

65 ***And thus*** he was baptized, and the Spirit of God descended *upon him*, **and thus** he was born of the Spirit, and became *quickened in the inner man* [emphasis added]. ["***And thus***" means, "this is how it's done" and "this is the pattern to follow." This same "and thus" language was also used by Alma the younger in Mosiah: "All mankind … must be born again, yea born of God, changed from their … fallen state … *being redeemed of God…. And thus* they become new creatures" (Mosiah 27:24-26; emphasis added). This is the baptism or immersion in spiritual fire and the Holy Ghost. This is the sign given by God, in answer to our sign to Him by our immersion in water, that He has accepted our offering of a broken heart and a contrite spirit (an absolute requirement per 2 Ne. 2:6-7), tied to our willingness and wholehearted commitment to follow Him thereafter, even to the degree of willingness in risking everything, including the offering of our very lives in His service, and/or the offering up of our mortal lives if called upon so to do. This is when we are "quickened in the inner man" and are born of God.

This is the gate that Christ said few would find. And fewer still will "endure to the end," meaning, few will stay by the tree of life, continuously partaking of its fruit and doing His will throughout the remainder of their days in mortality. This ongoing spiritual nourishment is the "living waters" to which Christ often referred. The reason that we are "quickened in the inner man" is to enable us the ability to enter the Divine Presence while in our flesh, as well as in that eternal world. We must be prepared in advance and remain protected by and through His quickening influence, which is one of the main purposes for the First Comforter. Notice these verses: "And no man can behold all my glory, and afterwards remain in the flesh on the earth" (Moses 1:5); "For no man has seen God at any time in the flesh, *except quickened by the Spirit of God*" (D&C 67:11; emphasis added); "For without this no man can *see the face of God*, even the Father, and live" (D&C 84:22; emphasis added).

In the Guide to the Scriptures, the definition of the word *quicken* is, "to make alive… to change a person ***so that he can be in the presence of God***" (Guide to the Scriptures, Study Helps, "Quicken"). Said another way, one of the purposes of the First Comforter is to prepare us to obtain the Second Comforter spoken of in scripture. And the purpose of the Second Comforter, at least in part, is to redeem us from the Fall of Adam so we can meet the Lord in this life and later be shown the Father by Christ Himself.]

66 And he heard a voice out of heaven, saying: *Thou art baptized with fire, and with the Holy Ghost.* This is the record of the Father, and the Son, from henceforth and forever (emphasis added). [In addition to being filled with a member of the Godhead as on the day of Pentecost, many who go through this spiritual rebirth will experience a voice coming to their minds, or even an audible voice, reaffirming unto

them that they are either being born of the Spirit or baptized with fire and the Holy Ghost. This is the "voice out of heaven." This "record of the Father" of how we may become "one in [Him]" and of the necessity of being "baptized with fire, and with the Holy Ghost" is part of that record pertaining to the doctrine of Christ that should never be modified or changed, stemming from an immutable decree by Father Elohim Himself. This is why He specifically issued the words, "***from henceforth and forever***" (emphasis added). Paul also spoke to this when he said, "there be some that … would pervert the gospel [i.e., doctrine] of Christ," and added, "but though we, or an angel from heaven, preach ***any other gospel*** unto you than that which we have preached unto you, let him be accursed. As we said before, so say I now again, if any man preach *any other gospel* unto you than that ye have ***received***, let him be accursed" (Gal. 1:8-9; emphasis added). In other words, "This is the record of the Father, and the Son, from henceforth and forever," and the way to becoming one of His sons (including with regards to those same fruits of salvation arising therefrom) is not to be described *differently than what it actually is*, neither altered or changed by any man, including the ordinances of salvation. Joseph said, "*Ordinances* instituted in the heavens before the foundation of the world, in the priesthood, for the salvation of men, *are not to be altered or changed*" (*Teachings of the Prophet Joseph Smith,* p. 308; emphasis added). This likewise applies to the doctrine of Christ and the fruits arising therefrom.]

67 And thou art after the order of him who was without beginning of days or end of years, from all eternity to all eternity.

68 Behold, thou art one in me, a son of God; ***and thus*** may all become my sons. Amen (emphasis added). [Through spiritual rebirth, we experience a perfect knowledge of God's existence and reality (beyond that of faith) and a oneness with the Father, Son, and seemingly all other living creations, at least in our immediate environment. We become filled with God's love, or charity. We become one of His sons, because through our whole and authentic faith and repentance, issuing forth the cry of the soul for mercy to be redeemed and cleansed (tied to that requisite "willingness" of sacrifice and determination to serve Him to the end), we are spiritually adopted by God and become a living "epistle of Christ ... written not with ink, but with the Spirit of the living God, not in tables of stone, but in fleshy tables of the heart" (2 Cor. 3:3).

I'd like to close this chapter by sharing the lyrics from one of our LDS hymns entitled "Behold Thy Sons and Daughters, Lord," which references the experiential *hour* of our redemption:

> Verse 1: Behold thy sons and daughters, Lord, on whom we lay our hands. [This is the promise of the Father that is confirmed upon us by the laying on of hands.] They have fulfilled the gospel word, And bowed at thy commands. [Through *fulfilling* the gospel word, we are justified by the Holy Spirit of Promise.]

> <u>Verse 2</u>: Oh, now send down the heav'nly dove [symbol of the Holy Ghost], And overwhelm their souls [baptism of fire], With peace and joy and perfect love [the fruit of God's love received at the time of the rebirth], As lambs within thy fold [metaphor for those of His sheep that can now "go in and out and find pasture"].
>
> <u>Verse 3</u>: Seal them by thine own Spirit's pow'r [This is when the Lord's name is written on our hearts through the Holy Spirit of Promise.], Which purifies from sin [this is the remission of sins by fire and the Holy Ghost], And may they find, from this *good hour*, They are adopted in. [This is when we are no longer a cucumber but a pickle, per Elder Bednar ("Ye Must Be Born Again," April, 2007 General Conference Talk)].

We are now sons of God, begotten sons unto God. King Benjamin said that "*this day* he hath spiritually begotten you" (Mosiah 5:7). Notice that in the hymn below, Elder Parley P. Pratt also refers to "*this good hour*." Let us now also consider the lyrics of the hymn, "Now Let Us Rejoice."

"Now let us rejoice in ***the day*** *of salvation.*
No longer as strangers on earth need we roam.
Good tidings are sounding to us and each nation.
And shortly ***the hour*** *of redemption will come,*
When all that was promised the Saints will be given"
("Now Let Us Rejoice," Hymns, p. 3).

Whether referring to the day or the hour, the author of these words is referring to an actual experience in power by the Holy Ghost wherein we are "redeemed of the Lord." This is when we experience a full conversion and obtain *the knowledge of God* beyond that of faith. Referring to this experience, the Lord said: "At that ***day*** ye shall know that I am in my Father, and ye in me, and I in you" (John 14:20). As we receive this gift, we are born again into the family of Christ, having been adopted as a member of His family, ***and we know it, or at least understand that something deeply transformative has happened to us—no question***. Even, we are told by the apostle Paul, "the Spirit Himself bears witness with our spirt that we are children of God" through "the Spirit of adoption" by whom we cry out, 'Abba, Father'" (Romans 8: 15-16).

And now we return to our hymn:

> <u>Verse 4</u>: Increase their faith, confirm their hope [i.e., confirm their hope from the promise they received at the time of their rebirth, reaffirmed to them by way of that more sure word of prophecy], And guide them in the way [the way, in this context, is personal revelation through the Spirit, and growing in the

knowledge of God], with comfort bear their spirits up, Until the perfect day [Comfort them through the Comforter and through the knowledge of having been sealed up unto eternal life, counting all things as dross but for the excellency of the knowledge of Christ until the perfect day when we shall see "eye to eye" in mortality]. (See chapter 12, "Rending the Veil and Knowing God"; Text: Parley P. Pratt, 1807–1857, Music: Alexander Schreiner, 1901–1987. © 1948 IRI.)

Chapter 8

Seven Born Again in Our Latter Day

In the Doctrine and Covenants section 124, given during the early years of the Church, the Lord directed the Prophet Joseph Smith to pen a "solemn proclamation" to all the leaders and nations of the world. This responsibility ultimately ended up wresting on Parley P. Pratt, who is thought to have written most of the document with the help of the other members of the Quorum of the Twelve Apostles. It was entitled "Proclamation of the Twelve Apostles of the Church of Jesus Christ of Latter-day Saints." It speaks to our *unchangeable gospel*. I'd like to share with the reader the first two pages of that proclamation:

To all the Kings of the World; To the President of the United States of America; To the Governors of the several States; And to the Rulers and People of all Nations: Greeting: Know ye:—

That the kingdom of God has come: as has been predicted by ancient prophets, and prayed for in all ages, even that kingdom which shall fill the whole earth, and shall stand for ever. The great Eloheem Jehovah has been pleased once more to speak from the heavens: and also to commune with man upon the earth, by means of open visions, and by the ministration of Holy Messengers. By this means the great and eternal High Priesthood, after the Order of his Son, even the Apostleship, has been restored; or, returned to the earth. This High Priesthood, or Apostleship, holds the keys of the kingdom of God, and power to bind on earth that which shall be bound in heaven; and to loose on earth that which shall be loosed in heaven. And, in fine, to do, and to administer in all things pertaining to the ordinances, organization, government and direction of the kingdom of God. Being established in these last days for the restoration of all things spoken by the prophets since the world began; and in order to prepare the way for the coming of the Son of Man.

And we now bear witness that his coming is near at hand; and not many years hence, the nations and their kings shall see him coming in the clouds of heaven with power and great glory. In order to meet this great event there must needs be a preparation. Therefore we send unto you with authority from on high, and command you all to repent and humble yourselves as little children, before the majesty of the Holy One; and ***come unto Jesus with a broken heart and a contrite spirit, and be baptized in his name****, for the remission of sins (that is, be buried in the water in the likeness of his burial and rise again to newness of life, in the likeness of his resurrection), and you shall receive the gift of the Holy Spirit, through the laying on of the hands of the Apostles and elders, of this great and last dispensation of mercy to man. This Spirit shall* ***bear witness*** *to you, of the truth of our testimony; and shall enlighten your minds, and be* ***in you*** *as the spirit of prophecy and revelation. It shall bring things past to your understanding and remembrance; and shall show you things to come. It shall also impart unto you many great and glorious gifts; such as the gift of healing the sick, and of being healed, by the laying on of hands in the name of Jesus; and of expelling Demons; and even of seeing visions, and conversing with Angels and spirits from the unseen world. By the light of this Spirit, received through the ministration of the ordinances— by the power and authority of the Holy Apostleship and Priesthood, you will be enabled to Understand, and to be the children of light; and thus be prepared to escape all the things that are coming on the earth, and so stand before the Son of Man. We testify that the foregoing doctrine is the doctrine or gospel of Jesus Christ, in its fulness; and that it is the only true, everlasting, and* ***unchangeable gospel****; and the only plan revealed on earth whereby man can be saved" ("Proclamation of the Twelve Apostles of the Church of Jesus Christ of Latter-day Saints," April, 1845; emphasis added).*

When we receive the *unchangeable gospel* referenced in this proclamation, whose fruits have been the same since ancient times—and will be from everlasting to everlasting—we shall be born of the Spirit even as those of old, and experience the same blessings that were experienced by them. We will then *be the children of light* ourselves and come to the actual knowledge of Him through that broken-hearted offering of the heart in complete surrender—being born again.

In the book *Born of the Spirit*, E. Richard Packham relates the story of an anonymous woman who had been born again. I include it here because it follows the pattern and experience of spiritual rebirth that is discussed in this work. It is similar in many ways to the accounts of the 7 born again in our latter day (and four of whom I know personally), and from whence came the title of this chapter. These four have each been invited to share their own very personal story as to how they were led to be born of God. For the record, none of these four is my own personal story. With that said, all experiences of spiritual rebirth are miraculous in my view, and have an underlying commonality between them.

In studying the below accounts, see if you can find the pattern in their experiences. For example, you'll find that in each case, the individual experiences a major crisis, preceded and/or accompanied by an unquenchable desire and willingness to sacrifice all to know God, before obtaining the "mighty change of heart." The Light of Christ leads us to a profound, heart-felt repentance with a broken heart in a spirit of contriteness and complete submission so that we might fall down, cry out for mercy, and subsequently partake of the "exceedingly great joy" spoken of in scripture.

Born Again Experience #1 in Our Latter Day

I will not recount the entire story that Packham shares of this beloved sister who had been born again but instead have chosen to highlight the important points using her own words, added to occasionally with personal commentary:

"All of my life I have had a love of the scriptures. I have enjoyed reading all the standard works.... However, I have never understood the Atonement.... For several years as I have taken of the sacrament, I have prayed that I could understand the Atonement, but no understanding came to me.... I could not comprehend how the Savior could cleanse us. Would we simply say to Jesus, 'Here, take my sins!' and then we would be clean?

"My teacher began to rehearse for me the great suffering of our Lord ... of both the body and spirit to the extent that it caused him, even God, to bleed at every pore! It was a suffering which he willingly took upon himself, and he paid the penalty for each sin committed, even from the fall of Adam to the end of the Millennium. It was a suffering both physical and spiritual, which was so terrible that *it caused his great heart to break.* And to think that all the time he could have withdrawn!

"To realize that my own sins were amongst those which gave him pain brought me down into the depths of sorrow. I wept because of my sins ... not only because I was sorry that I had had them (for I had always been sorry before), *but because I knew that I had added to my Savior's suffering...* My heart was born down into the dust with this new realization, and I cried.... I did not realize that by my wicked ways I added to the incomprehensible suffering of him on that dreadful day! [C.S. Lewis, in his book *Mere Christianity,* said: 'When Christ died, he died for you individually just as much as if you had been the only person in the world'. Christ is a God who is constantly working on our behalf, individually and undividedly. Only a God could do that! He is our mediator and constant advocate with the Father.]

"Suddenly, there stood before me a bright picture of all my sins.... I was painfully aware of all my carelessness—yes, of even blasphemy! For I now realized how irreverent I had been in remembering the emblems of his death!

"How many times had I prayed during the sacrament (for ever since I was a little girl I had been taught to pray during the sacrament) and said, 'Dear Lord, I thank thee for all that I have and now please give me this, and give me that.' And ***never once did I thank him for his gift to me—or ask his forgiveness of my sins.*** "Or how many times had I come to the sacrament table and asked forgiveness for my own transgressions, *and still held a grudge against those who had transgressed against me*! All these things and many, many others stood bright and clear before me, and I was weak and sick with shame!

"*Then, suddenly*, that light flashed on bright and perfect and as clear as crystal. 'This is it!' I exulted. This is the love of God! My heart leaped with joy! My heart leaped up, and I wept again, but this time not with sorrow and shame, but with joy, for I had tasted of his love and forgiveness, and now I knew what it was!... I had indeed been 'born again' ... of the Spirit. *My first reaction beyond my pangs of joy was of astonishment (emphasis added).* Even though it was late at night, I wanted to run out and pound on the doors of the houses and shout, " I know about these things, I know about it—do you know about it?' I restrained myself, however, and instead of running and shouting, *I sat and meditated.* But I still could not, and cannot to this day, get over my surprise, for *I had been in the Church all my life, and had loved the gospel, and had not dreamed that there was so much more to be had.*

"The first thing which came to my mind *during my meditation,* was that I had never before known the real meaning of the fourth Article of Faith. Faith in the Lord Jesus Christ and repentance now means: ***a knowledge** (and I do not say belief because I had always believed*) ***of our Savior*** and his atonement to the extent that we are brought down into the depths of repentance, thus to plead for his mercy upon us; *for this is **the only way** we can enter again into the presence of the perfect God!* [Notice the similarity of her words to Alma's words: *"Never, until I did cry out unto the Lord for mercy, did I receive a remission of my sins" (Alma 38:8)].* And *I know* that he can purify us, *for I have felt his cleansing power*." [Notice that this dear sister "never once did ... ask for His forgiveness." To "ask" fulfills a divine law which cannot be made void or circumvented. There are many scriptures that point to this requirement (such as D&C 42:61; 46:7, and 1 Nephi 15:11).

Nephi often referred to the above ***knowledge*** of salvation as "a perfect brightness of hope." It is not mere belief. In this context, it is the knowledge given that we have received a remission of our sins, been promised eternal life, and obtained the knowledge of God. This anonymous sister defines the endowment of power called *faith* as that which leads to that knowledge of God. After her rebirth, she understood faith and repentance to now mean that process by which she had come to "***a knowledge of our Savior*** and his atonement (i.e., '*the knowledge of God*')." She did not use the word "belief," for as she had mentioned, she had "always believed." And this actual ***knowledge of God*** received during her spiritual rebirth ties into the words of Christ pertaining to all who are saved: "and *if they know me*...they shall have a place eternally at my right hand" (Mosiah 26: 24; emphasis added). "*If ye receive me in the world then shall ye know me*" (D&C 132:23; emphasis added). "The names of the righteous,... unto them will I grant an inheritance [of eternal life] *at my right hand*" (Alma 5:58; emphasis added). "And he shall set the sheep on his right hand, but the goats on the left. Then shall *the King* say unto them on his right hand, Come, ye blessed of my Father, inherit the kingdom prepared for you from the foundation of the world" (Matthew 25:33-34; emphasis added). *Said now in plainness, all those who receive the **sure knowledge and witness of God** by passing through "the gate" (which is to receive and be purified by the baptism of fire and of the Holy Ghost while "in the world" or during "the day of this life"), and who thereafter endure to the end, shall inherit eternal life,* which is to be saved in the highest degree of the celestial kingdom of God. Fellow seeker and sojourners, the actual ***knowledge*** [of God] that this dear sister obtained could only have come to her through a bestowed, living faith, received through compliance with the law upon which the promised blessing of this cleansing had been predicated. Said the Prophet Joseph, "*For there is a great difference between believing in God and knowing Him—knowledge implies more than faith*" (*Lectures On Faith,* p. 77; emphasis added). Our dear sister then reaffirms how this ***sure knowledge [of God]*** comes: "*And it is the **faith*** [i.e., this perfect, living faith bestowed] which we have had *that has brought us to this **great knowledge**"* *(Packham, "Born of the Spirit," p. 61; see also Mosiah 5:4, emphasis added).]*

Our good sister continued: "Then there flooded into my mind verse after verse of scripture—scripture which I had known since childhood, scripture that I had loved and repeated. And to my surprise *they had a new meaning*. In the light of the ***new knowledge*** which I received, these scriptures had taken on a new significance... they all had bearing on this one thing—the Atonement. [Even though her focus here is on the Atonement, it is clear to me that what she was trying to convey was that "this one thing" that "these scriptures" are directing us towards *is to experientially be born of God ourselves*, which is made possible through the Atonement of Christ, and, more specifically, through His power to make us a new creature—changing our very natures].

"I had felt this power (His power) and witnessed this presence [i.e., His "glory," which is the presence of God as perceived by humans], and for the first time I understood how we are cleansed by the refiner's fire [cleansed by an immersion in spiritual fire; emphasis added], how the gift of tongues comes, how Joseph Smith could prophesy in the name of the Lord, how the lame are made to walk, the blind to see, the dead raised [i.e., the gifts that follow them that believe]. I even understood how the brother of Jared could remove the veil so that he could see Jesus. And all these things I could see, because at last I'd been able to exercise my faith as a 'grain of mustard seed'.

"The next day…I could not resist the urge to sit down and read the scriptures, and to my astonishment the *true meaning of these things flooded into my understanding. I suddenly knew what all these things meant—and I knew that I knew!* I saw for the first time what all these prophets were trying to say. And they were all trying to say one thing—that Jesus died that we might live! [Jesus died that we might live, and not just physically but spiritually—to come alive unto a spiritual resurrection wherein Christ is made anew in us so that we too might say as did the apostle Paul, "Nevertheless I live; yet not I, but Christ liveth in me" (Galatians 2:20)].

"Now I know what it is that the writers would say again and again: 'And it is marvelous before our eyes—and we were astonished *and the eyes of our understanding were opened and it is the faith which we have had that has brought us to* ***this great knowledge [of God]*** whereby we do rejoice with *exceedingly great joy*' [which is the joy we experience at the time of our spiritual rebirth] (Packham, "Born of the Spirit," p. 61; see also Mosiah 5:4, emphasis added).

"As I went about my day's duties, my heart swelled up in an *unsurpassable love for those about me [i.e., the "love of God" or promised fruit of the Tree of Life]*, even the strangers whom I passed on the street. My heart went out in love to them, and I couldn't help looking at them and wondering *if they knew what I knew.*

"To my surprise not only had my spirit been quickened, but all of my senses also. I found a new enjoyment in the landscape about me. I saw beauty in all the commonplace things which had meant nothing to me before. The same old songs now seemed new and beautiful. And even colors seemed brighter and more vibrant because my senses were quickened so that I could enjoy them more! [This is the experience of oneness with all living things heretofore spoken of in Putting on Christ, which occurs during spiritual rebirth].

"I thought to myself, 'This is the means by which all things (i.e., spiritual knowledge) come—not by man's own [intellectual] knowledge but by the Holy Ghost which bears record of Him!' [This is the "learning by faith" discussed in holy writ. It follows the diagram from chapter 1. This living faith or "power to become the sons of God" yields knowledge unto salvation, and salvation includes being filled with God's love during the Rebirth, or in other words, "faith," "hope," and "charity."].

"And I must sing like Job of old—'I know that my redeemer liveth, and that he shall stand at the latter day upon the earth'; and if I am true and faithful and endure to the end, 'though after my skin worms destroy this body, yet in my flesh shall I see God" (E. Richard Packham, *Born of the Spirit,* pgs. 56-62; all bracketed, parenthetical additions, references in bold and/or italics above are mine and have been added for emphasis).

We must consistently practice the affirmation referenced above: "***Yet in my flesh shall I see God***" (Job 19:26; Moses 5:10). Ultimately, all it takes to realize or "make real" this blessing for ourselves is to hold to the ***desire*** within us to obtain (while removing the weeds of doubts and fears in the garden of our hearts), which we would never thereafter allow to be extinguished. This, together with the diligent and steadfast practice of daily loving God and seeking Him, will bring us to that encounter of all encounters. We need only imagine or "image in" our obsession of obtaining Christ through our imagination, visualization, and "eye of faith." Keep hope alive, for if we do, we shall experience being filled with the love of God, which hope or "spiritual knowledge" arises out of a bestowed, perfect living faith in Christ, even a perfect knowledge, and should we be so fortunate, later seeing "eye to eye"!

Born Again Experience #2 in Our Latter Day: Lorenzo Snow

Of all the stories of spiritual rebirth, I personally feel the most connected with that of Lorenzo Snow. His experience gives us an amazing pattern to discover where we might currently find ourselves on our journey to conditional salvation. These are his own words:

"Some two or three weeks after I was baptized, one day while engaged in my studies, I began to reflect upon *the fact that I had not obtained a knowledge of the truth* of the work … and I began to feel very uneasy [this is part of our "awful situation" which develops]. I laid aside my books, left the house, and wandered around through the fields *under the oppressive influence of a gloomy, disconsolate spirit, while an indescribable cloud of darkness seemed to envelope me.* I had been accustomed, at the close of the day, to retire for secret prayer, to a grove … but at this time I felt no inclination to do so. *The spirit of prayer had departed and the heavens seemed like brass over my head.* At length, realizing that the usual time had come for secret prayer, I concluded I would not forego my evening service, and, as a matter of formality, knelt as I was in the habit of doing, and in my accustomed retired place, but not feeling as I was wont to feel.

"I had no sooner opened my lips in an effort to pray, than I heard a sound, just above my head, like the rustling of silken robes, and immediately the Spirit of God descended upon me, completely enveloping my whole person, filling me, from the crown of my head to the soles of my feet, and O, the joy and happiness I felt! No language can describe the almost instantaneous transition from a dense cloud of mental and spiritual darkness into a *refulgence of light and knowledge*, as it was at that time imparted to my understanding…. It was a complete baptism, *a tangible immersion in the heavenly principle or element*, the Holy Ghost; and *even more real and physical in its effects upon every part of my system than the immersion by water;* dispelling forever, so long as reason and memory last, all possibility of doubt….

I cannot tell how long I remained in the full flow of the blissful enjoyment and divine enlightenment, but it was several minutes before the celestial element which filled and surrounded me began gradually to withdraw. On arising from my kneeling posture, … 'I *knew* that He had conferred on me what only an omnipotent being can confer—that which is of *greater value than all the wealth and honors worlds can bestow.* That night, as I retired to rest, the same wonderful manifestations were repeated, *and continued to be for several successive nights.* The sweet remembrance of those glorious experiences … impart[s] an inspiring influence … and I trust will to the close of my earthly existence" (*Biography and Family Record of Lorenzo Snow,* comp. Eliza R. Snow, pp. 7-9; all italics added for emphasis are mine, excepting the word "knowledge" which was made by Eliza R. Snow or Lorenzo Snow).

Born Again Experience #3 in Our Latter Day: Thankful Halsey Pratt

Thankful Pratt, the first wife of Parley P. Pratt, had a miraculous rebirth a few days before her death (in my opinion, all rebirths are miraculous). During this time, she "had a vision in open day while sitting in her room. She was overwhelmed or immersed in a pillar of fire, which seemed to fill the whole room as if it would consume it and all things therein; *and the Spirit whispered to her mind, saying: 'Thou art baptized with fire and the Holy Ghost.'* It also intimated to her that she should have the privilege of departing from this world of sorrow and pain, and of going to the Paradise of rest as soon as she had fulfilled the prophecy in relation to the promised son. This vision was *repeated on the next day* at the same hour, viz;—twelve o' clock. She was *overwhelmed* with a joy and *peace indescribable*, and seemed *changed in her whole nature* from that time forth" (*Autobiography of Parley P. Pratt,* pp. 352-53; emphasis added).

After delivering her promised son, who had been promised to her by prophecy, Thankful dressed her son, looked on him, embraced him, and three hours later ceased to live in the flesh. She had accomplished the most important thing that she had come to this earth to experience and receive: she had been spiritually born again and adopted into the family of Christ by taking upon her His name. This was when she was cleansed and "*overwhelmed with a joy and a peace indescribable* [or what the Lord refers to in the Doctrine and Covenants as the "unspeakable gift of the Holy Ghost"], and seemed *changed in her whole nature*, from that time forth" (ibid; emphasis added).

Born Again Experience #4 in Our Latter Day, by One Personally Known to Me

"This is an account of my rebirth experience. I was born into a family belonging to the Church of Jesus Christ of Latter-day Saints as so many are. I am one of five brothers and two sisters. I was baptized at the age of eight years old like most LDS members, and as is accustomed, given the Lord's directive to be baptized at the age of accountability. I continued to live, attending Church and taking part in family home evenings until I was 14 years old. At this time, my parents made the decision to move to northern Utah and become members of an LDS fundamentalist Church. My eldest brother had been serving a mission in Perth Australia at the time. I believe, and feel it is important to note that if my parents had not made this abrupt decision, all of my brothers and I would have served missions in the Church. However, God has his way of making miracles happen despite what our circumstances may look like at any particular time.

"After my family left Southern California and moved to Northern Utah, things started to change rapidly. There was no more Sunday service or family home evening. We did not pray together as a family that I can recall. In fact, one of my older brothers and I were able to get our hands on alcohol and made a fairly regular habit of getting drunk. It is so clear for me to see in hindsight how the adversary was seizing the opportunity to bring my family completely away from the Church, by driving a wedge between us and our relationship with Heavenly Father. As the years went on, I continually drew further and further away from having any spiritual sensitivity in my life. Alcohol turned into other drugs and I was exposed to groups of people that were involved in criminal behavior.

"There was an immense darkness that surrounded and persuaded me in making decisions that were contrary to my conscience. I was led into situations that nearly took my life on several occasions. It was only by the grace of God that I was eventually snatched up and separated from the dark circle of influence that was constantly all around me. I was literally rescued by being arrested by law enforcement. The events that led up to my arrest involved several days of hard drinking and drug use.

"At the time of the arrest I was extremely combative with the police, which led to a harsh beating in order to subdue me. Upon arrival at the police station I was placed in what they referred to as 'the chair'. Years later I learned that this specific chair treatment was the cause of many fatalities and that treatment had now been outlawed. Any combative spirit that was left in me was extinguished after being in 'the chair' and having been slid into a tiny, concrete, box-shaped room for several hours, having what seemed to be a perforated potato bag over my head during this time. When I was removed from the chair, I was informed I was being charged with a long list of felonies. I was only 18 years old and the decisions I had made that night led me to being charged with reckless driving, aggravated arson, possession of an incendiary device, assaulting a police officer among several other felonies. I was informed that I was looking at a minimum of five years to life in prison. I was then stripped naked and escorted to a cell where the floor was covered with vile substances, where I sat naked and alone on ice cold concrete during the winter month of January in Utah. After a long cold night, the next day I was given clothes and placed in solitary confinement. It was in this separation from the other influences in my life, drugs, alcohol and associates, that I was able to have a moment of clarity and awareness. I could finally see what had become of my life. It was at this time that I could not ignore how far I was from any type of peace and happiness. I remember realizing that the cell I was being held in was actually underground and might as well have been a coffin. I might as well have been dead. It had no windows leading to the outside world and only a small fluorescent light lit the tiny jail cell. I could now see that the life I was living had brought me nowhere. In fact, I was allowing myself to be led to certain destruction. I could see that the precious gift of life that I had been given had been wasted and defiled beyond description. I was contributing nothing to the world in any way. My future was dead, my freedom was gone, I was alone and there was no hope left inside me.

"Then my thoughts were reflected back to my early childhood and I remembered what I had been taught in my primary and Sunday school classes so many times in my youth. I have a Heavenly Father that loves me and I am never alone. Jesus Christ was my Savior. I could cry out to God in prayer. This became more than a hope. It became an actual remembrance of the truth and the true reality of God. ***My faith was profoundly awakened.*** [This is the endowment of a "*living faith*" spoken of in earlier chapters, or "*power* to become the sons of God."] There alone in my jail cell, *I cried out to God, believing* that he would hear my cry, exercising a pure faith, standing before God, acknowledging all of my imperfections, hoping that my unworthy and wretched cry would be heard. *I placed my heart upon the altar of the Lord* and asked for his help and mercy. I reached my *breaking point* and could not stand to be trapped alone in that room any longer. There was a palpable *desperation and despair* accompanied by a spiritual panic.

"Immediately the room filled with light and the presence of Jesus Christ, as if I could see him face to face, yet shrouded by the veil, came to me and my soul was filled with a peace I cannot describe even to this day. I was comforted by an unspeakable power as I physically felt the arms of the Savior wrap around me and fill my soul with his grace and mercy. I now had an everlasting, experiential witness of Christ. My soul had been renewed. Then a few moments later my cell door was opened and I was released for no apparent reason, other than the one that was perfectly obvious to me. My prayer was answered beyond my ability to comprehend. I made my way home and when I arrived, I found there was a dark cloud surrounding my bedroom. When I entered my room, I was nearly paralyzed by a thick presence of darkness. I felt an enormous amount of guilt for all that I had done wrong in my life. As I acknowledged these things, *I felt my sins being burned out of me*. I could only describe this at the time as a *baptism of fire*. I didn't know there was such a thing at the time. My sister found me and saw that I did not look normal. She brought my mom to me and asked her to pray. As my mother prayed, I heard an actual, audible voice which said, 'everything will be OK'. As the prayer ended, there was no more cloud of darkness and I arose filled with a great power and a surety that I could not be harmed by any evil influence that had overpowered me before. I was now protected and enveloped by the Spirit. Every moment of my day was a walking, living, breathing prayer with our Father in Heaven. I was in a state of constant acknowledgement of God and of his love and I could feel the direction and influence of the Spirit at all times. My sensitivity had been heightened to the highest level possible. It was as if I had *new eyes and ears and all my senses were born again* and I was able to see and interpret the spiritual nature of all things. The trees, the air, the water, the birds, the clouds, the flowers, even the entire world was speaking to me. I knew that I would never be the same person I was before my Rebirth. I had no disposition to do anything except that which was righteous and pure before God. Through the unspeakable power and sanctification of the Holy Ghost, the reality of our Savior Jesus Christ was witnessed to me through the pure grace of the Father and of the Son, who is my Lord and King. I love him with all my heart and I have dedicated my life to serving him as he directs me according to his will.

"No personal testimony or witness of any natural man can even come close to explaining the witness we can all receive through this gift of the Holy Ghost. I have only shared my experience in the hopes that someone will take the chance and cry out to God and find the everlasting peace that they will receive through the unspeakable witness of the Holy Ghost for themselves. I witness that our Savior Jesus Christ is the resurrected Son of God. He is our Redeemer and the way to an eternal life of never-ending peace and happiness beyond any understanding or description. I am now 40 years old and the witness I received many years ago has never faded or left me and never will" (emphasis added).

We notice in this rebirth experience that the person who received it was not seemingly worthy to have received it. He had been living a riotous lifestyle, like that of Alma the younger. And yet, I wanted to bring a principle to light that will give us both the hope and belief to cry out to God, irrespective of where we may spiritually find ourselves or what we might have experienced by way of sin and transgression. This candidate for spiritual rebirth had not confessed his sins to his bishop, for example. But keep in mind that God sees things in eternity, and He knew that this candidate for salvation would, after his rebirth, find his bishop and confess all his sins—and he did. Cornelius, for example, received the Holy Ghost prior to his baptism of water—a rare exception. The sequence did not matter to God, since He knew all things from the beginning and that all laws would be complied with by this young man in order to receive His promised blessing.

Here's the key to keep in mind, however. Although this candidate for salvation was not worthy just prior to his rebirth, he was still able to find the gate of salvation. How? I'll explain. Keep in mind that he had already received the laying on of hands for the concurrent or future reception of the Holy Ghost by priesthood authority. This endowment came to him through broken-hearted repentance, having a willingness to sacrifice all things to follow God until the end of his days without any reservation in his heart, standing figuratively naked before Him, repenting of his sins, and crying out to God with his whole soul. The Lord's words to Peter concerning Cornelius apply here: "What God hath cleansed, that call not thou common [meaning, unclean]" (Acts 10:15).

Alma reminds us that those who are saved are not just the penitent, but verily, the "*truly penitent*" (Alma 42:24; emphasis added). As a direct result of his having been *truly penitent in a broken-hearted state*, he was given an endowment of a living faith, bestowed as a gift from a loving God, in order that he could be justified and "made worthy" through Christ, and subsequently saved! And although prior to this he was not yet worthy or righteous, the Father and Son made him instantaneously righteous by way of justification and sanctification through the candidate's repentance and *sole reliance and faith* upon Christ's merits, mercy, and grace.

"And we know that justification through the grace of our Lord and Savior Jesus Christ *is just and true*. And we know also, that sanctification through the grace of our Lord and Savior Jesus Christ is just and true, to all those who love God" (D&C 20:30; emphasis added). Paul said to the Philippians, "And be found in him, not having mine own righteousness, which is of the law, but that which is through the faith of Christ, *the **righteousness** which is of God **by faith**"* (Phil 3:9; emphasis added).

Hugh Nibley also spoke to the above. "Who is righteous?" he asks. "Anyone who is repenting. No matter how bad he has been, *if he is repenting, he is a righteous man*. There is hope for him. And no matter how good he has been all his life, if he is not repenting, he is a wicked man. *The difference is which way you are facing.* The man on the top of the stairs facing down is much worse off than the man on the bottom step who is facing up. The *direction we are facing, that is repentance"* (*Approaching Zion,* pp. 301-2).

Theodore M. Burton teaches us that "punishment is not repentance. Punishment follows disobedience and precedes repentance.... Confession is not repentance. Confession is an admission of guilt that occurs as repentance begins.... Remorse is not repentance. Remorse and sorrow continue because a person has not truly repented. But if suffering, punishment, confession, remorse and sorrow are not repentance, what is repentance? ***Repentance is a turning back to God!*** ("The Meaning of Repentance," BYU Speeches, 1985; emphasis added). This is the same principle, in essence, that the Prophet Joseph reinforced. He said, "Repent! Repent! Obey the Gospel; ***Turn to God, for your religion won't save you*** ... and you will be damned" (Teachings of the Prophet Joseph Smith, p. 361; emphasis added).

As to the above experience, notice that there was a complete and absolute willingness in the heart of this man to first *turn to God with full purpose of heart*, having an *ironclad committed willingness* to love, follow, and serve God the remainder of his life. He *cried out* and was heard because he fulfilled the law upon which the promised blessing of spiritual rebirth was predicated! He was "all in" and *wholly willing*! "That they are *willing* to take upon them the name of thy Son" (Moroni 4:3; emphasis added). Peter referenced the level of willingness required in his words to Christ: "Behold, ***we have forsaken all***, and followed thee; what shall we have therefore?" (Matthew 19:27; emphasis added). Fellow seeker, the Lord may not require that we forsake all to know Him, but to fulfill the law, we must at least be *willing* to forsake all. This is the test. There are no short cuts and there is "none other way" (2 Ne. 9:41) of getting through this gate of spiritual rebirth, for the Holy One of Israel is its keeper, and He employeth no servant there. He "searcheth the reins and hearts" (Rev. 2:23). He alone will know who is *willing to forsake all* and who is not, who passes through the gate and who does not, "for he cannot be deceived, for the Lord God is his name" [2 Ne. 9:41]).

*The candidate for salvation whose story we have just read served as elders quorum president in his home ward in Chandler, Arizona, and has since been released.

Born Again Experience #5 in Our Latter Day by One Personally Known to Me

"I have put off writing this story for many years because of how painful I knew it would be to recall and share. But when Steven asked me if I would do it, I knew I had to. What I share, I do with the hope that it may benefit any other spiritual seeker who may be going through an extremely difficult trial.

"The experiences I wish to share began contextually with the birth of our first child (I'll call him Michael) over 30 years ago. I suppose most fathers yearn to have a son, someone they can do 'guy stuff' with, someone they can relate to. I was no exception, so when my wife gave birth to our firstborn son, I was ecstatic. I envisioned taking Michael to sporting events in the not-too-distant future and teaching him how to throw a football, hit a baseball and dribble a basketball. I knew I would someday teach him how to fly fish and shoot a shotgun and how to appreciate *Star Wars* and the legends of classic rock and everything else I loved. And of course, he would love the Lord, as I did.

"Michael was an extraordinarily bright little boy. He was a quick learner and his mind developed rapidly. He was very artistic and creative. His dexterity and hand-eye coordination were striking. At one year old he could recite numbers and letters. By 2, his artistic talent was very evident, and he grew to become a talented sketcher. By 3, he was building intricate objects with Legos and hitting a baseball with exceptional prowess. And by the time he was 5, he was reading everything and anything he could. In the 3rd grade, he read all my *Star Wars* novels. As soon as I heard about the first *Harry Potter* book, I got it for him, and he read it voraciously. By the time the last book came, he could read it in one day, despite its length.

"But from the very beginning of his life, Michael struggled with some sort of mental defect which was not obvious to most people. Later in life, he tried to describe to me the noise that was constantly in his head. This may explain why he learned to love to play the drums in his early teenage years—to overpower the inner noise he heard and felt. With instruction from a neighbor, and through countless hours of practice, Michael became an amazing drummer. He learned to play songs from some of my favorite rock bands. When he was a 10th grader, I signed him up to take the ACT test, knowing that he would do well, based upon his near-genius intellect and photographic memory. Though he refused to do a single minute of study for the test, and despite staying out late the night before playing video games with his friends, he absolutely aced the test. He scored a 35 out of 36 on the reading comprehension part, missing only one question.

"I do not explain all of this about Michael to brag in any way. As his parents, we couldn't take much credit for his inborn talents and abilities. But along with his incredibly high IQ and cognitive abilities, Michael possessed an extremely contrary and oppositional temperament. From the moment he was born, we knew something was not right, but we could never clearly identify what it was. As a baby he cried incessantly. As a toddler, he screamed every time there was a change in his life: when it was time to take a bath and when it was time to get out—when it was time to get into the high-chair or car seat, and when it was time to get out, etc. As new parents, we were clueless about how to help him, even to the point of accepting that it was a normal thing for a child to naturally always refuse to comply with anything his parents needed him to do. But when he was 2, we left him with my wife's parents for three weeks to take a tour of the Middle East. When we returned home and met them at the airport, my mother-in-law's words confirmed to us how difficult Michael was. She said, 'I raised 8 children, but I never had one try my patience like this boy. You guys really have your work cut out for you.' By the time he was 8 and we had 3 other children, we could see just how tough it was to try to raise him, compared to his siblings. My wife used to joke about it by saying, 'At the judgement bar, the only question I will be asked is: "Did you commit infanticide," and I will answer "No," and I will be exalted!"

"I do not explain all of this to in any way excuse myself as a father. Although my wife was, and is, an angel of a mother, full of Christ-like patience and motherly love, I did not know how to be a patient, gentle father to my oldest son. The author Mitch Albom has written in his book *The Five People You Meet in Heaven*, 'All parents damage their children. It cannot be helped.' I know I damaged my son, though I didn't really realize how I was doing it at the time. I remember my wife enrolling us in a day-long 'Love & Logic' type parenting seminar called 'Let's Fix the Kids.' I soon realized that the material presented there, and the instruction manual and tapes we brought home, were all designed to actually 'fix the parents.' I was upset to be told that *my* personality and parenting style was a huge contributing factor to Michael's behavioral problems. Of course, deep down, I had always suspected this was true. I was not always living the gospel the way I knew I should have at that time. Thus, I was not as close to the Lord as I needed to be, and I lacked the close companionship of the Spirit. So, I did not always exemplify the gospel I was trying to teach my children. I felt like a hypocritical example of a Latter-day Saint, often speaking and acting one way in public, but not the same way in my home. At times I would be so full of anger and rage at Michael's actions that I would yell at him, lecture him and even physically punish him in ways that were hurtful and harmful, just the opposite of the teachings of Christ. I was still an immature, young father who didn't know how to be selfless, how to discover who my son really was and what *he* needed and wanted to become.

"Consequently, as Michael was growing up, I was continually frustrated with him. I didn't know how to deal with his nature and behaviors. Instead of patiently loving him and trying to understand him and gently teaching him, I grew increasingly irritated by him. I was often critical and negative instead of being encouraging and positive. Consequently, my oldest son and I seemed to grow further apart, which added to my selfish frustration. Although my wife and I are very active in the church and have always tried to teach our children the truths of the gospel, I can look back now and recognize that due partially to my lack of deep love and patience with him, Michael did not grow to embrace our love of the Lord, His doctrines and His church. I don't put the entire blame for this on myself, since I know that all children have free will.

"From a young age Michael began to struggle with the concept of faith; he had a hard time believing in things which couldn't be seen or proven. When he was 6, he began pestering me about the existence of Santa Claus. I wanted to have the spirit of Father Christmas in our home, remembering how I believed in it as a child, probably even up until the 5th grade or later. But Michael was doubting the whole thing by the 2nd grade. Finally, after weeks of his incessant pestering, I told him the truth: I was the guy behind all of the mysterious presents and the whole idea of Santa was make-believe. He was angry and frustrated and saddened by the news. In retrospect, like most 'problems' with Michael, I didn't handle it very well. I think that somehow this may have been a turning point in his life. Whereas before he had been relatively happy going to church with us, I could sense that he was now beginning to question the very existence of God. We sometimes had deep discussions about the nature of God (not the usual topic of conversation between a father and 7-year-old son), and I could feel serious doubt coming into his young mind. One Sunday around that time, he announced to me that he wasn't going to church, and I couldn't make him. My first instinct was to say something my father would have said to me in that situation, but instead, the Spirit settled upon me and I simply said, 'Michael, it's not my church. Go tell Heavenly Father and Jesus that you don't want to go to their church.' Almost immediately he said, 'Fine. I'll go.' He was asserting his agency, but I could tell he still wasn't thrilled about going to church. By the time he was 8, he somewhat reluctantly decided to be baptized. The baptismal day of my first child was not the pleasant experience for both of us that it should have been.

"I feel like a large part of Michael's falling away from his childhood faith was due to my hypocrisy. I would often say the words 'I love you' to Michael, but to him, I think my love felt feigned, because my actions often didn't match my words. Since I had always wanted my children to get along with and love each other, and because I felt Michael often lacked the effort or even ability needed to do this, I began to separate him from the family when there was contention between himself and anyone else in the family. It was quicker and easier than teaching him how to resolve conflict, but the result was that he gradually withdrew himself from us, and I didn't encourage him strongly enough otherwise, preferring the peace his separation provided us. As I look back now, I can see that he wanted to change, but didn't know how, and I didn't believe he was sincere. How unjust and unforgiving I was with him.

"In his early teenage years, Michael's church, seminary and family home evening attendance grew increasingly sporadic. In high school, he gradually stopped hanging out with his friends in the ward and started associating with a different friend-group at school, many of whom did not share gospel standards. I could see how he was distancing himself from the church and even further from our family, and I was extremely sorrowful. I started to 'wake up' to the reality of the situation for which I was partly responsible. Wondering if it was too late to change, my prayers became much more authentic at this time, and I cried to the Lord many times for the strength to change and for increased love for and help with my son. It was so painful to watch him make choices I knew would hurt him in the future. I felt like I had failed him.

"One day when Michael was 16, he approached me privately and kindly informed me that, although he knew it would break my heart, he just did not believe the same things I did, and he wouldn't be coming to church anymore. This news, though not entirely unexpected, wrenched my heart to the breaking point—for up to that point in my life, I had never known sorrow like this. I'm ashamed to admit that some of my sadness was based on embarrassment; I was almost as worried about what people would think of me as a father as I was about my son's welfare. In any event, I didn't know what to do. As his parents, we knew we couldn't force the issue. Trying to force him into obedience would have backfired. Michael completely stopped attending church, seminary and most family-related functions. He was spending more and more time with his new friend group, some of whom seemed to have a very real darkness about them. Unbeknownst to us at the time, Michael and some of these friends were becoming involved with a form of pagan witchcraft which has elements of Satanism. He had purchased a large book containing instructions for myriads of incantations and rituals.

"But a glimmer of hope came one Monday night, when Michael unexpectantly attended our Family Home Evening. We welcomed him, of course, and he stayed the whole time. After it was over, and everyone else had left the room, Michael approached me privately. He informed me that he had a serious problem and needed my help. I assured him I would do anything for him. He then informed me that he was unable to go downstairs to his bedroom. When I asked him why, he said that there was an evil spirit in his bedroom. When I asked him how he knew that, he told me that he had seen the spirit and that it had spoken to him face to face. One can only imagine the feelings I had at that time. Fear began to creep into my heart. When I questioned him further, he explained about the book, etc. and told me what he had been doing. This was a dreadful revelation. However, because of some things I had been studying recently, I did not react instinctively as I might have in the past. Instead, I said a silent, urgent prayer in my heart and immediately felt inspired to begin to teach my son some things from the scriptures. I had just read the First Presidency message in the *Ensign* that month, a message about how to overcome the power of the adversary. Not coincidentally, I had also just finished reading an autobiography of an emeritus General Authority, in which he had shared an experience about overcoming an evil spirit by using the principle found in 1 John and Moroni 7—namely, that 'perfect love casteth out fear.' I spent the next hour teaching and reading spiritual truths together with my son, something we hadn't done in a very long time. At that point, he asked me a question he had never asked before. He said simply: 'Dad, would you give me a blessing?'

"I had been in the habit of giving each of my children a father's blessings annually at the start of every school year, but Michael hadn't wanted one for many years. But now his need was urgent, and his request was sincere. I said another silent prayer, asking the Father to fill me with love for my son. Of course, I had always loved him, but I absolutely hated some of his recent choices. As I laid my hands on his head, I was overcome with feelings of love for him. I pronounced a priesthood blessing of comfort and love, as directed by the Spirit. When I was finished, he stood and hugged me, grabbed some scriptures and headed down to his room. I was shocked but did not feel the fear that I had experienced just an hour earlier. The light in his room stayed on late that night as he read scripture and prayed. The next Sunday was the monthly Fast Sunday, and Michael attended Church with us for the first time in several months. He shocked me again when he went to the stand to bear his testimony. He told about having a serious problem (he didn't say what it was) and about asking for a blessing. He then described a miraculous experience. He said that he had been full of fear and anxiety, but that the moment I laid my hands on his head and spoke his name, he felt an intense warmth start from the top of his head, which eventually enveloped him with an overpowering feeling of peace and comfort that he had never before experienced. All fear and worry left him, and he felt happy and comforted. This was something I had not known until he said it at the pulpit.

"For the next couple of weeks, Michael was different. He was pleasant and agreeable. He came to church with us and participated in family prayer and scripture study. Sadly, this change was short-lived. A few weeks later when he didn't come to church with us, I asked him why. He told me that he didn't believe anymore. I asked him how this could be, considering his miraculous experience. He said that he had shared his experience with his friends, and they explained to him how it wasn't real, that it was a figment of his imagination, that it was all in his head, like a sort of psychological illusion. I didn't really know how to respond. I was helpless to convince him otherwise. He never came back to church again. He became distant and brooding, and we started to feel like we couldn't trust him. We were increasingly apprehensive and uneasy around him.

"By the time Michael turned 19, the tension in our home had become quite difficult to manage. My wife and I agonized over the decision of whether to ask him to move out on his own. He wasn't going to college, wasn't going on a mission, obviously, and he wasn't living a lifestyle compatible with allowing the Spirit to be with him. Eventually we helped him to get a good-paying job and arranged for him to move into a house owned by one of our friends, whose own son was living there also. In the beginning, this seemed to work out well, and we felt like our relationship with Michael began to improve. Over time however, he was losing more and more light. He seemed cut off from anything spiritual, and his life choices, personality traits and whatever mental defect he suffered with, together with the lack of genuine love he undoubtedly felt from me, all combined to trap him into what probably seemed to be a hopeless situation. We could sense he was in trouble, but he wouldn't respond to us or allow us to help him in any way. In hindsight, I fear he felt alone and abandoned. At some point after turning 21, he bought a handgun. Shortly after that, he quit his good-paying job for no apparent reason. His boss could not get ahold of him and called us instead. He went so far as to tell me how trusted and loved Michael was at work, how they planned to help him go to college and pay him a lucrative salary someday. I sadly informed him that we couldn't get ahold of Michael either. I had even tried to stop by his house and talk to him. His car was parked out front signifying he was home, so when nobody answered the door, I let myself in and knocked on his bedroom door. He was not happy to see me and even mentioned that I was lucky he hadn't pulled his gun on me. After a brief, uncomfortable chat, I left. I never did that again. He stopped coming to yearly family functions and seemed to be growing even more distant and dark.

"The last time I ever saw Michael was in the fall of that year. He uncharacteristically answered a text from me one day and agreed to hang out with me. If only I had known it would be my last chance to talk to him, as I took him to lunch that day, and drove him to the gun range to shoot his pistol, and said good-bye to him at his house, I would have looked him in the eyes multiple times and sincerely expressed how much I truly loved him, how smart and capable and kind he was and how proud I was of him. I would have assured him that everything could work out in his life, and he would by okay if he would just keep trying. I would have told him that he could move back in with us and start over again, that we would help him with school, that we could help him get counseling if he wanted to, and that his mother and I could help figure out his life and who he was. We would have done anything for him. But instead, thinking I had a lifetime ahead of us to work things out, I simply told him I loved him, and we said our final goodbyes.

"November came and went. Michael didn't come to our extended family Thanksgiving celebration, despite pleading texts from his parents, siblings and cousins. In early December, I sent him a text one Sunday morning asking what he wanted for Christmas, but still received no reply. That afternoon, after attending church and eating lunch, I laid down for a nap. Little did I know that it would be the last time I would be able to sleep soundly for a long time. At about 4 o'clock, my wife woke me up with a terrified look in her eyes. Two police detectives had arrived at our house. We sent the other children downstairs so we could speak with the officers. After asking us a few questions, they gently broke the news to us that, sometime in the early morning hours of that day, Michael had ended his life. It was almost surreal. I felt like I was still asleep, having a lucid dream, a nightmare, where I realized I was dreaming but felt powerless to change the outcome. My head was swimming. A thousand thoughts swirled through my mind. I'm sure I was in shock. I'll never forget one of the officers kindly ask the question: 'Does this news surprise you?' My wife and I turned to look at each other and almost in unison, said 'no.' After giving us instructions about what to do next, the detectives left.

"At this point, the sudden recollection of an event that had occurred 16 years earlier was brought to my mind, no doubt by the Holy Spirit. I had attended the funeral of a boy I knew who had been violently and unexpectantly murdered. I distinctly remembered his father explain how that, after the police had informed him and his wife of their son's murder, he gathered his family around him and asked them all to pray. They prayed that this tragedy would not destroy their family or their faith in God. They prayed for peace, hope and love. It was one of the most powerful talks I had ever heard. And somehow, I knew that I needed to be there that day to hear it. Now, 16 years later, I found myself calling the children back upstairs, giving them the crushing news, and saying similar things to them. But saying something and doing it are two different things.

"We did pray as a family and ended up crying together. We didn't know what to do. We knew we needed to call our extended family, but we didn't know what to say to them. Thankfully, within 20 minutes of the police leaving our home, our bishop arrived to offer his help. He along with a member of our stake presidency gave us some much-needed priesthood blessings. Our family and ward members rallied around us and showered us with love and service. Friends from work rushed to our home to be by our side. The Ward's Primary children (including our Sunbeam class we were then teaching) came to our home the next night, holding luminaries and singing songs and Christmas carols on our front yard in the cold. It was truly a remarkable, Zion-like outpouring of charity. So many friends and neighbors brought us flowers and gifts by the dozens. Our stake president wrote us the most beautiful, comforting and inspired 3-page letter one could ever imagine reading. I could never recount all the acts of service and Christ-like love that were rendered in our behalf. But despite this incredible outpouring of ministering, I felt a *deep despair* gradually increasingly in my soul. My wife and I would try to pray together but just ended up crying in each other's arms. I could not sleep at night. Every time I closed my eyes, memories of my mistakes and failings as a father flooded into my mind. I felt like the worst father ever. I felt like I had failed my son. As the week wore on, despite the support being given to us, I was becoming more and more lost and hopeless. I searched the scriptures and words of the prophets, and found some measure of solace, but I could still feel myself spiraling down into a pit of deep depression. Misery and despondency soon overwhelmed all other feelings, and I was growing suicidal myself.

"By the middle of the week it was time to plan the funeral. After yet another sleepless night, I arose at 4 am to write the obituary. It took me 3 hours to write 600 words. It was one of the most agonizing experiences of my life. That morning, my friend who owned the house where Michael had been living, came over to drop off his earthly possessions. Looking at each item only increased my heartache. Then the man from the funeral home came over to help us with the funeral arrangements—another 2 hours of sadness. By the time he left, I had become physically, mentally, emotionally and in all other ways exhausted. I retreated to my bedroom, locked the door and threw myself onto my bed in a desperate act of total despair. For three previous days and nights I had been tormented with all kinds of pain and guilt. I feared for my son's future and for my own eternal salvation, because of what I had done to him. Satan had been pulling me down to hell, and I was beaten, finished and crushed.

"I began to *cry to the Lord from the depths of my agony*. I was drowning in guilt, torment and grief. I begged and begged for forgiveness. I cried in anger, asking God how He could have let this all happen. I pleaded for help, like a person hanging on to the edge of a cliff, but without the strength to hold on one second more. Just at the moment I was ready to give up, *feeling totally and completely abandoned, hopeless and desperate*, the most incredible miracle of my life occurred: *The Lord spoke to me*. His voice was clear, audible, and unmistakable. His words were the same ones heard by the Prophet Joseph Smith in Liberty jail. He said simply: 'My son, peace be unto thy soul.' No sooner as he had spoken those words, my soul was flooded with the most incredible feelings of peace and love imaginable. It was an overwhelming influence of the Savior's atoning grace—I don't know what other power it could have been. It swept over me and filled me, doubtlessly conveyed by the Holy Ghost, the Comforter. I received a sure witness of the Father and the Son. From that moment on, I felt myself being lifted up out of hell, and filled with marvelous and indescribable feelings of peace and hope. *It felt as if I had been spiritually reborn*. I'm sure it still seems weird for some to hear me say this, but from *that instant* onward, I felt happy—I had no more despair. My son had taken his own life, but I was full of joy. It was such an ironic paradox that it felt almost humorous. I felt like nothing else that could ever happen to me could ever cause me pain again. I still felt sad over the loss of my son, but that bereavement was accompanied by an incredible feeling of hope for my son as well.

"There just is no way to describe the power that came into my life at this time. It was as Paul says: a "peace which passeth all understanding." Or as Nephi says: "He hath filled me with his love, even unto the consuming of my flesh." I tried to explain this feeling to some of my close friends and family members at that time, but words failed me. When they suggested I record my feelings and experience, I knew I would be incapable of explaining it, even as I am now. All I know is that I was filled with an indescribable feeling of love for everyone, and I had no fear of the future, or even of dying at that time. I knew that everything would be alright, that somehow, through Christ's atonement, everything could be fixed, and all the mistakes of the past could be corrected. I remember driving to the cemetery to pick out a plot and thinking "I should be grieving miserably and mourning terribly" but I was feeling joy instead. The crazy reversal of feelings in my heart, mind and soul could not have been more real or dramatic. Later that week at the funeral and viewing, I was in an unexpected position: I found myself comforting those who had come to mourn with me. I did not feel awkward or uncomfortable at all. Some of my friends whom I had not seen for a long time, or whom I had never seen express strong emotions before, were so sad that they could barely speak without crying. I simply smiled and hugged them and told them that everything would be okay. I distinctly remember some of Michael's friends from high school—the ones he had gotten into some serious trouble with—coming through the line at the viewing. They were not of our faith and seemed to be inconsolable and without hope. I also believe that they felt as if I may have hated them for years (which, to be honest, I had not loved them like I should have, back when Michael had hung out with them). But on that day, I felt nothing but love for them as I hugged each one and reassured them that everything would be okay.

"Michael's funeral and graveside service were amazing. Everything about that day was beautiful and inspiring, and the feeling of love that was there was overwhelming. The whole chapel and cultural hall were absolutely packed with people who had come to show support and to mourn with and comfort us. My daughter gave an amazing eulogy of her brother. She felt so uplifted by the Comforter and the Savior's atonement during the meeting that it was a turning point in her own life, one which caused her to desire to serve a mission so she could share the hope she felt with others. The next day was Sunday, and we were emotionally spent. It was difficult to envision taking the sacrament in the same chapel where we had just had the funeral. The bishop sensed this and told us to stay home and that the priests would come and administer the sacrament in our home. We were surprised when the whole priest quorum, all their leaders and the entire bishopric arrived to give us the sacrament. It was the single most sacred and memorable sacrament service I have ever participated in. The room was thick with feelings of love and hope because of Christ's atonement. The Comforter is real.

"For several weeks afterward, I was filled with feelings of intense love and peace. I could drive on the freeway, have another motorist cut me off or make some other rude gesture and my response was a smile, instead of anger. Gradually these feeling subsided and I was brought back down to earth. But for a time, I felt like I was in a celestial state. Temptations were inconsequential. But I still felt sadness over the tragic loss of my son. I cried seemingly endless tears. As things got back to normal in January, I could start to sense a waning in the intense feelings of hope and love I had been experiencing. My wife sensed this and suggested we go to the temple. We hadn't been in many weeks, partly because our temple is only 1500 yds from our house, and it is almost impossible to go there without seeing someone we knew. It had been 6 weeks since Michael's passing, and I was beginning to dread uncomfortable conversations I might have with stake members or other acquaintances I might see who didn't know our situation who might ask innocent questions like, "How is your family?" I had no idea how to answer that question briefly, honestly and sincerely.

"We decided to go to the temple in the middle of the afternoon when we knew there would be fewer patrons there so the chance of seeing someone we knew would be diminished. After changing into our white clothes, we sat in the back of the chapel, hoping to remain inconspicuous. To my chagrin, the officiator conducting that endowment session saw us from the stand and made a beeline for us. I almost dreaded his anticipated question, but we agreed to be the witness couple, putting us in a situation where we would surely be seen by everyone in the session. Looking back on it now, I know the officiator was inspired. Had we not been chosen as the witness couple that day, there is no way we would have participated in the prayer circle. But the Lord wanted us there because he had a tender message for us. The other officiator who spoke the prayer that day was a much older brother, probably in his mid to late 80s. I did not know him and I'm sure he did not know us, but it was obvious from his prayer that he knew the Lord. I shall never forget that prayer. I have probably attended over 500 endowment sessions in my life, and I have been in the prayer circle many times, but I had never heard a prayer like this. His voice was deliberate, solemn and earnest. Toward the end he uttered these inspired words, which I have never heard before or since in any temple prayer. He said: "Dear Father, please bless those who are here, mourning the loss of a close loved one."

"It was a tender mercy of the most powerful kind imaginable, a sure reminder of the Lord's love and constant mindfulness of us. My wife and I simply wept together, unable to speak. I was reassured once more of the infinite power of Christ's atonement. For many months, I could not speak of the incident without an uncontrollable flowing of tears of gratitude and joy. Speaking of tears, I can honestly say that I wept every day for at least a year after Michael's death—probably even 18 months—every single day. Sometimes they were tears of joy, but often they were tears of regret and mourning. I missed him and the future events we could have shared together in this life. Three years before he died, a brother in our ward had taken his life in a very similar and tragic way. I had been the family's hometeacher years earlier, and when we went to the home to give our love and condolences to his widow, I asked if there was anything I could do. She immediately asked me to speak at his funeral. It was a supremely difficult task. I did my best. The one thing I remembered most from the funeral was a statement from our bishop. He said that he KNEW that this brother currently regretted the decision he had made to end his life. I knew that his statement was true, and it haunted me when I remembered it. I knew it was doubtless true in Michael's situation as well.

"Perhaps the Lord could see how concerned I was for my son's welfare in the Spirit world, because yet another remarkable thing happened to me. A few months before I was able to go through the temple for Michael's endowment, maybe 9 months or so after he died, I had a dream. I will conclude my story with this experience. It is sacred to me, but I feel permission from the Lord to share it. I should start by saying two things. First, I am not a dreamer. I have had dreams, like most people do, strange nonsensical dreams that may or may not hold any real meaning. But significantly, at that specific time in my life I was taking a medication for a neurological condition, and one of the side effects was deep, dreamless sleep. The second point is this, and it may make it sound like I was a bit faithless or skeptical, but maybe because I hadn't ever experienced a dream like this before, it was difficult for me to believe that others did or had. Needless to say, my dream was very unexpected and certainly unanticipated.

"It was near the morning, after another night of very sound sleep, when my dream occurred. I keep using the word "dream," but I know it was more than that. It was in actuality, a real occurrence. I suddenly found myself in a very familiar place downtown, a place I know well and have visited multiple times. It is a small, grassy area, surrounded by tall buildings. But in my dream, there was an alley between two of the buildings, that doesn't exist there in this world. As I stood on the grass, facing the entrance to this alleyway, Michael suddenly walked out. At first, I couldn't believe my eyes—it really was him and he really was alive. It was so real that I remember thinking to myself in my dream "he must have faked his death. But how? I KNOW he was dead in his casket—how did he fake his own death?!" He walked up to me with a smile on his face, seeing how shocked and surprised I must have looked, and gave me a hug. I hugged him tight and could really feel him! I looked in his eyes and cried, "Michael, you're not dead! He answered matter-of-factly, "No dad, I'm not dead, but I'm in a hurry and I have to go." He turned, walked back down the alley, and I woke up. The whole thing probably lasted 30 seconds—30 of the most incredibly real seconds I have ever experienced in a dream. I started to weep, realizing what had just occurred. I had not asked for it, but the Lord had given me another tender, merciful message of hope. Death is not the end. My son is still alive. The Spirit World is real, and through the atonement of Christ, there is still a hope that our departed loved ones can be "delivered out of bondage" and receive of God's grace, "according to his own will and pleasure" (Mosiah 7:33). Michael's agency is still in force and he must make correct choices, but taking his name through the temple a few months later was a more peaceful, hopeful experience than I had thought possible.

"I feel that my very *nature* has been permanently changed through these experiences, beginning when I had been redeemed by Christ and filled with His love. Scriptures and doctrinal concepts which were once theoretical are now real to me. I have much less doubt and much more hope. I have been blessed beyond measure and certainly beyond merit. I also know that where much is given, much is required. Thus, one verse of scripture has become especially significant to me. It is in the Book of Mosiah, chapter 24, vss. 13 & 14: "And it came to pass that the voice of the Lord came to them in their afflictions, saying: Lift up your heads and be of good comfort, for I know of the covenant which ye have made unto me; and I will covenant with my people and deliver them out of bondage. And I will also ease the burdens which are put upon your shoulders, that even you cannot feel them upon your backs, even while you are in bondage; and this will I do **that ye may stand as witnesses for me hereafter, and that ye may know of a surety that I, the Lord God, do visit my people in their afflictions."**

"I am *a witness* of the reality and power of Jesus Christ and of His atoning grace. He has heard my cries and has saved me from a real hell. His grace is sufficient, as long as I continue to put my trust in him. I know He has the power to save anyone and everyone who will ask from the depth of their soul, with a broken heart, with a contrite spirit and with faith in Him. I can bear witness to these truths, and in fact, *I must.* I know the salvation I have experienced is real. I will never doubt my Savior's power."

*The candidate for salvation whose story we have just read has worked professionally as a seminary teacher most of his adult life and has since worked for many years as a beloved institute teacher.

Born Again Experience #6 in Our Latter Day by One Personally Known to Me

"I was six months into serving a mission for The Church of Jesus Christ of Latter-Day Saints when I stopped believing I was beautiful. I had been showered with 'compliments' my entire life in regards to my naturally thin and petite frame and body. Then the unexpected happened. I gained forty pounds in a mere six months. I was no longer thin, and therefore (at least in my mind), no longer beautiful.

"I would not be able to label or address the actual problem until much later. At that time, my problem was simply that I wanted to be skinny. The solution was to do whatever it took to get 'there,' wherever 'there' was. Eventually, I would learn that 'there' did not even exist at all.

"My immediate solution consisted of regular exercise and paying attention to what I ate. When that didn't seem to work, I exercised MORE frequently and MORE intensely. I paid MORE attention not only to what I ate, but precisely how MUCH I ate. I was slowly binding myself with flaxen cord, and did not even realize it.

"One of my darkest moments followed after going out for Mexican food with a group of missionaries. My favorite! I was starving. I had been starving for weeks. I ate a plate of food. And then another. And then another. I could not stop. Heavy and unshakable guilt followed that meal. 'Why can't I master self-control? Why am I so quick to give in? What is wrong with me?' These were a few of the shame-loaded questions racing through my mind that I truly believed were healthy and came from a place of good intention to improve.

"I relived every bite I took trying to somehow calculate how and where it would stick to me. The fear spiraled out of control until I locked myself in the bathroom, grabbed my electric toothbrush, looked myself in the eyes through the mirror, and proceeded to shove my toothbrush down my throat—an act completely new to me. It was an act I heard about girls doing, but could never understand why until this moment. I started to vomit. A feeling of thrill and disappointment, warped into one, overcame me. I went back for a second try. This time my toothbrush shut off for no explicable reason, and I felt a distinguished and powerful warning from the influence of the Holy Ghost. He reminded me that my body was a gift, and that I should not treat such a wondrous gift so poorly. I melted into a puddle on the floor and cried out to my God for forgiveness. I felt the warm embrace of familiar angels surrounding me. I vowed to never purge again.

"The purging stopped, but I saw no problem with cutting my portion sizes smaller and smaller, and pushing my body harder and harder. I thought I was gradually gaining greater control over myself. In actuality, my agency was withering away and my health right along with it. Although the battles I was fighting quietly were continuous, I fell in love with being a missionary for Christ's church. The joy was unlike anything I had ever before experienced. The most wonderful friendships were created. I witnessed the Holy Spirit work in the hearts of people I had come to love. I immersed myself in scripture and prayed consistently with real intent. I thanked my God for each and every day. As I learned more about my Heavenly Father and Jesus Christ, I developed a greater and greater desire to give my heart to Them. *I desired to give everything to Them.*

Curiously, however, I always felt deep down like I had been withholding one thing: My body. I had a body of flesh and bones, made after the image of God. This was my gift for choosing to come to earth! A glorious, marvelous, beautiful, tangible gift! I believed the doctrine. I taught it every day. But I could not see it so simply. I was blind. Somehow, no matter how hard I wrestled, I couldn't seem to give up my obsession with the journey to attain the 'perfect' body. This only added fuel to my fire of shame. I was put through heaven and hell through the next year. I fondly refer to my heaven as my 'vacation,' and my hell as 'Liberty Jail.'

"My vacation took place over a period of six weeks. I was placed in a trio with two other sisters. We lived in the most charming apartment across the street from the mall. My companions strived to live consecrated obedience, and attempted to teach me to stop obsessing over the destination-less journey to achieve perfection in every aspect of my life and missionary work. We talked to everyone we came in contact with and shared the message of the restored gospel unapologetically. We knew angels prepared the way before us, and as a result we witnessed hundreds of miracles in that short time.

"I remember convincing them to work out with me one night. In the process, they fell to the floor laughing at their attempt to mimic the strange moves the woman on our workout video performed. This too made me fall to the floor laughing! Our favorite form of exercise consisted of riding bikes in circles around the mall, while singing Josh Groban at the top our lungs. It was refreshing to have a break from taking life so seriously! Their body size was comparatively larger than mine, but it never stopped them from eating a midnight snack, or indulging in a slice of chocolate cake. They were happy! I often stood in fascination watching them do what I defined as 'careless.' During this time, I believe a subconscious light bulb flipped on in my mind, no doubt having arisen from the Spirit. 'What if I could be happy with how I am, right now? What would it feel like to eat a slice of chocolate cake and enjoy it?' Even if I wanted that, I no longer knew how. Despite this, a hope of one day returning to normalcy sprouted within me.

"My Liberty Jail lasted quite a bit longer. Eight months longer. I moved to a little doublewide trailer in the South Carolina forest. After my first day in the area, I felt exhausted! I was so excited to climb into my freshly cleaned sheets. When I pulled down my bedding, I saw cockroaches crawling everywhere. The horrific pest infestation would prove to be the least of my problems during this time.

"I loved my companions dearly, but they all struggled to love the work. I trained new missionary after new missionary. It was no longer like my little vacation where the work energized us and brought us together. Nevertheless, I was firmly committed to continue sharing my faith in Christ's gospel, and I continued to do it to the best of my ability. My best in those days was nothing compared to what it had once been, and I was all too aware of it. I was weak. I was always shivering. I was colorless. I hadn't menstruated in a year. My hair was falling out in gobs. My companion brushed it for me after my showers, as I cried and asked her to throw it all away before I could see how much I was losing. I never attributed this to my lack of nutrition. It never even occurred to me. I was convinced I had some unknown medical disease. The questions in my mind always seemed to go unanswered. The world went bland and colorless. It wasn't long before I became numb to sensing joy altogether. My heart had inadvertently become 'less feeling.'

"I continued on, and made it to the final months of my mission. My toxic perfectionism quickly grew into every aspect of my life. Social anxiety ruled my thoughts. I convinced myself others were judging me through my own distorted lenses. I believed when others looked at me, they only saw disappointment. I felt the same towards God. I no longer viewed my Heavenly Father as a perfectly loving and empathetic parent, but now a boss I worked for who was always focused on my shortcomings. I still believed He was loving and merciful to everyone else, but that I was the exception. I felt that I was not worthy of His love. I was thinner and more brittle than I had ever been in my life, but I still wasn't 'there.' Instead, I sat in a pit of complete hopelessness. I had dug myself into a dark pit, and had decided to take responsibility for climbing out of it myself, seemingly all alone.

"Notwithstanding the darkness that I was going through at the time, I was determined to finish my mission strong. I hoped for a companion that was independent and well- adjusted to the rhythm of mission life. I was in no place for anyone to rely on my strength. I could not even take care of myself. I knew I just could not train another missionary. There was no way I had it in me! These exact thoughts rolled through my brain right as my mission president called me. 'Sister Johnson, I've prayed about it, and I would like you to train a new missionary.' My heart sank. Out of a desire to please him and irrespective of my personal struggles at that time, I reluctantly agreed.

"The weight of this calling didn't sit well with me. I knew that I had been only trying to survive. No way was I in a position to help a young missionary learn the ropes and push herself. I didn't want my feelings of inadequacy to affect the start of her mission. The next day at a meeting, I pulled my mission president aside and told him I was not in a place to fulfill such a calling. I felt unworthy and incapable. To my surprise, he responded with, 'Sister Johnson, I know you are supposed to train this missionary. If you sustain me, you will trust me.' Taken aback, I agreed with not a word more.

"My dear friend in the ward, Julie Carson, drove me to pick up my new companion early one spring morning. I loved Sister Young from the moment I met her. She was beautiful, but not the kind of beautiful I was seeking to obtain. She was half Caucasian, half Japanese and truly got the very best physical traits of both. She had long, thick brown hair, milky white skin, freckles, and legs that went on forever. Above all, she was kind. Kindness is exactly what I needed.

"'By small and simple things do great things come to pass,' was the mantra I kept playing in my mind those final months. I wanted to teach Sister Young to be an obedient, and confident missionary. I wanted her to witness her own miracles, just like I had. My best attempt was clumsy and imperfect, but I hoped God would make up the difference for her sake. I just wanted to give every drop of oil I had left in my lamp.

"But one night the oil in my lamp ran out completely. Julie suggested I take a quiz on her phone to identify if I had an eating disorder. This is something people always alluded to for months, but I refused to acknowledge. I took the test, and the score came back blinking red.

"We headed home. The apartment door swung open and I immediately fell to my knees in complete and utter heartbreak. I was broken! Beyond broken. Beyond repair. I couldn't hold it in any longer. I unloaded to Sister Young EVERYTHING that transpired in silence over the past year. I unloaded my dark moments. I unloaded my fears of going home to a family that would not even recognize me. I unloaded about the monster I had created. I admitted for the first time, not only vocally but also to myself, that I wanted to return to normal, but was not capable of doing it on my own.

"She sat calmly and still. Not a word came out of her mouth. This surprised me. Not a, 'Wow! Really? Why would you do that?' Not a single, 'Oh my,' not even a widening of the eyes. She just listened as if she had lived through it all with me and already knew.

"Once it was all out in the open, I just cried. A couple minutes of this went on when unexpectedly, Sister Young opened her mouth. I knew almost immediately, however, that her words were not, in fact, hers. *"Sister Johnson. I've known since the minute I met you that you were anorexic. I have fought this same battle. I have overcome this. And I can help you overcome it too."* These words changed my life forever. My tears immediately subsided and my soul was filled with amazement.

"I recognized where these words came from. They came from the Savior Himself. He was manifestly there. I did not see His physical body, and frankly it would not have made a difference if I had, for I believe the **knowledge** could not have been any greater. He was there and I knew it. I could feel it beyond description! It was an undeniable truth.

"His Presence was absolutely glorious. I even knew exactly where He was standing in our tiny little apartment. The Holy Ghost testified to me of His divinity with a surety. The room filled of His warm light. Love encircled me. And at once, even instantaneously, it all became "known." Like a puzzle of complex pieces that comes together in the snap of a finger, the focus of the gospel all made absolute, beautiful and perfect sense.

"The truth about my Heavenly Father and my Savior was unmistakably revealed to me in a heavenly moment that I could never be able to successfully describe, even if I spent my entire life in the attempt. Heavenly Father was not obsessing over my shortcomings and failures like I had been. He was perfectly grateful for the offering I had unknowingly given Him at the time. *It was everything I had.* He knew it, and accepted it graciously. He was weeping with me all along through my darkest moments, even when I felt completely alone. He wanted me to be whole and provided a way to accomplish just that, through His Son.

"Just as He did in days of old as He walked the streets of Palestine, the Savior made me whole. I was blind, and He caused me to see. I was sick, and He healed me. I was deaf, and He caused me to hear. The most exciting part of all was that He was anxious to do it. I knew it! It was as if He were simply waiting for me to acknowledge myself that I needed power beyond my own, and permission for Him to heal me. He did not expect me to give anything I was not capable of giving. Just like the parable of the bicycle by Stephen E. Robinson, *I gave everything I possessed and it was enough.* "That moment made every minute of my suffering and pain worth it. The joy was indescribable.

"The next couple of weeks continued on the same level of glory and joy. Color was restored to the world in an even brighter and more beautiful way than it had ever before. I relished in feeling the sunshine on my skin, as if I had never felt it before. A plain bowl of cheerios tasted so delicious! It felt so amazing to have a full stomach. Peace was restored to my life. I was clean! I was light! I was free!

"I spent my nights for the next couple of weeks lying awake for hours in pure amazement of how merciful my Savior is. He heard the subconscious cries of my heart. Every morning, when I thought I had finally processed my experience, I would reattempt to tell Sister Young the entire story. I never could explain it in a way to capture the magnitude of the miracle. She would just smile and nod.

"'If ye then, being evil, know how to give good gifts unto your children, how much more shall your Father who is in heaven give good things to them that ask him?' Sister Young was also my gift. She taught me how to listen to my body. She taught me to eat when I was hungry, and what I was hungry for, and stop when I was full. I got better quickly and miraculously. I went home feeling 'normal.'

"Upon returning home, I learned that I still have to occasionally battle the natural consequences that come from having lived a life of toxic perfectionism, although I have never once struggled with my eating habits since Christ healed me. The difference is, I now never wonder if I am fighting the battle alone. In fact, I know the battle is already won.

"Years have passed, but this transformative experience I had with my Savior and the knowledge that I now have of Him will forever remain with me. His redemptive power and grace fill my heart with gratitude every single day. A dear friend I have recently come to know mentioned that her father, Steven Bishop, was already several years deep into the process of writing a book on Spiritual Rebirth. In fact, the night before his writings went to the publisher, and at his invitation, I gave him my story to add to His manuscript—a manuscript called, "Putting On Christ." I was thrilled and honored to do so. I always assumed the scriptural phrase "Spiritual Rebirth" had referred to the ordinance of baptism. Fascinated, I asked his daughter to explain more. What she then described to me rang absolutely true, and not only true, but I, in fact, knew that I knew it because I had experienced it myself.

"I remember weeping in gratitude for several weeks after my experience which had lasted several days and nights. I have never been the same since. I later confided in this same dear friend one day and said: "Although I did not know what it was called at the time, I am confident I have had my spiritual rebirth." Upon reading accounts of others who experienced a similar manifestation of Christ Himself and their subsequent ascension into a higher state of being, I knew without any doubt, confirmed by the Spirit, that the Lord had in fact, adopted me into His family. The Spirit had told me to write my story over a year ago, and I straightway obeyed. Now I know why. I am now finally able to put a name on my transformative experience. I had been spiritually Born Again."

*Fellow Seeker: Here is another person who had experienced an indescribable transformation in her inner person through a manifestation of God which gave her the knowledge of Him beyond that of faith. And notice the price paid in her own words: *"It was everything I had."* This is the pearl of great price referenced by apostles and prophets that comes in a miraculous way. And if we are to obtain the same endowment, we too must make the "all in" commitment to God and give *everything we have* as well. The candidate of salvation whose story we have just read is currently enrolled as a full-time college student in Salt Lake City, Utah.

Born Again Experience #7 in Our Latter Day by One Personally Known to Me

"I was baptized and confirmed a member of The Church of Jesus Christ of Latter-day Saints when I was 8 years old. During most of my life, however, I remained inactive and not interested in religion. I did, however, maintain a love for Jesus. I remember smoking marijuana as a youth, because to me, smoking it made me feel peace and love, and this peace and love is what I thought of as Jesus. In a confused, erroneous way of thinking, I saw smoking marijuana as a way I could be more like Jesus.

"Later in life, I married my girlfriend who delivered our only child. Right after my son was born, however, I was sent to prison for a 2-year period for illicit activity. After getting out of prison, I was able to be with my son for about 8 months before my wife issued a restraining order against me and later filed for divorce. Through this and other means, I was able to see my son only on a very limited basis. In 1997, I learned that my son had been murdered by a rival gang member. At that time, he was only 23 years of age. I was completely devastated and as a result, I chose to harden my heart.

"When he died, even though he was now a 23-year-old (adult), in my heart and mind, he was still that little 2-year-old because that's when I saw him the most. In fact, the only picture that I have of him to this day, is a picture of when he was 2 or 3 years old. My wife attempted to raise our son but as a result of her own personal challenges, she ended up having him taken care of by her mother. When my son turned 12 (I had learned quite a while later, even after his death), he had been legally adopted by my ex-wife's sister and her husband.

"In 2002, I was diagnosed with cancer and through aggressive radiation, chemo, and a surgery on my throat, was able to remain alive, by the grace, miracle, and will of God. Approximately five years later is when my Dad passed away. That too, was devastating. But I am sad to say that because my heart had become so hardened from my son's death, I couldn't even shed a tear for my father at that time. And I truly loved my father. It wasn't until 2012, that I experienced unimaginable and inexpressible sorrow, grief, and pain. I had lost my best friend, who had been my best friend since childhood. And when this happened, it opened up all the old wounds of my son's and father's deaths. My best friend had died a few days before October 4, 2012, which was the date of his funeral.

"Several years prior to my friend's death, my friend had started a Christian rock band out of his garage and was able to do some recordings. He left me with a copy of his music when I had visited him last in the hospital 2 years prior. I had never listened to his music until I learned of his death. I was not at his funeral because I was financially destitute and didn't have the funds to fly there since he lived out of State. I also continued to struggle with addiction during this time. I wanted somehow to feel close to my friend who had just passed, so I put his CD in the stereo player on the day of his funeral and started listening to it. I was completely broken—spiritually, emotionally, and in every way. I couldn't see myself going any further in this world. This is when the unexpected and unimaginable happened. A song came on, played and sung by my friend's band, which had these penetrating and life-changing lyrics, seemingly intended for only me:

Broken hearts and shattered dreams, I can't find out what life really means. And I don't want this darkness over me. It seems like only yesterday, things in life were going my way. And now I'm lost; lost in a haze. I need to know who I am. I need somewhere to make my stand. Won't somebody help me? Help me please!

Something inside said, 'Kneel and pray'. A still soft voice said, 'I'll show you the way. This is my Son…the price already paid. Just give your heart and he will stay. Through thick and thin, he's the only way. So just put all your trust in Him'.

If there is One, show me the way. To lift me out of this maze. Won't somebody please cover me!

Jesus my lord, come into my life. I give you my heart. You are my life. Jesus my lord, my God, I praise your holy name!

"At this point during the song, I dropped to my knees by my bed in a completely broken state, with every intention of saying the words, 'Save me, Lord', crying from the depths of my entire soul. No sooner than my knees had hit the ground, I became overcome by a powerful influence I can only describe as God's glory, through a *heavenly manifestation* from beyond this mortal world. I had received the unspeakable witness and power of the Holy Ghost. For 3 days and nights, I stayed within this unspeakable influence and most of the time, I remained alone in my room being tutored by this unseen power. My mother had entire bookshelves of LDS books downstairs by my bedroom. My aunt, who had previously died, had loaned her generously marked copy of the scriptures to my mother. When I would have a question come to my mind, I would, without thinking, go to the bookshelf and take a book seemingly at random, and I would open to the exact page and look to the exact place where the answer to my inner question was revealed. Most of these answers came from my aunt's well marked scriptures. This miraculous process continued for 3 days and nights, while being filled with this glorified Member of the Godhead. I was taught and filled by the Holy Ghost and nothing can now ever be the same. I had been born again, completely changed in my inner person. I call this experience "my manifestation." My whole nature had been changed from a sinful man into a man of God. There are no earthly words to even begin to convey the light that entered my being at that time. I am now His forever; adopted into His family. I pray that this witness may rest upon those who read it, that they might turn to God with their whole souls and exercise faith in Christ and be rescued and saved as I had been. Glory and praise be to God. I am His forever.

"After my Rebirth, I wanted to tell everybody. I called the parents of my deceased friend, who were Catholic, and I said, 'Hey, the Father, the Son, and Holy Ghost are real. They were with me in my home! I wasn't able to be at the funeral but that's OK, I spent it with the Holy Ghost.' Yes, I get it now. Although I was sincere, they thought I had gone crazy. I soon learned that I had to be very careful with whom I shared my experience, as there were many who were not in the right space to believe or understand what had happened to me. Unfortunately, I had to learn this the hard way.

"A few years before my Rebirth, a friend of mine by the name of Steve, said, 'I've been to every Church and have been looking to find the true Church, but I'm convinced that none of them are true.' Anyway, with Steve in mind, I prayed to God to know if I should share anything with Steve about my experience. Before I spoke to Steve, however, I asked God, 'Is the Mormon Church true'? The answer came back, 'Yes'. I thought, 'Great'. But then I inquired, 'Wait a minute. Do I need to go to the Mormon Church then too?' The answer was the same. Prior to inquiring of God for this answer, I wholly believed that I didn't need to go to Church because God was with me in power. Why would I need a Church? Or so I thought. Anyway, through this process I learned differently. I am now a very active member within the restored Church of Jesus Christ of Latter-day Saints."

The same day on which John's deceased friend's life was being celebrated at a funeral, John was celebrating a new life in Christ. John's friend left him a gift that was the catalyst which seemingly saved him. And all that occupies John's mind is to do the same for his friend by doing his temple work for him. This is how the Lord works. He allowed two best friends to be involved in each other's salvation. As one spirit was leaving through the portals of death, a new spiritually reborn spirit had been "made alive" (Eph. 2:1) in Christ, through putting on Christ.

*The candidate for salvation whose story we have just read, currently lives in Kaysville, Utah, and is heavily involved in temple and family history work.

Fellow seeker: ***The most troubled of souls may most often be the closest to salvation.*** I believe this to be the case for the individuals found in this chapter because "they had fallen to the earth" and had "viewed themselves in their own carnal state, even less than the dust of the earth" (Mosiah 4:1-3) prior to crying out for His mercy. Christ taught of leaving the ninety and nine and seeking after the one. He is perfect at rescuing and saving "the one." And at some time in our lives, we ourselves will be that *one*. He truly looks upon the heart. One of the biggest takeaways from receiving the spiritual rebirth for me personally was that the depth of my sins and transgressions did not matter. That had been made manifestly clear to me by God. All had been obliterated in one holy instant through exercising whole reliance upon Christ on the level that if I were wrong about Him, I would have preferred to not even exist.

Christ despises the prideful and the self-righteous. Those who have a sense of entitlement to God's grace will never receive this level of grace unless they consider themselves "fools before God" (2 Ne. 9:42). We may feel entitled to this grace because we belong to the true Church. That said, I'd like to make the following point abundantly clear. The true Church is not a perfect Church because it is filled with imperfect mortals. The true Church is the Church which holds and administers the ordinances through perfect priesthood authority and keys by which man can obtain the knowledge of God in power, come into His Presence, and be made like Him.

The danger in continuing with any feelings of entitlement to salvation through belonging to the Church of God is that we may not fall down and cry out with that sufficiency of faith to do His will throughout our lives, which appears to be part of the law irrevocably decreed that is tied to the promised blessing of "receiving" the Holy Ghost. Steeped tradition can skew the reality and power inherent in the actual gift and enjoyment of the Holy Ghost. "And that wicked one taketh away light and truth through *disobedience* and *because of the tradition of [our] fathers*" (D&C 93:39; emphasis added). This same principle is reaffirmed in Alma: "For it is because of the traditions of their fathers that caused them to remain in their state of ignorance…" (Amla 9:16).

Another stumbling stone for us as the children of Zion is that many of us are either subconsciously or unconsciously trying to save ourselves by our many good works alone. This directly conflicts with one of the requirements to spiritual rebirth, which is to "rely wholly upon the *merits* of Him who is mighty to save" (2 Ne. 31:19).

Notice again the pattern offered by Alma:

> *"I remembered also to have heard my father prophesy unto the people concerning the coming of one Jesus Christ, a Son of God, to atone for the sins of the world.*
>
> ***Now, as my mind caught hold upon this thought, I cried within my heart: O Jesus, thou Son of God, have mercy on me****, who am in the gall of bitterness, and am encircled about by the everlasting chains of death" (Alma 36:17-18; emphasis added).*
>
> *Of this experience, Alma later testified that "**the knowledge** which I have is **of God**," meaning, of the experiential reality of God Himself—of His existence (Alma 36:26; emphasis added). In other words, to be born of God is to obtain the knowledge of God, even on the same level as many recipients of a near death experience obtain.*

I'd like to close this chapter with some of the points that are put forth in Exhibit "D" and taken from the book *The Worth of a Soul*. These points, written by Steven A. Cramer, are addressed to all members of the Church for our prayerful consideration:

1. "Mormons have a need to understand that *everyone must be born again*—even righteous, life-long members who have not been guilty of any major transgression."
2. "Some of the people who marvel most over the need to be changed by God, instead of getting into heaven by their own good works, are righteous

Church members who are sincerely trying to live the gospel and who do not feel guilty of any major sins. '*Mere compliance with the formality of the ordinance of baptism does not mean that a person has been or will be born again*'" (Bruce R. McConkie, *Mormon Doctrine,* "Born Again").

3. "It is the difference between relying on the mortal plan of merely *controlling* our bad habits, and allowing Christ to change our heart and give us a new birth so that we no longer *want* the sins. And nothing but the blood, Atonement, and grace of Jesus Christ can do that."

4. "No matter how valiant and sincere we are, no matter how earnestly we try, *no one* can change their own carnal nature by their own efforts, for 'only Jesus Christ is uniquely qualified to provide that hope, that confidence, and that strength to overcome.'"

5. "He waited until I realized *with all of my being* that I was never going to cure myself by myself, because only then could I open my heart to his power."

6. "The mortal part of us may cry, 'But I have tried everything I know to overcome my faults—and still I fail.' Think about this: Jesus Christ never fails. Therefore, we may be certain that if we continue to fail, it is because we are relying more upon our own power than upon *His.*"

Chapter 9

After the Rebirth: Now What?

We'll begin this chapter with a review of the seven steps to spiritual rebirth:

1. We must receive the ordinances of God by proper authority and have a diligence in seeking Christ with an unrelenting desire, faith, and will to find Him.

2. We must offer up on the altar of our souls a broken heart and contrite spirit, having the determination to serve Him until the end, which is to make the "covenant of obedience."

3. We must view ourselves not as righteous Latter-day Saints but in our own carnal state, even less than the dust of the earth. This allows us to see the truth of our unsaved or "awful situation" and the true state of our spiritual cris-is, so we can truly know that Christ-is.

4. We must repent fully and wholly, standing figuratively naked before God, hiding nothing. Seeing the truth of our "awful situation" and knowing our need to be right with God at any and all costs allows us to truly repent with Godly sorrow.

5. We must possess a willingness to give up all that we possess, including our very lives if necessary, to forsake all that we have and are, and do so from the depths of our hearts. The key here is the willingness, not that we would be necessarily required to sacrifice on this level. Remember: Abraham walked down the mountain together with his son, but he was willing to make that walk alone if God wanted him to.

6. We must bow down and cry out mightily in faith for mercy to be redeemed and to know Him, believing that He will hear our cry. A cloud of desperation, despair, or darkness will likely precede our rebirth. When this happens, we must fight through it and cry out in exceeding faith until the darkness is lifted. Our spiritual crash site (or our own mini-Gethsemane) will give us this sufficiency of faith to cry out. When we do so, it will be done mightily, with the exceeding faith necessary to be heard and answered. This crying out needn't necessarily be vocal or audible. It is the cry of the soul that only God can hear and must be tied to the previously mentioned covenant of obedience, which is our willingness and determination to serve Him until the end.

7. Lastly, we must rely alone or wholly upon the merits of Christ in order to be conditionally saved. We do so while acknowledging His divine mercy and grace. To rely in any degree upon our own merits disqualifies us from receiving this level of grace which offers the sure promise of eternal life, a complete remission of sins, and the accompanying gift and companionship of the Comforter to abide in us. This gift is given as "the promise of the Father," received through confirmation by the laying on of hands after the baptism of water.

The Fourth Book of Nephi has only one chapter, but it provides a description of the state of the people who had been born of God through the baptism of the Holy Ghost and who had received a perfect knowledge of Him, many "eye to eye" through His visit and the remainder thereafter through obtaining the heavenly gift, having exercised faith in the words of others who had seen Him. "And as many as did come unto [His disciples], and did truly repent of their sins, were baptized in the name of Jesus; and they *did also receive the Holy Ghost.* And it came to pass… *the people were all converted unto the Lord*, upon all the face of the land…. They had *all things common among them*, therefore … *they were all made free, and partakers of the heavenly gift*" (4 Ne. 1:1-3; emphasis added). "And they did not walk any more after the performances and ordinances of the law of Moses, but they did walk after the commandments which they had received from their Lord and their God, *continuing in fasting and prayer*, and in meeting together oft, both to pray and to hear the word of the Lord. And … there was no contention among the people, in all the land, but there were mighty miracles wrought" (4 Ne: 12-13; emphasis added).

Fellow seeker: The end game for all God's people is to receive the Holy Ghost and be "made free, and partakers of the heavenly gift"— even as the record says, to become "delightsome." To receive the Holy Ghost is to be freed from "the performances… of the law of Moses" or *the law as our schoolmaster* (i.e., a checklist mentality) until such time as we are *justified* against the bar of God's law and the demands of His justice through our faith in Christ—thereby becoming *new creatures.* "Wherefore the law was our schoolmaster to bring us unto Christ, [to what end?] that we might be *justified by faith*" (Gal. 3:24) and be made free of these demands through the grace of God.

Once we are *justified*, we receive the Holy Ghost and are then led directly by God alone, to the end that "every man might speak in the name of God the Lord, even the Savior of the world … that the fulness of [His] gospel might be proclaimed by the weak and the simple unto the ends of the world" (D&C 1:20, 23). As we proclaim this fulness, even the fulness of His gospel, we seek to become holy ourselves through enduring in the sanctifying light of His Spirit so that we too may become partakers of the heavenly gift, *seeing eye to eye.* This is the path of enduring to the end; this is our pattern to follow.

Surely You Must Know It Was All for You

While contemplating the chapter headings of this work, and as I sat preparing for a stake priesthood leadership meeting to commence, I prayed that God would give me wisdom and direction regarding what principles were to go where and in what precise order. Then the order came, as if I were taking dictation: "Chapter 1, Ground Zero, The Battle Over the Heart"; "Chapter 2, The Light of Christ"; "Chapter 3, The Creation, Fall, and Atonement"; and so on. As they came then, they stand today in this work. Only now, instead of the experience of three born again in Chapter 8, we have the experience of seven.

Many months later, while thinking on this very chapter along with the first and great commandment, the words contained in one of the last scenes of *Pride and Prejudice* came into my mind. In it, Mr. Darcy speaks to his beloved, and soon to be, fiancé:

> *"How could I ever make amends for such behavior. You must know. Surely you must know, it was all for you. You are too generous to trifle with me. I believe you spoke with my aunt last night and [that] has taught me to hope as I had scarcely allowed myself before. You have bewitched me, body and soul, and I love... I love... I love you. I never wish to be parted from you from this day on" (transcribed from the movie).*

Although these words are from what I believe to be one of, if not *the* greatest love stories of all time, they are a type, pattern, and likeness for the love that we are to develop with our Heavenly Father and with our Lord. The feelings that we develop for Them stem from a gratitude for all of the blessings received; disasters averted by Their guiding hands; Their constant patience, tutelage, and loving direction; and even those times of necessary chastening of us in love. The words of Mr. Darcy are part of the spiritual and tender conversation between us and the Father and the Son. Through awareness and pondering on the magnitude of the blessings we have received throughout our lives, we will undoubtedly "hear" a loving conversation similar to this one, which will come tearfully into our view:

Us: *"How could I ever make amends for such behavior?"* We can scarcely believe that given all that we have done that is far beneath our privileges and birthright, our Father in Heaven and His Son have continued to love us immeasurably. It's too much for us to fully take in, and we are left bewildered and mystified at the magnitude of their grace and love.

The Father and Son: "*You must know. Surely you must know, it was all for you.*" Our life flashes before our eyes, and we see His hand so plainly and clearly now as we look back on our journey, including the moments when They interceded on our behalf. We gaze in reverent awe at the magnitude of Their love. The sheer reality of these words stands revealed: "You must know. Surely you must know, it was all for you." The fullness of our gratitude becomes just too much to take in. Our cup runneth over. The Spirit maketh intercession with inner groanings. We fall down in raw humility and amazement.

Us. "You are too generous to trifle with me. I believe you spoke with [me] last night and [that] has taught me to hope as I had scarcely allowed myself before. You have [changed] me, body and soul, and I love… I love… I love you. I never wish to be parted from you from this day on."

There is no way that we can have these things come into our view and at the same time hold back the tears from flowing. We develop a love for God that is similar to but much greater than an *all-consuming love story*. It is pure; it is wholesome; it is the most loving, tender, and sweet relationship that can be had, forged in sacrifice, pleadings, and tears.

We love Them, because They first loved us. Our love becomes so full and all-encompassing for both the Father and Son. It extends to all our brothers and sisters, both known and unknown. We receive the knowledge that we are not only accepted in Their sight but that we are profoundly and ineffably loved beyond measure—a knowledge revealed to us in unmistakable power. Our response to them from our hearts is immediate and unequivocal: "You have [changed] me, body and soul, and I love…I love…I love you. I never wish to be parted from you from this day on." These words can only be understood by way of the Spirit through the sacredness of the soul. When we approach it thus, we will taste of this love and desire all to receive it, even someone we may have previously considered a most ardent enemy.

After spiritual rebirth, the prophet Nephi speaks in plainness as to what is next, which is to continue doing the same things that delivered us to and through the gate, only now we move forward with the Comforter and the amplified endowments received when we were filled with the love of God:

> *"Wherefore, ye must press forward with a steadfastness in Christ [faith], having a perfect brightness of hope, and a love of God [charity] and of all men" (2 Ne. 31:20).*

Faith, hope, and charity. It is important for us to understand that we serve others, not because of our *duty* but instead, for the love of our *Deity*. We love all because that has become our very nature, through Their grace.

Continue with What Got You Here. Follow the Amplified Endowment of the Comforter.

"For behold, again I say unto you that if ye will enter in by the way ["the way," meaning the gate of spiritual rebirth], and receive the Holy Ghost, it will show unto you all things what ye should do" (2 Nephi 32:5).

Through an introduction to Gracie Jujitsu in the early 1990s, I met one of Rickson Gracie's students named Pedro at their academy in Torrance, California. I was somehow able to convince Pedro, who had earned a black belt, to move to Utah to start Gracie Jujitsu in my home town in Utah, and I helped him establish his Jujitsu school.

During years of being around and training with Pedro, I was amazed to watch him practice and train in his Brazilian-style of Jujitsu. Early on, I noticed something that became very apparent to me. While training, *Pedro almost always had his eyes closed.* He would "feel" the movements and intentions of his opponent, almost as if he could perceive their thoughts and movements beforehand. Through this developed feel, Pedro could thereby counter whatever moves were thrown at him just as they were being executed. This feel required some type of contact with an unseen force or "knowing," which he must have developed and honed over many years of training. In contrast, his beginning and moderate students "memorized moves," and they practiced them again and again. There was only one problem, however. When one of his students found himself in a position that he had not found himself previously, the student would become prey to the practitioner who worked more from feel than by memorized moves. Through my training and personalized instruction from Pedro almost daily for over two years, I was able to develop and hone my gift for this type of sensitivity or feel as well.

The memorization of the various Jujitsu moves reminds me of the law and the schoolmaster discussed in chapter 7. They initially had a purpose, like training wheels on a bike when we are first learning to ride. Like Pedro, through purposeful practice we develop a feel for connecting with God's Light. We learn to feel our way by noticing the intimations, peace, and stillness that comes through the Spirit and the guiding influence and personal revelation we receive as we turn inward and feel for answers. I have noticed that this Spirit is most easily contacted with our eyes closed as we intentionally shut out the tangible world to more effectively connect and focus on the intangible spiritual world. Remember, a portion of God's light is within us. And as we connect with *It*, we can feel our way back to Him, one personal revelation at a time.

This sensing and feeling after God's Light with our eyes closed, just as Pedro would do in practicing his Brazilian style of Jujitsu, is akin to following the Light of Christ. We close our eyes and turn inward through meditation and sense or feel for the Lord's guiding hand to direct us. Looking back, I am now able to clearly see that most of my life's important decisions involved this type of sensing or feeling for an answer to my heart's petition. I would often study a problem out in my mind, feel for direction, and then make a decision that felt right to me. Once the decision had been made, my heart would move in the direction of my decision. Then I would (time permitting) spend the next several days, weeks, or even months feeling for a spiritual confirmation, which came as a feeling of overall peace, or in some cases, a feeling of *relief*, as if I had become unexplainably unburdened. On some rare occasions, the peace didn't come until I had already begun moving forward in my decision. This peace and sense of relief was my green light or divine approval to continue to press forward in faith with the decision I had made. **One word of caution:** If our hearts are hardened, it will be more difficult to feel our way. This is why chapter 1 is so important, and why it is absolutely crucial that we first obtain, and then continue to maintain a soft, tender, and open heart.

In the event this peace did not come after having made the decision, I would revisit the decision and reverse course. I'd start the whole process anew with an alternate decision or course correction after studying it out in my mind once again and doing the proper studious spiritual and mental due diligence. I would then pursue the new course until the confirming peace would ultimately find its way into my soul. Personal revelation is not as simple as just asking. Sometimes the answers come through much sacrifice. Stay the course. God is there. In fact, "the Lord" is inside us. Turn inward and continue to feel for His influence.

The Parable of the Sower

Christ said, "When any one heareth the word of the kingdom. and understandeth it not, then cometh the wicked one and catcheth away that which is *sown in his heart"* (Matt. 13:19). It's important for all of us to grow roots of lasting conversion—true conversion. Those roots are sown in our hearts *by the Savior Himself.* Elder Bradley Foster said, "If our children merely hear but do not understand the gospel, then the door is left open for Satan to remove these truths from their hearts" (General Conference, Saturday Afternoon Session, Oct., 2015). Notice intently and purposefully the Diagram once again from Chapter 1:

*Desire →Tender/Open Heart →Spiritual Sight/"Seeing" →Belief (Light) →Acting in Gospel Belief→**Faith** →Spiritual Knowledge/Understanding **(Hope)** →Salvation **(Charity)****

**Salvation includes an experience of being filled with the Love of God [charity], an actual knowledge as to the reality of the Father and the Son manifested in power, receiving a remission of sins as though by spiritual fire, and receiving the sure promise of Eternal Life, subject to enduring to the end.*

Concentrated longing, as Maharaj says—which is the ***diligent, steadfast seeking of Christ*** and following His light within (i.e., "obedience to every word which proceedeth forth from the mouth of God")—joined with an awareness and acknowledgement of God's hand in ***all things*** (i.e., which brings overflowing gratitude that increases our love for Him experientially), repenting with godly sorrow and doing the compassionate works of kindness that He did, garners the bestowal and infusion of faith as an endowment from on high. Noticing or sensing this faith is when we begin to believe. As it is being bestowed, the buildup of additional belief and faith in us erupts like a volcano unto a living faith which overflows. We can then see the kingdom of God and ourselves in it! What flows are the tears instead of lava, in a seemingly never-ending stream of increasing gratitude until we are spiritually filled and emotionally spent.

Loving God through Praise and Gratitude

The greatest thing we can do to help us "endure to the end" is the daily experiential exercise, through prayer and meditation, of the great and first commandment of loving God with all our heart, might, mind, strength, and soul. It takes practice, just like any other art. Just as we would set aside time to practice playing the piano or any other instrument, we are to set aside time to daily practice the art of loving God. ***Keep in mind that we don't love God for hope of reward. We love God because loving God is the reward.*** "For how knoweth a man the master whom he has not served, and who is a stranger unto him, and is far from the thoughts and intents of his heart" (Mosiah 5:13)?

One of my dearest friends, a Catholic priest, does the same hourly ritual, which he calls his "holy hour." Whether it is a holy hour or holy half hour is not important. What is important is that we set apart a portion of each day with the intention of drawing near to and connecting with God. I find that the greatest tool to aid us in our "holy hour" is using sacred music, especially music of praise towards God, to get us in touch with Him. [Author Commentary: As mentioned in Chapter 1, spiritual, soul-enlivening and uplifting music which points to and enhances our love for God (and singing along to the same with eyes closed), is one of the greatest tools I have found to obtain and maintain a pliable, tender, and open heart towards God. As we purposefully and intentionally incorporate spiritually-grounding music which points us to Christ, while incorporating desire and faith as a catalyst, the "heart walls" that we will have allowed to develop as a natural consequence of living and interacting within a fallen world will begin to melt and be systematically torn down. This highly effective and life-long musical journey and tool in our spiritual arsenal will assist our efforts in maintaining a connection to the Light of Christ and facilitate our arriving to the "promised land" of salvation and "enduring to the end" thereafter].

Praise fulfills the law of gratitude and the law of love for God, all in one. Are we not expressing both love and gratitude for God as we are praising Him? We must focus our intention by directing our *feelings* of praise, love, and gratitude towards God with all the spiritual "umph" we can muster. Trust me, He knows us. When we practice this "art" by using holy and sacred music of praise, we too will come to know Him on deeper and deeper levels. The author of the Odes says, "My art and my service are *in His hymns*, because His love has nourished my heart, and His fruits He poured unto my lips. For my love is the Lord; hence I will sing unto Him. For *I am strengthened by His praises*, and I have faith in Him" (The Odes of Solomon 16:2-4; emphasis added).

Have you ever noticed the "weird" people you see at Christian concerts with uplifted hands? Have you ever felt to do the same? It is my opinion that these brothers and sisters are following the Light of Christ in their souls and are not concerned with what the people in the great and spacious building may be thinking of them. The act of the uplifted hands is a sign of peace, worship, and surrender. For me, raising my hands to heaven is a type of reaching for our heavenly parents, just like a little child will often reach for his earthly parents. This uplifting of the hands was a predominant exercise once found within the Church of Jesus Christ during the early days of the Restoration. In fact, when blessing the holy sacrament in the early days of the Church, the one performing the ordinance would often put his hands to the heavens during the speaking of the ordinance.

In the School of the Elders during the days of Kirtland, the brethren would great each other with a holy salutation, with uplifted hands in praise. Notice the following verse from the Savior's own lips: "That your incomings may be in the name of the Lord; that your outgoings may be in the name of the Lord; that *all your salutations* may be in the name of the Lord, ***with uplifted hands*** unto the Most High" (D&C 88:120; emphasis added). These same words were revealed to Joseph to be used during the dedication of the Kirtland temple. (Please don't tell anyone, but I frequently praise God with uplifted hands while listening to sacred music in my holy room at home. It's how I often worship, according to the dictates of my own conscience. Please keep this little secret between us.) "We claim the privilege of worshiping Almighty God according to the dictates of our own conscience, and allow all men the same privilege, let them worship how, where, or what they may" (Articles of Faith 1:11).

Praising God can also be used as an effective practice when we experience sad or gloomy moods in ourselves or in those around us. My youngest daughter, Aneesa, came home from school very down one day. I took her with me for a ride in the car to visit a brother in the hospital. I played an upbeat song of Christian praise and sang along to it with full-fledged "gusto." She at first just listened but then soon joined in with her dad. Her countenance completely changed within 10 minutes of playing and singing to this music. I have an experiential testimony that it works. If you haven't already tested this, try it and you will know.

Worshipful praise inclines the ear and heart of God towards us. If our hearts are initially hardened, we can still choose to speak forth the words of praise in song *until we begin to feel the words of praise* we are singing, and thereby, "begin to believe" (Alma 33:22).

Singing along to music of praise is a great tool we can use to get us into the spirit of praise. After praising in this way all the day long, our soul will then reverberate this love and praise until it becomes a continual prayer ascending up as incense to our God. Eventually, we can actually become that living, breathing light and love that will be felt by soft-hearted people with whom we come in contact. This is how we can, at least in part, "let [our] light so shine." We may unknowingly bless other people's lives because as we carry the pure love of Christ within us, His light will have an unseen calming and healing effect upon those we meet.

Captain Dale Black, in his book *Flight to Heaven,* shared the following regarding music of praise during his near-death experience in heaven:

> *"Next I heard the faint sound of water rushing in the distance. I couldn't see the water, but it sounded as if it were rivers cascading over a series of small waterfalls, creating music that was ever-changing.* ***Music was everywhere. The worship of God was the heart and focus of the music, and everywhere the joy of the music could be felt****. The deepest part of my heart resonated with it, made me want to be a part of it forever. I never wanted it to stop.* ***It swelled within me*** *and without me as if it were inviting me into some divine dance. The music was a seamless blend of vocals and instrumentals, the voices enhancing the instruments, and the instruments enhancing the vocals. Neither diminished the other but rather enriched the other. There was no competition, only cooperation.* ***Perfect harmonic order."***

Captain Black continued:

> *"The* ***music of praise*** *seemed to be alive and it passed through me, permeating every cell. My being seemed to* ***vibrate like a divine tuning fork....*** *The music there, like the light that was there existed in everything, and everything felt in perfect harmony. There was not a note of discord. Not a trace of someone playing his own music. Not a bit of competition anywhere. This was* ***perfect unity****. Expressed toward one focus—God. It was as if all of heaven knew the beat, the tempo, the words, the pitch, the tone, and all participated in their unique way but in a way that all was united into* ***one song****. There were not different songs playing together; it was all* ***one song*** *sung by everyone, simultaneously. It was beautiful beyond*

belief. And it was blissful beyond belief. I never felt such overwhelming peace" (Flight to Heaven, pp. 102-103).

Fellow Seeker: This *one song* referenced was the music of praise for God. Music can bypass the intellect and go straight to the heart. Remember also Captain Black's words of having to "get out of his head," as it were, for the revelations to continue coming. So it is with us.

Notice what must be present to be with God in heaven, according to Captain Black's story:

1. *All loved, worshiped, and praised God with all heart and soul. (Notice the importance in heaven of the first and great commandment, as all loved and worshiped God).*

2. *Everything and everyone obeyed the light of God, which is His law. Obedience to this light is the first law of heaven. This is one of the purposes for this life, which we are to learn and practice while here—following the light.*

Next to using music of praise and sacred art, another great tool to draw nearer to God is to spend as much time as possible in nature. Nature is filled with Christ's light and influence. My preferred location in nature is near the ocean or near the sound of a waterfall or water rushing through a small river or creek. The sounds of water are soothing and spiritually healing to the soul. And according to Captain Black's story, isn't it interesting that he heard what sounded like the continuous cascading of small waterfalls?

Almost immediately following my rebirth, I was led to what I refer to as my rebirth song. It is a song by Fernando Ortega, now one of my favorite artists, and is called, "I Stretched Out My Hands," together with the Riverbend Choir, found on *The Odes Project* CD set. During my rebirth, I played it several hundred times. Perhaps this song will become your rebirth song as well. The lyrics are taken from Ode 37 of "The Odes of Solomon." The spiritual gold I have found in the Odes cannot be overstated.

The Comforter's Influence May Inevitably Withdraw at Times, by Design.

In my view, we are not intended to have the strength of the Comforter's abiding influence within us without interruption until the end of our lives. Remember, although we may have been born again, we will still be living in a fallen world, and the adversary will continue to be very shrewd in dragging us out of our peace. Gautama Buddha purportedly said, "Before enlightenment, chop wood, carry water. After enlightenment, chop wood, carry water." The same applies to spiritual rebirth. Even though we may have been filled with the love of God and had communed with seemingly all of God's creation through an indescribable peace and oneness during spiritual rebirth, we too may become "entangled again in the vanities of the world" as had Joseph Smith himself (see D&C 20:5). We will still need to pay the bills, provide for our families, perform our civic and religious duties, counsel our children, endure the Lord's chastening on occasion, and yes, *chop wood and, carry water.*

We will likely experience bouts where it will become hard to believe that we could have ever drifted so far from His Spirit. I can relate to this personally. But take heart, this is specifically designed to get us to dig deeper and seek God again in earnest. Hence the question asked by Alma, "If ye have felt to sing the song of redeeming love, I would ask, can ye feel so now?" (Alma 5:26). Brigham Young spoke to our ability (or lack thereof) to maintain the companionship of the Comforter in our post-rebirth state of being:

> *"Will this state of feeling always remain? Will passion ever rise again? Yes; for* ***you then commence a warfare,*** *though the Comforter fills your heart, making you rejoice in God your Savior, with the atmosphere of your existence clear and unclouded;* ***this is not to continue,*** *but soon the day of trial and temptation darkens the fair prospect,* ***to teach you to lean on the Lord, and to overcome the world****" (Effects and Privileges of the Gospel, Etc., JD, Vol. 1, pp. 240-241).*

This warfare is real. As discussed in Chapter 1, the battle is over the heart—both before and after we have been born of God. At times, the journey can be spiritually pounding, excruciating, and soul bending. At times we will feel as though the heavens are as brass, but as we keep our focused attention and clear intention on the Lord, continuing in fasting and prayer, the connection to His Spirit will once again become more easily felt and we will once again know that we are found within His grace. We will know this by the return of His Spirit back into our lives, which resurfaces as we turn again to Him and repent of our sins, both those of omission and commission.

Remember, before every peak, there is a valley preceding it. And before moving upward, there is, on occasion, a noticeable fall back. This is part of the process of overcoming the world. Those who have overcome in and through Christ have experienced the same thing many times over. Joseph exclaimed, "O God, where art thou? And where is the pavilion of thy hiding place?" Christ Himself, exclaimed, "My God, my God, why hast thou forsaken me?" It is necessary that we all endure such adversity and trials, but we are to never give up. We are to "press forward."

Below is a personal journal entry of mine which speaks to the necessity of our pressing forward:

> *This last week, the adversary had been kicking me while I was down, while I had a nasty cold. I didn't feel like going to Ward*

Council or to Church yesterday. Rebecca [my wife] told me that that was totally unlike me, and it was. I knew it must have been the adversary's influence. Then the words "press forward" came to my mind. I began to understand, on a deeper level, what those two words meant:

Pressing forward is moving forward even when we feel like we may have been completely forsaken by God—even though in all reality, we have not been. Pressing forward is to do the things that Christ did, even when we may not feel like it. Pressing forward is to fight through the wall of adversity and of the adversary, even though or perhaps especially when we may feel like we are totally "going it alone." As we press forward in faith, at some point ... because of a certain, previously unknown law of mercy that always eventually kicks in, spiritual relief and divine aid always comes. But in my experience, it always comes after the eleventh hour—after the trial of our faith. "And we will prove them herewith, to see if they will do all things whatsoever the Lord their God shall command them" (Pearl of Great Price, Abraham, 3:25). This "proving herewith" is all about finding out if we are going to "press forward" towards God, even during those times when he is seemingly, at least, nowhere to be found. It is to find out if we will still press forward, even when His Spirit may not be filling our souls with a million gigawatts of power. It is to press forward especially when we may not feel like it. Because when we do, we will have passed a certain unspoken, perhaps unwritten test. And always without fail, after we have endured the travails of darkness, the light of the "Son" shines brightly forth through our desire and tenacity in seeking Him.

Fellow seeker, we find God in our extremities. We will either press forward through the wall of adversity or the same lesson will continue being served up until we learn the lesson. Each wall of adversity that we press through opens us up to grace and spiritual endowments on the other side of that wall. Once we receive the spiritual gifts on the other side of that wall, we will then be able to more easily feel gratitude for having experienced the adversity. This pattern will continue until we arrive at that point when we are able, through awareness, to recognize (and actually embrace) the gift, together with the accompanying expressions of gratitude from our hearts in the initial moment that the adversity were to rise its ugly, yet glorious head. To "press forward" is an exercise of faith. Part of the endowment or gift on the other side of each "adversity wall" is a removal, by degree, of certain increments of unbelief and darkness. This too is part of God's grace. And this removal of unbelief and darkness is replaced with additional portions of His light and truth, by grace. And this light and truth contains His attributes that become infused into us. Elder Quentin L. Cook says it this way:

> *"The refiner's fire is real, and qualities of character and righteousness that are forcing the furnace of affliction perfect and purify us and prepares us to meet God" ("The Refiner's Fire," Mormon Messages).*

John Taylor spoke similarly on this topic with these words:

> *What if we have to suffer affliction! We came here for that purpose: we came in order that we might be purified; and this is intended to give us a knowledge of God" ("Trials, etc.," John Taylor, Delivered in the Tabernacle, SLC, November 13, 1859; JD 7:194).*

Adversity, sacrifice, and opposition are part of that refining process which sanctifies, through His grace. When we find ourselves stuck and can't seem to figure out a problem, try something different. Troubleshoot. Throw your spiritual spaghetti at the wall to determine what sticks. And by "sticks" I mean, simply stay with what works for you—that which uplifts and enlivens you and makes you get into a positive "flow." Positive change that feels good to us inside will inevitably manifest positive results.

Breaking through the Psychological and Mental Wall

I'd like to forewarn you as to one of the adversary's repeated tactics throughout this journey along the path. The following thoughts may flow through your mind, including with those who have passed through the gate of spiritual rebirth. The adversary will try to get us to believe that we are just "mind tripping" ourselves—that what we experienced was not real. We will hit a psychological wall at times through his ongoing lies. Let me assure you that these thoughts stemming from the adversary are his attempt to shut our progress down. Don't be sidetracked by this. In fact, when it comes, tell the adversary, "Thank you for your witness and testimony."

In order to combat these lies and the wiles of the adversary, I find it best to keep a "miracle" or "tender mercies" journal. Have you ever noticed how certain smells can take us back to our childhood or teenage years? Well, our miracle journal is similar. It takes us back to the moment of the experience, as if it were happening again.

Keep a journal that highlights the spiritual experiences you are encountering along your journey. Then when the adversary rears his ugly head and tells you that you're misremembering things or just making these things up in your mind, you can turn back to your miracle or tender mercies journal and read all about your experiences leading up to your rebirth and all that has transpired since. As you do so, just pause, then notice what you feel. These words in your journal can become as powerful as scripture because they are, in a very real way, personal scripture. They are evidences of God's power and reality specifically made available to us individually. I promise you that as you read your own personal "scripture," the Spirit will reaffirm to you that what you are experiencing and have experienced is absolutely real and that there is even more along the journey to be had, even unspeakably so.

The Bread and the Water: "Types" Leading Both to and from Spiritual Rebirth

I like to think of the ordinance of the sacrament, beginning with the bread, as leading up to the Rebirth through striving to obtain the First Comforter. I like to think of the blessing on the water (or wine) as the "hope" of having received the same through our striving thereafter to maintain the Comforter's ongoing companionship and influence in our lives. There are, of course, deeper meanings that can be highlighted as well, as is the case with all gospel principles. For now, however, I will offer brief commentary only on these aspects.

"O God, the Eternal Father, we ask thee in the name of thy Son, Jesus Christ, to bless and sanctify this bread *to the souls* [Author Commentary: The whole purpose of asking God to both bless and sanctify the bread is so that the sanctified bread might sanctify *our souls*, made possible only by grace, through our faith] of all those who partake of it, that they ***may*** eat in remembrance of the body of thy Son [Author Commentary: Some may be able to eat in remembrance of his body, and some may not], and witness unto thee, O God, the Eternal Father, that they are ***willing*** to take upon them the name of thy Son [Author Commentary: To 'witness' as to our own individual willingness to take upon us the name of His Son is to witness to our willingness to be born of God or born again every time we partake of the sacrament. This happens by making the actual covenant of obedience, or 'all in' commitment, tied to the requisite disposition to sacrifice all that we have and are. This commitment will inevitably include the perpetual 'cry of the soul' discussed repeatedly throughout this work], and always remember him and keep his commandments which he has given them [Author Commentary: This covenant of obedience will obviously include making Christ the center and focus of our lives—to 'always remember Him' and to keep His commandments, including the commandment to enter the depths of repentance in order to offer our broken hearts to Him. When we fulfill this 'all in' commitment through our actions out in the world, and that commitment is joined profoundly with our hearts and we continue to 'call upon His holy name,' we will be adopted into His family. When this occurs, we will receive the First Comforter in fulfillment of 'the promise of my Father']; that they may *always* have his Spirit to be with them [which is when we obtain the reception and companionship of the Holy Ghost through a baptism of fire]. Amen" (D&C 20:77; emphasis added).

Now to the water or wine, which again, I like to think of as being symbolic of the hope that the blood of Christ has already cleansed and sanctified us during *the Rebirth.* After spiritual rebirth, there are steps we can take to retain a remission of sins by striving to preserve the sanctifying influence of the Comforter or Holy Ghost in our lives.

"O God, the Eternal Father, we ask thee in the name of thy Son, Jesus Christ, to bless and sanctify this wine [symbolic of the blood of Christ which has hopefully already sanctified us] *to the souls* of all those who drink of it [Author Commentary: Again, the whole purpose of asking that the Father bless and sanctify the water (or wine) is to ultimately sanctify our immortal souls], that they ***may*** do it in remembrance of the blood of thy Son, which ***was shed*** for them [Wow! This is full of gold, is it not? The prayer is that the candidates of salvation *may* be able to actually witness that the blood of Christ had already been shed on his or her behalf (hence the terms "may" and "was shed"). Now comes the hope part. Some *may* be able to witness to this if they have been reconciled to God and born of Him. Some *may not*. And if they are successful in being born of Him, they will be in a new station]; that they *may* witness unto thee, O God, the Eternal Father, that they ***do*** always remember him [Author Commentary: Notice the word "do" here. Its usage is not given in a past or future tense. The hope is that the candidates of salvation ***do*** always remember Him, which is made possible *after* Christ writes His name on their hearts, making it possible for them to always remember him in this way, to the end] that they may have his Spirit to be with them. [Author Commentary: If we are able to witness or become witnesses ourselves as to the living reality of Christ and the Father because we have been born of God and have come to know Him, which is to 'enjoy the words of eternal life *in this world'* (Moses 6:59), it means we will have received the *ongoing companionship* of the First Comforter—hence the phrase "always have his Spirit to be with them." And in fulfilling this objective of receiving and maintaining this companionship, we will retain a remission of our sins, which occurred at the time of our spiritual rebirth, thereby giving us the benefit of the Comforter's ongoing, sanctifying influence. And if we endure to the end within His sanctifying influence, we can also have the privilege and blessing of seeing the face of the Lord while in mortality]. Amen" (D&C 20:79; emphasis added. See also D&C 93:1).

Receiving the Comforter during Spiritual Rebirth Truly Qualifies Us to Preach the Word

The reception of the Holy Ghost or First Comforter appears to be a prerequisite to preaching the word of God. To me this makes sense, although when I served a full-time mission, I had not truly understood the doctrine of Christ nor had I received the Holy Ghost. But this much I can say, had I received the First Comforter prior to my mission, I would have been a much more effective missionary. I know now that I had not been truly prepared nor effectively qualified. Elder Charles W. Penrose, an early member of the Council of the Twelve, said, "If any man desires to act in the holy ministry he must first be baptized for a remission of sins and receive the gift of the Holy Ghost, otherwise he cannot be a teacher unto others" (*Journal of Discourses,* 21:80). He also said:

> *On that day (Pentecost) Peter preached that great gospel sermon which we read about in the second chapter of the Acts of the Apostles. He did not teach the people anything in regard to his opinion. He told the people that which he knew, that which had been made manifest to him, that which he understood, and he did it under the influence and power of the Holy Ghost, the same spirit which rested upon the ancient prophets, the same spirit by which Jesus spoke... No man has a right to preach in the name of the Lord,* ***unless he is endowed as were those Apostles*** *" (Discourse by Elder Charles W. Penrose, delivered in the Tabernacle, Salt Lake City, Sunday Afternoon, May 20, 1883; JD 25:39; emphasis added).*

This may give us added insight into the revelation which says, "And if ye receive not the Spirit [meaning, the gift, enjoyment and companionship of the Holy Ghost] ye shall not teach" (D&C 42:14). We are told that in Alma's day, the priests waxed "strong in the Spirit, *having the knowledge of God* [code for having been born of God], that they might [what?] *teach with power and authority from God*" (Mosiah 18:26; emphasis added).

During the early days of the Restoration, many were told by the Lord to remain where they were, at least until they were prepared and qualified to preach the restored gospel. This preparation included being filled with God's love and Spirit so that the knowledge of the "hidden" gems of the gospel could be discovered and effectively taught. Notice the following scripture:

> *"And it shall come to pass, that if you shall ask the Father in my name, in faith believing,* ***you shall receive the Holy Ghost****, which giveth utterance,* ***that you may stand as a witness*** *of the things of which you shall both hear and see, and also* ***that you may declare repentance unto this generation*** *" (D&C 14:8; emphasis added).*

"Faith, hope, and charity" is code for one having received spiritual rebirth and the First Comforter. Remember, this is when we are *filled with the love of God*, having tasted of the fruit of the tree of life and salvation. Notice the following scripture, perhaps with new eyes:

"Therefore, if ye have desires to serve God ye are called to the work;

For behold the field is white already to harvest; and lo, he that thrusteth in his sickle with his might, the same layeth up in store that he perisheth not, but bringeth salvation to his soul;

***And faith, hope, charity and love**, with an eye single to the glory of God, **qualify him for the work**" (D&C 4:3-5; emphasis added).*

This is what Joseph was talking about when he and Oliver received the Holy Ghost. The gospel passages previously hidden from their view then came alive. This is what was witnessed to as well by the young woman who had been born of the Spirit in the beginning of Chapter 8. The subsequent enlightenment of Joseph and Oliver's minds is what qualified them to be able to understand the revealed intention behind the written word of God on a level not attained to previously so that it could be effectively taught with an elucidated and correct understanding—to every nation, kindred, tongue, and people:

"We were filled with the Holy Ghost, and rejoiced in the God of our salvation.

Our minds being now enlightened, we began to have the scriptures laid open to our understandings, and the true meaning and intention of their more mysterious passages revealed unto us in a manner which we never could attain to previously, nor ever before had thought of" (Joseph Smith—History 1:73-74).

Becoming Fully Qualified to Preach the Word

Passing through the gate of spiritual rebirth and receiving the actual Holy Ghost is the single most important and effective way to prepare and become qualified to both understand and preach the word of God to the nations of the world:

"Behold, I speak unto you, and also to all those who have desires to bring forth and establish this work;

*"**And no one can assist** in this work <u>except</u> he shall be humble and **full of love, having faith, hope, and charity (code phrase for 'born of God')**, being temperate in all things, whatsoever shall be entrusted to his care.*

"Behold, I am the light and the life of the world, that speak these words, therefore give heed with your might, and ***then you are called****. Amen" (D&C 12:7-9; emphasis added).*

All those who have had *His name upon them*, which is preceded by a willingness to take upon us His name, are said to be fully qualified to go forth with the convincing power of God, having obtained the knowledge of Him. When we experience faith, hope, and charity through spiritual rebirth, we most definitely will have His name upon us, even, "in fleshy tables of the heart" (2 Cor. 3:3).

The below comes from the dedicatory prayer of the Kirtland temple. Notice the words "that thy name may be upon them." There is power in having had this name placed on us or having been born of Him:

"And we ask thee, Holy Father that thy servants may go forth from this house ***armed with thy power****, and* ***that thy name may be upon them****, and thy glory be round about them, and thine angels have charge over them" (D&C 109:22; emphasis added).*

The foundational rock on which the ancient Church was built (and on which we too must be built) is the rock of revelation *imparted by the Comforter* given to abide in man. From this understanding, one could easily make the assertion that the rock upon which the ancient Church was built was and is the Comforter. The *Holy Ghost or Comforter* gives us the knowledge of God and *is that which showeth and revealeth all things*, once the endowment of the Holy Ghost is received. Lorenzo Snow confirmed the above:

"Peter, at Pentecost, promised the Holy Ghost to all who would be baptized (Acts 2:38), or in other words, obey the Gospel. ***The Holy Ghost [i.e., Comforter] would impart the knowledge which would constitute the rock of revelation*** *upon which the Savior said his people should be established" (Journal of Discourses, 13:284; emphasis added).*

So often my Catholic friends refer to Peter as the rock, or in the Church of Christ as "the rock of revelation." But how does this revelatory gift come to us? It is clear to me that His gift comes when we receive the First Comforter and are grounded upon this rock which gives revelation upon revelation. "Peter told the people, *on the day of Pentecost*, they should receive... ***the gift of the Holy Ghost****... and wherever this principle exists,* ***the principle of revelation and the knowledge of God exists****—*" (A Discourse by John Taylor, "The Gospel," Delivered in the Tabernacle, Great Salt Lake City, January 15, 1860).

So what is this rock? Is it Peter himself? Is it revelation itself? Or does this revelation proceed from a gift? President Snow taught that the *principle of revelation*, this rock, is given through the gift and enjoyment of the Holy Ghost or First Comforter:

> *"This gift of the* ***Holy Ghost is a different principle*** *from anything that we see manifested in the sectarian world.* ***It is a principle of intelligence, and revelation****. It is a principle that reveals things past, present and to come, and these gifts of the Holy Ghost were to be received through obedience to the requirements of the Gospel....* ***It was upon this rock [of the Holy Ghost or Comforter given to abide in man] that their faith should be grounded****" (Journal of Discourses, 13:284; emphasis added).*

As to the gift of revelation through the Comforter, notice this verse with new eyes:

> *And upon this rock I will build my church [meaning, upon the reception of the Holy Ghost which "showeth all things" will I build my Church]; yea,* ***upon this rock <u>ye are built</u>****, and if ye continue [upon this rock, and maintain the Comforter's influence within you], the gates of hell shall not prevail against you (D&C 33:11-13; emphasis added).*

Elder Alma Sonne, a former assistant to the Twelve and General Authority of the Church, also spoke of this "rock" or "spirit of revelation" being *the Comforter:*

> *"****The Holy Ghost ... is the spirit of revelation*** *upon which the true Church is founded.* ***He is the Comforter*** *... referred to by the Lord Jesus" ("The Gospel Restored," Conference Report, April 1968, pp. 40-42; emphasis added).*

The Holy Ghost is the spirit of revelation (i.e., "the rock") upon which the true Church is founded, and this same "spirit of revelation" is the Comforter. Said another way, "the rock" is the Comforter which provides the spirit of revelation upon which we must be built. How did people gain knowledge in the early days of the Church in ancient times? They received the Comforter, which "showeth all things." They did not have a well-oiled organizational machine and ways of electronic and digital communication as we have today. They were taught of God through the Comforter. It is this Comforter which imparts the knowledge of God and of His mysteries and is received concurrently with the baptism of Fire. The Comforter reveals all things and prepares us to once again enter the presence of the personage of the Lord Jesus Christ, which is when we are redeemed from the Fall of Adam. When we receive the promised blessing of the Holy Ghost, He then becomes the great revelator and revealer of all things to us, which includes *the revelation of the absolute reality and knowledge of Himself to us*. Thereafter we are given here a little, there a little, growing in the knowledge of God through our faith, knowledge, and steadfastness in Christ. And it is upon the reception of the Comforter that we become *true witnesses of His reality*. Hence, "No man can [truly] say that Jesus is the Lord, but by the Holy Ghost" (1 Cor. 12:3; emphasis added). As a side note, Joseph Smith taught that this phrase "No man can say that Jesus is the Lord, but by the Holy Ghost," should be translated "no man can ***know*** that Jesus is the Lord, but by the Holy Ghost" (See Teachings, p. 223).

The Apostle Delbert L. Stapley said it this way:

> *"Without this spiritual endowment [of the Comforter], Christ's disciples could not become true witnesses to testify that Jesus was their Redeemer, Savior, Lord, and God. The need of this same blessing applies to each of us, or we will be without conviction and faith of Christ's reality" (Conference Report, October, 1966, pp. 111-114; emphasis added).*

Notice that this same blessing of becoming "true witnesses," just as Christ's disciples, *"applies to each of us,"* for God is not a respecter of persons. The receipt and enjoyment of the Holy Ghost or First Comforter, given ultimately as a gift of grace, is how the ancient Church of Christ was originally built. They had the witness of Christ through the Holy Ghost, became *living witnesses themselves*, and were tutored by God Himself through this gift. They sought by faith, and by faith they obtained the greater knowledge. And it is accomplished of course through this rock of the Comforter that is given to abide in man, which *reveals* to him "all things which pertain to life and godliness." This is why we are told repeatedly that the rock on which the Church would be built, and that we ourselves must be built on, is *revelation*. But without this Comforter, the molding of ourselves unto *the measure of the fulness of the stature of Christ* cannot happen. This is the importance of receiving the gift of the Holy Ghost and why this book and the gospel itself is ultimately about coming to partake of or experience of this unspeakable gift in our lives.

In the end, our greatest objective is to be fully redeemed from the Fall, which occurs when we come into the Lord's literal presence while in mortality. But to get there, our hearts must first be purified: "The pure in heart shall see God." This is a literal, spiritual purification of the heart. We can never accomplish this purity of heart without the reception and *ongoing enjoyment* of the promised gift and blessing of the Father—the Holy Ghost. It is through this Comforter that "men got the knowledge of all things which pertain to life and godliness" (*Lectures On Faith*, 7:19).

Elder McConkie said that to obtain the knowledge of God (which I witness happens by way of a heavenly manifestation of the Lord's Spirit) was the rock foundation on which our religion was based, and that without it we could not hope for the glories of eternity:

> *The knowledge of God ... is the rock foundation upon which all true religion is based, and without that knowledge and without revelation from him, it is not possible for men to hope for or gain the blessings, honors, and glories of eternity ("This Is Life Eternal," Conference Report, April 1952, pp. 55-57).*

Do we all now sufficiently understand that obtaining "the knowledge of God" is "code" for receiving a manifestation in power of the Lords' Spirit, which is likewise when we receive the Baptism of Fire and are given the Comforter to abide in us as a gift? And that without this gift and knowledge, we cannot progress unto "the blessings, honors, and glories of eternity," per Elder McConkie? This is why, fellow seeker, *the primary purpose of this work*—Putting On Christ, is to ***highlight the patterns that lead to spiritual rebirth***. Thereafter, God Himself will teach us. Nothing is more important in mortality than receiving this gift, because without it, we cannot be conditionally saved, nor continue in our progression towards overcoming the world.

Greater vs. Lesser Portion of the Word

For the purposes of better understanding the following verses, I will substitute the word *Spirit* or *the Spirit* for any reference to *the word* or *Him*.

9 And now Alma began to expound these things unto him, saying: It is given unto many to know the mysteries of God; nevertheless they are laid under a strict command that they shall not impart only according to the portion of his [Spirit] which he doth grant unto the children of men, according to the heed and diligence which they give unto [the Spirit].

10 And therefore, he that will harden his heart, the same receiveth the lesser portion of the [Spirit]; and he that will not harden his heart, to him is given the greater portion of the [Spirit], until it is given unto him to know the mysteries of God until he know them in full. [Author Commentary: Changing out these words makes it so simple and plain for us to understand. If there is an obstruction in any degree degrading the love and light of God from entering our hearts, we will receive a smaller portion of it, will we not?]

11 And they that will harden their hearts, to them is given the lesser portion of the [Spirit] until they know nothing concerning his mysteries [for as it is written, "my Spirit shall not always strive with man"]; and then they are taken captive by the devil, and led by his will down to destruction. Now this is what is meant by the chains of hell (Alma 12:9-11)

[Remember, the "word" here refers to the God Light or Light of Christ ("for my word is Spirit") which is constantly being broadcast to all of us at the same time and at all times. Why do some sense or feel different portions of this light, word, or Spirit? Because our portion received directly corresponds to the heed and diligence we pay to it. We must act on that word of Spirit. And that's why the degree of the "film," "plaque," or "wall" that we have developed over our hearts is crucial to monitor and clear out. Hence the constant need for removing the heart walls and maintaining open hearts is so critical. These verses directly correlate with chapter one, do they not? Ground Zero of the battle is over our hearts.]

11 He answered and said unto them, because it is given unto you to know the mysteries of the kingdom of heaven, but to them it is not given. [And why? Because they had chosen to further harden their hearts instead of seeking God's grace in healing their hearts.]

12 For whosoever hath, to him shall be given, and he shall have more abundance: but whosoever hath not, from him shall be taken away even that he hath [through a hardened heart] (Matthew 13:11-12).

In other words, "my Spirit shall not always strive with man." If a man chooses to harden his own heart and stiffen his own neck against his Creator, then that is a choice of individual agency, which not even God will confront in man, as free agency is an unassailable gift.

The Lord reinforced these greater and lesser portions of His word or "Spirit" when He visited the Nephites. "And if it shall so be that they shall *believe these things* then shall the greater things be made manifest unto them. And if it so be that they will *not believe these things*, then shall the greater things be withheld from them, unto their condemnation" (3 Nephi 26:9-10). Notice how unbelief or those that "will not believe these things" are led to condemnation as outlined in the antithesis of our Diagram found in Chapter 1. Notice also that to "not believe" is tied to a hard or closed heart:

Apathy →Hard/Closed Heart →Spiritual Blindness →Unbelief (Darkness) →Acting in Unbelief→Fear →Loss of Spiritual Knowledge/Understanding →Condemnation.

The Diagram shown above is the same as the parable of the sower in that those who rejected the word or seed that had been planted did not receive the blessings that could have been theirs. It is important to recognize that both the lesser portion of the word and the greater portion of the word are essential within the gospel program. The prior is preparatory and can lead to the latter, much like the Aaronic is preparatory for the Melchizedek. I like to think of them in the context of outward and inward performances.

The Lesser Portion of the Word. (The lesser portion of Christ's Light or Spirit given to man is arrived at through mostly outward performances without those ordinances being justified by the Holy Spirit of Promise).

1. Little awareness of hearing and heeding the voice of the Spirit or Light of Christ. Little awareness of this Light residing within themselves. "The light shineth in darkness, but the darkness comprehended it not."
2. Belief in the Lord Jesus Christ
3. Confession, and perhaps lacking whole-hearted repentance
4. Baptism by water
5. Receiving the ordinance called "the gift of the Holy Ghost" without the actual reception and enjoyment of the gift.
6. Aaronic Priesthood ordination (for young men)
7. Melchezedek Priesthood ordination (for adult men)
8. Washing and anointing ordinance
9. Temple endowment
10. Temple sealing (sometimes referred to as marriage)

The Greater Portion of the Word (The greater portion of Christ's Light or Spirit is arrived at through mostly *inward performances* of the soul and is subject to having previously received the *outward ordinances* by proper authority, which yields having those ordinances justified by the Holy Spirit of Promise. Joseph tells us that the plan of salvation was a system of faith and that "it begins with faith, *and continues by faith*; and **every blessing** which is obtained in relation to it **is the effect of faith**" (Lecture 7:17; emphasis added.)

Notice that "*every blessing ... is the effect of faith.*" Notice also that faith is a common denominator of every rung on salvation's ladder and is involved throughout the entire journey until we receive the knowledge of God. Thereafter, we will continue to then grow in the knowledge of the Lord to more of a fulness of that knowledge where unbelief is no more. And when unbelief is no more, the veil is no more, and when the veil is no more, we are permitted to see the Lord. The process looks something like this:

1. Belief and faith in Christ through predominantly hearing and heeding the voice of the Spirit or Light of Christ.
2. Belief and faith in Christ through confession and wholehearted repentance. We approach the throne of grace with full purpose of heart, without hypocrisy or deception before God.
3. Belief and faith in Christ through entering the waters of baptism.

4. Belief and faith in Christ through receiving "the promise of the Father" via our confirmation, which is performed by Melchizedek Priesthood authority and which provides the key to the knowledge of God, subject to fulfilling the law tied to that promised blessing.

5. Belief and faith in Christ through offering our broken heart on the altar of our souls with complete surrender and submission. (This is a law. There is no getting around it. Our Redeemer's heart broke. Ours too must break and then be consecrated as an offering to Him (see 2 Nephi 2:6-7).

6. Belief and faith in Christ through calling on His name with a longing, yearning, and desire in our souls to find and know Him, which is to also obtain or find the knowledge of God (not just "about" God, for there is a monumental difference). Remember Alma's words: "***and <u>never, until</u> I did cry out unto the Lord for mercy, did I receive a remission of my sins***" (Alma 38:8; emphasis added).

7. Belief and faith in Christ unto an endowment of receiving a living faith (that "power" or "perfect faith" to become the sons of God), which is to be able "to see" the kingdom of Heaven and ourselves in it. This opens the door to immediate *justification and subsequent sanctification by grace*, through the bestowal of a living power of faith needed, as referenced repeatedly throughout *Putting on Christ.*

8. Faith in Christ in obtaining justification through the Atonement of Jesus Christ wherein the justice of God's law is offset by the mercy of Christ through the shedding of His blood, thereby holding the sinner harmless.

9. Faith in Christ unto the obtaining of *the knowledge of God*, which is accompanied by the purification of the heart and soul through the baptism of fire and of the Holy Ghost, which is made possible through the "shedding of the blood of Christ." This baptism of fire cleanses us of all sin and removes from us the desire to sin at all. This is also when we are born of God, no longer struggling to overcome the natural man in us, at least for a long season. This is when we are also adopted spiritually into the family of Christ and become "begotten sons and daughters" unto Christ (Mosiah 27:25, 26). Through this spiritual cleansing and purification by the Deity, we are in that moment prepared "to enter" the kingdom of heaven, should we in that moment be called home to our heavenly abode.

10. Faith and growing in the knowledge of Christ and the Father while successfully passing through our own Abrahamic test. *We can prepare for this test by practicing the art of the First and Great*

Commandment of loving God with all the heart, might, mind, and strength.

Abraham becomes our father in fulfillment of the oath that God swore, that through him all of humanity who has ever lived and ever will live could receive the full blessings of salvation. At our rebirth, we become the "seed of Abraham," per Joseph Smith's own words. The Lord said, "Therefore, they must needs be chastened and tried, even as Abraham, who was commanded to offer up his only son. For all those who will not endure chastening, but deny me, cannot be sanctified" (D&C 101:4-5). Joseph Smith, as quoted by John Taylor, said, "We must be tried even as Abraham." And, said he, "God will ***feel after you*** and will take all of you and arrange your very heart strings" (*Journal of Discourses,* 24:196). Joseph stated that "it will be a trial of our faith ***equal*** *to that of Abraham*, and that the ancients will not have whereof to boast over us in the day of judgement, as being called to pass through heavier afflictions; that we may hold an even weight in the balance with them" (*Teachings of the Prophet Joseph Smith,* p. 137). Brigham Young said, "God never bestows upon his people, or upon an individual, superior blessings without a *severe trial* to prove them, to prove that individual" (*Discourses of Brigham Young,* p. 338).

11. Faith and growing in the knowledge of Christ and the Father until the candidate of salvation comes to "an actual knowledge… that the course of life which he pursues is according to the will of God" (Lecture 6:2). The *Lectures On Faith* state that through this knowledge, our faith "becomes sufficiently strong to lay hold of the promise of eternal life" (Lecture 6:11).

12. Faith and growing in the knowledge of Christ and the Father unto the ministering of angels (see Moroni 7 and Mosiah 13). We are Adam or Eve, respectively, looking for further light and knowledge delivered through messengers from the Father to aid us to know Him by entering His Presence and seeing His face. Part of this light and knowledge may be given to us through the ministering of angels. Angels can prepare us for future endowments. Angels may include those both seen and unseen. Brigham Young taught: "I wish that every man would live so that he could have communion with angels—so that Jesus would come to visit him. I wish I could see this people in such a position; but there is yet too much sin in our midst: our traditions cling to us so strongly, that we cannot yet break through into that liberty; but we will see the day, if faithful, in which we can converse with angels. There are persons in this congregation that will converse with angels just as freely as we converse with each other" (J.D. 5:258).

13. Faith and growing in the knowledge of Christ and the Father unto receiving the (nearly) unconditional promise of eternal life, which is to have our calling and election made sure (also known as the more sure word of prophecy and promise of eternal life). This prophecy is about the candidate's future and is given directly from God to the individual recipient. It is about the more sure promise of a future fulness of immortal glory we are to obtain in the resurrection and world to come. This knowledge brings peace in this world and allows the candidate for salvation "to endure all his afflictions and persecutions, and to take joyfully the spoiling of his goods" while still in this life (see Lecture 6).
14. Faith and growing in the knowledge of Christ and the Father to a dissipation of all unbelief in us unto the reception of the Second Comforter. This is the endowment of the visitation of the personage of Jesus Christ to the candidate of salvation.
15. Other spiritual endowments known only between the candidate of salvation and God Himself.

It is my opinion that these 15 waymarks along our spiritual path are part of *the greater portion of the word* that may be obtained by faithfully executing the doctrine of Christ. Nephi says that, "there will be no more doctrine given until after he shall manifest himself unto you in the flesh" (2 Ne. 32:6).

Fellow seeker. This is my view of the greater versus the lesser portions of the Word or Christ Light. They could also be viewed as ***a linear depiction of the straight and narrow path*** to the tree of life and beyond while in mortality, although ***they can come in any order in which God chooses***. Which portion of His word or Spirit will we choose and seek? Remember, the only requirement to receive the greater portion of the word is to "diligently seek" in faith, beginning and continuing with a burning, inner desire. *This diligently seeking and desiring to find and know Him and to always do His will* ***must become a way of life***. And if it does, there is no question about it, you and I will inherit eternal life, by the Father's own word and promise.

To diligently seek means that we must recognize the urgency of this endeavor and take on us the personal responsibility of finding the gate for ourselves through seeking by faith. Part of this enduring will be to assist those of our family members and loved ones to find the gate for themselves as well. Receiving the Holy Ghost or First Comforter is the most critical endowment to obtain in mortality. Without it, we cannot be led to the subsequent endowments given through the Comforter. For "then cometh the night of darkness wherein there can be no labor performed" (Alma 34:33). Let us not become numb through the constant consumption of the "All is well in Zion" prescription and succumb to this unaware, unawake, comatose state of being. For this is how he "cheateth their souls and leadeth them away carefully down to hell"

(2 Ne. 28:21). We must arise and stand forth, even in the faith of Him who created us.

The True Seekers and True Saints Will Come under Steady Opposition.

I wanted to share a musical recipe for those times in which we may be feeling opposition from the adversary. It includes a musical play list that will change the atmosphere and increase light. I recommend a music device so that the vibrations and resonance of the music fill the air in your room. The first song I'd recommend to play out loud is the song "Hallelujah," from Handel's Messiah, performed by the Mormon Tabernacle Choir on their Ring Christmas Bells CD. Feel free to turn the volume up and sing along with gusto. The forces of darkness do not enjoy hanging out with us while we praise God, nor do they want anything to do with praising God. Not even a little bit. So as we seek spiritual relief, in addition to priesthood blessings, prayer, and the like, may I suggest listening to the Tabernacle Choir at Temple Square" as one of our first countermeasures. As a rotating three-song playlist, may I recommend next, "I Believe in Christ" from the *This Is the Christ* CD, and lastly the song, "Alleluia," found on the *Men of the Mormon Tabernacle Choir* CD. After this third song plays, feel free to repeat the playlist and then at the end, leave the "Alleluia" song on repeat. This holy trifecta I have found to be very effective in combating the forces of darkness who desire to rob us of our peace. When you feel any negative energy, darkness, or heaviness of any kind, you'll know an effective recipe and remedy. Try it. It has worked repeatedly for me.

The Cycle of Sanctification by Faith and Spiritual Knowledge unto Holiness

After we have found the gate," the pattern in our Diagram remains the same for acquiring additional faith and spiritual knowledge in a never-ending cyclical loop of living faith (power) and hope (spiritual knowledge). So long as we maintain a soft and open heart and continue to do the things out in the world that our Savior did, we will receive additional portions of faith as an endowment, which will yield additional spiritual knowledge. As the scriptures instruct us, this is hope "which … cometh of faith" (Ether 12:4). These spiritual "knowledges" accumulated over time allow us to "grow in grace and in the knowledge of the truth" (D&C 50:40). Remember, Christ is the Truth. As we grow in the knowledge of the truth through faith, we will arrive at an overall "knowledge of God" and the "mysteries of godliness," void of any unbelief whatsoever. We receive the "more sure" knowledge from God Himself that we will receive eternal life, which "maketh an anchor to the souls of men, which would make them sure and steadfast, … being led to glorify God (Ether 12:4). This is where the brother of Jared arrived. He attained an overall perfect knowledge of God, His plan of happiness, and his own place and standing in that plan. And because of this perfect knowledge (which likewise gave him a "hope" for a future endowment of exaltation), he could not be kept from within the veil. And so it is with us. We are to go and do likewise.

This cyclical pattern of acquiring spiritual knowledge and understanding by faith, or what the scriptures refer to as seeking and "learning by faith," is how we acquire this additional "perfect knowledge" and "grow in the knowledge of God." The Bible Dictionary says it this way: "*The principle of **gaining knowledge by revelation** is the principle of salvation*" *(See "Revelation," LDS Study Helps, Bible Dictionary). This knowledge is primarily spiritual knowledge, obtained by spiritual means. And the preeminent knowledge we are to receive is the knowledge of God, whom to know is eternal life.*

"Learning by faith" means to turn to God from the soul, being persistent and consistent in asking over and over again for the desired answer we are seeking, with the feeling of expectancy that God can and will answer our pleading for this confirmed "hope" or spiritual knowledge, all in His timing. In my experience, this desire to know must be submerged within our feelings, even deeply into the emotions to be most effective. We've got to really desire the answer and turn to Him repeatedly. This is learning by faith. Learning by faith is not obtained from books or from the words of others. President Harold B. Lee taught, "From heavenly instructions and … the *experiences* of almost anyone who has sought diligently for heavenly guidance, one may readily understand that *learning by faith requires the **bending of the whole soul** through worthy living to become attuned to the Holy Spirit of the Lord*" ("The Iron Rod," general conference, April 1971; emphasis added).

The prophet Alma reaffirms this principle of faith turning into a perfect knowledge: "Now, if ye give place, that a seed may be planted in your heart, behold, if it be a true seed, or a good seed, *if ye do not cast it out by your unbelief*, that ye will resist the Spirit of the Lord, behold, it will begin to *swell within your breasts*; and when you feel these *swelling motions*, ye will begin to say within yourselves—It must needs be that this is a good seed, or that the word is good, for it beginneth to *enlarge my soul*; yea, it beginneth to *enlighten my understanding*, yea, it beginneth to be *delicious* to me. "Now behold, would not this increase your faith? I say unto you, Yea; *nevertheless, it hath not grown up to a perfect knowledge*" (Alma 32:28-29; emphasis added).

Notice at this point, it is not a perfect knowledge, but as we continue to grow, we reach a point in which our faith is no longer faith. It becomes a perfect knowledge "in that thing." "And now, behold, is your knowledge perfect? *Yea, <u>your knowledge is perfect</u> **in that thing**, and **your faith is dormant**; and this **because you know**"* (Alma 32:34; emphasis added). This is how we grow in the knowledge of the mysteries of God and godliness. These cumulative "perfect knowledges" acquired "here a little and there a little" (2 Ne. 28:30; Isa. 28:10) are what allows us to eventually rid ourselves of all unbelief. ***And where there is no unbelief, there is no veil, because the veil is unbelief.*** We can then come to know God in the form of His personage. The preeminent knowledge we can receive in mortality is to have a perfect knowledge of God; which is not faith, nor belief. We come to "know" God when we receive the First and/or Second Comforters and other endowments. In each of these experiences, faith is no longer, because our "***knowledge is perfect*** ***in that thing and [our]*** ***faith is dormant;*** ***and this because*** ***[we] know***" (Alma 32:34; emphasis added).

The process of accumulating spiritual "knowledges" parallels acquiring additional light and truth. Joseph said, "Add to your faith knowledge, etc. The principle of knowledge is the principle of salvation. This principle can be comprehended by the faithful and diligent; and every one that does not obtain *knowledge sufficient to be saved* will be condemned" (Teachings of the Prophet Joseph Smith, p. 297). Joseph then added that, "the principle of salvation is given us through *the knowledge of Jesus Christ"* (ibid; emphasis added).

Acquiring light and truth is to receive more and more of God's glory, which contains His attributes. Accruing light and truth is primarily acquired through grace by Christlike, selfless service. It is to "do the things that ye have seen me do" (2 Ne. 31:12). As we continue to learn by faith, which is to turn directly to God for personal revelation, we receive additional spiritual knowledge.

We must needs receive a fulness of both God's mind (which is the Holy Spirit) and glory in order to become like our Father in Heaven and our perfect exemplar in Christ. This fulness of the Spirit and glory of the Father is our end objective, for as Christ received a fulness of the Spirit and glory of the Father centered in His Father Elohim, so are we to receive a fulness of the same Spirit and glory which is centered in Christ. This is how we become "saved" to the fullest extent, even as intended by our Father Elohim.

Chapter 10

Faith vs. Unbelief: Spiritual Keys from the Lectures On Faith

The Lectures On Faith were "designed to unfold to the understanding the doctrine of Christ" (Lectures On Faith, Lecture First).

Christ says, "Behold, I stand at the door, and knock: if any man hear my voice, and open the door, I will come in to him, and will sup with him, and he with me" (Revelation 3:20). In other words, the Lord is saying, "Desire (to come to the knowledge of God and His Glory)…. Ask, Seek, Knock—Receive. Then Repeat." This is the model we are to follow.

Notice that man himself must not only *hear* His voice, which is His Spirit, but in fact must also "open the door." How do we open this door? We do so by *eradicating ourselves of all unbelief* and growing by degrees of faith and endowments of light and truth, through the power and grace of Christ, made possible through the act of His atonement. ***In my opinion, this "eradication of unbelief" is the primary purpose for the Lectures On Faith***, a neglected treasure by most within our LDS community. Through personal, sacred experiential knowledge, I have come to view, understand, and value the *Lectures On Faith* like scripture for my own personal journey. They have been *that* impactful. The Lord Himself said, "And if it so be that they will not believe these things, then shall *the greater things* be withheld from them, unto their condemnation" (3 Ne. 26:10). Learning by faith as patterned for us in these lectures is what I believe yields these "greater things" or "the greater portion of the word," referenced both by Christ directly and in scripture.

Incorporating in our lives the information contained within the *Lectures On Faith* may in fact lead us through faith to the greatest blessings we can receive in mortality, including the actual knowledge that we are accepted in God's sight, thereby giving the added endowment of faith to lay hold of that more sure word of prophecy and subsequently, that of rending the veil of unbelief altogether in order to see the face of God. Elder Bruce R. McConkie referred to the *Lectures On Faith* as follows: "In my judgment, it is the most comprehensive, intelligent, inspired utterance that now exists in the English language—that exists in one place defining, interpreting, expounding, announcing, and testifying what kind of being God is. It was written by the power of the Holy Ghost by the spirit of inspiration. It is, in effect, *eternal scripture*; it is true. I will only read part of it, and even then, because of the deep content that is involved in the words, we cannot measure or fathom their full intent. We need to study and ponder and analyze the expressions that are made" ("The Lord God of Joseph Smith," discourse delivered January 4, 1972, Provo, Utah, p. 4). President Joseph Fielding Smith considered the Lectures "to be of EXTREME VALUE in the study of the gospel of Jesus Christ" (Joseph Fielding Smith, "Seek Ye Earnestly," Deseret Book, 1970, p. 194). If Elder McConkie, an apostle of the Lord, has referred to the *Lectures On Faith* as eternal scripture, I feel comfortable in seeing them as such for my own personal journey.

It is important to realize that every quorum of the Church approved the *Lectures On Faith* by common consent in a general assembly of the Church as *the doctrine* for "The Church of the Latter Day Saints." This is found on pages 255-257 in the original 1835 edition of the Doctrine and Covenants, which is available as part of the Joseph Smith Papers. Joseph Smith and the entire First Presidency appended their names to the lectures as outlined in the preface. To quote the original 1835 preface: "There may be an aversion *in the minds of some* against receiving any thing purporting to be articles of religious faith… but if men [specifically, the First Presidency] believe a system, and ***profess that it was given by inspiration***, certainly, the more intelligibly they can present it, the better" (pp. iii-iv).

The Prophet Joseph and other members of the First Presidency affirm that these lectures were given them *by inspiration* from God and also speak with solemnity of spirit as to the serious nature (and perhaps sacred nature) in which they had approached its inclusion and publication within the Doctrine and Covenants, with the lectures comprising "the doctrine" of that work. In Joseph Smith's own writings, he states: "During the month of January, I was engaged in the school of the Elders, *and in preparing the lectures on theology for publication in the Book of Doctrine and Covenants*, which the committee appointed last September were now compiling" (*History of the Church,* Vol. 2, p. 180).

In the 1835 preface, it reads: "We [meaning, the First Presidency] do not present this little volume [referring to the Lectures] with any other expectation than that *we are to be called to answer to [God, for] every principle advanced*, in that day when the secrets of all hearts will be revealed, and the reward of every man's labor be given him" (D&C, 1835 Preface, p. iv; emphasis added). To assert that they will be called to answer to God "for every principle advanced" instills in this bosom the knowledge that they did not consider its inclusion in the Doctrine and Covenants to be taken lightly or as something inconsequential. To me, this provides the broader context of the work as having been "given by inspiration," not to mention the fact that it had been adopted by common consent by the entire body of the Church at that time, even quorum by quorum during a general assembly. As stated in the Introduction of this work, "These lectures were considered as doctrine when published as part of the Doctrine and Covenants until 1921. Though they were removed as canonized scripture then, they are still available worldwide and published as a separate booklet" (see Introduction, *Putting on Christ*). I'm grateful that the lectures are widely made available to us even now. They were given for a reason.

Notwithstanding the above, through God's grace, the diligent seekers shall always become finders. The below points are 16 spiritual keys which are provided to aid the spiritual seeker in eradicating all unbelief as to meeting our Lord in mortality. The spiritual keys I have chosen to highlight from the lectures are as follows:

Spiritual Key #1: Faith Is the Principle of Power in Man as Well as in Deity.

God works by faith. Everything He does is by faith. And "it is by reason of this *principle of power* existing in the Deity, *that all created things exist*" (Lecture 1:15; emphasis added). "All these things were done by faith. It was by faith that the worlds were framed. God spake, chaos heard, and worlds came into order by reason of the faith there was in Him. *So with man also*" (Lecture 1:22; emphasis added).

"Faith, then, is the first great governing principle which has power, dominion, and authority over all things; by it they exist, by it they are upheld, by it they are changed, or by it they remain, *agreeable to the will of God.* Without it there is no power, and *with out power there could be no creation nor existence*!" (Lecture 1:24; emphasis added).

Faith is "*the assurance we have of the existence of unseen things.*" This being the case, it is also "*the principle of action* in all intelligent beings," which includes us (*Lectures On Faith*, p. 10; emphasis added).

Spiritual Key #2: Adam and Eve Never Lost Their Memory of Having Seen God, even after Expulsion from the Garden, Thereby Allowing for Personal Human Testimony.

"Though [Adam] was cast out from the garden of Eden, his knowledge of the existence of God was not lost, neither did God cease to manifest his will unto him" (Lecture 2:20). This put Adam in the same place as we find ourselves in mortality in our day (with the exception of our not retaining our prior knowledge of God), subject to having received the ordinances of baptism by water and confirmation. Through an angel, God gave Adam commandments and told him to "repent and call upon God in the name of the Son for evermore. And in that day, the Holy Ghost fell upon Adam, which beareth record of the Father and the Son" (Lecture 2:24). When the third member of the Godhead falls upon a candidate of salvation, that candidate receives the perfect knowledge of God, even though the same may be separated from the presence of God by a veil. This is how Adam's posterity (including us) are "first made acquainted with the existence of a God; *that it was by a manifestation of God to man*" (Lecture 2:30). Adam, through his earlier memory and knowledge of God prior to the Fall, and through his being spiritually reborn of God, "communicated the knowledge which he had unto his posterity… which laid the foundation for the exercise of their faith [in Him], through which they could obtain a knowledge of his character and also of his glory" (Lecture 2:31).

Spiritual Key #3: The Essential Nature of Human Testimony: A Common Prerequisite to Seeing the Face of God.

When I first read the first two lectures of the *Lectures On Faith,* I "zoned out" in part when I arrived at all the "begats." Adam begat Seth, who begat Enos, who begat Cainan, who begat Mahalaleel, who begat Jared, who begat Enoch, who begat Methuselah, who begat Lamech. And Lamech begat Noah, who built the ark. Are you still with me? A total of 1,056 years passed between Adam and Noah. There was another 1,000 or so years between Noah and Abraham. Here is why it matters and why it is crucially important.

First, Adam and Eve were the only ones at the commencement of their traversing the path laid out for them (and as participants in the newly formed world that God had created for them) who had walked with, talked with, and seen God face to face. And Adam sought to bring his posterity into the presence of God to behold His face, just as he had previously seen Him. In fact, not only did Adam behold Him prior to the Fall, his objective, intention, and continuous affirmation was to do it again. To use Adam's words, he affirmed that "again in my flesh, I shall see God" (Moses 5:10). "The evidences which these men (Adam's posterity) had of the existence of a God, was the testimony of their fathers in the first instance" (Lecture 2:33).

Secondly, Adam sought to bring his entire posterity into the presence of God the same way we are to obtain it, and that was by providing the necessary ordinances of salvation through the Melchizedek Priesthood, *and (now this is crucial!) by providing direct,* ***human testimony*** *as to his having seen the face of God prior to the Fall, as well as a manifestation of God through the reception of the Holy Ghost after the Fall.* "For previous to the time that any of Adam's posterity had obtained a manifestation of God to themselves, Adam, their common father, had testified unto them of the existence of God, and of his eternal power and Godhead" (Lecture 2:35).

"Where there is no vision, the people perish" (Prov. 29:18). If we see ourselves "dwindling in unbelief," it is because our vision is getting distorted or hazy. Our vision must start with the first principle of the gospel, which the Prophet Joseph says is "to know for a certainty the Character of God, and to know that we [yes, that means you and I] may converse with Him as one man converses with another" (*Teachings of the Prophet Joseph Smith,* p. 345). This is where we start with our vision. It starts with the mental video of our encounter with the Son of God and the constant replaying of that video in our mind's eye until we meet Him while in the flesh.

Prior to a real estate developer's breaking ground in building a skyscraper, or prior to even turning over the first shovel of dirt, he would have already "seen" it in his mind's eye. It will have already been created, spiritually first, through believing it with his entire being, even "as though" or "as if" the building had already been built.

Now, I can't think of anything of less importance to me personally than visualizing a skyscraper being built. But I can think of something that *is* of utmost importance, and that is the vision of winning Christ by entering His Presence. This, my brothers and sisters in Christ, is one of our first steps on our path to Godhood and eternal life in its fullest sense.

In the *Lectures On Faith* we are given **the only vision that truly matters**:

> *"Let us here observe, that after any portion of the human family are made acquainted with the important fact that there is a God, who has created and does uphold all things, the extent of their knowledge respecting his character and glory will depend upon their* ***diligence and faithfulness in seeking after him, until****, like Enoch, the brother of Jared, and Moses,* ***they shall obtain faith in God, and power with him to behold him face to face****" (Lecture 2:55; emphasis added).*

This is a vision beyond words, is it not? Our knowledge of God will depend on our diligence and faithfulness in ***seeking after Him***. But what is it that would get us excited about seeking after Him? Because there is always the remote chance that we might be seeking that which is unobtainable, correct? We might actually wonder if we are setting ourselves up for a serious disappointment. So what gets us to that point of desire and belief to chase after this vision? It is revealed in the next paragraph what the motivation was for the children of Adam and Eve:

> *"It was human testimony, and human testimony only, that excited this inquiry, in the first instance, in their minds. It was the credence they gave to the testimony of their fathers [who had already obtained the knowledge of God for themselves], this testimony [i.e., 'the witness'] having aroused their minds to inquire after the knowledge of God" (Lecture 2:56; emphasis added).*

And when this human testimony was received and acted on by the candidate of salvation, it "***always terminated when rightly pursued, in the most glorious discoveries and eternal certainty***" (Lecture 2:56; emphasis added). **This eternal certainty**, in the context of Lecture 2:55, **is to see the face of God.** But there is one slight problem. As a general rule, no one, unless he is cleansed and sanctified by the Deity beforehand, can see the face of God and live (D&C 84:22). We must be prepared for such an event in our lives. It requires being wholly cleansed as though by spiritual fire and further sanctified unto holiness. We must be made *like unto Him* before entering His Presence. What are we to do? We start by following the directive at our confirmation to "receive the Holy Ghost" by faithfully executing the doctrine of Christ.

Let's take a walk now, back to the "begats." Why were we told of all the begats? And why did the second lecture list the "begats" later from Noah until Abraham. One reason was to demonstrate that for 930 years, Adam lived on the earth and would have easily witnessed to his first-hand account and knowledge. It was to also demonstrate that all the way through Abraham, there were others who saw the face of God and could give a first-person account of having seen Him. That's over 2,000 years wherein there was a first-person individual witness as to the reality of God through having seen Him. Again, why was it important that Adam lived 930 years? Because Adam would have been able to speak personally and directly to his children, grandchildren, great-grandchildren, great-great-grandchildren, great-great-great-grandchildren, great-great-great-great-grandchildren, and so on for 930 years. ***They would have all had the opportunity to receive a first-hand personal witness to themselves individually from Adam of his experiences of having walked and talked with God***. Any who have played the game called Telephone will understand why this direct communication was important. To play the game, one person whispers something to another person, and then that person whispers it to another, and that person to another, and so on, until that message has progressed to a dozen or more people. When the last person in the game divulges what he or she believes was originally said, it isn't a surprise that the original message wasn't anywhere close to the accuracy of the original statement or message.

Outside of the loss of accuracy as a message progresses through multiple people, there is always more power when the person delivering a specific message is able to deliver it in power directly to the hearer, especially in light of having had first-hand knowledge. This is even more applicable when it concerns the knowledge of God, because the Spirit would also witness to the reality of this individual's having seen the face of God directly. And you could look the person straight in the eyeballs and know if they were telling the truth, especially when combined with the witness of the Spirit.

As mentioned, from Noah to Abraham others also obtained a face-to-face knowledge of God and could then give first-person knowledge of Him, which they had obtained through the testimony of their father Adam. Looking to our day, why is the Prophet Joseph's witness so powerful? *Because his was a first-hand witness also*.

When I listened to Bruce R. McConkie's last testimony eleven days before he died, I knew that he had seen the Lord. Almost everyone knew it. Some will take that testimony and ride it home all the way to eternal life. Others will dwindle in unbelief. But the testimony was needed, and continues to be essential, and not just from him. I have met Elder McConkie personally on several occasions. I know his witness was and is true. I also know another man who has seen the Lord. He is living today. I know his witness is also true. And I know that we can all take the witness of McConkie, and others, and allow their witness to "excite this inquiry… in [our] minds" (Lecture 2:56). And by giving credence to these witnesses, we may likewise seek to so obtain. "And this is life eternal, that they might know thee, the only true God, and Jesus Christ whom thou hast sent" (John 17:3).

To know Him on this level requires a sincere heart, like that of a little child. To find Him will depend on our "diligence and faithfulness in seeking after him," until we behold Him. Desire and Faith must become the persistent and diligent beat of our drum.

Spiritual Key #4: Three Things Are Necessary to Exercise Faith in God unto Life and Salvation.

a) The idea that He actually exists.

b) A correct idea of His character, perfections, and attributes.

c) An actual knowledge that the course of life which one is pursuing is according to God's will (see Lecture 3:2-5; Lecture 6).

You have read repeated references to the word ***actual*** as I described the type of knowledge required to be with God. Actual knowledge is just that: actual knowledge. With actual knowledge, there can be no guesswork nor ambiguity in the heart and mind of the recipient who receives this knowledge from God directly. In lecture 3, we are told that without the understanding of a & b above, and the actual knowledge of c above, our faith will be "imperfect and unproductive" in leading to "life and salvation." But with it, our faith "can become perfect and fruitful … unto the praise and glory of God the Father, and the Lord Jesus Christ" (Lecture 3:5).

We'll review the simple list given in Lecture Third of God's character, perfections, and attributes. I'll leave it to you to go deeper into what these entail on your own.

The correct idea of the character of God involves the following (see *Lectures On Faith* 3:12-18):

i. "That he was God before the world was created, and the same God that he was after it was created."

ii. "That he is merciful and gracious, slow to anger, abundant in goodness, and that he was so from everlasting, and will be to everlasting."

iii. "That he changes not, neither is there variableness with him; but that he is the same from everlasting to everlasting, being the same yesterday, to-day, and for ever; and that his course is one eternal round, without variation."

iv. "That he is a God of truth and cannot lie."

v. "That he is no respecter of persons: but in every nation he that fears God and works righteousness is accepted of him."

vi. "That he is love."

Now to an understanding of the correct idea of God's attributes, which "is essentially necessary, in order that the faith of any rational being can center in him for life and salvation" (*Lectures On Faith* 3:19). These "attributes" of God are found in Lecture Fourth (see *Lectures On Faith* 4:5-10):

i. Knowledge, meaning that God knows all, "declaring the end from the beginning."

ii. Faith or power. As God hath "sworn" or "thought," so shall it come to pass.

iii. Justice. God is a just God.

iv. Judgment. God executes perfect and fair judgment.

v. Mercy. God is merciful and gracious, always ready to pardon.

vi. Truth. God is a god of truth and cannot lie.

Without the knowledge of these attributes in the Deity, it would not be possible to exercise faith in God unto life and salvation. God never changes. His attributes and character remain forever the same. This foundational understanding gives all men an equal privilege to exercise faith in Him until they receive a knowledge of all things that pertain to life and salvation.

Spiritual Key #5: Those Who Overcome, Receive a Fullness of the Glory of the Father, Possessing the Same Mind with the Father, Which Mind Is the Holy Spirit.

To overcome the world is to become exalted by the Father in the resurrection. The Holy Spirit, we are told in the Lectures, is the mind of God. This spirit or mind is the light which already fills the immensity of space. This is how our Father Elohim is connected, in a way incomprehensible to mortal man, to all things. That is because this spirit is in and through all things. Through this spirit or mind, God is omnipotent, omniscient, and omnipresent. I like to think of this fullness of the Father as being connected to the matrix of all light that fills the immensity of space. This is why, when we pray, He can hear us before we can even whisper, and even before the thought even surfaces within us to pray.

The Son is filled with the same mind (Spirit), glory, and power of the Father. We too can be filled with the same fullness of the mind, glory, and power of the Father. If we believe on Christ's name and keep his commandments, we can receive a fullness of the spirit (i.e., mind) of the Father and become "joint heirs with Jesus Christ; possessing the same mind, being transformed into the same image or likeness, even the express image of him who fills all in all; being filled with the fullness of his glory, and become one in him, even as the Father, Son and Holy Spirit are one" (Lecture 5:2).

This oneness, then, becomes a permanent endowment and not just a taste as is experienced during spiritual rebirth. The purpose of the taste of oneness through spiritual rebirth is to give man the foreknowledge as to what he can strive for and realistically expect in the eternities, only then with a fulness of that previous taste or experience obtained upon receiving the actual gift of the Holy Ghost. Joseph asks in the Lectures, "Do the believers in Christ Jesus, through the gift of the Spirit, become one with the Father and the Son, as the Father and the Son are one?" His answer: "They do" (Lecture 5:19). If we "endure to the end," this endowment experienced in part can become a fullness in the resurrection.

Those who overcome will experience a fullness of the glory of the Father. Remember, glory is light and truth, also known as intelligence. We partake of this fullness, we are told, through some type of connectivity in full with this spirit which already fills the immensity of space. We become one with this spirit, just as this spirit becomes one with and in us. "As the Son partakes of the fullness of the Father through the Spirit, *so the saints are, by the same Spirit, to be partakers of the same fullness*, to enjoy the same glory; for as the Father and the Son are one, *so, in like manner, the saints are to be one in them*" (Lecture 5:3; emphasis added). This spirit is what all the gods in eternity abide in. These are the "everlasting burnings" spoken of in holy writ.

Spiritual Key #6: To Obtain Actual Knowledge That Our Lives Are Acceptable in the Sight of God or That the Course of Life We are Pursuing is in Accordance with His will.

The Lectures teach that the candidate of salvation may, through faith, obtain the ***actual knowledge*** *that he or she is accepted in God's sight* (see Lecture 6:2-3).

The Lectures add that those who obtain this actual knowledge of God's acceptance "will have faith to lay hold on the "more sure" promise of eternal life, and will be enabled, through faith, to endure unto the end, and receive the crown that is laid up for them that love the appearing of our Lord Jesus Christ. *But those who do not make the sacrifice (i.e., a holy consecration or "offering"), cannot enjoy this faith,* because men are dependent upon *this sacrifice* in order to obtain *this faith*" (Lecture 6:11; emphasis added).

Spiritual Key #7: Faith unto Manifesting the Resurrected Lord into Our Lives, Subject to His Holy Will and Timing.

This manifesting may include one or more of the following: To visualize or imagine an encounter with our Lord. To hold to the desire to know God with tenacity until He manifests Himself. To spiritually create our encounter with Him through having an eye of faith, by enduring in seeing Him who is invisible in our mind's eye according to the divine will of God. To continuously speak and affirm His appearance to us personally until we prevail, subject to His grace, holy will, and timing.

This protocol explains that if we were to continually visualize an encounter with the Living Son of the Living God, while continually removing the weeds of doubt (which is darkness), we would attract (in accordance with the Lord's timing, will, and grace) that which we have beheld with an eye of faith and which we will have affirmed through the spoken word. The Prophet Joseph stated: "When a man works by faith, he works *by mental exertion* instead of physical force [this is the visualizing portion or 'eye of faith']. It is *by words* [this is the affirmation or affirmative statement portion], instead of exerting his physical powers with which every being works when he works by faith" (Lecture 7:3; emphasis added). Then the Prophet gave an example of God using His faith: "God said, 'Let there be light: and there was light'" (ibid.).

For years I have used the following affirmation. I share it so that you might use it as a template in developing your own:

"I feel the unbelief dissipating in me and being constantly replaced with endowments of faith. Through the grace, will, and timing of God, I shall know and see the face of my Lord, while in my flesh."

Spiritual Key #8: A Perfection of Faith Leads to Becoming Like God.

Many would believe that in order to become more like God, we would need to become more righteous. But how many of us have equated the level of our faith with the level of our righteousness? To perfect our faith is to become more righteous. It is a law. In fact, in Lecture First, we are taught that the foundation of all righteousness is faith (see Lecture 1:1; 1:27): "When men begin to live by faith they begin to draw near to God; *and when faith is perfected they are like him*" (Lecture 7:8; emphasis added).

Spiritual Key #9: As All the Visible Creation Is the Effect of Faith, So Is Salvation Also.

"It is by reason of this [spiritual element and] power [called 'faith'], that all the hosts perform their works of wonder, majesty, and glory" (Lecture 7:4). It is also by faith that men obtain salvation. "And as God desires the salvation of men, he must, of course, desire that they should have faith" (Lecture 7:7).

This means that the same way we may attract any abundance into our temporal lives is the same way that we might attract the Lord into our lives. When Wayne Dyer in Maui, Hawaii, was manifested in my life (through God's will, timing, and grace), it was through my visualizing an encounter with him and affirming it out loud. In other words, it was through "**mental exertion**" and **affirming** "**words,**" instead of working by physical labor. The same is true in having an encounter with the Living Son of the Living God. Do we see how the First and Great Commandment fulfills all other laws and facilitates coming to know the Lord? This First and Great Commandment will fill us with so much desire in our hearts to know the Lord that we will manifest Him in our lives or we will never be satisfied or at rest. If we truly love Him, we will keep His commandments. And His commandments include the directives to "come unto Him" and to "seek the face of the Lord always."

Joseph informs us that "the real difference between a saved person and one not saved is—the difference in the degree of their faith—one's faith has become perfect enough to lay hold upon eternal life, and the other's has not" (Lecture 7:9). Notice again that the criteria for salvation is founded on faith, and not on our supposed righteousness alone. Why is this? Because as we surrender all to Him with that eternal covenant of the soul during our repentance process, we can subsequently receive of that endowment of a living faith as a gift of perfect faith which is bestowed in power, which then allows us to be justified against the bar of God's justice and to be sanctified through the blood of Christ. When this happens, would we not be made instantaneously worthy and "righteous" through and in Christ?

Spiritual Key #10: Whatever Constitutes the Salvation of One Will Constitute the Salvation of Every Creature Which Will Be Saved.

Joseph Smith clarified: "It is also necessary that men should have an idea that he [God] is no respecter of persons, for with the idea of all the other excellencies in his character, *and this one wanting*, **men could not exercise faith in him**; because if he were a respecter of persons, they could not tell what their privileges were, *nor how far they were authorized to exercise faith in Him, or whether they were to do it at all*, but all must be confusion; but no sooner are the minds of men made acquainted with *the truth on this point, THAT HE IS NO RESPECTER OF PERSONS*, than they see that they have authority by faith to lay hold on eternal life, the richest boon of heaven, BECAUSE GOD IS NO RESPECTER OF PERSONS, and that every man in every nation has an equal privilege" (*Lectures On Faith,* 3:23; emphasis added).

Fellow seeker: How one is saved is how all are saved. This is the general rule. Of course, there are always exceptions to this rule. And that exception has everything to do with God's rule—His will. As a general rule, for example, the remission of sins for one person will be the same way that the next person receives a remission of sins. And according to what our scriptures say, that general rule is that we will receive a remission of sins *by fire and the Holy Ghost* through the manifestation of the Lord's Spirit.

The same would be true of our calling and election made sure or receiving the more sure word of prophecy. How one receives their calling and election is how all will receive it. Again, this is the general rule, and the Lord can make an exception as He deems fit to make.

As to the Second Comforter, there can be little dispute either in the scriptures or in the Church. The Second Comforter includes the personal visitation of the Lord Jesus Christ to the candidate of salvation. The First Comforter's role is to prepare the candidate to enter the Divine Presence by sanctifying him or her unto holiness, which is to become like Christ or Christlike. This happens grace for grace. *These "graces" come as periodic endowments and "portions" of His light and glory. They are received as we put aside our own comforts and extend compassionate works of service to others in doing the things that Christ would and did do, only in our own lives.* "And may God grant, in his great fulness, that men might be brought unto repentance and good works, that they might be restored unto *grace for grace, **according to their works***" (Helaman 12:24; emphasis added).

I find that whenever I sacrifice my own comforts in order to provide compassionate service to one of God's children, and then retire to my "sacred space" at home, I can feel it coming on—a spiritual shower of approval from the Father in the form of heavenly, inner vibrations of and from the Spirit, experientially felt from my head and down into the center of my being. It is undeniably real. And it lingers, while refining the soul. I like to think of this as the experiential "how" as to the way in which we grow in His Light.

This growing in the grace of God's light, grace for grace, is how we become partakers, at least in part or by degrees, of the attributes of God's divine nature. His attributes are found in His light. By the infusion of these incremental "graces," the light derived from God's grace expands within us, and we grow from one level of expanded light within us unto an increased, expanded level, until the perfect day.

Spiritual Key #11: To Become Assimilated into Their Likeness Is to Be Saved.

In Lecture 7, we are taught that "to become assimilated into their likeness is to be saved, and to be unlike them is to be destroyed: and on this hinge hangs the door of salvation" (Lecture 7:16). There is no way that we can become "assimilated into their likeness" without this assimilation stemming from gradual endowments of light and truth through grace, which comes from Them and arises out of our own desire, obedience, compassionate service, and faith.

Remember, *righteousness is not the foundation of righteousness.* Faith is "the foundation of all righteousness" (see *Lectures On Faith* 1:1, 27). Or as Paul taught, "Not having mine own righteousness, which is of the law, but that which is through the faith of Christ, the righteousness which is of God by faith" (Phil. 3:9). The above principle of becoming a replica of Their likeness was likewise reinforced by the Prophet Joseph when he taught that "salvation consists in the glory, authority, majesty, power, and dominion which Jehovah possesses *and in nothing else*; and no being can possess it but himself *or one like him*" (Lecture 7:9; emphasis added). Jesus Christ is "the great prototype of all saved beings" (Lecture 7:16). We must have a heart "like" His and make "like" offerings. He will make up the difference as we stumble, while doing all within our power to heed His directives.

And how did the Father and the Son propose to assimilate man into Their likeness? Through man's faithful execution of the doctrine of Christ, which is to lead the candidate of salvation to be born of God through spiritual Rebirth, and thereafter to endure to the end with the Comforter to abide within that candidate. To have the sanctifying influence of the Comforter is to prepare one to become like unto the Savior and enter His presence in the form of His personage in this life and the world of glory in the next. As previously mentioned in the introduction, to receive the gift of the Spirit (or gift of the Holy Ghost) is to experience the taste of the fruit of the tree of life, which includes not only being filled with the love of God but also with the taste of being "one with the Father and the Son, as the Father and the Son are one" (see Lecture 5:19). As we endure in Him through faith, we can expect to lay hold upon the more sure promise of eternal life, by way of grace through prophecy to us individually. This too cannot be earned, but it can be merited through tests of the heart and soul through offerings which yield endowments of faith. Of this path, the apostle Paul said: "Therefore it is of faith, that it might be by grace; to the end the promise might be sure to all the seed" (Romans 4:16).

Spiritual Key #12: Salvation Itself Is the Effect of Faith.

This could be considered a continuation of Spiritual Key #9. In Lecture 7, the Prophet Joseph inquires, "Who cannot see then that salvation is the effect of faith?" And as to this principle of faith, he then makes this declaration:

> *"And this is the lesson which the God of heaven, by the mouth of his holy prophets, has been endeavoring to teach to the world" (Lecture 7:17).*

And what is that lesson? *That salvation is the effect of faith.* This principle leads us to better understand that the people of the world have not been entirely successful in learning about the power, reality and saving influence of faith, because it has been our Father's *ongoing endeavor* since the beginning of the world. To *endeavor* for something is to toil, to do one's utmost, and to give one's all.

How is it that non-scholarly fishermen, many of whom were perhaps not able to read, were able to obtain salvation? Allow me the literary license to answer this, as delivered from the Lectures. In short, they didn't follow a checklist of what they were "supposed to do." They were not solely focused on the law of carnal commandments or performances under the Jewish law. They sought strictly "by faith, and by faith obtained" (*Lectures On Faith* 7:20). To seek ***by faith*** is to turn directly to God and to implore Him for spiritual knowledge from on high, while fully expecting to receive it and not relying solely upon the ***works of the law.***

> *"And that Israel, who followed after the law of righteousness, has not attained to the law of righteousness. Wherefore? [Why?]* ***Because they sought it not by faith, but as it were by the works of the law****; for they stumbled at that stumbling stone" (Lectures On Faith, 7:17emphasis added. See also Romans 9:32.).*

The Israelites, later known as the Jewish nation, focused on all of the things they were beholden to do throughout their day, which was a continuous list of things that were intended to direct them to God. They stumbled because with all of this, their hearts remained far from God. Their works became a monotonous and mindless series of actions that were mostly not accompanied by loving God or their fellowman, nor exercising faith in the true and living God unto salvation. *Faithless tradition* can lead us to the same type of monotonous, mindless, and heartless service—performing a checklist. In short, the only thing that was truly lacking was that of seeking by faith from the heart. The Lectures emphasize:

> *"All things that pertain to life and godliness are* ***the effects of faith and nothing else****; all learning [which would include all book and intellectual learning], wisdom and prudence* ***fail****, and everything else as a means of salvation* ***but faith****. This is the reason that the fishermen of Galilee could teach the world—* ***because they sought by faith, and by faith obtained****" (Lecture 7:20; emphasis added).*

Read and reread the above. Then close your eyes and connect with what you just read. Breath it in. Taste it. Feel it. Then desire it with tenacity until you experience it. This is how we can eventually become born again and later, "come to an innumerable company of angels, to the general assembly and Church of Enoch, and of the Firstborn."(D&C 76:67). Notice that it was ultimately through faith and faith alone that they obtained salvation. But most will not obtain salvation because most of us will not rely *alone* upon a being whom we have not beheld with our natural eyes.

The children of Israel stumbled at the stumbling stone of trying to work out their salvation through the "checklist"— "the law of performances" and hearing or reading the word of God alone—without relying wholly and solely upon their Redeemer from whom they could receive the knowledge of salvation through faith. In contrast, those who truly followed Jesus in His day turned to God in full from their hearts in faith for their knowledge and salvation, relying alone upon the merits of Christ. Only in this way could they attain the kingdom of heaven. And if we too are to obtain His blessings, it will be accomplished through the same pattern.

President Kimball taught that "man cannot discover God or his ways *by mere mental processes*.... Why, oh, why do people think they can fathom the most complex spiritual depths without the necessary experimental and laboratory work accompanied by compliance with the laws that govern it? Absurd it is, but you will frequently find popular personalities who seem never to have lived a single law of God, discoursing ... [about] religion. How ridiculous for such persons to attempt to outline for the world a way of life.... One cannot know God nor understand his works or plans unless he follows the laws which govern [obtaining that knowledge]" (Spencer W. Kimball, "Absolute Truth," BYU Devotional address, Sept. 6, 1977).

In the Lectures we are taught to add FAITH UPON FAITH, filling our "faith cup," if you will, until we receive that sufficiency of faith to obtain ***the knowledge of God*** (beyond that of faith), the salvation of our own souls, and ultimately overcome the world and its enticements. This is how "the just" are to live, moment to moment. "For [the gospel] is the power of God unto salvation to every one that believeth. For therein is the righteousness of God revealed ***from faith to faith***; as it is written, the just shall live by faith" (Rom. 1:16-17; emphasis added). And I would add, the just become the just by the same—namely, faith. They become "just" by first becoming justified by the Holy Spirit of Promise through an accrual of this spiritual element called faith unto spiritual knowledge and ultimately salvation. They did not obtain through books alone or the works of the law alone. This is where we miss the mark. At some point, our book knowledge must be accompanied with seeking by faith through direct experience. The just seek by faith and by faith obtain, just as Christ's disciples did. The just obtain by turning directly to God, for there is one, and one only, who can save us. Salvation is not performed by our Church, nor by our religion (although the ordinances by the higher priesthood provided by the same are a prerequisite to being saved). Salvation comes from our God, and our God alone, by turning to Him directly.

This accrued sufficiency of faith is also in fact the central purpose of all holy writ. Elder D. Todd Christofferson says that the central purpose of all scripture is "to come to know the only true God, and Jesus Christ, whom he has sent." Notice he did not say, "to come to know about God," but in fact, to KNOW GOD:

> *"In the end, the central purpose of all scripture (and every Christlike act of service within the Church and gospel) is to fill our souls with faith [through the reception of periodic endowments of faith] in God the Father and in his son Jesus Christ—Faith that they exist; faith in the Father's plan for immortality and eternal life; faith in the atonement and resurrection of Jesus Christ, which animates this plan of*

happiness; faith to make the gospel of Jesus Christ our way of life; and ***faith to come to know the only true God, and Jesus Christ, whom he has sent*** *(John 17:3)" ("The Blessing of Scripture"; emphasis added).*

Faith is also intertwined with the "law, irrevocably decreed in heaven before the foundation of this world, upon which all blessings are predicated" (D&C 130:20). That law is the law of restoration, also known as the law of the harvest. The thoughts or "seeds" of belief and faith that we plant in the soil of our own hearts and souls through adhering to the word of God must produce after their own kind. In other words, that which we visualize and hold to in our thoughts, especially when coupled and enhanced with deep desire and emotion, will (when rightly performed over time) materialize, so long as we remove the doubts and fears (i.e., weeds) of unbelief, "for where doubt is, there faith has no power" (*Lectures On Faith* 3:44). Unfortunately, if I plant thoughts of darkness, despair, and failure, I may also unknowingly create or manifest in my life more of the same.

Spiritual Key #13: The Plan of Salvation Is a System of Faith.

Too often when discussing the doctrine of Christ, we think that faith is a component or necessary ingredient only in its beginning. For example, we check the box of faith in Christ and then move on to the next steps of repentance, baptism of water, and so on. We don't understand that we must *continue in faith* as part of our own process of becoming a perfect replica of Christ, which will occur well into the next life. As previously addressed in this work, faith is a common denominator to all things that are manifested in our world, whether temporally or spiritually, including that of salvation. Everything that we do in our world must involve faith, or "no thing" happens. The Lectures say it this way:

> The plan of salvation is "a system of faith—it begins by faith, and *continues by faith*; and every blessing which is obtained in relation to it is the effect of faith" (Lecture 7:17; emphasis added).

Spiritual Key #14: Every Man Receives According to His Faith.

The Lectures state that "every man received according to his faith—according as his faith was, so were his blessings and privileges, and *nothing was withheld from him when his faith was sufficient to receive it*" (Lecture 7:17; emphasis added). Notice the words "nothing was withheld." There are some who might feel or even suggest that we cannot receive the Holy Ghost as on the day of Pentecost, which is how the original apostles received the Holy Ghost. If this were the case, then this part of the Lectures would have to be false. "Nothing [i.e., no promised blessing] was withheld" so long as their "faith was sufficient to receive it." This might also include faith to obtain heavenly dreams, visions, or visitations. It might include having our calling and election made sure. It might include meeting the Savior of the world and falling at His feet. "Nothing was withheld"! Said another way, anything withheld would be a direct result of our own unbelief.

Spiritual Key #15: It Is Through Faith That We Obtain the Knowledge of God. And It Is Through Obtaining the Knowledge of God That We Obtain All Other Things That Pertain to Eternal Life and Godliness.

This is one of the last spiritual keys that I have chosen to highlight within the Lectures. You should of course seek out other gems through your own diligent study. This spiritual key is the foundational principle of this book of *Putting on Christ.* I have continually asserted and affirmed that our heroic journey does not truly start in earnest until we first obtain the knowledge of God. Why is this? Because it is through obtaining this endowment that faith is replaced with something more enduring—that of actually knowing of the Deity. It is also because when we receive this level of knowledge, we receive a remission of sins and are given the Comforter to abide in us, whose calling and charge it is to *lead us into all truth.* Or as Moroni said, "by the power of the Holy Ghost, [we] may know the truth of all things" (Moro. 10:5).

Throughout this work and as an exercise in awareness, I have had the reader pay close attention to the number 3. There are other perfect numbers as well. If you look intently at the last two pages of the *Lectures On Faith,* you will notice that the synonymous phrases "Knowledge of God," "Knowledge of Him," and "Knowledge of Christ" are mentioned ten times. If you were to search for the next "closest" reference of the phrase "Knowledge of God," you would find it in the Lecture Second. Isn't it interesting that at the completion of the *Lectures On Faith,* these synonymous phrases are mentioned ten times in the last two pages of that work? What is the Lord wanting to demonstrate with this?

I believe He wants us to know and understand that in order to obtain the completeness of our own salvation, we must first obtain the knowledge of God (i.e., through spiritual rebirth), which can only come by faith, and then subject to obtaining that knowledge, continue to seek by faith (and added knowledge) and by faith obtain "like" blessings and privileges, just as the apostles of old. How did Paul see into the third heaven? He sought for and obtained the privilege by faith and by no other means. He learned by faith by turning directly to God for his spiritual knowledge, wholly believing that God would deliver, and he persisted in it. But he had to have first received the knowledge of God and the Comforter to abide in him in order to see into the third heaven, which is part of the "all other things" referenced in the Lectures that were pertaining to eternal life and godliness.

"And if the question is asked, how were they to obtain the knowledge of God? (for there is a great difference between believing in God and knowing him—knowledge implies more than faith. ***And notice that all things that pertain to life and godliness were given through the knowledge of God)*** *the answer is given—**through faith they were to obtain this knowledge**; and, having **power by faith to obtain the knowledge of God**, they could with it obtain all other things which pertain to life and godliness" (Lectures On Faith 7:18; emphasis added).*

Are we seeing this? All things pertaining to life and godliness arise out of first having obtained the actual knowledge of God through having received an endowment by God Himself of that spiritual power and element called "faith." For it is written, "To them gave he power [a perfect, living "faith"] to become the sons of God" (John 1:12). And as the Lectures state, "This knowledge [of God] was the effect of faith," including "all things which pertain to life and godliness" (Lecture 7:19). This information reinforces the preamble to *Putting on Christ* at the beginning of this work. To wit, that once we have complied with all other prerequisites under the law, "it is ultimately his bestowal of faith as an endowment of power that saves" (see *Putting On Christ*, Preamble). To be saved and redeemed is to obtain the knowledge of God and vice versa. The above sheds further light as to Joseph Smith's statement in the Preface of this work:

"The principle of knowledge is the principle of salvation. The principle of salvation is given us through ***the knowledge of Jesus Christ****" (Teachings of the Prophet Joseph Smith, p. 297).*

As we grow in the knowledge of Jesus Christ (i.e., the knowledge of God the Son), we will arrive at a place where all unbelief will dissipate and become nonexistent. We will then continue waiting on the Lord to appear. What I am speaking to here now is literal. We will continue to speak affirmations of His appearance and visualize the encounter of all encounters, thereby facilitating the creation of a spiritual blueprint from the intangible world of the "unseen," which will attract that which we most desire into our tangible world of the "seen." This is what it means to have an eye of faith. All things come by faith, whether temporal or spiritual. These keys from the Lectures will aid us in obtaining the "more sure" promise of eternal life. And with that "more sure" promise, we will be given the added faith and knowledge to thereafter pierce the heavenly veil and know God the Son, even eye to eye. And once known, He shall reveal the Father. This, we are told, is eternal life, even in the simplest of terms, that we "might know [Him]" (John 17:3).

Chapters 11 and 12 will highlight the remaining ingredients of our knowing God on this level.

Spiritual Key #16: Authority by Faith.

Somehow, I missed including this last key much earlier, but in hindsight I believe it was by design. Joseph Smith, including every quorum of the priesthood who supported and ratified the *Lectures On Faith* as Church doctrine through a vote of common consent (see pp. 255-257 of the original printing of the 1835 D&C), clarified that

> *"it is also necessary that men should have an idea that he **[God] is no respecter of persons**, for with the idea of all the other excellencies in his character, and this one wanting, **men could not exercise faith in him**; because if he were a respecter of persons, they could not tell what their privileges were, nor how far they were authorized to exercise faith in Him, or whether they were authorized to do it at all, but all must be confusion (Lectures On Faith, 3:23; emphasis added).*

Then came this gem:

> *"But no sooner are the minds of men made acquainted with the truth on this point, that he is no respecter of persons, than they see that they have **authority by faith** to lay hold on eternal life, the richest boon of heaven ... and that every man in every nation has an **equal privilege**" (Ibid.; emphasis added).*

When I read this the first time, it didn't hit me. Where does our authority (especially as "unworthy creatures") come from to approach the throne of God for His grace when we are not feeling worthy? Does it come from righteousness? Does it come because of our good works and deeds alone? No, it ultimately comes through our faith and sole reliance upon Christ, our intercessor and mediator. It is *our faith* and complete reliance upon Christ and his merits alone which *gives us the authority* to approach the Father.

One day my daughter Aneesa came to me and told me that she was feeling spiritually "in the dumps." We knelt down by her bedside, and I asked her if she would like to pray. She said, no. I asked her why, and she told me that she felt unworthy to pray. Anyone who knows Aneesa will attest that rarely would she feel "unworthy" to pray. But her honesty and authenticity revealed how most of us feel when things are not going right in our lives. Most of us will turn away from God because of these times of feeling unworthy. But this is the adversary's trap. He wants us to shy away from praying by whispering to us that we are not worthy. And, of course, we would be being real, authentic, and honest to acknowledge that we do indeed feel this way at times, especially given that we will continue to live in a fallen world. Even the Savior of the world said during His ministry, "Why callest thou me good. There is none good but one, that is, God" (Mark 10:18).

Here's my point, fellow seeker. None of us are worthy, at least not in and of ourselves! If we had to wait to be worthy in order to pray, God would never hear from any of us. Do we understand this? We all have ***authority by faith*** to approach the thrown of grace through our complete reliance upon the One who is worthy, relying alone upon His merits, mercy, and grace, and supported by the foundational Atonement which has already been wrought on our behalf.

When we are feeling unworthy and not "able to pray," try this type and pattern of prayer: "Father, I approach Thee this day, even as an unworthy creature before Thee. I have no authority in and of myself to even look in Thy direction, as I am full of filth and shame at this time. So that is why I approach Thee this day through the authority that I have *by faith* and full reliance upon Thy holy Son, even Jesus Christ, the one who *is* worthy and whose very Atonement was wrought so that I could still have the means whereby I could approach Thee." You get the idea. Regardless of how we may be feeling, please recognize that this is perhaps the most important time for us to approach God, our Heavenly Father. And we can do so with full confidence, even in our unworthiness, because we are not approaching Him in and of ourselves. We are approaching Him in and through Christ, in whose worthiness we know we can have full confidence.

Overcoming the Wall of Feeling Undeserving

Fellow seeker: Overcoming the negative self-perception and doubt which may arise out of either guilt, shame, unworthiness (or perhaps just our own inadequacy) as to our ability to lay claim upon forgiveness of sin or even salvation can feel overwhelmingly challenging, daunting, and even unobtainable. It is challenging because we will all inevitably hit a seeming brick wall of not feeling worthy or deserving (a form of unbelief) of His glorious, unspeakable blessings. And the reality is, we would be right. We are not worthy, *nor will we ever be able to make ourselves worthy, in and of ourselves*. Not ever! These feelings are completely normal and are to be understood and expected.

Now here's the fixity of focus that both saves and redeems. HE IS! HE IS WORTHY! HE IS DESERVING! We all have the authority to approach the throne of grace through that authority given us by our faith—in Him! And that faith which gives us this authority is the faith which relies solely upon Him as our Savior, and in *His merits*. It is the focus of His deservingness alone (and none of our own), devoid of any doubt, that allows us to approach the Father at all times, because we are not approaching Him through *our own merits* in any degree. We have authority because He has authority. We are approaching the Father in and through Him, who *is* the worthy One. Are we seeing this? In Alma 33 it references the phrase, "because of thy Son," four times. Whenever the Lord repeats something this many times, we already know the answer. How are we able to receive this experience of redemption? Because of [His] Son! Or rather, because of our faith in His Son's redeeming power.

This is what gives us the faith to receive of this, His gift of grace, to receive of His offering to us, so long as we have fully committed in our hearts to do His will. Through the infinite power of Christ, made possible through His atonement, His deservingness can completely obliterate the lack of our own. *This is what holds the power! It is faith in the Lord Jesus Christ and the power of HIS offering to the Father while relying solely upon His merits! But we have to receive the gift! We have to receive it with all of our hearts and not turn away from Him because of our feelings of unworthiness!* He would not have the desire nor incentive in giving a gift that we wouldn't wholeheartedly receive with overwhelming gratitude and value above all the gold and treasure in the world. "For what doth it profit a man if a gift is bestowed upon him, and he receive not the gift? Behold, he rejoices not in that which is given unto him, neither rejoices in him who is the giver of the gift" (D&C 88:33).

We can overcome this, our unbelief, when we acknowledge that it is only in and through the grace of God, made possible by the Son's Atonement, that these blessings are permitted to be bestowed, as a glorious, redeeming, pass-through to us! It is important for us to understand that we cannot earn our own salvation through our own good works, the law of performances, or works of the law. What a relief this is to know, is it not? This is what Elder Uchtdorf meant when he said, *"Salvation cannot be bought with the currency of obedience"* ("The Gift of Grace," April 2015 General Conference). There is no amount of works that we could possibly perform to earn His grace. If we could earn our way into His kingdom, in and of ourselves by our own works, why would we need a Savior?

A dear friend of mine says that the desiring or hoping (with persistent effort) *is* the actual exercising of faith. We are to believe (*be* and *live*) the promises that are available to us individually! All that is necessary is for us to increasingly *desire* them and turn to God with all our hearts, while never letting go of that desire, in order to receive them. This ever-increasing and expanding desire shall fuel our journey to the promised land of salvation. God is our genie, only His "bottle" is the immensity of space. His Light extends throughout the immensity and is in and through all things, including us. And His wish for us is to give us the desires of our hearts. He only hopes that our desires match His desires for us.

The Power of Visualization—Having an "Eye of Faith"

The idea of visualization is to create an inner reality which can then create a *spiritual blue print* or pattern from that which our desired intention may bring forth and become manifest. Shakti Gawain and many others have taught this most of their adult lives.

So has Jesus. It is not a new principle. *This spiritual blue print then attracts that which we most desire into our world* of "external reality," if you will. When it manifests, we will witness the miracle which will have of necessity been preceded by faith. Notice the Savior's words and how they relate to our discussion:

> *"What things soever ye **desire**, when ye pray, believe that ye receive them, and ye shall have them" (Mark 11:24).*

The Imagination of a Child

Imagination is the ability we all have to create a mental picture or image in our mind's eye. In creative visualization, which is really a component of "faith," we use our imagination to create not just a clear image of what we'd like to create, but we use it to create the feeling of it as though it were already happening or even had already arrived. This "seeing it" and "feeling it" actually aids in "attracting it." In other words, through our continuous and unrelenting focus on the righteous desire of our hearts, and through perpetually asking God for it, we will eventually (through His grace and will) achieve the desires of our hearts. "For we know that … we must call upon thee, *that from thee we may receive according to our desires*" (Ether 3:2; emphasis added).

The fantasy of a child is very closely related to visualization and imagination, only with fantasy we have this belief that it's not true. Whereas with visualization and imagination, we actually do believe in the depths of our being that which we have seen with an eye of faith, similar to the faith of a little child. Perhaps this is why we are, at least in part, admonished by Jesus to become as little children.

The Unlimited Shopping Spree

Dr. Joe Dispenza speaks about how his daughter (15 years old at the time) was the greatest "manifester" he had ever met. He tells a very heartfelt and funny story about how his daughter specifically intended to create an unlimited shopping spree through the power of visualization. I won't go into many of the details here, but suffice it to say that she manifested it. It became a reality in the world of form. The miracle was preceded by her having visualized the experience during her morning meditation spanning a period of time that was undisclosed. When Dr. Dispenza quizzed her on how she did it, this is what she said:

> *"I'll tell you what I do. I move into a state of being where I convince my brain and body it's already done. And then I get up and **live as if my prayer is already answered…** The moment I start to analyze and try to figure out where it's going to come from, I just returned back to the old self. The new self would*

never think that way" (see YouTube, https://www.youtube.com/watch?v=n6pqcS2Nli0).

Childlike imagination and visualization, then, is the practice which allows that which we gaze upon to come alive or become real for us. Imagination trumps our own, puny willpower by an exponential degree. Keep in mind that the most powerful nation on earth is not the United States, China, or Russia. The most powerful nation on earth is the "Imigi" nation. The Imagi nation allows us to "image in," or hone in on the object of our desire, which for our purposes is not a shopping spree but Christ. Could there possibly be anyone more worthy of our consideration, adoration, or obsession than Christ (and the Father)? And this new nation we create in us through imagi-nation must come from a pure space and with overflowing gratitude to God. See the difference? We give God all the glory all the time. We are able to "manifest," because God gives us the desires of our hearts according to His divine will and timing. But He wants us to learn this principle of faith while we're here. It's one of the most important principles we are to practice as we journey through our mortal lives. The above example also demonstrates why we must approach the endeavor much as a little child would, with a pure intention yoked with wonderment, curiosity, and awe. By doing so, and relying upon His holy will and timing, there is nothing that is impossible for us to achieve.

One crucial practice is to "see ourselves" doing the works of Jesus. We simply choose to go out into the world and do those compassionate works we know He did. We can practice this by first imagining these compassionate works in meditation. Our brain and body can't tell the difference between what is real and what is imagined. Look at what happens with your emotions at a movie theater. When you combine thought, feeling, and emotion, there is great power of creation. Imagination is the spiritual womb where conception and creation begin and flourish. The key is to attempt to make our inner world even more real than our outer world. New spiritual experiences create new feelings which become buried within our emotions. And our desires, joined by our deep feelings and emotions, through faith, can create a beautiful new external reality which is on par with our inner reality. Our new reality is then what generates new spiritual experiences until we come to the knowledge of God ourselves. The cycle is then repeated. Clear intention buried deep in the feelings and emotions is what helps us create a new reality. We don't just think about it. We attach emotion to it. This leads to new heightened thoughts, new heightened experiences, and new elevated feelings and emotions that attract more of the same, including new and enhanced knowledges of God—sacred experience after sacred experience with Him. This is how we are to grow in the spiritual knowledges, which collective knowledges ultimately remove all unbelief, thereby aiding us in eventually rending the veil of unbelief in totality and knowing God as we are known (see Chapter 12: "Rending the Veil and Knowing God").

Now, in order to know if this visualization and spiritual imagination works, we must first gain a witness, or as we often say in our latter-day Church, gain a "testimony." We do this by first test-ing it out in our own lives. The first step is that of pure intention through involving the Savior Jesus Christ in the faith that we exercise. The witness begins by turning inward through meditative visualization and creating that spiritual blueprint. As we hold to this "pure and true imagination" (as a child would) through visualization or "the eye of faith," we will attract that which we most desire over time. In the very least, let me say this: By using a Christ-centered intention during our visualization, we will most definitely increase our chances of seeing those things we desire to show up in our reality. This is the realm where, if rightly pursued, we will see miracles.

Affirmations and meditative visualization create a spiritual blueprint in our inner world which yields a *spiritual expectancy* (a "feeling"), thereby creating a catalyst (or spiritual attraction) for change in our outer world. As with the temporal, so it is likewise with the spiritual. This is all part of exercising faith. I like to think of faith as a spiritual element, "*the substance* of things hoped for" (Hebrews 11:1). When that *expectancy* is joined by concentrated longing and desiring, which are buried deep within our emotions, and in effect experiencing it on every level in our being through imagination, visualization, and "the eye of faith" before it shows up, then it could be said that we are "practicing" faith or coming into a joint venture with God in spiritual creation. Then it is that we begin to anticipate and even *expect* that which we have visualized to appear "outwardly," having originated from the unseen world of Spirit. In other words, it becomes "created spiritually first."

When we fulfill the law associated with any promised blessing, the gift of faith is bestowed and the blessing is thereby granted. "Things which are *seen* were not made of things which do appear" (Hebrews 11:3). In other words, things which are *seen* (with an eye of faith) were not made of things which do appear—meaning, they come not from our temporal or material world of the seen but from the spiritual world of the unseen—kind of like the fishes and loaves "created" by Jesus. And they will have originated from the spiritual blueprint created through our visualization, imagination and the law of expectancy. Alma referred to this law as "looking forward to the fruit thereof" (Alma 32:41).

There are many scriptures that build upon this *seeing with an eye of faith with expectancy*. And of course, all good endowments are subject to God's holy will and timing. And this truth is part of that which we are supposed to find as a diligent, honest seeker. This seeking is a lifetime pursuit. It becomes the true seeker's (and the truth seeker's) way of life. These truths are validated by the word of God and by personal experience. Hence Christ's comment, "If any man will do his will, he shall know of the doctrine, whether it be of God, or whether I speak of myself" (John 7:17). Desire…Ask, Seek, Knock…Receive. Then repeat.

What Things Soever Ye Desire

Pay close attention again to the Savior's words here. Everything begins with desire. And from desire arises faith, just as our Diagram demonstrates:

> *"Whosoever shall say ... and shall* ***not doubt in his heart****, but shall believe that those things which he saith shall come to pass;* ***he shall have whatsoever he saith****. Therefore, I say unto you, What things soever ye desire, when ye pray,* ***believe that ye receive them****, and ye shall have them" (Mark 11:23-24; emphasis added).*

Notice again the law of expectancy here. If he "shall not doubt in his heart ... he shall have whatsoever he saith." And also, "Believe that ye receive them!" Now notice the subtle change in the Revised Standard Edition of the Bible:

> *"Whatever you ask in prayer, believe that you* ***have received it****, and it will be yours" (Mark 11:24).*

Believe (and submerge the feeling deep within the emotions) that ye have received it already. Immerse yourself by experiencing the joy in advance of having already received it, while expressing gratitude and recognizing from whom all blessings flow. And if we do so, we shall have it.

Notice likewise the power of the words "*even as you desire of me*":

> *"Verily, verily, I say unto you,* ***even as you desire of me so it shall be done unto you ... if thou wilt desire of me in faith****, with an honest heart, believing in the power of Jesus Christ, or in my power which speaketh unto thee" (D&C 11:8, 10; emphasis added).*

Know that there is a force from the infinite and eternal realm of Spirit from which arises that which we intensely desire from the unmanifest into the manifest as we hold to this, our righteous desire, until it comes into fruition. In other words, we are to expect and fully anticipate that which we hold most dear to show up and look for signs of it manifesting from the "unseen world" into our "external" world of form or reality, without doubt in our hearts. That said, we've been cautioned to only seek for those things which are "expedient" for us. And again, as it is with the temporal, so it is with the spiritual. This includes coming unto Christ, seeking His face, *and seeing His face.*

Remember, belief leads to faith, which leads to a perfect knowledge. As pertaining to faith unto salvation, we are told that,

*"If you will not nourish the word, **looking forward with an eye of faith** to the fruit thereof, you can never pluck of the fruit of the tree of life" (Alma 32:40; emphasis added).*

Or said another way,

*"If you will nourish the word, **looking forward with an eye of faith** to the fruit thereof, you can surely pluck of the fruit of the tree of life."*

As we cultivate the word of belief and light in our hearts through desire, our faith develops and builds over time, then yields sacred experiences, thereby generating in us *spiritual knowledge upon knowledge* (or what I call "the knowledges of God" or what the scriptures reference as "growing in the knowledge of the Lord"), ultimately resulting in the dissipation of all unbelief. This is where the unbelief specific to Christ is completely removed, and the veil progressively "thins" and is in time lifted altogether in order to ultimately view the face of God. Can any other understanding or principle be of more value or worth, whether in time or in eternity?

What precedes this Heavenly Gift is the ultimate of all stillness and the birth of the holiest of atmospheres in our sacred space, created in accordance with the foreknowledge of God. It will be preceded by many "practice runs" leading up to it. As a general rule, no one will accidentally "happen upon" entering the Divine Presence. Those who have seemingly happened upon it, such as Saul in the New Testament and Joseph Smith in the First Vision, received it for a specific purpose in God. Those who build on the foundation of desire and faith, and hold to both, will inevitably prevail. It is absolutely certain! "And there were many whose faith was so exceedingly strong, even before Christ came, who could not be kept from within the veil, ***but truly saw with their eyes the things which they had beheld with an eye of faith***" (Ether 12:19; emphasis added). In other words, they visualized it (with eyes closed) in meditation, time and time again, even over a period of years—even decades. And as a result, they "truly saw with their eyes" that which they visualized and wholly expected to show up. They expected it because *they could feel it on the level as if it had already happened.* It all begins and endures by adopting the imagination of that little child hidden in all of us.

The "eye of faith" is a component of "visualizing," and visualizing is a component of exercising an "eye of faith." It is this intense longing, desiring, and yearning that is the actual "exercising of faith" spoken of in holy writ. This longing and intense desiring of the heart, and never letting go is the key ingredient in the diligent seeking required to find and know Him by way of both Comforters here in mortality.

Unbelief is truly the veil we must rend in order to ultimately view the face of God. In the case of salvation, the veil is the unbelief that the precious promises referenced by the apostle Peter are intended for you and me, personally and individually. This is the great wall. This is the great hurdle. This too becomes our great overcoming! It's easy to believe that prophets and apostles receive these endowments, is it not? Now notice:

> *"Behold, when ye shall rend that veil of unbelief [as to your obtaining the precious promises of God for yourself] which doth cause you to remain in your awful state of wickedness, and hardness of heart, and blindness of mind,* ***then*** *shall the great and marvelous things which have been hid up from the foundation of the world from you ... be unfolded in the eyes of all the people [including you]" (Ether 4:15-16; emphasis added).*

Our unbelief is what causes us to remain in wickedness, hardness of heart, and spiritual blindness. This is straight out of Chapter 1. Note that this unfolding of the marvelous things of God are to occur in the eyes of "all the people," which includes you and me. It will happen once we individually rend the veil of our *own* unbelief as to our *own obtaining* of these "marvelous things." The beginning of this "rending of the veil" first occurs, not just before meeting the Lord in mortality, but when we offer unto Him the sacrifice of a broken heart and a contrite spirit. This offering is what precedes the new day that will dawn when God will be unveiled to us in power while still in the flesh.

The Three Key Knowledges Leading to the Second Comforter

Below is my list of the three key knowledges that permit us to see the Lord:

1. The personal knowledge that we have been redeemed and born of God, having obtained a knowledge of Him on the same level "as though he had already come among us" (Mosiah 3:13).
2. The personal knowledge that we have been "accepted of [Him]" or "accepted in the sight of God" (see Lectures 3 & 6).
3. The personal knowledge that we have been "sealed up unto eternal life, by revelation and the spirit of prophecy, through the power of the holy priesthood," for "it is impossible to be saved in ignorance" (D&C 131:5-6).

Fellow Seeker. As a general rule, if and when we will have received these three "knowledges," we are permitted to see the Lord, in His own due time. And when we see the Lord, we will be ordained of God and sent forth to do a work and calling as directed personally by Him.

Joseph told us that "the key to salvation is knowledge." He also taught that "knowledge of these things [i.e., God and the things of God] *can only be OBTAINED*

BY EXPERIENCE [made possible] through the ordinances of God set forth for that purpose" (*Teachings of the Prophet Joseph Smith,* p. 335; emphasis added). These three "knowledges" unto salvation are not book knowledge, but spiritual knowledge. It is actual knowledge given from the Deity to us directly via personal revelation in a manner that is absolutely certain, void of any doubt or guess work whatsoever. We will know.

Having these three knowledges, which in each case is to obtain actual knowledge with absolute certainty, allows for the eradication of doubt and unbelief. Why is that? Because "where doubt is, there faith has no power" (*Lectures On Faith* 3:44). And when we understand that we are saved ***through faith as an act of grace***, we understand why these three knowledges are so important to obtain. They rest all doubt and unbelief because it is actual knowledge—not just once but three impactful times, interspersed with other tests and assurances through the Spirit. Remember, ***unbelief*** is the veil. When we remove all unbelief, we remove the veil, which is to then have the greatest of all gifts unveiled to us—the Heavenly Gift, who is Christ the Lord Omnipotent.

The Acceptable Offerings

We are commanded to practice the art of loving God with all our heart, all our soul, all our mind, and with all our strength. Why? Because all the tests of mortality are tests of our willingness to sacrifice, which is designed to prove the authenticity of this love—our love for God on this level. If we do not love on this level, we will not pass the requisite tests of sacrifice that most surely will come our way. These sacrifices will surround that which we value. But anything that takes up our heart space that does not put Him first and foremost must be sacrificed. The Lord said, "And we will prove them herewith, to see if they will do all things whatsoever the Lord their God shall command them" (Abr. 3:25). This begins with loving God with all we are and will be. The fulfillment of these commandments must require the heart instrument or we will not be found to be acceptable before the Lord.

When the Lord appeared to Joseph Smith, He said, "They draw near to me with their lips, but their hearts are far from me" (JS—H 1:19). Why did Christ despise the self-proclaimed righteous of His day? Because it was all a show. It was an act. They wore a mask—the perfection mask. They were not authentic. They had no authentic love for God. They were checking boxes. They sought the high callings and approval of men. They wanted to appear spiritual. ***We must authentically love God with all that we have and are, or we will not stand. This is my witness.***

To receive the knowledge of God and His mysteries in power by the Holy Ghost, we must endure in the first and great commandment to love God with our all, which is demonstrated in large degree by diligently seeking Him. If we truly love Him, we will seek to find and know Him. The journey is an epic love story of the highest and purest order. This seeking is where we will spend our time. This is what we will put first and foremost in our lives. For the true disciple, everything else but seeking Him will be viewed as a complete nuisance and waste of time. We are commanded to "seek the face of the Lord always" (D&C 101:38). This is not figurative. It is literal. We can know the Lord, here and now, once we have accumulated the faith and spiritual knowledge of the brother of Jared.

Revelation states, "Neither is man capable to make them [the mysteries of godliness] known, for they are only to be seen and understood by the power of the Holy Spirit, which ***God bestows** on those who love him*" (Doctrine and Covenants 76:11, 12, 116; emphasis added). Notice that the power of the Holy Ghost and the accompanying mysteries of godliness are bestowed as an act of grace to those who practice the art of the First and Great Commandment—for those who love Him. And those who love Him will seek Him. Nephi says that the Holy Ghost "is a gift of God unto all those who diligently seek him" (1 Ne. 10:17). So not only must we seek, but we must seek ***diligently***. Diligently is defined as "constant in effort; attentive and persistent in doing; painstaking." In Hebrews it says that God "is a *rewarder* of them that diligently seek him" (Hebrews 11:6). What does He reward them with? The Holy Ghost, as a gift, which sanctifies, shows, and teaches all things.

There are acceptable offerings and then there are unacceptable offerings. The Lord gives us a hint in Moroni 7:9 as to how prayer can be acceptable: "Wherefore it is counted evil unto man if he shall pray *and not with real intent of heart"* (emphasis added). Notice the instrument that is required. Abel gave of the firstlings of his flocks and the Lord found his offering acceptable. Cain's offering was rejected. The difference was that one did it from the heart; the other was checking a box, devoid of the heart instrument.

The Father made an offering through sacrifice of the Son of God because of His love for the world. That was an excruciating ordeal for Him, even God, but He did it to save us by giving us an opportunity to return to live in His presence. There needed to be a perfect Lamb sacrificed in order to satisfy the demands of justice. Abraham went through a test that was similar to this offering. The Father was so touched by Abraham's offering that He promised Abraham that all those who would obtain salvation must of necessity come through His seed. This is literal and is what the gathering of Israel is all about. Those who are "adopted in" become his literal seed. As one member is adopted in through spiritual rebirth or by being born of the Spirit, he or she becomes the actual seed of Abraham and is added to the family of Abraham and of Christ.

Consider the offering by the Son of God of Himself as the unblemished Lamb. He willingly chose this offering of Himself because of His love of the Father and His love for us. "Behold, he offereth *himself* a sacrifice for sin, to answer the ends of the law, unto all those of a broken heart and a contrite spirit, *and unto none else*" (2 Ne. 2:6-7).

In the law of man, any attorney could tell us that for a contract to be valid, we must provide consideration. Consideration is something of value that is acceptable to both parties, which is then exchanged and relinquished to the other for the contract to be binding. This contract in the gospel is a covenant. This consideration on our end is the offering of a broken heart in the spirit of complete surrender to Christ. Christ has already tendered his consideration in Gethsemane and on the cross.

So not only did Christ endure a brutal scourging and pass through unimaginable pain on the cross, this was preceded by much more. Out of his love for us, He endured emotional and spiritual suffering incomprehensible to mortal man. He was willing to do all of this in exchange for us, to save us—and did it out of his deep love for us. How could we contemplate such an offering and not feel the profoundest of love for Him, breaking down emotionally as a result of His act of kindness towards us unworthy creatures? During those hours of excruciating emotional and spiritual suffering and pain, He bled from every pore, a suffering that we will never be able to understand or fully relate to ourselves. Through the Savior's offerings, salvation is made available to all mankind. But it requires conditions on our part. And this is key: ***It requires offerings of our own***.

All tests that we encounter in mortality will be tests of our willingness to make offerings through sacrifice, for it is only in and through this sacrifice that we are able to prove our love to and for Him and the Father. "We will prove them herewith," God has said. The true disciple of Christ will have many tests placed before him and will be required to make offerings which are types of His and the Father's offerings through sacrifice. Although one of the keys here is of our willingness to make these consecrated offerings, not that the Father would necessarily require them all at our hand. Remember the words of the sacrament ordinance: "That they are willing to take upon them the name of thy Son" (D&C 20:77). This statement is speaking to our willingness (or not) to make a specific, acceptable offering through sacrifice which is tied to the promised endowment of the Holy Ghost, received during spiritual rebirth. There are offerings which begin with the smaller and lead to the greater.

What are we willing to sacrifice as an offering? What does He require in our offerings in order to become joint heirs with Him? Are they not "types" of His offering? He said, "Follow thou me," and "Do the things which ye have seen me do." He meant what He said.

Christ made the offering of a broken heart in Gethsemane to the Father in complete submission, in a spirit of contriteness. When our hearts break, which they inevitably will, we will be given each time the test (the chance and opportunity) to make an offering of that broken heart to God in complete, eternal allegiance to Him and His will and in complete submission and surrender. "Where is the quiet hand to calm my anguish? Who, who can understand?... He answers privately, *reaches my reaching in my Gethsemane*" ("Where Can I Turn for Peace?" Hymns, no. 129; emphasis added). This *reaching* spoken of is from the soul level and occurs during a personal crash of our own. In following the rod of iron of personal revelation, there will come a time in our lives when our knees will buckle and we will fall down. This will come right before partaking of the fruit of the tree of life. This is when we will join Him symbolically in His Gethsemane, and when He literally joins us in ours.

When we make this offering, which is to go into the depths of repentance, or, as Alma says, "repenting nigh unto death," we will pass through our own mini-Gethsemane and be born of Him by way of a personal visit through a heavenly manifestation of His Spirit. This is when we will experience a oneness with the Father and the Son. This is when we first come to truly know Him and experience that "peace that passeth all understanding." We will then have eyes to see and ears to hear. We will see things as they really are. This is when He changes our hearts mightily and we are awakened out of a deep sleep unto God. We will come to know God and His reality with absolute certainty in power.

The Lord speaks to the visit of Himself, through the manifestations of His Spirit: "But he that believeth these things which I have spoken, ***him will I visit*** *with the manifestations of my Spirit*, and he shall know and bear record" [Ether 4:11; emphasis added]. He said, "And behold, whosoever believeth on my words, ***them will I visit*** with the manifestation of my Spirit; and they shall be born of me, even of water and of the Spirit" (D&C 5:16; emphasis added). Fellow seeker, this is the gate. I bear solemn witness of this heavenly manifestation lasting days and nights. When we are all in with Him, He is all in with us.

When we partake of the fruit of the tree of life and are *redeemed* of the Lord, we will become a new creature in Him. Our hearts will be changed in a mighty way. This is when we are born of God. Physical birth is preceded by a gestation period—a process. And this process leads to an actual birthing. It is the same with spiritual rebirth. Yet after we are spiritually birthed, we must still grow up in Christ.

The straight and narrow path will involve other offerings of sacrifice to test our love of God and of our resolve to follow Him. What else will we be required to offer? Would we be willing to offer our firstborn child? Would we be willing to offer our only child? Now this would be a test, would it not? This would be a gut-wrenching, soul-wrenching test. Keep this in mind. This is a test of our willingness, not that God would necessarily require it our hands. And the devil will likely use this as a tool to scare us away from coming unto Christ. Remember, Abraham walked down the mountain together with His Son.

For some, the Lord will require more than our willingness. My dear friend Doug was one of those. He lost his small son. And what did he do? He consecrated his son as an offering to God. Others reading these words may have lost children. I can't imagine this kind of pain. These offerings, however, are there to demonstrate our real, authentic, and true love for God. Doug had a choice. He could have hardened his heart against God, but instead, he made one of the ultimate offerings. This is why we must "practice" the art of loving God. This practice is to prepare us for these tests of sacrifice. The best way to practice loving God is to quiet the inner workings of the mind, or as the scriptures say, to "be still and know that I am God." Spiritual meditation grounds us in this stillness. It is in the stillness where we most easily hear His voice. And His Spirit will lead us to make these offerings of sacrifice through a holy communion that can be attained. The Spirit will also reveal to us the specific type of offering to make on each occasion when the time comes.

So, what about all of these distractions we notice in life? Why all the distractions? Why do many of them come in waves and barrages? Would you like to know the answer? They are tests to see if we will take the time to still put God first in the midst of these barrages. And what is the underlying foundation of these tests all about? The love of God. The Lord is saying, "How much do you really love me? Do you love me with all that you have and are? What are you willing to offer to prove this love?" Do we love God enough to put the business of our world on hold and make everything else wait? Are we willing to take the considerations that occupy our time and put them in a subordinate or subservient role to our love and attention to God? What are these distractions doing? They are testing our resolve and love for God through seeking Him first and often. When we forego our perceived needs and wants in the moment for what the Lord wants, we are sacrificing and passing the test. We are making an offering.

Our willingness to sacrifice for God develops into offerings we will each make. We demonstrate our love through these offerings. To make these offerings requires great faith, but we begin with the small ones until we are ready for the greater. What is keeping the Sabbath day holy, at the end of the day? It's an offering through sacrifice. What is a decision to let go of a vice or addiction? It's an offering through sacrifice. What is it to not watch TV or the Super Bowl on Sunday? It's an offering through sacrifice. What is fasting? It's an offering through sacrifice. What do these offerings demonstrate and prove to God? Our deep and abiding love for Him. His love for us is without question. But it is our love for Him that is in question and needs to be proven through our actions. Ultimately, Christ redeems those only who love Him with all that they have and are, surrender in full to Him, and diligently seek Him in their hearts. The Spirit will lead us from simple to mighty offerings in similitude of the Savior's offerings when we are seeking and are spiritually prepared. And when we do, what we are doing is demonstrating our love for Him through our willingness to sacrifice, made possible through sacred, consecrated offerings, not of animals, but ultimately that which is truly "ours" to give.

In the Odes of Solomon, an ancient text that may have been written as early as the 1st century, there is a hidden gem revealed. It reads, "Because I love Him that is the Son, I shall become a son" (The Odes of Solomon, 3:7). The author of the Odes also wrote these two statements by the Savior, "And I became useless to those who knew me not.... *And I will be with those who love me*" (Ibid., 42:3-4; emphasis added). "My elect ones have walked with me, ***and my ways I will make known to them who***

seek me; and I will promise them my name. Hallelujah" (The Odes of Solomon 33:13; emphasis added).

In other words, the Lord is saying, "Those who love me enough to diligently seek me and are willing to sacrifice their all for me, will be redeemed. And I will grant unto them a remission of sins and adopt them into my family." Here's another thing He may say: ***"Although I have the power to make you into me, I cannot make you love me."*** As we diligently seek, He will lead and guide us to make the offerings that are types of His offerings and that of the Father's. ***When we actually make these offerings that we will be led to make through the Spirit, endowments of further sanctification are bestowed.***

If and when we demonstrate (through tests and offerings) our love for God, then God will demonstrate His immense love for us by granting us the desire of our hearts to know Him and to stand in His Presence forever. But we must first truly repent and offer up the broken heart in complete surrender, and then He will give us the conditional yet sure promise of eternal life. As we pass one test and make an offering that is accepted, an opportunity for another offering will be granted to us. As we continue to make these offerings which are accepted, we will be led to a like test of Abraham. Joseph Smith said, "We must be tried even as Abraham." He also said, as quoted by John Taylor: "God will *feel after you* and will take all of you and wrench your very heart strings," (John Taylor, Deseret News: Semi-Weekly, Aug. 21, 1883, p. 1.). Joseph also taught that "it will be a trial of our faith *equal to that of Abraham*, and that the ancients will not have whereof to boast over us in the day of judgement, as being called to pass through heavier afflictions; that we may hold an even weight in the balance with them" (*Teachings of the Prophet Joseph Smith,* p. 137). The Lord said, "For I did it, saith the Lord, TO PROVE YOU ALL, as I did Abraham, and that I might require AN OFFERING at your hand, BY covenant and SACRIFICE" (D&C 132:51; emphasis added). Joseph Smith has said: "He (God) could not organize His kingdom with twelve men to open the Gospel door to the nations of the earth, and with seventy men under their direction to follow in their tracks, unless He took them from a body of men who had offered their lives, and who had made as great a sacrifice as did Abraham. Now the Lord has got His Twelve and His Seventy, and there will be other quorums of Seventies called, who will make the sacrifice..." (D.H.C. 2:182).

Brigham Young said, "God never bestows upon his people, or upon an individual, superior blessings without a severe trial to prove them, to prove that individual" (*Discourses of Brigham Young,* p. 338). What is being "proven"? Our primary love for God above every other consideration, including that of friends and family members or any other desire or consideration of this world.

Joseph Smith spoke to the importance of obtaining the knowledge of God's favor of us through an offering or sacrifice, in order that we might obtain the added faith (and spiritual knowledge) to lay hold on eternal life.

"It is vain for persons to fancy to themselves that they are heirs with those, or can be heirs with them, who have offered their all in sacrifice, and by this means obtained faith in God and ***favor with Him*** *so as to obtain eternal life, unless they, in like manner, offer unto him* ***the same sacrifice****, and through that offering* ***obtain the knowledge that they are accepted of Him****"* *(Lectures On Faith 6:8; emphasis added).*

The Lectures teach that if we are to obtain the added faith (and spiritual knowledge) to lay hold on the "more sure" promise of eternal life, we must make a "like" spiritual offering (i.e., "the same sacrifice") even as those who have gone before us. The lectures add that those who obtain this "testimony" (i.e., knowledge) that, "their course is pleasing in the sight of God," will have faith to lay hold upon (the "more sure" promise of) eternal life (Lectures On Faith, 6:10; emphasis added). This was the same promise—the "more sure" word of promise of eternal life by prophecy that the brother of Jared obtained by faith (see Ether 12:20-21). This is when he saw God. This is when I believe Christ became the finisher of the brother of Jared's faith. The seeker is encouraged to seek the above-referenced **knowledge** (obtained through "that offering") from the source of all Truth.

As an exercise in awareness, it is essential to realize the depth of spiritual knowledge which can be made available (through faith), arising out of Lecture Sixth. It is also essential to realize that this specific Lecture was of such importance, that it is the only one of the seven Lectures wherein the spiritual student and aspirant was, "instructed to commit the whole to memory" (see post Lecture 7 afterword comment).

I close this chapter with words spoken in humility and love for everyone reading these words. I have come to intimately know of Christ's love and redemption. It is not obtained because of our worthiness, but because of His. It is a gift. Paul said, "By grace are ye saved, through faith, and that not of yourselves. It is the gift of God." We qualify for this grace through falling on our faces in broken-hearted repentance and throwing all that we are upon His altar as an offering, in complete surrender and love, tied to an unyielding and unbreakable willingness to do His will forever. The word *willingness* in 2 Nephi 31:13 is cross-referenced with the word *commitment* in our Church-produced scriptures. To receive and experience faith, hope, and charity when we are born of God, we must first make the eternal *commitment* to follow Him and do His will forever. We will not cry out with the requisite sufficiency of faith for His grace if we view ourselves as "righteous" Latter-day Saints. Why? Because then we may see ourselves as, perhaps, "deserving of His grace" arising out of our works, or worse, feeling *entitled to it.* We must ***rely alone upon His merits***, mercy, and grace. In order to cry out in whole faith, we must know of our awful situation, which is our unsaved or unsafe condition. We must see ourselves as spiritually destitute and come to know of our inability to deliver ourselves—even with all of our being. We must view ourselves like unto those who saw themselves in King Benjamin's day, "even less than the dust of the earth" (Mosiah 4:2). Our hearts must break and be offered up. We must know that we need His saving grace and desire it like a drowning man wants air, or deliverance may elude us.

Jesus is perfect at saving and fixing broken things and people. When we perform the offering of ***our all*** in our brokenness, which is the only acceptable offering, He offers us His. This is when we obtain the knowledge of God. And all other endowments and knowledge unto life and godliness available to man can only come through having first obtained this knowledge. I bear witness as to the "eternal certainty" that can be ours through obtaining the knowledge of Their living reality, even that same knowledge and accompanying fruits given the early apostles, or as Joseph Smith said, "***The same*** as given on the day of Pentecost" (*Teachings of the Prophet Joseph Smith,* p.149; emphasis added. See also Acts 2.). It is available to the least saint, for God is not a respecter of persons.

That we might know Him, the only true God, and Jesus Christ, whom He has sent, whom to know is Eternal Life. That we might all come to this knowledge made available through the ordinances of God set forth for that purpose, together with the consecrated offerings through sacrifice to be revealed to each one of us who is seeking to know Him. That we might become aware and avail ourselves of the miracles, powers, and blessings of Christ and His atoning sacrifice. Christ is risen. He lives! And because of Him, we can all live with Him in immortal glory through obedience to His Light. This has been witnessed to my soul in a manner unspeakable. And because He lives and because of His Atonement wrought in perfect love for us, we can all have the hope of becoming like Him, beginning with a spiritual resurrection in this life as well as a physical one in the next. This is all made available because of the Father's offering of His Son, and the Son's offering of Himself. This is my witness, my perfect brightness of hope obtained from Him in loving kindness, and which is available to all of us, in the worthy name of He who is mighty to save, the enduring friend we all have in Jesus—He who truly brings rest to the broken and a yearning soul in all of us.

Chapter 11

The "More Sure" Word of Prophecy

"Therefore, having so great witnesses, by them shall the world be judged, even as many as shall hereafter come to a knowledge of this work. And those who receive it in faith, and work righteousness, shall receive a crown of eternal life" (D&C 20:13-14).

The fairy tale stories of kingdoms, princes, princesses, and the like, along with movie blockbusters containing their symbolism, draw our hearts to them because they have an element of eternal truth to them. We resonate with these ideas and feelings because there is something to them that is so familiar. We are to be part of a kingdom. If we are true and faithful in all things, we are to be crowned kings and priests, queens and priestesses unto the Most High God, to rule and reign alongside Them forever and ever. This is the "happily ever after" we have been so enamored with through fairytales and other wholesome plays and heart-warming movies. We are innately princes and princesses, although currently living in a fallen world. Largely removed from our consciousness is the awareness of our true, divine identities, an awareness that inspires us to act instead of being acted upon and to choose wisely through our faith in God. We are all being enticed by both the prince of darkness and the Prince of Peace. We become more like one or the other depending on which one we "listeth to obey" (Mosiah 2:33; Alma 3:26-27; D&C 29:45). It is all subject to the choices we make using our free will. The lyrics to "Only Make Believe" ("Bread For The Journey" CD; Shaina Noll with Russell Walden) expresses this notion perfectly:

Once upon a time,
There were castles and kings
Fairy tales and horses with wings.

Once upon a time
There were witches and gnomes
Beauties and beasts
And gingerbread homes.

But you know,

It's only make believe
It's only make believe
Just imagination running wild
And unless you're still a child
It's only make believe.

Once upon a time
There was magic untold
Turning princes to frogs
And straw into gold

Once upon a time
There were dragons to slay
Kingdoms to win and gods to obey.

But you know,
It's only make believe
It's only make believe
Just imagination running wild
And unless you're still a child
It's only make believe.

What's become of the dragon slayers?
Did they claim the Holy Grail?
And as for the wizards
And the soothsayers
Now they tell a new tale...

Once upon a time
In a kingdom afar
On a beautiful sphere
Circling a star.

Everyone in time
turned to the sun [the Son]
Finally saw
The world as one.

And you know,
It isn't make believe
It isn't make believe
It's just a vision running wild

A prayer for every child

It's not *only* make believe.
It's just a vision running wild
A prayer for every child
It's not *only* make believe...

When we visualize and capture this vision with an eye of faith and obtain through grace the "Holy Grail," even *the prize of Christ*, we will have come to know God, whom to know is eternal life. It's not only "make believe" but rather the pure truth of our future reality. It is the prayer of every child which is forgotten when "sin conceiveth in [our] hearts" and we become the natural man. In order to recognize that "it isn't only make believe" anymore, but real, we must come into the light of the sun (or Son of God) so that we may "finally see" the reality of that which lies in store for us beyond the veil, even unto all those who "love and serve God with all their mights, minds, and strength" (D&C 20:31).

In this work, we have discussed in great detail the importance of following the "God" within, otherwise known as the Light of Christ. This same Light (an extension of our Father) can lead us, if we will allow Him, to spiritual rebirth or being born of Him, other personalized endowments, and eventually that dawn of our lives referenced by the Apostle Peter, when the day star (Christ's like heart) arises in our hearts. Paul taught that God "hath also sealed us, and given the earnest of the Spirit in our hearts (2 Cor. 1:22). The Odes state it beautifully: "You have given Your heart, O Lord, to Your believers" (the Odes of Solomon 4:3).

Elder Jeffrey R. Holland has spoken in plainness as to the reality of not just the "sure word" that we receive at the time of spiritual rebirth but also of the reaffirmation of that same "word," only now a "more sure word" of promise by prophecy. This promise is the same, even as before, only this time, it is delivered with an irrevocable decree from the Father, saving only that circumstance in which we were to shed innocent blood, or deny the Holy Ghost. I pray his words will bring comfort and a further assurance that this endowment which Elder Holland has received is available to us as well, personally and individually:

> *"**These things I declare to you with the conviction Peter called 'the more sure word of prophecy.'** What was once a tiny seed of belief for me has grown into the tree of life, so if your faith is a little tested in this or any season, I invite you to lean on mine. I know this work is God's very truth, and I know that only at our peril would we allow doubt or devils to sway us from its path. Hope on. Journey on. Honestly acknowledge your questions and your concerns, but first and forever fan the flame of your faith, because all things are possible to them that*

believe" ("Lord, I Believe," general conference, April 2013; emphasis added).

I love Elder Holland, and I cherish as pure gold his words. He spoke these words, coincidentally, the same month and year that I became a member of the family of Abraham through Spiritual Rebirth. All those called and elected must come through the lineage of Abraham. This is why when we are first born of God, we are thus chosen and become "actually of the seed of Abraham," per Joseph Smith's teaching and witness. All of our tests are to ultimately see if we are willing to first obtain and then remain faithful to the testimony (witness) of Jesus obtained in mortality. It has already been revealed that those "who are not *valiant in the testimony of Jesus…* obtain not the crown over the kingdom of our God" (D&C 76:79). President Joseph F. Smith, in his vision of the redemption of the dead, gives us some insight into the consecrated sacrifice offered by those deemed "faithful to the testimony of Jesus."

"And there were gathered together in one place an innumerable company of the *spirits of the just*, who had been *faithful in the testimony of Jesus* while they lived in mortality." Then President Smith reveals the following:

*"And who **offered sacrifice in the similitude of the great sacrifice of the Son of God**, and had suffered tribulation in their Redeemer's name" (D&C 138:12-13; emphasis added).*

In the same revelation of the redemption of the dead, we learn the simplicity of this journey in obtaining a "more sure" salvation or that more sure promise of eternal life, which is so beautiful in its simplicity and so clear as to the purpose of practicing the first and great commandment of loving God with our all. In speaking of the just men made perfect, or those who are inheritors of eternal life, the revelation continues: "These the Lord taught, and gave them power to come forth, after his resurrection from the dead, to enter into his Father's kingdom, there to be *crowned with immortality and eternal life*" (D&C 138:51; emphasis added). Then notice the simplicity of to whom this gift is offered:

"And continue thenceforth their labor as had been promised by the Lord, and be partakers of all blessings which were held in reserve for them that love Him" (D&C 138:52; emphasis added).

Notice the three simple, initial ingredients required to obtain the faith necessary to lay hold of eternal life: love, obedience, and sacrifice. **Love**, on the level that our bodies can become emotionally spent through the practice and process of experientially loving God and even communing with Him. Through this communing, we also come to the absolute knowledge of Their love for us as well, causing once again (since our rebirth), "[our] mouths should be stopped that [we] could not find utterance, so exceedingly great was [our] joy" (Mosiah 4:20). We set the table for this communing by being inwardly quiet, "getting still" in meditation.

Next, we choose **obedience** in living by *every word* revealed to us experientially by way of the rod of iron (i.e., "word of God" or Holy Spirit) through personal revelation. And we obey simply out of love, because it has now become our nature.

And the last of the three mentioned is our willingness to **sacrifice** all things. This level of willingness to sacrifice all things, stemming from love and obedience, is what the Lord is constantly monitoring in our hearts. In the beginning, we may demonstrate our obedience to God and His word out of a perceived duty, even perhaps, as part of a checklist. After we receive the perfect knowledge of God and have "felt to sing the song of redeeming love," our obedience will then transition and be performed strictly out of a pure love for Him. How could we experience redemption in Christ, and not be immersed in an all-consuming love and gratitude for Him, even eternally?

For those with eyes to see and hearts wide open, the magnitude, breadth, and scope of the Father's love is revealed to our hearts in undeniable power. The world and everything in it shall pass away. Nevertheless, this pure love of His shall endure forever. It is breathtakingly real and the only thing that truly matters. The following are the Prophet Joseph's words pertaining to the "more sure" word of prophecy, together with some commentary (all citations and commentary in the following section come from *Teachings of the Prophet Joseph Smith, with brief emphasis added for clarity*).

They Who Endure to the End

Section Two 1834-37, p. 63

"That those who keep the commandments of the Lord and walk in His statutes to the end, are the only individuals permitted to sit at this glorious feast, is evident from the following items in Paul's last letter to Timothy, which was written just previous to his death,--he says: 'I have fought a good fight, I have finished my course, I have kept the faith: henceforth there is laid up for me a crown of righteousness, which the Lord, the righteous Judge, shall give me at that day: and not to me only, but unto all them also that love His appearing.' No one who believes the account, will doubt for a moment this assertion of Paul which was made, as ***he knew****, just* <u>*before*</u> *he was to take his leave of this world [and his mortal body]. Though he once, according to his own word, persecuted the Church of God and wasted it, yet after embracing the faith, his labors were unceasing to spread the glorious news: and like a faithful soldier, when called to give his life in the cause which he had espoused, he laid it down, as he says, with an assurance of an eternal crown. Follow the labors of this Apostle*

from the time of his conversion to the time of his death, and you will have a fair sample of industry and patience in promulgating the Gospel of Christ. Derided, whipped, and stoned, the moment he escaped the hands of his persecutors he as zealously as ever proclaimed the doctrine of the Savior. And all may know that he did not embrace the faith for honor in this life, nor for the gain of earthly goods. What, then, could have induced him to undergo all this toil? It was, as he said, that he might obtain the crown of righteousness from the hand of God. No one, we presume, will doubt the faithfulness of Paul to the end. None will say that he did not keep the faith, that he did not fight the good fight, that he did not preach and persuade to the last. And what was he to receive? A crown of righteousness. And what shall others receive who do not labor faithfully, and continue to the end? We leave such to search out their own promises if any they have; and if they have any they are welcome to them, on our part, for the Lord says that every man is to receive according to his works. Reflect for a moment, brethren, and enquire, whether you would consider yourselves worthy a seat at the marriage feast with Paul and others like him, if you had been unfaithful? Had you not fought the good fight, and kept the faith, could you expect to receive? Have you a promise of receiving a crown of righteousness from the hand of the Lord, with the Church of the Firstborn?" Joseph continues, "Here then, we understand, that Paul rested his hope in Christ, because he had kept the faith, and loved His appearing and from His hand he had a promise of receiving a crown of righteousness.

A Crown for the Righteous

Section Two 1834-37, p. 64

"If the Saints are not to reign, for what purpose are they crowned? In an exhortation of the Lord to a certain Church in Asia, which was built up in the days of the Apostles, unto whom He communicated His word on that occasion by His servant John, He says, 'Behold, I come quickly: hold that fast which thou hast, that no man take thy crown. And again, 'To him that overcometh will I grant to sit with Me in My throne, even as I also overcame, and am set down with My Father in His Throne' (see Rev. 3). And again, it is written, 'Beloved, now are we the sons of God, and it doth not yet appear what we shall be: but we know that, when He shall appear, we shall be like Him' for we

shall see Him as He is. And every man that hath this hope in him purifieth himself, even as He is pure" (1 John 3:2, 3). (Author Commentary: Notice the words, "...in Him purifieth himself." What or who is this "Him" through whom we are to purify ourselves? Answer: It is the Light of His Glory! We are further sanctified in Him through endowments of His Light and Glory as we do the works of love and compassionate service that He did! This is what it means to grow grace for grace and grace to grace). How is it that these old Apostles could say so much on the subject of the coming of Christ? He certainly had once come; but Paul says, To all who love His appearing, shall be given the crown: And John says, When He shall appear, we shall be like Him; for we shall see Him as He is. Can we mistake such language as this? Do we not offer violence to our own good judgment when we deny the second coming of the Messiah? When has He partaken of the fruit of the vine new with His ancient Apostles in His Father's kingdom, as He promised He would just before he was crucified? In Paul's epistle to the Philippians (3:20, 21) he says: 'For our conversation is in heaven; from whence also we look for the Savior, the Lord Jesus Christ: who shall change our vile body, that it may be fashioned like unto His glorious body, according to the working whereby He is able even to subdue all things unto Himself.' We find another promise to individuals living in the Church at Sardis who had not defiled their garments: 'And they shall walk with me in white: for they are worthy. He that overcometh, the same shall be clothed in white raiment; and I will not blot out his name out of the book of life, but I will confess his name before my Father, and before His angels.' John represents the sound which he heard from heaven, as giving thanks and glory to God, saying that the Lamb was worthy to take the book and to open its seals; because he was slain, and had made them kings and priests unto God: and they should reign on the earth (see Rev. 5). In the 20th chapter we find a length of time specified, during which Satan is to be confined in his own place, and the Saints reign in peace, all these promises and blessings we find contained in the law of the Lord, which the righteous are to enjoy: and we might enumerate many more places where the same or similar promises are made to the faithful, but we do not deem it of importance to rehearse them here, as this epistle is now lengthy; and our brethren, no doubt, are familiar with them all."

The Ancient Saints Obtained Promises

Section Two 1834-37, p. 65

"Most assuredly it is, however, that the ancients, though persecuted and afflicted by men, obtained from God promises of such weight and glory, that our hearts are often filled with gratitude that we are even permitted to look upon them while we contemplate that there is no respect of persons in His sight, and that in every nation, he that feareth God and worketh righteousness, is acceptable with Him. But from the few items previously quoted we can draw the conclusion that there is to be a day when all will be judged of their works, and rewarded according to the same; that those who have kept the faith will be crowned with a crown of righteousness; be clothed in white raiment; be admitted to the marriage feast; be free from every affliction, and reign with Christ on the earth, where, according to the ancient promise, they will partake of the fruit of the vine new in the glorious kingdom with Him; at least we find that such promises were made to the ancient Saints. And though we cannot claim these promises which were made to the ancients for they are not our property, merely because they were made to the ancient Saints, yet if we are the children of the Most High, and are called with the same calling with which they were called, and embrace the same covenant that they embraced, and are faithful to the testimony of our Lord as they were, we can approach the Father in the name of Christ as they approached Him, and for ourselves obtain the same promises. These promises, when obtained, if ever by us, will not be because Peter, John, and the other Apostles, with the Churches at Sardis, Pergamos, Philadelphia, and elsewhere, walked in the fear of God, and had power and faith to reveal and obtain them; but it will be because we, ourselves, have faith and approach God in the name of His Son Jesus Christ, even as they did; and when these promises are obtained, they will be promises directly to us, or they will do us no good. They will be commandments and walking uprightly before Him. If not, to what end serves the Gospel of our Lord Jesus Christ, and why was it ever communicated to us?" (Teachings of the Prophet Joseph Smith, pp. 61-64; emphasis added).

(Author Commentary: The Prophet elaborated clearly how we can obtain the same promises as the ancients—by approaching God the same way as they did. And if we do so, "***they will be promises directly to us, or they will do us no good.***" This is straight from the mouth of the Prophet Joseph Smith. Now we turn to a section in the same book, wherein the Prophet Joseph additionally describes the witness we must receive from the Father as to being sealed up unto eternal life.)

Calling and Election

Section Six 1843-44, p. 298

"Now, there is some grand secret here, and keys to unlock the subject. Notwithstanding the apostle exhorts them to add to their faith, virtue, knowledge, temperance, etc., yet he exhorts them to make their calling and election sure. And though they had heard an audible voice from heaven bearing testimony that Jesus was the Son of God, yet he says we have a more sure word of prophecy, whereunto ye do well that ye take heed as unto a light shining in a dark place. Now, wherein could they have a more sure word of prophecy than to hear the voice of God saying, This is my beloved Son.

Section Six 1843-44, p. 298

"Now for the secret and grand key. Though they might hear the voice of God and know that Jesus was the Son of God, this would be no evidence that their election and calling was made sure, that they had part with Christ, and were joint heirs with him. They then would want that more sure word of prophecy, that they were sealed in the heavens and had the promise of eternal life in the kingdom of God. Then, having this promise sealed unto them, it was an anchor to the soul, sure and steadfast. Though the thunders might roll and lightnings flash, and earthquakes bellow, and war gather thick around, yet this hope and knowledge would support the soul in every hour of trial, trouble and tribulation. Then knowledge through our Lord and Savior Jesus Christ is the grand key that unlocks the glories and mysteries of the kingdom of heaven."

This knowledge to ourselves directly from God of having received of this "more sure" word is exactly as was revealed to the Prophet Joseph: "The more sure word of prophecy means *a man's knowing* that he is sealed up unto eternal life, by revelation and the spirit of prophecy through the power of the Holy Priesthood" (D&C 131:5). In other words, it appears a man cannot receive it and not have a keen awareness as to having received it.

The Experience in Poetic Form of a Dear Sister Born of God and Given the More Sure Word of Prophecy

I'd like to share the account of an individual personally known to me—a dear sister and friend of mine who has received the "more sure" word and whom I have been fortunate to know during part of my mortal journey. I asked her to share her story of redemption which she does most eloquently below in the form of a poem she wrote on March 10, 2009. You will feel the Spirit in her words. It is entitled "Immersed in Mercy":

> **"**I'd thought that God was probably just a way to see the whys,
> But learned one day that He exists, which came as a surprise.
> I'd read, then prayed and pondered, like Moroni had admonished,
> And felt God's presence so intensely, I was just astonished.
>
> Ever since that time, I've never doubted He was there,
> And I've been glad for prophets, scriptures, gospels truths, and prayer.
> Then since I'd learned we'd all have tests and trials in mortality,
> I didn't look at pain or hardship as an abnormality.
>
> My testimony helped me feel both cared for and protected,
> Until I reached a time beyond whatever I'd expected.
> "This **can't** be right!" I'd cried about the awful situation.
> This wasn't just a trial--it was nearer devastation.
>
> He **wouldn't** want for something so destructive to continue.
> *That* seemed as clear as truths you feel instinctively within you.
> But where **was** He in all of this? I couldn't see His hand,
> When I had such a desperate need to somehow understand.
>
> Didn't He love me? Didn't He hear? I *knew* He did, no doubt.
> I also knew His power could bring **anything** about.
> Wasn't I "good enough" in faith or in striving to obey?
> I felt bereft as years wore on, and more worn down each day.
>
> But though I wouldn't choose to get to live it all again,
> I felt profoundly grateful later, that I'd lived it then.
> I recognized the ways my soul had deepened and matured,

And had a new compassion from some things that I'd endured.

I saw our times of trial could become, with heaven's surety,
Refining fires, heating gold to purge away impurity.
Both time and outcomes came to pass before I'd understood,
He can indeed make **all** things work together for our good.

And after that, no matter what went on, and come what may,
I trusted Him completely that my world was still okay.
Though sometimes things were trying, and a time or two felt terrible,
Just knowing He would tend the fires, made the heat more bearable.

I knew *He* knew where I must go and what my soul yet lacked.
He loved me more than *I* did, never-endingly, in fact.
I also found, (surprised by this miraculous reality),
That Christ could heal the vast and varied sufferings of mortality.

The self-inflicted wounds of sin were only just a start.
He'd heal a broken life, or broken dreams or broken heart.
And tragedy could change to gift, if just from that alone--
His hallowed touch could leave souls blessed in ways they'd never known.

I'd pled for mercy and His power, to heal my grieving soul.
It finally came, and in that hour, made me healed and whole.
The wonder of it left me stunned, surpassing exclamation,
And bound my heart to His in praise and reverent adoration.

Years passed, which brings the time to where it touches my today—
A time where love and mercy change my world in every way.
My journey for a while now, had led to some progression
In what has ever been my life's "magnificent obsession."

I've spent some time considering my prayers and Who they're to,
Combining that with counsel from the prophets, old and new.

I wanted to increase the time I spent in prayer and pondering,
While making sure my thoughts were staying focused and not wandering.
Something which had helped my preparation quite a lot,
I took from thoughts of Elder Maxwell and from Elder Scott--

I kneel and think about my Father; think of things He's done;
That He's created endless worlds, and still knows every one.
But at this moment, it's as if He listens just to *me.*
It's my belief that this is how He's patterned prayer to be.

I think how I am speaking with the Author of creation--
And we are spending time now, **one on one**, in conversation.
This image makes each empty word or phrase dissolve away.
And then, I reach for Him, to feel His closeness as I pray.

I draw from what I find within, and try to search my heart,
And often wait to feel for words, before I try to start.
And sometimes, I will tell Him that I don't know what to say,
But still, would like to be with Him in prayer a while that day.

Carving out the time most days to pray with this intent,
Quite quickly changed my concept of what praying really meant.
Praying now is not too much like "saying prayers" was then.
It's not a constant stream of statements, ending in amen.

I've learned to "press" within myself to help my soul be still—
And feel the Spirit easier within me if I will.
I ponder more in prayer, and spend more time now, simply waiting.
It's almost like some different way to do communicating.

I still desire to know His will and have the strength to do it.
I still seek those impressions on my heart which lead me to it.
I ask more questions, and at times, discern more clear replies,
But sometimes, I'm just "there" with Him, with no "I wants" or "Whys?"
I love this time, including parts of it where I don't speak.

Prayer isn't just for *words*—it is *His presence* that I seek.

Then one reply that shifts my prayers in such a priceless way,
Is brought about when I respond to what I read one day.
I read a sweet account regarding God, from one who knew.
I ponder it, then ask in awe, "Is what that said there true?

Is that the way Thou art, and can Thy children be Thy friends?"
There's stillness, then a flow of power and sweetness soon descends.
I don't know what to think at first except, "I'm undeserving!"
The feeling's heavenly, but its immenseness is unnerving.

This love's too much. Unmerited. My startled soul resists.
I'm foolish, weak, and… "*wonderful,*" the sweetness there insists.
But still, I almost shrink away. I don't deserve this feeling.
The tears slide down my face as I stay bowed and humbly kneeling.

This can't be so. I ask Him for a clear cut confirmation,
For why should **I** feel this amazing love and validation?
"Father… help…. Am I deceived? If so, *please,* let me know!"
Why **would** He do this thing for me? It's hard to trust it's so!

Or could I do **all this** myself? Create it all somehow?
"**Please** help me, so I understand what I should do right now."
It's **not** the beauty of this feeling that I doubt—it's ***me***.
I've yearned for heaven, yet I feel such insufficiency.

Then in response, the feeling swells, **more** sweet and strong and pure,
And there's a "settled" feeling, too, which helps my heart feel sure.
He lets me stay, immersed in all this loving, pure intensity,
Until I leave, still awed by its incredible immensity.

He makes it clear this wondrous love I'm feeling now is charity—
The love **He** has for **us**, and can bestow. This comes with clarity.

He does this for **true followers** of His beloved Son.
I guess my question really was, "Does He see **me** as one?"

He owns my heart, and I don't choose to purposely do wrong,
But probably let Him down sometimes, as things go on along.
My totaled "shoulds" would likely get a mediocre rating.
I feel *so* blessed, but **why** I am, will take some contemplating.
This bless-ed state lasts on and on! For months I feel immersed
In love so pure and sweet and huge it seems my heart might burst.

Then after, when I pray and take the time, that power and sweetness
Is almost always there, along with peaceful, pure completeness.
And He is just *so* loving and so nurturing and tender,
But with an unexpected, unassuming sort of splendor.

This isn't like whatever I'd expected, once I found Him.
There'd *have* to be some aura of "supremacy" around Him.
He's *God.* He's the *Almighty*, many million miles above me.
He *wouldn't* feel like someone who'd just **be** with me and **love** me!

And yet, it somehow seems He's pleased that He is here with *me*.
It's never rushed, like there's some other place He needs to be.
It seems our time together is a joy and not a bother;
Like I'm a favored daughter with my kind and tender Father.
It's just so very humbling that He'd feel so close at all!
My gratitude is infinite; all sense of merit, small.

And then, I go to Him when I feel bad about a day,
To tell Him I'm so sorry—I'll do better in that way.
I have no thoughts on what He'll do... (I go because I *should...*)
Perhaps I feel He'll be let down, but I'm not sure He would.

But **how** He is, completely changes how ***I*** live, forever,
Quite likely more than any moment, item or endeavor.
He shows no disappointment, disapproval, condemnation;
I don't feel shamed or blamed; there is **no** hint of accusation.

That love I've felt before is there. It's powerful. Intense.
It blesses all my being with a might that's *so* immense!
He's tender and **so** kind... He wants me ***not*** to be discouraged...
It's like a soul-deep hug of hope... I feel *beyond* encouraged...

A pure, "I **know** you'll do it..." and, "I **love** you. You're so good!"
From the **most** amazing Someone I have ever known, or could.
And mostly, He **believes** in me. It fills the very air—
The sense of this **ennobled me** He sees—so strongly there.

It lifts me up with strength to want to **be** the way He **feels**.
It blesses and inspires me; enlightens and reveals.
And through it all, is glowing love, which melts my heart with His.
I **long** to be this person who He sees already "is."

I yearn to do this now **for Him**. And then… I know! I "see"—
That He'll *be pleased* by what ***I*** do! Joy rises up in me!
I feel it grow within me. It's a beautiful, sweet fire.
To **please** the Source of Love and Light becomes my life's desire!

To know that **I can please Him** brings a joy I can't compare,
Along with thoughts that He may even **tell** me so in prayer!
My love for Him expands until it fills me and surrounds me.
I have **a way to show my love for Him**! The hope astounds me!
Consuming longing, both to **know** and **do** His will, comes though—
Like nothing more is needed, but that nothing less will do.

Then, different from the joy and sweetness coming from this feeling,
The very **nearness** of Him is emotionally healing.
Love **SO** intense it melts a heart, can melt a shattered soul!
In being wholly close to Him, the nearness **makes** things whole.

Like water that evaporates one bright and blazing day,
Within my soul, the shadows simply evanesce away.

I wouldn't say I see Him, but it's almost like I do,
As if I see Him smiling and it melts me through and through.

~*~

And though most things aren't different now, from how I'd lived each day,
They're changed by **why** I do them, in an elevating way.
It's not because "it's right," or "a commandment," or "it's best,"
For blessings, or eternal life, or any of the rest.
I do it since **IT PLEASES HIM**, and lets me show **I *LOVE* HIM!**

And everything that's done can **all** be in **remembrance** of Him.
It consecrates and blesses all decisions, every action,
'Til even daily chores become a joy and satisfaction.

My gratitude's profound for how He's made my life so sweet.
I'm grateful also for a peace that makes me feel complete.
I'm awed by the affection, love and the tenderness I find
In each exchange I've had with Him, no matter what its kind.

I've always heard that "God is Love," a truth I didn't doubt,
Not even when some righteous purpose didn't come about.
I've seen His love ten thousand times, ten thousand different ways,
And felt His hand on awfully great *and* greatly awful days.
I've known His love through righteousness as well as through repentance,
Yet simply hadn't known the fuller meaning of that sentence.

But now, as I come closer, almost close enough to touch,
I realize what I hadn't comprehended very much.
I think how negativity and darkness disappear,
Replaced by how it always feels whenever He's so near.

And how--apart from goodness, peace and power—the emotion
I feel from Him is mostly sweetness, kindness and devotion,

Affection, caring, interest, fondness and appreciation,
Tenderness and cherishing, warmth and dedication,
Nurturing, benevolence, comfort, affirmation,
Mercy and encouragement, delight and validation.

And I **know** I don't deserve it, still, the Savior's boundless grace
Has generously, wondrously, allowed me to this place,
So full of love and power that I almost cannot bear it--
Consumed with gratitude for more than I could ever merit.

And I think the reason **why** it always feels the way it does,
Whenever He's so close to me, is simply just because--

God *IS* Love...

...a truth which I have just begun to see,
but one which has transfigured the **entire world** for me.
~*~
I know that more awaits as well, before this life is through,
And I can hope to know Him even better than I do.
While I **haven't** been to heaven, I can **almost** touch it now...
I know it feels more beautiful; I'm wondering just how.

I haven't fully entered in His presence, but I've **found** Him,
And love that nameless feeling there, which radiates around Him;
How, just to reach for Him one moment as I contemplate,
Will fill me with the sweet and perfect beauty of that state.

For now, I ever seek for Him, that I might reach that place
My lifelong dream's fulfilled as I am brought to His embrace.
Perhaps it might be after death—but if it's now or then—
I seek the perfect day that brings us face to face again.

I'm honestly amazed my life is "good enough" to "count"!
He sends us blessings in a disproportionate amount!
I marvel at how generous and merciful He is;
How once we let Him have **our** hearts, then **He** lets *us* feel **His**!

To those who haven't felt this love—

He sweetly waits there *for* you,
To teach and tutor, help and lift, to cherish and restore you.
He reaches out to **every** soul; He **offers all** the same,
Who leave their sins, obey His voice, and call upon His name.

And I believe—
that if you seek Him, He will make a way
For you to surely find Him, if you'll only just obey.

And I believe—
He calls to us, if we will hear His voice,
And waits for every one of us. ***Go find Him*** and rejoice!

~*~

I wish that I could write with power, like the prophets do.
I have but one small gift, to bear my one small witness through.
I feel His hand upon my heart, as I am writing here.

Of things for which no words exist, and trying to make them clear.
I pray, and then I contemplate what I would hope to share—
Just earnestly **keep seeking Him**
For He is **truly there**!

I write the "feeling" of Him down, and hope I can explain it.
Then, once again, I'm overwhelmed 'til I cannot contain it.
I feel that wondrous love, and all His tenderness and grace,
And cannot write; my eyes are blurred, and tears run down my face.

I'm overcome by kindness and how sweet He is, once more,
And feel that adoration for Him, often felt before.
I know I can't deserve this much—I only know it's so—
But I will bear my witness of His love that we can know.

Then as I write, that wonderment anew is what I feel.
And peace-filled sweetness comes again, to tell me,

"Yes, it's real."

I finish now, and contemplate His kindnesses once more,
Poured down on me throughout my life, and still, I see them pour.
I read these pages one last time, and ponder all this through;
Amazed He'd feel such love for ***me***...

...then feel again,
"I do."

The More Sure Word of Promise by Prophecy from God Gives Us Courage to Endure All Adversity

Fellow seeker, the ability that those having received this more sure endowment to endure unspeakable adversity and turmoil is also referenced in Lecture 6 of *Lectures On Faith:* "It was this [more sure promise] that enabled the ancient saints to endure all their afflictions and persecutions, and to take joyfully the spoiling of their goods, knowing [not believe merely] that they had a more enduring substance." Part of this more enduring substance was this more sure word of promise by way of prophecy which they had received directly from God to themselves. The Lectures then add that these elect ones could not only take joyfully the spoiling of their goods, "but also to suffer death in its most horrid forms; knowing [not merely believing] that when this earthly house of their tabernacle was dissolved, they had a building of God, a house not made with hands, eternal in the heavens" (2 Cor. 5:1).

This more sure word of promise by prophecy of eternal life (or that more sure word of prophecy) is what provides the key to then pierce the heavenly veil and know God, "not with the carnal neither natural mind, but with the spiritual. For no man has seen God at any time in the flesh, except quickened by the Spirit of God. Neither can any natural man [i.e., a man not having been sanctified by the Spirit, as a general rule] abide the presence of God" (D&C 67:10-12). It is the same pattern as given us by the brother of Jared in Ether, chapter 12. Notice that this more sure word of promise, which was prophesied to him, came *before* he obtained the additional faith (and added knowledge) to pierce the heavenly veil.

*For so great was his faith in God, that when God put forth his finger he could not hide it from the sight of the brother of Jared, because of **his word** which he had spoken unto him, **which word he had obtained by faith**.*

*And after the brother of Jared had beheld the finger of the Lord, **because of the promise [i.e., more sure word of promise]***

> ***which the brother of Jared had obtained by faith**, the Lord could not withhold anything from his sight; wherefore he showed him all things, for he could no longer be kept without the veil" (Ether 12:20,21; emphasis added).*

What promise is this? It is the same "more sure" word of promise that the brother of Jared had obtained by faith unto a *more excellent way,* which is to see eye to eye:

> ***But in the gift of his Son** hath God prepared **a more excellent way**; and it is **by faith** that it hath been fulfilled,... wherefore, he showed not **himself** until after their faith (Ether 12:11-12; emphasis added).*

This same "word" was received by the apostle Paul regarding the *assurance* that had been given to him *before* he surrendered his mortal tabernacle, having fought the good fight. It is that *more sure* word, promise, or assurance of eternal life made known to the candidate of salvation of eternal life that can never be undone, excepting the shedding of innocent blood and denying the perfect knowledge received of the Holy Ghost which was obtained at the time of spiritual rebirth. This *assurance* is that more sure word of prophecy, ***delivered as a more sure promise of eternal life***, given by and from God to the candidate of salvation as direct, spiritual knowledge that cannot be misinterpreted. That is why it is sure. As a general rule, this *more sure word of promise* must be obtained prior to entering the Divine Presence of the Christ. In fact, it is what gives that added knowledge that we are, in fact, invited "to see and hear and touch and converse with the heavenly person," per Elder McConkie.

Moving along in our discussion, Joseph Smith said that our "anointing and sealing" (speaking of those additional ordinances received in the temple) is to be "called, elected, and made sure." Said another way, our anointing and sealing received in the temple must be justified by the Holy Spirit of Promise. When they are, we receive this "*more sure*" promise by prophecy from God to us personally and individually in an unmistakable manner. When He has done so, we will have obtained this knowledge from God with certainty, or as Joseph says in the Lectures, "*knowing* [not believing merely]." (Lecture 6:2).

Those of us who have followed the plan outlined by Elohim, which was sustained by Jehovah in the pre-existence, and have come to this earth and have received His ordinances by proper authority, have been given a glorious opportunity. We will be tried and tested to see if we will do all that is necessary to seek and find the Lord while in mortality. In this sense, we have all been *called.* When we are actually born of the Spirit, we are then *chosen or elected* and have found the gate. This is when we receive the baptism of fire and of the Holy Ghost and are cleansed by the Deity. As we "endure to the end" *in this election* by abiding in the true Vine and not dropping the "fruit" we have already tasted of God's glory, our election can then be made *more sure.* This is "the promise which the brother of Jared had obtained by faith," referenced in Ether. And with this additional knowledge, we are enabled to rend the veil in totality and know God as we are known, having abolished in ourselves all unbelief. Ridding ourselves of *all unbelief* is what enables us to open the door when He knocks.

> *"Behold, I stand at the door, and knock: if any man hear my voice, **and open the door**, I will come in to him and will sup with him, and he with me" (Revelation 3:20; emphasis added).*

I have a dear friend who received of his "more sure" endowment. He told me: "When our calling and election is made sure, it is as if we are now on autopilot in that we feel as if we are no longer steering our own vehicle. It is as if all decisions are now being made for us which feels as a relief and blessing versus one of control. This is because in a very real way, we have surrendered or completely aligned our personal will with God's. I say personal will and yet it feels as though there is not as much of a personal 'me', only more of a Oneness in God. It is more as though God is now living our life for us and in us. We will still need to take joyfully the spoiling of our goods but with this spiritual tethering, if you will, that never goes away and is ever present and self-evident, we feel constantly embraced by God's love." Then as if to further clarify the above, he added: "It feels somewhat accurate to say that we are no longer steering our own vehicle, but we still are. It would be more accurate to say that we now have the ability to properly steer our vehicle with surety, and because of this surety there is no desire to do anything unrighteous. In other words, there is an increased clarity, untainted by the desires of the natural man. It is as if a certain layer of the veil has been removed making it that much easier to see truth and make the best choices."

I want to make it clear, that although we may have received this *more sure* promise by prophecy from God, the occasional (even sometimes crushing) opposition we will encounter will never cease so long as we continue to live in this fallen world. We are then just given the courage to take joyfully the spoiling of our goods, together with an enhanced spiritual strength to endure and overcome the trials and opposition.

The mind of the natural man is filled with mists of darkness and must be constantly held in check through awareness as it continually tries to steal away the righteous desires and faith arising in our hearts and the belief that we ourselves can obtain of these precious promises of God. As depicted in Lehi's dream, we can become lost in the mist.

Joseph quotes the Savior and says, "I will put *promises in your hearts*, ***that will not leave you***, that will seal you up." The Apostle Paul likens this as part of that "day star" (the like heart of Christ) that arises in our hearts when our calling and election is made sure. Joseph then adds: "We may come to the General assembly and Church of the firstborn, spirits of just men made perfect, [and] unto Christ. The innumerable company of angels are those that have been resurrected from the dead; the spirits of just men made perfect are those without bodies. ***It is our privilege to pray for and obtain these things.***" Joseph continues, speaking for the Lord, "*he [meaning, the Holy Ghost] shall teach you until ye come to me & my Father.* God is not a respecter of persons, ***we all have the same privilege. Come to God, weary Him until He blesses you...we are entitled to the same blessings,*** Jesus...Angels...not laying again the doctrine of Christ, go on unto perfection. Obtain that holy Spirit of promise--Then you can be sealed to Eternal Life" (Andrew F. Ehat, *Words of Joseph Smith,* pp. 14, 15; emphasis added). It is clear here that we are to seek receiving that more sure word of prophecy, yet with the following understanding and caution from Joseph Smith:

> *As Joseph Smith here defines it, making one's calling and election sure is the crowning achievement of a life of righteous devotion. However, the Prophet apparently senses that, "if this concept is too commonly taught it could easily generate within the Church a misguided devotion to a principle that could divert the Saints' energy from the equally important principle of selfless devotion to others. Seeking blessings for oneself* ***only*** *is contrary to the principle that 'He that loseth his life for my sake shall find it'" (Andrew F. Ehat, Words of Joseph Smith, note 7, p. 18; emphasis added).*

In other words, it is okay to seek these blessings for ourselves as long as it is accompanied with the equally necessary and important devotion of alleviating the suffering of others through compassionate service and sharing the gospel of love. But if we are filled with the love of God through spiritual rebirth and have our election made sure, why would we not have this same desire? Our job is to "endure" in this love and not allow the adversary of our souls to harden our hearts thereafter. This is the center of the ongoing battle, "ground zero," which is to maintain soft, open, sensitive, and pliable hearts towards God and all men.

Those Having Received the More Sure Word of Prophecy May See the Lord

When a man has "his calling and election made sure, then it will be his privilege to receive the other comforter":

> *Now what is this other comforter? It is no more nor less than the Lord Jesus Christ himself; and this is the sum and substance of the whole matter; that when any man obtains this last comforter, he will have the personage of Jesus Christ to attend him, or appear to him from time to time, and even he will manifest the Father unto him, and they will take up there abode*

with him, and the visions of the heavens will be opened unto him, and the Lord will teach him face-to-face, and he may have a perfect knowledge of the mysteries of the kingdom of God; and this is the state and place the ancient Saints arrived at when they had such glorious visions—Isaiah, Ezekiel, John upon the aisle of Patmos, St. Paul in the three heavens, and all the saints who held communion with the general assembly and Church of the Firstborn ("Teachings," pp. 150-151).

Chapter 12

Rending the Veil and Knowing God

"He has allowed Him to appear to them that are His own; in order that they may recognize Him that made them, and not suppose that they came of themselves" (Odes of Solomon 7:12).

The simplicity of the straight and narrow path entails receiving the Holy Ghost and subsequent revelation through His influence, giving us the requisite knowledge for our journey back to the Father, made possible through the ordinances of God set forth for that purpose. These ordinances must be performed by the authority of the Melchizedek Priesthood, which together *through justification* contain "even the key of the knowledge of God" (D&C 84:19). The Holy Ghost or Comforter is necessary for us to be led into all truth and knowledge in addition to the further sanctification of our hearts unto holiness necessary to enter God's presence *here* and return to Him in the eternities *there*.

Once we arrive at this station, like the ancients, we shall experience the things that they experienced. We shall rend the veil of unbelief and come into His presence, here and now, while in mortality. ***Those who receive the ordinances by priesthood authority, believe in the promises and hold to them through pure intent, tenacity, diligence, true vision, unyielding desire, and faith, shall obtain the associated blessings.*** President Kimball bore witness to this:

> *"I have learned that where there is a prayerful heart, a hungering after righteousness, a forsaking of sins, and obedience to the commandments of God, the Lord pours out more and more light until there is finally power to pierce the heavenly veil and to know more than man knows. A person of such righteousness has the priceless promise that one day he shall see the Lord's face and know that he is" ("Give the Lord Your Loyalty," Ensign, Mar. 1980, p. 4; emphasis added).*

I have repeatedly shared Sri Nisargadatta Maharaj's that echo the seedlings of a true and core principle: "What is imagined and willed [i.e., intensely desired and acted upon] becomes actuality." This principle contains the foundation for the divine blueprint for obtaining the Second Comforter. But it takes a persistence and diligence in keeping the weeds of doubt from entering or taking root in the garden of our hearts, which destroys the belief, faith, and light that must be constantly nourished and nurtured in order to obtain the Heavenly Gift—even the appearance of the very Christ. The primary and quintessential question we must first ask ourselves is not only "Do I believe?" but rather *"Do I believe it for myself?"* Do I desire to meet the Lord in mortality, do I believe that I can obtain such an endowment, and am I willing to accept the responsibility of living the lifestyle of a covenant disciple? In short, *do I believe Him and in His promises... given to me and for me?* If the answer is no, then this unbelief is the wall that must be torn down. This involves an ongoing process. If the answer is yes, then we must hold to this initial belief, constantly imagining it, expecting it, "willing it," experiencing it emotionally through visualization, looking for evidences of it, living a life of discipleship as if it had already happened, and constantly building faith in it until it manifests into our world of the "seen" here in mortality, originating from the world of the unseen. In other words, "things which are seen are not made of things which do appear" (Heb. 11:3). Jesus said, "But he that believeth not is condemned already" (John 3:18). Ultimately, our ability to nurture our faith along the path of this earthly journey stems from whether we believe God (and in His promises), not just for "anyone," but *for ourselves individually and personally.*

A perfect, whole and living faith, delivered from our perfect, whole, and living God, leads to a perfect knowledge of God's reality as part of the First Comforter. After we are born of God, as we continue to press forward in faith and knowledge of Him through the quickening influence of His Spirit and obedience to His directives, additional "knowledges" come to fruition, line upon line, and are made manifest. This is how we *grow in the knowledge of God* we received at the time of our rebirth. These additional knowledges lead us ultimately to the removal of all *unbelief.* And *unbelief* is the veil that separates us from the presence of God. When all *unbelief* dissipates and we are filled with faith and knowledge, and our hearts are pure, we shall then know God according to His perfect timing, eye to eye, just as the brother of Jared knew Him. For "when men begin to *live by faith*, they begin to draw nigh to God; and when *faith is perfected*, they are *like him*" (*Lectures On Faith,* 7:8). "The real difference between a saved person and one not saved is—*the difference in the degree of their faith*—one's faith has become perfect enough to lay hold upon eternal life, the other's has not" (Ibid., 7:9).

But before this time, we will have been tried and tested in the fire of adversity multiple times. Orson Pratt taught:

> *"Before you can see the Father, the Savior, or an angel, you have to be brought into close places in order to enjoy this manifestation. The fact is,* ***your very life must be suspended on a thread****, as it were. If you want to see your Savior,* ***be willing to come to that point where no mortal arm can rescue, no***

***earthly power save**! When all other things fail, when everything else proves futile and fruitless, then perhaps your Savior and your Redeemer may appear" (Orson Pratt, Journal of Discourses, 1:124; emphasis added).*

Somewhere in Time

In pondering this chapter and how to open this most beautiful of endowments to our collective view, I repeatedly felt the words "Somewhere In Time" coming to my mind. I found that odd. I remember seeing the movie by the same name over 30 years ago. The Spirit would not let it go, however, so I decided to investigate what it was that the Lord wanted me to portray. As I jumped in with both feet, the beauty of this movie's symbolism became all-consuming and could not be ignored. As I read the synopsis of the movie, I came across these words presented in the very beginning of the movie: "Come back to me." As soon as I read these words, I wept. I instantly knew why the Lord had put this movie's title in my mind. He intensely wants us all to return or "come back to [Him]." And it goes without saying that we can't return to a familiar home unless we've already lived there.

"*Somewhere in Time*" is a love story of epic proportion. It is a story symbolic of our own love story between God and us—of our yearning and love for God and of our journey back home. It is a story of going back in time to an era much grander than this one. Somewhere in time, we once lived in spiritual union and love for God. Our objective in this life is to "come back to Him" and experience that union once again, even eternally. He longs for our return. In the movie by the same name, Richard Collier (played by the actor Christopher Reeves) embarks on an incredible journey into another realm, another lifetime, *in search of a love that he had once enjoyed.* Through it emerges a symbolic link between man and his Eternal Father somewhere in the past, beyond time. Similarly, throughout scripture we see the symbolism of this spiritual and pure love between ourselves—the true seeker and truth seeker—and our resurrected Lord. He refers to us in scripture as His "jewels." In other places, He calls us the bride and Himself the Bridegroom. The story of finding our true love in the Lord truly is a heroic journey, and one that is certifiably epic.

In the movie, the journey begins in 1980 when a stranger to Collier, an old woman (played by Jane Seymour), places a beautiful, vintage pocket watch in Collier's hand as a gift. All she says to him is, "Come back to me." Collier appears to have been in his early thirties at the time. The gift is given as a *token of remembrance*—something to remind him of the former love these two had once shared, although Collier had no memory of it. He is confused by her intrusion and eventually shrugs it off. Fast forward eight years later, and Collier is going through a heart break stemming from a breakup with his girlfriend. Nothing is going his way personally or professionally. As a playwright, he experiences writer's block, and something inside tells him to leave town and just "get away." Unbeknownst to Collier, he is at his *personal crash site*, trying to find the purpose and meaning of his life. He ends up at the Grand Hotel in Mackinac Island, Michigan. During his *wandering* about the hotel, he happens on the historical museum of the hotel and notices an old photo of a young woman, Elise McKenna, and he becomes entranced with her. Something in the photo spoke to his soul.

Miss McKenna (who is the same stranger and old woman who had given him the vintage pocket watch as a gift eight years earlier), had been a popular young actress in 1912 (some 68 years or so earlier) and had performed at this very same hotel. Coincidentally, Collier was a playwright (again, from the 1980's) and often sought the very talent this woman possessed back in her heyday.

To me, the young woman in the old photo represents our Father. This Father could represent either Christ as our Father, who adopts us when we are spiritually "born" and adopted into His family, or our Father Elohim. Either way, we know that the Father and Son are One. Collier ***obsesses*** about this figure—this woman who is representative of our Father and the love we once shared with Him. He takes the same action as one who is obsessed with any person. He first learns everything that he can about her. He can't stop thinking about her. He goes to the local library and reads everything that he can find about her. Is this not a type and pattern for us as well for finding our spiritual Father?

Collier recruits the help of one of the librarians to track down some old articles about the actress that were not accessible to the public and had been stored away in the back of the library. Notice what it took for Collier to obtain this information. He first had become a private investigator (of sorts) of both his own life and the life of this young woman (representative of our Father). He had to *diligently seek* her. The seeking was born of an inner yearning in his soul, which later led to an encounter, which then led to a subsequent gift of remembrance (i.e., a beautiful pocket watch made in the early 1900s, likened unto the Light of Christ given to every man who enters the world), which led to further inquiry, which led to investigation and further seeking, which led to the belief that he had actually known this person before. Fellow seeker, do we not see the parallels here for our own journey?

This *feeling that he could not let go of*, that he had actually known this person before, led to further investigation and seeking. And in that investigation, the Spirit whispered to him to *seek actual knowledge* as to whether he himself had been at this same hotel back in 1912, even though he had been born decades after that date. He recruited the help of an older gentleman who had been an employee of the hotel and who had lived there since the days in which his father had worked there when he was just a little boy. This little boy, now an old man perhaps in his 80s, had met this actress Miss McKenna himself. He allowed Collier entrance to an old attic within the hotel that contained many old hotel relics and records. And in Collier's seeking, he found a guest registration book. Collier went to a specific date in 1912 and, lo and behold, found his own name and signature in the book. This blew Collier's mind since he himself had been born in the 1950s. In finding his own signature, Collier had received another gift of remembrance. This time, this gift gave him *actual knowledge* that irrespective of when he was born, he had actually been at this same hotel back in 1912.

Fellow seeker, this knowledge is part of the initial knowledge of God—the actual knowledge of a previous encounter with a true friend and love found "somewhere in time." It is followed by the experiential "knowledges" of God and His mysteries that we receive line upon line and build increasing knowledge and faith to a more sure salvation and the appearance of the Lord of glory Himself.

Collier continues his obsession and investigation about this figure—his true love. He now knows without any doubt that he had once known this actress. He knows he was at this very hotel. He visited an older woman and friend of Miss Mckenna in the 1980s after receiving the mysterious watch. Collier saw a book in her home on time travel through self-hypnosis. She mentioned that Miss Mckenna had frequently read this same book and had obsessed about it but didn't know why. Collier's quest to seek his true love, led him to another piece of evidence of their prior encounter and relationship. Does this seeking by Collier not remind us of the required awareness regarding similar clues, evidences, and tender mercies that we too must receive in our quest to find and know the love we once had for Christ and our Father?

Collier subsequently departed the friend's home to seek the advice of the book's author, who now happened to be a professor at a local university. Upon meeting the professor, Collier asked him if time travel was possible. The professor had told him that he himself had accomplished it, but only for a short moment. (Note: This is symbolic of the testimony given by those who have actually obtained a perfect knowledge of God through the First and Second Comforters, and which gives us the belief and hope that we too, might obtain this experience. It is also a pattern referenced in the *Lectures On Faith* that "it was human testimony, and human testimony only that excited this inquiry…to inquire after the knowledge of God" [Lecture 2:56]). This instilled a strong belief in Collier that he could do the same by exercising immense faith through this meditative practice of self-hypnosis described by the professor.

Through *the foundation of desire and faith* that he could accomplish such a task, and through the "human testimony" of the professor who had accomplished it himself, Collier set out to do just that. He immersed himself in everything he could find from Miss Mckenna's day. (Note: This is our charge as well. We must immerse ourselves in "all things Christ" to find Him.) Everything visible in his room had to be of that same time period, and *there could be* ***no present-day distractions***. The intensity of his focus was all consuming. And as spiritual seekers ourselves, we must match this intensity. The symbolism here is surprisingly accurate. Collier's obsession to find and know Miss Mckenna (our true love in our "Father") led to his arrival into her presence and subsequent spiritual union or oneness with her. We are to go and do likewise, only with our Lord, in order to find and obtain the spiritual oneness and experiential "knowledges of God" for ourselves.

It is on *the foundation of desire and faith* that we obtain all spiritual endowments subject to having received God's ordinances by proper authority. A soft heart accompanied with honest, inner, self-inquiry leads to belief in truth, which is light. This light in our hearts that is speaking to us, if followed, leads us to act in our newfound belief in gospel principles. When we act in the doctrine and gospel belief, including through broken-hearted repentance and being truly penitent while yearning to find and know God (and do His Will) in the midst of our own mini-Gethsemane, we are able to receive an endowment of faith unto knowledge and salvation through crying out or "calling on His name." The circular interplay of faith and knowledge then repeats itself until we receive additional "knowledges" of God's reality, void of any unbelief or doubt whatsoever, enabling us to (at least at some point), rend the veil in totality and enter the Divine Presence ourselves.

Notice it is a living faith, bestowed by grace, which leads to hope, a synonym of knowledge. It follows chapter one in this work. It involves the last three on our Diagram: Faith --->Hope (Spiritual Knowledge of God and of our own salvation, and of "the hope" in His promise to us of eternal life) --->Charity (or the love of God we become filled with—which is the fruit of "Salvation"). Faith upon faith upon faith, yielding spiritual, experiential knowledge upon knowledge upon knowledge. As Joseph truly said, "A man is saved no faster than he gets knowledge." This is the path of acquiring the spiritual knowledge of God's reality and portions of His glory until the overall knowledge gets to be so much that we say to ourselves and to the Lord: "It is enough! I need not see any more evidences of thy reality, goodness, and love. Will you now please come out from behind the curtain" (i.e., "veil")? This overall spiritual knowledge (or knowledges of God) and accompanying endowment becomes so SURE in us that it even becomes *expected.* This is when the Lord says to us, as he did the brother of Jared: "Because thou knowest these things ye are redeemed from the fall. Ye are brought back into my presence; therefore I show myself unto you" (Ether 3:13).

Joseph said, speaking of our own privileges, that "many of us have gone at the command of the Lord in defiance of everything evil, and obtained *blessings unspeakable*, in consequence of which our names are sealed in the Lamb's book of life, for the Lord has spoken it. It is the privilege of every Elder to speak of the things of God; and could we all come together with *one heart and one mind in perfect faith* the veil might as well be rent today as next week, or any other time" (*Teachings of the Prophet Joseph Smith,* p. 5; emphasis added).

Prophets of All Ages Have Sought to Bring Their People into the Presence of God While in Mortality

After the Fall, Adam and Eve's primary objective was to come back into the presence of God and see Him once again in their flesh. Adam, after the Fall, declared once again his intention when he said, "***and again <u>in the flesh</u> I shall see God***" (Moses 5:9-10; emphasis added). Is this not an affirmation of Adam's faith? Fellow seeker, we are all as Adam and Eve, respectively. Our doctrine is clear. Adam sought that his posterity, "through the exercise of their faith ... could obtain a knowledge of His character *and also of his glory*" (*Lectures On Faith*, 2:31; emphasis added).

This was made clear when Joseph Smith spoke further about Adam's objective for his posterity in that they were "to feel after him—to search after a knowledge of his character, perfections, and attributes, until they became extensively acquainted with him, and not only commune with him and behold his glory [First Comforter], *but be partakers of his power and* ***stand in his presence*** [Second Comforter]" (Ibid., Lecture 2:34; emphasis added). Fellow seeker: Once the First Comforter is experientially made manifest or "real" (unto the praise and glory of God), would not the fulfillment of the Second be as equally real?

> *"Now this Moses plainly taught to the children of Israel in the wilderness, and sought diligently to sanctify his people* ***that they might behold the face of God****" (D&C 84:23; emphasis added).*

Notice the intention of Moses. He wanted them to experience what he had experienced. He knew that it was possible or else he would not have sought diligently for his people to obtain this objective. Joseph Smith spoke to Adam's intention and affirmed it was the same as Moses's:

> *"This is why Adam blessed his posterity;* ***he wanted to bring them into the presence of God****. They looked for a city, etc., 'whose builder and maker is God' (Hebrews 11:10.)* ***Moses sought to bring the children of Israel into the presence of God****, through the power of the Priesthood, but he could not (Teachings of the Prophet Joseph Smith, p.159; emphasis added).*

Everything in the scriptures is there to lead us first to a sure salvation by obtaining the knowledge of God through a manifestation of the Lord's Spirit in power, followed by receiving the more sure word of salvation by prophecy, followed by entering the Divine Presence. So why were most of the Israelites unsuccessful? As we continue reading, it becomes clear. Notice the similarities to Chapter 1, "Ground Zero: The battle over the heart":

> *"****But they hardened their hearts*** *and could not endure his presence; therefore, the Lord in his wrath, for his anger was kindled against them, swore that they should not enter into his rest while in the wilderness, which rest is the fulness of his glory" (D&C 84:24; emphasis added).*

Fellow seeker, a hard heart is an unbelieving heart. And what was the consequence of the Israelites' unbelief resulting from their hardened hearts? "He took Moses out of their midst, and the Holy Priesthood also" (D&C 84:25). And He replaced all of this with the "law of carnal commandments." Notice that the Lord's "anger was kindled against them," because He so much wanted the Israelites to qualify to come into His Presence, but they would not. Not only is He desirous for us to come into His Presence, but it is clear to see that it affects Him when we desire otherwise. Notice these verses below:

21 And ***without*** the ordinances thereof, and the authority of the priesthood, the power of godliness ***is not*** manifest unto men in the flesh;

22 For ***without*** this [manifestation] ***no man can*** see the face of God, even the Father, and live (D&C 84: 21-22; emphasis added). Now let's read the same words when stated positively rather than negatively:

"And with the ordinances thereof, and the authority of the priesthood, the power of godliness is manifest unto men in the flesh. For with this, man can see the face of God, even the Father, and live."

When we strip ourselves of jealousies and fears and humble ourselves before the Lord, He promises us that "the veil shall be rent and you shall see me and know that I am—not with the carnal neither natural mind, but with the spiritual. For no man has seen God at any time in the flesh, *except quickened by the Spirit of God*" (D&C 67:10-13; emphasis added). This is another reason why we must receive the baptism of the Spirit and be "quickened in the inner man." This quickening experience is the first step of the overall process which prepares us to enter the Divine presence and see God—and remain alive. As a general rule, no natural man is able to endure His presence. We must first be changed mightily and then become further sanctified unto holiness. This is the preparation. This is the process.

As it was with Moses in his day, so it was in every dispensation in which the fullness of the gospel of Jesus Christ has been in existence, including our own dispensation. In fact, bringing man into the presence of God was Joseph's objective as well for a Zion people in this dispensation of the fulness of times, which brings together in one all earthly dispensations. This includes the winding up scene wherein the city of Enoch shall come down from above and unite with the Zion from below, with each party falling upon each other's necks with tears of joy and praise for the God of their salvation.

Joseph Smith's objective was the same for the Latter-day Saints: "All who are prepared, and are sufficiently pure to abide the presence of the Savior, will see Him in the solemn assembly" (Teachings of the Prophet Joseph Smith, p. 91). He also said: "In the first ages of the world they tried to establish the same thing; ***and there were Eliases raised up who tried to restore these very glories***, but did not obtain them…;

but they prophesied of a day when this glory would be revealed" (Teachings of the Prophet Joseph Smith, p. 161).

Fellow seeker: That day is today. That day is ours. That day is now. And it is all made available through the ordinances of God by proper priesthood authority, then striving to have those ordinances justified and "sealed" by the Holy Spirit of Promise. It arises by desiring to draw nearer and nearer to God, through the art of practicing our love for Him, facilitated by getting quiet—really quiet—and connecting with Him through the deep recesses of our souls.

Subsequently we learn from Joseph that "the extent of [our] knowledge respecting His character and glory will depend upon [our] diligence and faithfulness in *seeking after Him*... ***until [we] shall obtain faith in God, and power with Him to behold Him face to face*** " (*Lectures On Faith* 2:55; emphasis added). But to behold Him face to face, we are first to be made "like [unto] Him" so "that when he shall appear we shall be like him, for we shall **see him as he is...** that we may have this hope [i.e., revealed knowledge]; that we may be purified even as he is pure. Amen" (Moroni 7:48; emphasis added). Why is it important that we be "purified even as he is pure," and in this manner be made "like him"? Because, as Joseph has said, "to be assimilated into their likeness is to be saved, and to be unlike them is to be destroyed; and on this hinge turns the door of salvation" (Ibid, Lecture 7:16).

If we pay close attention to the words of the prophets in holy writ, we will clearly see that the pattern of obtaining *the prize of Christ* is to enter His presence while in our flesh. This is also the pattern to being fully redeemed from the Fall, as was the case with the brother of Jared. This is the very purpose for the fullness of the gospel. This has been the case since the foundation of this world. The personage of Christ is *the Heavenly Gift* we are entitled to receive, if we but will have faith that this endowment is available to us personally and individually *and if we hold to that vision with an undeviating eye of faith.* Moroni declared, "But because of the faith of men he has shown himself unto the world, and glorified the name of the Father, and prepared a [more excellent] way that thereby others [i.e., us] might be partakers of the heavenly gift [i.e., Christ's appearance to us personally] that they might hope for those things which they have not seen [yet]" (Ether 12:8).

The *Lectures On Faith* poses both the question and the answer:

> *"How do men obtain a knowledge of the glory of God, his perfections and attributes? By devoting themselves to his service through prayer and supplication, incessantly strengthening their faith in him [i.e., fully filling their "faith cup"), until like Enoch, the brother of Jared, and Moses, they obtain a manifestation of God to themselves" (Lectures On Faith, 2:20).*

And the ability to obtain such a manifestation is reinforced in the Lectures as being "founded upon [mark it well] ***human testimony alone***, until persons receive a manifestation of God unto themselves" (Ibid., 2:203). This is why those who have received the actual knowledge of God have been commanded to bear record (see Ether 4:11). As for my part, I can witness that the added fuel and desire to seek a more excellent way came from the human testimony of Bruce R. McConkie, whom I have met personally on several occasions and one other dear friend who has received this very personal endowment. Listen to Elder McConkie's final testimony in general conference before his death entitled, "The Purifying Power of Gethsemane." One cannot listen to that address and not know that Elder McConkie had seen the Lord. There can be no mistaking it:

"And now, as pertaining to this perfect Atonement, wrought by the shedding of the blood of God—I testify that it took place in Gethsemane and at Golgotha, and as pertaining to Jesus Christ, I testify that He is the Son of the living God and was crucified for the sins of the world. He is our Lord, our God, and our King. This I know of myself, independent of any other person. I am one of His witnesses, and in a coming day I shall feel the nail marks in His hands and in His feet and shall wet His feet with my tears. *But I shall not know any better then than I know now* that He is God's Almighty Son, that He is our Savior and Redeemer, and that salvation comes in and through His atoning blood and in no other way" (general conference, April, 1985).

Elder McConkie, in his talk "The Seven Christ's" in 1982, said:

"Thanks be to God that the heavens have been rent, that the Father and the Son appeared to Joseph Smith, that revelation and visions and gifts and miracles abound among the true Saints.

"Thanks be to God that ***in our day many have seen the face of his Son*** and that he has poured out the gift of his Spirit upon an even greater number."

The Almighty God desires that we enter and endure His Presence so that we might obtain the kind of joy which He both lives and experiences. This is eternal life—***to know God***. This is His work and His glory. ***This is the ongoing, eternal struggle, which is to bring men into His Presence***. It happens by faith. It commences with faith and endures by faith. And faith yields the knowledge of God. And the knowledge of God yields "all things that pertain to life and godliness" (*Lectures On Faith* 7:13). As we unite to God's message and purpose, we work lock step with Him in the same spiritual endeavor involving the salvation of mankind.

The Culmination of the Entire Path in Mortality Is to Enter the Divine Presence and Become the Friends of God

Having a culminating experience of entering the Divine presence here in mortality could certainly be considered controversial in many circles within our LDS faith. But let's not toss it out without at least considering it in a deeper or more meaningful way. I believe that one can be saved and even have that salvation made "more sure" without seeing the Lord in mortality. But I also know that those with a more abundant faith can obtain a more excellent way. This more excellent way is plainly taught in the scriptures. And this more excellent way is to reach that sufficiency of faith (which is an absence of any doubt or unbelief whatsoever) that we are not only entitled to see His face but as Elder McConkie has suggested, we expect "to see and hear and touch and converse with the Heavenly Person."

Moroni professed a path which included many endowments given through faith, and then added, "but in the gift of his Son [to us personally and individually] hath God prepared *a more excellent way* [which is to see the Son by rending the veil of unbelief and entering His presence]; and it is by faith that it hath been fulfilled,... wherefore, *he showed not **himself** until <u>after</u> their faith*" (Ether 12:11-12; emphasis added).

We Are Commanded to Seek the Actual Face of the Lord

Many have obtained the endowment and privilege of seeing the Lord, face to face. These include Adam, Seth, Enoch, Noah, Abraham, Moses, Elijah, Elisha, Ezekiel, Isaiah, Jacob of old, Lehi, Nephi, Jacob, Alma, Moroni, the brother of Jared, the Nephite Twelve, and hundreds of others. Then there many others, both known and unknown, including Joseph Smith and apostles and prophets of our dispensation. Elder Bruce R. McConkie, whom I have frequently quoted in this book, is one of them.

The Lord commanded: "And **seek the face of the Lord always**, that in patience ye may possess your souls, and ye shall have eternal life" (D&C 101:38; emphasis added).

Fellow seeker. This is a commandment. Ever since I was a little boy, Nephi's admonition has sounded loudly in my ear. His admonition is perhaps one of the most quoted from the Book of Mormon:

> *"I will go and do what the Lord hath commanded, for I know that the Lord giveth no commandments unto the children of men, save he shall prepare a way for them that they may accomplish the thing which he commandeth them" (1 Ne. 3:7).*

There are many spiritual and symbolic dress rehearsals for the real thing, prior to the actual endowment or heavenly gift being made manifest. Elder McConkie tells us that "He is there waiting our call, ***anxious to have us seek his face***, awaiting our importuning pleas to rend the veil so that we can see the things of the Spirit" (*The Promised Messiah*, p. 582).

The lyrics for "Came to the Rescue," by Hillsong, possess this same truth as it was delivered to its writers through the Light of Christ:

Falling on my knees in worship
Giving all I am to seek your face
Lord, all I am is yours

My whole life I place in your hands
God of mercy, humbled I bow down
In your presence, at your throne

I called, you answered
And you came to my rescue
And I want to be where you are...

The Lord's word to "seek the face of the Lord always" was not just a helpful suggestion for us to follow. It was a commandment from the Almighty God. And it was given with an eye towards our own best interest and overall happiness. The Prophet Joseph has said:

"As God has designed our happiness—and the happiness of all His creatures, he never has—He never will institute an ordinance or give a commandment to His people that is not calculated in its nature to promote that happiness which He has designed, and which will not end in the greatest amount of good and glory to those who become the recipients of His law and ordinances" (Teachings of the Prophet Joseph Smith, p. 256).

This commandment was given by the Lord Himself, together with the recipe for its fulfillment:

"Verily, thus saith the Lord: It shall come to pass that every soul who forsaketh his sins and cometh unto me, and calleth upon my name, and obeyeth my voice, and keepeth my commandments, ***shall see my face and know that I am****" (D&C 93:1).*

Latter-day Apostles, Prophets, and Saints Have Seen the Lord

Fellow Seeker: Where there is no striving, there is no arriving. In the following statements, I have added bold and italic for emphasis. Pay attention.

Oliver Cowdery said:

*"**Never cease striving until you have seen God face-to-face**. Strengthen your faith; cast off your doubts, your sins, and all your unbelief; and nothing can prevent you from coming to God. Your ordination is not full and complete till God has laid his hand upon you. We require as much to qualify us as did those who have gone before us; God is the same. If the Savior in former days laid his hands upon his disciples, why not in the latter days?... Therefore call upon him in faith and in mighty prayer till you prevail, for it is your duty and your privilege to bear such a testimony for yourselves" ("Minutes and Blessings, 21 February 1835," in Minute Book 1, 160–61).*

"***For we saw him, even on the right hand of God***; and we heard the voice bearing record that he is the Only Begotten of the Father" (D&C 76:23).

"And the day cometh that ***you shall hear my voice and see me***, and know that I am" (D&C 50:45).

"For they will hear my voice, ***and shall see me***, and shall not be asleep, and shall abide the day of my coming; for they shall be purified, even as I am pure" (D&C 35:21).

"To whom he grants ***this privilege of seeing*** and knowing for themselves" (D&C 76:117;).

"Therefore, sanctify yourselves that your minds become single to God, ***and the days will come that you shall see him; for he will unveil his face unto you***, and it shall be in his own time, and in his own way, and according to his own will" (D&C 88:68).

"Yea, and my presence shall be there, for I will come into it, and ***all the pure in heart that shall come into it shall see God***" (D&C 97:16).

"***We saw the Lord*** standing upon the breastwork of the pulpit, before us; and under his feet was a paved work of pure gold, in color like amber" (D&C 110:2).

The Experiences of Apostles and Prophets Can Be Our Own

We have been taught repeatedly to liken the scriptures unto ourselves, holding out hope that their experiences can be our own. Many prophets and apostles in the scriptures have witnessed to having seen the Lord:

*Nephi said, "**For he verily saw my Redeemer, even as I have seen him**. And my brother, Jacob, also has seen him **as I have seen him**" (2 Ne. 11:2-3).*

King Lamoni stated after his spiritual rebirth, "For as sure as thou livest, behold, ***I have seen my Redeemer***; and he shall come forth, and be born of a woman, and he shall redeem all mankind who believe on his name" (Alma 19:13).

Alma stated, "Behold, ***many*** have been born of God, and have *tasted as I have tasted, **and have seen eye to eye as I have seen***; therefore they do know of these things of which I have spoken, as I do know; and the ***knowledge*** which I have is ***of God***" (Alma 36:26).

> *"And then shall ye know that **I have seen Jesus**, and that he hath talked with me **face to face***, and that he told me in plain humility, even as a man telleth another in mine own language, concerning these things" (Ether 12:39).
>
> "Wherefore I know that ye know that our flesh must waste away and die; nevertheless, ***in our bodies we shall see God***" (2 Ne. 9:4).
>
> "Blessed are the pure in heart: ***for they shall see God***" (Matt. 5:8).
>
> "And when he had said these words, behold, the Lord showed himself unto him, and said: Because thou knowest these things ye are redeemed from the fall; ***therefore ye are brought back into my presence; therefore I show myself unto you***" (Ether 3:13).
>
> "***And he saw God face to face***, and he talked with him, and the glory of God was upon Moses; therefore Moses could endure his presence" (Moses 1:2).
>
> "And I saw the Lord; and he stood before my face, and he talked with me, ***even as a man talketh one with another, face to face***" (Moses 7:4).
>
> "Thus I, Abraham, ***talked with the Lord, face to face***, as one man talketh with another; and he told me of the works which his hands had made" (Abraham 3:11).
>
> "And Jacob called the name of the place Peniel: ***for I have seen God face to face***, and my life is preserved (Gen. 32:30).
>
> "And upon the nobles of the children of Israel he laid not his hand: ***also they saw God, and did eat and drink***" (Exodus 24:11).

"And though after my skin worms destroy this body, ***yet in my flesh shall I see God***" (Job 19:26).

"Then said I, Woe is me! for I am undone; because I am a man of unclean lips, and I dwell in the midst of a people of unclean lips: ***for mine eyes have seen the King, the Lord of hosts***" (Isaiah 6:5).

"And said, Behold, **I see** the heavens opened, and **the Son of man** standing on the right hand of God" (Acts 7:56).

"***And when I saw him, I fell at his feet*** as dead. And he laid his right hand upon me, saying unto me, Fear not; I am the first and the last" (Rev. 1:17).

"Now this Moses plainly taught to the children of Israel in the wilderness, *and sought diligently to sanctify his people* ***that they might behold the face of God***" (D&C 84:23).

The Fulness of the Gospel Provides Man the Opportunity to Enter the Divine Presence While in Mortality

Speaking of the experience of the brother of Jared who pierced the veil of unbelief with his faith, Elder McConkie made these faith-promoting comments:

> *From these revelations we learn that there are* ***no limitations placed upon any of us****. Revelations are not reserved for a limited few or for those called to positions of importance in the Church. It is not position in the Church that confers spiritual gifts. It is not being a bishop, a stake president, or an apostle that makes revelation and salvation available. These are high and holy callings which open the door to the privilege of great service among men. But* ***it is not a call to a special office that opens the windows of revelation to a truth seeker****. Rather it is personal righteousness; it is keeping the commandments;* ***it is seeking the Lord while he may be found*** *(Isa. 55:6). God is no respecter of persons (Acts 10:34). He will give revelation to me and to you on the same terms and conditions. I can see what Joseph Smith and Sidney Rigdon saw in the vision of the degrees of glory—and so can you.* ***I can entertain angels and see God… and so can you*** *("Rock of Salvation," Conference Report, October 1969, pp. 79-84).*

The fullness of the gospel incorporates the ability of man to come back into the presence of God and thereby be fully redeemed from the Fall. This gospel fullness was obtained in the days of Moses by Moses himself, Aaron, Nadab, Abihu, and seventy others, but the majority of the Israelites squandered their privilege and opportunity. This gospel fullness was also made clear by Joseph Smith, John Taylor, and others in the early days of the Church, and the same principle continues and is made available in our day. And what is that? To once again enter the presence of God and thereby be fully redeemed from the Fall. John Taylor explains:

"The Israelites had the Gospel preached to them in the wilderness"; but, as the Apostle says in speaking of them, 'The word preached did not profit them, ***not being mixed with faith*** in them that heard it' (Heb. 4:2). But Moses did lead some of them into the presence of God (Ex. 24:9-11), which were those who were prepared to receive it; the others, when they heard the thunders and saw the lightning (Ex. 20:18) and heard the voice of God (Ex. 19:16-19), they said unto Moses, 'Speak thou unto us, and we will hear: but let not God speak with us, lest we die' (Ex. 20:19); we are not prepared for this glory, for this kind of manifestation which has been given unto us."

Taylor continues, "Well, they were foolish; they departed from correct principles, they violated the laws of God and therefore incurred his displeasure, and his Spirit was withdrawn from them, and the Gospel [fullness] was taken from them and they were left under a law of carnal commandments [D&C 84:23-27], and the law was given them as a schoolmaster, we are told, until Christ came [Gal. 3:24]. And what did Christ do? ***He restored the fulness of the Gospel that they had forfeited,*** because of their former transgressions" (*Journal of Discourses* 20:219).

We are told that the "Melchizedek Priesthood, is to hold the keys of all the spiritual blessings of the Church—To have the privilege of … the heavens opened unto [us], to commune with the general assembly and Church of the Firstborn, ***and to enjoy the communion and presence of God, the Father, and Jesus the mediator of the new covenant***" (D&C 107:18-19; emphasis added). Elder McConkie tells us that "if and when the holy priesthood operates to the full in the life of any man, he will receive its great and full blessings, which are that ***rending of the heavens and that parting of the veil of which we now speak*"** (*The Promised Messiah,* p. 588).

Whenever the fullness of the gospel has been on the Earth, people have entered into the presence of God. In modern-day revelation to the Prophet Joseph, we learn that Moses, through the ordinances delivered by the authority of the Melchizedek Priesthood, could bring people of faith and obedience to experience "the power of godliness" ***while in the flesh.*** That was God's entire objective for them, and it is His objective for us today. But without the justification of these ordinances by the Holy Spirit of Promise, which was administered by proper authority, "no man can see the face of God, even the Father, and live" (D&C 84:22).

I'd like to introduce an article that was written and provided by Ivan J. Barrett. Barrett was an associate professor of Church history and doctrine at Brigham Young University at the time and served as patriarch to the BYU Tenth Stake. The name of his work is called, "He Lives! For We Saw Him!" He wrote it in 1975, and it can be found on LDS.org as presented originally in the *Improvement Era,* 33:726. It is filled with experiences surrounding those who came to know the Lord in the form of His personage. It is an amazing compilation that must be read by all true seekers. When finished reading it, please continue below. Ready?

As to the reality of entering the Lord's presence on this level, John Pontius had this to say:

> *Begin where you are. Take the Holy Spirit for your guide. Be faithful in all things. Be as fearless and constant and obedient as you're able, constantly moving toward the light. Do this, and you will, in the due time of the Lord, arrive in His presence (John Pontius, The Triumph of Zion, p. 176).*

The Diagram found throughout "Putting on Christ" involves waymarks or guideposts which coincide with the gradual increase of our faith over a lifetime in a parallel path to that increase of light and truth over a lifetime. It is faith, however, that is the catalyst for receiving the periodic "downloads" of those endowments of light and truth—until the perfect day.

Receiving light and more light sanctifies (or makes holy) a person degree by degree through an endowment of light and truth (or God's glory) through grace (resulting from obedience and an authentic love for God; see Helaman 3:35), until we receive in the resurrection a fulness of light and truth which is centered in Christ. Our souls can be upgraded and we can be adopted in as Sons of God the Father. This is how we could become joint-heirs with Jesus Christ.

That light shall grow brighter and brighter within us, having been upgraded by God through grace, as we thereby become more like God through endowments of light and truth, becoming purified and sanctified, until we arrive at that station of becoming holy men and women. When this occurs, we cannot be kept from without the veil.

Sacred Writings on Seeing God

8 Blessed are the pure in heart: ***for they shall see God*** (Matthew 5:8).

21 He that hath my commandments, and keepeth them, he it is that loveth me: and he that loveth me shall be loved of my Father, and I will love him, ***and will manifest myself to him.***

22 Judas saith unto him, not Iscariot, Lord, ***how is it that thou wilt manifest thyself unto us***, and not unto the world?

23 Jesus answered and said unto him, If a man love me, he will keep my words: and my Father will love him, and ***we will come unto him, and make our abode with him*** (John 14:21-23).

3 John 14:23—The appearing of the Father and the Son, in that verse, is ***a personal appearance***; and the idea that the Father and the Son dwell in a man's heart is an old sectarian notion, and is false (D&C 130:3).

20 Behold, I stand at the door, and knock: if any man hear my voice, and open the door, ***I will come in to him, and will sup with him***, and he with me Revelation 3:20).

"I [i.e., through faith] was the door to everything" (The Odes of Solomon 17:10).

44 Wherefore, I am in your midst, and I am the good shepherd, and the stone of Israel. He that buildeth upon this rock shall never fall.

45 And the day cometh that ***you shall hear my voice and see me***, and know that I am.

46 Watch, therefore, that ye may be ready. Even so. Amen (D&C 50:44-46).

10 And again, verily I say unto you that it is your privilege, and a promise I give unto you that have been ordained unto this ministry, that inasmuch as you strip yourselves from jealousies and fears, and humble yourselves before me, for ye are not sufficiently humble, the veil shall be rent and ***you shall see me and know that I am***—not with the carnal neither natural mind, but with the spiritual.

11 For no man has seen God at any time in the flesh, ***except quickened by the Spirit of God.***

12 Neither can any Natural man abide the presence of God, neither after the carnal mind.

13 Ye are not able to abide the presence of God now, neither the ministering of angels; wherefore, continue in patience until ye are perfected (D&C 67:10-13).

114 But great and marvelous are the works of the Lord, and the mysteries of his kingdom which he showed unto us, which surpass all understanding in glory, and in might, and in dominion;

115 Which he commanded us we should not write while we were yet in the Spirit, and are not lawful for man to utter;

116 Neither is man capable to make them known, for they are only to be seen and understood by the power of the Holy Spirit, which God bestows on those who love him, and purify themselves before him;

117 To whom he grants this ***privilege of seeing and knowing for themselves***;

118 That through the power and manifestation of the Spirit, while in the flesh, they may be able to bear his presence in the world of glory (D&C 76:114-118).

19 And this greater priesthood administereth the gospel and holdeth the key of the mysteries of the kingdom, even the key of ***the knowledge of God*** (D&C 84:19).

68 Therefore, sanctify yourselves that your minds become single to God, ***and the days will come that you shall see him***; for he will unveil his face unto you, and it shall be in his own time, and in his own way, and according to his own will.

69 Remember the great and last promise which I have made unto you; cast away your idle thoughts and your excess of laughter far from you

75 That I may testify unto your Father, and your God, and my God, that you are clean from the blood of this wicked generation; ***that I may fulfil this promise [of manifesting myself to you],*** this great and last promise, which I have made unto you, when I will (D&C 88:68-69, 75).

The Pure in Heart Shall See God in His Temples

15 And inasmuch as my people build a house unto me in the name of the Lord, and do not suffer any unclean thing to come into it, that it be not defiled, my glory shall rest upon it;

16 Yea, and my presence shall be there, for I will come into it, and ***all the pure in heart that shall come into it shall see God.***

17 But if it be defiled I will not come into it, and my glory shall not be there; for I will not come into unholy temples (D&C 97:15-17)

The Pattern of the Brother of Jared

19 And because of the knowledge of this man he could not be kept from beholding within the veil; and he saw the finger of Jesus, which, when he saw, he fell with fear; for he knew that it was the finger of the Lord; and he had faith no longer, for he knew, nothing doubting.

20 Wherefore, having this perfect knowledge of God, he could not be kept from within the veil; therefore ***he saw Jesus***; and he did minister unto him (Ether 3:19-20).

The Son Reveals the Father

27 All things are delivered unto me of my Father: and no man knoweth the Son, but the Father; neither knoweth any man the Father, save the Son, ***and he to whomsoever the Son will reveal him*** (Matthew 11:27).

Apostles and Elders Should See God

Elder McConkie taught the following: "Apostles and prophets are named as examples and patterns of what others should be. The quorum of the 12 should be a model quorum after which every Elders quorum of the Church might pattern its course. I repeat: apostles and prophets simply serve as patterns and examples to show all men what they may receive if they are true and faithful. There is nothing an apostle can receive that is not available to every elder in the kingdom." Elder McConkie adds, "Every Elder is entitled and expected to seek and obtain all the spiritual blessings of the gospel, including the crowning blessing of ***seeing the Lord face-to-face***" (*The Promised Messiah,* pp. 594-595).

"Any person who will search the scriptures, keep the commandments and ask in faith will get his heart so in tune with the Infinite that there will come into his being, from the still small voice, the eternal realities of religion. And as he progresses and advances and comes nearer to God, there will be a day when he will entertain angels, when he will see visions, and the final end is to view the face of God" (Bruce R. McConkie, "How To Get Personal Revelation," New Era, June, 1980).

The Prophet Joseph taught: "God hath not revealed anything to Joseph, what he will make known unto the Twelve and even the least saint may know all things as fast as he is able to bear them" (*Teachings of the Prophet Joseph Smith,* p. 149).

"The other comforter spoken of is a subject of great interest, and perhaps understood by few of this generation. After a person has faith in Christ, repents of his sins, and is baptized for the remission of his sins and receives the Holy Ghost, by the laying on of hands, which is the first comforter, then let him continue to humble himself before God, hungering and thirsting after righteousness, and living by every word of God, *and the Lord will soon say unto him, son, thou shalt be exalted. When the Lord has thoroughly proved him, and finds that the man is determined to serve him at all hazards, then the man will find his calling and his election made sure,* ***then it will be his privilege to receive the other comforter***, which the Lord has promised the Saints....

"Now what is this other comforter? It is no more nor less than the Lord Jesus Christ himself; and this is the sum and substance of the whole matter; that when any man obtains this last comforter, ***he will have the personage of Jesus Christ to attend him, or appear to him from time to time, and even he will manifest the Father unto him***, and they will take up their abode with him, and the visions of the heavens will be open unto him, and the Lord will teach him face-to-face, and he may have a perfect knowledge of the mysteries of the kingdom of God; and this is the state and place the ancient Saints arrived at when they had such glorious visions—Isaiah, Ezekiel, John upon the Isle of Patmos, St. Paul in the three heavens, and all the saints who held communion with the Gen. assembly and Church of the firstborn" (*Teachings of the Prophet Joseph Smith,* pp. 149-51).

Deceptive Tools of the Adversary

"New Age" and "personal power" alone, outside of Christ, are merely deceptive tools used by the adversary to rob God of His glory and ourselves of salvation. Another cunning tool used by the adversary is when he convinces us to say within ourselves, "I consider myself 'spiritual,' not 'religious'." Well, if indeed you are "spiritual," you will follow the light of Christ found in your soul, which will lead you to the study of God's word. And in studying that word, you will realize that we must come under heavenly contract with God through His ordinances in order to be born of both water and the Spirit to obtain the knowledge of God and redemption in Christ. And after we have come under contract with Him, we will do the things which we have seen Him do in our mind's eye and as outlined in scripture. This realization will be confirmed by those who truly are spiritual because they will be in tune with His light. Even Jesus Christ was baptized in obedience to the Father. Are we greater than He? Being "spiritual" should not be a pretext or back door into becoming a *law unto ourselves* and doing our own thing. Sorry, but that just won't cut it. That is the natural man's way. God has the spiritual gold. And He who has the spiritual gold makes the rules. His "rules" are the doctrine of Christ, "the only and true doctrine of the Father, and of the Son, and of the Holy Ghost." His doctrine is "the way; and there is none other way" (see 2 Ne. 31:21). Anyone who "climbeth up some other way, the same is a thief and a robber" (John 10:1).

Fellow Seeker: It is our own connection to heaven that matters. It does not matter if others attain salvation, if we ourselves do not (see Ether 12:37). Please do not delay your broken-hearted repentance as I had nearly done, even until I thought I was to experience an early death. Now is the time for man to prepare to meet God. There is very strong evidence to suggest that those ordinances not sealed by the Holy Spirit of Promise in this life will have no efficacy or power in the next (see D&C 132:7, 22-24). We are to desire to know Him with all our hearts and be willing to surrender our all, including our very lives if necessary. It takes faith in a Being whom we have not seen with our natural eyes, though nevertheless is real. ***Whatever we may value more than Him is what stands in the way of Him. Surrender it all.*** We must fall on our knees and partake of the fruit which is most desirable to the soul. This experience and subsequent fruits will sanctify us and prepare us for the encounter of all encounters.

Notice with your heart instrument the following lyrics of the song entitled, "Captivate Us," by WaterMark.

Your face is beautiful
And Your eyes are like the stars
Your gentle hands have healing
There inside the scars
Your loving arms they draw me near
And Your smile it brings me peace
Draw me closer oh my Lord
Draw me closer Lord to Thee
Captivate us Lord Jesus, set our eyes on You
Devastate us with Your presence, falling down
And rushing river draw us nearer
Holy fountain consume us with You
Captivate us Lord Jesus with You

Your voice is powerful
And Your words are radiant bright
In Your breath and shadow
I will come close and abide
You whisper love and life divine
And Your fellowship is free
Draw us closer oh my Lord
Draw me closer Lord to thee
Captivate us Lord Jesus, set our eyes on You
Devastate us with Your presence, falling down
And rushing river draw us nearer
Holy fountain consume us with You
Captivate us Lord Jesus with You

And let everything be lost in the shadows
Of the light of Your face
And let every chain be broken from me
As I'm bound in Your grace
For Your yoke is easy, Your burden is light
You're full of wisdom power and might
And every eye will see You
And captivate, captivate us Lord Jesus with You
Captivate us...

Rending the Veil and Knowing God Conclusion

When we are captivated by His presence, our knees will buckle and we will fall down. We will wet His feet with our tears, and He shall cause us to stand and embrace us. The Second Comforter is the greatest experience (beyond that of spiritual rebirth) that we can have while in mortality—and it is even *expected* of us. It is available through the ordinances of God given through priesthood authority, and these can be made efficacious and manifestly "real" through our unrelenting desire, faith, and knowledge unto piercing the heavenly veil.

My dear fellow seeker: This book has been my life's calling from God to write, and I consecrate it to the glory of God the Father, God the Son, and God the Holy Ghost from the fullness of my heart. The same night that I finished this last chapter, even to the minute, my son-in-law Mark sent me a text with the name of a song appended, asking if I had heard it. It is called "Rescue Story." It was a tender mercy from God. God wanted to communicate something to me that I will explain. This song has lyrics that include these words:

There I was empty-handed, crying out from the pit of my
despair, There You were in the shadows, Holding out Your hand

You met me there.... Lifted me up from the ashes, carried my soul from death to life, Bringing me from glory to glory, You are my rescue story.... ***You were writing the pages before I had a name...*** *" and "**you never gave up on me**" ("Rescue Story" by Zach Williams).*

This is what I then texted back to Mark: "Long story short, but long before my Rebirth and while living in filth, shame and sin, my prayer would always include these words: '*Don't ever give up on me Father! Don't ever give up on me*!'" These lyrics completely coincided with perhaps a decade-long prayer! Notice the timing of this communication. The Father was showing me that He never did give up on me! He was in fact *writing the pages before I had a name*—before I came to be here in mortality. Tears and praise.

The Heart Attack That Wasn't

Sometime around September of 2019, I felt as though I were having a full-blown heart attack—even as though my heart would explode within my chest cavity. I still had not finished writing chapters 10-12. I pled out loud all the way to the emergency room for God to spare my life until such time as I were able to complete this work. Here's what I would like to say to my family, and I pray that they take it as serious as they would a heart attack. If I were kidnapped and held at gunpoint, about to be sacrificed, and had only three words of counsel to relay to them before my impending demise, it would be these:

DILIGENTLY... SEEK... CHRIST!

Desire Him; long for Him; yearn for Him; seek Him! Those who do, *shall* find Him. It is a promise from a God who cannot lie! But we must *make seeking Him a way of life*. We must latch on as with a vice grip and never let go. We are to plead with the Father that He will never let go of us as well. Moroni says it this way:

"And now, I would commend you to ***seek this Jesus*** *of whom the prophets and apostles have written, that the grace of God the Father, and also the Lord Jesus Christ, and the Holy Ghost, which beareth record of them, may be and abide in you forever. Amen" (Ether 12:41; emphasis added).*

We must prepare to meet God through gut-wrenching repentance. This is facilitated through a realization of our current standing before Him—our "awful situation." This realization can be followed by the decision to "die before we die," if you will. We must offer it all up to be born of Him. Then, like Collier from "Somewhere In Time," we are to remove all idols and distractions. We are to go to Him in our mind's eye with all our heart. We are to meet Him "there" over and over

… and over again: we act it out spiritually and feel it so much so that we profoundly taste of the experience beforehand. Then He will knock, and we will open the door.

As we draw closer and closer to the Lord, He too will draw closer. Through this process, we will undoubtedly come to experientially "taste" of His holiness—Holiness to the Lord. Why these tastes of holiness? They come as gifts from a benevolent God, ***as a reward for our diligent seeking*** (Heb. ll:6), made available to increase our faith, ***dissolve unbelief***, and ultimately prepare us for the unveiling of all unveilings. And although I have yet to experience ***my fondest dream***, I shall continue pressing forward with a steadfastness of faith in (and perfect knowledge of) Christ with all that is in me, until that blessed, ***perfect day*** is made manifestly "real" while yet in this life. Of this fondest dream, the Lord revealed: "The veil shall be rent and you shall see me and know that I am…. in my own due time" (D&C 67: 10, 14). I earnestly pray this fondest dream be fulfilled in the lives of all sincere, diligent seekers.

Of his yearning to know the living God eye to eye and to experience the same in his own life, Parley P. Pratt's words stand as a pattern and beacon of light for us to follow:

> ***For my part I never can rest until my eyes have seen my Redeemer. Until I have gazed like Nephi upon the glories of the Celestial world. Until I can come into full communion and familiar converse with the angels of glory and the spirits of just men made perfect through the blood of Christ. And I testify to all, both small and great, both male and female, that if they stop short of the full enjoyment of these things, they stop short of the blessings freely offered to every creature in the Gospel (Parley P. Pratt in a letter to John Taylor, November 27, 1836; spellings and punctuation corrected).***

Dr. Hawkins spoke about surrendering to "the Ultimate," which can only rightly be understood as our surrendering to God Himself. As to this surrender, Hawkins states: "The devotion to the Truth becomes overwhelming. It isn't that you're driving it. You're being *pulled* by your own destiny; it is by your own *karmic commitment that you've chosen the ultimate destiny"* (*Letting Go,* p. 333 [notice the page number]; emphasis added). I have often felt the tug and beckoning of God through what I refer to as *a spiritual tractor beam*, although I struggle to understand the depths of how or why this is. It is experienced as a celestial force or energetic pull towards God. It is difficult to describe, yet nonetheless undeniably real. Elder Paul E. Koelliker references this celestial force—God's spiritual beckoning this way:

> *"As we remove the distractions that pull us toward the world and exercise our agency to seek Him, we open our hearts to a*

celestial force which draws us toward Him" ("He Truly Loves Us," Ensign, May 2012, 18).

I think we would all agree that there could not be anything more "ultimate" or of a greater "ultimate destiny" than becoming reacquainted with our Lord while yet in mortality. The priceless endowment of salvation is directly tied to the *intensity and tenacity* with which we ***diligently seek Him***. Those whose hearts have already made this "*karmic commitment*" to obtain the Heavenly Gift in that premortal world and who open their hearts to it again here will sense they seemingly have no other choice but to know Him now, even as we are known. These will find that *they just have to know Him* and may not fully understand the origins of this unquenchable desire and need. This is what the author of the Odes meant when he said,

"And He who created me when yet I was not, knew what I would do when I came into being" (The Odes of Solomon 7:9).

The Lord will grant a view of these glorious promises to all who are true seekers and truth seekers. As spiritual beggars, unrelenting in our pursuit of Him, the *highlighted patterns* found in this work can lead all to the perfect knowledge of Him, but it may require the bending of the soul to achieve it. And this includes the journey of finding Him through *persistent and unrelenting desire and faith*, delivered as an act of grace. Remember the pattern: "Desire… Ask, Seek, Knock—Receive. Then Repeat." We are to press forward and obtain the "knowledges" and things of God through direct experience *until all unbelief is completely dissolved.*

Those who "just have to know Him" will fall under this *spiritual tractor beam*, feeling an irresistible and indefensible, energetic pull towards Him in knee-collapsing worship, adoration, and overflowing love in tears. Then it is that we shall once again encounter our true love within the play of our own love story that we will have been unknowingly writing alongside Him the entire journey home. We shall feel the seven emblems of His body and sacrifice, and speak the very words spoken by Abraham. These words shall then become our own property, as if spoken for the very first time:

Now, after the Lord had withdrawn from speaking to me, and withdrawn his face from me, I said in my heart: Thy servant has sought thee earnestly; now I have found thee (Abr. 2:12).

If you have been born of God, even as on the day of Pentecost, Steven Bishop would love to hear from you. Please share your story with him at PuttingOnChrist.com

About the Author

Steven Anthony Bishop

Steven Anthony Bishop was born on the seventh day of the seventh month in Southern California yet considers Utah as his "home base." He has worked as an entrepreneur most of his professional life and is a seasoned real estate investor.

Steven is best known for having obtained the first ever granted exclusive worldwide license to replicate Michelangelo's incomparable "La Pieta" sculpture from the Vatican Observatory Foundation. His company, "Vescovo Buonarroti Art," has made the viewing of its replicas available to Catholic Churches throughout the United States, as well as internationally (see www.LaPieta.com).

Steven has served in many callings in his Church, beginning as a young missionary for The Church of Jesus Christ of Latter-day Saints in the Seville, Spain (now Malaga) Mission. Since his mission, Steven has worked in various callings including serving as a Priest Quorum Advisor, Elders Quorum President, in a Bishopric, and as Director of Public Affairs for Tempe and Chandler, Arizona.

When not serving in The Church of Jesus Christ of Latter-day Saints, Steven can be found doing missionary work and finding the Lord's elect. Steven is a witness to the reality of our risen Savior, Jesus Christ, and shares this message to all who will listen. Steven joyfully welcomes opportunities to promote building faith in Jesus Christ, including volunteering to speak at firesides, or other faith promoting events.

Steven and his wife Rebecca recently moved from Arizona to Utah, and have raised four daughters along with a little yorkie dog named "Gracie," who they all swear is an actual person.

Follow Steven

Puttingonchrist.com

Instagram.com/puttingonchrist

Facebook.com/puttingonchrist

Linkedin.com/company/putting-on-christ

Appendix A

The Holy Ghost as on the day of Pentecost
(See PuttingOnChrist.com for the future release of this material)

Appendix B

Born of God Synonyms
(See PuttingOnChrist.com for the future release of this material)

Appendix C

Music Therapy to Comfort and Soften the Heart
(See PuttingOnChrist.com for future release of this material)

Made in the USA
Monee, IL
07 August 2023

40644485R00234